First Ten Annual Reports of the American Board of Commissioners for Foreign Missions

American Board of Commissioners for Foreign Missions

FIRST TEN

ANNUAL REPORTS

OF THE

AMERICAN BOARD OF COMMISSIONERS

FOR

FOREIGN MISSIONS,

WITH

OTHER DOCUMENTS OF THE BOARD.

———

BOSTON:
PRINTED BY CROCKER AND BREWSTER,
1834.

CONTENTS.

MINUTES

OF THE

FIRST ANNUAL MEETING.

———

At a meeting, in Farmington, (Ct.) September 5th, 1810, of the Commissioners for Foreign Missions, appointed by the General Association of Massachusetts Proper, at their sessions in Bradford, June 27th, 1810, present—

His Excellency John Treadwell, Esq
Rev. Dr. Joseph Lyman,
Rev. Dr. Samuel Spring,
Rev. Samuel Worcester,
Rev. Calvin Chapin.

The meeting was opened with prayer, by Dr. Lyman.

Voted, That the doings of the General Association of Massachusetts Proper, relative to the appointment and duties of this Board, shall be entered on the minutes of the present sessions. Those doings are expressed in the following words, viz.

"Four young gentlemen, members of the Divinity College, were introduced, and presented the following paper.

'The undersigned, members of the Divinity College, respectfully request the attention of their Rev. Fathers, convened in the General Association at Bradford, to the following *statement* and *inquiries.*

'They beg leave to *state,* that their minds have been long impressed with the duty and importance of personally attempting a mission to the heathen; that the impressions on their minds have induced a serious, and they trust, a prayerful consideration of the subject in its various attitudes, particularly in relation to the probable success, and the difficulties attending such an attempt: and that, after examining all the information which they can obtain, they consider themselves as devoted to this work for life, whenever God, in his providence, shall open the way.

2

'They now offer the following *inquiries*, on which they solicit the opinion and advice of this Association. Whether, with their present views and feelings, they ought to renounce the object of missions, as either visionary or impracticable, if not, whether they ought to direct their attention to the eastern or western world, whether they may expect patronage and support from a Missionary Society in this country, or must commit themselves to the direction of a European society; and what preparatory measures they ought to take, previous to actual engagement.

'The undersigned, feeling their youth and inexperience, look up to their fathers in the church, and respectfully solicit their advice, direction and prayers.'   ADONIRAM JUDSON, Jun.
SAMUEL NOTT, Jun.
SAMUEL J. MILLS.
SAMUEL NEWELL.*

"After hearing from the young gentlemen some more particular account of the state of their minds, and their views, relative to the subject offered to consideration, the business was committed to the Rev. Messrs. Spring, Worcester and Hale.

"The committee on the subject of Foreign Missions, made the following report, which was unanimously accepted.

"The committee to whom was referred the request of the young gentlemen, members of the Divinity College, for advice relative to missions to the heathen, beg leave to submit the following report.

"The object of missions to the heathen cannot but be regarded, by the friends of the Redeemer, as vastly interesting and important It deserves the most serious attention of all who wish well to the best interests of mankind, and especially of those who devote themselves to the service of God in the kingdom of his Son, under the impression of the special direction, 'Go ye into all the world, and preach the gospel to every creature ' The state of their minds, modestly expressed by the theological students, who have presented themselves before this body, and the testimonies received respecting them, are such as deeply to impress the conviction, that they ought not to renounce the object of missions, but sacredly to cherish their present views, in relation to that object: and it is submitted whether the peculiar and abiding impressions by which they are influenced, ought not to be gratefully recognized, as a divine intimation of something good and great in relation to the propagation of the gospel, and calling for correspondent attention and exertions.

"Therefore, *Voted*, That there be instituted by this General Association, a Board of Commissioners for Foreign Missions, for the purpose of devising ways and means, and adopting and prosecuting measures, for promoting the spread of the gospel in heathen lands.

"*Voted*, That the said Board of Commissioners consist of nine members, all of them, in the first instance, chosen by this Association; and afterwards annually, five of them by this body, and four of them by the General Association of Connecticut —*Provided, however*, that, if the General Association of Connecticut do not choose to unite in this object,

* The history of the rise and progress of the missionary spirit of which this communication was a result, may be seen in the Life of Samuel J. Mills *Editor* 1834.

the annual election of all the Commissioners shall be by this General Association.

"It is understood, that the Board of Commissioners, here contemplated, will adopt their own form of organization, and their own rules and regulations.

"*Voted*, That fervently commending them to the grace of God, we advise the young gentlemen, whose request is before us, in the way of earnest prayer and diligent attention to suitable studies and means of information, and putting themselves under the patronage and direction of the Board of Commissioners for Foreign Missions, humbly to wait the openings and guidance of providence in respect to their great and excellent design."

"Pursuant to the report of the Committee, the Association proceeded to institute a Board of Commissioners for Foreign Missions, and the following gentlemen were chosen :—His Excellency John Treadwell, Esq., Rev. Dr. Timothy Dwight, Gen. Jedidiah Huntington, and Rev. Calvin Chapin, of Connecticut; Rev. Dr. Joseph Lyman, Rev. Dr. Samuel Spring, William Bartlet, Esq., Rev Samuel Worcester, and Deacon Samuel H. Walley, of Massachusetts

"*Voted*, That the gentlemen of the commission, belonging to Newburyport, Salem and Boston, consult with the other members, for the purpose of appointing a time and place for the first meeting of the Board."

The Board then formed and adopted the following Constitution:

1. The Board shall be known by the name and style of the American Board of Commissioners for Foreign Missions.

2. The object of this Board is to devise, adopt, and prosecute, ways and means for propagating the gospel among those who are destitute of the knowledge of Christianity.

3. This Board shall, at every annual meeting, elect, by ballot, a President, Vice-President, and a Prudential Committee of their own number, also a Recording Secretary, and a Corresponding Secretary, a Treasurer, and an Auditor of the Treasury, either of their own number, or of other persons, at their discretion

4. The annual meetings of this Board shall be held alternately in Massachusetts and Connecticut, on the third Wednesday of every September, at ten o'clock, A. M. The place of every such meeting is to be fixed at the annual meeting next preceding. The President shall call a special meeting at the request of a majority of the Prudential Committee, or of any other three members of the Board. Five members of the Board shall constitute a quorum, a majority of whom shall be competent to the transaction of ordinary business.

5. The Prudential Committee, under the direction of the Board, shall have power to transact any business necessary to promote the object of the institution; and shall, in writing, report their doings to each annual meeting.

6. The Auditor, by himself, or with such others as may be joined with him, shall annually audit the Treasurer's accounts, and make report to the annual meeting of the Board.

7 It shall be the duty of the Commissioners to receive all donations of money, other property and evidences of property, and the same deliver

to the Prudential Committee; and the Committee shall deliver the same to the Treasurer, to be managed by him for the interest of the funds.

8. The Treasurer, in keeping his accounts, shall distinguish such monies as may be appropriated, by the donors, for immediate use, from such, the interest of which is alone applicable to use, and the principal is designed to form a permanent fund; the surplus of the former, which may, at any time, be in his hands, he shall place at interest, on good security, for such limited period as the Prudential Committee shall direct; and the principal of the latter he shall place and keep at interest, or vest in stock, as he shall be ordered by the Board, or by the said Committee.

9. The Prudential Committee shall keep an account of all monies and other property, or evidences of property, by them received, and of all payments by them made either to the Treasurer, or for other purposes; and of all orders by them drawn on the Treasurer: and their accounts shall be annually audited and reported to the Board.

10. The Commissioners shall be entitled to be paid their necessary expenses incurred in going to, attending upon, and returning from, meetings of the Board; and all officers of the Board shall be, in like manner, entitled to be paid their necessary expenses, as they shall, in each case, be liquidated and allowed by the Board; but no commissioner or officer shall be entitled to receive any compensation for his personal services.

11. The appointment of missionaries, their destination, appropriations for their support, and their recal from service, when necessary, shall be under the exclusive direction of the Board.

12. A report of the transactions of this Board shall annually be made, in writing, to the respective bodies, by which the commissioners are appointed.

13. This Board will hold correspondence with Missionary and other Societies for the furtherance of the common object.

14. This constitution shall be subject to any additions or amendments, which experience may prove necessary, by the Board at an annual meeting; provided the additions or amendments be proposed, in writing, to the Board at the preceding meeting.

JOHN TREADWELL,
JOSEPH LYMAN,
SAMUEL SPRING,
CALVIN CHAPIN,
SAMUEL WORCESTER.

The Board then proceeded to the choice of officers for the year ensuing, and the following were elected:

His Excellency JOHN TREADWELL, Esq. *President.*
Rev. Dr. SPRING, *Vice President.*
WILLIAM BARTLET, Esq. ⎫
Rev. Dr. SPRING, ⎬ *Prudential Committee.*
Rev. SAMUEL WORCESTER, ⎭
Rev. CALVIN CHAPIN, *Recording Secretary.*
Rev. SAMUEL WORCESTER, *Corresponding Secretary.*
Deacon SAMUEL H. WALLEY, *Treasurer.*
Mr. JOSHUA GOODALE, *Auditor.*

Voted, That the Prudential Committee prepare a Report, and submit the same to the Board; and that the Board submit it to the General Association of Massachusetts Proper, and to the General Association of Connecticut.

Voted, That the Prudential Committee and Corresponding Secretary be requested to obtain the best information, in their power, respecting the state of unevangelized nations on the western and eastern continents, and report at the next meeting of the Board.

Voted, That the Board highly approve the readiness of the young gentlemen at Andover, to enter upon a foreign mission; and that it is advisable for them to pursue their studies, till further information relative to the missionary field be obtained, and the finances of the institution will justify the appointment.

Voted, That the next annual meeting of this Board be in Worcester, (Mass.) at such place as the Prudential Committee shall provide.

Voted, That five hundred copies of the doings of the present meeting be printed; that thirty copies be transmitted to each of the commissioners; and that the remaining copies be put into the hands of the Prudential Committee for circulation; and the Prudential Committee will draw upon the Treasurer for reimbursement of the expense.

Voted, That the Recording Secretary be requested to procure the printing and distribution of the doings of this meeting, as stated in the preceding vote. The meeting was concluded with prayer by Dr. Spring.

By order of the Board.

JOHN TREADWELL, *President.*

Attest. CALVIN CHAPIN, *Recording Secretary.*

The following Address and form of subscription were then prepared, read, and adopted, viz.

The American Board of Commissioners for Foreign Missions, solicit the serious and liberal attention of the Christian public.

The Redeemer of men, who, although "he was rich, for our sakes became poor," just before he ascended up on high to give gifts unto men, gave it in special charge to his disciples to "go into all the world, and preach the gospel to every creature." Almost eighteen centuries have passed away since this charge was delivered, and yet a great proportion of our fellow men, ignorant of the gospel, are "sitting in the region and shadow of death." The promise, however, is sure, that the Son "shall have the heathen for his inheritance, and the uttermost parts of the earth for his possession," and that the world "shall be filled with the knowledge of the glory of the Lord." The long expected day is approaching. The Lord is shaking the nations; his friends in different parts of christendom are roused from their slumbers; and unprecedented exertions are making for the spread of divine knowledge, and the conversion of the nations. In our own country, the missionary spirit is excited, and much has already been done for imparting the gospel to the destitute in our new and frontier settlements. But for the millions on our own continent and in other parts of the world, to whom the gospel has never been preached, we have yet those exertions to make, which comport with the Savior's emphatical directions, and our distinguished advantages for promoting the great object, for which he came down from heaven and labored and suffered. A new scene, with us, is now opening. It is ascertained that several young men, of good reputation for piety and talents, under sacred and deep impressions, hold themselves devoted for life to the service of God, in the gospel of his Son, among the destitute, and are ready to go into any part of the unevangelized world, where providence shall open the door for their missionary labors. Is not this a divine intimation of something great and good? And does it not call, with impressive emphasis, for general attention and exertion? In the present state of the world, Christian missions cannot be executed without pecuniary support. Shall this support be wanting? When millions are perishing for lack of knowledge, and young disciples of the Lord are waiting, with ardent desire, to carry the gospel of salvation to them; shall those millions be left to perish, and that ardent desire be disappointed? Is there, then, in those who are favored with the gospel, the same mind that was in Christ, when he freely gave his own blood for the redemption of men? Should not this reflection come home to the hearts of the rich, and of all who, by the bounty of the Savior, have it in their power to contribute even their mites, for the salvation of those for whom he died?

The commissioners hold themselves sacredly bound to use their best endeavors for promoting the great design for which they have been appointed; and solemnly pledge themselves to the Christian public faithfully to appropriate, according to their best discretion, all monies which shall be contributed and committed to their disposal, for aiding the propagation of the gospel in unevangelized lands.

For promoting the object of their institution, we the subscribers, engage to pay to the American Board of Commissioners for Foreign Missions, the sums annexed to our respective names.

MINUTES

OF THE

SECOND ANNUAL MEETING.

———

PURSUANT to the constitution of the American Board of Commissioners for Foreign Missions, the following members of that Board convened in Worcester, (Mass.) September 18, 1811, viz.

> The Hon. JOHN TREADWELL, Esq.
> Rev. SAMUEL SPRING, D. D.
> Gen. JEDIDIAH HUNTINGTON,
> Rev. JOSEPH LYMAN, D. D.
> Rev. JEDIDIAH MORSE, D. D.
> Rev. SAMUEL WORCESTER,
> Rev. CALVIN CHAPIN.

The meeting was opened with prayer by the Vice President.
Certificates of appointment for the ensuing year were exhibited.
Minutes of the last session were read.

The Hon. JOHN TREADWELL, was elected *President of the Board;*
> The Rev. Dr. SPRING, *Vice President;*
> WILLIAM BARTLET, Esq. ⎫
> Rev. Dr. SPRING, ⎬ *Prudential Committee.*
> Rev. SAMUEL WORCESTER, ⎭
> Rev. CALVIN CHAPIN, *Recording Secretary;*
> Rev. SAMUEL WORCESTER, *Corresponding Secretary.*
> JEREMIAH EVARTS, Esq., *Treasurer,*
> Mr. JOSHUA GOODALE, *Auditor.*

The Rev. Dr. Morse, the Rev. Dr. Lyman, and Gen. Huntington, were appointed a committee to consider whether any, and if any, what, alterations of the Constitution may be expedient.

The Prudential Committee presented their report, which is as follows:

REPORT.

Agreeably to the direction of the Board, the doings of their meeting at Farmington, together with their address to the public and the form of subscription for promoting the object of their institution, were printed without delay, and extensively circulated. Though a disposition favorable to the great object was very soon discovered on the part of charitable individuals, yet the Committee perceived, that considerable time must elapse, before they could be in possession of funds adequate to the support of a mission upon a promising scale, in any part of the heathen world. Four young brethren, however, viz Messrs. Adoniram Judson, jun., Samuel Nott, jun., Samuel Newell, and Gordon Hall, held themselves in readiness for the service, and only waited to be sent where Providence should direct. Under these circumstances, that as little time as possible might be lost, and with a view to the missionary interest at large, the Committee, after consultation on the subject, judged it advisable to send one of the four brethren to England, to confer with the Directors of the London Missionary Society. Mr Judson was designated for this purpose; but as a precautionary and preparatory measure it was thought proper, that the four missionary brethren should all be examined by the Committee relative to their qualifications for the service, to which they held themselves devoted. Accordingly they attended a session of the Committee, and were examined, and approved. In the mean time, arrangements were made for Mr. Judson's special mission to England; and he was fitted away with all convenient despatch. The precise views of the Committee, in this measure, will more distinctly be seen by the letter of instructions which was given to Mr. Judson, and which in this place the Committee beg leave to submit.

Mr. ADONIRAM JUDSON,—As you and your brethren, Samuel Newell, Samuel Nott, and Gordon Hall, have professed to hold yourselves sacredly devoted to the service of Christ, in some part or parts of the heathen world, as in Divine Providence a door may be opened to you, and as, with reference to this important object, you have chosen to place yourselves under the superintendence and direction of the American Board of Commissioners for Foreign Missions; the Prudential Committee of the said Board, after obtaining satisfaction in regard to your qualifications severally for the contemplated service, and seriously consulting on the subject at large, have judged it advisable to have a full and distinct understanding with the Directors of the London Missionary Society, in relation to the general object. For this purpose they have determined on sending you, dear Sir, to England, under the following instructions.

Agreeably to arrangements made, you will sail for England in the ship Packet; and on your arrival at her port of destination, you will proceed, as soon as convenient, to London, and deliver your letter of introduction to the Rev. George Burder, Secretary of the London Missionary Society. Mr. Burder, we doubt not, will receive you with Christian courtesy, and from him, and his brethren of the Board of Directors, you will receive such notices as will enable you to accomplish in the best manner the design now in view. A principal object of your attention will be to ascertain, as distinctly as possible, whether any and what arrangements can be made for a concert of measures in relation to Missions, between the American Board of Commissioners and the London Missionary Society. Particularly, whether, if circumstances should render it desirable, you and your brethren can be supported in Missionary service for any time; by the London funds, without committing yourselves wholly and finally to the direction of the London Society. Or whether it may be in any case consistent for the mission to be supported partly by them, and partly by us   And if so, under whose direction it must be held. On these points you will possess yourself of the views of the Directors of the London Society, and receive their propositions for our consideration. You will, also, during your stay in England, avail yourself of your opportunities and advantages for obtaining ample and correct information, relating to missionary fields, the requisite preparations for missionary services, the most eligible methods of executing missions, and generally, to whatever may be conducive to the missionary interest; and the most important parts of such information as you may obtain, you will commit to writing, for the use of the American Board.

As it is not expected that you will be at your own charge in this engagement, you will keep a full account of your expenditures, for adjustment on your return.

We commend you, dear brother, to the Providence and the grace of God, with fervent prayers for your safety, your success, and your happiness. In behalf of the Prudential Committee of the American Board of Commissioners for Foreign Missions.

Yours, dear brother, with great affection,   ,SAMUEL WORCESTER.

The instructions were accompanied by an official letter from the Corresponding Secretary to the Secretary of the London Missionary Society, which, for the further satisfaction of the Board, it may be proper in this connection to exhibit.

Salem, January 3, 1811.

REV. AND DEAR SIR,—Inclosed with this you will receive a printed paper, in which you will see in general what has recently been done in this country in relation to foreign missions. Four young gentlemen, Messrs. Adoniram Judson, jun., Samuel Newell, and Samuel Nott, jun , whose names you will find in the paper referred to, and Mr. Gordon Hall, have offered themselves as candidates for missions to the heathen, under a solemn profession that they have devoted themselves to God for this arduous service, wherever in his Providence he may see fit to employ them. These beloved brethren have all passed through a course of collegial education and received a collegial degree Since leaving the universities they have completed a course of studies at the Theological Institution in this vicinity, where they have acquitted themselves to the high satisfaction of their instructors and friends. According to our established order, they have been regularly licensed for the Christian ministry; and for a considerable time they have all preached in our churches to good acceptance. Their moral and Christian reputation is good, and their talents and attainments are respectable. Before the Prudential Committee of the American Board of Commissioners for Foreign Missions they have passed an examination in form, relative to their religious sentiments, their religious feelings, and their views in offering themselves for the missionary service: and their answers and declarations throughout were highly satisfactory. They profess their full belief in the articles of faith which are established in the Theological Institution, a copy of which you will receive, and the Prudential Committee have great confidence that they have received the truth in love; that they are persons of sincere and ardent piety; that they have offered themselves for the missionary service from the best motives; and, in a word, that they have qualifications for distinguished usefulness. The manner in which these young men have come forward, together with a similar disposition manifested by several others, has made, extensively, a deep impression, and excited a lively interest. It is gratefully hailed as an indication that the Lord is about to do something by his friends in this country, in furtherance of the great design in which their brethren in England have been so nobly and so exemplarily engaged.

On our own continent, indeed, there are many millions of men "sitting in darkness and in the region and shadow of death," and our brethren in England may wonder that, while such is the fact, we should turn our views to any other part of the world. But the attempts which have been made to evangelize the aboriginal tribes of the North American wilderness, have been attended with so many discouragements, and South America is yet in so unpromising a state, that the opinion very generally prevalent is, that for the Pagans on this continent but little can immediately be done. Hence, though the hope is entertained, that the time is coming when the benevolent exertions of the Redeemer's friends here, for spreading the knowledge of his name, may be successfully employed nearer home; yet at present the Eastern world is thought to offer a more promising field.

As yet however, we have no adequate funds established, for the support of distant and expensive missions. What may be done in the course of a short time we know not. It is the desire and the prayer of many, that American missionaries may have American support; and we are not without hope that He, to whom the silver and the gold belong, will open the hearts of the rich among us for this interesting purpose. Should this hope be realized, and missionary funds to any considerable amount be raised, they will probably be placed under such an arrangement as to be employed either in the East or on our own continent, as Divine Providence may direct.

Under existing circumstances, the American Board are desirous to open a communication with the London Missionary Society, whose knowledge of missionary concerns is ample, and the praise of whose liberality and persevering exertions is in all parts of the world. For this purpose Mr. Judson, one of the missionary brethren, of whom you have already some knowledge, and who has been favored with a letter from you, has been appointed to go to London. To your courtesy and Christian attention he is most affectionately and respectfully recommended; and for the particular objects for which he is sent, I beg leave to refer you to his letter of instructions.

Besides the official testimonial contained in this letter, Mr. Judson will carry with him others, and particularly one from the Faculty of the Theological Institution at Andover; an Institution which, though young, is fast rising in importance, and in which, both on account of the principles on which it is founded, and the ability and piety with which it is conducted, great confidence is reposed. Should these testimonials be satisfactory, and should it in the event be thought best that our young brethren should be resigned to the patronage and direction of your Society, your venerable and highly respected Board of Directors will judge, whether, after the course of studies through which they have passed, it will be expedient for them to spend any time at your school at Gosport, and whether, for any purpose, it will be necessary for the other three to go to England, before they shall be actually engaged in your service.

It may not be improper to state, that some of the young men propose to take wives with them to the missionary field. If this meet the approbation of your Board, as we are not unapprized of the laudable care which you take in regard to the character not only of your missionaries themselves, but also of their wives, we shall certainly consider it important that similar care be taken here.

With great personal consideration, and in behalf of the American Board of Commissioners for Foreign Missions, I tender to you, dear Sir, and through you to your brethren of the Board of Directors, the most affectionate and respectful salutations.

SAMUEL WORCESTER, *Corresponding Secretary.*
Rev. George Burder, Secretary of the London Miss. Society.

Agreeably to his instructions Mr. Judson sailed in the ship Packet of Boston, about the first of January. On her passage out, the Packet was captured by a French privateer. Mr. Judson was taken out and carried first to Passage in Spain, and thence to Bayonne in France, where he was cast into close prison. By the favor of Providence, however, he soon obtained a release from his confinement; but it was so long before he could obtain permission to depart from France for England, that he did not arrive in London until May, just in season to be present at the annual meeting of the London Missionary Society. He staid in England about six weeks, had repeated conferences with the Directors and the Secretary of the London Society, and returned to this country in August. His reception by the Directors, and the result of conferences with them, will appear in part by the official letter which he brought with him from their Secretary to the Corresponding Secretary of this Board, which it may be proper to introduce in this place.

TO THE REV. MR. WORCESTER.

London, June 11, 1811.

REV. AND DEAR SIR,—With peculiar pleasure I received your letter of January 3d, by the hands of our worthy young friend, Mr. Judson, who happily obtained his liberty just time enough to be present at our annual meeting.

I rejoice greatly, with my brethren in the Direction of the Missionary Society, in the disposition which has been manifested by Messrs. Judson, Newell, Nott, and Hall, towards the poor heathen in the East. We hail it as a token for good, that the Lord has mercy in store for myriads, when he thus inclines young men of talents, piety, and education to consecrate themselves to the service of Christ among Pagan nations; and the Directors, feeling the most perfect satisfaction with the full and decided testimonies given by you, Sir, your colleagues, and other reverend gentlemen, to the character of the young men, have most cordially received them as Missionaries, and they unite with them in wishing that they may proceed with all convenient despatch, from your shores to those of India.

By the official letter of instructions which I hope will be ready for Mr. Judson before his departure, (which we lament is so hasty) you will perceive that the Directors wish they may proceed to Calcutta (or rather to Madras, if possible,) and from thence to Vizagapatam, which we consider as our Head-Quarters; and there to abide for a time, as various advantages, we think, will accrue from conversation with those who have been sometime there. We have thought it a matter of too great importance hastily to be decided upon, in what particular place they shall labor, and after all that we are now able to say on the subject, we must allow some latitude to the brethren, to determine, upon the most deliberate consultation, what stations may probably be found the best and most promising.

We have long had in view the great city and populous neighborhood of Surat; but have been repeatedly disappointed in our attempts to send missionaries thither Mr. Spratt, one of our missionaries lately gone from America, has been thought eligible for that station; but he must not go alone.

We have also had in view, for some years, Prince of Wales's Island (or Penang,) which has lately become a place of great consequence, and promises to be the key of Asia, especially of the vast countries of the Malays, the importance of which has appeared to us, since our acceptance of your young friends, in a stronger light than ever, in consequence of what Dr. Buchanan has just published on that subject.

But we must intreat, that the young men be advised by you, as well as by us, not to think of going all together to any one station, in the first instance. We are too well aware of the jealousy entertained against missions by many gentlemen both in India and in Britain, to venture on a step which might excite unnecessary alarm. Such is the good sense of the young men, and such their regard to the ultimate success of their endeavors, that we confidently hope they will be satisfied in observing the apostolic pattern; and proceed to their work, two and two.

The young men have expressed their inclination to enter into the married state before their departure. On some accounts this is certainly desirable; but where *new* stations are attempted, we have always been of opinion that it is safest and best for a missionary to go alone: this, however, would not be insisted upon in the present case, as they are going to a civilized country, where they will enjoy the protection of a regular government.

But it is of immense importance that the females chosen for their companions, should be truly pious persons, of tried integrity and unblemished character; prudent, domestic, humble, not looking for great things in this world; such as will be willing to deny themselves, and take up their cross and follow the lowly and diligent Son of God: it is also proper, that they should be persons who have manifested some zeal for God, in their attention to the education of poor children, visiting the sick, or in some other way; for without some ardent love to Christ and religion, we cannot expect that they will prove helpers to missionaries, but miserable hindrances

Now, my dear Sir, on you and the other gentlemen of the Prudential Committee, or others who may be thought adequate, the Directors must and do rely with confidence, that the greatest care and caution may be observed, and that, if any doubts arise, a reasonable time be allowed more fully to develope the character, even though the union should be for a time deferred, and the young woman afterwards go out to join her intended partner. But such, Sir, appears to have been the prudence and care with which your committee have proceeded with regard to the missionaries, that we feel confident equal care will be employed respecting their partners.

So many are the objects of our attention, that we are obliged to pay a sacred and constant regard to economy, in order that we may support missions already established, and if possible commence many more. Already our expenditure is about £7,000 annually, and it is likely that this year we shall expend £10,000. Whether the liberality of the British public will keep pace with our exertions, we know not. We hope it will. We cannot, therefore, but wish that prudent and zealous endeavors may be made in America for the support of Foreign missions, and we entertain so favorable an opinion of our good friends in the United States, that we cannot suppose they will permit the London Society to serve alone; and we stand fully prepared to hear of general and liberal contributions, as soon as it is known in the American churches, that four of their brethren, "flesh of their flesh and bone of their bone," and animated with their own spirit of independence, are engaged in this service. We hope the religious public will come forward, and so fill your funds, that not four only, but forty may go forth with apostolic zeal—with the zeal of Eliot, Mayhew, Brainerd, (names dear to us as to you), and spread abroad in many places, the sweet savor of the name of Jesus—ours and yours.

Indeed we have just heard that a pious lady, one of the first promoters of Foreign Missions among you, has bequeathed a noble sum for this purpose. Ere this, I doubt not the example has been followed by others, and a foundation laid for the most generous exertions.

However, should the Commissioners not find it convenient at present to undertake the support of the four brethren, the Directors will agree to allow them the same annual salaries as are given to their missionaries: viz. £100 a year to a single, and £150 a year to a married missionary; that is, until they are able, by some means, not incompatible with their missionary engagements, to procure their own support; which we consider to be the bounden duty of every missionary to attempt, as soon as possible; and without which missions can never be very widely extended.

We shall be happy, dear Sir, to hear from you as fully, and as frequently, as possible.

Be pleased to present the cordial respects of the Directors, to all the ministers and gentlemen of the Board, or who are otherwise engaged in this good and great work.

I am, Sir, with sincere esteem, your affectionate brother and fellow laborer.   GEO: BURDER, *Secretary.*

The Board will perceive, that though the London Directors gave the most favorable reception to our messenger, and shewed the most Christian zeal towards the general object; yet in this letter of the Rev. Mr. Burder, nothing is said in direct reference to the points on which Mr. Judson was instructed to confer with the Directors, relating to a co-operation in the support and conduct of missions.   Though the Committee have not received any written communication from Mr. Judson, yet they have learned from him in general, that the London Directors are of opinion, that a joint conduct of missions will not be practicable; and that although they are ready to receive our young brethren under their patronage, and would gladly have aid from us in respect to their support, yet they do not think it consistent to admit this Board to a participation with them in the direction of the mission.   The Prudential Committee have always perceived, that a co-operation between the London Society and this Board, in the conduct of a mission, must be attended with difficulty. They thought it possible, however, that the Directors of the London Society, with their more perfect acquaintance with missionary concerns, might point out some way in which a co-operation might be practicable and useful; and if not, yet a hope was entertained, that it might be consistent with the views and means of the Directors to afford some pecuniary aid to a mission to be directed by this Board, until adequate funds could be raised in this country.   It now appears, that nothing of this kind is to be expected; the plans of the London Board are so extensive as to require all the funds at their command; and if any concert of measures be had with them, it must be in the way of our giving pecuniary aid to missions under their direction, rather than to that of receiving aid from them to missions under our own direction

On the whole then, it now rests with this Board to determine, whether it will be expedient to resign the four missionary brethren, or any of them, to the London Directors; and in that case what aid, if any, it will be proper to give towards fitting them out for the mission and supporting them in it, or whether it will be better to retain the young gentlemen under the direction of this Board, and trust, under Providence, in the liberality of the Christian public in this country for the means of supporting them.   It is the opinion of the Committee, which they beg leave respectfully to submit, that the latter is to be preferred.   The grounds on which this opinion rests are briefly the following.   By raising up young men among us endowed with the spirit and qualifications for missions, Divine Providence seems distinctly to call on the Christian public in this country for the requisite means of their support, and upon this Board to apply the means and direct the missionary labors.   From this view of the subject, and from what has already come to our knowledge of the disposition of individuals towards the object, the Committee feel a confidence that He, to whom the silver and the gold belong, will open the hands of the rich and liberal among us, so as shortly to provide the means for supporting a foreign mission upon a promising scale.   Though at present the Eastern world appears to hold out the most favorable prospects for missionary efforts; yet the Committee presume, that this Board will not lose sight of the heathen tribes on this continent, but will make it an object in their arrangements to be in readiness to meet the openings of Providence for imparting the knowledge of the gospel to them.   And, finally, it is believed by the Committee, that if the missionary brethren are retained under the direction of this Board, a greater interest will be excited in the American public, greater liberality for the support of missions will be displayed, and greater exertions for the missionary cause will be made, and, on the whole, more will be done for the spread of the gospel and the promotion of the Redeemer's kingdom.

The Committee have expressed a confidence that adequate missionary funds may be raised in this country; not indeed because funds to any considerable amount have been actually realized. But the Committee feel themselves bound thankfully to express, that, for the time which has intervened since the institution of this Board, they think the encouragement good. It is known to this Board, that a bequest to the amount of thirty thousand dollars for the foreign missionary use, was left by the late Mrs. Norris of Salem. That bequest indeed is at present under litigation. In addition to this, several smaller donations have been made to the amount of about fourteen hundred dollars, making the whole amount of the funds already given to this Board, about thirty-one thousand and four hundred dollars. This, given in the short space of a few months after the Board became known to the public, presents itself to the Committee in the light of a providential intimation, that a reasonable reliance may be placed on American funds for the support of American missionaries. The London Missionary Society have for some years past expended about £7,000 sterling, annually, in the support of foreign missions; and this year it is expected that they will expend £10,000. Shall the four American missionaries then be cast upon the London funds? Is not the American public as well able to supply £600 annually, the sum estimated to be sufficient for the support of four missionaries, as the British public is to supply £10,000? Would it not indeed be a reproach to our character as a Christian nation, as well as shew an ungrateful distrust of Providence, should we resign our missionaries to the London Society, under an apprehension that we could not support them?

If, however, it should be determined to retain the missionary brethren with a view to employ them in a mission to be supported and directed by this Board, it readily occurs, that exertions must be made upon an extensive scale, and with zeal and perseverance, for raising the requisite funds. In conformity with the views of the Board at their former meeting, the Committee are still of opinion that the best way to raise the funds will be by application to individuals, especially to the rich, but not to the neglect of the less wealthy, in all parts of the country. And it is respectfully submitted whether some measures may not be taken by the Board to engage the clergy and other influential characters, extensively, to attend zealously to this subject.

The Committee have made it an object of their attention and inquiry, to obtain information with respect to the best stations for missionary establishments. The Eastern world, especially Hindoostan, the Malayan Archipelago, and the Birman empire, presents most extensive fields for missionary labors; fields which appear to be fast whitening for the harvest. All those vast regions are full of people *sitting in darkness and in the region and shadow of death,* and by experiments already made, it has been abundantly evinced that it is by no means a vain thing to attempt to spread the gospel of salvation among them. But the most favorable station for an American mission in the East would probably be in some part of the Birman empire. The population of that empire is great and somewhat advanced in civilization; the character and manners of the people are perhaps as favorable to the reception of the gospel as will be found in any part of the heathen world; and what deserves particular consideration, they are not within the limits of the British empire, and therefore not so much within the proper province of the British Missionary Societies.

On our own continent, it is well known to the Board, there are many tribes of men in Pagan darkness. Notwithstanding the discouragements which have hitherto attended the efforts which have been made to evangelize the American Indians, there are many reasons which forcibly press upon an American Missionary Board a very tender and serious attention to this portion of the Pagan world.

On the whole, therefore, the Committee beg leave to submit, whether it would not be best for this Board to fix upon some place in the Birman empire for a missionary station in the East, and upon some place within the territories of the Indians of this continent for a missionary station in the West; and direct their attention to these two points, with a view to follow the intimations of Providence in regard to them, respectively, and to establish missions in them as soon, and upon as extensive a scale, as their means will admit.

The mission of Mr. Judson to England was attended with expense; to what amount exactly the Committee are not able to state, as the want of a Treasurer, and the shortness of the time since Mr. Judson's return, have rendered it impracticable to complete a seasonable adjustment of his accounts.

In the close of this report, the Committee would devoutly congratulate the Board on the evident smiles of Providence upon the design of this infant institution. The cause is God's, and it must succeed. The object is the salvation of men; the furtherance of the great purpose for which the Redeemer came down from heaven and died, the extension of his kingdom and the advancement of his glory. In this cause, therefore, we have every Christian inducement to be *steadfast and immovable, always abounding in the work of the Lord, for as much as we know, that our labor will not be in vain in the Lord.*

SAMUEL SPRING,
SAMUEL WORCESTER, } *Prudential Committee.*

DONATIONS TO FOREIGN MISSIONS,

In the foregoing report, the sum of *fourteen hundred dollars* is mentioned as having been given to be expended in Foreign Missions. The particulars of this sum are as follows :

Money collected in Hadley, received by the hands of the Rev. Dr. Lyman, - -	47 98
From individuals in the Society of West Brook, (Ct.) received by the Rev. Mr. Chapin, - - - - - - - - - -	8 00
Donation from a friend to Foreign Missions, received by Mr Chapin, -	410 20
Donation from William Woodbridge, Stonington, (Ct.) by the hands of Gen. Huntington, - - - - - - - - -	10 00
From two young ladies, New London, - - - - - -	4 00
From Rev. Doctor Wolworth, Long Island, - - - -	15 00
From a friend to missions, New London, - - - - -	50 00
From another friend to missions, New London, - - - -	250 00
From a friend to missions, Norwich, - - - - -	50 00
From sundry persons unknown, - - - - - - -	9 72
From individuals, by the hands of the Rev. Mr. Huntington of Boston, -	212 00
From Deacon Samuel H. Walley, Boston, - - - - -	100 00

$1,166 90

Mr. Bartlet, Mrs. Norris, and others, gave to fit out Mr. Judson, more than sufficient to make up the sum specified.

ADDRESS TO THE CHRISTIAN PUBLIC.

NOVEMBER, 1811.

Immediately after their first organization in September of the last year, the American Board of Commissioners for Foreign Missions respectfully solicited the serious and liberal attention of the Christian public to the great object of their appointment. They are now happy in having it in their power to acknowledge, with gratitude to the Father of all good, that the solicitation was not in vain. Many have viewed the object with deep interest, and some have embraced the earliest opportunity of promoting it by their pious liberality. The name of the late Mrs. Norris in particular, is endeared to thousands; and what she has done will be told for a memorial of her in distant lands, and in generations to come. Animated by the encouragement given them, and impelled by a regard to their high responsibility, the Commissioners have made an important advance in the prosecution of their design. At their late annual meeting they resolved to establish, as soon as practicable, a Christian mission in the East, and another in the West. In the East, their attention will first be directed to the Birman empire; and in the West, to the Caghnawaga tribe of Indians.

The Birman empire, which lies on the farther peninsula of India, between Hindoostan and China, comprises within its present limits the native country of the Birmahs, together with the ancient kingdoms of Arracan and Pegu, a considerable part of Siam, and several smaller territories, all which, though formerly subject to their own independent princes, are now reduced under the power of one Imperial chief. The population, according to the most probable estimate, amounts to not less than fifteen millions, and the people are considerably advanced in civilization. They are vigorous, intelligent, and tractable, and in many respects superior to the Hindoos; yet not less deeply immersed in the darkness and corruptions of Paganism. On the whole, it is believed, that scarcely any part of the world presents a more inviting or a more important field for Christian missionaries, than does the Birman empire.

This nation, it is true, is at a great distance from us; but is it not composed of our brethren, descended from the same common parents, involved in the consequences of the same fatal apostacy from God, and inhabiting the same world, to every creature in which the Savior has directed that his Gospel should be preached? And by whom is this direction to be obeyed, in regard to them, if not by us? The Christians of Great Britain are, indeed, ardently engaged in the glorious work of evangelizing the nations; but in imparting the word of life to the hundreds of millions ready to perish in Asia and Africa, they need and they desire our help.

Though the field is distant, it is not unknown, and as reasonable calculations can be made with respect to success in this region, as we can ordinarily hope to make with respect to an untried object of this nature. Distance of place alters not the claims of the heathen, so long as the means of access to them are in our power. Christianity is equally a blessing to the inhabitants of the polar circle, and to those of the torrid zone. The salvation of the soul is all-important to the heathen natives of the Indian peninsulas, as well as to the Christian descendants of pious ancestors Wherever the knowledge of Christ can be spread, *there* is the field for Christian exertions. A few years ago, our countrymen sent a donation to the Baptist Missionaries in Bengal, to assist them in translating and printing the Bible. Though the place was distant, the remittance soon arrived, and was immediately appropriated to its destined object; and the natives of Hindoostan, to a greater extent than would have been otherwise practicable, are now reading the word of God in their own languages, in consequence of this very donation. It is not too much to hope, that those pious persons who shall enable the Commissioners to establish a permanent mission in the East, will, in a few years, hear a good report from the scene of their liberality; that they will read of Christian schools, and Christian churches, casting a mild and salutary light through dark regions, and affording a happy presage of the latter day-glory.

But while the Commissioners view with deep interest the populous regions of the East, they are not unmindful of the Pagan tribes on our own continent. Among these, no tribe perhaps bids fairer to give the Gospel a favorable reception, and eventually an extensive spread, than the Caghnawagas in Lower Canada. Their situation is of easy access; they are well disposed towards the white people, and have great influence with their red brethren of other tribes. And a fact not to be disregarded among the indications of Providence is, that a native of that tribe, a pious young man, whose heart burns with a desire to carry the Gospel to his countrymen, is now in a course of education, and gives promise of eminent usefulness.

Here, then, are presented two great fields for missionary labors; fields rich in hopeful prospects, and offering ample scope for Christian benevolence and exertion. Laborers are also ready to enter the fields, and impatiently wait for the means of conveyance and support. Can these means be withheld? Can the Christians of this favored land be willing, that, for the want of these means, millions of their fellow-men should remain in darkness, and perish for lack of knowledge?

To be impressed with the importance of the Gospel to the character and condition of man, even in the present world, we need only glance at a comparative view of Pagan and Christian nations; we need only look, indeed, at the difference, as exhibited by the excellent Dr. Buchanan, between the Pagan natives at Benares and Juggernaut, and the Christian natives at Tranquebar and Cande-nad. The infinite importance of the Gospel to the character and condition of mankind with reference to the world to come, no sound believer in Divine revelation can doubt. The gospel is the grand instrument, ordained by infinite wisdom "to turn men from darkness unto light, and from the power of Satan unto God." It is, in effect, the power of God unto salvation "to every one that believeth, to the Jew first, and also to the Greek."

How, then, is the Gospel to be imparted to men in the dark places of the earth, if not through the instrumentality of missions? Is not this the very way which the glorious Author of the Gospel has himself seen fit to appoint? Is it not the way, and the only way, in which any part of the world has ever been evangelized? What were the apostles and first preachers of the Gospel, by whom so many nations were converted, but Christian missionaries? Was it not by missions that the Gospel was made known, according to the commandment of the everlasting God, for the obedience of faith, to the nations in the west and north of Europe, in the sixth, the seventh, and the following centuries; and that our own remote ancestors were turned from their idols to serve the living God, and to transmit the knowledge of salvation to their posterity? Had it not been for missions, the British islands, in which so many immortal spirits have been sanctified by the truth and prepared for heaven, and in which so much Christian beneficence is now displayed; these very islands, from which we derive our origin, our language, our laws, and our religion, might still have been inhabited by savages worshipping in the groves of the Druids, or offering human sacrifices to their false gods.

In later times, Ziegenbalg and Swartz in the East, and Eliot and Brainerd in the West, have given illustrious examples of what might be done by patient and persevering zeal in missionary labors, and not only shall their memory long be blessed on earth, but their witness is in heaven, and their record on high.

By means of the single missionary establishment at Tranquebar, first commenced by Ziegenbalg about a century ago, and afterwards conducted by his worthy successors, particularly by the venerable Swartz, not less, it is estimated, than *eighty thousand* Pagans, "forsaking their idols and their vices, have been added to the Christian Church." If not so much can be said of the missions of Eliot and Brainerd, it is to be considered, that their labors were among a people scattered in the wilderness, and that men of a like spirit were not found to succeed them in their work, and prosecute their pious design. Still, however, there were precious fruits of their labors, which will remain for joy and praise, in the kingdom of the Redeemer, when this world shall be no more. The general history of such missions as have at any time been conducted on Christian principles, and with a real regard to the salvation of the heathen, affords abundant encouragement to proceed with vigor, in the same glorious cause.

But if so much has been done by a few men, and in ordinary times, what may we not expect from united and extensive exertions in the present extraordinary period of the world? For sometime before the Messiah came, a light to lighten the Gentiles and the glory of his people Israel, an expectation extensively prevailed, that a glorious luminary was about to arise, and an important change to commence. Prophecies to this effect were on record, and the providence of God strikingly indicated their approaching fulfilment. Something very similar to all this is manifest in the present age. If the Messiah was then the Desire of all nations, his millennial reign is no less so now. If the seventy prophetic weeks of Daniel were then drawing to a close, the 1260 mystical days of the same Jewish prophet, and of the Christian prophet John, are now hastening to their completion. If the providence of God strikingly indicated the approach of the glorious change then expected, not less strikingly do the unusual events, which now astonish the nations, indicate the approach of a change still more glorious, because more complete and universal. The Lord himself has arisen *to shake terribly the earth,* and *to plead his own cause* with the nations. But though *the day of vengeance is in his heart, the year of his redeemed has come.*

Prophecy, history, and the present state of the world, seem to unite in declaring, that the great pillars of the Papal and Mahommedan impostures are now tottering to their fall. The civilized world is in a state of awful convulsion and unparalleled distress. At the same time, Christians are awakened to a perception of their peculiar duties, and to correspondent labors and sacrifices. New facilities are afforded for the dispersion of the Scriptures in many languages, for the establishment of missions, and the general promulgation of the Gospel. The enormity of the heathen superstition, and the unutterable evils which march in its train, stand forth to view in all their hideous proportions. Now is the time for the followers of Christ to come forward, bodly, and engage earnestly in the great work of enlightening and reforming mankind. Never was the glory of the Christian religion more clearly discernible; never was the futility of all other schemes more manifest; never were the encouragements to benevolent exertion greater, than at the present day. In the great conflict between truth and error, what Christian will refuse to take an active part? Satan has long deceived the nations, and held in ignorance and idolatry much the greater part of the human race. When his empire is assailed, and his throne begins to crumble under him, what friend of the Redeemer will refuse to come *to the help of the Lord, to the help of the Lord against the mighty?* Ultimate victory is secure, as it is promised by Him *who cannot lie, and in whose hands are the hearts of all men.* What Christian will not esteem it a privilege to become instrumental, though in a humble degree, in accomplishing the glorious and beneficent purposes of Jehovah, by extending the influence of the Gospel?

It appears from what has been stated in this address, and would more fully appear from a sketch of missionary exertions made during the last century, and especially during the last twenty years, that a *great and effectual door* for the promulgation of the Gospel among the heathen is now opened to all Christian nations· but to no nation is it more inviting, than to the people of New England. The truth of this declaration will be easily manifest from the following considerations·

First· No nation ever experienced the blessings of the Christian religion more evidently, and uniformly, than the inhabitants of New England, from its first colonization till the present time, through nearly two centuries. Of all our social and civil enjoyments, scarcely one is worthy to be mentioned, which is not derived directly, or indirectly, from this holy religion; and all the enjoyments, which concern us as immortal beings, spring directly from this source. If we were deprived of all the civilization and liberty, all the present consolations and future hopes, which we receive from the Gospel, what should we have left? Where is the Christian who would not mourn day and night, were he told, that at some future time, this favored land should sink into the superstition, corruption and impiety of Paganism; that the Sabbath should become extinct, our churches moulder to ruin, no voice of supplication ascend to Jehovah, no children be dedicated in baptism to the triune God, and no memorial be observed of the Redeemer's sufferings, atonement, death, and resurrection; that instead of the rational worship of Christian assemblies, future generations should behold some horrible idol receiving the adoration of deluded millions? Where is the person of common humanity, who would not lift up the voice of lamentation, at the certain prospect of such an apostacy from the truth, and such a debasing fall into the cruelties and debaucheries, the sins and miseries, of heathenism? If we should feel so intensely at the prospect of these evils befalling our own country, can we avoid being touched with compassion at the sight of many populous nations, which have been subjected for ages, and are still subjected, to the power of the most degrading idolatry? Are we not called upon in a peculiar manner, to exert ourselves in dispelling this worse than Egyptian darkness?

Let us reflect for a moment on the tendency of missionary exertions to promote religion among ourselves. The Rev. Mr. Grout, in his sermon before the Hampshire Missionary Society, observes, that "what seems to be peculiarly worthy of attention is, the unusual effusion of God's Spirit in and near the places where the missionary spirit has prevailed." "About nine years have elapsed," he adds, "since the establishment of this Society. In what other period of that length, have we witnessed in this country so many instances of the refreshings of Divine grace?" The preacher then pertinently inquires, "Do not these things, like the pillar of the cloud and of fire in the camp of Israel, betoken the Divine presence to have attended the course of missionary labors?" We press this question upon the consciences of Christians, and ask them to decide, from their own observation and experience, whether this is not a just view of the subject. It is an unchangeable law in the Divine government, that *it is more blessed to give than to receive*, and that *he that watereth, shall be also watered himself*. As we regard the salvation of our neighbors, our friends, our families, let us send the Gospel to the heathen.

Secondly: If all the circumstances of the case are considered, we are more able to take an active part in evangelizing the heathen, than any other people on the globe. With the exception of Great Britain, indeed, no nation but our own has the inclination, or the ability, to make great exertions in the prosecution of this design. Great Britain is engaged in a conflict for her existence, with a power which threatens to subjugate the civilized world; yet, beside all the expenses of this unexampled conflict; beside the millions paid for the support of the parish poor, and the immense aggregate of the sums given in occasional charity; beside the vast annual expenses of charity schools, hospitals, and many other benevolent institutions; beside the support of the regular Clergy, both of the Establishment and among Dissenters; beside these and many other expenses, Great Britain spends *hundreds of thousands of dollars*, annually, in distributing the Bible, employing Missionaries, translating the Scriptures, and other extraordinary methods of dispensing the Gospel to mankind. Our public burdens are light compared with those of England, and there is among us wealth sufficient, abundantly sufficient, to employ all the instruments which will be offered to our hands. We are accustomed to hear many encomiums on the liberality of Christians in England; let it be remembered, that these very encomiums will condemn us, unless we *go and do likewise*.

Let it not be supposed, that the embarrassment of our public affairs, and the consequent derangement of private business, and loss of private property, are forgotten. With these things in full view, it may still be truly said, that wealth enough can be spared from among us for the vigorous prosecution of this transcendently important purpose.

Nor should it be omitted, that there is no need of withholding a single dollar from the numerous Missionary and Bible Societies, and other charitable institutions, which are already in operation in our country. Our Missionary Societies have been for a number of years incalculable blessings to the new settlements and destitute places of the United States; and though our Bible Societies have been but lately formed, their prospects of usefulness are most encouraging. May the means of all these benevolent institutions increase continually; and may the same beneficence which patronizes them, be extended to satisfy the pressing calls of Foreign Missions.

The public will perceive, that a considerable sum of money is necessary before a mission to Asia can be commenced with any prospect of success; and that money is the only thing which is still wanting. Need another word be said to ensure liberal and extensive donations?

JEDIDIAH MORSE,
SAMUEL WORCESTER,
JEREMIAH EVARTS,

November, 1811.   *Committee appointed by the Board.*

MINUTES

OF THE

THIRD ANNUAL MEETING.

———

THE annual meeting of the American Board of Commissioners for Foreign Missions, was held at the house of Mr Henry Hudson, in Hartford, on Wednesday and Thursday the 16th and 17th days of September 1812;—Present,

Gen. JEDIDIAH HUNTINGTON,
Hon. JOHN TREADWELL, Esq. LL. D.
Rev. JOSEPH LYMAN, D. D.
Rev. TIMOTHY DWIGHT, D. D. LL. D.
Rev. SAMUEL SPRING, D. D.
Hon. JOHN HOOKER, Esq.
Rev. JEDIDIAH MORSE, D. D.
Rev. CALVIN CHAPIN.
Rev. SAMUEL WORCESTER, D. D.

The meeting was opened with prayer by the Rev. Dr. Dwight.

During the session the following gentlemen were unanimously elected members of the Board, viz. the Hon. JOHN LANGDON, LL. D. Esq., and the Rev. SETH PAYSON, D. D. of New Hampshire, the Rev. HENRY DAVIS, D. D. of Vermont; JEREMIAH EVARTS, Esq. of Massachusetts; His Excellency, WILLIAM JONES, Esq. of Rhode Island; the Hon. JOHN JAY, Esq. LL. D., the Rev. SAMUEL MILLER, D. D., the Hon. EGBERT BENSON, Esq. LL. D., and the Rev. ELIPHALET NOTT, D. D., of New York; the Hon. ELIAS BOUDINOT, Esq LL. D , and the Rev. JAMES RICHARDS, of New Jersey; and the Rev. ASHBEL GREEN, D. D., and ROBERT RALSTON, Esq , of Pennsylvania.

The following gentlemen were elected officers of the Board, viz.

The Hon. JOHN TREADWELL, Esq. LL. D. *President*.
Rev. SAMUEL SPRING, D. D. *Vice President*.
WILLIAM BARTLET, Esq.
Rev. SAMUEL SPRING, D.D.
Rev. SAMUEL WORCESTER, D. D. } *Prudential Committee*.
JEREMIAH EVARTS, Esq.
Rev. SAMUEL WORCESTER, D. D. *Corresponding Secretary*.
Rev CALVIN CHAPIN, *Recording Secretary*.
JEREMIAH EVARTS, Esq. *Treasurer*.
SAMUEL H. WALLEY, Esq. *Auditor*.

The Treasurer's accounts were exhibited. Mr. Goodale, the late Auditor, having removed to a distant part of the country, these accounts could not be audited before the meeting of the Board; but were referred to the present Auditor.

The Rev. Dr. Morse, the Rev. Dr. Worcester, and Mr. Evarts, were appointed a committee to prepare and publish an address to the public on the behalf the Board.

Voted, That the Prudential Committee pay an immediate and particular attention to the circulation of the Holy Scriptures in the various languages of the unevangelized nations; and that, as soon as expedient, they expend upon this object as much at least of the funds of the Board as the Act of Incorporation requires.

The report of the Prudential Committee was read and accepted.

The instructions of the Prudential Committee to the Missionaries, who lately sailed for India under the direction of the Board, were read and approved.

Voted, That the Prudential Committee annually transmit a copy of the doings of this Board, to the General Association of New Hampshire, the General Convention of Congregational and Presbyterian ministers in Vermont, the General Association of Massachusetts Proper, the General Association of Connecticut, and the General Assembly of the Presbyterian Church in the United States.

Voted, That the Treasurer be requested to return the thanks of this Board, as far as practicable, to all those who have heretofore contributed for the purposes of the institution.

Voted, That the Hon. John Hooker, Esq. and the Rev. Dr. Lyman be a committee to procure the printing, in the Iroquois language, of such Christian writings as, in their judgment, may be expedient for the use of the Iroquois Indians; and that they distribute them according to their discretion.

Voted, That the Treasurer give bond to the Board for the faithful discharge of the duties of his office, in the sum of twenty thousand dollars, with sufficient sureties, to be approved by a major part of the Prudential Committee.

Voted, That this Board will receive Mr. Eleazer Williams under their patronage, and support him in completing his education for the ministry; provided, he shall consent to submit himself to the direction of the Board:

Voted, That the President of this Board, the Rev. Dr. Lyman, and the Rev. Mr. Chapin, be a committee to consider, and report upon, that part of the report of the Prudential Committee, which regards an intercourse between this Board and the Auxiliary Foreign Mission Societies.

The Editor of the Panoplist, made a written proposition to the Board to the following effect:—That all the profits of that publication, after a reasonable allowance for his services as Editor shall have been deducted, be devoted to the promotion of the missionary cause under the direction of this Board; and that the amount of such reasonable allowance be fixed, at the close of each volume, by a committee mutually agreed upon between himself and the Board. This arrangement to commence with the next volume,* should the work be continued as usual.

---

* A similar arrangement exists with respect to the current volume; though the Board, not being in session when it was formed, could not be made a party to it.

To prevent misconception, it was expressly stated, that the Editor did not wish to have such an arrangement considered as an approbation of the Panoplist on the part of the Board, or as connecting the Board in any manner with that work; but simply as a method mutually agreed upon to find what are the real profits of the publication.

It was also stated, that it shall always be in the power of the Committee to designate the specific objects to which said profits shall be applied, and which shall always be such as said Committee shall judge to be peculiarly important to the missionary cause.

The foregoing proposition was accepted, and the following gentlemen were mutually agreed upon as the Committee, viz. the Rev. Joshua Huntington of Boston, the Rev. John Codman of Dorchester, Dr. Reuben D. Mussey of Salem, Henry Gray, Esq of Boston, and the Rev. Moses Stuart, Professor in the Theological Seminary at Andover.

Voted, That the Treasurer loan or invest the money in the Treasury, or such part of it as may be judged expedient, with the concurrence and under the direction of the Prudential Committee.

Voted, That the next annual meeting of the Board be held at Concert Hall in Boston, on the third Wednesday of September, 1813, at 10 o'clock, A. M.

The Rev. President Dwight was appointed to preach on the occasion, and the Rev. Mr. Chapin was appointed his substitute.

Voted, That the President and the Recording Secretary present the thanks of this Board to Mr. Henry Hudson for the proof of his regard to the cause of Foreign Missions, manifested by the very hospitable and generous manner in which he has provided for the members during the present session.

The session was closed with prayer by the Vice President.

REPORT.

WITH high sensibility, and with lively gratitude to the Redeemer and King of Zion, the Prudential Committee of the American Board of Commissioners for Foreign Missions meet their Brethren on the present occasion, and make their annual Report.

The purposes of the Board, distinctly expressed at the last meeting, it has been the desire and endeavor of the Committee to carry into effect as early, and to as great an extent, as practicable. As soon as convenient, an address to the public on the subject of missions to the heathen was prepared and printed, and care was taken to give to it an extensive and efficacious circulation. In the separate sheet, and in the Panoplist and Missionary Magazine, it has found access to the different parts of our country; and there is reason to believe that its effect, in exciting attention to its great object, and in awakening and spreading the missionary spirit, has been very considerable. The Committee, however, could not entirely rely on the address, or any other means which had been put in operation, for the immediate and permanent supply of funds requisite to answer their wishes and those of the Board. Four missionaries were waiting, and had long been waiting, with a degree of impatience, to be sent out with the everlasting gospel to the perishing millions of the East; and the Committee were earnestly desirous to relieve their

5

impatience, and to embrace the earliest opportunity for conveying them to the destined field of their labors. But for this purpose thousands of dollars were wanting.

When contemplating possible ways and means, no plan presented itself to the Committee as more eligible, than to institute in the principal towns in New England and in other states, as far as practicable, societies auxiliary to this Board, and whose special business should be to aid in procuring funds. This plan, it was hoped, would bring immediate help in the existing exigency, combine extensively the influence of the friends of missions, give increase and efficiency to the missionary spirit, and open durable sources of supply to the treasury. The plan was adopted early in the winter. Mr John Frost, a licentiate preacher, in whom the Committee had great confidence, was appointed an agent, and invested with a commission to assist in carrying it into execution; and the success has exceeded the most sanguine expectations. About twenty societies have been formed, more than four thousand dollars have been remitted from them to the treasury; and the annual subscriptions in them, though they cannot be accurately estimated at present, amount to a very considerable sum. These societies cannot but be regarded as vastly important to the general concern, and as claiming very particular attention; and the Committee would respectfully submit, whether some measures should not be adopted to extend, to animate, and to strengthen them; and to establish between them and this Board a regular and permanent intercourse.

Though the Committee were very desirous to be in a state of preparation to send out the waiting missionaries by the first conveyance; yet, such were the commercial embarrassments, but little expectation was entertained that a conveyance would soon occur. But He, who has the times and the seasons in his hands, and whose, especially, is the missionary cause, knew the day and the hour. In the latter part of January, Messrs. Newell and Hall, the two missionary brethren, who had resided for some time at Philadelphia on account of the medical advantages there enjoyed, returned in haste with the intelligence, that a ship called the Harmony was shortly to sail from that port for Calcutta, and would afford accommodations for the missionaries This return was by the particular advice of Robert Ralston, Esq, a name well known, and greatly endeared to the friends of missions, in Europe and India, as well as in this country; and from him they brought a letter, presenting the opportunity in a very favorable light, and kindly offering assurances of his attention and aid. The Committee immediately met, and the moment was an important one. The Harmony was to sail in about a fortnight; if that opportunity were not embraced it could not be foreseen when another would occur; but the funds then at the disposal of the Committee did not exceed twelve hundred dollars. After serious deliberation, however, the Committee were impressed with the persuasion that divine Providence called for an immediate and great effort; and they resolved to send out the four missionaries by the Harmony, and took their measures accordingly.

It was on Monday the 27th of January that this resolution was taken. The ordination of the missionaries was appointed to be on the Thursday of the next week, the latest day, which would leave time for them to get on to Philadelphia in season. Notice was immediately given to the friends of the mission in the vicinity, and means were put in operation with all possible activity, and to as great an extent as the limited time would allow, for raising the requisite funds.

In the mean time, Mr. Luther Rice, a licentiate preacher from the Theological Institution at Andover, whose heart had long been engaged in the missionary cause, but who had been restrained from offering himself to the Board by particular circumstances, presented himself to the Committee with good recommendations, and with an earnest desire to join the mission. The case was a very trying one. The Committee were not invested with full powers to admit missionaries, and they still felt a very heavy embarrassment from the want of funds. In view of all the circumstances, however, they did not dare to reject Mr. Rice; and they came to the conclusion to assume the responsibility, and admit him as a missionary, to be ordained with the four other brethren, and sent out with them. This responsibility still rests upon the Committee. But with the pleasing consciousness that they acted in the case under an impressive sense of duty, and with a sacred view to advance the great design of this Board, they cheerfully submit themselves to the inquiry and to the judgment of their brethren.

While the preparations were making, it came to the knowledge of the Committee, that the brigantine Caravan, of Salem, was to sail for Calcutta in a few days, and could carry out three or four passengers; and, after attention to the subject, it was deemed advisable, that two of the missionaries, with their wives, should take passage in that vessel. This lessened the general risk, and was attended with several advantages.

According to appointment, on the sixth of February, the missionaries were ordained, at the Tabernacle in Salem. A season of more impressive solemnity has scarcely been witnessed in our country. The sight of five young men, of highly respectable talents and attainments, and who might reasonably have promised themselves very eligible situations in our churches, forsaking parents, and friends, and country, and every alluring earthly prospect, and devoting themselves to the privations, hardships, and perils of a mission for life, to a people sitting in darkness and in the region and shadow of death, in a far distant and unpropitious clime, could not fail deeply to affect every heart, not utterly destitute of feeling. Nor less affecting were the views, which the whole scene was calculated to impress, of the deplorable condition of the Pagan world, of the riches of divine grace displayed in the gospel, and of the obligations on all, on whom this grace is conferred, to use their utmost endeavors in making the gospel universally known. God was manifestly present: a crowded and attentive assembly testified, with many tears, the deep interest which they felt in the occasion; and not a few remember the scene with fervent gratitude, and can say, it *was good to be there.*

After the public solemnities, arrangements for the departure of the missionaries were made with all possible despatch; and, on the evening of the same day, brethren Nott, Hall, and Rice, took their leave in haste, that they might not fail of arriving at Philadelphia, in season for taking their passage in the Harmony. Those who remained were expected to sail early in the next week. Circumstances occurred, however, by which both the vessels were detained for several days; and it was not until the 19th of February that brethren Judson and Newell with their wives sailed in the Caravan from Salem; and about the same time brethren Nott, Hall, and Rice, with the wife of Mr. Nott, and several missionaries from England, left the Delaware in the Harmony.

The delay of the vessels was highly auspicious: and the Committee would do violence to their feelings, and be greatly wanting in attention to a subject for high thankfulness to God, should they refrain from expressing the deep impression which they have felt of his particular providence in the whole business of preparing and sending out the mission. When the resolution was taken to embrace the opportunity by the Harmony, the utmost which the Committee expected to be able to do was, to fit out the four missionaries then engaged without their wives; or, if their wives should go, to advance to them only a half year's, instead of a whole year's, salary; or else to retain only two of them in the employment of this Board, and resign the other two to the London Missionary Society. Probably, indeed, the resolution could not have been taken at all, but for the commission which had been obtained from that Society. For the Committee cast themselves upon divine Providence in the case, with the alternative distinctly in view, that should they fail of seasonably obtaining the funds to enable them to send out the missionaries in the employment of this Board, they could, in the last resort, let them go under the London commission. Having this alternative, they ventured upon a measure, which otherwise, (so doubtful was the prospect of obtaining the pecuniary means,) they probably would have judged presumptuous. And they acted upon the same principle, when they added Mr. Rice to the mission. Nor was it until after the solemnities of the ordination, that they felt themselves warranted decisively to resolve on sending all the missionaries in the service, and at the expense, of this Board; and even then, their expectations extended no further than to an advance for each missionary of a half year's salary. But the Lord made it to be remembered that *the silver and the gold are his.* The hearts of the people were wonderfully opened; money flowed in from all quarters; and by the time that the Caravan sailed, the Committee were able to meet all the expenses of fitting out the missionaries, and to advance for each of them a whole year's salary. In addition to this, collections were made at Philadelphia, during the same interval of delay, and delivered to the brethren who sailed from that port, to such an amount, as to make the whole which was paid to the missionaries in advance, equal to their stipulated salary for a year and a quarter nearly. This deserves very grateful notice; for had our brethren been sent out, as it was expected they must be, with provision only for six months, such is the obstructed state of commercial intercourse, and the uncertainty of making remittances to India, that not only the Committee and this whole Board, but the friends of the mission generally, must have been distressed with apprehensions of the sufferings to which, for want of the means of support, they might have been exposed. GOD WILL PROVIDE; *God did provide.* Within about three weeks, reckoning from the commencement of the special arrangements, more than six thousand dollars were collected for the mission Several societies, and many individuals, shewed a liberality, which entitles them to the very grateful acknowledgments of this Board, and of all the friends of the Redeemer's cause; and which, it is devoutly to be hoped, will be a precious memorial of them, in his kingdom forever. While contemplating the providence of God in these transactions at large, it should not be overlooked that, had not our brethren been sent out at the very time they were, as no opportunities have since occurred, and as none are now likely soon to occur, the mission must have been delayed for a long time, and perhaps even till the close of the present deplorable war.

Since their departure, no intelligence has been received from the missionaries. As they were commended to the grace of God, with many prayers and tears, they will not cease to be so commended; and to Him, under whose signal auspices they went out, and whose own glory is the ultimate object of all sincere attempts to spread the gospel and to save the heathen, the whole disposal of the mission may be safely referred. And it becomes all who feel an interest in it, to hold themselves prepared devoutly to bless his name, whether he crown it with success answerable to their hopes, or in his inscrutable wisdom disappoint their expectations, and make it a subject of severe trial to their faith.

The instructions given to the missionaries were necessarily drawn up in great haste: but they will be submitted, with leave, to the consideration and for the revision of the Board.

Under the direction of the Committee, Messrs. Richards and Warren, who were accepted by the Board at the last annual meeting, have been favored with advantages of medical instruction in the intervals allowed by the Theological Institution of which they are members; both of them at Dartmouth College the last autumn, and one of them since, with Dr. Miller of Franklin, and the other with Dr. Mussey of Salem. And the particular thanks of this Board are due to the gentlemen Professors of the Medical Institution at Dartmouth, and the two physicians who afforded their private instructions, for their ready liberality. The two brethren hold themselves still at the direction of this Board, with a readiness of mind to enter into active service, as soon as Providence shall open the door for the purpose.

Mr. Eleazer Williams, the Indian youth proposed for an Indian mission, and who is in a course of education for this purpose, partly at the expense of this Board, made a visit, in the course of the last winter, to his tribe, a journal of which has been seen by the Committee. It is an excellent journal; affords great evidence of the piety and good sense of Mr. Williams; and details some facts highly favorable to his reception among his red brethren, when the time shall come for him to be sent to them. When that time will come, is known only to Him who has all events under his sovereign direction. At present, the prospect regarding the contemplated mission to the Caghnawaga Indians, and that regarding the missions to the East, are darkened by war; but this darkness may be dissipated, and brighter scenes open than men can foresee.

For reasons, which will be obvious to this Board, it was judged advisable to apply to the Legislature of Massachusetts for an act enduing the Board with corporate powers and privileges. An application was accordingly made, which ultimately succeeded. The act will be submitted to the consideration of the Board.

On a review, the Committee are persuaded that their brethren, as well as themselves, will recognize many precious reasons of thankfulness to God; many impressive tokens of his gracious regard to our great design;

many signal encouragements to prosecute the design with renewed and increased devotedness and activity. The war may embarrass our operations, but should not restrain our efforts. If the sure word of prophecy warns us of perils and calamities, of *distress of nations with perplexity;* it gives us assurance also, that in these *troublous times,* the gospel shall be extensively propagated, and that in *overturning, and overturning, and overturning,* the Lord is making way for the establishment in all the earth of that kingdom which cannot be shaken. *If the Day of vengeance is in his heart, the year of his redeemed is come.* Great Britain, while sustaining a conflict unexampled in the history of the world, is displaying a liberality, a zeal, and a spirit of enterprise, for imparting the word of life and the blessings of salvation to all people, to enemies as well as to friends, not less strikingly unexampled. And in this glorious work, so far from being checked by any pressure of burdens or difficulties, she continues without remission, and abounds more and more. By her admirable example, America should be provoked to emulation. Under no circumstances should we faint or be discouraged; but, trusting in God, in whose cause we are engaged, if difficulties present themselves, our zeal should rise, and our efforts be augmented. The word is sure; He, who reigns on the holy hill of Zion, shall have *the heathen for his inheritance, and the uttermost parts of the earth for his possession.* We hail him LORD OF LORDS, AND KING OF KINGS; we rejoice in the opening prospects of his kingdom; and to be instrumental in extending his dominion, and the blessings of his salvation, will be our highest glory.

INSTRUCTIONS

GIVEN BY THE PRUDENTIAL COMMITTEE OF THE AMERICAN BOARD OF COMMISSIONERS FOR FOREIGN MISSIONS, TO THE MISSIONARIES TO THE EAST, FEBRUARY 7, 1812.

"*To the Rev. Adoniram Judson, Samuel Nott, Samuel Newell, Gordon Hall, and Luther Rice, Missionaries to the East, under the American Board of Commissioners for Foreign Missions.*

"VERY DEAR BRETHREN,—As in divine Providence, we are specially charged with the weighty care of the Mission in which you are engaged, it devolves on us, as a sacred duty, to give some instructions for your observance. These instructions, owing to a pressure of circumstances, and the want of certainty in regard to some important points relating to the mission, will, doubtless, be more imperfect than otherwise they might have been; and it will rest with us, or with our successors in this care, hereafter to make them more complete.

"1. Your first concern, dear Brethren, must be *personal.* As you have given yourselves to the service of God in the gospel of His Son among the Gentiles, it will be of the utmost importance, not only that you be sincere and without offence, but also that your hearts be kept constantly burning with love to God, to the Lord Jesus Christ, and to the souls of men. In order to this, you will be much in the exercises of devotion; in reading, meditation, and prayer; you will be religiously observant of all the precepts, ordinances, and instructions of the gospel; and you will 'exercise yourselves to have always consciences void of offence, both towards God, and towards men. Keep under your bodies, and bring them into subjection. Keep your hearts with all diligence. Live by faith in Christ Jesus. Walk before God, and be perfect.'

"2. 'Have fervent charity among yourselves. Let there be no strife among you, which of you shall be accounted the greatest: but he that is greatest among you, let him be as the younger; and he that is chief, as he that doth serve. Ye have one Master, even Christ; and all ye are brethren. Be watchful over one another, in the spirit of meekness; and provoke one another only to love and good works.'

"3. The Christian Missionaries of every Protestant denomination, sent from Europe to the East, you will regard as your brethren; the servants of the same Master, and engaged in the same work with yourselves. With them your only competition will be, who shall display most of the spirit, and do most for the honor, of Christ; with them you will be ready to cultivate the best understanding, and to reciprocate every Christian and friendly office; and with them you will cheerfully co-operate, as far as consistently you can, in any measure for the advancement of the common cause. However it may be with others, let it never, dear Brethren, be your fault, if among the converts to Christianity in the East, every one shall say, 'I am of Paul, and I of Apollos, and I of Cephas, and I of Christ;' but remember, that there 'is one body, and one Spirit, even as believers are all called in one hope of their calling: one Lord, one faith, one baptism, one God and Father of all, who is above all, and through all, and in them all.'

"4. Wherever your lot may be cast, you will withhold yourselves most scrupulously from all interference with the powers that be; and from all intermeddling with political concerns. You will sacredly remember who has said, 'Render unto Cæsar the things that are Cæsar's, and unto God the things that are God's. Render unto all, therefore, their dues: tribute, to whom tribute is due; custom, to whom custom; fear to whom fear; honor, to whom honor. Submit yourselves to every ordinance of man, for the Lord's sake.'

"5. 'As much as in you lies live peaceably with all men.' You go, dear Brethren, as the messengers of love, of peace, of salvation, to people whose opinions and customs, habits and manners, are widely different from those to which you have been used; and it will not only comport with the spirit of your mission, but be essential to its success, that, as far as you can, you conciliate their affection, their esteem, and their respect. You will, therefore, make it your care to preserve yourselves from all fastidiousness of feeling, and of deportment: to avoid every occasion of unnecessary offence, or disgust to those among whom you may sojourn; and in regard to all matters of indifference, or in which conscience is not concerned, to make yourselves easy and agreeable to them. In this, as well as in most other things, you will do well to hold in view the example of Paul, the first and most distinguished missionary to the heathen; who, 'though he was free from all, yet made himself servant unto all, that he might gain the more; and became all things to all men, that by all means he might save some.' When you behold the superstitions and abominations of the heathen, your 'spirits,' indeed, 'will be stirred in you,' and you will be very jealous for your God and Savior. But even then, you will take heed that your zeal be according to knowledge, and tempered with the meekness of wisdom. In all things, it will behove you, dear Brethren, 'to be harmless and blameless, the children of God without rebuke;' to show to the Gentiles the excellent character of the religion of the gospel, and to let them see in you a living example of 'whatsoever things are true, of whatsoever things are honest, of whatsoever things are just, of whatsoever things are pure, of whatsoever things are lovely, of whatsoever things are of good report.'

"6. From the best views, which we have been able to obtain, our present desire is, that the seat of this mission should be in some part of the empire of Birmah. After your arrival in India, however, you will make it an object to avail yourselves of information relating to that empire, and also relating to other parts of the East; and after due deliberation, you will be at your discretion as to the place where to make your station. It will also, in a similar manner, rest with you to determine, whether the great object of the mission will probably be best promoted, by your residing together in one place, or by occupying separate stations. In regard to those very important points, however, it is expected that you will act with unanimity; certainly, that you act only with a due regard each to the views and feelings of the rest, to our known desire and expectation, and to the essential interests of the Mission.

"You will perceive, dear Brethren, the very urgent importance of observing strict economy, in regard both to your time and expenditures. You will therefore, make it your care to get to the field, or fields, of your labors, as soon and with as little expense as possible.

"7. For yourselves and for the object of the mission, it will be important that you adopt, as early as possible, some plan of polity, or social order. The office of presiding in your little community should, for very obvious reasons, we think, be held in rotation. You will have a treasurer, and a secretary or clerk, that your financial concerns may be conducted, and the records of your proceedings kept, with regularity and correctness. The rules and regulations which you adopt, you will transmit to us for our consideration. Of the journals of the mission, also, to which you will pay very particular attention, and in which you will regularly note whatever may be interesting to you, or to us, you will, as often as convenient, transmit to us copies

"8. No time should be lost in forming yourselves into a church, according to the order divinely prescribed, that you may attend in due form upon the worship and ordinances of Christ's house. This will be of great importance, both to yourselves, and to the people among whom you dwell. The ordinance of the Lord's supper should be administered, we think, as often at least, as once in every month; and you will freely reciprocate the privilege of communicating in this ordinance with other Christians in regular church standing.

"In all places, and especially among people superstitiously observant of their own sacred times and seasons, a very exemplary observance of the Sabbath is of the very first importance to Christianity. This, dear brethren, you cannot too deeply feel; and it will be your care that Pagans shall not have occasion to say, or to think, that Christians have no reverence for the ordinances of their God. It is by their eyes, not less than by their ears, that you are to gain access to their hearts. In regard, also, to the time of beginning the Sabbath, you will perceive it to be not of little consequence, that you be conscientiously agreed.

"9. The great object of your Mission is to impart to those who sit in darkness, and in the region and shadow of death, the saving knowledge of Christ. In order to this it will be a matter of primary attention to make yourselves acquainted with the language of the people, with whom you are to converse, and to whom you are to preach. You will not, however, neglect any opportunity or means of doing them good, even before you can use their language; but you will give yourselves wholly to your work, and use all care that you 'run not in vain, neither labor in vain.' The deplorable ignorance of the poor heathen will constantly be in your minds, and deeply affect your hearts. To them you are to make known the 'words by which they and their children may be saved.' To them you are to teach, not the commandments, or the dogmas of men; but the pure doctrines of the gospel, drawn directly from the Scriptures of truth. You will most religiously beware of that 'philosophy, and vain deceit, which is after the tradition of men, after the rudiments of the world, and not after Christ, and avoid questions and strifes of words, whereof come envy, strife, revilings, evil surmises, and perverse disputings of men of corrupt minds.'

"In teaching the Gentiles, it will be your business, not vehemently to declaim against their superstitions, but in the meekness and gentleness of Christ, to bring them as directly as possible to the knowledge of divine truth. It is 'the truth, THE TRUTH AS IT IS IN JESUS, which is mighty through God to the pulling down of strong holds, casting down imaginations, and every high thing, which exalteth itself against the knowledge of God; and bringing every thought into captivity to the obedience of Christ.' So far as the truth has access so as to produce its effect, the errors, and superstitions, and vices of Paganism will fall of course. You will beware of the rock on which Missionaries have too often split; and not at once advance upon the uninstructed with things beyond their power to understand. Beginning with the 'first principles' of the doctrine of Christ, you will proceed in your instructions gradually, with patience and wisdom, feeding the people with milk, until they have strength to bear meat. And for their good unto salvation, it will be your delight, as it will be your duty, to be 'instant in season, and out of season; to be their servants for Jesus' sake, and to spend and be spent.'

"10. If God, in his infinite grace, prosper your labors, and give you the happiness to see converts to the truth, you will proceed in regard to them, at once with charity and caution. You will allow sufficient time for trial, and for the reality of conversion to be attested by its fruits; that, as far as possible, the scandal of apostasy may be prevented. You will admit none as members of the church of Christ, but such as give credible evidence that they are true believers; and none to the ordinance of baptism, but credible believers and their households. The discipline of Christ's house, you will charitably and faithfully observe.

"11. As in Christian lands, so in all lands, the hope of the church is principally from the rising generation. Youth and children, therefore, will be objects of your very particular solicitude and attention; and no pains will be spared either by yourselves, or by our dear sisters, your wives, for their Christian education.

"12. It will be your desire, as it is ours, to lighten as much as possible the expenses of the Mission; that by the pious liberalities of this country, your establishment may be enlarged, and other missions supported. So far, therefore, as you can consistently with your missionary duties, you will apply yourselves to the most eligible ways and means of procuring a support for yourselves and families, agreeably to the example of European missionaries, and even of the apostles.

"*Dearly beloved brethren,*

You cannot but be sensible of the vast responsibility under which you are to act. Yo are made a spectacle to God, to angels and to men. The eyes of the friends, and of the enemies, of Christ and his cause will be upon you. You are the objects of the prayers, and of the hopes, and of the liberalities, of many. On your conduct in your mission, incalculable consequences, both to the Christian and to the Pagan world, are depending. "Be strong in the Lord, and be faithful. Count not even your lives dear unto yourselves, so that you may finish your course with joy, and the ministry which you have received of the Lord Jesus, to testify the Gospel of the grace of God." With fervent prayers for your safety, your welfare, and your success, we commend you, dear brethren, to God, and to the word of his grace.

A true copy from the Records of the Prudential Committee,

  Attest,   SAMUEL WORCESTER,

Salem, Feb. 7, 1812.   *Clerk of the Prudential Committee.*

PECUNIARY ACCOUNTS

The American Board of Commissioners, in account current with Jeremiah Evarts, their Treasurer, Dr.

To cash paid in conformity to orders, from No. 1 to No. 22, inclusive, signed by the clerk of the Prudential Committee, between the annual meeting in September, 1811, and the passing of the Act of incorporation, June 20, 1812, viz. for,

Expenses incurred in the prosecution of the objects of the Board,	9,327 04	
Payment of money borrowed,	360 00	9,687 04
To losses by counterfeit money received in donations,		12 33
		9,699 37
To balance carried to new account,		4,091 63
		$13,791 00

Contra Cr.

By cash remaining in the hands of the Prudential Committee, at the annual meeting in 1811, and since accounted for to the Treasurer,	843 64
By cash borrowed by the Prudential Committee in Feb. 1812,	360 00
By cash received in donations between the annual meeting in Sept. 1811, and June 20, 1812,	12,587 36
	$13,791 00

ACT OF INCORPORATION.

COMMONWEALTH OF MASSACHUSETTS.

In the year of our Lord One Thousand Eight Hundred and Twelve.

An Act to incorporate the American Board of Commissioners for Foreign Missions.

Whereas WILLIAM BARTLET and others have been associated under the name of the American Board of Commissioners for Foreign Missions, for the purpose of propagating the Gospel in heathen lands, by supporting Missionaries and diffusing a knowledge of the Holy Scriptures, and have prayed to be incorporated in order more effectually to promote the laudable object of their association.

SEC. 1. *Be it enacted by the Senate and House of Representatives in General Court Assembled, and by the authority of the same,* That WILLIAM BARTLET, Esq. and SAMUEL SPRING, D. D. both of Newburyport, JOSEPH LYMAN, D. D. of Hatfield, JEDIDIAH MORSE, D. D. of Charlestown, SAMUEL WORCESTER, D. D. of Salem, the Hon. WILLIAM PHILLIPS, Esq. of Boston, and the Hon. JOHN HOOKER, Esq. of Springfield, and their associates, be, and they hereby are incorporated and made a body politic, by the name of the AMERICAN BOARD OF COMMISSIONERS FOR FOREIGN MISSIONS; and by that name may sue and be sued, plead and be impleaded, appear, prosecute, and defend, to final judgment and execution; and in their said corporate capacity, they, and their successors forever, may take, receive, have and hold in fee-simple or otherwise, lands, tenements, and hereditaments, by gift, grant, devise, or otherwise, not exceeding the yearly value of four thousand dollars; and may also take and hold by donation, bequest, or otherwise, personal estate to an amount, the yearly income of which shall not exceed eight thousand dollars; so that the estate aforesaid shall be faithfully appropriated to the purpose and object aforesaid, and not otherwise. And the said corporation shall have power to sell, convey, exchange, or lease all or any part of their lands, tenements, or other property, for the benefit of their funds; and may have a common seal which they may alter or renew at pleasure. *Provided,* however, that nothing herein contained shall enable the said corporation, or any person or persons as trustees for or for the use of said corporation, to receive and hold any gift, grant, legacy, or bequest, heretofore given or bequeathed to any person in trust for said Board, unless such person or persons, could by law have taken and holden the same, if this act had not passed.

SEC. 2. *Be it further enacted,* That the said Board may annually choose from among themselves, by ballot, a President, a Vice-President, and a Prudential Committee; and, also, from among themselves or others a Corresponding Secretary, a Recording Secretary, a Treasurer, an Auditor, and such other officers as they may deem expedient; all of whom shall hold their offices until others are chosen to succeed them; and shall have such powers and perform such duties, as the said Board may order and direct; and in case of vacancy by death, resignation, or otherwise, the vacancy may in like manner be filled at any legal meeting of the said Board. And the said Treasurer shall give bond with suf-

ficient surety, or sureties, in the judgment of the Board, or the Prudential Committee, for the faithful discharge of the duties of his office.

SEC. 3. *Be it further enacted,* That all contracts, and deeds, which
the said Board may lawfully make and execute, signed by the Chairman
of said Prudential Committee, and countersigned by their Clerk, (whom
they are hereby authorized to appoint,) and sealed with the common seal
of said corporation, shall be valid in law to all intents and purposes.

SEC. 4. *Be it further enacted,* That the first annual meeting of the
said Board shall be on the third Wednesday of September next, at such
place as the said William Bartlet may appoint; and the present officers
of said Board shall continue in office until others are elected.

SEC. 5. *Be it further enacted,* That the said Board, at the first annual meeting aforesaid, and at any subsequent annual meeting, may
elect by ballot any suitable persons to be members of said Board, either
to supply vacancies, or in addition to their present number.

SEC. 6. *Be it further enacted,* That the said Board shall have
power to make such bye-laws, rules, and regulations, for calling future
meetings of said Board, and for the management of their concerns, as
they shall deem expedient; *provided* the same are not repugnant to the
laws of this Commonwealth.

SEC. 7. *Be it further enacted,* That one quarter part of the annual
income from the funds of said Board shall be faithfully appropriated to
defray the expense of imparting the Holy Scriptures to unevangelized
nations in their own languages. *Provided,* that nothing herein contained
shall be so construed as to defeat the express intentions of any testator,
or donor, who shall give or bequeath money to promote the great purposes of the Board: *Provided,* also, that nothing herein contained shall
be so construed, as to restrict said Board from appropriating more than
one quarter of said income to translating and distributing the Scriptures,
whenever they shall deem it advisable.

SEC. 8 *Be it further enacted,* That not less than one third of said
Board shall at all times be composed of respectable laymen; and that
not less than one third of said Board shall be composed of respectable
clergymen; the remaining third to be composed of characters of the
same description, whether clergymen or laymen.

SEC. 9. *Be it further enacted,* That the legislature of this Commonwealth shall at any time have a right to inspect, by a Committee of their
own body, the doings, funds, and proceedings of the said Corporation,
and may at their pleasure alter or annul any or all of the powers herein
granted.

In the House of Representatives, June 19th, 1812.—This bill, having
had three several readings, passed to be enacted.

TIMOTHY BIGELOW, *Speaker.*

In the Senate, June 20th, 1812.—This bill, having had two readings,
passed to be enacted.   SAMUEL DANA, *President.*

June 20, 1812.—By the Governor, Approved,   CALEB STRONG.

Copy—Attest, ALDEN BRADFORD, *Secretary of the Commonwealth.*

N. B. The *Associates,* alluded to in the foregoing act, were the Hon.
JOHN TREADWELL, Esq. LL.D., the Rev. TIMOTHY DWIGHT, D.D. LL.D.
President of Yale College, Gen. JEDIDIAH HUNTINGTON, and the Rev.
CALVIN CHAPIN, all of Connecticut.

BYE-LAWS.

At a meeting of the Board held by adjournment, in Boston, Nov. 9, 1812, the following Bye-Laws were adopted.

CHAPTER I. *Of the Duties of the Officers.*

SECTION 1. It shall be the duty of the President, and, in his absence of the Vice President, and, in the absence of both President and Vice President, of the oldest member of the Board present, to preside at each meeting of the Board, and to perform such official acts, either during the session of the Board, or at any other time, as shall be assigned to him by any future bye-law, or any future vote of the Board.

2. It shall be the duty of the Prudential Committee to carry into effect all votes and orders of the Board, the execution of which shall not have been assigned to some other Committee;—to superintend all the missions instituted or patronized by the Board;—to examine, counsel, instruct, and direct, all missionaries approved by the Board;—to beep the Bond given by the Treasurer to the Board, in pursuance of the Act of Incorporation;—to draw orders on the Treasurer, authorizing the payment of all monies which shall be expended under their direction;—to prescribe the place where the money of the Board shall be deposited;—to direct the loaning of monies, or the purchasing of productive stock, as they shall judge most conducive to the interests of the Board;—to ascertain the state of the Treasury at least twice a year, and oftener if they see cause;—to appoint, or authorize the appointment of, such agents at home and abroad, as may, in their opinion, be necessary to secure a safe remittance and a faithful expenditure of monies, and for such other purposes as in their judgment the interest of the Board may require;—and to perform any other duties, which shall be necessary, in their opinion, to carry into effect the foregoing powers, or to promote the interests of the Board, provided the same shall not be contrary to any vote or bye-law of the Board, nor to the Act of Incorporation.

The Prudential Committee shall appoint one of their number to be their Clerk, whose duty it shall be to keep a full record of their doings, and to sign all their orders and other official acts. The records above described shall be always open to the inspection of the Board

3. It shall be the duty of the Corresponding Secretary to act as the organ of the Board in conducting the written correspondences between this Board and similar institutions, and between this Board and individuals, at home and abroad, generally; and to make such written communications as the Board or the Prudential Committee shall particularly direct

4. It shall be the duty of the Recording Secretary to keep accurate minutes of the proceedings of the Board, and to enter the same in a book of records, and to certify all such doings of the Board as are to be known only by an inspection of the records.

5. It shall be the duty of the Treasurer to receive all monies or other property given, contributed, or paid to the funds of the Board,

and to give receipts therefor;—to keep safely all the monies of the Board, and all notes, bonds, deeds, and other evidences of property,—to pay out monies according to the orders of the Prudential Committee signed by their Clerk, or of the Board signed by the Recording Secretary;—to keep fair and accurate accounts of all monies received and expended;—to make up particular annual accounts, and estimates, for the information of the Board;—to loan and invest monies, and make remittances, according to the direction of the Board, or of the Prudential Committee,—to exhibit his accounts, whenever required, to the Board or the Prudential Committee,—and to do such other acts as experience may prove to be necessary, in order to a faithful execution of the duties of his office.

6. It shall be the duty of the Auditor to examine the Books of the Treasurer thoroughly and particularly, at least once a year; and, if he shall find the accounts correctly kept and accurately computed, the payments well vouched for, and the balance satisfactorily stated and accounted for, to give his certificate accordingly; which certificate he shall enter at large in the Treasurer's books, and transmit a duplicate thereof to the Recording Secretary.

CHAPTER II.   *Of the meetings of the Board.*

SECTION 1. There shall be an annual meeting of this Board, on the third Wednesday of September in each year, until the Board shall, at any annual meeting, fix upon some other day for that purpose. The place of holding each annual meeting shall be fixed by vote at the annual meeting next preceding. The officers of the Board shall be chosen at each annual meeting, and shall hold their offices until others are elected.

2. It shall be the duty of the President, or (in case of his death or inability) of the Vice President, or (in case of the death or inability of both President and Vice President) of the oldest member of the Board, to call a special meeting of the Board, on the written application of the Prudential Committee, or any three other members of the Board. The time and place of holding the meeting shall be such as the officer who calls the meeting shall appoint. On receiving an application as above described, the officer to whom the same is directed shall give each member of the Board notice of the time and place of meeting, by transmitting to each member a letter by mail, in such season that, by the ordinary course of the mails, each member may receive his notification at least thirty days before the day of said meeting.

3. All adjourned meetings shall be notified as follows: The Recording Secretary shall transmit written notice of any adjourned meeting to every member of the Board, as soon as practicable after such meeting shall have been agreed upon by the Board.

4. At any meeting of the Board, three members shall form a *quorum* to adjourn or dissolve the meeting; and five members shall form a *quorum* to transact business.*

---

* These Bye-Laws were incorporated in, and superceded by, the Laws and Regulations of the Board, adopted at the Annual Meeting of 1832, and printed in the Appendix to the Report of that year. EDITOR, 1834.

ADDRESS TO THE CHRISTIAN PUBLIC.

NOVEMBER, 1812.

The American Board of Commissioners for Foreign Missions, at their late annual meeting, appointed the subscribers a committee to prepare and publish an address to the Christian Public, in the name and on the behalf of the Board. The favor shewn to the objects in view by the liberal and pious in different parts of the country, as manifested by their free-will offerings, their active exertions, and their prayers, cannot with propriety be passed over in silence; nor should the smiles of Divine Providence upon the first attempts to send the gospel from America to Asia, be received without distinct and grateful commemoration.

For a particular history of the events in which the Board have been intimately concerned during the past year, it is sufficient to refer the reader to the Report of the Prudential Committee herewith published. The two most prominent of these events, however, it is proper to mention briefly in this place

The first is the actual commencement of a mission to Asia, by the ordination and embarkation of five missionaries in the month of February last. The magnitude of this event, if estimated by its probable consequences, and the nature of the cause intended to be promoted by it, is such as to form a new era in the history of American churches. While saying this, however, we do not forget, that the immediate consequences may be such as to disappoint the hopes and try the faith of Christians. But that the ultimate consequences of *all* attempts to diffuse the Gospel among mankind will be glorious, the explicit promises of God forbid us to doubt.

The other event referred to is the passing of an act, by the Legislature of Massachusetts, incorporating the Board, and giving them power to hold, in their corporate capacity, funds sufficiently large to answer all the present purposes of the institution. The advantages of perpetual succession, and of holding funds under the immediate protection of the law, which could be obtained only by an act of incorporation, are highly important to secure the confidence of the American public. For this instance of the fostering care of the Legislature, the friends of religion, generally, will unite with the Board in expressing thanks.

The two great objects which the Board have in view, and to which they would direct the attention of their brethren, are the establishment and support of missions among the heathen, and the translation and publication of the Bible in languages spoken by unevangelized nations. That these objects are transcendently important, it would be a waste of time to prove; that they are admirably calculated to go hand in hand seems, also, undeniable. Neither the Bible without preachers, nor preachers without the Bible, will ever effect any great change among ignorant and idolatrous people. The majesty, glory, and divine authority of the Bible, are immediately acknowledged by some, at least, among the heathen, whenever this sacred Book speaks to them in their vernacular tongue; and Providence seems to indicate very clearly, that the great renovation of the world, which is so ardently desired by good men, and so explicitly promised by God himself, will be produced by a universal preaching and reading of the Scriptures, accompanied by a like universal operation of the Holy Spirit.   Instruments will be used in the accomplishment of this mighty work, and these instruments God will provide, in his own manner, and at the proper season.   Happy the Christian who shall be found worthy to contribute in any degree, however humble, to that blessed consummation, which is daily remembered with joyful anticipation in his prayers.

The two objects, which have been mentioned are sufficiently great, extensive, and attainable, to solicit, nay to command, exertions and sacrifices from every benevolent person throughout the Christian world.

These objects are *great*.   Every thing which has a direct tendency to promote the salvation of immortal souls is great beyond the power of language to express, or imagination to conceive.   Who shall describe the happiness to be enjoyed by a single redeemed sinner during a blessed eternity? or the miseries, the unutterable and never ending horrors, escaped in consequence of being made wise unto salvation?   Who shall adequately declare the magnitude of an attempt to evangelize whole nations, and ultimately to renovate a world; an attempt to disenthral the slaves of Satan, and bring them into the glorious liberty of the sons of God; an attempt to diffuse peace and joy throughout the abodes of men, and to people the regions of immortal life with redeemed and sanctified spirits?   In an attempt thus noble and sublime does every man engage, who aids in sending the heralds of salvation to the heathen, and in putting the word of truth into their hands.

The objects are *extensive*.   They admit, they *require*, the labors of multitudes.   The glorious employment of being fellow laborers in the cause of God, is an employment in which all, who are so inclined, may at all times engage.   But the support of missions, and the publication of the Scriptures, in all nations, are enterprises in which the efforts of multitudes can be united with peculiar facility.   Christians in both hemispheres, and of every denomination, can direct their exertions to produce one result,—a result of the highest conceivable importance. Combined efforts, whether of a good or evil character, are incomparably more powerful than single efforts can be.   How delightful, how enrapturing the sight, to behold good men of every rank and condition, in all parts of the world, uniting in one vast labor of love.

It is not only practicable for multitudes to unite in the great purpose of evangelizing the world; but such a union is absolutely necessary, in order to bring about this event in the shortest time.   All the power and influence of the whole Christian world must be put in requisition, during the course of those beneficent labors which will precede the millennium. What expenses, what privations and sacrifices must be incurred, before six hundred millions of heathens can read the word of God in their own languages, and possess it in their own families; and before preachers can be furnished to direct this countless host into the path of life!   The utmost exertion of every Christian now living, so far as his other duties will permit, is required in this glorious service.   How boundless must be the field of labor which admits, and will continue to admit, the labors of all benevolent persons, in every region of the habitable globe!

But the most animating consideration still remains—these objects are *attainable.* To deny the practicability and usefulness of missions, and translations of the Scriptures, would manifest a total ignorance of the subject, or a deep hostility to the progress of Christianity. Twenty years ago, objections to these extraordinary efforts might have been formed much more plausibly than at present. Happily for the world, such objections did not then stifle those beneficent attempts, which have already given the Bible to nations in the heart of Asia, in their own languages. Whether Providence shall bless the efforts of this Board, it is not in the power of man to determine. Let us wait with humility and submission. But that the objects in view will be attained, and by human instruments too, will not be doubted by those, who expect the final prevalence of true religion over error and sin. If the faith of Christians in America should be tried at the outset, it is no more than has frequently been experienced by Christians in every age. Such trials have often preceded the most signal success, and far from disheartening, should stimulate to more animated and faithful labors.

While on this part of the subject, it is proper to mention, that, since the Board was incorporated, unexpected and most auspicious intelligence has arrived from Asia. An Auxiliary Bible Society has been formed at Calcutta, which in a short time raised funds to the amount of above thirty thousand dollars, and at the last dates was printing the whole Bible in one language, and the New Testament in two others, for immediate and extensive distribution. A regular succession of large editions of the Scriptures, in the common languages of Asia, may now be expected, if the liberality of Christians shall equal the occasion for its exercise. All that the people of America now have to do, in order to share in this exalted undertaking, is to remit their money to Calcutta, the centre of Eastern missions and translations, where suitable agents will easily be provided to superintend the expenditure. The Board will endeavor, as soon as possible, to arrange a system of safe and regular remittances to India, so that the donations of the benevolent in this country shall reach the place of their destination, and the field of usefulness, without any considerable delay. At present there seems to be no difficulty in making remittances by the way of London.

It is also worthy of consideration, that the Board are not confined in their operations to any part of the world, but may direct their attention to Africa, North or South America, or the Isles of the sea, as well as to Asia. If unsuccessful in one place, they can turn to another; and can seize, (according to their means,) upon any promising opportunity to do good to any portion of the heathen world.

It is an obvious reflection, and a pretty common one, that Christians of the present generation are greatly favored. While their eyes have seen most astonishing and unparalleled displays of human wickedness, they have also beheld innumerable trophies of divine grace. From nations betrayed, enslaved, weltering in their blood, and shrouded in a starless night of infidelity and profligacy, their attention has been turned with transport to the light which has encircled the dwellings of the faithful, and to the rising glories of the Sun of Righteousness. Their ears, for a long time stunned by the outcries, blasphemies, and unutterable confusion of a wicked world suffering the vengeance of God from the

7

hands of cruel men, have found a happy relief in hearing the glad sounds of salvation reverberating through heathen lands, and in listening to the songs of converted idolaters, soon to be exchanged for the songs of the blessed.   Already they hear, or seem to hear, the commencement of that celestial hymn, *Arise, shine; for thy light is come, and the glory of the Lord is risen upon thee;* a hymn in which all tribes and nations will hereafter unite with joy unspeakable, and which will be re-echoed from the realms of immortality in one boundless chorus of rapture and praise.

To be silent and inactive spectators of these animating scenes, if that only were permitted, would be a grand felicity. But Christians need not be silent and inactive spectators.   Indeed they ought not, they must not.   They are now favored with opportunities of promoting the cause of Christ not enjoyed by preceding generations.   No age since that of the Apostles has afforded so great encouragement to engage with zeal and activity in the best of all causes, as the present day affords.   How would the saints of former times, the Baxters, the Beveridges, the Wattses, the Edwardses, have rejoiced to see this day?   They looked forward to it, and to the more delightful scenes still future, with joyful anticipations; how would they have exulted to join in its employments, and mingle their labors and prayers with those of the great multitudes, who now incessantly labor and pray for the universal establishment of the Redeemer's kingdom?

It is now generally seen and felt, by those who have any claim to be considered as proper judges, that Christianity is the only remedy for the disorders and miseries of this world, as well as the only foundation of hope for the world to come.   No other agent will ever control the violent passions of men; and without the true religion, all attempts to meliorate the condition of mankind will prove as illusory as a feverish dream. The genuine patriot, therefore, and the genuine philanthropist, must labor, so far as they value the prosperity of their country and the happiness of the human race, to diffuse the knowledge and the influence of Christianity, at home and abroad.   Thus will they labor most effectually to put a final period to oppression and slavery, to perfidy and war, and to all the train of evils which falsehood, ambition, and cruelty have so profusely scattered through the world.   Infidelity seems abashed, and in the attitude of retiring from every place where her hideous form and features can be compared with the symmetry and beauty of religion. She seeks concealment and obscurity, and is half ashamed of her votaries, who, in their turn, are cordially ashamed of her.   Over infidelity and every abuse of religion the Captain of our salvation will triumph. Wise are they who enlist under his banner, fight his battles, and share in the joys of his victory!

Possibly it may be thought by some, that the present times are unfavorable to the objects above described, so far as pecuniary contributions are needed; and that it would be best to defer charitable designs till our national calamities shall have been removed.   We cannot yield for a moment to reasoning of this sort.   It might receive many answers; a few brief hints will be sufficient.

God alone is the deliverer from public troubles, and must be regarded as such by all who have any just views of his providence.   He can change scenes of national distress into scenes of joy and gratulation. He can cause light to spring up out of darkness, and educe good from evil. To him must the eyes of all be turned, who long for the happiness of mankind and the prosperity of the Church. What method so likely to secure the favor of God, as that of obeying his commandments? And it is his commandment, that the Gospel should be preached *to every creature.*

Besides, it would be adding immeasurably to all the necessary evils of war, if every charitable enterprise were to cease during its continuance. The interests of truth and beneficence would thus lose more in a short war than could be regained in a long peace. National calamities, instead of producing national repentance and reformation, would be the signal for letting loose the malignant passions, while all the charitable virtues were to lie dormant. What would be the result of this but a return of the ages of barbarism? Let the people of this country rather imitate the multitudes of good people in the country to which we now stand in the relation of a public enemy, who in circumstances of great national anxiety, and while pressed with uncommon burdens, are more and more stimulated to devote their influence, their example, and their property, to the service of their Lord.

Again; by engaging in any course of beneficence we consult our present happiness. The devotees of pleasure and dissipation are not deterred from their pursuits by the present aspect of the times. Millions are annually expended for their temporary gratification; and the greater part of these enormous sums is directly subservient to the cause of sin. Shall Christians refuse their thousands? Shall *they* be the only persons who plead national calamities as a reason for withholding their money, when that money will contribute, if wisely laid out, to bring these very calamities to an end, and to build up that cause by the prevalence of which all calamities would cease? Let them rather supplicate the favor of God for every human being; and strive earnestly to extend the boundaries of that kingdom which is *righteousness, and peace, and joy in the Holy Ghost.*

While thanks are returned to all the benevolent societies and individuals, by whose distinguished liberality the Board have been encouraged and supported in their first attempts, it is with pleasure we are able to add, that the other benevolent institutions of a similar nature, in our country, have been unusually favored with respect to their funds during the past year. This was confidently expected, and should be acknowledged with devout gratitude. All benevolent societies, conducted on Christian principles, are sisters. They flourish or languish together. Occupying different fields of usefulness, and acting advantageously by adopting the principle of a division of labor, they promote the success of each other, and accomplish vastly more than could be done by the same pecuniary means under the direction of one Society. They possess all the advantages of combination; and yet do not become unwieldly and embarrassed by the multiplicity of their concerns. Let the peculiar friends of each unite in promoting the success of all. Let there be no jealousy between them but a godly jealousy; and no rivalry but a holy emulation in one grand attempt to extend the gospel through the world.

While soliciting the prayers of the pious, and the pecuniary contributions of all who are able and willing to contribute, it behoves us explicitly to disclaim any desire to profit by mere appeals to the passions. We trust that the addresses and other public papers of the Board, have never partaken of this character. Convinced that the work of evangelizing mankind is the noblest work in which men ever engaged, that the encouragements to prosecute it are at all times abundant, and that its completion is certain, nothing more can at any time be needed to interest the hearts of Christians in it, than to open a promising field of labor.

At the present time, the call for renewed and increased exertions is so loud, that it has been heard and obeyed by thousands in different parts of the world. The friend and patron of missions, far from acting by the blind impulse of passion, is supported by the plainest dictates of reason, the decisive experience of ages, and the infallible declarations of Scripture. He who embarks in such a cause, and whose heart approves the conclusions of his reason, will not easily relinquish the object of his hopes and prayers.

It is worthy of particular notice, that there has been a uniform progress, for the last twenty years, in the number, magnitude, and success of the attempts to preach the Gospel, and to impart the Scriptures, to the ignorant and destitute, both in Christian and heathen lands. God grant that this progress may continue and increase; and that those who offer, and all who read, this address, may have some humble share in promoting a cause, which aims directly and supremely at the glory of God, and the salvation of the whole human race.

We are unwilling to conclude, without addressing a few words particularly, and very respectfully, to the Clergy, the reverend pastors of the American churches.

FATHERS AND BRETHREN,—From the performance of your professional duties, especially from the study of the sacred Volume, you derive most affecting considerations with respect to the worth of immortal souls, and the divine efficacy and glory of the Christian religion. When you look around upon a world *lying in wickedness*, and reflect on the many discouragements and very partial successes, which attend your best and most highly favored exertions, you cannot but sigh for the advent of that blessed day, when "they shall not teach every man his neighbor, saying, KNOW THE LORD, for all shall know Him, from the least to the greatest." Lamenting the sins, and feeling for the miseries of mankind, you habitually regard with deep interest all attempts to extend the influence of the Gospel. Without the good wishes and cordial aid of a serious and enlightened clergy, no great attempt of a religious nature will ever succeed; but every such attempt, judiciously made and conscientiously persevered in, will be countenanced by these good wishes and this aid.

The Board whose duty it is to superintend the first American mission to foreign parts, and to expend with fidelity such monies as may be committed to their disposal, deeply feel their responsibility. They wish for all information which can be had, relative to the subjects which will come before them. Any communications, therefore, from the Clergy, either in their individual or associated capacities, will be received with respect and thankfulness. It will be the desire and aim of the Board so to conduct their affairs, as to secure the confidence of all Christians throughout the United States, of every denomination; and they venture to hope for the countenance of all, who admit the utility of missions and translations.

Among the numerous claims upon the public liberality, you will doubtless recommend those objects as worthy of especial regard, which have a direct tendency to make men happy here, and to fit them for heaven. That all such objects may be promoted, and that they all may harmonize in producing one grand result, the universal triumph of truth and benevolence, you will not cease to labor and pray. Thus laboring and praying, and exciting others to a course of beneficent actions, a more devout attention will accompany your weekly ministrations. They who are urged to feel for the souls of the perishing heathen, will be apt to feel that they and their families have souls to be saved or lost for ever. Such has generally been the effect hitherto, and there is every reason to believe that such will be the effect in future.

Let us all remember, Fathers and Brethren, that the time allotted to our earthly labors is short, that the spiritual wants of the heathen imperiously demand attention and relief; and, while urging each other and our fellow sinners to deeds of charity, let us never forget *the words of the Lord Jesus, how he said, It is more blessed to give than to receive.*

In behalf of the Board,

JEDIDIAH MORSE,
SAMUEL WORCESTER, } *Committee.*
JEREMIAH EVARTS.

Boston, Nov. 10, 1812.

MINUTES

OF THE

FOURTH ANNUAL MEETING.

———

The Annual Meeting of the Board was held at Concert Hall in Boston, on Wednesday, Sept. 15, 1813. Present,

  The Hon. JOHN TREADWELL, Esq. LL. D.
    Rev. JOSEPH LYMAN, D. D.
    Rev. TIMOTHY DWIGHT, D. D. LL. D.
    Rev. SAMUEL SPRING, D. D.
     WILLIAM BARTLET, Esq.
    Rev. SETH PAYSON, D. D.
    Hon. JOHN HOOKER, Esq.
    Rev. CALVIN CHAPIN,
    Rev. JAMES RICHARDS,
    Rev. SAMUEL WORCESTER, D. D.
     JEREMIAH EVARTS, Esq.

The meeting was opened with prayer by the Vice President.

Minutes of the last annual meeting, and of two adjourned meetings, were read.

The following gentlemen were chosen officers for the year ensuing, viz.

  The Hon. JOHN TREADWELL, Esq. *President.*
  The Rev. Dr. SPRING, *Vice President.*
   WILLIAM BARTLET, Esq. ⎫
  The Rev. Dr. SPRING,   ⎬ *Prudential Committee.*
  The Rev. Dr. WORCESTER, ⎪
   JEREMIAH EVARTS, Esq. ⎭
  The Rev. Dr. WORCESTER, *Corresponding Secretary.*
  The Rev. Mr. CHAPIN, *Recording Secretary.*
   JEREMIAH EVARTS, Esq. *Treasurer.*
   CHARLES WALLEY, Esq. *Auditor.*

The Rev. Dr. Spring laid before the Board a seal, which had been presented to the Board by Robert Ralston, Esq. Whereupon,

Voted, to accept the said seal as the seal of this corporation.

Voted, that the thanks of this Board be presented to Mr. Ralston for his generous donation.

The Rev. Dr. Lyman and the Hon. Mr. Hooker, were appointed a committee to revise the bye-law respecting the powers of the Prudential Committee.

The Rev. Mr. Chapin and the Rev. Dr. Payson, were appointed a committee to report on the case of Messrs. Judson and Rice, who have withdrawn themselves from the service of the Board.

The Rev. Dr. Spring had leave of absence the remainder of the session.

Adjourned till 9 o'clock to-morrow morning.

Thursday, Sept. 16. Met according to adjournment, and the business of the day was opened with prayer by the Recording Secretary.

The Rev. JEDIDIAH MORSE, D. D. took his seat at the Board.

Voted, That this Board consider the relation between this Board, and the Rev. Adoniram Judson, jun., as having been dissolved on the first day of Sept. 1812, when, in a letter to the Corresponding Secretary, he announced his withdrawment of himself from under our instructions.

Voted, That this Board consider the relation between this Board and the Rev. Luther Rice, as having been dissolved on the 23d day of October, 1812, when, in a letter to the Corresponding Secretary, he signified, that it was no longer compatible with his sentiments to follow our instructions.

Voted, That the following be adopted as a part of the bye-laws, chap. I. sect. 2.

All applications to be employed as missionaries shall be made to the Prudential Committee; and said committee shall carefully inquire and examine into the qualifications of any applicants; and in case thereupon they are well satisfied of the propriety of employing such applicants, they are authorized to expend any sums of money necessary for fully qualifying the applicants for the mission to which they may be designated, or on which they may be proposed to be sent; and when, in the judgment of said committee, the applicants may be suitably qualified, the said committee are authorized to send them on such missions as they may think proper.

And the Prudential Committee are authorized to suspend any missionary, whenever, in their judgment, he shall violate the instructions given him, or shall fail to perform the duties reasonably required of him, until the next meeting of the Board.

The Prudential Committee shall regularly report their proceedings to the Board.

At 11 o'clock, A. M. attended public worship, when a sermon was delivered by the Rev. Dr. Dwight from John x. 16.

Voted, That the thanks of this Board be presented to the Rev. Dr. Dwight for his sermon this day delivered, and that a copy be requested for publication.

The Rev. Dr. Morse, Mr. Evarts, and the Rev. Dr. Worcester, were appointed a committee to carry the above vote into effect.

The Report of the Prudential Committee was accepted.

The Treasurer's accounts were exhibited, as examined and certified by the Auditor, and accepted.

The Rev. Drs. Dwight, Morse, and Lyman, were appointed a committee relative to the connection between Mr. Eleazer Williams and this Board.

Voted, That Mr. Evarts be requested to present the thanks of this Board to Mr. Duren, and the choir of singers under his direction, for their very acceptable services in the public exercises of this day.

Voted, That the thanks of this Board be presented to the committee of the First Church in Boston, for the use of their church for public religious exercises.

Voted, That the Prudential Committee be directed to make inquiry respecting the settlement of a mission at St. Salvador, Brazil; at Port Louis, in the Isle of France; and on the island of Madagascar.

Whereas it has been stated to this Board by the Prudential Committee, that a gentleman, who wishes his name not to be mentioned, has offered to this Board a printing-press, whenever it shall be needed to publish the Scriptures under the direction of the Board,—

Voted, That the Clerk of the Prudential Committee be requested to present the thanks of the Board for this liberal offer, and that the donation be accepted.

Voted, That this Board approve of the measures taken by Messrs. Richards and Warren, as reported by the Prudential Committee; and that the thanks of this Board be presented to Robert Ralston, Esq., Drs. Dorsey, James, Chapman, Hewson, Davis, and Billings, the Rev. Drs. Staughton and Rogers, Mr. Patterson, and others, for the kindness and patronage which they have respectively extended to Messrs. Richards and Warren.

Adjourned till nine o'clock to-morrow morning.

Friday, Sept. 17.   Met according to adjournment, and the business of the day was opened with prayer by the Rev. Dr. Payson.

The committee to whom was referred the case of Mr. Eleazer Williams, presented the following report, which was accepted:

That Eleazer Williams, upon satisfying the Prudential Committee with respect to his departure from the course prescribed to him by the Board,* and engaging to place himself fixedly under their direction, may again be received under the patronage of the Board.

Voted, That the Treasurer be allowed three hundred dollars for his official services the last year.

A communication was received from the Hon. Elias Boudinot, Esq., a member of the Board, enclosing, as a donation, a bill of exchange on London for one hundred pounds sterling; Whereupon

Voted, That the thanks of this Board be presented to the generous donor.

---

* He had prematurely joined his brethren, the Iroquois Indians, in New York and Vermont, near the frontiers of the United States.

Voted, That the next annual meeting of this Board be held in the Philosophical Chamber of Yale College, on the Thursday next after the second Wednesday of September, 1814, at 10 o'clock, A. M.

Voted, That the Prudential Committee be authorized to allow the missionaries of this Board such incidental and unforeseen expenses, as have been necessary.

Voted, That the thanks of this Board be presented to Samuel H. Walley, Esq. for his services as Auditor.

The Rev. Drs. Morse and Worcester, and Mr. Evarts, were appointed a committee to prepare and publish an address to the public on the behalf of the Board.

Voted, That it be the duty of the Prudential Committee to compile and publish a report, including the address to the public, the report of the Prudential Committee, a statement of the Treasurer's accounts, such accounts of donations as may be found expedient, extracts from the minutes of the present session, and such other information as they may deem useful.

During the session, the Rev. ALEXANDER PROUDFIT, D. D., of New York, and Gen. HENRY SEWALL, and the Rev. JESSE APPLETON, D. D., President of Bowdoin College, of the District of Maine, were unanimously elected members of the Board

The Rev. Dr. Miller was appointed to preach at the next annual meeting; and the Rev. Mr. Richards was appointed his second.

Voted, That the Recording Secretary give immediate notice to all the members of the Board, who are not now present, of the time and place of the next annual meeting.

The meeting was closed with prayer by the Rev. Mr. Richards.

REPORT.

BRETHREN,—When Jesus of Nazareth was going about doing good, despised and rejected of men, little was it expected by the world, and little did it comport with human probability, that he would ascend to the right hand of the Majesty on high, be invested with all power in heaven and earth, and reign until every knee should bow to him, and every tongue confess him to be Lord, to the glory of God the Father. As he himself, on his way to *the joy set before him*, passed through scenes apparently the most inauspicious; so his servants, whom he has been pleased to employ in great designs and enterprises for advancing his kingdom, have generally been subjected, especially in their initiatory attempts, to trials and adversities, painful in their nature, and unpropitious in their aspect. But often has he shewn that his thoughts and ways are not like those of men. Often has he displayed the plenitude of his power, wisdom, and goodness, in causing light to shine out of darkness, in carrying small beginnings into great results, and in crowning designs and enterprises, held for a time under discouraging circumstances, with unexpected and glorious success. Always, indeed, there is perfect safety in confiding in him; and happy are they, whether for the present successful or unsuccessful, who are truly engaged in his cause. Under these impressions, the Prudential Committee now meet their brethren, and submit their report with lively sentiments of gratitude and hope.

8

It was not until about three months after the last meeting of this Board, that the first intelligence from our missionaries sent out to the eastern world, was received in this country. In the mean time, however, they were not forgotten by the Prudential Committee. As the ordinary intercourse with India was obstructed by the war, it became necessary to establish a special channel, through which communications and remittances might be made with safety. For this purpose, the Committee assigned to Samuel Williams, and Junius Smith, Esqrs., of London, and to the Hon John Herbert Harrington, Esq., the Rev. David Brown, D.D. and the Rev. William Carey, D. D., at Calcutta, such agencies, as might be requisite in those places respectively for securing remittances to our missionaries, and for furthering generally the objects of this Board. To the gentlemen designated as agents at Calcutta, was entrusted, very particularly, the application of the means forwarded to India by this Board, for aiding in the translation and distribution of the Holy Scriptures.

Pursuant to arrangements made by the Committee, a remittance of one thousand dollars for the support of our missionaries, and another of the same amount for aiding in the translation and distribution of the Scriptures, were forwarded by the Treasurer to our agents in London in the month of November. About the same time fifty pounds sterling were remitted to the Rev. George Burder, to refund what had been advanced from the treasury of the London Missionary Society, to Mr. Judson, when in England, in 1811. In February, another remittance was made for the support of the missionaries to the amount of twenty-two hundred dollars. Of the receipt in London of these several remittances, the Treasurer has been duly advised, and assurances have been received from our agents there, in terms very gratefully to be acknowledged, of their cheerful acceptance of the trusts confided to them. For the translation of the Scriptures, another remittance of about thirteen hundred dollars, (more than five hundred of which were specially appropriated to the repairing of the loss sustained by the fire at the Mission House at Serampore,) was made in May; and another of about a thousand dollars, in July. Of the receipt of these two remittances, it is not yet time to have received advice.

At the meeting of the Board in 1811, a sum, not exceeding three hundred dollars, was appropriated to the purchasing of books for the use of the missionaries. As our brethren, when they were fitted out, were furnished with but few books, the Committee thought it important to embrace the earliest opportunity of conveying to them an additional supply. Accordingly, as an unexpected opportunity was presented in November, a purchase was made of such books as were supposed to be the most suitable, to the amount of about two hundred dollars. These books were put on board the schooner Alligator of Salem, bound to Arracan; were directed to our agents in Calcutta, and committed, with special instructions, to the care of the supercargo, who was also constituted an agent for this Board. The Alligator sailed from Salem about the first of December; and by her, official letters were forwarded from the Corresponding Secretary and the Treasurer, to our missionary brethren, communicating to them such advices and directions as were deemed expedient; and to the Hon. Judge Harrington and Drs. Brown and Carey, respectfully soliciting their assumption of the agencies entrusted to them, referring them to documents accompanying the letters, by which they would be made acquainted with the institution, design, and transactions of this Board, and the instructions under which our missionaries were sent out—and soliciting their good offices in favor of the missionaries, especially in reference to the difficulties and dangers to which they might be exposed on account of the war. These letters, with leave, will be submitted to the Board. From the Alligator no intelligence has been received since her departure.

The substance of the information respecting our missionaries, collected from the letters which have been received, is comprised in the following statement:

Our brethren were all highly favored in their passages. The Lord had them under his gracious care—kindly preserved their health—rendered their situation on board the ships agreeable—and conveyed them in safety to their destined port. Messrs. Newell and Judson, with their wives, arrived at Calcutta in the Caravan, on the 17th of June, and Messrs. Hall, Nott, and Rice, with the wife of Mr. Nott, in the Harmony, on the 8th of August, 1812. By Christian people there, of different religious denominations, they were received in a manner the most courteous and affectionate; and their letters very pleasingly testify their deep and grateful sense of the divine goodness to them, and of the cause which they had to "thank God and take courage."

Soon after their arrival, however, Messrs. Newell and Judson, received an order from the government, requiring them to return to this country by the Caravan; and signifying, that the Caravan would not be allowed to depart without them. By this order they were thrown into great perplexity and distress. Their Christian friends at Calcutta and Serampore entered with great sympathy into their situation; earnest solicitations were employed in their behalf with the officers of the government; and special and united prayers were offered up to Him who reigns in Zion, and turns the hearts of men. After some time the order was relaxed, and liberty was granted to the two brethren, to depart, by any conveyance which might offer, to any place, not within the jurisdiction of the East India Company. It then became a weighty question whither they should go. Respecting Birmah, which had been contemplated by us, and by them, with particular desire and raised hope, as the field of the mission, they had received such information, as decisively to deter them from attempting an establishment in any part of that empire. China, still farther east, they supposed to be absolutely closed against them. Seeing no door open, or likely to be opened, in countries eastward of British India, they had only to turn their eyes westward. While in this state of anxious suspense, they received letters from their brethren of the Harmony, dated at the Isle of France, with the intelligence that the governor of that Island was friendly to missions, and very desirous of having missionaries employed there, and in the neighboring Island of Madagascar. As the Isle of France, Bourbon, and the more easterly Island of Ceylon, are not within the jurisdiction of the East India Company; but belong to the *crown* of Great Britain, and are under separate governments; in them the policy of the East India Company does not prevail. Messrs. Newell and Judson, therefore, at length concluded to embrace the first opportunity of a passage to the Isle of

France; considering that, should they not find it expedient to attempt an establishment either there, or at Madagascar, they would at least be out of the reach of that government which had hedged up their way, and at liberty to go thence wherever Providence might direct them.

Accordingly, on the 4th of August, Mr. and Mrs. Newell embarked for the Isle of France, in a vessel which could not afford accommodations for any more passengers; and the expectation then was, that Mr. and Mrs. Judson would soon follow them.

Four days after the departure of Mr. Newell, the Harmony with Messrs. Hall, Nott and Rice, arrived at Calcutta. After going through a process, similar to that to which the two brethren before them had been subjected, these brethren came also to a similar determination. They were providentially, however, detained at Calcutta, until the latter part of November

This interval of delay was marked with some changes, which should have been little to be expected, and which cast a new cloud upon the affairs of the mission. On the 27th of August, Mr. Judson addressed a note to the Baptist Missionaries at Serampore, informing them that he and Mrs. Judson had changed their sentiments on the subject of baptism, and signifying their desire to be immersed. Accordingly, on the first Sabbath in September, they were immersed. In his note, Mr. Judson says, "It is now about four months since I took the subject into serious and prayerful consideration." Mr. Newell, however, who was his companion on the passage to Calcutta, and after his arrival there until within about three weeks of the date of this note, appears to have left him without any knowledge of the change. His other brethren, also, who were at Calcutta, when he went from that place to Serampore, on the 27th of August, appear to have been unapprized of the object of his visit there, and to have received their first intelligence on the subject two days afterwards from Dr Marshman.

In a joint letter, written about twenty days after Mr. Judson's immersion, his brethren, referring to the fact, say, "In consequence of this trying event, it has appeared to him and to us, and to those with whom we have conversed, expedient that we should separate and labor in different fields." This letter had the signature of Mr Rice. About four weeks after this a letter was written by brethren Hall and Nott, in which they say, "You will be surprised to receive a letter written by us alone: we are surprised and distressed that it is so. Brother Rice has been led to change his sentiments on the subject of baptism; and brother Judson and he will probably attempt a mission to Java. What the Lord means by thus dividing us in sentiment, and separating us from each other, we cannot tell. This we know, the Lord seeth not as man seeth; and it ill becomes us to be dissatisfied with what he does. We hope and pray that these unexpected things may not damp the missionary spirit which has been kindled, but that it may burn with a brighter and purer flame." Mr. Rice, in a letter of the same date, professes to have examined the subject, "with prayerfulness, and in the fear of God, and with no small impression of the delicacy and high responsibility of his situation."

Aware of the fallibility of the human mind, and of the frailty even of good men, the Prudential Committee have no disposition to impeach the sincerity of these two brethren. It cannot, however, but be regarded with regret, if they had not, "with prayerfulness and in the fear of God," examined that subject, before so late a day:—before they assumed engagements of so high and responsible a character;—before they were placed in circumstances rendering it nearly impossible for them to preserve an equable state of mind, while examining as doubtful, a question which ought long before to have been settled with them, and in regard to which a change of sentiments would entirely change their relations, and open to them new and very different prospects,—before, in fine, they were in a situation, peculiarly exposing them, as the case might be, to mistake impulses for arguments, and an act, in which there would be "a shew of wisdom, in will-worship and humility," for an indispensable effort of Christian self-denial. *Nevertheless the foundation of God standeth sure:* and on this foundation, the instances of instability, which we lament here to record, but against which no human foresight could provide, should lead us more entirely to repose our hopes. They shew us that missionaries are but men; and forcibly inculcate the importance of great caution, and great fidelity in examination, on the part, not only of this Board, but of all who would offer themselves for the missionary service. Instead, however, of inducing discouragement, they should rouse the holy zeal, and quicken the pious exertions, of all the friends of truth; and should they, in the wisdom of God, be so overruled, as to bring an accession of strength to the missionary cause, the event would be joyous.

During their stay at Calcutta, Messrs. Hall and Nott obtained such information, and such views of probable events, as induced them to relinquish the design of returning to the Isle of France, in the hope that they might yet find it practicable to establish themselves at Bombay, Surat, or some other eligible place in India. Early in November, therefore, they engaged a passage for Bombay, obtained their passport from the police, and were contemplating their prospects with high satisfaction and encouragement. But here, on a sudden, another trial was interposed. After their effects were on board for Bombay, they had notice from the police, that it was the pleasure of the government to have them conveyed to England, and that a passage would be provided for them in the fleet then under despatch. They were greatly perplexed; but, as their passports were not revoked, they at length concluded, that they might be warranted in going on board the ship in which they were regularly entered as passengers, and had paid their passage, and await the event. Accordingly, on the 20th of November, they went on board. The ship remained in the river, a little below Calcutta, five or six days, during which they were not without fear of being ordered back by the officers of the police, who well knew where they were; but on the 27th, the ship dropped down the river, and on the 29th she was out at sea. This was the date of our last intelligence from them. Under this date, Mr. Nott writes, "We are now past all the danger which we feared. As far as we can judge, if we are favored with good weather, we shall have a pleasant passage. We hope soon to have a home. If we do not go to Bombay, we shall either stay at Ceylon, or go to some place where we shall certainly stay."

About the time that these two brethren left Calcutta, Mr. and Mrs. Judson and Mr. Rice took passage thence for the Isle of France, where they arrived about the middle of January. On the 15th of March, Mr. Rice took passage in a Portuguese vessel for the Brazils, with a view to return to this country on special business, deemed by himself and Mr. Judson important to their contemplated separate mission. He has just reached this place from New York; and from him the Board may probably receive some further communications. He left Mr. and Mrs. Judson at the Isle of France, waiting for a passage to Penang, or Prince of Wales's Island, where they intended, if practicable, to effectuate an establishment.

Mr. and Mrs. Newell's passage from Calcutta to the Isle of France was long, perilous, and distressing. After leaving Calcutta, on the 4th of August, they were driven about in the Bay of Bengal for a month, in which time Mrs. Newell was sick with a fever. On the 5th of September the ship put in at Coringa in distress. Thence they sailed on the 19th of the same month, and arrived at the Isle of France in the fore part of November.

About three weeks before their arrival, they were called to the mournful office of consigning to the waves an infant daughter, whom but five days before, they had joyfully received at the hand of God, and whom with mingled vows and tears, they had solemnly devoted to him in baptism. Soon after this, symptoms of a consumption began to shew themselves in Mrs. Newell. The disease baffled all medical skill; and on the 30th of November at Port Louis in the Isle of France, she fell asleep.— "During the whole of her sickness," says her mourning husband, "she talked in the most familiar manner of death, and the glory that was to follow." She wished it to be distinctly made known to her friends, that "she had never regretted leaving her native land for the cause of Christ." "God calls me away," said she, "before we have entered on the work of the mission; but the case of David affords me comfort: I have had it in my heart to do what I could for the heathen, and I hope God will accept me." When told that probably she would not live through another day; "O joyful news," said she, "I long to depart."

Precious in the sight of the Lord is the death of his saints. Precious to the hearts of many is the memory of this amiable and excellent woman. Her superior and cultivated mind, her enlarged and active benevolence, her solid and elevated piety, her steady and cheerful fortitude, her enlightened and sacred devotedness to the missionary cause, adorned with all the endearing virtues of the female character, had raised her high in Christian estimation, and given no ordinary promise of distinguished usefulness. But He, from whom all these excellences proceeded, and to whom they were consecrated, best knew how long to employ them in this world, and when to raise their possessor to perfection for higher employment in a better. Mrs. Newell neither lived to herself, nor died to herself. Her witness, we believe, is in heaven, and her record on high; and we trust that her fervent prayers, her readiness to forsake all for the service of Christ, and her exemplary life and death, will not be lost to her friends, or to that sacred cause to which she was so ardently devoted.

Her bereaved husband feels her removal as an unspeakable loss; yet appears to bow to the dispensation with a truly resigned spirit, and to be sustained under it with the consolations of God. He will be remembered by this Board in his affliction, with tender sympathy and with fervent prayers; and He, whose servant he is, and who will never be unmindful of him, knows how to make his trials redound to the furtherance of the great design in which he is engaged, and to work for him a far more exceeding and eternal weight of glory.

On the 24th of February Mr. Newell left the Isle of France, in a vessel bound to Bombay, intending to join his brethren Hall and Nott there, or at Ceylon, as Providence should direct.

In regard to the difficulties, experienced by our brethren from the government at Calcutta, it may be proper to state, that they do not appear to have been in any respect peculiar to American missionaries. They were only such as English missionaries have had to encounter; and they proceeded from the general policy of the East India Company, which, on the principle of mercantile monopoly, goes, excepting in cases of connivance, to exclude from their territories all persons, of whatever profession, not licensed by the Directors at home. To this policy the Directors of the London missionary Society, in their Annual Report, last May, have repeated reference. One of their Missionaries, a Mr. Thompson, on his way to the Missionary station at Belhary, arrived in March, 1812, at Madras; where, "when it was found that he came from England without a license from the East India Company," he received an order from the superintendant of the police as follows:

"Rev. Sir,—I am directed to inform you, that the Honorable the Governor in Council is precluded, by the orders of the Supreme Government, from permitting you to reside in any place under this Presidency; you will, therefore, return to the Isle of France, or to Europe, by the first opportunity."

No revocation of this order could be obtained. But Mr. Thompson in a letter, says, "I have nothing to complain of the government here, for they act agreeably to the letter of their instructions; nor of the government at home, as, when the Charter was given to the Company, there was little regard to such an accession of territory, and it had no view to the religion of the people: and when the Toleration Act was passed, the Parliament did not anticipate that the British dominions would be so extensive, or that Christians would feel it their duty to communicate the gospel to foreign lands, and therefore no provision was made for such a purpose." In reference to the case of Mr. Thompson, the Directors of the Missionary Society, say, "It is impossible not to feel, on this recital, the most painful regret, that regulations, which were originally made for commercial purposes only, should now be employed to impede the progress of Christianity, or place under the control of the East India Company a subject so intimately connected with the present and eternal happiness of many millions of the human race. For the removal of such unrighteous restrictions, the Society applied to his Majesty's ministers; has petitioned the Legislature; and will continue importunately to address the Throne of Grace."

As the Charter of the East India Company is about expiring, petitions not only from the London Missionary Society, but from other bodies, and meetings composed of highly respectable members of the Established Church, clergymen and laymen, as well as of other religious denominations, and in the different parts of Great Britain, have been poured in upon the Legislature; praying, that, in the new Charter, there may be some effectual provision in favor of the propagation of the Gospel in the Company's extensive and populous territories. If these petitions have failed, or shall ultimately fail of success, the failure will be greatly lamented by the true friends of the gospel and of the best interests of mankind, both in Great Britain and in this country.

The information, which our missionaries obtained at Calcutta respecting Birmah, and by which they were deterred from proceeding thither, was probably more particularly detailed, in letters which have not yet arrived, than in those which have been received. It appears, however, that war, both civil and foreign, was raging in that empire; and that the missionaries, who had been sent thither from London, and the Baptist Missionary Societies, had been obliged to leave the country. These are strong facts, and doubtless will appear to this Board sufficient to justify our brethren, in relinquishing, for the present, a design which had been entertained with great fervency of hope, and in regard to which no small disappointment is felt. The committee, however, do not abandon the hope, that a door may yet be opened, at no very distant period, for the propagation of the gospel in Birmah.

Though disappointed in regard to the Birman empire, and obstructed in British India, our missionaries, at their last dates, were by no means discouraged. They still had hope of obtaining footing at Bombay, or Surat, in a way similar to that in which missionaries had obtained footing, notwithstanding the difficulties always presented in different parts of India. And should they fail there, they had assurance of being allowed to establish a mission at Ceylon; where a field of no small extent or promise would be open to them. Of this Island, as a field for missionary labors, the Directors of the London Missionary Society, in their last report, give a very favorable representation. A gentleman resident there, as quoted by the Directors, says,' "I hope the Missionary Society, and all other societies for promoting the glorious cause, will strain every nerve to send some able teachers to this country. Never was such a harvest as is here prepared for the reapers."

Our missionaries mention, in very grateful terms, the courtesy, hospitality, and generosity, which they experienced from many persons at Calcutta, Serampore, and Port Louis. At Calcutta, in addition to various other acts of liberality, collections were made for them, in money, of upwards of seven hundred rupees—more than three hundred dollars. For these collections, they express very particular obligations to the Rev. Mr. Thomason, an Episcopal clergyman, who on all occasions had acted towards them the part of a Christian and a friend. And when Mr. Newell left Calcutta for the Isle of France, he had a letter of credit, from Dr. Carey to a house in the latter place, to be used, in case of necessity, until he should receive from us the means of repayment.

The Prudential Committee have not lost sight of the design of this Board, respecting a mission to the Iroquois, or Caghnawaga Indians. It is a design peculiarly near to their hearts; but they have to lament, that, on account of the war, it cannot at present be carried into effect. May the God of mercy grant, that the present obstructions may soon be removed, and a door yet be opened for the Gospel to be imparted to our pagan brethren of the wilderness, whose claims for commiseration are most unequivocal and affecting; and in regard to whom, before the great Parent of all, a responsibility the most awful rests upon the people of these States.

Messrs. Richards and Warren, who for two years have been under the particular patronage of this Board, soon after they had closed their studies, a year ago, at the Theological Institution, went, under the direction of the Prudential Committee, to Philadelphia, for advancement in medical science. They have been in that city about ten months; and have there received marks of courtesy and liberality, which are mentioned by them in terms of fervent gratitude, and which claim the grateful acknowledgments of this Board. From regard to the service to which they are devoted, they have been admitted, gratuitously, to an entire course of lectures in the celebrated Medical Department of the Pennsylvania University, and, recently, have been placed in very eligible situations, one in the Pennsylvania Hospital, and the other in the Philadelphia Almshouse—situations not only exempting them from a principal part of the expenses of living, but affording them advantages for medical improvement, not exceeded, probably, by any in the United States. Besides attending to their medical studies, they have been employed, for a considerable part of the time, by the Missionary Society in Philadelphia, and have performed jointly, in the city and vicinity, the duties of one missionary: thus favoring the funds of this Board, improving themselves as preachers, and doing good, we devoutly trust, to the souls of many. They will be ready for our service abroad, whenever it shall be judged expedient to send them.

Notwithstanding the embarrassments of the times, the liberality of the Christian public towards the objects of this Board has been such, in the course of the year, as highly redounds to the praise of Divine grace. Our brethren and friends in the Auxiliary Societies in the different parts of our country, have exerted themselves with very exemplary and animating zeal, and are entitled to the most affectionate and grateful recognition on this anniversary. The donations to the Board have been published as they were received. The amount received from Sept. 1, 1812, to August 31, 1813, exceeds eleven thousand dollars, as will appear more particularly by the Treasurer's annual accounts. Several Auxiliary Foreign Mission Societies have been formed within the year past; but the exact number cannot be stated, as it is frequently some months after these societies are formed before authentic information is received from them.

In the close of this Report, the Prudential Committee would deliberately say, that, in a general review, they see no reason for discouragement, or for a remission of activity, on the part of this Board or its friends; but abundant cause of thankfulness, and increased exertion. If, when we engaged in our great design, we were not prepared for trials—if we did not lay our account for occurrences apparently adverse, and calling for the utmost firmness of faith, steadiness of purpose, and energy of action; we had profited but little by the experience of ages, had observed to little purpose the unvaried course of Divine dispensations, and were but ill qualified for an undertaking of this arduous and momentous kind. Hitherto our trials have been comparatively light; and our encouragements many and great. It is only three years since the first meeting of this Board, then only a voluntary association, feeble, destitute of funds, and unassured of any adequate patronage. It is not time to have achieved much in the pagan world· if any thing has been done in the way of preparation—in giving stability and efficiency to the institution—in gaining the attention and favor of the Christian public to the design, obtaining the requisite funds for its support, and devising and maturing plans for carrying it into effect;—we have not labored in vain, but may reasonably hope to reap in due time. That the heathen world is to be converted to Christ is as certain, as that the word of God is true: that this is to be effected by the instrumentality of Christians is as evident, as the Divine institution of the Christian ministry is unquestionable· that the time for its accomplishment is near, both the word and the providence of God unequivocally declare. Preparations for this great event have been commenced upon a vast scale; and, amidst the portentous commotions of the world, are advancing with astonishing constancy and celerity. Not to discern the signs of the times, were a proof of most deplorable blindness, not to hail with grateful joy the advance of HIM to whom the kingdom of the whole earth belongs, were a fearful indication of inward hostility to his cause; not to be zealously engaged in the great design of bringing all nations under his benign dominion, were to betray a deadness of heart, an unbelief, a devotedness. to the world, or a pusillanimity, unworthy the Christian name. With humble reliance on HIM, may this Board be *steadfast and unmovable, always abounding in the work of the Lord.*

PECUNIARY ACCOUNTS.

The American Board of Commissioners for Foreign Missions in account current with Jeremiah Evarts, their Treasurer, Dr.

To cash paid from Sept. 1, 1812 to Aug. 31, 1813, in conformity to orders from
  No. 25 to No. 52 inclusive, signed by the clerk of the Prudential Committee,
  for expenses incurred in the prosecution of the objects of the Board $8,603 05
To losses by counterfeit bills received in donations   -   -   -   8 00—8,611 05
To balance carried to the credit of new account, Sept. 1, 1813   -   -   -   8,077 59
                                                                              ————————
                                                                              16,688 64

Contra Cr.
By balance brought to the credit of new account, Sept 1, 1812, as appears by
  the Auditor's certificate of Oct. 8, 1812   -   -   -   -   -   -   - $5,252 46
By cash received in donations, as particularly published in the Panoplist, from
  Oct. 1812 to Sept. 1813   -   -   -   -   -   -   -   -   - $11,284 90
By avails of a dollar, which proved to be genuine, though supposed to be
  counterfeit, and charged as such in last year's account   -   -   -   94
By interest on money lent   -   -   -   -   -   -   -   -   -   150 34—151 28
                                                                              ————————
                                                                              $16,688 64

ADDRESS TO THE CHRISTIAN PUBLIC.

OCTOBER, 1813.

IN behalf of the American Board of Commissioners for Foreign Missions, the subscribers, a committee for the purpose, beg leave to solicit the attention of the Christian public to the cause in which the Board is engaged, and for the promotion of which it was originally instituted, and has been since incorporated. We are not backward to state, at the commencement of this address, that we shall lay before the reader, with great satisfaction, some of the facts and reasons on which our attachment to this cause is founded, and which, we are sure, will not fail to commend themselves to every enlightened conscience, and to make an impression on every pious heart. The cause itself is transcendently glorious, and deserving of the warmest approbation of all men, however imperfectly, or feebly, we may state its claims. To doubt, or hesitate, in regard to the urgency of these claims, and the duty of keeping them habitually in view, would be equally repugnant to our feelings, and dishonorable to our profession as Christians. Can it be a matter of doubt, or of indifference, to any man, who has the Scriptures in his hands, and has profited by perusing them, whether Christianity is to become, at some future day, the religion of all mankind?—whether its transforming power is universally to influence the hearts and the lives of men?—whether the word of God is to be read, understood, and obeyed, by the nations now sunk in idolatry and ignorance?—whether this grand consummation is to be effected by the means which men are voluntarily to supply?—or whether there is an imperious necessity that Christians should zealously co-operate in this great work of the Lord?

The object of the Board is *one*—the promulgation of Christianity among the heathen. The means, by which this object is designed to be effected, are of two kinds;—the publication and distribution of the Scriptures in the different languages of the nations; and the support of faithful missionaries to explain, exemplify, and impress on the mind, the great truths which the Scriptures contain.

In regard to the distribution of the Scriptures, the Board is in fact, though not in name, a FOREIGN BIBLE SOCIETY; and, under this aspect, we earnestly request that its advantages may be considered by all, who would joyfully place the Bible in the hands of Pagans. Confined in its operations to no part of the globe in exclusion of other parts, the Board can extend the sovereign balm wherever there are spiritual maladies to be healed; enjoying the benefit of established plans of correspondence and co-operation, the result of its proceedings can be more prompt than could otherwise be expected; and having its attention long fixed on the most promising fields of exertion, its agents will acquire a facility of action, which can never be applied to single, insulated, and sudden efforts. Through the instrumentality of the Board, every charitable person, however retired or obscure, has it in his power to send the Bible to those very heathens, than whom none of the human race can need it more, and on whom there are peculiar encouragements to bestow it. A known, regular, uninterrupted channel will be kept open, (with the blessing of Providence,) through which the streams of American beneficence may flow into the centre of the Pagan world, and contribute to fertilize regions which have long been dreary and barren of all moral good. And shall not these streams increase, till they form a mighty river, flowing with a steady and resistless current, and bearing on its bosom the immortal hopes of restored Jews, and the imperishable riches of converted Gentiles? Will not many of our countrymen esteem it a high privilege, that their contributions, at whatever season bestowed, may, in a few months and without care or trouble to themselves, be so applied, even in the remote eastern hemisphere, as to commence a series of good effects, which shall never end, and the number and magnitude of which no human powers can calculate? A single Bible given to a Hindoo or a Ceylonese, may be the means of enlightening a family, of arousing the attention of a neighborhood, of withdrawing a multitude from idolatry, leading them to procure the Scriptures for themselves, and turning them from darkness to light, and from the power of Satan to the living God.

It is a fact highly gratifying to the Board, that the liberality of Christians has devolved on them the duty of remitting, in the course of the year past, bills of exchange to the amount of about *eight hundred and sixty pounds sterling*, to aid in the translation and distribution of the Scriptures in Asia; a sum which will produce as much in India, according to the present rates of exchange from London to Calcutta, as would be produced by remitting four thousand dollars in specie, after deducting from that sum the peace rates of freight and insurance. Though it is a pleasing reflection, that some part of this money may even now have been expended, and contributed to supply the spiritual wants of numbers, yet we are not to forget, that a few thousand Bibles cannot suffice for many millions of inhabitants; that the demand for the word of God will be more urgent, the more a knowledge of it is disseminated, and that the united efforts of all Christians, in all parts of the world, are demanded, and will be demanded for many years to come, in this single branch of charity.

We might state a multitude of facts, all tending to prove, that the encouragement to distribute the Scriptures in Asia is continually increasing. From the journal kept by Peter, a native missionary of the cross, it appears, that throughout a long journey in Orissa, a part of Hindostan, performed in the autumn of 1811, he found great numbers of persons, who heard him with attention when he preached, and were very anxious to receive from him copies of the Scriptures. In stating his labors on a particular Lord's day, he says, " Some sat down with me for two hours at a time, reading the New Testament and hearing it explained. Others earnestly entreated for a Testament, or a tract; and when they had obtained their request seemed as glad as if they had gained some rich prize." "At Bhudruka, as well as in the way to it," says the same writer, "I preached Jesus to multitudes. The people seemed so eager for books, that I think I could have distributed a thousand, if I had had them." On a subsequent day, he writes thus: "I sat from twelve o'clock till seven in the evening, reading and explaining the word of God. I gave away many tracts; also two Testaments to two very sensible Ooriyas, [i. e. natives of Orissa,] one of whom appeared very serious and attentive, and, after I had departed to my lodgings, came and inquired very particularly about the way of salvation."

Two other missionaries write thus: "The poor heathen are much surprised to hear the gracious news of eternal life through Jesus Christ our Lord. You would admire to see with what gladness they accept the Orissa Testaments at our hands. They say they never thought the Firingees* had such a good book! We have distributed a considerable number of Testaments in the country, and have had the pleasure of sending one to Pooree, and the Brahmins of Jugunnath [Juggernaut] received it gladly. They wanted to pay for it; but we strictly charged the bearer to present it without taking any thing for it."

Important, however, as the distribution of the Scriptures among the heathen, in their own languages, is held to be by us, and by the Christian public generally, it should never be forgotten, that the *preaching of the gospel* in every part of the earth, is indispensable to the general conversion of mankind. Though the Scriptures alone have, in many individual cases, been made the instrument of regeneration, yet we have no account of any very extensive diffusion of Christianity, unless where the truths of the Scriptures have been preached. Were the heathen generally to receive the Scriptures, and anxious to learn divine truth, they would, like the Ethiopian eunuch, apply for instruction to those who had been previously acquainted with the same Scriptures; and when asked if they understood what they had read, would reply, *How can we, except some man should guide us?* The distribution of the Bible excites inquiry, and often leads those who receive that precious book to attend public worship in the sanctuary. But *the preaching of the gospel* is, after all, the grand means appointed by Infinite Wisdom for the conversion and salvation of men. Without this, the Scriptures, however liberally distributed, will have comparatively little effect among any people, whether Pagan or nominally Christian. This assertion is not only approved by reason, but abundantly confirmed by the history of the Church, and the express declaration of God's word. "Whosoever," says the great apostle to the Gentiles, "shall call upon the name of the Lord shall be saved. How then shall they call on him in whom they have not believed? and how shall they believe in him of whom they have not heard? and how shall they hear without a preacher? and how shall they preach except they be sent?" i. e. how shall they proclaim the gospel to the heathen, or the Jews, unless they go as missionaries? And, as if to show that the circulation of the Scriptures, and the preaching of the gospel, should go hand in hand, the apostle comes to this conclusion *"So, then, faith cometh by hearing, and hearing by the word of God."* The countries in which heathenism now prevails, will doubtless be able to furnish themselves with preachers, after Christianity shall have made extensive progress in them; but at the commencement of the gospel dispensation to those who are entirely ignorant of it, they must for many years receive preachers from Christian nations.

So far as the Board has been engaged in the attempt to establish missions, some unexpected impediments have been thrown in the way. It has been ascertained, however, that Ceylon is open to our exertions; and

---

* "That is, the *unclean,* a name given by them to all who were without cast."

this is certainly one of the most promising fields in the world for missionary enterprise. At the Isle of France, also, a useful station might be fixed; and hopes are entertained, that a door will be opened for the preachers of the gospel in the populous regions near Surat and Bombay. It may also be reasonably hoped and believed, that the missionaries who remain in the service of the Board, will be improved, and rendered fit for eminent usefulness, by the trials which they have experienced. So far as can be judged from their letters, the painful dispensations to which we refer, have added to their patience, fortitude, and humility, and have attached them more strongly to the cause which they have espoused.

Disappointments in the great work of evangelizing the world are to be expected; but they should never dishearten us, nor cause us to intermit our labors; nor should they induce us to relinquish a particular object, unless they are of a decisive character, or have been many times repeated. Christians have been too ready to faint and grow weary under discouragements, in almost all ages of the church. They would do well to take lessons on this subject from the men of the world. Does the loss of one ship, or of a whole convoy, deter enterprising merchants from entering on a new commerce, which promises, so far as probability is regarded, to become lucrative and successful? Do our farmers abandon fields, which had been prepared for cultivation with great labor, merely because the first crop has not answered their most sanguine expectations? The Christian should feel persuaded, that though a single attempt, or even a series of attempts, to send the gospel to the heathen, should fail; yet, not only the experience of the church from the first promulgation of Christianity to the present time, but the express promises of God in relation to times still future, afford the strongest encouragement to persevering labors in this cause.

Some persons speak of *missions*, as though they were a new thing in the world; or at least as though they had never done much good to mankind. These persons forget, that Christianity has always been extended by missions, wherever it has been extended at all, with the exception of what has been done in this way by colonization. They forget that all Europe, and large portions of Asia and Africa, have been converted to Christianity by missions; that the primitive preachers of Christianity were almost all missionaries; that the disciples who composed our Lord's household, to whom Matthias and Paul were subsequently added, were named *missionaries*, and have been gloriously distinguished in all succeeding ages, as the *missionaries of Jesus Christ*. They seem ignorant that the word *apostle*, introduced into our language from the Greek, is precisely of the same meaning as our word *missionary*; and that learned divines have regretted, that the word was not translated instead of being thus introduced. They forget, that our ancestors in Britain were wretched idolaters, offering human sacrifices, and clinging to the most degrading superstitions, till they were delivered from their miserable bondage by the instrumentality of missionaries. If such mighty transformations were wrought by the labors of missionaries, when printing was unknown, and there was but little intercourse between nations; when most barbarous nations were subdivided into a multitude of petty states, hostile to each other; when science was in its infancy, and the restraints of law and order were but partially enjoyed; when commerce had but just begun to produce its civilizing effects;—how much more encouragement is there to proceed with vigor in the establishment and support of missions, in these highly favored times, when the art of printing will enable us to multiply copies of the Scriptures so as to supply the wants of every human being; when commerce visits every part of the world; when wealth is abundant, and the means of supporting distant expeditions of benevolence are easily supplied; when the number of persons engaged in this good work is great and increasing; and above all, when the day is not far distant, as we trust, in which the word of the Lord shall have free course, and its influence be felt from the rising to the setting sun?

It is to be remembered that, when any great design is to be accomplished for the church and the world, God sees fit to try those who are engaged in it, by many adverse occurrences. Through what a series of difficulties did Moses conduct the Israelites before they were permitted to enter Canaan? Through what disheartening scenes were the immediate disciples of our Lord called to pass, before and after his resurrection? How dark and mysterious must it have appeared, that Paul, with his illustrious qualifications, should have spent so large a part of his life in prison, and in laboring with his own hands for his support: and should have been so perpetually exposed to the rage and persecution of ungodly men? In the time of the Reformation, also, how numerous were the difficulties to be encountered,—and frequently how unexpected,—before the truth could be preached with safety in a single nation in Europe? How often did the nations, which had been partially reformed, relapse into Popery, and re-kindle the flames of persecution? When our ancestors first came to this country, and sacrificed their ease and comfort to establish churches in the wilderness, how many and various were their hardships? How often did they suffer under the frowns of Providence, and how severely were their faith and hope tried? Yet, in all these instances, God was preparing his people for success and prosperity. So in most of the modern attempts to send the gospel to the heathen, the discouragements, which at first presented themselves, have been overcome by zeal and perseverance. If the Moravians had yielded to discouragements, of which they experienced a great variety, they never could have had, as they now have, one hundred and fifty missionaries, some of them in the most inhospitable climates, and *twenty thousand* hopeful converts. If the Missionary Society in England had given over their labors, at the loss of the ship Duff, they never could have had, as they now have, missionaries at twenty different stations; nor could they receive, as they now do, most gratifying intelligence of the progress made in communicating instruction, and of conversions from idols to Christ. If Zeigenbalg and his associates had been deterred by temporary hindrances, they could not have planted the gospel, more than a century ago, in southern India; nor could a long succession of missionaries and pastors have ministered to churches, whose light has shone in that region with double splendor, in contrast with the surrounding darkness.

In estimating the success of missionaries, we must regard the stage of the mission, the difficulties to be met in the beginning, the value of an establishment among the heathen, and many other things, beside the number of converts made by the personal exertions of the first laborers in a new field. The man who shall learn a new language, conciliate the regard of even a few natives to the cause in which he is employed, add facilities to the acquisition of the language, begin a translation of the Scriptures, and prepare the way for others to labor with greater advantages, may, eventually, be the instrument of bringing more souls to heaven, (though he should never be so happy as to see any fruit of his toil with his mortal eyes,) than the most honored servant of Christ in a Christian country.

They who urge against missions to the heathen the small immediate success which usually attend the first attempts in a new region, would do well to consider, that without a beginning there can be no progress,— without a progress no consummation. And shall there never be a beginning? Will Christians fold their hands, and leave the heathen to grope in Egyptian darkness, without an effort to enlighten them? Or, if this melancholy determination is not allowed, when shall the beginning be made? Can a more favorable time to institute new missions ever be expected? If this favorable crisis, when the Christian world is awake on the subject, should be suffered to pass away unimproved, who can ensure the return of another? But it will not pass away in this manner; it has already been seized by multitudes who will not relinquish the object. In regard to many missions, the beginning is past; the progress is cheering beyond expectation or hope; and a glorious consummation may be reasonably anticipated.

To those who allege that little has been hitherto done in the great work, it may be replied, that in most instances, quite as much has been done, as was expected by any man who considered the means employed. In some instances, more has been done than the most enthusiastic ventured to hope. Who would have dared to predict so salutary and speedy a change, as has been experienced at Bavian's Kloof and Bethelsdorp in South Africa, by the wild, ferocious, and besotted Caffres and Hottentots? From a state of the most deplorable ignorance and brutism, several hundred families of these degraded people have been delivered, by the preaching of the plain truths of the gospel. Industry has taken the place of vagrancy; honesty the place of fraud and theft; cleanliness and decency have been introduced, where the most sordid and loathsome habits prevailed; *the love of Christ has been shed abroad in hearts*, which had been the residence of stupidity, sin and guilt; and the Christian graces and virtues have supplanted the selfish, malignant, and sensual passions and vices.

When Carey planned and entered upon a mission to Hindostan, about twenty years ago, he did not believe it credible, in his most sanguine moments, that his own eyes would ever witness such a progress as they have already witnessed. It appeared to him an object worthy of the most strenuous labors of a whole life to translate the New Testament into a single language; an object, which, if he might live to accomplish it, would furnish ground of everlasting gratitude and praise to God. What then must be his emotions, to see translations now carrying on in ten languages, in an establishment of which he was the founder; to see the publication of the New Testament in several languages, and a third edition of the whole Bible printing in one? What ought to be the emotions of Christians generally, while beholding these things, and the kindred efforts of other individuals and associations aiming at the same great end? How animating the thought that translations of the Scriptures are commenced in thirty Asiatic languages? Though we have to lament the early death of a Leyden, and a Martyn, yet others will be raised up to supply their places, and complete their benevolent designs.

The progress which has been made in obtaining a knowledge of the religious character of the Asiatics, and of the necessary qualifications of a missionary, in ascertaining the manner in which many classes of the heathen are disposed to treat Christian instructors, and in establishing the fact, that the great doctrines of our holy religion produce their proper benign effects, wherever preached in simplicity, may be regarded as highly important and satisfactory. The most common and popular objections to missions are found to be utterly groundless; and the day seems to have nearly arrived, when, with all *who love the Lord Jesus Christ in sincerity*, there shall be but one opinion on the practicability and duty of engaging in missionary enterprises.

Are we to reason, and act, as though all these advances were unworthy of consideration? Is the progress already made to be accounted as nothing? Is it nothing, that missionaries are stationed in New Holland; at many places in Hindostan; in Ceylon, at five or six places in Africa; in Tartary; in South America; in Labrador and Greenland; and in the islands of the Pacific ocean? Is it nothing, that such a man as Dr. Buchanan has travelled, and published the result of his researches, in order to show the progress of Christianity in the east, and to press upon Christians the duty of activity in this great work? Is it nothing, that the caverns of the Inquisition at Goa have been thrown open, and the wretched captives suffered to go free? and that this victory of religion over superstition has been achieved in consequence of the benevolent attempts to extend the light of the gospel to Asia? Is it nothing, that we are enabled, by intelligence received while we are writing, to celebrate the triumph of the friends of missions in the British Parliament? a triumph which unbars India to the missionaries of the cross? Is it nothing, that the executive government of Great Britain is strongly in favor of communicating religious instruction to sixty millions of Asiatic subjects? Is it nothing, that the voice of the English nation was raised, in the course of three months, to a louder note of intreaty in favor of sending Christianity to the east, than it had been raised for a century past, on any moral or political subject whatever, not excepting the abolition of the slave trade for which the nation struggled twenty years? Is it nothing, that nine hundred petitions loaded the tables of each House of Parliament, signed by nearly half a million of individuals,—a greater number than ever before offered petitions in their own hand-writing, for one common purpose, to any government on earth? Is it nothing, that these petitions flocked together from every part of England, Ireland and Scotland, as if moved by the same impulse; that they were every where encouraged by the wise, the considerate, the benevolent, the pious; and that their success was earnestly desired by all classes of persons from the prince to the peasant,—from the learned divine to the amiable child?

We are anxious to fix your attention, Christian brethren, on the great object of evangelizing *all* nations, an object more glorious, more wor-

10

thy of universal patronage and admiration of the people of God, than the tongue can express, or the heart conceive; and an object of sure and no very distant accomplishment. To this object the eyes of Christians in many countries are already most earnestly directed. The Christian world is now, for the first time, reaching forward to its attainment, and even grasping it by anticipation. In Great Britain, the promulgation of true religion in every part of the earth, and the publication and distribution of the Scriptures in every language, are topics of general and familiar allusion, as though these stupendous events were at hand, and were even now hailed with demonstrations of joy. When we notice that the wisest and the best informed men in that empire, and in our own country, partake of these joyful anticipations, and that a similar crisis in the state of the church has never before been known; when we observe, that this tone of public feeling has been excited not by a sudden impulse of enthusiasm, but by a patient comparison of the word of God with his providence, of prophecy with history, by an attentive consideration of the peculiar *signs of the times*, and by the gradual operation of causes above the powers of man to contrive or combine; we are forced to believe, that God has great things to be accomplished by the men of this generation, and that, after punishing the nations for their sins, he is about to deliver them from the wretched bondage in which they have been held. To this day the ancient prophets looked forward with holy rapture; for this day the persecuted congregations of the faithful prayed, during the gloomy reign of popish superstition; for this day the Reformers labored and suffered; for this day the most devout aspirations of pious souls have in every age ascended. Shall we, who are so happy as to see this day, neglect to do *our* part? Other times have been times of preparation; the present age is emphatically the age of action. Shall we remain idle in this harvest time of the world?

Some may inquire; What shall we do? What are the duties peculiarly incumbent upon Christians at the present time? To these questions the following answers are respectfully submitted.

Christians should *pray* constantly and fervently for the advent of the latter-day glory. This topic should never be forgotten in the public assembly, the social circle convened for prayer, the family, or the closet. It is uniformly in answer to prayer, that Christ appears in his glory to build up Zion. It is in consequence of prayer, that spiritual blessings are ever to be expected. Were it possible that prayer should cease to be offered for the millennium, that blissful period would never arrive; and the creation would groan under the prevalence of sin without hope of deliverance. Daniel understood *by books** the time appointed for the restoration of his captive countrymen to their native land, and set his face to seek the Lord God by prayer and supplication. So Christians should understand by the *sure word of prophecy*, the time of general deliverance, and should engage in earnest and united prayer. They should pray, in order to awaken their sympathy for the immense multitude of sufferers throughout the world; to enkindle their own zeal, and stimulate others to the good work of the Lord, and to prepare themselves for all the sacrifices and active services, which the momen-

* Dan. ix, 2.

tous crisis demands. They should pray, that Christians may all be united in the greatest effort, which ever claimed their aid; and that smaller points of difference may be forgotten in the great contest between Christ and false gods. They should pray that all Missionary Societies, and all individuals who have an influence in the direction of missions, may be prudent, faithful, and guided by Infinite Wisdom; that the Missionaries whom they send may be humble, prayerful, courageous, and persevering, full of faith and of the Holy Ghost, and may happily exemplify the doctrines wich they teach, that a great and effectual door may be opened for their entrance among the heathen, and that Christ may speedily become *the power of God and the wisdom of God* to many who shall believe through their instrumentality; and that a divine blessing may rest on all who contribute by their influence, their example, their property, or their personal labors, to extend the limits of the true Church, and gather Christ's wandering sheep into the one fold.

We take the liberty of stating, in this place, that many Christians in Great Britain have, since missions were fitted out from that country, observed the first Monday evening in each month, as a season of peculiar prayer, both social and secret, for the success of missionaries and the spread of the Gospel. The same time has been devoted to the same purpose, by Christians in some of our towns, since the mission was fitted out from this country to Asia. Concert is pleasing in the pursuit of any desirable object. Let Christians who are accustomed to assemble for social prayer, consider whether this concert may not be further extended. But whether this season be equally convenient for all, or not, we earnestly urge upon all the duty of stated, particular, persevering prayer for missionaries and those to whom they are sent. Let Christians raise their voices in unison, and adopt the language of the prophet, "For Zion's sake will I not hold my peace; for Jerusalem's sake I will not rest; until the righteousness thereof go forth as brightness, and the salvation thereof as a lamp that burneth. And the Gentiles shall see thy righteousness, and all kings thy glory."

Another obvious duty binding upon all Christians, is to *show the sincerity of their prayers by their practice.* None, who have read their Bibles, ought to be ignorant, that they are stewards of whatever they possess; that all their means and opportunities of doing good are recorded in the book of God's remembrance; and that an account must be rendered of the manner in which this stewardship has been exercised. Who, in this favored land, can say, that he has not been entrusted with at least *one* talent? Who can be willing to hide that talent in a napkin? How many are there, who have their five, their ten, their fifty, their hundred talents? And how unhappy will be their case, if all this liberality of Providence shall be found at last to have been wasted upon them; to have produced none of the good to which it ought to have been applied; and to have proved its earthly possessors guilty of unfaithfulness to the rightful Proprietor?

The proportion of his property, which each Christian should devote to public and charitable purposes, differs according to the different circumstances in which he is placed, and must be left to the decision of his own conscience instructed by the word of God. But however difficult it might be to determine the exact amount which each one should give, there can be no hesitation in declaring, that it should, in all circumstances, and at all times, be so great as to be really valued by him who gives it, and thus be a real sacrifice in his estimation. For a poor widow to give her two mites, *even all her living*, is a great sacrifice; but for a wealthy man to give two hundred mites can be no sacrifice at all; for it would not cause him a moment's uneasiness, nor be considered as a loss worthy to be mentioned, if he were to lose ten times that sum in the bottom of the sea. That Christians may act with system, and yield to each charitable claim its proper regard, they will do wisely to ascertain, each one for himself, how large a sum he ought to bestow from year to year; always remembering, that it is safer to err on the side of generosity than on that of parsimony, that few err in giving too much, many in *withholding more than is meet*; and that his decision is to be re-examined at the *judgment-seat of Christ*.

Still less would we venture to intimate the proportion which is due to the various charitable purposes now existing in this country. We are confident, however, that where the public have the means of information in relation to such purposes, where no invidious comparisons are made between the claims of different charitable associations, and no rivalship exists but that which provokes to love and to good works, there is reason to believe that Providence will direct to a proper distribution of pecuniary means. There are many charitable institutions, on each of which every good man ought to implore the divine blessing. Perhaps no one of them receives so much patronage as it deserves, and might very usefully employ. Let it be the endeavor of the particular friends of each to increase the general stock of benevolence, trusting, that if this be done, *all* benevolent designs will receive a rapidly increasing patronage.

There is one objection to sending missionaries abroad so common, and so plausible at first view, that it ought to be mentioned here. It is this. That many ministers of the gospel, more than can at present be supplied, are imperiously needed at home. This objection states a melancholy truth, but proceeds on a mistaken principle. If the apostles had argued thus, they never would have quitted Judea; the Gentiles would never have heard the gospel till many ages after the Christian era; our ancestors in Britain would never have been converted. The same objection could have been applied, nay, was applied, to sending missionaries from Connecticut and Massachusetts to our new settlements, when the domestic Missionary Societies first began their operations.

But not to dwell on this consideration, there is another which settles the debate at once; which is, *That the readiest and most efficacious method of promoting religion at home, is for Christians to exert themselves to send it abroad.* On the most thorough examination, this position will be found strictly and literally true. When missions to the heathen were first contemplated in England, the above objection was strongly urged, and with as great plausibility as it ever can be urged here. What has been the event? The number of evangelical preachers and professors of Christianity has been increasing in that country, in an unexampled manner, during the whole time since the first missionaries sailed from England. The increase of faithful preachers alone has more than twenty-fold exceeded the whole number of missionaries sent abroad.

When it was objected on the floor of the Senate of Massachusetts to the act for incorporating the Board in whose behalf we speak, that it was designed to afford the means *of exporting religion, whereas there was none to spare from among ourselves;* it was pleasantly and truly replied, *that religion was a commodity, of which the more we exported the more we had remaining.* However strange this may appear to some, it will not seem strange to him who considers the import of these words: "There is that scattereth, and yet increaseth, and there is that withholdeth more than is meet, but it tendeth to poverty. He that watereth, shall be watered also himself. It is more blessed to give, than to receive." The government of God is a government of benevolence; and is intended to convince us, that he, who does good to others, is most secure of receiving good himself. The same remark, which was made respecting the increase of religion in England, will apply to this country, so far as it has been in similar circumstances.

The only remaining duty, which our limits permit us to urge upon Christians, in relation to this subject, is, *That they use all the means in their power for obtaining information, respecting, the wants of the heathen, and the encouragements to support missions.* Without information, no person can act understandingly; but when in possession of a simple statement of what has been done, and what is doing, with the motives for perseverance, Christians can act vigorously, unitedly, and to good effect. To be ignorant of the state and prospects of the Church, at this day, is criminal; especially as the means of information are within every person's reach.

We are unwilling to conclude, without addressing a few words particularly to our brethren in different parts of the country, who have associated in Foreign Mission Societies, and have committed their funds to the disposal of the Board.

BELOVED BRETHREN,—We consider it as a token of great good to our own country, and as a pledge of success in the attempt to convert the heathen, that so many ornaments of our churches and pillars of civil society, have united in devoting a yearly tribute to extend the knowledge of Christ in foreign lands. In every great cause union is necessary; in none more evidently so, than in the one to which all our remarks have reference. Union in this cause is peculiarly productive of happiness. We appeal to your own experience, brethren. Is not the thought of joining in a work of vast importance to the souls of men with multitudes of your fellow Christians, widely scattered through the world, a thought which dilates the heart with joy? which prompts to Christian activity? which animates to prayer and praise? which ennobles the soul, and powerfully reminds it of the *love of Christ which passes knowledge?*

The multitudes among us who have lent their influence, and their property, to assist in the mighty enterprise of converting the heathen, could not direct their operations to effect, unless they had some common bond of union,—some centre of action. If the American Board of Commissioners for Foreign Missions, secured as it is by an act of incorporation, can furnish this bond, and can so far be the servants of all, as to direct the offerings and benefactions of all to the end for which they are designed, the satisfaction thence arising will be a rich reward for the care and labor which so weighty a concern demands. That the Board shall in no case err, it would be presumptuous to engage; but that their designs are in a high degree interesting to all the disciples of Christ, may be safely affirmed; and that the measures adopted by them will, with a divine blessing, be greatly conducive to the happiest results, may reasonably be hoped.

It is respectfully recommended to Foreign Mission Societies, that this address be read at their next annual meetings, unless peculiar circumstances render it inconvenient.

The worthy and pious females in our country, who have associated to contribute to the funds of this Board, are deserving of particular and affectionate remembrance. Nor would we pass over other females of like character, whose situation does not permit them thus to associate, but whose cordial regards to the cause have been expressed by individual donations. From the time of our Lord's crucifixion to the present day, probably from the patriarchal ages, the larger proportion of his most faithful and devoted followers have been found in the female sex. Here is a scene of action, in which women may take a lively interest without overstepping the limits which a sense of propriety has imposed on female exertion. Here is an occasion, in which thousands of pious females may express the same affection with which the heart of Mary overflowed, when she anointed the feet of her Savior, and wiped them with the hairs of her head. *She* did it to honor the person of her Lord *before his burial; they* are invited to show the same affection, by furnishing the means of calling *to spiritual life in Him those who are dead in trespasses and sins.*

To conclude; the Board are deeply sensible that they need, and are earnestly desirous to receive, the co-operation, the good wishes, and the prayers, of the numerous friends of Christ, who have embarked in this cause. The considerate public will readily allow, that to examine the comparative claims of many distinct heathen countries;—to select the most promising fields of action;—to judge of the qualifications of missionaries;—to meet unexpected trials with fortitude and undiminished resolution;—to anticipate and supply the wants of distant laborers in the vineyard.—to keep up an extensive foreign correspondence;—to make prompt and regular remittances, in the changing state of the world;—to instruct missionaries in all the unforeseen and difficult cases which may occur;—to manage with skill and prudence the pecuniary affairs of the institution; —in short, to discharge with fidelity, and care, and from love to Christ and his disciples, all the various duties imposed upon the members, and especially upon the officers of this Board, is an arduous work; a work fraught with high and solemn responsibility, which requires much thought, constant attention, and frequent labor, and which makes it proper that they, to whom so weighty a charge is committed, should solicit the affectionate remembrance of their brethren, whenever they draw near to the mercy-seat. Enjoying this consolation amidst their cares, and relying on this source of strength and wisdom, the Board may hope to contribute something to the advent of the happy period, when God shall extend peace to his church *like a river, and the glory of the Gentiles like a flowing stream.*

JEDIDIAH MORSE,   }

SAMUEL WORCESTER,   } *Committee.*

JEREMIAH EVARTS,   }

Boston, October 25, 1813.

MINUTES

FIFTH ANNUAL MEETING.

———

THE Board met according to appointment, at the Philosophical Chamber of Yale College, on Thursday, September 15, 1814, at 10 o'clock, A. M.—Present,

The Hon. ELIAS BOUDINOT, Esq. LL. D.
Hon. JOHN TREADWELL, Esq. LL. D.
Rev. JOSEPH LYMAN, D. D.
Rev. SAMUEL SPRING, D. D.
Hon. JOHN HOOKER, Esq.
Rev. JEDIDIAH MORSE, D. D.
Rev. CALVIN CHAPIN,
Rev. JAMES RICHARDS,
Rev. SAMUEL WORCESTER, D. D.
Rev. HENRY DAVIS, D. D. and
JEREMIAH EVARTS, Esq.*

The Vice President opened the meeting with prayer.

The following gentlemen were chosen officers for the year ensuing, viz.

The Hon. JOHN TREADWELL, Esq. *President.*
The Rev. Dr. SPRING, *Vice President.*
The Rev. Dr. SPRING,
The Rev. Dr. WORCESTER, and } *Prudential Committee.**
Mr. EVARTS,
The Rev. Dr. WORCESTER, *Corresponding Secretary.*
The Rev. Mr. CHAPIN, *Recording Secretary.*
JEREMIAH EVARTS, Esq. *Treasurer.*
Mr CHESTER ADAMS, *Auditor.‡*

* The Rev. Dr. Dwight was prevented by College business, from attending till near the close of the meeting.
† William Bartlet, Esq., declined a re-election.
‡ Charles Walley, Esq., who was chosen Auditor last year, declined accepting the office.

Voted, That the thanks of this Board be presented to William Bartlet, Esq., for his services as a member of the Prudential Committee, and for the generous entertainment which, on several occasions, he has afforded the Prudential Committee.

The Hon. Elias Boudinot communicated an extract from a letter, stating an earnest request from the Delaware Indians, that missionaries be sent among them; which extract was referred to the Prudential Committee.

Voted, That it is the opinion of this Board, that the independent and unevangelized tribes of Indians, occupying their own lands, whether without or within the limits stated in the treaty of peace between the United States and Great Britain, are, with other objects, embraced by the Act of their Incorporation.

The Prudential Committee exhibited their Report, which was accepted.

At 3 o'clock, P. M., public divine service was attended, in the church of the United Society, and a sermon was delivered by the Rev. Mr. Richards, from Ephesians iii, 8. "Unto me, who am less than the least of all saints, is this grace given, that I should preach among the Gentiles the unsearchable riches of Christ."

Voted, That the thanks of this Board be presented to the Rev. Mr. Richards for his sermon delivered this day, and that a copy thereof be requested for publication.

The Hon. Mr. Boudinot and the Rev. Dr. Davis were appointed a committee to carry the foregoing vote into effect. The printing of the sermon was referred to the Prudential Committee.

Voted, To request De Lauzun Deforest, Esq, to audit the Treasurer's accounts for the year now closed.

Friday, September 16. The Rev. Dr. Davis opened the meeting with prayer.

The Treasurer's accounts were exhibited, as examined and certified by the Auditor, and accepted.

Voted, That the next annual meeting be holden at Salem, (Mass.) on the third Wednesday of September, 1815, at 10 o'clock, A. M.

The Rev. Mr. Chapin was chosen preacher for that meeting, and the Rev. Dr. Davis second preacher.

Voted, That the Recording Secretary transmit to every member of the Board, information of the time and place of the next annual meeting.

The following by-law was adopted, in addition to chapter second, section first, of the By-laws:

If, in the opinion of the Prudential Committee, it shall at any time be dangerous to the health of the members of the Board, or on any other account highly inexpedient, to meet at the place appointed for any annual meeting, the Prudential Committee are authorized to appoint some other place for such meeting, by giving notice of such place to the Recording Secretary, in season for him to give notice to each member of the Board.

Voted, That the thanks of this Board be presented to the President and Fellows of Yale College, for the convenient accommodation afforded them, during their present session, in the Philosophical Chamber appertaining to said College, and that the Recording Secretary transmit a copy of this vote to the President.

Voted, That the Prudential Committee be directed to prepare and publish the annual Report of the Board, including such parts of the Report of the Prudential Committee as they shall judge most useful, an abstract of the Treasurer's accounts, a statement of donations, and such other information as they shall deem proper and expedient.

The Rev. Dr. Lyman closed the session with prayer.

REPORT.

BRETHREN,—The last annual Report of your Committee left our missionaries in the East, on the mighty waters, uncertain where they should land, and still more doubtful where they should abide. During the year, great solicitude has been felt for them; but at length that solicitude is considerably relieved. For a long season they were held in anxious suspense, painfully fluctuating between fear and hope; but at length that suspense appears to have come nearly to an end. Our last letters from them were received, by the way of England, about ten days ago, the latest date from Mr. Newell being the 20th of last December, at Columbo, in the island of Ceylon; and from Messrs. Hall and Nott, the 23d of the same month, at Bombay. The principal facts and circumstances, related in their several communications, your Committee will report in order.

Messrs. Hall and Nott, as reported at our last anniversary, left Calcutta on the 20th of November, 1812, under circumstances not very pleasant, and embarked for Bombay, expecting to touch at Ceylon, and doubtful whether they should proceed any further. It appears, however, that they touched not at Ceylon, but at Pondicherry, where they staid about five weeks. The reason of this they probably assigned in a letter written at Pondicherry, to which in a subsequent letter they refer, but which has not been received. They arrived at Bombay on the 11th of February, 1813, about eleven weeks after leaving Calcutta. On their arrival, they immediately found that intelligence concerning them, forwarded from Calcutta, had reached Bombay, intelligence, disadvantageous to them, and accompanied with an expression of the will of the supreme government, that they should be sent to England. They were permitted to submit to Sir Evan Nepean, governor of Bombay, a very respectful and judicious memorial, which, together with accompanying documents, declared the views with which they came to India—made known the patronage and instructions under which they had been sent forth—gave a narrative of their proceedings at Calcutta—explained the misunderstandings which had arisen between them and the supreme government there, and the reasons of their departing thence for Bombay, under circumstances so liable to misconstruction—referred their case to the well known clemency and candor of the Governor, and implored his favor and protection. Their memorial was very kindly received and considered; and every thing relating to their object and their proceedings, appeared to the Governor in so satisfactory a light, that he not only allowed them to remain for the present at Bombay, but assured them of his disposition to render them every favor in his power; and even took upon himself the trouble to write a private letter in their behalf to Lord Minto, the governor general at Calcutta, with a view to remove the unfavorable impressions respecting them, which had been made on his Lordship's mind, either by misrepresentations or unexplained circumstances, and to obtain permission for them to reside at Bombay, or to go, unmolested, in pursuit of their object elsewhere. Thus encouraged the two brethren sat down to the study of the Mahratta language, under the tuition of a Brahmin; in the hope of having the satisfaction, in due time, of preaching in that language to the natives at Bombay, and in the extensive and populous regions in which the language is vernacular.

Sir Evan Nepean's letter appears to have been successful in satisfying the governor general's mind in regard to the character and proceedings of the two missionaries. The war, however, between the United States and Great Britain, intelligence of which had been received in India, gave rise to new difficulties. On the 25th of June, the brethren were informed by Dr. Taylor, a gentleman from whom they received many friendly offices, that the Governor, Sir Evan Nepean, had expressed his fears that, on account of the war, he should be under the necessity of sending them to England; though, as they state in their journal, "the Governor expressed to Dr. Taylor his firm confidence in their integrity, and the excellency of the character of those gentlemen by whom they were patronized."

On the 18th of August, by the advice of a Mr. Money, another gentleman to whom they were indebted for many offices of kindness, they drew up another memorial to the Governor, which was to be presented along with certain documents of a purport to shew decisively, that their mission had no connection with the war. Mr. Money, they say, "urged us to do this immediately, as he had observed our names down at the marine office as passengers to England in the Caarmarthen, which was to have sailed about this time, but having sprung a leak will be detained a month or two." From this memorial, that something of the spirit and feelings of the brethren may be perceived and felt, the following passages are extracted —

"Right Honorable Sir,—When we consider that both English and American Christians are interested in our success—that already much time and money have been expended in our enterprise, and that much more must be expended if we are sent from this place;—that we must then be in perfect uncertainty, whether we shall ever be allowed to preach to the destitute the unsearchable riches of Christ;—and especially when we consider the command of that ascending Lord, in whom we all hope, and whom we would obey,—we feel justified, we feel compelled, by motives which we dare not resist, to entreat your Excellency's favor. To ourselves it cannot but be supposed, that to fail in our object must be in the highest degree trying. Our feelings are deeply interested, it may well be supposed, in our object, to which we have been looking for so many years—for which we have left our country, our prospects, and our dearest friends—to which we are conscientiously, and, by the help of God, unalterably devoted—in which the hearts of Christians are universally engaged, without distinction of country, and which we cannot doubt, is under the favorable eye of our Lord and Master."

"Your Excellency's well known desire for promoting Christian knowledge, and the certainty that we should be in future, as really under the direction and at the disposal of your Excellency, as at the present moment, encourage us in requesting that we may be allowed to remain, at least till it may be learned whether there will be a speedy termination of the unhappy war."

On the next day they write, "Having prepared the preceding memorial, we went with it to Mr. Money, being desirous to forward it as soon as possible, on account of a report which we last evening heard, that we were to go to England in the Sir Godfrey Webster, to sail on Sabbath next. At breakfast with Mr. Money, we saw the superintendant of embarkation, who told us, that he had, by order of the Governor, yesterday settled every arrangement for our going in the Sir Godfrey Webster, and that every pains had been taken to make us comfortable, and that we had been provided for suitably to our ministerial character. We were much distressed by this intelligence, and especially as we were entirely unprepared for such a voyage. Mr. Money immediately waited on the Governor, to tell him our unprepared state, and to hand him the above petition. On his return he informed us, that the Governor's orders from Bengal were such, that he would be unable to allow us to remain; but, as he was unwilling to put us to any inconvenience, he would allow us to stay until the sailing of the Caarmarthen, which is to be in about six weeks. We then waited on the Governor ourselves, and expressed our thanks for his kindness now, and on former occasions. He told us, that he had supposed us prepared on the ground of what he had told Dr. Taylor; and endeavored to justify the Supreme Government in sending us away on account of the war. He declared his perfect confidence that we were innocent and harmless men, whose weapons of warfare were not carnal but spiritual. He likewise told us that he had succeeded in removing the unfavorable impressions which had been made on the mind of the Governor General, to effect which he had written to Lord Minto a private letter. Thus it pleases the Lord to deal with us We have never been covered with so thick a cloud."

Things remained in this posture until about the middle of September. At that time the brethren received from Calcutta the letters which, about ten months before, had been sent out for them from this country by the Alligator; and which, they say, "afforded us a pleasure which we cannot describe." With the advice of particular friends, they submitted to the Governor's inspection the official letter to them from the Corresponding Secretary, accompanied with a note, in which they say, "We extremely regret that the accompanying letter did not come to hand at an earlier period. Though received at so late an hour, we should not feel that we were faithful to our Patrons, to a numerous body of Christian friends, and to the Savior's cause, were we not to beg the liberty of presenting it to your Excellency for perusal. Its general tenor, and particularly the information which it gives of the appointment of a Committee at Calcutta to co-operate in our mission, seems to us fully to declare, that our Society is simply engaged in the great work, dear to English and American Christians, of spreading Christian knowledge and Christian hopes. The gentlemen, whom we now understand to constitute the Committee, are the Rev Dr. Carey, the Rev. Mr. Thomason, Chaplain, and George Udny, Esq.; the latter two in the place of Dr. Brown, and J. H. Harington, Esq. To this Committee we yesterday made known our unhappy situation; and we beg leave to express our desire to your Excellency, that our departure from this Presidency may be so long delayed, as to give them an opportunity of acquainting the Governor General with their relation to us, and of removing, if possible, the objections to our stay arising from the unhappy war."

The next day after this note was delivered, they write in their journal, "Mr. Nott waited on the Governor this morning at his request. He mentioned that he felt greatly embarrassed on account of yesterday's letter to him; that he wished to do all in his power for us; that he would think on the subject, and give an answer in two or three days. He did not hesitate in saying, that were he left to himself, he could not send us away."

The Committee of Agency for our affairs in India, appointed by the Prudential Committee, as this Board will recollect, were the Hon. John H. Harington, Esq. and Drs. Carey and Brown. But when our communication arrived at Calcutta, Dr. Brown was dead, and Judge Harington was absent. Under these circumstances, Dr. Carey thought fit to appoint the Rev. Thomas Thomason,* in the place of Dr. Brown, and they unitedly requested George Udny, Esq † to act in the place of Mr. Harington. Intelligence of this arrangement was duly communicated to the two brethren at Bombay; and they, perceiving the advantage which it offered them, immediately addressed the letter, referred to in the above cited note to Governor Nepean, to the Committee at Calcutta, for the purpose of engaging their good offices with the Governor-General in their behalf.

About five days after this, the two brethren received letters from Mr. Newell at Columbo, and from the Rev. Mr. Thomson, Chaplain at Madras, from which the following extracts are given. Mr. Newell, under date of Aug. 18th, 1813, writes, "I have had repeated assurances from the Hon. and Rev. Mr. Twistleton, senior Chaplain, and from Mr. Brisset the other Chaplain, the Governor's brother-in-law, that as many of my friends as choose to come here shall be safe, and have liberty to go to any part of the Island." Mr Thomson, under date of Sept 7th, writes, "You have, I believe, received notice from Mr. Newell, that you will be welcomed at Ceylon. I am warranted by letters from the Hon and Rev. Mr. Twistleton, to confirm it. I think you should lose no time in submitting this to the Governor, Sir Evan Nepean, and requesting leave to retire thither, instead of being sent to England."

Accordingly, after prayerful consideration, Messrs. Hall and Nott, on the 22d Sept. submitted the communications from Messrs Thomson and Newell to the Governor, accompanied with a memorial, in which they say, "After having read them, we beg your excellency to regard with a favorable eye, the pure, peaceful, inoffensive, Christian character of our mission, proved incontestibly by our instructions, by our letters, and by the appointment of a committee of British gentlemen of the clergy and laity to co-operate in the mission, which we have had the happiness of

* The Prudential Committee, before receiving this communication, had appointed the Rev. Mr. Thomason to supply the vacancy occasioned by the death of the Rev Dr. Brown
† George Udny, Esq. has been for many years a member of the Supreme Council in the Bengal Government, and has been uniformly favorable to the diffusion of Christianity in India The Supreme Council consists of four members, with the Governor General at their head.

making known to your Excellency; and to bestow an indulgent consideration on our present distressing situation, which must be aggravated in a severe degree, if we are sent across the seas to a foreign land, divided from our own by an unhappy war, the commencement of which we have sincerely deprecated, and for the conclusion of which we earnestly pray."—"It is still our highest wish to remain here, and render ourselves useful as instructors of youth and preachers of the gospel, under the protection of your Excellency's government, where the spiritual miseries of thousands call so loudly for the blessings of Christianity, where there are so many facilities for diffusing those blessings, and from which we cannot be sent without so much grief to numerous Christians, and so much discouragement to others, who are desiring to leave their own country, and go to preach Christ in Pagan lands. It is only therefore in the last resort, and with the hope of preventing the entire defeat of our pious attempt, that we implore your Excellency's sanction to remove ourselves from this place to Ceylon, where we have such assurances of a favorable reception, where we cannot but be under the superintending eye of a British government, and where, we trust, our conduct will be unobjectionable to his Excellency Governor Brownrigg."

In their journal, Oct 2, the brethren write, "Mr. Money having, at our request, conferred with the Governor concerning our petition, received this day from his Excellency a note nearly as follows: 'I find myself awkwardly situated relative to the two missionaries whom I wish to serve. On the 20th of August I wrote to Lord Minto, and I ought to have received his Lordship's answer some days since, and am now in daily expectation of it. I told his Lordship, that I understood he had changed his plan concerning missionaries, and allowed one in similar circumstances to remain in Bengal, and that now there was time for him to shew the same favor to Messrs. Hall and Nott; but that if I should receive no new commands from his Lordship, I should send them to England by the next ships. I had thought of another plan for them, which was, that in case Captain Digby should arrive in season, I should request him to give them a passage in the Cornwallis, which, as that ship will stop at Ceylon, would give Governor Brownrigg an opportunity to take such measures relative to them as he might judge proper." Nine days afterwards they write, "This day dined with the Governor. He added nothing to what he had said in Mr. Money's note. He repeated that he must send us in one of these ships, unless something new should take place." And five days after this, that is, on the 16th of October, they say, "This afternoon we received a note from our friend W. T. Money, Esq. informing us, that the Governor had failed in his application to Captain Digby. He says, 'Sir Evan sincerely regrets his ill success. I am sure he felt, and does now feel, much interest for you. Under these inauspicious circumstances, nothing now remains, but to prepare for your departure in the Caarmarthen.'"

The Caarmarthen was, at this time, on the eve of sailing, and there remained to Messrs. Hall and Nott scarcely a gleam of hope that they should avoid being sent to England. On the 18th of October, however, they had information of a vessel going to Cochin; learned that she would give them a passage, if they could be ready to go on board in about four or five hours; and understood, that from Cochin she would shortly convey them to Columbo in Ceylon. The time for deliberation was short They concluded to go; and accordingly taking some of their most necessary things, they embarked; leaving Mrs. Nott with her child, and some notes hastily written to acquaint their friends at Bombay with the fact and the reasons of their departure. On the 30th of the same month they arrived at Cochin, where they were kindly received, and during their stay very generously entertained, by Mr. Pearson, magistrate of the place.

On the 5th of November they write in their journal. "For five days we have been laboriously employed in travelling among, and inquiring about, the Jews and Christians. We have visited the college at Valipoli, and several Catholic churches; Candenade the see of the late Syrian Bishop: and the synagogues of the Jews at Cochin We have carefully committed to paper what information we could obtain, having been kindly furnished with such facilities as the place affords."

The vessel which had conveyed them to Cochin could not, as they had expected, convey them thence to Columbo While waiting and seeking for a passage, and just as one seemed to be presenting itself, an order arrived from Bombay, requiring them to be sent back to that place. They accordingly returned, after an absence of almost a month. With their private departure from Bombay, Sir Evan Nepean was not well pleased, as it might, from the favor which he had shewn them, subject him to censure from the General Government, for imputed connivance or delinquency. In a respectful and able memorial to him, however, after their return, they justified the procedure on the broad principle, that the authority of the Lord Jesus, under which they had been sent forth to preach the gospel to the heathen, was paramount to any civil authority, which would frustrate, or counteract their mission; and the Governor at length was so far satisfied, as to allow them to leave the ship in which they had been brought back to Bombay, and which for several days after their arrival they were not allowed to leave, and, free from all duress, to occupy a house provided for their accommodation in the city. Still he considered himself as required by the Supreme Government to send them to England; and as under particular obligations, from assurances which he had given the Governor General, to send them by the earliest regular conveyance.

On their return into the city, the two brethren were received by their worthy friends there with great joy, and with expressions and tokens of undiminished affection, confidence, and respect. Very soon afterwards, on the 10th of Dec. they received, from the Rev. Mr. Thomason of Calcutta, the last of three letters, bearing date Oct. 8th, and 13th, and Nov. 19th, 1813, in answer to theirs of Sept 15th, addressed to our agents at Calcutta. In these letters Mr. Thomason, with strong expressions of Christian affection, and of desire to promote the great object of their mission, related to them the measures which he and his colleagues in the agency had taken in their behalf with the Government, and the success with which those measures had been attended. "The last letter, in particular," say the brethren, "filled us with joy and thanksgiving to God. We immediately sent a copy of it to brother Newell, and to Mr. Money on the Gauts. Our friends advise to wait a day or two in hopes of something more full from Calcutta; and if nothing should come, to lay them, before the Governor." Accordingly, on the 13th of December, they sent to the Governor the following note, enclosing the two last letters from Mr. Thomason.

"RIGHT HONORABLE SIR. "Having always been convinced that the resolution to send us from this country emanated solely from the orders of the Supreme Government, and not from the disposition of your Excellency, which we know to be friendly to the evangelical object of our mission; and having received letters from Calcutta, evincing a change of sentiments in the late Governor General, and the conviction of Lord Moira the present Governor General, "that our intentions are to do good, and that no conceivable public injury can arise from our staying," and that his Lordship "spoke very decidedly about our being allowed to stay;" we beg to submit to the perusal of your Excellency two letters, dated 13th Oct., and 19th ult., addressed to us by the Rev. Thomas Thomason, a most respectable minister of the Church of England, resident at Calcutta. We trust that your Excellency will consider these letters as containing decisive evidence of the favorable inclinations of Lords Minto and Moira in regard to our present circumstances, and future views: and that with this proof of the light in which our mission is now regarded by the supreme British authority in India, you Excellency will have no difficulty in permitting us to remain in this place.

"It is with inexpressible satisfaction that we are enabled, by a kind and overruling Providence, to present these communications to your Excellency, at this very interesting moment.

We have the honor to be, &c. &c.

"*Bombay, Dec,* 13, 1813."

On the 16th Dec. their friend Mr. Money informed the two brethren, "that he had just been with the Governor, who mentioned, that no orders having been received from Calcutta concerning their stay, and he being still under the positive orders of the Supreme Government to send them away, he must now send them." And on the 20th, R. T. Goodwin, Esq. the senior magistrate of police, officially notified them, "that a passage was to be provided for them to England on board the Charles Mills."

The Charles Mills was then under orders to sail on the 22d of the same month, only two days after this note was given. At this critical moment they drew up a memorial to the Governor, as their last appeal: a memorial which they considered as a private communication, addressed to his Excellency, not as a Governor only, but as a man, and a Christian; which was written with the feelings and the solemnity of the occasion; and which, as they are careful to note, they viewed as of a confidential nature, but that the worthy Governor was pleased himself to give it publicity. It appears to have been generously received by the Governor, according to his accustomed goodness, and to have had its desired effect.

On the next day after sending this letter, the brethren write in their journal, "We continued our preparations. By two o'clock, (the same day) our things were packed and labelled; by three the Coolies (porters) were all here; the things were all carried below; the boats were engaged to carry them on board ship, and the carpenter to go and fasten them The friend who had charge of the things, then went to the Captain for orders to have them received on board   The Captain went to the pay office for the money for our passage, the money was refused, and it was reported that we were not to go.   The friend returned with this information, and the things were all put into a room below, and the coolies dismissed.   About five, Mr. Goodwin, the senior magistrate of police, called upon us to say, that our letter had been communicated to the Council; and that upon examination, it had been found, that no orders of any kind had been received from Bengal, of a later date than the 19th of November, and that the government would allow us to remain until they should receive further orders from Bengal concerning us. This intelligence, at this decisive moment, has filled us with great joy, and given us great hopes, that we shall yet be allowed to remain at Bombay.   How wonderful and how merciful are God's dealings with us!"

The next morning, 22d Dec. they received the following official note

"To the Rev. Gordon Hall, and the Rev. Samuel Nott, American Missionaries.

"GENTLEMEN, I am directed by the Right Honorable the Governor in Council, to acquaint you, that under the expectation of receiving some further instructions from the Supreme Government respecting you, he has determined to defer the carrying the directions he has received into execution, until such instructions shall arrive.

"I am, gentlemen, your obedient servant,

W. NEWNHAM, *Sec. to Government."*

"Bombay Castle, Dec. 21, 1813.

Our last letters from these brethren appear to have been forwarded to England by the same ship, in which they themselves expected to have been conveyed thither, and which sailed from Bombay on the 23d of December.   Later than this date we have no intelligence from them. From the facts and circumstances now communicated, however, your Committee derive a pleasing confidence, that our mission may obtain an establishment at Bombay and they are persuaded that this whole Board, and the Christian public extensively, will unite with them in adoring the goodness of the Lord, so remarkably displayed in the signal interpositions of his providence in behalf of our missionaries.   Under Providence, grateful acknowledgments are due to the Right Honorable Sir Evan Nepean, for the candor, magnanimity, and kindness, exhibited in his treatment of the missionaries, so creditable to his character, as a magistrate and a Christian.   Nor can the Committee forbear to express their high sense of the admirable spirit and conduct shewn by the missionaries themselves, in the circumstances of severe trial in which they have been called to act.   The evidence here exhibited of their firmness, their perseverance, their wisdom, and their devotedness to the great object of their mission, cannot fail to raise them in the estimation and affection of this Board, and to secure to them the confidence and favor of the Christian public.

On the 24th of Feb. 1813, Mr. Newell embarked at the Mauritius, on board a Portuguese brig, bound to Bombay, but destined to touch at Point de Galle in the Island of Ceylon. At the latter place he expected to meet one or both of the other brethren; but on his arrival, he learned that they were both gone to Bombay. Supposing, however, that they would not be allowed to remain there, he thought it best for him to stay in Ceylon, where he was assured of the protection and favor of Governor Brownrigg, and other principal officers of the government. He immediately despatched a letter to the brethren at Bombay; and by the return of the mail he received an answer from them, from which he learned, that, though their situation at Bombay was quite precarious, yet they had considerable hope that they should be allowed to establish themselves there, and thought it advisable for him to direct his studies with a view to that place. Accordingly, as soon as he could make arrangements for the purpose, he commenced the study of the Sangskrit, Hindoostanee, and Persian languages, and quietly pursued this study until some time in November, when, from information received from the brethren in Bombay, he felt himself compelled to give up all hope of the establishment of the mission at that place. From the time of his arrival in Ceylon, however, till the date of his last letter, he preached in English constantly, once, twice, or three times a week, to English and half-cast people; of whom, he says, "there are thousands in and about Columbo, who stand in need of instruction as much as the heathen," and among whom he hoped his labors would not be in vain. At the date of his last letter, Mr. Newell supposed that his brethren were actually on their passage to England, and that he was left alone. "Stript," says he, "of all my domestic enjoyments, by the death of my wife and child, and separated from all my dear missionary associates, I find myself a solitary pilgrim in the midst of a heathen land. My heart is sometimes quite overwhelmed with grief. But my prevailing desire is, and my determination, to try to do something for the wretched heathen around me. My conviction of the duty and practicability of evangelizing the heathen has not been diminished, but greatly increased, by all that I have witnessed in this part of the world." Thus circumstanced, he was undetermined in regard to the field in which to fix his mission, whether to remain in Ceylon, or attempt an establishment at Bussora at the head of the Persian Gulf. The reasons which weighed in his mind for the one and for the other, he states at large, and in a manner which indicates much attention and reflection. His trials, though different from those of his brethren, have been not less painful; and appear to have been sustained in a manner not less creditable to the character of a Christian missionary. He must have been greatly rejoiced to learn, as he doubtless did in a short time, that his brethren had not been sent to England, as he supposed, and if they have been permitted to remain at Bombay, he has probably joined them there, to the great joy of them all.

Messrs. Richards and Warren, who, at the time of our last annual meeting, were, as then reported, in very eligible situations at Philadelphia, have just completed their respective periods of engagement there; and, so far as appears, very much to their own satisfaction, and to the satisfaction of those with whose patronage and friendly offices they have been favored.

12

Soon after our last annual meeting, Messrs. Benjamin C. Meigs, Burr Baldwin, Horatio Bardwell, and Daniel Poor, were admitted by the Prudential Committee, as candidates for our missionary service; and since, after such a period and measure of trial as the Committee judged suitable, they have all, excepting Mr. Baldwin, been formally received as Missionaries, to be under the patronage and direction of this Board. Mr. Baldwin has been prevented from being thus received, by feeble health, which the Committee greatly lament, and from which they devoutly hope he will ere long be recovered.

Messrs. Richards, Warren, Meigs, Bardwell, and Poor, will hold themselves in readiness to go forth to forth to the heathen with the glad tidings of salvation, as soon as Providence shall open the door for their being sent. At present the door at every point seems to be closed by the war; but this Board and the friends of Christian missions will not cease to pray, that the war may soon be terminated; nor are the Committee without hope, that, should it continue, some way will nevertheless be found out for the conveyance of the waiting missionaries to their destined fields of labor.

From three other young gentlemen, one now a practising physician of distinguished promise, another a student at the Theological Seminary at Princeton, and the other a student at the Theological Seminary at Andover, the Committee have received very pleasing communications, expressing their desire to be engaged in the missionary service, under the direction of this Board. But upon these applications, as they are yet quite recent, no decisive act has been passed,

It will appear, by the statements which the Treasurer will furnish, that the liberality of the Christian public toward this Board is continued and extended. New associations are formed for the purpose of contributing their aid. The number of pious persons, who are becoming acquainted with the wants and the miseries of the heathen world, and who are desirous of uniting their efforts to remove these wants and alleviate these miseries, is evidently on the increase. Your Committee have reason to believe, that should Providence soon prepare the way for the establishment of missionary stations in different pagan countries, an adequate number of pious, able, devoted servants of Christ would offer themselves as heralds of the gospel to the heathen, and the means would not be withheld of supporting them in their most laborious, as well as most benevolent, undertaking. It is a pleasing thought, and one which may be indulged without presumption, that the Redeemer will graciously bestow upon Christians in America the honor of becoming joyful instruments in promoting his cause, and advancing the progress of the millennium, not only within our own borders, but extensively also in foreign lands. How noble will be the distinction, should we be known as a people, to the inhabitants of distant continents and islands, not as covetous of territory,—not as ambitious of political dominion,—not as engrossed by commerce and swallowed up by the cupidity of avarice;—but as the liberal dispensers of unsearchable riches, as cheerfully and zealously imparting to others God's unmerited bounty to ourselves.

While regarding the subject in this point of light, your committee cannot refrain from expressing their joy, that this glorious work has been begun;—that it has been formally and systematically entered upon by

Christians in this country;—that missionaries, in the employment of this Board, have been engaged on the shores of Asia, in preparing to preach to the people in their own languages;—that the Scriptures, in the common tongues of the countries, have been purchased and distributed, as free-will offering to God, from our *honorable women*, our *young men and maidens*, our *old men and children*.

It ought to be thankfully noticed, that many enlightened persons in India,—men of enlarged views and great acquaintance with the world;—dignified magistrates and persons of professional eminence;—have most unequivocally and earnestly expressed their conviction of the necessity of missionaries, and their sense of the deplorable condition of the people in a moral point of view. Persons of this description have joyfully hailed the co-operation of America, in the great work of evangelizing mankind, as a most desirable event. They have expressed an anxious wish that our efforts may be greatly and indefinitely increased. The limits of this Report, already too long perhaps, will not allow your Committee to specify all the facts on the authority of which these assertions are made. Many such facts have appeared, in the course of the preceding narration, and the accompanying documents.

It is evident also from every page of the correspondence of the missionaries, that notwithstanding all their discouragements and perplexities, they have been more and more convinced, by all they have seen and heard, not only of the practicability and duty of supporting missions, but of its being their particular duty, as it is evidently their highest pleasure, to consider themselves as unalterably devoted to this work. They are also convinced, as their repeated discussions of this topic abundantly prove, that whatever may be the design of Providence in regard to themselves or their mission, it is the duty of Christians to take it for granted, that the cause of missions will prevail, and to resolve, that by the help of God, and with all reverential submission to his holy dispensations, it *shall* prevail.

The agents of this Board in London have remitted to Calcutta, by the earliest opportunities, the avails of our several remittances to them. We had calculated, that our missionaries would have received our first remittance at an earlier date than that of their last letter, as this remittance was sent from London by the earliest spring ships of 1813. It could not, we think, be much longer delayed. But, through the kindness of friends whom Providence had raised up for them in every place they had visited, there was little danger that our brethren would be put to serious inconvenience by any accidental delay of remittances.

At the conclusion of their Report, the Committee would direct their respectful attention to the Christian public. They need not solicit, what will be granted of course and without solicitation, a candid perusal of this their annual communication and of the papers which follow it. All who have contributed to send the blessings of the gospel to the heathen; all who love the prosperity of Zion; will feel a deep interest in the history of our infant mission, and, we doubt not, will perceive the necessity of continued and persevering exertions. The object in view is so transcendantly important, as not to admit of any halting or hesitation in the pursuit, while any prospect of success remains. Such a prospect will remain, we are persuaded, without suffering even a temporary eclipse, till the gospel [shall shed its benign influence on every land. With thankful acknowledgment of the many favors shewn by the Christian public to this object, and of the many prayers offered in its behalf, the Committee would animate their fathers and brethren, as well as themselves, with the exhortation, *Be not weary in well doing; for in due season we shall reap, if we faint not.*

New-Haven, Sept 15, 1814.

PECUNIARY ACCOUNTS

The American Board of Commissioners for Foreign Missions in account current with Jeremiah Evarts, their Treasurer, Dr.

To cash paid from Sept. 1, 1813 to Aug 31, 1814, in conformity to orders of the Board, and of the Prudential Committee, from No 53, to No. 79, inclusive for expenses incurred in the prosecution of the objects of the Board $7,071 62

To losses by counterfeit bills received in donations   -   -   -   6 00—7,077 62
To balance carried to the credit of new account, Sept. 1, 1814   -   -   -   13,467 53

$20,545 15

Contra Cr.

By balance brought to the credit of new account, Sept. 1, 1813, as appears by the Auditor's certificate of Sept. 11, 1813   -   -   -   -   -   -   - $8,077 59
By cash received in donations, as particularly published in the Panoplist, from Sept. 1, 1813 to Aug 31, 1814, inclusive   -   -   -   -   -   12,008 91
By cash received as income of stock and interest on notes, during the year preceding August 31, 1814,   -   -   -   -   -   -   -   -   -   458 65

$20,545 15

APPENDIX TO REPORT.

[On the day after their arrival at Bombay, Messrs. Hall and Nott, after taking suitable advice, put into the hands of Mr. Money, a gentleman of that place, the following petition to his Excellency, the Governor.]

To the Right Honorable Sir Evan Nepean, Governor of Bombay, &c.

Right Honorable Sir,—The undersigned, lately arrived from America by way of Bengal, beg leave to state to your Excellency, that having been ordained to the Gospel ministry, they have come to this country with a desire of being useful, by translating the Scriptures, by aiding in the education of children, and ultimately by making known the gospel to some who are now ignorant of it.

Humbly trusting that these objects will meet with your Excellency's approbation, they most earnestly beg, that they may be allowed to pursue them. At the same time, they cherish the hope, that should they be permitted to remain in the country, an orderly and prudent conduct will show, that your Excellency's indulgence has not been misplaced.

They are happy indeed, Right Honorable Sir, in thus presenting the advancement of our holy religion to a Christian governor;—one, too, who has given so many proofs of a desire for the diffusion of the Scriptures, and the promotion of happiness among mankind.

They have the honor to be, with the highest respect, right Honorable Sir, your most obedient and most humble servants,   GORDON HALL,

Bombay, Feb. 12, 1813.   SAMUEL NOTT.

[On visiting the police office, the same day on which the preceding petition was forwarded, the missionaries were told, that they would not be permitted to remain, and that unfavorable impressions concerning them had been made upon the mind of this government. They found themselves charged with having broken their word, in not going from Calcutta to the Isle of France; and with having concealed themselves at Calcutta, while the police officers were in search of them to put them on board ship for England. For the purpose of refuting these charges, and explaining their conduct, they drew up and presented, by his Excellency's permission, the following memorial.]

To the Right Honorable Sir Evan Nepean, Governor of Bombay, &c.

Bombay, February 18, 1813.

Right Honorable Sir,—We have heard with the deepest concern, that your Excellency has received from Bengal, intelligence deeply injurious to our character, as men, as Christians, and especially as Ministers of the Gospel. Our concern is the more distressing, when we consider our solemn responsibility to the great Head of the Church, and the high importance that the missionary character should stand without reproach; especially in a region like this, where the forfeiting of that character must be attended with circumstances so truly deplorable. We beg, therefore, your Excellency's indulgent consideration of the following statement of our conduct.

When we left America, as your Excellency will perceive by our letter of instructions, a copy of which we take the liberty of sending herewith, our destination was not precisely fixed; but was left for our subsequent decision. On arriving at Calcutta, our first object was to obtain such information as would enable us to decide with discretion. But from representations made to us at that time, we were induced to believe, that we should not be allowed to remain in the Honorable Company's dominions. An order from government, received about a week after our arrival, which order included Messrs Johns, Lawson, and May, three English missionaries, and Mr. Rice, an American, increased our fears. We doubted whether we should be allowed to leave the Honorable Company's dominions for any place east of the Cape of Good Hope; and, if for any, supposed it would be for the Isle of France alone. With these views we presented the petition marked No. 1.*

When this petition was handed, Mr. Martin† objected to the presenting of it; and said, that the order of government was positive for our return to America,—that we must depart upon our own ship, but that she might carry us whither she liked.

In the course of a week from this, we received an answer from government, stating, that our assurances of going to the Isle of France were accepted; but that we must expect to be at the disposal of the government of that island.

After this, we continued in the expectation of going to the Isle of France, for about two months. We were endeavoring to obtain a passage, when we were taken sick. As soon as we recovered, we renewed our endeavors, engaged our passage in the ship Adele, and paid for it as early as the 17th of September, at which time we were expecting the Adele to sail in a few days, though she did not till about the middle of the following month.

---

* See No. 1. at the close of this Memorial.
† Mr. Martin was the chief magistrate of police.

During our delay at Calcutta, the causes of which we have now explained, we were led by observation to believe, that our fears had been premature· for we found Missionaries, who had been ordered away, no less positively than ourselves, nevertheless residing quietly in Bengal; and we ascertained the same to be true of others in India. We therefore began to hope, that, had we pursued a different plan, we might have been allowed to go to the place, which our inquiries should incline us to choose. Several reasons at length inducing us to desire to go to Ceylon, rather than to the Isle of France, we prepared the annexed petition, No. II;* but, lest we should presume too much on the indulgence of government, we at the same time pursued our arrangements, intending, should that petition be rejected, to proceed, according to our original plan, to the Isle of France. The petition, when delivered at the Police, was carried by the clerk to Mr. Martin, who was on the opposite side of the room, and who replied, through the same clerk, "that it was unnecessary to present that petition, and that he would give us a pass at any time." The question was asked by Mr. Hall, 'Should we go to Ceylon, instead of the Isle of France, would that be equally acceptable to government?' and was answered in the affirmative

The petition was withdrawn; and we did all in our power to obtain a passage for Ceylon. But before we could obtain one, we were summoned to the Police, and our reasons were demanded for not having gone to the Isle of France. Our reply was, that we had been endeavoring to go thither, till we had learnt from the Police, that a pass might be obtained equally well for Ceylon; and that we were then seeking for an opportunity to depart for that island. We did not at this, or at any other time, say, at the Police, nor to any person whomsoever, that our delay of going to the Isle of France was for want of opportunities. Nor could we have said this without obviously appearing to many, who well knew our proceedings, to be totally destitute of every principle of honor and religion.

Notwithstanding all our efforts, we found no opportunity of going to Ceylon; nor could we hope for one, we were told, earlier than the January fleet. In the mean time, it had been suggested to us, that Mr. Martin would probably give a general pass from Bengal, without specifying any particular place. We supposed, from what he had said respecting his giving a pass, that a pass from him, and not a formal permission from government, was a regular departure. Whether such a pass could be obtained we did indeed doubt; but we were encouraged to make the attempt in the confidence, that to fail could not injure us, and that, should we succeed, in the voice of the police we should have the voice of government; particularly as the police had been the only organ of government to us.

Our application succeeded; and on the faith of our passes, "to depart in the ship Commerce, Capt. Arbuthnot," we proceeded to make our arrangements; esteeming it a great favor that we had obtained permission to depart, though it gave us no right of remaining in the place to which we intended to go. Our friends expressed their happiness at our success; among whom were some, in whose judgment we thought it safe to confide.

* See No. II., at the close of this Memorial.

The passes now in the hands of R. T. Goodwin, Esq.,* were obtained on the 10th of November, with the expectation that the ship would sail in four or five days. On Saturday the 13th, a part of our baggage was put on board. On Tuesday morning, the 16th, we paid our passage to the captain's agent, and, in the afternoon of the same day, we were unexpectedly summoned to attend at the Police, which we did the next morning, with Messrs. Rice and Judson, who had received a like summons. We then received a communication from government, stating, that on account of our having failed to go to the Isle of France, we were considered as having forfeited all claim to the further indulgence of government; and directing the Police to correspond with the Marine Board, concerning the provision for our departure for England, in the fleet under despatch. The fleet, we were informed, was to sail within five days, which would allow no more than three days to prepare for a voyage to England.

After reading the order, Mr. Nott mentioned to Mr Martin his circumstances, and asked, whether the order of government would interfere with his previous arrangements, and prevent his departing according to his pass? The reply was, "Certainly; the order of government is positive." Mr. Martin then mentioned the opportunities there had been of going to the Isle of France, which had been neglected; and added, that he had always told him, that he would have to go to the Isle of France or England. Neither of us, however, had heard our going to England mentioned before.

We were directed by the person who went with us from the Police, to give information should we change our place of residence; and were also advised by him to write to Mr. Martin concerning our families, as they had not been noticed in the orders of government. This advice, however, we did not follow, as we immediately formed the plan of making the annexed address to the Right Honorable the Governor General.

Concluding from the unexpected orders, that, if we applied, we should not perhaps be permitted to proceed to Bombay, we resolved to attempt to obtain liberty to go to Point de Galle, where the captain was so obliging as to promise to put us on shore. With these views we prepared the petition, No. III.†

After this paper had received the approbation of some of our friends, we went on Thursday morning to Barrackpore, for the purpose of presenting it to his Lordship. The Hon. Mr. Elliot, his Lordship's private secretary, upon reading the first sentence, observed, that as it related to an order in council, his Lordship would not receive it in his private capacity. We mentioned the urgency of the case, and requested him on that account to deliver it; but he refused, and advised us to hand it to the secretary to whose department it belonged. We left him without his probably knowing who we were, and returned to Calcutta.

Having found upon inquiry, that the meeting of the council was postponed till after the time appointed for the sailing of the fleet, we did not hand our petition to the secretary, according to the Hon. Mr. Elliot's advice; but resolved to embrace the doubtful but only alternative of

---

* Mr. Goodwin is chief magistrate of police at Bombay.
† See No. III, at the close of this Memorial.

embarking on board the Commerce, according to our previous arrangements and our passports, should we find, that the captain had reported us to the police as his passengers and obtained the port-clearance for his ship. Upon inquiry we found that he had not. We therefore delayed our embarkation till Friday noon, when the captain showed us his certificate, (which he can doubtless now show,) that he had reported us to the police, agreeably to the orders of the Governor General in Council; and likewise told us, that the ship was cleared out at the custom-house, and would probably sail the next day We then completed our arrangements, and went on board the same day. Till we went on board, we were either at our known place of abode, or moving publicly about Calcutta on our necessary business. We did not give information of our going on board to the Police, because our having obtained a pass, and the captain having reported us on that very day as his passengers, furnished them, we supposed, with sufficient means of knowing where we were.

Though both the captain and the agent had told us, that the ship would sail the next day, yet she remained at her moorings till Monday morning, when we proceeded down the river. We imputed our not being sent for to the intention, and not to the ignorance, of the Police.

On this statement of the circumstances of our leaving Calcutta, we beg leave to remark, that we did diligently endeavor to obtain an audience from government till it appeared that no audience could be obtained before too late an hour; that considering our passes, and particularly the captain's report to the police, which was made after the same police had communicated the orders of government to us, we did consider ourselves as acting with regularity, and presumed, when we found ourselves suffered to proceed, that the police, as we were now manifestly on the point of leaving Bengal, were not disposed to carry their inquiries any further.

Though we had not succeeded in presenting the above-mentioned petition to Lord Minto, we still intended to stop at Ceylon, supposing that a fresh departure from that island might be more favorable to our reception in Bombay, than to arrive directly from Bengal. But as Bombay continued to be the place of our desire; as the government of Bengal had suffered us to proceed, while considering us, as we supposed, bound to Bombay; as we met with a long and unexpected delay on the coast; and as our funds were low; we concluded to proceed directly to this place.

We beg leave to express our fears, that some appearance of inconsistency in us may have arisen from a mistaken connexion of us with our two brethren;* from whom we lived at considerable distance apart; with whose plans we were unconnected; and from whose business at the Police ours was generally distinct and different. Your Excellency will readily perceive, that such a connexion, though the conduct of each, severally, might be explained, would give an appearance of inconsistency to both.

The above we declare to be a full statement of our conduct, in relation to the government of Bengal; the truth of which is known to many

---

* Messrs. Rice and Judson. Ed.

of our friends, with whom our conversations have been frequent and particular. That we have acted with integrity, we have the testimony of our own consciences. That we have guided our affairs with discretion, we will not say. But if the above statement exhibits indiscretions, we hope they will appear to be such as have arisen, not from rashness and obstinacy, but from an honest zeal in what we considered as laudable objects, and from the ignorance of strangers in a strange land. Above all, we hope, Right Honorable Sir, that our intentions will appear to have been good, and our conduct such as not to have cast a deserved reproach upon our holy religion, nor to have destroyed our character as ministers of Jesus, in the interests of whose church we believe your Excellency to feel deeply concerned.

Having said these necessary things, respecting our characters and conduct, we beg your Excellency's further indulgence, while we submit at large the objects we desire to pursue in this place.

Our great and general object is the diffusion of Christian knowledge and Christian morals. In attempting this, we should consider our first step to be the acquisition of the language of the country, which, in a tolerable degree, we suppose, must occupy the greatest part of our time for two or three years. During this time we should hope to be useful, by the instruction of schools composed either of European or half-cast children, or by teaching the English language to the natives themselves. While engaged in the acquisition of the language, we should hope to be useful in our intercourse with the people, particularly the lower classes; giving religious instruction to such as should be inclined to receive it, and, finally, should we be allowed to remain, it would be our intention to do all in our power to forward the translation of the Scriptures into the Mahratta language; and, perhaps, should our lives be spared, into the Guzerattee likewise; with the hope that by our feeble endeavors some might be induced to embrace them as the word of life, and become partakers of the unsearchable riches of Christ, which are such an inestimable blessing to Christian countries.

This statement we cheerfully submit to your Excellency, hoping that our conduct has not forfeited, and that our object claims, your Excellency's indulgence; and that we shall not be under the painful necessity of relinquishing an object, in which so many Christian friends are so deeply interested.

With sentiments of the highest respect, Right Honorable Sir, we are your Excellency's most obedient, and most humble servants,

GORDON HALL,
SAMUEL NOTT.

No. I.

To the Honorable the Governor General, in Council.

WE the undersigned, passengers lately arrived on board the American ship Harmony, having received an order to depart out of the country on board the same ship, beg leave to state, that agreeably to our intention, stated at the Police on our arrival, of leaving the Company's

13

dominions, we request liberty to depart, by the earliest opportunity, for the Isle of France; and therefore that the Harmony may not be refused a clearance on our account.　　　　　　　LUTHER RICE,

　　　　　　　　　　　　　　　　　　　　　　　GORDON HALL,

Calcutta, Aug. 21, 1812.　　　　　　　　SAMUEL NOTT,

No. II.

To the Right Honorable Lord Minto,* Governor General, in Council.

THE undersigned, having been detained by sickness and other causes from going to the Isle of France, as permitted about two months ago, and now wishing to depart to Ceylon, beg permission to pass out of the Honorable Company's dominions to that island.　　　GORDON HALL,

Calcutta, Oct. 17, 1812.　　　　　　　　SAMUEL NOTT.

No. III.

To the Right Honorable Gilbert Lord Minto, Governor General.

THE undersigned, having read at the Police the orders respecting their going to England, wherein they are said to have forfeited all claim to the further indulgence of government, by not having gone to the Isle of France, beg leave to solicit your Lordship's attention to the causes of their delay, and to their present circumstances.

As early as the middle of September, and as soon as they had recovered from the sickness into which they fell on their arrival, they engaged their passage on the ship Adele, bound to the Isle of France, which was to sail in the course of that month, but was detained till sometime after the date of the enclosed petition.†

Information received during this delay led them to wish to go to Ceylon; and two days after its date they conveyed the enclosed petition to C. F. Martin, Esq. to be presented to government; intending to proceed immediately to the Isle of France, if that petition should be denied. They were informed by Mr. Martin, that it was unnecessary to present that petition, and that he would give them a pass at any time. Accordingly the petition was withdrawn, the design of going to the Isle of France relinquished, and they endeavored to find an opportunity to go to Ceylon. Not finding any prospect of a ship going directly to Ceylon, they made application on the 10th inst. at the Police for a pass to depart on the ship Commerce, which pass was granted them, and on the faith of it, they have paid their passage, put part of their baggage on board, and are expecting daily that the ship will sail.

After what had been said on presenting the enclosed petition to the Police, and after having obtained the pass, they supposed they might in-

---

* Lord Minto administered the government of Bengal for six years. His term of office expired sometime in 1813, and he sailed for England probably in December last. Late English papers mention his death soon after he reached home, aged 53. About the year 1788, then Sir Gilbert Elliot, he was an active member of the British House of Commons. He is succeeded, in the government of the Company's dominions, by Lord Moira, known as Lord Rawdon in the American revolutionary war

† See No. II.

nocently and safely make their arrangements for departure. The arrangements are made; the ship is ready to drop down the river, and convey them to Point de Galle, where she would leave them.

We humbly beg of your Lordship, that in consideration of our present circumstances, the order of government may not be carried into effect on us, and that we may be freed from the very serious inconvenience of a voyage to England.

Your Lordship's most obedient and most humble servants,
GORDON HALL,
Calcutta, November 18, 1812. SAMUEL NOTT.

[When the missionaries were brought back to Bombay, they heard that they had been considered as prisoners of war, and were charged with having violated a parole. This charge they refute in the first part of the following memorial. The refutation proved to be unnecessary, as the Governor explicitly declared, after reading it, that he had never considered them as prisoners of war, nor as bound by a parole. They were judicious, however, in meeting a charge of so serious a nature, and which they had reason to suppose had received some sanction from persons in authority. It had even been surmised in Bombay, that they were political spies.

The concluding part of the memorial will speak to the understanding, the conscience, and the feelings, of every reader]

Copy of a Letter to the Right Honorable, the Governor, dated Bombay Harbor, on board the Honorable Company's cruiser Ternate, Dec. 4, 1813.

To the Right Honorable Sir Evan Nepean, Baronet, Governor, &c. &c. &c. of Bombay.

RIGHT HONORABLE SIR,—It has pleased a wise and Holy Providence to return us to this place, and in circumstances on many accounts extremely unpleasant. But we have learnt with peculiar distress, that your Excellency, besides having felt officially obliged to interrupt our voyage, on which we were well advanced towards the Island of Ceylon, has conceived our conduct to have been inconsistent with the duties of our profession, and with the obligations arising from the indulgence and attentions, which we had the honor to receive from your Excellency, during our stay in Bombay.

Did the present case concern ourselves merely, and were the consequences depending on its decision to fall on us alone, we are happy in the belief, that your Excellency is not one of those ungracious rulers, who condemn without allowing the accused to be heard in his own defence. But with how much greater confidence ought we to hope and pray for an indulgent and attentive hearing, while we stand so highly impeached as the ministers of Jesus—the living God. If we have departed from the path of Christian simplicity and innocence;—if we have prostituted the confidence, inspired by our sacred office, to the base purpose of deception;—if, under the cover of zeal for God, we have dared to engage in the infamous designs of political intrigue, we have wounded our Savior, in the house of his friends,—we have brought an awful scandal on the Christian name, and done what tends to destroy all confidence in the missionary character, and to delay that period, which is the object of Christian hope, when the heathen shall all be gathered unto Christ.

As these mournful consequences must follow necessarily upon our guilt, we should be uncharitable indeed to believe, that your Excellency, whose standing is so high, not only in the political but in the religious world, and whose decision on the subject is of such great importance, would not, like ourselves, earnestly desire that our characters, if possible, should stand without reproach.

Whether we can say any thing to remove, or even extenuate, our imputed crime and guilt, is not for us to decide. It is the prerogative of Him, who has seen all that we have done, and before whom our conduct is sealed up for judgment and eternity. We do, however, hope, that after having read what we now desire to offer, your Excellency will at least believe we have acted with Christian honesty, integrity, and zeal, though our zeal should still seem to have been inordinate, and our measures indiscreet.

We have understood that we are charged with having violated the obligations of a parole—obligations so universally held sacred, and which so materially mitigate the calamities of war. We confess, that, we are in a great measure ignorant of the laws of nations; and are sensible, that ever since we have been in this country, we have been exposed to numerous though involuntary errors in those painful transactions relative to Government, which, as ministers of peace, we had little reason to expect. If we have violated the obligations of parole, we have certainly done it through ignorance; though we did not act without careful consideration.

We had been warned, as your Excellency has seen, by our Reverend and beloved Patrons at home, and we were disposed most entirely ourselves, to be particularly cautious in our conduct, on account of the unhappy war in which our country is engaged. We felt therefore under peculiar obligations to examine the subject according to our ability; and it appears to us in the following light.

We were originally ordered to leave the country, long before any intelligence of the war had arrived in India, and the same orders included unimpeached and well recommended English missionaries, in precisely the same terms as ourselves: for both which reasons we could not consider these orders as having any relation to our national character, and much less as making us prisoners of war, or afterwards to be exercised upon us as such.

On our arrival at Bombay, we were informed by R. T. Goodwin, Esq. the chief magistrate of Police, that Government would not allow us to remain in the country, on account of orders which had been received from Bengal. These orders must have left Calcutta before any intelligence of war had reached that place, having then but just arrived overland at Bombay. Mr. Goodwin's communication to us therefore did not, as we conceive, regard us as prisoners of war, nor did he intimate, that we were to be considered as such. He directed us to procure ourselves a passage to England, and to give him information of our place of residence. We replied, that we had not the means of procuring ourselves a passage to England. We certainly did not suppose, that what passed at this time amounted, either to an express, or an implied, parole; that we had laid ourselves under any of the obligations, or that we were to enjoy any of the peculiar privileges of a parole. Nor did we suppose, that the liberty, with which we left the office, resulted from any thing which had been transacted there; much less from any peculiar confidence reposed in us, as we were then under severe censure.

We had other reasons for supposing we were entirely free from the obligations of a parole We did indeed think, that no one could consider us to be under such obligations, while we did not enjoy the provision usually made for prisoners of war, while we were defraying expenses exceeding our means, and while expecting to be sent to a land of strangers, without the prospect of a provision there

Besides, we have been led frequently to inquire, whether peaceably behaved gentlemen, being found in a civilized state, at the commencement of a war between that state and their own, are usually considered as prisoners of war.—We were uniformly answered "*No*."—And from the nature of the case, as well as numerous facts, we supposed "No," the only rational answer.

But we certainly had a higher reason for believing that we were not to be considered as prisoners of war. We had declared ourselves—and our declaration had received the confidence of your Excellency, and of the Governor General—to be the Ambassadors of the Prince of Peace, employed in his service, and devoted to that alone. We knew that we were parties in no war, and we believed that we were the friends of all men. We thought we could not be considered as prisoners of war, while adhering to the peaceable maxims of our Divine Lord—the common Redeemer—the God of England and America, before whom both nations, and all nations, are as one.

Shortly after our arrival in Bombay, we presented to your Excellency a statement of our proceedings in Bengal, and of the object of our mission; accompanied by the official instructions under which we were to act The liberality and kindness, with which your Excellency was pleased to view these documents, exacted our gratitude, and animated our hearts. Distressing as our circumstances had been, and conscious as we were of the integrity of our hearts, and the sacredness of our object, we received your Excellency's favor as a blessing from Heaven, we indulged the most pleasing hopes; *we thanked God, and took courage.*

The attention your Excellency was pleased to bestow upon our subsequent addresses, we thankfully acknowledge. The indulgent confidence with which you viewed us, and the kind attentions which we continually received, were flattering to our hearts, and increased our desire of doing that, and that only, which should be agreeable to you But while they attached our hearts, we should have mistaken their intention, had we considered them as shown for our personal merits, and not as the effusions of a pious and liberal mind, and to us as ministers of the gospel, for our work's sake.

While, however, in all our requests to your Excellency, we solicited what we thought would be for the honor of Christ, we never had occasion to ask for a greater degree of personal liberty, than we at first enjoyed. From the time of our first visit to the Police, we were not aware that any additional liberty was granted, any new restrictions added, any old one removed, any pledge required, or that any act of our own laid us under any restraining obligation, not to be found in the nature of our character as Christians, or our office as ministers of the gospel. We were not aware of any other difference made in our relation to Government, than that which arose from an orderly and Christian conduct, and from those high and unsolicited attentions, which were never due to us as men, but only to the ministerial character, which we hope was unsullied before we left Bombay.

Your Excellency will allow us to express our honest belief, that the liberty we had, when we left Bombay, was the same that was given us before we had made any communications to you, or had received those kind attentions which we most thankfully acknowledge. We of course felt ourselves under obligations to act, not as American prisoners on parole, but as missionaries of Jesus, and to regulate ourselves by the inspired directions and holy examples, which are to guide the ministers of the cross.

In thus considering ourselves, we felt indeed as having in general terms the sanction of your Excellency; whom we had understood to say, that we were not prisoners of war, but harmless, inoffensive men, whose weapons of warfare were not carnal but spiritual.

We have observed, that we felt under obligation to regulate ourselves by the inspired directions and holy examples of the Bible. If we know our own hearts, these, and these alone, influenced our minds, not with the delusive force of novelty, but with the permanence of a conviction settled by meditation, and unaltered in the midst of delay and trials, and the darkest prospects.

Long before we were ordained to the gospel ministry, it became with us a solemn inquiry, in what part of the world it was the will of Christ we should preach his gospel. In Christian countries we saw thousands of ministers, innumerable Bibles and other religious books, to guide immortal souls to everlasting life.

We looked upon the heathen, and alas! though so many ages had passed away, three fourths of the inhabitants of the globe had not been told, that Jesus *had tasted death for every man.* We saw them following their fathers in successive millions to eternal death. The view was overwhelming—the convictions of our own duty were as clear as noon, and our desire was ardent to bear to the dying heathen, *the glad tidings of great joy*—to declare to them Him who had said, *look unto me and be ye saved, all the ends of the earth;* and who, after he had brought from the grave the body crucified for men, said—*Go—teach all nations—he that believeth shall be saved, and he that believeth not shall be damned.*

Affected and convinced as we were, though fastened to our country by the strongest ties,—though we had aged parents to comfort, and beloved friends to enjoy;—though urged by affectionate congregations to stay and preach the gospel to them;—we were compelled to leave all and come to this land, with the prospect of no temporal advantage, but with the prospect, the certainty, of much temporal loss, and even of suffering too, should our lot be cast under a heathen government, as the experience of all ages warned us to expect. We were determined, as we thought, to deliver our message at the hazard of every personal convenience or suffering, trusting in God, who guides the ways of all men, and willing to abide his allotments.

Right Honorable Sir, thus we were devoted to a work of which we are, and ever shall be, infinitely unworthy;—devoted for reasons which can never lose their force, but whose weight in our own case had been increasing by all the preparations we had made, and by all the information we had acquired. Before we left Bombay we had spent more than a year in different parts of India;—had conversed with many gentlemen, clergy and laity, on the subject of missions;—had learnt much of the language, manners and customs of the people; and had become more deeply impressed with their wretchedness, and the duty of publishing to them the blessings of the gospel. While we enjoyed these advantages, we trusted we had acquired a valuable degree of preparation for a prudent and useful management of a Christian mission; which made it more than ever our duty to preach to the heathen.

We were standing on heathen ground. We were surrounded by immortal beings, polluted by idolatry, dead in sin, and exposed to hell. There was not one messenger to a million, among all the idolaters of India, to preach Jesus to them. There was enough before our eyes to convince us, that the command of Christ to teach all nations had not been thoroughly fulfilled; and we knew that it had never been revoked. We had for years been preparing; and we had come to this country for no other purpose than to obey this command. But now we were called upon to relinquish the purpose which had been so long conceived—to abandon the work for which we had been so long preparing—and to depart, not only from the particular field which we had entered, but from the heathen altogether. We were commanded by a government we reverenced, a government exalted, as an enlightened and a Christian government, among the nations of the earth—a government, under which Christian people have been active beyond a parallel in modern ages, in their efforts for the universal diffusion of Christian knowledge; and, what was peculiarly distressing, your Excellency had considered it your official duty to execute upon us orders, which would remove us from this *field white already to the harvest.*

Thus situated, what could we—as ministers of Christ, what ought we to have done? The miseries of the heathen were before us. The command of Christ remained in full force We had hoped, and prayed, and waited—till almost the day on which the orders for our going were to be executed, our work defeated, and our prospect of preaching to the heathen destroyed. We ask again what could we—We appeal to your own Christian feelings, what ought we to have done? That the gospel should be preached to these heathen we knew was according to the will of Christ. If by any means we could do this, though we had been forbidden, we thought, (we say it with all possible deference,) that we ought to obey God rather than man.

There did seem to be a way authorized by the Holy Scriptures, which, though doubtful in its issue, furnished, we thought, considerable prospect of success. It was to escape and reach Ceylon, where we had been assured of protection and encouragement. Paul and Barnabus escaped from Thessalonica; and again Paul was let down in a basket by the wall of Damascus, while he knew that the highest civil authority of the city was waiting to apprehend him.

We stand far behind apostles, those venerable messengers of the Lord; but, though so far behind them, yet, as ministers of the same Lord, we feel bound in duty to plead their example, especially when we consider ourselves, if prevented from doing our work in one city, under a command of our Lord *to flee to another*.   This we attempted, but without success; and for this attempt we now stand so highly impeached.

Amidst the distress which unavoidably results from the imputation of guilt, it affords us consolation to reflect, that until we left Bombay, our character, by a fair testimony, both here and at Calcutta, stood unimpeached.

If this single act does really bring guilt upon our souls; if it does justly destroy the confidence previously reposed in our characters; how can we justify apostles and others, of whom the world was not worthy, who in like manner fled from city to city rather than abandon their work?

Such, Right Honorable Sir, is the statement which we have thought it our duty to submit to your serious consideration.   We should be happy indeed, should it remove from our characters the imputation of guilt. Confident as we are of none other than the best intentions, we most earnestly hope, and anxiously desire, it may, and pray that the time may not be distant, when we shall be freed from the painful duty of vindicating ourselves, and when we shall enter with joy and thanksgiving upon that work, for which we are literally strangers and pilgrims, and have no certain dwelling place.   But the matter rests with God.   On Him we will endeavor quietly and patiently to wait; to Him we will look to bear us through our present trials—to publish his own gospel to the dying heathen, and to honor his dishonored Son among all nations.

We have the honor to be, Right Honorable Sir, with the highest respect, your Excellency's most obedient and most humble servants,

GORDON HALL,
SAMUEL NOTT.

[Letters from the Rev. Thomas Thomason of Calcutta, addressed to one of the missionaries at Bombay, the last of which was received December 10, 1813.]

Oct. 8, 1813.

MY DEAR SIR, I have been favored by your two letters, and to save the post of this evening, write in haste to say, that Mr. Udny seems to think that some attempt may be made with Earl Moira to interest him in your favor; but how, or of what nature, he has not intimated.   I am now going to wait upon him.   No time will be lost in doing what can be done; nor, if any thing is to be done effectually, ought a moment to be thrown away.   You shall hear as soon as any thing may be concluded.

We are deeply concerned in all your motions, and shall feel most happy and thankful to God, if any thing should arise favorable *to all our desires.* It will be from Him.   Vain is the help of man.

Yours affectionately,   THOMAS THOMASON.

Oct. 13, 1813.

MY DEAR SIR, It has been no easy matter to know how to proceed in your business.   At first we determined on an address to Lord Moira, to be signed by Mr. Udny, Dr. Carey, and myself.   After preparing the letter we demurred about the expediency of addressing Lord Moira, on so delicate a business, so soon after his entering on the government, especially as we had to plead, not for missionaries merely, but for *American* missionaries; and moreover to urge *a revocation of a government order*, even while Lord Minto, the Ex-Governor General, was upon the spot.

On the whole, we thought it best to apply first to Lord Minto; and this morning I have had a long interview with him. I showed him a copy of your last letter, and also of the letter of the Board of Commissioners for Foreign Missions, appointing us to act in India. This I did in order to explain why we interested ourselves individually in this matter.

His Lordship was very gracious—professed the highest opinion of your intentions—but could not give a decided answer without consulting with his late colleagues in council. For his own part, however, he seemed to think that Sir Evan Nepean could judge as well as they could, and that the business might be left to him to act as he thought proper.

I told him, that we petitioned only for a relaxation of the order, which *bound* Sir Evan Nepean to send you away. He said he would inform me, as soon as he had had an opportunity of conversing with the council. If they can be persuaded to relax in their views of the subject, the way will be cleared for Lord Moira to act without any indelicacy to his predecessor.

Thus the matter rests. It may be several days before you hear the result. But as there is a hope that it may be favorable, I hope you may obtain *permission to stay until you hear again*

But we look above councils and governors in this matter. We have a gracious Head, who is not unmindful of his Church. To Him let us commit the matter in faith and prayer.

Yours affectionately,   THOMAS THOMASON.

Nov. 19, 1813.

MY DEAR SIR, After much delay I have at length received a favorable intimation from government, which grants all that you requested. Lord Minto was long in giving me his judgment of the case. So I wrote again, enclosing in my letter a copy of a letter from a Mr. Erskine, of Bombay, to his friend Dr. Hare. A copy was at the same time sent to Lord Moira by Dr. Hare. In that letter Mr. Erskine spoke very candidly and kindly of you both. No answer, however, was sent by Lord Minto to *this second* communication; but *he called* upon me, and said, that he thought I should find no difficulty in obtaining the permission of this government. Our address to Lord Moira, signed by Mr. Udny, Dr. Carey, and myself, was accordingly sent in without delay.

Yesterday I had an audience of Lord Moira. He spoke very decidedly about your being allowed to stay, and expressed his conviction that you meant to do good, and that no conceivable public injury could arise from your staying. But, he added, your letter will come before Council in a day or two, and will be publicly answered.

Thus the matter stands. In a short time I hope to write again. Meanwhile, Sir Evan Nepean may be assured, that the government here has a friendly disposition towards you. May this arrive in time to prevent any decisive steps for your leaving India; and may you be abundantly blessed in all your plans and labors.

I have the inexpressible satisfaction to observe, that Lord Moira has come out with every laudable desire to do all the good he can, and with the determination to extend the efficient aid of government in forwarding

14

plans of general instruction and improvement. I am now preparing the materials of a very extended plan of operation, which, in the course of a month, I hope to submit to him. You shall hear from me on the subject more at large, if nothing unforeseen prevent me from writing.

My kindest regards to your colleague, and to Dr. Taylor, to whom I am in arrears, and hope to write shortly.

Yours affectionately,　　　THOMAS THOMASON.

To the Right Honorable Sir Evan Nepean, Governor, &c. &c.

RIGHT HONORABLE SIR,—We understand that the final arrangements for our being transported to England are now made. At this decisive moment, we beg to submit to your Excellency the following considerations.

That exercise of civil authority, which, in a manner so conspicuous and determined, is about to prohibit two ministers of Christ from preaching his Gospel in India, can be of no ordinary consequence; especially at the present moment, when the Christian public in England and America, are waiting with pious solicitude to hear how the religion of the Bible is welcomed and encouraged among the Pagans of this country. Our case has had so full and conspicuous a trial, that its final decision may serve as a specimen, by which the friends of religion may learn what is likely to befall, in India, those evangelical missions, which they are laboring to support by their prayers, and by their substance.

Had the decision been favorable to missions, it would have encouraged the hearts of thousands to increase their exertions for the enlargement of the Redeemer's kingdom; it would have brought thanksgivings to God and blessings to the heathen. But if the decision must be unfavorable, it will tend to deject the hearts of Christians; it will cast a new cloud of darkness over this heathen land, and discourage many from attempting to rescue the poor Pagans from the doom which awaits idolaters. This momentous decision, Right Honorable Sir, rests with you.

Now we would solemnly appeal to your Excellency's conscience and ask: Does not your Excellency believe, that it is the will of Christ that his Gospel should be preached to these Heathens? Do you not believe, that we have given a creditable testimony that we are ministers of Christ, and have come to this country to preach his Gospel? and would not prohibiting us from preaching to the Heathen here be a known resistance to his will? If your Excellency finally exerts civil authority to compel us from this heathen land, what can it be but a decided opposition to the spread of the Gospel among those immortal beings, whom God has placed under your Excellency's government?* What can it be but a fresh instance of that persecution against the Church of Christ, and that opposition to the prevalence of true religion, which have so often provoked the indignation of God, and stamped with sin and guilt the

---

* It is manifest, from the whole history of this business, that this question, and the succeeding one, were meant to apply to the system of measures adopted by the East India Company and the Bengal government, and not to Sir Evan Nepean in his individual capacity; for he appears to have been favorably disposed toward the missionaries.

history of every age?   Can you, Right Honorable Sir, make it appear to be otherwise to your own conscience—to that Christian public who must be judges in this case—but especially can you justify such an exercise of power to your God and final Judge?

Your Excellency has been pleased to say, that it is your duty to send us to England, because you have received positive orders from the Supreme Government to do so.   But, Right Honorable Sir,   *

      *   *   *   *   *

      *   *   *   *   *

were it even admitted, that whatever is ordered by a superior authority is right to be done, would not our case stand thus: Several months ago, your Excellency received from the Supreme Government positive orders to send us to England; but repeatedly expressed a deep regret that you were obliged to execute such orders upon us.   But a few days since we had the happiness to present to your Excellency such communications from Bengal, as were acknowledged to evince such a change in the mind of Lord Minto, as that he was willing we should remain in the country, and that Lord Moira was also favorable to our staying.   May not your Excellency therefore presume, that notwithstanding the previous orders of the Supreme Government, it has since become their pleasure that we should remain in the country?

Besides, those communications further state, that the subject was soon to come before the Council for a formal decision.   But delays are so liable to occur in such cases, that at this moment a reasonable time has hardly elapsed for the arrival of an official decision, though we have reason to expect it daily.

Under such circumstances, could your Excellency be judged unfaithful to your trust, should you at least suspend our departure until a further time were allowed for official communications to be received from Bengal?   By so doing could you be thought to take upon yourself an unjustifiable responsibility; especially when it is considered what a discussion the spreading of the Gospel in India has undergone in England, and how great is the probability, that something decidedly in its favor will soon be announced in this country?   *   *   *   *   *

It is our ardent wish, that your Excellency would compare, most seriously, such an exercise of civil authority upon us with the general spirit and tenor of our Savior's commands.   We most earnestly intreat you not to send us away from these Heathens.   We intreat you by the high probability, that an official permission from the Supreme Government for us to remain here will shortly be received; and that something more general, and to the same effect, will soon arrive from England. We intreat you by the time and money already expended on our Mission, and by the Christian hopes and prayers attending it, not utterly to defeat its pious object by sending us from the country.   We intreat you by the spiritual miseries of the Heathen, who are daily perishing before your eyes, and under your Excellency's government, not to prevent us from preaching Christ to them.   We intreat you by the blood of Jesus, which he shed to redeem them:—As Ministers of Him, who has all power in Heaven and on earth, and who with his farewell and ascending voice commanded his Ministers to *go and teach all nations*, we intreat you not to prohibit us from teaching these Heathens.   By all the principles of our holy religion, by which you hope to be saved, we intreat you not to hinder us from preaching the same religion to these perishing idolaters By all the solemnities of the judgment-day, when your Excellency must meet your Heathen subjects before God's tribunal, we intreat you not to hinder us from preaching to them that Gospel, which is able to prepare them as well as you for that awful day.

  *   *   *   *   *

We intreat your Excellency not to oppose the prayers and efforts of the Church, by sending back those whom the Church has sent forth in the name of the Lord, to preach his Gospel among the Heathen; and we earnestly beseech Almighty God to prevent such an act, and now and ever to guide your Excellency in that way, which shall be most pleasing in his sight.

  *   *   *   *   *

We have the honor to be, Right Honorable Sir, Your Excellency's most obedient and most humble servants,   GORDON HALL,
Bombay, Dec. 20, 1813.   SAMUEL NOTT.

[Extracts of a letter from Mr. Newell to the Corresponding Secretary, dated Colombo, Ceylon, Dec. 20, 1813. This letter is very copious, and, lest preceding letters should have miscarried, contains many facts which had before been communicated. The introduction of the letter, and the comparison of Jaffna and Bussora, as missionary stations, are selected to accompany the Report of the Prudential Committee]

REVEREND AND DEAR SIR,—Nearly two years have elapsed, since you sent us forth to carry the glad tidings of salvation to the perishing heathens in the East. Our Christian friends in America will perhaps expect, that before this time we have chosen our station, arrived at the field of our labors, commenced the study of the language or languages of the place, and made considerable progress in our work It would be no less pleasing to me, than to you or them, to be able to communicate such intelligence But I rejoice, dear sir, to see, by your report for the last year, that you are prepared, and that you have endeavored to prepare the minds of the Christian public, to hear of our disappointments. It has pleased God, in his inscrutable wisdom, to call us, in the very outset, to pass through the depths of affliction, and to experience the disappointment of our dearest hopes. Perhaps God intends by these trials to humble us; to purify our hearts from pride and ambition, to crucify us to the world, and make us more sensible of our dependence on his grace, that we may be better prepared to serve him, in the kingdom of his Son, among the heathen. If tribulation work in us *patience,* and patience *experience,* and experience *hope,* we shall have reason to bless God that we have been so early and so deeply afflicted. Pray for us, fathers and brethren, that the things which have befallen us in Asia may turn out *for the furtherance of the Gospel* of Christ; that as *the sufferings of Christ abound in us,* so *our consolation may abound* by Christ, that we may be able to comfort them, who are in any trouble, *by the comfort wherewith we ourselves are comforted of God.*

  *   *   *   *   *

[At the time of Mr. Newell's writing this letter, he took it to be certain, beyond a doubt, that Messrs. Hall and Nott had been sent from Bombay to England, and that the British government over the dominions of the East India Company was inexorably opposed to missions   He does not appear to have been informed of the great exertions, which had been made in England, to open India to the preachers of the Gospel. He considered himself as obliged to act alone, at least till he could be joined by fellow-laborers from this country. In this state of things, he looked around for the best place to establish an infant mission. His views on that subject are as follows]

I have also written to our Committee at Calcutta for advice. I am wavering between two places, Ceylon, and Bussora at the head of the Persian gulf They both have their advantages and disadvantages. I will give you a summary of my reasoning with respect to each.

The reasons for establishing our mission at Ceylon are these:

1. The country is the king's, and his majesty's government is friendly to missions. His Excellency, General Brownrigg, the present Governor of Ceylon, has been pleased lately to say, that he is authorised by the *Secretary of State*, (Eng.) to encourage the efforts of all respectable ministers.* Sir Alexander Johnstone, the chaplains, the Hon. and Rev. Mr. Twistleton and the Rev. Mr. Bisset, and indeed every influential character in the place, is favorably disposed.

2   There is here a very considerable scope for missionary exertions. The population of the island is variously estimated, from a million and a half to three millions. It is probably somewhere between these limits.

3   There are very great facilities for evangelizing this people. There are but two languages spoken in the island, so that when a missionary has acquired these, he may preach to several millions of people. The natives can read and write. The whole of the Bible has been translated into the Tamul, the language spoken in the north of the island, and the New Testament into the Cingalese,† which is spoken in the south and the interior There are, at the lowest computation, 200,000 native Christians, as they are called, but who are totally ignorant of Christianity. "They have no objection to the Christian religion," says Mr. Twistleton, "but for their amusement are apt to attend the Budhist festivals." Under the head of facilities may be reckoned the schools. There are about 100 already in operation, and the government is establishing others in every part of the island. Here we should be perfectly secure, under the protection of the British government, from all those dangers to which we should be exposed in the Burman country.

4. There are but two missionaries in the whole island, Mr. Errhardt, a German, from the London Society, and Mr. Chater, from the Baptist Society, the same that was four years in the Burman country. Mr. Vos,

---

* This is an exceedingly important fact Mr. N also states, in another part of his letter, that Gov. Brownrigg had interceded with Sir Evan Nepean in behalf of our missionaries, and that Sir Alexander Johnstone, Chief Justice, had also written to Bombay in their favor. These kind applications either had not reached the Bombay government, at the date of our last letters from that place, or the applications, if received, had not been made known to our missionaries. The Christian public in this country may draw a favorable conclusion, as to the importance of this mission, when they consider, that the Governor of Bombay, the Governor and Chief Justice of Ceylon, and a member of the Supreme Council of Bengal, together with a considerable number of very respectable gentlemen, chaplains, missionaries, physicians, and others, of different religious denominations, at Calcutta, Madras, Colombo, and Bombay, places many hundred miles from each other, not only *desired* that our missionaries might fix themselves within the British dominions in Asia, but exerted a *gratuitous and active influence* to promote such an event.

* This translation is thought to be so imperfect, as that a new version is necessary. This appears by the fifth topic of this discussion.

who was sent hither by the London Society, has left the place, and gone to the Cape, where he is settled in a Dutch church. Mr. Palm, another of the missionaries from the London Society, has left Jaffna, where he resided eight years, and has been appointed by government to the Dutch church here in Colombo, so that he ceases to act as a missionary. Mr. E. has not yet acquired the Cingalese language; nor has Mr. C. yet had time to acquire it, so that there is not at this time one missionary on the island, who can speak to the people in their own tongue.

5. Mr. Chater has told me, that Mr. Talfrey, (who has been engaged in translating the New Testament into Cingalese,) has repeatedly expressed a desire, that I would apply myself to the study of Cingalese, and qualify myself to carry on the translation. Mr. C. has also expressed the same wish. There seems to be no jealousy on this point. Mr. C. himself wishes me to stay here. He is somewhat advanced in the acquisition of the Cingalese, having been here a year and a half, and it is his intention to engage in the business of translation; but he wishes that more than one may be engaged in the work.

6. If we take our station at Jaffna, where the Tamul language is spoken, we have an immense field before us; for the same language is spoken just across the channel, on the neighboring continent, by seven or eight millions of people. The intercourse between the island and continent is nearly as easy and frequent, as if they were contiguous. Besides, on the little island of Ramisseram, between Ceylon and the continent, is one of the most famous Hindoo temples, that is to be found in all India. Sir Alexander Johnstone recommended this place to me, as a missionary station, on account of the crowds of pilgrims, who resort to this temple from all parts of the continent. The Brahmins here are said to have the power of restoring *cast*, when it is lost, a prerogative which is not claimed by the priests of any other temple in India. I visited this place in September, on my way to Jaffna, upon the recommendation of Sir Alexander. The result of my inquiries was a conviction that much good might be done here by distributing tracts and portions of the Scriptures, among the pilgrims who would carry them to the various parts of the continent from which they came, and thus divine instruction would be conveyed to many places, where no European missionary might go for a hundred years to come. *We* cannot be allowed to settle on the continent at present, perhaps never. But a station at Jaffna is in fact the same thing, as one any where in the south of India. Our personal labors can extend but a little way around us, wherever we fix our station. There are a hundred and twenty thousand natives in Jaffna, and this is more than we can instruct ourselves. We might establish an institution for the religious education of youth, to raise up and qualify the natives themselves for schoolmasters, catechists, and itinerating missionaries; and if Christianity be once firmly established in Jaffna, it must from its nature spread into the adjoining continent Then, if some of us learn the Cingalese language too, we may prepare and send forth missionaries in that language also, to carry the Gospel up into the Candian country in the interior of the island These are the principal arguments for establishing our mission here.

[Mr. Newell briefly enumerates his objections to a mission any where in the British dominions; which objections we hope are now obviated by the favorable issue of the decision of the British Parliament on the subject.]

I will enumerate particularly my reasons for a mission to Bussora, on the Euphrates, near the Persian gulf.

1. Bussora is a commercial town, the great emporium of western Asia, through which the merchandise of the east is distributed to Persia, Arabia, and Turkey. It is situated on the confines of these three extensive countries, and the Persian, Arabic, and Turkish languages are, I believe, all spoken there.

2. In the whole of western Asia, containing a population of forty or fifty millions, there is not one protestant missionary. The Karass mission, (which is certainly a most important one,) is, I believe, within the limits of Europe.* The Turkish and Tartar languages are the proper sphere of this mission; the Arabic and Persian, that of a mission to Bussora.

3. It is an object of primary importance to procure correct translations of the whole Bible into Persian and Arabic. The Arabic alone was said by the late Rev. Mr. Martyn to be of more importance than three fourths of all the translations now in hand. This gentleman had undertaken to superintend the translation of the Scriptures into these two languages, with the assistance of N. Sabat, the converted Arabian, and Mirza Fitrut, a learned Persian. Mr. M. died in December last, on a tour through Persia and Arabia, having only completed the New Testament in both languages. Whether any other person in Bengal will take up the work, and finish it, I do not know. I have written to ascertain. But even if the Bible were completed in both languages, it would be of little use, until some person would go and carry it to them, and say to the people, *Hear the word of the Lord.*

4. There are numerous bodies of Christians, of different sects, scattered through these countries, who have sunk into the grossest darkness for want of instruction, but who would gladly receive the Bible. These Christians might be made instrumental in diffusing the light around them, but would never take the lead in such a work. How many ages did the Syrian churches in Travancore live in the midst of an idolatrous people without ever thinking of giving them the Bible, or even of translating it into the vulgar tongue for their own use. But no sooner was the thing proposed by Dr. Buchanan, than the Syrian bishop himself sat down to the work, and the Malayalim Gospels have already been published. It is highly probable that in the Syrian and Armenian churches in those western regions, men may be found qualified and disposed to assist in spreading the light around them.

5. The Persians and Arabians rank as high in the scale of intellect, as any people in the world, and, if truly converted, would become very useful to the cause of Christianity.

6. There are several considerations, which, at the present time, seem to furnish a high degree of probability, that the gospel may be spread through these hitherto benighted regions. In the first place the Mussulmans are a kind of heretical Christians. They profess to believe in one God; in Moses and his law, David and his Psalms, Jesus and his Gospel; though they say these books have been corrupted by the Christians. And besides, the Persians profess so lax a system of Mahometanism, that

---

* Karass is in Russian Asia.—ED.

they are considered by some other Mussulmans as a kind of heretics. It is certain that Christians are, and ever have been, tolerated in Persia. When I was in Bengal, Mr. Sabastiana, a Catholic missionary, arrived there, who had been ten or twenty years in Persia, and reported that the Christians in that country were numerous. The story, which Dr. Buchanan has related, of Nadir Shah's attempt to get the Gospels translated into Persian, is a proof that they are not very scrupulous about admitting new religions into the country. When the late Mr. Martyn was last year at Shiraz, the seat of the Persian court, he wrote, that "the men of Shiraz had offered to assist him in translating the Bible into Persian."

All these circumstances seem to indicate the dawn of gospel day on those regions where the star, which led to Bethlehem, first appeared. Especially the progress of *Wahhabbe*, the Arabian conqueror, seems to portend the speedy downfal of the Mahometan power. The creed of this adventurer is simply this. *There is no other God but God.* He denies the divine mission of Mahomet, and the authority of the Koran, and destroys all the monuments of Mahometan superstition, which fall into his hands. He is said to show more favor to Christians than to Mussulmans; but he sets himself up as a prophet, or rather pretends to a divine commission.

But after all it must be confessed, a mission to these parts would be attended with considerable hazard. If the gospel should spread, and be embraced by persons of consequence, persecution would most probably follow. Already the streets of Bucharia have been stained with the blood of a martyred Christian. In that bigoted city, Abdallah, the noble Arabian convert, witnessed a good confession, and, in the presence of a wondering crowd, laid down his life for the name of the Lord Jesus. But Abdallah was a nobleman, and filled an office of the highest dignity in the Persian court. The common people, I believe, are not persecuted for changing their religion. But shall we wait till Persia and Arabia *are willing* to change their religion before we offer them the gospel. Great and discouraging difficulties lie in our way, wherever we would attempt to propagate the Christian religion. In China Mr. Morrison is translating and publishing the Scriptures, in opposition to an *imperial edict,* which renders him every moment liable to be seized and put to death.

Finally, a mission to western Asia would be all our own; and it would be free from the objections which I stated to establishing our mission in British India. We should be in the neighborhood of Mesopotamia, Syria, Palestine, and Egypt, those interesting theatres, on which the most wonderful and important events, recorded in sacred history, took place. There are Christian churches in all these countries. Might we not, by giving them the Bible, of which they have long been destitute, rekindle their zeal, and lift up in the midst of them *a great light,* that will dart its cheering beams far into the regions of thick darkness, by which they are surrounded. When I think of these things, I long to be on my way towards Jerusalem. But, dear Sir, I stand alone; I have no missionary associate to advise with, and I am afraid to rely on my own judgment. What would I not give to be one half hour with you. We could settle the business at once. Could I know that it would meet the approbation of the Society at home, I think I should be decided.

A consideration of minor importance, which makes me desirous of engaging in the mission is, I have been at very considerable expense in procuring Persian and Arabic books, and have devoted several months to the study of the Persian language. This I did with a view to Bombay, which I must now give up.

I am sorry that I cannot say to you in this letter precisely what I intend to do. I fear our disappointments and delays will prove a severe trial to the faith and patience of our Christian friends. But you will be able to inform them that nothing has befallen us but what is common to similar attempts in the first outset. The Baptist mission, which is now so flourishing, was severely tried for a time. They got no permanent establishment for six or seven years after the first missionaries came out. In two instances, where they have attempted to plant new missions, their missionaries have spent four or five years, and many thousands of rupees, and after all have abandoned the attempt and gone to other places. The same discouragements have been experienced by some of the missionaries of the London Society.

In the mean time, I hope I am not altogether useless. I have preached in English constantly, once, twice, or three times a week since my arrival in Ceylon. There are thousands of half-cast people, in and about Colombo, who stand in need of instruction as much as the heathens, and who understand the English language. Mr. Chater has a place of worship here, in which we preach alternately twice a week. We also keep the monthly prayer meeting, and a private prayer meeting every Monday evening. While I was at Jaffna, I (with the permission of Mr. Twistleton, senior chaplain) performed divine service in the fort for the few civil and military officers and soldiers there, as they have no chaplain at that station. For this month past, since I have been obliged to give up the hope of going to Bombay, I have laid aside the study of the eastern languages, until I am determined where I am to labor; and I am at present reviewing my Greek and Hebrew, with the study of critical works on the Bible.

[Mr. N. specifies the letters which he had previously written, and observes in reference to the probability that the letter he was then writing would be examined at the London post-office. "The worst thing I have to say, (relative to national affairs) is, that I am under the greatest obligations to his majesty's government, and that I do most deeply lament the existence of the present unhappy war between the two countries." He proceeds thus]

I have deposited in the letter-box at Galle two parcels directed to you. One contains two printed documents, Mr. Bisset's sermon before the Colombo Bible Society, and a specimen of the eastern translations now in the mission-press at Serampore. The other is a manuscript of six sheets of letter paper, containing extracts from Mrs. Newell's letters and diary, and an account of her sickness and death. In this communication you will find much information respecting our affairs, which I have not repeated in my letters to you. I shall enclose in this a letter to Mrs. Atwood, which I wrote some time ago. All these are left open for your perusal. The letter and the manuscript, when you have read them, I wish you to send to my dear mother, Mrs Atwood. I received letters by the Alligator—did not get them till the first of November. Your official letter, and that of Mr. Evarts, the brethren Hall and Nott have. I have not seen them.   The books are at Calcutta.   We have received no order from the Committee at Calcutta respecting supplies, but expect one soon. The Rev. Mr. Brown is dead, and Mr. Harrington is absent.   The Rev. Mr. Thomason, (a good man,) has taken the place of Mr. Brown, and G. Udny, Esq. (another good man,) the place of Mr. Harrington.

[Mr. N. gives a statement of his pecuniary affairs, adds several articles of intelligence, and concludes as follows.]

I expect another opportunity of sending letters in about a month, **and** shall write again at that time, and mention such things as do not occur to me now.   I hope then to be more particular respecting my future prospects.   This letter must serve for all my friends, for this time.   The brethren Hall and Nott, I trust, will immediately return from England and join me.   Some more will probably come out with brother Rice.

Rev. and dear Sir, I am your servant for Jesus' sake.

SAMUEL NEWELL.

MINUTES

OF THE

SIXTH ANNUAL MEETING.

The Board met in Salem, (Mass.) according to appointment, on Wednesday, September 20, 1815, and was continued by adjournment to Friday, the 22d.—Present,

Gen. JEDIDIAH HUNTINGTON,
Hon. JOHN TREADWELL, Esq. LL. D.
Rev. JOSEPH LYMAN, D. D.
Rev. SAMUEL SPRING, D. D.
Gen. HENRY SEWALL,
Rev. SETH PAYSON, D. D.
Rev. JEDIDIAH MORSE, D. D.
Rev. JESSE APPLETON, D. D.
Rev. CALVIN CHAPIN,
Rev. SAMUEL WORCESTER, D. D.
Rev. HENRY DAVIS, D. D. and
JEREMIAH EVARTS, Esq.

The session was opened with prayer by the Vice President. On the subsequent days the meeting was opened with prayer by the Rev. Drs. Appleton and Lyman, and the session was closed with prayer by the Rev. Dr. Morse.

The minutes of the last meeting were read.

The accounts of the Treasurer, as examined and certified by the Auditor, were exhibited and accepted.

The annual report of the Prudential Committee was read and accepted.

The following gentlemen were appointed officers of the Board for the year ensuing, viz.

The Hon. JOHN TREADWELL, Esq. *President.*
Rev. SAMUEL SPRING, D. D. *Vice President.*
Rev. Dr. SPRING,
Rev. Dr. MORSE,
Rev. Dr. WORCESTER, and } *Prudential Committee.*
Mr. EVARTS,
Rev. Dr. WORCESTER, *Corresponding Secretary.*
Rev. Mr. CHAPIN, *Recording Secretary.*
JEREMIAH EVARTS, Esq. *Treasurer.*
Mr. CHESTER ADAMS, *Auditor.*

Whereas the President of this Board has stated, that a legacy of $500 has been given to this Board, by Sarah Norton, late of Farmington, (Ct.) deceased, in her last will and testament; and whereas the legacy is held at present in litigation;—

Voted, That the President and Recording Secretary be authorized to employ legal counsel, and to take all other proper measures to recover said legacy.

Voted, That the Corresponding Secretary present the thanks of this Board to the Church Missionary Society in England, for their donation of twenty sets of the Missionary Register, with sundry other communications on the subject of missions.

Voted, That twenty-five copies of the annual reports of this Board, and of the sermons delivered before this Board, or at the request of the Prudential Committee, which have been, or shall be published, be sent to the Secretary of the Church Missionary Society, for the use of said Society.

Voted, That the person appointed as second to preach before the annual meeting of the Board, shall be considered as appointed the preacher for the next succeeding year, unless he shall preach the sermon in the year for which he was appointed as second.

The Rev. Dr. Davis was appointed to preach at the next annual meeting of the Board, and the Rev. Dr. Appleton his second.

Public worship was attended in the evening, when the annual sermon was delivered by the Rev. Mr. Chapin, from Psalm xcvi, 10:—*Say among the heathen,* THE LORD REIGNETH.

Voted, That the thanks of this Board be presented to the Rev. Mr. Chapin, for his sermon delivered last evening, by appointment of the Board; that a copy be requested for publication; and that Dr. Lyman, Dr. Appleton, and Gen. Sewall, be a committee to carry this vote into effect.

The Corresponding Secretary was directed to express the thanks of this Board to the London Missionary Society, for the Chinese version of the New Testament, and the transactions of said Society, with other documents presented by them to this Board.

Voted, That it be distinctly provided, that every Missionary employed in the service of this Board, is to be considered as being, under Providence, dependent on this Board for support, according to such regulations as the Board, or Prudential Committee may, from time to time, recommend or approve; and that all the earnings which any Missionary, or Missionary's wife, shall in any way procure, shall be considered as the property of this Board, for the objects of the mission, and, as such, to be regularly accounted for to the Prudential Committee.

Voted, That at every missionary station, to which more than one missionary shall belong, the salaries and earnings of the missionaries, and presents made to them, or any of them, shall constitute a common stock, from which they shall severally draw their support, in such proportions, and under such regulations, as may, from time to time, be found advisable, and be approved by this Board, or by the Prudential Committee.

The Prudential Committee were authorized to allow the missionaries, at each missionary station, to take such a house for their common use, as may be suitable for their accommodation, and to charge the rent of said house to the account of the Board.

Voted, That a majority of the Missionaries on any station, shall, in their regular meetings, decide all questions, that may arise in regard to their proceedings and conduct, in which the mission is interested.

Upon the principles of the foregoing votes, the subject matter of policy or social compact, for the regulation of our Missionaries, was referred to the Prudential Committee.

Voted, That the Prudential Committee be authorized to make to the Missionaries in India, such further allowance for extraordinary expenses, as, upon their representation, on an account stated, shall be deemed reasonable and proper.

The Trustees of the legacy, given by the late Mrs. Norris, were requested to transfer the same to the Board.*

Voted, That nine sets of the Church Missionary Register, and other documents received with it, be disposed of in the manner following, viz. To Bowdoin College, Yale College, the Theological Seminary at Princeton, Middlebury College, Dartmouth College, Williams College, the Theological Seminary at Andover, William Bartlet, Esq, and Mr. Solomon Goodell,† one set each.

Voted, That the Prudential Committee be directed to employ some suitable person or persons to visit St. Louis, St. Genevieve, and any other places, as they shall deem expedient, to ascertain and report to this Board, what measures are most eligible for diffusing the light and benefits of Christianity among the Aborigines in the western and southern parts of our country.

Voted, That the Prudential Committee be directed to hold stated quarterly meetings, and to make a quarterly communication, in the form of a circular letter, to each association, which has been, or shall hereafter be, instituted in aid of this Board.

Voted, That the Prudential Committee be authorized to employ agents to assist in forming auxiliary societies; otherwise to excite the attention of the public to the objects of this Board; and to use their exertions in obtaining funds.

Voted, That the next annual meeting be holden at Hartford, (Ct.) on the third Wednesday of September, 1816, at 10 o'clock, A. M., and that the Recording Secretary be directed to make the necessary arrangements for that meeting.

The Recording Secretary was directed to transmit to every member of the Board, not now present, information of the time and place of the next annual meeting.

Voted, That the Corresponding Secretary present the thanks of the Board to Mrs. Elizabeth Bartlet, for the very convenient accommodations which she has furnished for the present meeting; and, likewise, to those gentlemen who have hospitably entertained the members during the session.

---

* This has since been done in the manner, and for the purposes, described in the will of Mrs. Norris.

† This distinguished friend of missions had left the world before the meeting of the Board, though his death was not then known. The copy of the Missionary Register, which was intended to cheer his heart in the decline of life, will be sent to his widow as a token of gratitude for the almost unexampled liberality of her late husband.

REPORT.

BRETHREN,—Our two last annual reports contained much of interesting narrative recitals of the pilgrimages and adventures, perils and deliverances, discouragements and consolations, of our missionaries in the East, seeking a door of entrance to the heathen, but obstructed, disappointed, and held in continued anxiety and suspense; "troubled on every side, yet not distressed; perplexed, but not in despair; persecuted, but not forsaken; cast down, but not destroyed." Those recitals were interesting, as they shewed in a very clear and gratifying light, the faith and patience, the firmnesss and prudence, the fortitude and devotedness of the brethren; and especially as they afforded many affecting and animating proofs of the wisdom and goodness, the faithfulness and mercy, the almighty protection and overruling providence of God. "The Lord God is a sun and shield; the Lord will give grace and glory; no good thing will he withhold from them that walk uprightly. Their place of defence is the munitions of rocks; their eyes shall see the King in his beauty; they shall behold the land that is very far off." If our present Report contain less of striking narrative and affecting incident, it is because our missionaries have found at length an open door and a resting place; and though they have scarcely commenced their public labors, yet they are quietly and diligently preparing themselves for activity in their great and arduous work.

At our last anniversary we had the hope, that the brethren Hall and Nott, after their severe trials, would be permitted to remain at Bombay. This hope has not been disappointed. Since the latest date of the accounts then communicated, they have experienced so far as appears, no molestation; nothing but protection and kindness from the government. That latest date was December 23, 1813.

As early as the 13th of the next month, January, 1814, Mr. Newell received from them such intelligence, as gave him a degree of assurance, that the mission might be established at Bombay; and he immediately took measures of preparation for leaving Ceylon. On the 20th of the same month he writes in his journal, "I engaged passage in a Portuguese ship bound to Goa, as there was no opportunity of going direct to Bombay. Before my departure I addressed the following letter to the Governor.

"To his Excellency General Brownrigg, Governor and Commander in Chief in the Island of Ceylon.

"Sir,—Having resided nearly a year under your Excellency's jurisdiction, and experienced during that time every indulgence from government which I could wish, I beg leave to express the deep sense I have of your Excellency's kindness to me; and to ask permission to depart in the Angelica, Portuguese ship, bound to Goa, in pursuance of my original intention of joining the mission in Bombay. I should esteem it an additional favor, if your Excellency would be pleased to give me a testimonial, that would satisfy the Governor of Bombay, that I leave Ceylon with your Excellency's consent and approbation.

"I have the honor to remain, &c.   S. NEWELL."

"I felt obligated," he says, "to notify the Governor of my departure, as he had intimated on my first arrival at Colombo that I was not to remove without giving him previous notice; and I felt a real pleasure in expressing my gratitude for his kindness both to me and my brethren." "The Governor informed me through Lord Molesworth, that he consented to my departure, and would write by mail to the Governor of Bombay in my favor."

After a residence in the island of Ceylon of about ten months, Mr. Newell left Colombo for Goa on the 28th of January; and on the 4th of February the Angelica came to anchor in the roads of Cochin, where she stopped three days, and afforded him an opportunity which, he says, "he had long wished for, but never expected to be favored with; that of seeing the Cochin Jews and the Syrian Christians." Of this opportunity he appears to have availed himself with great diligence. He visited the Jewish synagogues at Cochin, and the Syrian-church at Candenad, the residence of the late primate Mar Dionysius. The results of his inquiries and observations together with those of his brethren Hall and Nott, who visited the same places about three months before, may constitute an interesting part of an appendix to this report.

On the 7th of February Mr. Newell left Cochin, and on the 24th arrived at Goa; where he "visited most of the colleges, churches, and monasteries, saw the Vicar General of the Dominicans, dined with the Superior of the Augustinians, and called on Father *Josephus a Doloribus*, the late Inquisitor, mentioned by Dr. Buchanan." "The Inquisition of Goa," he says, in his journal, "is no more. It was lately abolished by order of the Prince Regent of Portugal. It is said, however, that the Archbishop retains all the power that was lodged in the Court of the Inquisition."

On the 2d of March Mr. Newell sailed from Goa, and on the 7th he writes in his journal. "Early this morning the harbor and town of Bombay appeared in full view, and at 11 o'clock I landed and went in search of my friends, whom I found in a short time. It was a joyful meeting to us all. We had been separated more than two years, had all of us passed through many trying scenes, and often given up the idea of ever meeting again on earth; but that unseen Hand that had guided us in all our perplexities, and led us in a mysterious way, had at length brought us together in the very place, which, in our conversations on the other side of the water, we had often contemplated as the probable seat of our then future mission. And what was peculiarly gratifying to us, we had reason to hope, that we should now be established in this place, and be allowed to enter on our work, which had been so long delayed. Yet we rejoiced with a mixture of fear; for it was not absolutely certain that we should all be allowed to remain here."

Soon after his arrival at Bombay, Mr. Newell had an attack of fever which confined him several days. On the 23d of the same month, however, he writes.—"We kept a day of fasting and prayer, preparatory to the Lord's supper, which we proposed to celebrate the next Sabbath. Saturday evening the 26th, we kept another season of special prayer with a view to the solemn ordinance which we expected to attend upon the ensuing day. Sabbath, 27th, we met at 11 o'clock, A. M. and engaged in prayer: brother Hall delivered an address, suited to the solemn occasion, and brother Nott administered the ordinance.   There was a variety of circumstances attending this transaction, which were peculiarly calculated to affect our minds.   We were naturally led to look back on all the way in which the Lord had led us, since we devoted ourselves to the missionary cause, and particularly since we came to this land   Two of our brethren, who came with us to this country, had been separated from us, and had gone to different and distant countries, and we expected to see them no more in this world.   One of our little number had finished her work and received an early release from the pain and toils of the missionary pilgrimage.   Though on our own account, we could not but mourn her absence, yet we had reason also to rejoice in the hope, that she had entered into her rest; and though she could not return to us, yet, if we were the children of God, we should go to her, and partake with her at the marriage supper of the Lamb.   In the afternoon I preached to our own family, and a few of our acquaintance, who usually unite with us in our family exercises on the Sabbath."

Soon after these refreshing scenes of joyous meeting and of holy communion, on the 8th and 9th of April the brethren wrote to the Corresponding Secretary. "Our hopes," say Messrs. Hall and Nott, "are strong, and we look on the prospect with great delight   We trust that God's wonderful and merciful dealings with us, are ere long to be crowned with the special blessings we have sought; that our merciful Father has a work for us to do here; and that his various dispensations have been allotted with fatherly tenderness and care, and intended to teach us lessons of humility, trust, and patience.   We would hope, that they may make us more prepared for our work   We are sensible that God alone can teach us to profit.   Pray for us.   The God to whom you pray dwells also in this land.   Here he dwells in his own almighty strength; and, in answer to prayer, accepted from your altars, can pour a blessing, yea, an immediate blessing, upon our heads.   He can, he may in the hour of darkness, light up our path, cheer our desponding hearts, dissipate our doubts, and fill us with faith and love,—because you pray for us. We have great reason to acknowledge the kind attention paid to our circumstances and wishes, by the Rev. Dr. Carey, the Rev. Mr. Thomason and George Udny, Esq., acting as your Committee in Calcutta.   To their efforts, under God, we are indebted for the hopes we now enjoy."—"We add a few lines," say the three brethren together, "to express our united gratitude to God for his kindness in bringing us all together, after more than two years separation, to the place of our choice, and with prospects so favorable.   God has visited us with judgments hard to bear, and with mercies for which no gratitude is sufficient.   Pray for us that we may be knit together in love; that we may be diligent in our calling; that God may dwell in us and walk in us, and that we may be faithful unto death. Hereafter we shall hope to write to you in our united capacity."

To these grateful and devout sentiments of our beloved Missionaries, your Committee are persuaded the hearts of this Board will unitedly and ardently respond.   Here then let us religiously record our thankful acknowledgment to the Father of mercies and God of all grace for his wonderful kindness to them and to us; and our fervent prayer, that his various dealings with them may contribute to furnish and to fit them more completely for their important work, turn out to the furtherance of the Gospel in realms of darkness and of the shadow of death, and redound to the glory of his adorable name through the thanksgivings of many.

Since the receipt of the communication of April, 1814, Letters have been received from the three brethren, bearing date, June 10 and 13, and December 29 and 30, together with their Journals down to about the time of their last date. From these communications it appears that they regularly performed divine worship, and preached, at their own house, every Sabbath day, at which a few persons besides their own family usually attended; that they kept a prayer meeting on every Wednesday evening, "to seek God's blessing on their mission," and "observed the first Monday of every month as a season of prayer for the Church, in unison with the friends of Missions, in India, Europe," and our own country; that they "applied themselves closely to the study of the Mahratta language, the vernacular tongue of the Hindoos of Bombay, and of many millions on the" hither "side of India;" that with much deliberation they had formed and adopted a system of polity or social order for the regulation of their little community, agreeably to the Instructions given them by the Prudential Committee; that they had opened a school which they hoped might be "so managed and modified as to embrace half-cast children of Europeans, and become a boarding school of considerable importance to the mission:—in a word, that they had been diligently employed in the requisite preparations and arrangements for the establishment of the mission, and for the eventual extension and success of their labors. In their joint letter of 29th of December last they say: "We are now drawing near the close of the third year, since you sent us forth with the message of peace and love to the heathen in the East. The solemnities of that interesting day, on which we were designated to this important work, are still fresh in our minds, with all the affecting circumstances of the parting scene—and though our country and our friends are still dear as ever to our hearts, and though we have experienced, as you taught us to expect, 'much adversity, much opposition, and many dark days in which our hearts have swelled with grief,' our purpose and our choice remain unaltered. We trust we do, at this moment, renewedly devote ourselves to the work, and rejoice that God has given us *this grace, to preach among the Gentiles the unsearchable riches of Christ.*—We hope that nothing which has befallen us will deter others for a moment from engaging in the work. Our trials on the whole have not been greater, than we had reason to expect, and our encouragements are great. We are at length delivered from the long and painful suspense, in which we have been held and are now, we have no reason to doubt, permanently settled in this place. Here there is work enough for a great many missionaries, within the compass of a few miles. We cannot walk the streets half a mile, without meeting with thousands of heathens, with whom we may mingle and converse about the way of salvation, without any fear of giving offence, or exciting the least alarm. We are daily becoming more familiar with their language and their ways, and hope soon to commence the great work of preaching to them the gospel of Christ. There are many facilities here for the prosecution of our work, among which we would mention with gratitude the perfect security to our persons and property, which we enjoy under the British government· an invaluable blessing, and one upon which we could never calculate under a heathen government."

Such was the situation, such were the occupations, the sentiments and prospects of our missionaries at Bombay, nine months ago. Later than that time we have no accounts from them; but we have reason, we think, with a good degree of confidence, that, ere this day, they have become so expert in the language of the country, as to be able to preach to the perishing natives the words of eternal life. The station in which, after many disappointments, Divine Providence has placed them, is a most important one, and peculiarly eligible for the permanent seat of a central mission. In the midst of an extensive and populous region, they have a field apparently open to them, sufficient for the employment of hundreds of laborers, nor do they seem to entertain a doubt that others of their brethren from this country would be permitted to join them, and take part with them in their work. And besides Bombay and the surrounding country, they respectfully but earnestly direct our attention to other fields. particularly to Cochin and its environs, where they think there would be little difficulty in establishing a mission, and where many interesting circumstances, some of them rendered doubly interesting by the glowing representations of Dr. Buchanan, invite to the attempt; and the island of Ceylon, where every facility to missionary enterprize is offered, and where an extensive field appears to be white already to the harvest.

To this last mentioned field the eyes of your Committee have long been turned, with ardent desire and hope. Immediately after the restoration of peace, an event most auspicious to every interest dear to the good man's heart, and claiming the most grateful acknowledgments to Him who sits as King on the holy Hill of Zion, it was resolved to lose no time in fitting out a new mission to the East. Of the five missionaries who had for a considerable time been held in an anxiously waiting posture, Messrs. Richards, Bardwell, and Poor, were designated for this mission, which was particularly intended for the Island of Ceylon. At the same time, it was proposed to send the other two, Messrs. Warren and Meigs, on an exploring mission to some of the Indian tribes, in the western and southern territories of this country. In pursuance of these resolves, the 21st of June was appointed as the day, for setting apart the five brethren for their sacred work, by solemn ordination.

On the appointed day the missionaries were ordained, at the Presbyterian church in Newburyport. Ten churches by their Pastors and delegates, together with the Rev. Professors of the Theological Seminary at Andover, assisted in the solemnities of the occasion. Propitious heaven smiled on the day. A vast concourse of people assembled, and gave every attestation of deep interest. After the usual ordination solemnities, about seven hundred communicants of different churches sat down together at the table of their common Lord and Savior, gratefully to commemorate that divine love which was displayed in the great propitiation for the sins of the whole world, solemnly to testify their joint participation in the heavenly design of imparting the blessings of salvation to the perishing heathen, and unitedly to set their seal to the prayers and thanksgivings, and vows, and sacred transactions of the day. The scene throughout was most interesting, impressive, and refreshing; and was a precious earnest, as we may devoutly hope, of immortal blessings to many in distant lands, and of the holy joys of that day when they shall come from the East, and from the West, and from the North, and from the South and sit down together in the kingdom of God.

Without delay, arrangements were made, in the hope that the Missionaries would soon depart to the scenes of their respective destinations. But unforeseen hindrances have occurred and Divine Providence, in the mean time, has overruled one considerable part of the Committee's original plan In two or three days after the ordination, Mr. Warren was affected with a bleeding at the lungs, which rendered it for some time painfully doubtful whether he would ever be employed in missionary labors, and decisively took him off from the contemplated western mission. Through the mercy of God, however, he soon appeared to be slowly convalescent, and in pursuance of special and very respectable medical advice, it was determined by your Committee to send him with his brethren to the East as the most hopeful means of re-establishing his health, and securing his future usefulness. The destination of Mr. Warren being thus providentially changed, it was judged expedient to change that also of his associate, Mr. Meigs; and they are now both of them destined to go out with the other three brethren to the East It is due to Mr. Warren and Mr Meigs distinctly to state, that although they had long contemplated India as the future scene of their labors and turned all their missionary desires and thoughts towards that interesting field, and although when it proposed to them to take a destination in all respects so different as that of a mission to the Western Indians, they felt at first no small degree of painful disappointment; yet, after attentively considering the subject, in the light in which it was presented to them by the Committee, they yielded to the proposal with a spirit of cheerful acquiescence, which afforded a highly gratifying evidence of their sincere devotedness to go whithersoever Divine Providence might direct.

The brig on board which the five missionaries, four of them with their wives, are to embark, is now in a state of advanced preparation, and is expected to sail from Newburyport, in three or four weeks, directly for Ceylon. There it is intended that the brethren should be left, with instructions to exercise their sound discretion, in view of the circumstances which may be presented to them upon the spot, whether to establish themselves in some station or stations upon that island, or to go, all or a part of them, to Bombay, Cochin, or elsewhere, as Divine Providence shall seem to direct. And to Divine Providence, infinitely wise and infinitely good, this Board will commit them with the most affectionate and devout benedictions.

Though, for the reasons before stated, your Committee have found it necessary to suspend, for the present, the design of a western mission; yet they would by no means have it understood that the design is ultimately relinquished. It is cherished indeed under a very sacred sense of duty and with increasing ardency of hope From the best information which the Committee have been able to obtain, and they have taken care to obtain such as they think may be relied on as substantially correct, they estimate that within the United States and their Territories, there are about two hundred and forty thousand Indians, divided and subdivided into about seventy tribes and clans. Nearly one hundred thousand of these Indians are on this side the Mississippi; and of these the four Southern tribes, the Creeks, Choctaws, Chickasaws, and Cherokees, comprise about seventy thousand; more than one fourth part of number of Aborigines within the jurisdiction of the United States.   These four tribes seem to claim very particular attention on account not only of their comparative numerical importance: but also of their geographical situation, in a fine country and climate, and in the neighborhood of a rapidly increasing white population; and moreover of the disposition and habits, especially of the Cherokees, Chickasaws, and Choctaws, tending towards a state of civilization, and favorable to the reception among them of missionaries and other instructors.   In 1804 the Rev. Gideon Blackburn, whose praise should be in all the churches, instituted, under the auspices of the General Assembly of the Presbyterian Church, a mission among the Cherokees, which he conducted in person and with very inadequate assistance and support;* and within about five years, between four and five hundred young persons of both sexes were so instructed as to be able to read with a good degree of facility in the English Bible; were proportionably advanced in spelling, writing, and arithmetic; and at the same time were taught the principles of the Christian religion.   Many Bibles and religious tracts were distributed, and several individuals, some young and some of mature age, became hopeful and exemplary Christians   The Cherokee tribe is estimated at twelve thousand souls.   If we suppose four thousand of them to be of an age, suitable for attending schools; and four or five hundred of these, nearly an eighth part, were brought forward to the state of improvement now described, in the short period of five years, by the exertions of one man· what might not be effected, with the blessing of God, by a combined, well supported, and well conducted effort?   Were schools to be established upon Mr. Blackburn's plan, at different stations, so as to accommodate the whole tribe, and these schools supplied with good instructors and placed under the superintendence of a few able missionaries, who, besides the care of the schools, should be employed in other missionary labors; would it be chimerical to calculate, that in a course of years not very long, the tribe at large would become English in their language, Christian in their religion, and civilized in their general habits and manners?   One rising generation being generally initiated in the rudiments of English learning, and the principles of Christianity; the next generation would come forward under vastly increased advantages; and the third might be able to carry on the design with little extraneous aid.   The Committee would respectfully submit to this Board, and beg that it may be submitted to the Christian public, whether the probability of success in such a design, together with the vast importance of the end, be not sufficient to justify and demand an earnest, vigorous, and persevering experiment.   That not only the Cherokees, but their neighbors, the Chickasaws and Choctaws, have dispositions and habits in no small degree favorable to such an attempt, we have very satisfactory evidence· and the plan once established among them, and the happy results of it made manifest, it might be extended, as Providence should open the way, to the less tractable Creeks, and other tribes, with increased facilities and augmented encouragement.   ·

Whether we turn our eyes to the East, or to the West, or to the South, we cannot avoid being deeply impressed with the conviction, that the harvest is truly great, but the laborers are few.   At the same time, there

* The Committee of Missions of the General Assembly appropriated annually only five hundred dollars·

is evidence which claims the most grateful recognition, that the Lord of the harvest is not unmindful of the present spiritual wants of mankind. Besides our eight missionaries, gone and now going to their scenes of labor, there are five who have offered themselves, with very satisfactory testimonials, to be employed by this Board: Mr. Burr Baldwin whose health has been so much impaired, as to keep him back from active employment, but is at present in a hopeful state, two students at the Theological Seminary at Princeton, (N. J.) and two at Andover. Nor should it be overlooked, that the late remarkable effusions of the Holy Spirit on our Colleges, afford the animating hope, that not a few young men will be inclined soon to offer themselves for the service of God in the Gospel of his Son, both in our churches at home, and among the heathen abroad.

The concerns of this board are becoming from year to year more and more weighty, and the care, the labor, and the expense are proportionably increasing. The care and the labor must be ours, with humble reliance on the all-sufficiency of God; for means of defraying the expense, we must chiefly depend under Providence on the liberality of the Christian public. This dependence, we have reason to believe, will not be in vain. Hitherto the annual subscriptions and occasional benefactions have exceeded our expenditures. There are at present, in the different parts of our country, more than thirty Auxiliary Societies, whose annual contributions have amounted on an average for four years past, to about five thousand dollars. Besides these there are about fifty female associations, formed under different names, for the same purpose of supplying funds for this Board. The benefactions otherwise contributed during the last year amount to more than $5,000; and the proceeds of our funds at interest to about $560. The legacy of thirty thousand dollars, bequeathed by our benefactress of grateful memory, the late Mrs. Mary Norris, and held so long under perplexing and expensive litigation, has at length been adjudged to the Trustees. and is now, with the deduction of the expenses of the suits, held by them, subject to the direction of the Board. This, if well invested, will constitute, together with our other stocks, a permanent fund, whose annual proceeds will be considerable. We have now, however, eight missionaries, instead of three, dependent on us for support. Our expenditures, therefore, for the year to come must be more than they have been in preceding years; and must increase with every addition to the number of our missionaries, and to the extension of our operations. With this consideration, it is highly important that the friends of missions throughout the country should be impressed; and what method should be adopted to make the due impression, and turn it to the best account for the security of a permanent supply of funds, may deserve the attentive consideration of the Board.

Your Committee and all the Members of this Board are aware that there are other objects, besides those which our institution directly contemplates, which demand and urgently demand, the charitable attention of the Christian. Domestic Missionary Societies, Bible Societies, and Societies for aiding the education of young men for the ministry, Tract Societies, and Moral Societies, have all of them objects of incalculable importance, objects, which we would by no means hinder, but by all means promote. These objects, indeed, together with ours, are all in their nature harmonious and closely allied. The cause is one; and by all who are engaged in it, in whatever department, it should be sacredly regarded as one. There need be no jealousy, no interference; no other strife than to provoke one another unto love and good works. There need be no fear that any one of these objects will exhaust the liberality of individuals or of the community. We have a noble example before us. The several Societies in Great Britain, besides their home missions, employ not less than two hundred missionaries abroad in different parts of the world. The British and Foreign Bible Society issues annually more than two hundred thousand Bibles and Testaments in various languages, and expends annually more than two hundred thousand dollars in promoting its great object in the four quarters of the globe. Besides the more magnificent institutions, there are in the same kingdom many others of similar spirit and of no inconsiderable consequence, among which is a Religious Tract society, which circulates among different nations and different languages, more than a million tracts in a year. The contributions to those societies, notwithstanding the incalculable expense of the wars in which that kingdom has been engaged, have from year to year been constantly increasing. In the last two years the annual receipts of the Church Missionary Society rose from about twelve thousand dollars to about fifty thousand: and this and the other principal Missionary Societies are continually receiving great accessions of strength and of resources, and continually extending their plans and their operations. A similar spirit is rising in this country, and by proper means may be advanced to a proportional activity and productiveness. Nor is there any danger that by this spirit of liberality the community will be impoverished. It is estimated that the total annual expenditures of all the Missionary and Bible Societies in England do not amount to the annual expense of supporting a single ship of the line. What we have most to fear is, that the principal functionaries of the Board will not be able, with their other occupations, to bestow upon the continually accumulating business, that attention which its augmenting importance will demand. In regard to this subject, however, as well as in regard to every other concern, pertaining to this institution, the wisdom of the Board will be exercised, under the direction of Him in whom all fulness dwells.

This Report the Committee beg leave to submit, in the full confidence that the Board will perceive in it many reasons of devout thankfulness to God, and many inducements to pursue our great object with unremitting zeal. Hitherto the Lord hath helped us. The work is in his hand, it depends for its success entirely upon his blessing.

SAMUEL WORCESTER, *Clerk of the P C.*

PECUNIARY ACCOUNTS.

The American Board of Commissioners for Foreign Missions in account current with Jeremiah Evarts, their Treasurer, Dr.

To cash paid from Sept. 1, 1814, to Aug. 31, 1815, in conformity to orders of the Board, and of the Prudential Committee, from No. 80 to No 112, inclusive,	$5,007 80
To losses by counterfeit bills received in donations,	19 00
To balance carried to the credit of the Board in new account, Sept. 1, 1815,	19,833 30
	$24,860 10

Contra Cr.

By balance brought to the credit of the Board in new account, Sept 1, 1814,		13,467 53
By cash received in donations, from September 1, 1814, to August 31, 1815,		10,812 22
By cash received as income of stock and interest on notes,	$577 14	
By postage, and discount on uncurrent bills, reimbursed,	3 21	580 35
		$24,860 10

MINUTES

OF THE

SEVENTH ANNUAL MEETING.

The seventh annual meeting of the Board was held in Hartford, (Ct.) at the House of Mr Henry Hudson, on the 18th, 19th, and 20th days of September, 1816. Present,

Gen. Jedidiah Huntington,
Hon. John Treadwell, LL. D.
Rev. Joseph Lyman, D. D.
Rev. Samuel Spring, D. D.
Rev. Jedidiah Morse, D D.
Rev. Calvin Chapin, D. D.
Rev. Jesse Appleton, D. D.
Rev. Alexander Proudfit, D. D.
Rev. Samuel Worcester, D. D.
Rev. Henry Davis, D D., and
Jeremiah Evarts, Esq.

The meeting was opened with prayer, on the three successive days, by the Rev. Drs. Lyman, Proudfit, and Morse, successively; and was closed with prayer by the Rev. Dr. Appleton.

The annual accounts of the Treasurer were exhibited, as examined and certified by the Auditor, and were accepted.

The annual Report of the Prudential Committee was read and accepted.

The officers of the Board are the same as last year; viz.

The Hon. John Treadwell, Esq. *President.*
Rev. Samuel Spring, D. D. *Vice President.*
Rev. Dr. Spring,
Rev. Dr. Morse,
Rev. Dr. Worcester, and } *Prudential Committee.*
Mr. Evarts,
Rev. Dr. Worcester, *Corresponding Secretary.*
Rev. Dr. Chapin, *Recording Secretary.*
Jeremiah Evarts, Esq. *Treasurer,* and
Chester Adams, Esq. *Auditor.*

A petition was presented by James Morris, Esq. and the Rev. Charles Prentice, signed by them and by the Rev. Joseph Harvey, on the subject of establishing a school in this country for the education of heathen youths, arriving here from various parts of the Pagan world.

The Rev. Drs Lyman, Morse, and Appleton were appointed a committee to confer with the gentlemen* just named, and to report to the Board.

Voted, That the Board highly approve of the services of Mr. Elias Cornelius, in soliciting aid for the support of schools to educate children in heathen lands, and recommend it to the Prudential Committee to continue him in this service.

Letters from the Rev. Presidents Backus and Brown, addressed to the President of this Board, concerning two Indian youths, were communicated, and referred to the Prudential Committee

The Committee, to whom was referred the petition respecting the establishment of a school for the education of heathen youths, presented a report, which, after amendment, was accepted, and is as follows.

That the establishment of such a school, as is described by these respectable petitioners, is expedient;—

That this school be located in such place, as the agents hereafter named shall designate;—

That the Hon. John Treadwell, the Rev. Dr. Dwight, James Morris, Esq., the Rev. Dr Chapin, and the Rev. Messrs. Lyman Beecher, Charles Prentice, and Joseph Harvey, be agents of this Board; that any three of them shall be a quorum for the transaction of business, when all shall have been notified; and that the Hon John Treadwell be authorized and requested to call the first meeting of the agents, at such time and place as he shall deem expedient;—

That the said agents be empowered and requested to form such a plan for establishing and conducting a school for the education of heathen youths in our country, for the purposes expressed in the petition, as to them shall appear most conducive to the attainment of the object of such school; subject, however, to revision by this Board;—

That all monies contributed, or hereafter to be contributed, for the support of said school, shall be remitted to the Treasurer of the Board, or deposited according to his direction;—and,

That the said agents make an annual report of their doings to this Board, and receive from them, from time to time, such instructions as they shall deem it expedient to give.

The Corresponding Secretary was directed to express the thanks of this Board to Mr. Edward Thompson, of Philadelphia, for his generous offer of a gratuitous passage to such missionaries, as the Board may soon wish to send into India.

The same officer was also directed to express the thanks of this Board to a distinguished member of the Court of Directors of the East India Company, for his able defence of the American Missionaries before that Court.

On Thursday evening the annual sermon was preached before a numerous and respectable audience, in the Brick Church, by the Rev. Dr. Davis, from Psalm cxix, 96. *I have seen an end of all perfection: but thy commandment is exceeding broad.*

Voted, That the thanks of this Board be presented to the Rev. Dr. Davis for his sermon delivered on Thursday evening, that a copy thereof

* These gentlemen were requested to lay the subject before the Board, by a large and respectable meeting of persons friendly to the education of heathen youths, which was convened at New Haven, during the session of the General Association, in June

be requested for the press; and that the Rev. Drs. Morse and Appleton, and Gen. Huntington be a committee to carry this vote into effect.

Voted, That this Board exceedingly regret, that their missionary, the Rev. Samuel Nott, who, in circumstances of arduous difficulty and severe trial, had acquitted himself in a manner highly creditable to the missionary cause, should afterwards have judged himself at liberty to abandon the mission at Bombay, on account of his health, without a previous reference of his case to this Board, when the case did not, as it appears to this Board it did not, require an immediate departure.

Voted, That the mission of the Rev. Samuel Nott, as far as pertains to his appointment by this Board, terminated when he finally left Bombay.

The Hon. Stephen Van Rensselaer, of Albany, was unanimously elected a member of this Board.

Voted, That the next annual meeting of this Board be held at Northampton, (Mass.) on the third Wednesday of September, 1817, at ten o'clock, A. M , and that the Rev. Dr. Lyman be requested to make the necessary arrangements.

The Rev. Dr. Appleton stands first preacher for that occasion, and the Rev. Dr. Spring was appointed to preach in case of his failure.

Voted, That the thanks of this Board be presented to Mr Henry Hudson for the very convenient accommodations and generous hospitality which he has furnished to the Board during the present meeting; to the other individuals and families in this city, whose hospitality has been experienced by the members of the Board; and to Mr. Eli Roberts, and the choir of singers under his direction, for their very acceptable services in the public religious exercises of Thursday evening.

Voted, That it be the duty of the Prudential Committee to compile and publish a report, including their annual report, a statement of the Treasurer's accounts, such a detail of donations as may be found useful, extracts from the minutes of the present session, and such other information as they shall deem expedient.

REPORT.

BRETHREN,—Refreshing, after an absence of a year, are the countenances of friends, and the greetings of brotherly affection; but still more refreshing are the grateful recollections of heavenly good will towards men, and the lively anticipations of promised mercy, fulfilled unto all the families of the earth, most intimately associated with this consecrated anniversary. These are indeed like the "dew of Hermon, as the dew that descended upon the mountains of Zion, where the Lord commanded the blessing, even life for evermore." May He graciously command his blessing on this meeting, and on all our deliberations, and measures, for the advancement of his glory, and the salvation of men.

Our last Annual Report brought down the history of our Eastern mission just to the close of the year 1814. At that period, our missionaries were in a good degree tranquillized in the persuasion, that they would be suffered, without further molestation, to remain at Bombay. Of this, however, they had no assurance; and the state of precarious sufferance in which they were held, was attended with very considerable inconveniences. But our last communications from them, bearing date Nov.

29, 1815, give us the gratifying intelligence, that they have been released from their embarrassments. "His Excellency, Sir Evan Nepean," they say, "has just personally communicated to us the result of our concerns with government. After briefly recapitulating what had taken place, he said that the whole business had been represented to the Court of Directors, and that they in reply had stated, that the communications from the Bombay government concerning us were such as led them to think our object was simply the promotion of religion; and that therefore he (Sir Evan) was at liberty to allow us to remain if he chose, and that they should acquiesce in such a decision." His Excellency added, "I can now assure you that you have my entire permission to remain here, so long as you conduct yourselves in a manner agreeably to your office. I shall feel no difficulty in allowing you to go to any part of this Presidency; and I heartily wish you success in your work." He repeated his expressions of confidence in us, his belief that we were doing good, and his attachment to the object. In replying on our part, it was said, that we were greatly obliged to his Excellency for the kindness which he had shewn us, the interest he had taken in our mission, and the measures which he had employed to promote it."—The brethren remark, "We had not been expecting any further communications from government, but supposed that we should merely be left undisturbed in the pursuit of our object. This assurance strengthens us. We praise the Lord, and implore grace to be faithful laborers in this vineyard which he has given us in a manner so remarkable. We are now relieved from our former restrictions, and acknowledged as residents in the country; and we think the manner in which this assurance is given appears favorable to the introduction of other missionaries here."

An event so auspicious to the mission, claims the grateful acknowledgments of this Board to the Supreme Disposer; and considered as the issue of a series of occurrences, for a long time of dark and disastrous aspect, may reasonably be hailed, with religious joy, as a hopeful presage of good to that important portion of the heathen world.

Little, therefore, should we be disheartened by an event of a different kind; which, however, could not but awaken very deep concern. We allude to the return of our missionary, the Rev. Mr. Nott. Soon after his arrival in India, Mr. Nott was attacked with a disease which is common in that country, and which often proves fatal to persons not inured to that climate. Afterward, from time to time, he was visited with similar attacks, and his health generally was not good. At length it became a question with him whether he ought not to abandon a country, where his prospect for health and for life was so dark. Upon this question he consulted his physicians, and had from them a decided opinion, "that the climate of the East Indies was very unfavorable to his constitution, and that he could not remain in the country without endangering his life, and that he should return to his native country, or to Europe, as the most effectual means of recovering his health." Judging it proper to comply with this advice, Mr. Nott took his measures accordingly; and by the kind favor of Providence has returned to his country and his friends in safety.

Amid the various difficulties which it has had to encounter, our mission at Bombay has been steadily advancing towards its great object, and in its utmost extremities the voice of Providence has seemed to be distinct: "Destroy it not; for a blessing is in it." It is no small satisfaction to hear the testimony of the worthy Governor, whose unrestrained protection and favor our missionaries now enjoy, that "he believes they are doing good." Their communications to us, indeed, are replete with evidence, that they have entered upon their work with deep and sound reflection, and proceeded with firm and vigorous purpose, with enlarged and enlightened views, and with very laudable industry and proficiency. "We have already," they say, in a letter of Sept. last, "We have already told you that we have made so much proficiency in the Mahratta language as to be able to commence our great work of preaching the Gospel to the heathen. We daily impart religious instruction to the people around us, in some form or other; and this we expect will be the great business of our lives from day to day. , We have commenced the work of translating the Scriptures into the Mahratta language We both employed some part of our time almost every day in translating These essays at translating we consider at present as very imperfect; and we have no expectation that we shall be able, in a year or two, to effect a complete and correct version of the Sacred Volume. Our situation, however, affords many facilities for the prosecution of this work; the principal of which is, our living in the midst of the people for whom the translation is designed. We hand our translations around in manuscript, and read them to the people in our excursions, and, in this way, we are enabled to detect the errors at once, and ascertain to our perfect satisfaction whether our version is intelligible and idiomatical or not." In their subsequent letter of Nov. 29, they further state: "We have translated a Harmony of the Gospels and several tracts, copies of which are now in circulation among the heathen; and we have daily opportunities of observing how far they understand them. Besides these, Matthew is translated as far as the 23d chapter, as are parts of the remaining chapters, and the whole will be finished in a few days. We have also translated a short Catechism. We do not mean to say, that as yet we have any thing fit for the press: but we think we could soon bring some small tracts to that degree of perfection, which would render it very desirable to commence printing without delay."

In a paper which they have sent us, entitled remarks on Eastern Translations, the brethren say: "It would seem to be a self-evident principle; that no person can translate correctly into any language which he does not understand as well, or nearly as well, as his mother tongue; and it seems to be no less evident, that no person can understand a foreign language as well, or nearly as well, as his mother tongue, without residing at least a number of years in the country, where that language is vernacular, and conversing habitually with all kinds of people who speak the language." From that paper at large, and from their other communications, relating to translations, our missionaries appear to your Committee to possess views of this momentous subject, in an eminent degree enlightened, correct and important, and worthy of the confidence of this Board and of the Christian public. They have a deep impression, that although a translation of the Scriptures might be made in a few months to answer a merely temporary purpose; yet a translation intended for permanent use, and to convey to a whole nation the entire Word of Life, correctly, fully, and intelligibly, must be a work of time, of labor, and of care. Under this impression they have resolved, with submission to this Board, not to proceed at once to a translation and publication of the Scriptures at large; but to take select portions, of primary importance, and, as soon as conveniently they can, to put them into circulation among the people. This plan, as suggested in one of the quotations already made from their letters, will afford the best opportunities and advantages for revision and emendation, and for producing at last a good version of the whole Sacred Volume. At the same time it enables them to proceed with the least possible delay, not only in preaching, but in distributing also the written Word; in portions indeed, but as fast and in such order and manner, as may be requisite at first for the best effect.

In this plan, of which your Committee have expressed to the missionaries their decided approbation, considerable advance has been made. One of the Evangelists entire, a Harmony of all the Evangelists, and other select portions of the Scriptures have been translated, and some of these portions, together with a short Catechism, and some other small tracts, are circulated in manuscript copies among the people. And the brethren express a strong desire of having it in their power to commence printing, that copies may be multiplied with greater facility and with less expense. Your Committee have therefore judged it important, that the printing press which has been offered for the service, by an individual of distinguished liberality, should be held in readiness to be sent out to Bombay by the earliest opportunity; and in letters both to Bombay and Ceylon it has been expressed as the particular desire of the Committee, that our missionary, Mr. Bardwell, who before leaving this country made himself acquainted with the printing business, should as soon as possible join the brethren at Bombay, and be ready to take charge of the printing establishment. A remittance also of one thousand dollars has been forwarded for the express purpose of promoting these translations, publications and distributions.

Besides what they have done in acquiring the language of the country, in making translations, in distributing portions of the Scriptures and other tracts, and in their great and daily business of preaching to the people as they have opportunity, and conversing with them from house to house; our missionaries have been particularly and earnestly engaged for the education of the youth and children, many thousands of whom they see around them in the most deplorable ignorance, corruption and wretchedness. Several miserable orphans and outcasts they have taken into their own family to "bring up in the nurture and admonition of the Lord;" and they have established a school, which, at their last dates, was in a flourishing state and promised great utility. For the instruction of European and half-cast children they receive a compensation which helps to lighten, in some degree, the expenses of the establishment. But their great concern is for the heathen children of heathen parents; and for the instruction of these no compensation is to be expected. The schools must be free, and be supported chiefly if not wholly, at the expense of the mission. It is estimated, indeed, that the total expense of a school, consisting of fifty children, need not exceed 150 dollars a year. This is comparatively a light expense. But the field is immensely wide, the numbers of heathen children are vastly great; and it must be the ardent desire of Christian benevolence to extend the benefits of education to as many as possible, and, for that purpose, to enlarge and multiply schools to the utmost extent of the means which can be obtained for supporting them. Our missionaries have felt, and expressed their feelings, very strongly on this subject; have deeply lamented the restraint and embarrassment which they have experienced from the scantiness of their funds; and have pleaded with pathetic earnestness for the supply of means, more commensurate with the amplitude of their benevolent wishes, and the extent of their well concerted plans.

Your Committee have attended to these representations with a very lively interest, and under the impression which they made, have judged it advisable to institute a specific charity under the denomination of the School Fund, or the Fund for the Education of Heathen youth and children. The monies of this fund, it should be distinctly understood, are intended to be applied to the maintenance of such young objects of Christian charity as may be taken into our missionary families, to the support of free schools for heathen children and youth in India, in America, and in any and every place where our missions may be established; to the supply of the schools and of individuals with copies of the Scriptures, and such other books and tracts as shall be deemed needful; and, also, if found necessary, to the defraying of the expenses incurred in supporting and educating such heathen youths as have been, or may hereafter be, brought into our own country, and may, with fair prospects of usefulness, be designated to be sent back as preachers or teachers to their respective native lands. In the success of a fund so interesting in its object to every Christian, every generous and philanthropic feeling, great confidence was entertained from the first. In this confidence it was said to the missionaries, in a letter written at the time, "While we would have you take your measures with wisdom and good economy, we wish you not to feel yourselves bound hand and foot. Open your hearts to enlarged and generous views; let your plans be comprehensive and well combined; act with system, with vigor, and with perseverance; and depend, under Providence, on us and on the Christian public for the requisite pecuniary means." The Committee have great satisfaction in being able to state, that their confidence has not deceived them; that the Fund for the Education of Heathen Youth and Children, has been, in different places and extensively, received with peculiar favor and interest; and that so far as appears it only needs attention on the part of this Board and its auxiliaries to render it a perennial and copious source of widely extended blessings.

Your Committee have to regret, that from our missionaries at Bombay no communications have been received of a later date than 29th Nov. last; and from those who sailed the last autumn, destined for Ceylon, only the bare intelligence of their arrival at that Island has been received. It is already well understood, that this last company, though directed to Ceylon, were not however restricted by their instructions to that island; but were left at their well advised discretion, as to the place or places, where they should fix their station or stations. From the first it was thought highly desirable, if practicable, that one or more of them should join the mission at Bombay. This appeared to the Committee still more desirable and important, when they were made acquainted with Mr. Nott's determination to relinquish the mission; and in the letters which have since been sent out, the desire has been earnestly expressed that no legitimate means should be neglected to procure access to Bombay for at least two of the last five. They are all, however, in the hands of Him, who is to have the heathen for his inheritance, and whose servants they are: and to this providential direction and disposal, with fervent prayers and with cheerful submission, they may safely be confided.

In regard to the Pagan Aborigines of our own country the measures of the Committee may not have advanced so fast, as the expectations of the Christian public, or even of this Board. The Committee are fully aware, that many friends of missions, not only in this country, but also in Europe, have thought it strange, that while so much has been doing for the distant heathen in India, so little should have been done for the not less destitute tribes on our continent, and within our own borders. The seeming neglect of these tribes, however, is not imputable to a forgetfulness of them on the part of the Committee, or to a want of an earnest desire to do something for their benefit But the measures which have been concerted for this purpose have from time to time been frustrated, or impeded, by causes utterly beyond the power of the Committee to control. At present, however, measures are in such a train as to animate the hope of a gratifying result. Our missionary, the Rev. Cyrus Kinsbury, who has devoted himself to the service, with a view especially to the American Indians, has been directed to proceed as soon as convenient from the State of Tennessee, where he has been employed under a temporary commission from the Connecticut Missionary Society, into the Cherokee country, for the purpose of making the requisite preparations for the establishment there of a mission, and of mission schools, agreeably to the plan exhibited in our last annual Report. When on his way to the westward, in pursuance of his instructions he communicated the design of the Board to the Heads of Departments, at Washington, and solicited their patronage. They gave him a favorable hearing, expressed their decided approbation of the design, and their disposition to render it every facility and aid which the laws would permit; and by order of the President of the United States, the Secretary at War stated, officially, that "In the first instance, the Agent (for Indian affairs) will be directed to erect a comfortable school house, and another for the teacher and such as may board with him, in such part of the nation as will be selected for the purpose. He will also be directed to furnish two ploughs, six hoes, and as many axes, for the purpose of introducing the art of cultivation among the pupils. Whenever he is informed that female children are received, and brought into the school, and that a female teacher has been engaged, capable of teaching them to spin, weave, and sew, a loom and half a dozen spinning wheels and as many pair of cards will be furnished. He will be directed, from time to time, to cause other school houses to be erected, as they shall become necessary, and as the expectation of ultimate success shall justify the expenditure. The houses thus erected, and the implements of husbandry and of the mechanical arts which shall be furnished, will remain public property to be occupied and employed for the benefit of the nation. If the persons, who are about to engage in this enterprise, should abandon it, the buildings and utensils which shall have been furnished, may be occupied by any other teachers of good moral character. The only return which is expected by the President is an annual report of the state of the school, its progress, and its future prospects."

At Washington Mr. Kingsbury had opportunity of conversing repeatedly with Col. Meigs, Agent for the Cherokees, and with a Chief and two other men of the tribe, then at the city. "The Agent," he says, "may be relied upon, as a firm and substantial friend to the object of the mission. The Indians also appeared to be pleased with the design, and said it would be highly gratifying to the nation; that they had long wished to have schools established, and had thought of devoting a part of their annuity to the object, but in consequence of some embarrassments had felt themselves unable."

Three young men have offered themselves, with very good recommendations, and been accepted by the Committee, to be employed in teaching the mission schools. One of them, Mr. Moody Hall, is now under the direction of the Committee, in a Lancasterian school, for the purpose of becoming well versed in that method of instruction, and all of them hold themselves in readiness for the service. As soon, therefore, as information shall be received from Mr. Kingsbury of the requisite preparations being in sufficient forwardness, these teachers may be sent out, and the business may be commenced.

Although the object of civilizing and christianizing the small and scattered tribes of American Indians bears no comparison in magnitude with that of evangelizing the vastly numerous and crowded population of the eastern world; yet it is an object of too great importance to be overlooked, deeply interesting in itself, and presenting very peculiar claims upon the consciences, the feelings, and the liberalities of American Christians. Nor should it be regarded as a hopeless enterprise. The history of missions records few instances since the apostolic age, perhaps, indeed none in proportion to the expense and exertion of greater success in the conversion of the heathens, than that which attended the labors of Eliot, the Mayhews, and Brainerd, among the Indians. It is no wonder that since their day little has been achieved; for little, very little, has been attempted. The spirit of Eliot, of the Mayhews, and of Brainerd, has for a long time slept. Never indeed has the work of civilizing and christianizing our Indian tribes been taken up on a well concerted and extended plan, and conducted with vigor and perseverance; never has such an experiment been made as is now contemplated. To establish schools in the different parts of the tribe under the missionary direction and superintendence, for the instruction of the rising generation in common school learning, in the useful arts of life, and in Christianity, so as gradually, with the divine blessing to make the whole tribe English in their language, civilized in their habits, and Christian in their religion; this is the present plan· and the more it has been contemplated, the more it has presented itself to the minds of the Committee, as being decidedly preferable to any other which has been adopted or proposed. Were the Bible now translated into all the languages of the Indian tribes, it would be of no more use to them than our English Bible; for they could read it no better. They might be taught to read the Bible in the English language with as much ease, as they could be taught to read it in their own; and having learned to read the English language, the sources of knowledge and means of general improvement then opened to them will be incomparably greater and more various than their own language could ever procure for them. Assimilated in language, they will more readily become assimilated in habits and manners to their white neighbors; intercourse will be easy and the advantages to them incalculable. The missionaries, mean while, will make themselves acquainted with the language of the tribe and preach to the aged as well as to the young; and they will avail themselves of the various and precious advantages, which the education of the children will afford, to gain the most favorable access to the parents; and to communicate the knowledge of salvation, and the blessings of civilized life to the people of every age.

Besides the missionaries already employed, five young men, three of them educated at the Theological Seminary at Andover, and two of them at the Theological Seminary at Princeton, and all of them licensed preachers of the Gospel, now hold themselves devoted to the service, to be employed under the patronage of this Board, as wisdom shall direct.

It is an interesting fact that several youths, brought from the Sandwich Isles, are now resident in this country. Four of them, having for a considerable time engaged the attention of liberal and active friends of missions, have by them been recommended to the notice of your Committee, and the Committee have thought it right to receive them under the patronage of this Board to educate with a view to their being sent back in due time to their own native Isles, qualified to be employed as preachers or teachers to their heathen countrymen. These four youths, by the grace of God accompanying the means which have been used with them, have renounced their heathenism, appear to have been brought to a saving knowledge of Christ, commend themselves to all around them as engaged and exemplary Christians, and testify a deep concern for their idolatrous parents, and brethren, and people, and an ardent desire to be instruments of imparting to them the blessings of the Gospel. Their faculties are vigorous; their proficiency in their studies is good, and the promise which they give of future usefulness is highly encouraging. Another, a son of a king in one of the Islands, has lately come to the knowledge of the Committee, and measures are taken to obtain his discharge from the naval service of the United States, that he also may be placed under advantages similar to those which his four countrymen enjoy. Your Committee cannot but gratefully recognize the hand of God in bringing these lately pagan youths to our shores, placing them within the influence of Christian benevolence, inclining their hearts to the Gospel, and producing in them the desire of making known the unspeakable grace to their countrymen. It is an intimation which deserves attention, and may lead to very important events; and it is submitted to the wisdom of the Board to determine upon a plan to be adopted for the education, not only of the youth already under our care, but of such others from heathen lands, as Providence from time to time may offer to our patronage and direction.

The Committee feel a great pleasure in acknowledging the continued and liberal benefactions, which have been received during the year past from numerous auxiliary societies, and individuals. More than ten thousand and eight hundred dollars have been paid into the Treasury, within the time just mentioned, beside the legacy of the late Mrs. Norris, which is now in a productive state. The particulars of all donations to the Board have already been published, and the summaries will appear in the Treasurer's annual statements. The Committee are deeply impressed with a sense of their responsibility, as almoners of that bounty which Christian benevolence has placed at their disposal, to be expended in promoting the salvation of the heathen world.

While the smiles of divine Providence on this infant institution, and the fruits of divine grace in the contributions to our treasury, are to be devoutly and thankfully recognized, the impression cannot be too deep upon this Board, nor upon the Christian public, that all that has yet been done is only a small beginning in a long neglected work of immense extent and importance. Long has the infidel reproached Christianity on account of the narrow limits within which it has been confined. The reproach belongs neither to our holy religion, nor to its adorable Author. Christianity is adapted in its nature, its institutions, its whole design, to the condition and necessities, to the relations and interests, temporal and eternal, of all mankind. and from the day of our Lord's ascension, his momentous edict has been in force, and binding upon Christians of every age and in every place. Go ye and make disciples of all nations:—Go into all the world, and preach the Gospel to every creature.—This command has not been fulfilled. Eighteen centuries have passed away, and three fourths of the inhabitants of the earth are yet without the Gospel! It is a reproachful, an awful fact. For this large portion of mankind, amounting by estimation to six hundred millions, the whole of Christendom at this day, after the powerful excitements of the last twenty years, supplies only about two hundred missionaries—only one preacher of the Gospel to three millions of souls, dwelling in darkness and the shadow of death. Were portions of the unevangelized people of the world to be assigned to the several Protestant Christian nations, according to their numbers and their means for supplying missionaries, not less doubtless than one hundred millions would fall to the share of our own nation. For these we now employ nine or ten missionaries; not more than one to ten millions of souls! Is it time then to slacken our hands,—to relax our exertions,—to caution those who are coming forward with their liberalities lest they do too much for this object? How then shall we answer for that hundred millions of souls to Him who, though he was rich, yet for our sakes became poor, and who is calling upon us with all the energy of his love, and all the majesty of his authority, to impart the Gospel of his salvation to them! The vast magnitude of the work of promulgating the Gospel in every region of the heathen world, and the pressing duty, which lies with such accumulated weight upon Christian nations, might almost overwhelm with despondency, instead of stimulating to exertion. But it can be shown, with unanswerable conclusiveness, that the energies of Christendom, if wisely directed and accompanied with a divine blessing, would be amply sufficient to send the Gospel into every dark corner of the earth, and supply a competent number of faithful preachers, within the short period of a quarter of a century. Let the friends of missions take courage; let them arise with one heart and a steadfast

18

purpose, and apply themselves to the great enterprise before them; and let each one resolve for himself, whatever others may do, that he will not forget the heathen, while he has hands to labor, a tongue to plead, or a heart to pray.

In behalf of the Prudential Committee,

SAMUEL WORCESTER, *Clerk.*

Hartford, Sept. 18, 1816.

––––––

PECUNIARY ACCOUNTS.

The American Board of Commissioners for Foreign Missions in account current with Jeremiah Evarts, their Treasurer. Dr.

To cash paid from Sept. 1, 1815, to Aug. 31, 1816, in conformity to orders of the Board, and of the Prudential Committee, from No. 113 to No. 149, inclusive, $15,906 33
To losses by counterfeit bills received in donations, 27 50
To balance carried to the credit of the Board in new account, Sept. 1, 1816, 44,277 69

$60,211 52

Contra Cr.

By balance brought to the credit of the Board in new account, Sept. 1, 1815, as appears by the Auditor's certificate of Nov. 21, 1815, 19,383 30
By cash received in donations, from September 1, 1815, to August 31, 1816, inclusive; viz. as published particularly in the Panoplist, $10,858 34
By cash received as interest of money and income of stock, during the year past; viz. on account of the Norris Legacy, $595 92
On account of other funds, 481 39—1,077 31
By cash received as a premium on bank notes, 2 78
By postage reimbursed, 1 75
By cash for sermons sold, 2 40——6 93——11,942 58
Oct. 18, 1816. By the avails of the Norris Legacy paid into the Treasury by the Trustees, 28,435 64

$60,211 52

MINUTES

OF THE

EIGHTH ANNUAL MEETING.

———

THE eighth annual meeting of the American Board of Commissioners for Foreign Missions was holden in Northampton, (Mass.) on the 17th, 18th, and 19th days of September, 1817. Present,

The Hon. JOHN TREADWELL, Esq. LL. D.
Rev. JOSEPH LYMAN, D. D.
Rev. SAMUEL SPRING, D. D.
Rev. SETH PAYSON, D. D.
Rev. JEDIDIAH MORSE, D. D.
Hon. JOHN HOOKER, Esq.
Rev. CALVIN CHAPIN, D. D.
Rev. JESSE APPLETON, D. D.
Rev. ALEXANDER PROUDFIT, D. D.
Rev. SAMUEL WORCESTER, D. D.
Rev. HENRY DAVIS, D. D. and
JEREMIAH EVARTS, Esq.

The meeting was opened with prayer by the Vice President, and, on the two following days, by the Recording Secretary, and the Rev. Dr. Proudfit.

The annual accounts of the Treasurer were exhibited, as examined and certified by the Auditor, and accepted.

The Report of the Prudential Committee was read and accepted.

The officers of the Board are as follows; viz.

The Hon. JOHN TREADWELL, Esq *President.*
Rev. SAMUEL SPRING, D. D. *Vice President.*
Rev. Dr. SPRING,
Rev. Dr. MORSE,
Rev. Dr. WORCESTER, and } *Prudential Committee.*
Mr. EVARTS,
Rev. Dr. WORCESTER, *Corresponding Secretary.*
Rev. Dr. CHAPIN, *Recording Secretary.*
JEREMIAH EVARTS, Esq. *Treasurer.*
Mr. ASHUR ADAMS, *Auditor.*

Resolved, That Dr. Morse, present the thanks of this Board to Chester Adams, Esq.* for his services as Auditor the last three years.

———

* Mr. Adams declined a re-election.

Resolved, That the Trial Balance of the Treasurer be annually delivered to the Recording Secretary, and by him recorded in his book of records.

The Report of the Agents for the Foreign Mission School, as prepared by their committee, was read.

Philo Swift, Esq., and the Rev. Timothy Stone, both of Cornwall in Connecticut, were appointed agents, in addition to those who had previously constituted the agency for the Foreign Mission School established in that town.

Dr. Spring, Mr. Evarts, Dr. Davis, and Mr. Hooker were appointed a committee to consider, and report on, the subject of compensation to the Corresponding Secretary.

The following report of the committee last named was read and accepted, viz.

It appearing to this Board, that the duties and labors of the Corresponding Secretary are such as necessarily occupy a great part of his time, and are essential to a successful accomplishment of the important and benevolent objects of the Christian public in their benefactions, and of the incorporation of this Board: Therefore,

Resolved, That measures be taken for an effectual discharge of the duties of the Corresponding Secretary; and that his Honor Lt. Gov. Phillips, Hon. William Reed, William Bartlet, Esq., and Jeremiah Evarts, Esq., be a committee to devise means for this purpose; which committee are requested to report their doings to the Prudential Committee, who are authorized to carry the same into effect.

Resolved, That it shall be the duty of the agents of the Foreign Mission School to report, every six months, a statement of the pecuniary concerns of said school to the Prudential Committee; and it shall be the duty of the Principal Instructor of said school, every three months, to report to the Prudential Committee the state of said school, and the Prudential Committee are authorized to give, from time to time, such directions as they shall think proper.

At 3 o'clock, P. M. on the 18th, attended public worship, when Dr. Appleton delivered a sermon, by appointment of the Board, from 1 Cor. i, 21.

Resolved, To authorize the Prudential Committee to take such measures as they shall judge expedient, relative to a missionary chapel and school house at Bombay.

Resolved, That the Board approve of the doings of the Prudential Committee in reference to the stations they have selected to which missionaries have been sent, and at which schools have been established; and do also approve of the extension of schools to other Indian tribes, as stated in the report of the Prudential Committee, under the patronage, or in concurrence with the authority of the government of the United States.

Resolved, That the thanks of this Board be presented to the Rev. Dr. Appleton for his sermon delivered this day by appointment of the Board; that a copy be requested for publication; and that Dr Morse, Mr. Evarts, and Dr. Chapin be a committee to accomplish the object of this vote.

The Rev. Jeremiah Day, LL. D., President of Yale College, was unanimously elected a member of the Board.

Resolved, That the thanks of this Board be presented to the Rev. Solomon Williams, and to those individuals and families in this town, whose hospitality has been experienced by the members during the session.

Resolved, That Dr. Lyman present the thanks of this Board to Mr. Levi Strong, and the choir of singers under his direction, for their very acceptable services in the public religious exercises on the 18th instant.

Resolved, that Dr. Lyman present the thanks of this Board to the Proprietors of the Town Hall, for the very convenient accommodations afforded to the members in that room during their session.

Resolved, That the thanks of this Board be presented, in such manner as the Prudential Committee shall judge most suitable, to such associations and individuals, male and female, as have contributed to the benevolent objects of the Board.

Resolved, That the Prudential Committee be authorized and directed to erect a monumental stone, suitable to the simplicity of the missionary character, and with an appropriate inscription, over the grave of Mrs. Harriet Newell, at Port Louis, in the island of Mauritius, as a testimonial of the affectionate and grateful remembrance of her sacredly cherished by this Board

Resolved, That the next annual meeting of the Board be holden in the Philosophical Chamber of Yale College, in New Haven, on the Thursday next succeeding the second Wednesday of September, 1818.

The Rev. Dr. Spring stands first preacher for that occasion, and the Rev. Dr. Payson was appointed in case of his failure.

Resolved, That it shall be the duty of the Prudential Committee to compile and publish a report, including their report for the last year; the report from the Committee of agency for the Foreign Mission School, a statement of the Treasurer's accounts; such a detail of donations as may be found useful; extracts from the minutes of the present session; and such other information as they shall judge expedient.

The session was closed with prayer by the Rev. Dr. Payson.

REPORT.

BRETHREN,—Shall we mourn, or shall we rejoice? One of our number, a greatly beloved and revered associate, rests from his labors, and is gone to receive his reward. His life was a shining light of increasing effulgence, his death was the setting of an autumnal sun without a cloud. This is not the place for ample eulogy. It is due, however, to the memory of the illustrious dead, and especially to the honor of the Eternal Spirit, here thankfully to record, that the lamented Dr Dwight was an ardent friend and strong supporter of missions. By his distinguished instrumentality in enlisting under the banner of the cross many young men, destined for public action; by his enlightened views and divine sentiments, impressed on many more; by his extended and powerful general influence; and by his counsels and exertions in direct connection with this Board, he probably did not less than any one of his survivors in this country has done, towards the advancement of this holy cause. And if he now rests with the apostles of the Savior, of all his works on earth, it delights him chiefly to remember, that he was disposed and enabled to do something for a cause so beneficent and glorious;—so dear to saints and angels in heaven, and to Him, whose immeasurable love to it is the continually opening theme of their most joyous and exalted praises. Is our late associate now an associate with the innumerable company before the throne of God and the Lamb? The thought will impart a sacred elevation to our views, and a celestial animation to our work. If we be faithful, we too shall rest in due time, and we too shall enter into the joy of our Lord.

The Report now to be submitted will be disposed under several distinct heads.

BOMBAY.—Our mission at Bombay claims our first attention. By our last Report the history of this mission was brought down to the close of November, 1815. It is now to be continued to the 20th of last May, within four months of the present time.

The period, thus defined, affords many reasons for gratulation and thankfulness, as a period of tranquillity and prosperity. Not only have the brethren Hall and Newell been quieted in their station, but the mission has received accessions of strength, and of means for extending its operations.

"This day," say the Brethren, in their Journal, November 1, 1816 — "This day has been made joyful to us by the arrival of our long expected brother Bardwell, his wife, and child. They arrived safe, after a voyage of twenty-seven days from Colombo. It was a joyful meeting to us all; and we heartily united in thanksgiving and praise to that all-directing Providence, that has so mercifully preserved and guided us in all our ways, and crowned us with goodness and loving kindness. Now our waiting eyes are unto the Lord, that he would grant our brother a quiet settlement here; that thus our hands may be strengthened, and our hearts encouraged." The Lord was gracious to their desires. Mr. Bardwell, accompanied with the other brethren, was soon presented, with a letter of introduction from governor Brownrigg of Ceylon, to the governor of Bombay. His excellency received them, they say, "with his accustomed kindness, and expressed to Mr Bardwell his readiness to shew them any favor." Accordingly Mr. Bardwell took up his residence in connection with the mission, and entered upon its labors with alacrity, and without apprehension of difficulty as to his remaining there

In a few weeks afterwards, Mr. Hall was married to an English lady, who had resided in the country so long as to have acquired a knowledge of the Hindoostanee, one of the principal languages spoken at Bombay, and who is considered by the brethren as no small acquisition to the mission.

Referring to these accessions the Brethren say, "The mission family at Bombay is now very different from what it was when brethren Hall and Newell were laboring in comparative solitude, uncertain whether any more would ever be added to their number. Our prospects are pleasing. We have great encouragement to go forward with increasing zeal, putting our trust for the time to come in the same infinitely wise, kind, and gracious God, who has hitherto blessed us."

In another communication, they say, "Agreeably to the recommendation of the Prudential Committee, we have revised the plan of polity which was forwarded to you in December, 1814, and have, with perfect unanimity, adopted the Rules and Regulations, a copy of which is enclosed." The Rules and Regulations thus adopted are in perfect agreement with the principles established by this Board, and are in the opinion of your Committee very judicious.

Thus happily circumstanced, the missionaries appear to have applied themselves with great assiduity to the several branches of their work; which are preaching, translating, printing, and establishing and superintending schools.

It is about two years since the Brethren Hall and Newell have been able to *preach*, with a good degree of facility, in the language of the country. "We cannot," they say, "expect immediately a regular assembly, at a stated place of worship. But while we indulge the pleasing hope of hereafter seeing such a congregation, we must, in the mean time, instruct the people in such dispersed and varied situations as we find them in."—"It is an unspeakable joy to us, that we can do something for the religious instruction of the heathen every day; and that we can assure our patrons and Christian friends at home, that through their pious liberality hundreds of their unenlightened fellow-creatures, are every week warned to flee from the wrath to come, and to lay hold on that eternal life which is in Christ Jesus our Lord." "It is probable that the manner of our preaching will continue to be much the same. We shall daily go among the people and preach to five, fifty, a hundred, or to more, as we may find opportunity; and these we shall meet in the streets and market places, in private houses and in their temples, at their weddings, festivals, and pilgrimages, as the case may be. Thus we expect to labor, in the hope that by and by, through the divine blessing, a congregation will be collected and a church planted."

In private journals, which they have sent to us, and some of which have been published, the brethren have given us some specimens of the manner in which they employ and acquit themselves in this part of their work: from which it appears, that they have little difficulty at any time in finding people collected, or in collecting them in considerable numbers; that favorable opportunities are frequently afforded them for exposing the absurdities and enormities of heathenism, and for displaying, in contrast with them, the excellencies of Christianity; and that they are often heard with attention, and not without manifest impression.

Besides thus preaching to the heathen, wherever and whenever they can find an opportunity, the brethren have certain regular exercises, statedly attended. On Sabbath morning they hold a meeting for poor Europeans and half-casts, whose situation renders them objects of particular compassion, and to whom they impart religious instruction. Regularly also on the Sabbath, they have public worship in English at their own house; and once a month they celebrate the Lord's supper.

On the last day of the year 1815, they commenced the public reading of the Scriptures at one of their school-rooms. The reading is in the language of the country, and upon the portions read expository remarks are made. At these exercises, which appear to have been holden twice a week, from the time of their commencement, a considerable number of Pagans and some Jews have attended. "We have as yet," they say, "found quite as much encouragement as we anticipated, in our first attempt of this kind. We hope, ere long, to have several such meetings in different parts of this great city and its suburbs."

Although, for reasons now obvious, the missionaries must continue to go out into "the streets and lanes of the city," and preach as they can find opportunity; yet they are strongly impressed with the importance of having soon a house for public worship, where people of all classes, disposed to attend may be accommodated "It will be needless," they say, "to adduce arguments to evince the expediency of a measure, so universally sanctioned and enforced, by the example of all Christian missionaries." In the opinion of your Committee, also, the measure is one which claims very particular attention; and the confident hope is entertained, that an appeal to the Christian public for the purpose of procuring the means of building a missionary chapel, or house of worship, for the benefit of the heathen in Bombay, will be promptly and liberally answered

Another important part of the work of our missionaries is that of *Translating*. Their general views, on the subject of translations, have been communicated to this Board; and are such, your Committee believe, as will meet the approbation of every considerate and judicious mind Deeply impressed as they are with the importance of a good translation of the Scriptures entire into a language spoken by millions of people, and at the same time of the difficulty of making such a translation, they are yet sanguine in the hope, that they shall be enabled in due time to accomplish the design. "We are in the midst," they say, "of the people who speak this language; we daily read their books in it, we hear them speak it, and we daily preach in it to the people. The study and use of this one language is to be the main business of every day of our lives" A portion of their time every day is devoted to the study of the Scriptures in the original languages of those holy writings. For reasons such as these, they very reasonably think themselves entitled to a degree of confidence in their qualifications for making a good translation; and they appear to give themselves to this part of their work with sacred zeal, and with intense application. Besides a harmony of the Gospels, they have translated the Evangelists separately, the Acts of the Apostles, several of the Epistles, and select portions of other parts of the Bible.

Another part of their work is *Printing* Their ardent desire of being able to commence this business was communicated to the Board in the Report of the last year. This desire, to their great joy, has been fulfilled. The printing press, for which this Board is indebted to the generosity of a gentleman in Boston, and which, with its appurtenances, was sent out to Calcutta, in December last, had not, of course, at our latest dates, been received at Bombay. But before they had intelligence, that a press would be sent to them from this country, they had made arrangements for procuring one from Calcutta; and by the kind aid of the Rev. Mr. Thomason, to whom they and this Board are indebted for many favors, they received from thence, on the 9th of December, a press, with a fount of Nagree types As Mr. Bardwell, who is acquainted with the printing business, had arrived at Bombay about a month before, no time was lost in preparing to get the press into operation. Various difficulties however occurred. In their fount several types were wanting; others were untrimmed, and considerable alteration was found necessary in their press. But their resolute perseverance prevailed; and on the 10th of March, they finished the printing of fifteen hundred copies of a Scripture tract of eight octavo pages. "Almost the whole of the work," they say, "from beginning to end, has been done with our own hands. Difficulties of various kinds, and such as could not well be described, have occurred; but we have been able so far to overcome them, that this first production of our press has greatly encouraged us. We now commend this little portion of God's word to his gracious disposal, beseeching him to make it the means of salvation to many of the heathen, and imploring his kind direction and assistance in all our future attempts to serve him in the work of this mission."

In another communication, they add, "After so many discouragements as our mission has experienced, you will, we doubt not, rejoice with us in our being enabled at length, through divine goodness, to commence the delightful work of printing the word of God in the language of a numerous heathen people. We expect to put the Gospel of Matthew to the press in a few days, but shall not probably have it ready for distribution under three months.

In connection with their printing the brethren say, "We deem it of great importance that the *paper* should be of a good quality. There is a plenty of country paper, which we might get *cheap*, and thus we might make the things that we print *cheap*. But we think that already, time and money enough have been worse than thrown away by printing the Scriptures on paper so bad as to render the impression in many places quite illegible, and of course useless. The ignorance and the indolence of the heathen, their indifference to all religions but their own, their being unaccustomed to reading, especially a *printed* character, the hostility of all their own moral sentiments and feelings, to the religion of the gospel, and the constant allusion in the latter to the things of which they are entirely ignorant, and the great and unavoidable difficulties in the way of their reading and understanding the Scriptures when put into their hands: if to all this be added a vexatious difficulty in *reading*, arising from the badness of paper and printing, what can be expected?"

The representation given by the missionaries, in reference to the quality of the paper to be used in the printing of the Scriptures, is sufficient to shew the reasonableness of their request, that paper may be sent to them from this country, or ordered from England. Accordingly, your Committee have made arrangements for sending out a hundred reams.

Conformably also to opinions expressed by the brethren at Bombay, our missionary, Mr. Graves, under the direction of the Committee, has been making himself acquainted with the business of founding types, and Mr. Nichols with that of binding books. And as there is much difficulty in procuring good workmen at Bombay, it will probably be judged expedient to send out ere long, some suitable persons to be employed in different branches of business, connected with the printing establishment, that the missionaries may not be too much occupied with manual labor.

The total expense of the printing establishment, when gotten into operation amounted to about $1,000. The press sent out to Calcutta, if not wanted at Bombay, will be sent to the brethren in Ceylon.

Another, and a most important part of the work of our missionaries is the *care of Schools*. Their views, and the views of your Committee on this subject at large, were submitted, and approved at our last anniver-

19

sary. The brethren at Bombay have under their care an English school, consisting of about forty pupils. This since the accession of females to the mission they hope to enlarge, upon the plan similar to the mission school at Serampore, and in such a manner as will render it a source of emolument to the general establishment. But their hearts are much more ardently engaged in free schools for the instruction of the native youth and children in their own language. Of these, they had, at their last dates, three for heathen and one for Jewish children, containing in all about three hundred pupils. The teachers of the schools for heathen children are natives; but are employed by the missionaries; and under their direction. In the first school the teacher, for some time, made it a part of his care to instruct his pupils in the rites of idolatry; but the missionaries interposed, and this part of his instructions was discontinued. As the schools are of recent date, it is not yet time to hear much of the progress of the pupils in learning; but the representations of the brethren are encouraging.

In one of their last communications they say, "Our press, we hope, will soon enable us to introduce improvements into the native schools. Hitherto they have not been supplied with books, except a few lessons prepared for them in manuscript. The tract, which we have just printed, has already been introduced into the schools, and it is pleasing to hear the name of Jehovah pronounced, without scruple, or fear, by hundreds of pagan children. We would not convey the idea, that the children have abandoned their own religion. Far from it. They still carry upon their foreheads the marks of idolatry, and are taught by their parents to worship the gods of the heathen Still we think there is abundant encouragement for endeavoring to imbue their tender minds with the principles of a purer religion. The seed thus sown, though it should lie buried, and apparently fruitless for a time, may yet spring up at some future period, and bring forth an abundant harvest A knowledge of the Holy Scriptures must necessarily precede the general prevalence of religion among the people; and the establishment of schools, in which the Scriptures are used as a school book, seems to be one of the most promising methods of disseminating a knowledge of the Bible. In this point of view we consider the native schools as a very important part of our missionary establishment. We shall carry our plans of education to the full extent of our means. We rejoice to hear by your last letter, that we may expect shortly to receive remittances for this object. The school department is now considerably in arrears. Had our funds been sufficient, we should before this time have increased the number of schools. We wish also, as soon as possible, to erect one or more buildings, which may answer the double purpose of school houses and places of public religious instruction for the heathen. This we think may be done at a moderate expense

It has before been mentioned, that at the stated meetings for the public reading and exposition of the Scriptures, several Jews have attended. It is gratifying to state here, that in one of the Free Schools for heathen children, there had been some time more than twenty Jewish children; and that there should be a school principally for Jewish children, the brethren more than a year ago, considered as being, for several reasons, very desirable. "The Jews themselves," they then wrote, "have solicited it. They are very poor, and but few of their children are at present taught to read and write. In such a school the boys could be taught without any scruple in the Scriptures of the Old Testament, at least. A number of heathen boys would belong to the school, who of course would be instructed free from idolatry, in the knowledge of the true God. It would also lead to such an intercourse with the Jews, as would be favorable to their instruction in the knowledge of Christ." Under these impressions, they resolved on establishing such a school, as soon as they could engage a suitable teacher. In the course of the last spring, a Jew of considerable attainments, and well acquainted with the language of the country, offered himself for the service. Accordingly the school was instituted. It consisted in May, soon after its establishment, of about forty Jewish pupils, who are instructed to read and write both Hebrew and Mahratta. "We think this," say the brethren, "an interesting school, and cannot but hope, that it will be the means of doing something towards bringing these ignorant, wandering Israelites to the fold of Christ." In this opinion, and this hope, all Christians will deeply participate.

Your Committee are persuaded, that it will be the delight of this Board and of the Christian public, to gratify, to the greatest possible extent, the benevolent desires of the missionaries in regard to the establishment of schools. Twelve hundred dollars for this object was sent out for Bombay about eight months ago, another remittance of a thousand dollars was sent about three months ago, and large remittances will be forwarded for the same object by the missionaries now soon to depart. An important consideration, in reference to this branch of beneficent exertion, is, that there is no limitation to the field now opened for the moral culture of children. All the charitable feelings of the pious and liberal can here find ample scope for exercise. It is to be observed, however, that some care is necessary, lest a peculiarly pleasing and popular kind of charity should so engross the feelings of the liberal, for a short season, as to leave other equally important objects unprovided for. These schools are a delightful and promising branch of Christian charity, but unless missionaries are supported, schools cannot be properly superintended.

Amid their numerous and urgent labors and cares, the brethren at Bombay have looked abroad upon the heathen world extensively, with most expanded feelings and views. They have collected and communicated much information, important particularly in missionary respects, concerning the different parts of India, Persia, Arabia, Syria, Palestine, and Egypt; in all which countries they believe that missionary stations might be established with fair prospects of success. They have proposed various plans, evidently the result of deep and enlightened reflection, for the advancement of the general cause. And from the shores of India, their voice has been heard in this country and in Europe, calling upon all Christians to engage in the heavenly design of imparting the blessings of the Gospel to the heathen. *The liberal deviseth liberal things, and by liberal things shall he stand.*

CEYLON. At our last anniversary, we had only the bare intelligence of the arrival of the missionaries, sent out two years ago by the Dryad, at Colombo in Ceylon.   Your Committee have now the happiness to report some particulars of a highly gratifying nature.

After a passage, during the whole of which they had only gratefully to acknowledge and to record the tender mercies of God, they arrived at Colombo on 22d of March, of the last year.   They were welcomed upon the shore most affectionately by the Rev. Messrs. Chater and Norton, English missionaries then at the place, and were received by the officers of the government with marked attention and kindness   On the next morning, a sermon was preached on board the Dryad, by Mr. Poor, in which the signal mercies experienced during the passage were devoutly recounted, and a very affectionate leave was taken of the officers and company of the vessel, to whom, and particularly to Capt. Buffington, the master, and Capt. Titcomb, the supercargo, very grateful acknowledgments were made

The dispositions of the Governor of Ceylon will appear in a letter, addressed by him to the Corresponding Secretary.   It bears date, "King's House, Colombo, June 13th, 1816," and in terms as follows:

"Sir,"—Your letter communicating the thanks of the American Board of Commissioners for Foreign Missions, in consequence of my reception of the Rev. Samuel Newell, and recommending five other missionaries to my notice, was lately delivered to me by those gentlemen upon their arrival at this place.

"To protect and encourage as far as lies in my power those who devote themselves to the propagation of Christianity, is so grateful a part of my duty, that I cannot lay claim to any merit for a service to which I am prompted by my own inclination.   Yet I confess that the mark of approbation from the Commissioners announced in your letter, has given me great pleasure; and I beg you will convey to the gentlemen, who compose that Board, my sincere acknowledgments of their kind and flattering attention.

"When Mr. Newell was in this Island I was a good deal embarrassed by the relative state of our countries, then unfortunately at war.   The peace which has been since restored, will I hope long remain, and remove every obstacle from the way of those who come so far to preach the Gospel of peace.

"I have read with much satisfaction the judicious instructions of your Board, wherein religious zeal is tempered with sound discretion.   If your missionaries conduct themselves according to the course that is there so distinctly marked out, their success will not be doubtful.   They have just received my permission to establish themselves in Jaffna, the northern province of this island, where in their opinion the fairest field is open to their labors; and I beg you will assure the Commissioners of my strong desire to do every thing to promote their Christian views, in all that is consistent with the safety and tranquillity of his Majesty's colony at Ceylon."

Similar dispositions towards the missionaries, and the great object of their mission, were, on various occasions, testified by other principal officers of the government.   In the fourth annual report of the Colombo Auxiliary Bible Society, made after the missionaries had been several months in the place, distinct mention is made of them; and the Report adds, "They certainly appear to be men of superior attainments and information, and in every respect well qualified for the benevolent office, which they have undertaken."

These testimonials must be highly gratifying to this Board and to all the friends of missions, and agreeable to the dispositions expressed in them, has been the uniform treatment received by our missionaries, from the principal men, not only at Colombo, but in other parts of the Island.

The brethren sojourned at Colombo about six months. A considerable time was requisite, for the purpose of obtaining, by correspondence with the brethren at Bombay and other missionaries in different parts of India, such information, as would enable them to determine, agreeably to their instructions, on the stations best for them to occupy; and after they had come to the determination, it was several weeks before the monsoon would allow of their departure to the places of their destination. During their stay, however, they were neither idle, nor uselessly occupied. Soon after their arrival, at the instance of the Hon. and Rev. T. J. Twistleton, Chief Secretary to the government, they took charge of the instruction of several young natives, designed for the Christian ministry; and as soon also, as conveniently they could, they opened an English school. In the forementioned Report of the Ceylon Bible Society, made about a year ago, notice is taken of the particulars now stated in the following terms: "In the beginning of last May, eleven young Cingalese, of the Vellale cast, and four Malabars, were placed under the tuition of the American missionaries, for the purpose of being instructed in the principles of theology and the doctrines of the Christian religion, as they are most of them intended for the profession of the church. They are from 14 to 24 years of age, and were all brought up under Mr. Armour, at the Seminary, where they learnt to read and write the English language.

"They receive also from one of the American missionaries regular lessons in geography, a science which is utterly unknown to the natives, and deserves a particular attention in the plan of their education, as it is certainly well calculated to enlarge their minds, and remove many of the prejudices, under which they labor. These young men were placed by the Hon. and Rev. T. J. Twisleton under the American missionaries, who gave them daily instruction without any pay or remuneration.

"The American missionaries have besides, a school consisting of 26 European children of both sexes; for they are in this department assisted by their wives, who are well qualified for the superintendence of female education." With these statements the accounts of the missionaries themselves perfectly accord.

Besides the attention given by them to the youths and children under their care, they afforded assistance to the English missionaries at Colombo, and in the vicinity, by preaching on the Sabbath and other days, from three to six sermons a week. It is gratifying to notice the harmony and brotherly affection which subsisted there between missionaries not only of different nations, but also of different religious denominations. Congregationalists, Episcopalians, Methodists, and Baptists were all in mutual fellowship; and on the day of communion at the Lord's table, in the chapel of the Rev. Mr. Chater, a Baptist missionary from England, the infant child of our missionary, Mr. Meigs, was baptized.

"We have the satisfaction," say the brethren in a joint communication, "We have the satisfaction to believe that the time we spent at Colombo was not lost to the missionary cause. By our preaching in English, the missionaries there were enabled to devote more attention to that part of their work, which relates to the natives. By imparting instruction to those, of whom our native school was composed, we used the most appropriate means, for promoting the object of our mission. By our European school, we did something toward defraying the expenses of the mission, and we hope, rendered some assistance to the children of those parents, by whom the school was supported. By residing at the seat of government, we experienced but few of those evils, arising from false reports and groundless suspicions, to which foreigners are generally exposed; and we may hope, that the acquaintance we formed with the principal characters at Colombo, will prove to be of lasting utility to us and to our mission."

The result of their inquiries in regard to the stations to be occupied, was that Mr. Bardwell, should go to Bombay, and, if permitted, settle with the missionaries there; that Messrs. Richards and Meigs should attempt an establishment at Batticotta, and Messrs. Warren and Poor at Tillipally, both in the Province of Jaffna in the northern part of Ceylon. This district was visited by Dr. Buchanan in Sept. 1806, and by our missionary, Mr. Newell, in July 1813; and by both of them it is represented as peculiarly interesting, in a missionary point of view. Mr. Newell, in his journal, says, "In case of our settling in Ceylon, the province of Jaffna seemed to be the most eligible spot for us. It is near to the continent, and the Tamul, spoken at Jaffna, is the language of eight or nine millions of people, separated from Jaffna only by a narrow channel." In this opinion of the eligibility of Jaffna, the principal gentlemen at Colombo, the Chief Justice, Sir Alexander Johnstone, particularly, who expressed himself at large on the subject, and the missionaries generally, were fully agreed. And in this eligible province, Tillipally and Batticotta are considered as decidedly the best missionary stations.

Having settled their determination, and obtained the permission of the Governor, the brethren judged it advisable, that Mr. Warren should go by land to Jaffna, without delay, for the purpose of making some preparatory arrangements there; and that the rest should take passage, with their effects, by water, as soon as the monsoon would permit. Accordingly Mr. Warren left Colombo on the 1st of July, and arrived at Jaffnapatam on the 11th. Mr. and Mrs. Poor took their departure by water, on the 20th of September, and arrived at Jaffna on the 26th; and Mr. Richards and Meigs with their wives followed on the 24th of the same month, and arrived after experiencing some dangers, on the 1st of October.

In a joint letter, bearing date Jaffnapatam, Oct 9, 1816, the Brethren say, "On leaving Colombo, such was the state of our families, and our mode of conveyance, we had many fears, that we should be subjected to some serious evils on our passage. But He, who had before protected us, dealt better with us than we feared. Our safe arrival at this place, and the favorable circumstances that surround us, lay us under additional obligations to serve our divine Master. We have visited the places, in which we hope to spend our lives, in opening the treasures of the Gospel to the heathen.   Tillipally is situated about 10 miles north, and Batticotta 6 miles northwest, of Jaffnapatam.   At each place, there are between three and four acres of land, on which stand a dwelling-house, a large church without a roof, and a variety of fruit-trees.   From the estimates that have been made, 12 or 15 hundred dollars would be necessary to make such repairs as a prosperous mission at these stations would require."

Both Tillipally and Batticotta are represented as being places of great amenity and salubrity of climate.   The glebes and buildings mentioned by the brethren are the property of the government.   The churches and mansion houses were built by the Portuguese, in the 16th century; they are chiefly of coral stone; and the churches are so large, that, when repaired, two-thirds of each, will be amply sufficient for the purposes of public worship, and the remainder will afford good accommodations for schools. Of the fruit trees, about fifty on each glebe are palmyras: of which tree the timber is much used in building: the leaves serve to cover the roofs of their houses, and form the olas, so generally used in the east, instead of paper; and the fruit constitutes the principal food of the natives for more than one half of the year.   Thirty or forty good palmyras, it is said, will, for that season, support a family of natives.

The brethren have been officially given to understand, that these glebes and buildings cannot be permanently secured to the mission, until the pleasure of the British government at home shall be known; yet they have thought themselves warranted, in entering upon the premises, and making such repairs as may be made with little expense, and as will render the buildings fit for temporary use; leaving the question of more thorough repairs to be determined hereafter.   At Tillipally, the repairs were in such forwardness, that Messrs. Warren and Poor took up their residence there, about the middle of October.   But at Batticotta, the requisite repairs could not be made before the rainy season came on; and Messrs. Richards and Meigs, at the latest date, 20th of January, 1817, remained at Jaffnapatam.   There they were employed in studying the Tamul language, preaching occasionally in English, and getting forward, as the season would permit, the preparations for their residence at Batticotta.

Since fixing their residence at Tillipally, the brethren Warren and Poor have regularly, on the Sabbath, preached by an interpreter there, and also at Mallagum, a place about two miles distant.   Their congregations have varied from thirty to eighty persons. No females attend. They have every day, also, at the time of morning prayers, an exercise of religious instruction, at which a considerable number of persons are usually present.   Early in December, they established a school for the instruction of native youth and children, both in English and Tamul, and another at Mallagum; and at their last dates, they were making preparations for establishing a third school at Milette, and a fourth at Panditeripo, places in their vicinity.

In the province of Jaffna, there are some relics of the Roman Catholic religion, which was introduced two or three hundred years ago, by the Portuguese; some traces of religious knowledge afterwards communicated by the Dutch; and some decaying fruits of the labors of the missionaries, Christian David, Mr. Palm, and others: yet the great mass of the people are Pagans. In the other provinces of Ceylon, the paganism is of the Budhist form, the same which prevails in the Burman empire; but in Jaffna, it is Hindoo, the same with that which prevails on the neighboring peninsula of India. In this district, however, the people generally, and even the Brahmins, are less devotedly attached to their idolatrous rites, have feebler prejudices against Christianity, and are more easily accessible by missionaries, than in almost any other part of the Pagan world. They are particularly fond of having their children instructed; and our missionaries represent, that there will be no difficulty in establishing schools among them, to the utmost extent of the means, which shall be afforded for the purpose; and that something towards supporting the schools may even be expected from the people themselves.

They also represent, that there is urgent want of Bibles and of school books. There is a good translation of the Scriptures into the Tamul, the language of the province, made by the Danish missionaries, in the last century; but copies of the Tamul Bible are extremely scarce. A considerable number of the people can speak, and some of them can read English; and many of them are particularly desirous of having their sons taught the English language: but the English Bible is also scarcely to be found, and the country, in a word, is almost entirely destitute of books. Our missionaries had applied to the Colombo Auxiliary Bible Society for some Tamul Testaments for their schools; and were in expectation of receiving a few; but they saw no prospect of a supply of books from any quarter, until they could be printed in Jaffna; and there is no printing press in the district. They therefore express an earnest desire to be furnished, as soon as possible, with a printing establishment, and with hands and means for putting it into vigorous operation. Whether it will be best to order to Jaffna the press already sent out, and intended for Bombay, or to send out another directly from this country for Jaffna, your Committee have not determined, but it will doubtless be the pleasure of this Board, that the desire of the missionaries should be accomplished, and their means of usefulness enlarged with the least unnecessary delay. And it is to be hoped, that the friends of the Bible in our country extensively will display a liberality towards the object here presented, in some proportion to its evident and urgent claims.

It is not in the district of Jaffna only, that Bibles and other books might be advantageously distributed. The island of Ceylon at large is in a state of peculiar preparation for the means of Christian instruction. It is blest with a government of most benign influence, which lends countenance and aid to every benevolent design; and upon its population, extensively, a very considerable impression has been made by the operations of missionary and Bible Societies. To this impression, the Chief Justice, Sir Alexander Johnstone, a most distinguished and enlightened friend of mankind and of missions, in a communication which he has done us the honor to make to this Board, expressly attributes the very interesting fact, that a plan, which he has had long at heart for the abolition of slavery in the island, has lately been adopted with wonderful consent. As so important an effect has been produced by means, in which this Board and this Christian community have had a share, the benevolent Chief Justice entertains the hope, that from us in this country aid will also be received, towards the improvement of the large numbers of children, who, in consequence of the abolition, will be placed in circumstances peculiarly interesting to public charity.

Nor should it be overlooked, in this general survey, that the language of the province, in which our missionaries are stationed, is also the language of eight or nine millions of people on the neighboring peninsula; and that the intercourse is such that, from Jaffna, Bibles and other books might with ease be extensively distributed in India.

Hitherto our Ceylon mission has been marked with signal favor; and its present prospects are most rich in promise. The field is white already to the harvest, and most active exertions, with humble dependence on the Lord of the harvest, are evidently and urgently demanded. The feelings and views of the missionaries appear to be such, as every friend to the cause would wish them to cherish.

"The events which have hitherto befallen us," they say, "would form a striking contrast with those, which happened to our dear brethren, who preceded us to this eastern world. As we may hope their disappointments and trials have wrought in them experience, patience, and hope, and will ultimately turn out to the furtherance of the gospel, we would make it *our* concern, that the goodness of God, manifested in our prosperity, may lead us to repentance, encourage us in our arduous undertaking, and inspire us with such confidence in God, as will enable us to endure the various trials, which every missionary is taught to expect."— "We are not making confident calculations on great and immediate success. In view of the deplorable condition, in which we see the heathen around us, and the many obstacles to be surmounted in their being raised from their superstitious and degraded state, we wish to have our own minds, and the minds of our friends at home, deeply impressed with the belief, that such patience and perseverance are to be manifested, such expense incurred, and, in a word, such exertions of various kinds made, as will in some degree correspond with the magnitude of the object we have in view. In seasons of prosperity and adversity, we would look to God for our principal support and consolation. Yet, we need, we greatly need, to be strengthened and encouraged by the friends of missions in our own country. We are sometimes ready to faint in view of the responsibility of our station, and the important consequences of our conduct. Here, in this dark corner of the earth, the moral aspect of things around us has a chilling influence upon our hearts, while we are deprived of those numerous excitements to active piety, which are felt by all who enjoy and prize the privileges of Christian society. Hence we need evidence that the Christian public in America are with us,—that they remember us in their prayers, and are forward to support that cause, to which we would ever consider ourselves most sacredly devoted."

AMERICAN ABORIGINES.—Attention is now to be devoted to objects nearer home. The general plan of the Prudential Committee for civilizing and christianizing the Pagan tribes of American Indians, has been fully submitted to this Board, and at the last anniversary, measures preparatory to an establishment in the Cherokee nation were reported. Your Committee have now the satisfaction to state, that those measures have gone into effect, in a highly gratifying manner.

20

In September, a year ago, our missionary, the Rev. Cyrus Kingsbury, made his first visit to the Cherokees. Early in October he attended a general council of the chiefs of the Cherokees and the Creeks, and laid before them the object of his mission. After consultation, a principal chief took him affectionately by the hand, and said. "You have appeared in our full council. We have listened to what you have said, and understand it We are glad to see you We wish to have the schools established, and hope they will be of great advantage to the nation " Another of the chiefs was appointed to go with Mr. Kingsbury, and select a suitable place for an establishment.

Cheered by these favorable dispositions, Mr. Kingsbury immediately applied himself to the requisite arrangements A plantation, which had for some years been occupied by a Scotchman, who had resided in the nation, and which appeared to Mr. Kingsbury to be well adapted to his purpose, was offered on what were considered very reasonable terms; and your Committee did not hesitate to authorize Mr Kingsbury to make the purchase

As the design is to form the young Indians to the habits of civilized life, as well as to impart to them the knowledge of Christianity, it is necessary to take them from their connections, and place them entirely under the direction and influence of their instructors. As they thus constitute not only a school, but a great family, means must be provided for their support and for their employment. Land, therefore, not merely for the accommodation of the requisite buildings, but for all the purposes of rural and domestic economy, is evidently essential to the plan. And though the expense may be considerable in the outset; it may reasonably be expected, that when the establishment shall get well into operation, it will go far towards supporting itself.

Having fixed upon his station, Mr. Kingsbury's next care was to lay in a stock of provisions, intending to open his school in the course of the winter, or early in the ensuing spring. Having made these arrangements with great industry, and as your Committee believe, with excellent judgment, he returned to fulfil some engagements in Tennessee.

Meanwhile the Committee lost no time in doing what was necessary on their part, for the proposed commencement of the establishment. As soon as they were apprized of the purchase of the plantation, they requested Messrs. Hall and Williams, two of the young men who had been engaged as teachers, to get themselves in readiness for departure to the station, with all convenient despatch. They obeyed the summons with great gladness of heart, and great activity in preparation. They sailed from New York on the 22d of January, and arrived at Savannah on the 30th; thence proceeded to Augusta, and thence across the country to Chickamaugah, the place of their destination, where they were welcomed by Mr. Kingsbury with great joy

Here your Committee cannot satisfy their own minds better than by giving Mr. Kingsbury's narrative, bearing date 30th June.

"I arrived at this place," says he, "on the 13th of January. The weather for sometime after was extremely cold for this climate, and I felt the want of comfortable lodgings, having only a skin spread upon the floor, and a thin covering of blankets; but my health was kindly preserved. Immediately on my arrival I commenced making preparations to cultivate the land, and to open the school on the plan proposed.   On the 7th of March, I had the great satisfaction of welcoming the arrival of brethren Hall and Williams, with their wives.   A kind Providence preserved them through many dangers, and brought them to their destined place in safety.   Since their arrival we have all, when health would permit, been employed from Monday morning till Saturday night, either in hard labor, or on journies for the mission.   We have had to provide for a numerous family, and to make preparations for supplying the wants of a still more numerous one.   In such a situation, we felt it to be our indispensable duty, to labor as far as health and strength would permit, that we might not be chargeable.

"Soon after our arrival in the nation, we opened our doors to receive children into our family, to teach them the rudiments of the English language, the principles of the Christian religion, and the industry and arts of civilized life.   The present number is twenty-six; of different ages, from four to eighteen years   Some are full blooded Cherokees, others three fourths white.   Six of the native children had been at school before, and regularly read a portion of Scripture at our family worship. On the whole, we must say, that our children give us great satisfaction; they labor when out of school much more cheerfully and constantly than we had reason to expect: and could the friends of this mission look into our school, and see these tawny sons and daughters of the forest listening to our instructions, sitting at our table, and bowing around our family altar, we do not believe they would grudge the money they have given to commence this establishment."   "The school is much approved in the nation, and many are wishing to send their children as soon as we can take them."   "We expect six or seven more in a few days."

"Besides this school we have on the Sabbath a school for black people, in which there are generally from twenty to thirty, mostly adults, two Cherokee men, and three white men.   The conduct and improvement of all these is very pleasing; making in all fifty-six, that are either constantly or occasionally our pupils.

"We have preached on the Sabbath, and our congregation is respectable and constantly increasing.   Last Sabbath there were nearly a hundred, most of whom could understand our language.   After a sermon in English I endeavored to speak by an interpreter to those who did not understand it.   The audience appear attentive and solemn, and much more regular than many where I have attended in the settlement among the whites."

"So many have been our inconveniences, and so much labor has been upon our hands, that we could not have that division of duties, which we hope hereafter to observe.   Previous to the arrival of my brethren, the business of the mission had all been conducted by myself.   This circumstance, together with their feeble health, made it necessary that I should still continue to bear the burden of cares and of the business abroad. This has left me no time for study, or for writing.   My brethren have always felt anxious to relieve me from so much attention to secular business; and a few days since I gave the oversight of the business entirely to brother Williams.   This has relieved my mind from the weight of cares, which, together with my other duties, I found too great to bear. Brother Hall has from the first had the charge of the school, and, when out, he assists us in the work we have to do."

It will be recollected, that Mr. Kingsbury had assurance from the Secretary of War, that the government would erect for the benefit of the mission a school-house and a dwelling house, besides providing various implements of husbandry and domestic manufacture. Owing, not to any fault of the government or of the agent, but to a failure of the person who had contracted to erect the buildings, they had not been erected, nor were they likely to be for a considerable time "This," says Mr Kingsbury, "has subjected us to great inconvenience and much expense. We have been obliged to build four long cabins for dwelling houses. These will accommodate our school when our other houses are erected. We are now engaged in making and burning about 20,000 bricks for our chimnies; must soon burn lime for the same, and dig two cellars and a well. All this business comes upon us when we are most busy on our plantation. But it was work, which was indispensable, with our numerous family, and we thought it better to do it at once than to be two or three years about it We now have our meal to transport forty or fifty miles, and we use near a bushel a day. This rendered it necessary that we should have a mill immediately, and we are in daily expectation of a man to build it."

"Agreeably to our instructions, we have endeavored to lay the foundation of the establishment "broad and lasting" Though expensive at first, it is sound economy We have exerted ourselves to get in a crop, have between twenty and thirty acres in corn, some cotton, flax, potatoes, &c. All the money we could spare has been devoted to the purchase of stock." In a letter to the Treasurer Mr. Kingsbury says, "There are now belonging to the mission 3 horses, 1 yoke of oxen, 5 steers, 14 cows and 11 calves, 22 sheep, and about 30 swine. It would be greatly to the advantage of the mission to enlarge our stock, particularly in cows.

"My dear brethren Hall and Williams, and their wives, cheerfully bear their proportion of our labors, though they have not been favored with so good health as myself."

From these details, which your Committee have thought it important to the object of their report to exhibit thus at length, this Board, and through them, it is hoped, the community at large, will receive some just impressions of the indefatigable exertions of Mr Kingsbury and his faithful assistants, of the prosperity with which by divine goodness, those exertions have been attended, and of the nature, the principal features, and the high importance of the mission. "We have indeed," says Mr. Kingsbury, "had much labor and many cares; but in a remarkable manner, we have experienced the truth of that precious promise, "as thy day is so shall thy strength be;" and we feel more than compensated for all our labors, by the cheering prospects of usefulness, which are opening before us. But we rejoice with trembling; and would resign ourselves, and the cause of Christ in this nation, to the hands of Him, who does all things well."

Mr. Kingsbury is confident, that it would be highly gratifying to the Cherokees to have more schools established among them, and expresses a strong hope that the Board will soon be able to establish more. Should a considerable part of the nation, in consequence of the arrangement recently made for an exchange of lands, remove to the west of the Mississippi, the event, he thinks, should not be regarded as inauspicious; as a missionary establishment in that more distant region would be highly important, and would furnish many facilities for extending the Gospel over an immense wilderness.

But the Cherokees are not the only tribe of Pagan Aborigines, which demands benevolent attention. Such information has been received, as strongly impresses the belief, that establishments, similar to the one now reported, would be very acceptable to the Choctaws, Chickasaws and Creeks. Indeed, an ardent desire has been expressed by chiefs of these several tribes, and by government agents in them, that schools might be established among them. And it is peculiarly gratifying, that your Committee have it in their power to state, that the general government regards this design with highly propitious dispositions; that the officers of government are particularly desirous, that the instruction of the four nations now named should go on at the same time; and that official assurance has been given, "that the same patronage will be extended to any establishment made within those nations for the objects stated, as have been given to the establishment for similar purposes, made under the direction of Mr. Kingsbury in the Cherokee nation. "The limited appropriations," adds the Secretary at War, "The limited appropriations for the Indian department will, for the present, preclude the executive government from extending a more liberal patronage to the Board in their laudable efforts for the accomplishment of objects so very desirable."

For the liberal patronage which the executive government has extended and engaged to extend, and the favorable dispositions which the officers and agents of the government, have, in the kindest manner, testified towards the objects of the Board, your Committee beg to express, in behalf of the Board and its numerous coadjutors and friends, the most sincere thanks, and to invoke the most substantial blessings. They devoutly hail these gratifying indications as eminently auspicious tokens; and under a deep and grateful impression, they have placed on record the solemn resolve, that they "will take and perseveringly pursue measures for the establishment of missionary stations and schools in the Choctaw, Chickasaw, and Creek nations, as soon and as fast as Providence shall open the way and supply the means;" and measures in pursuance of this resolve are now in progress.

The Committee, indeed, have a strong and animating persuasion, that the time has come for a great and vigorous effort for bringing up, in part, the long and heavy arrears of our country to those poor and diminished tribes of our fellow beings, whose fathers once called their own the widely extended territories, over which our prosperous dwellings are now spread, and continually spreading. And they cherish the hope, that all classes of the community will feel the generous impulse, and give, with sacred emulation, their hearts and hands to the beneficent work.

Besides the Cherokees, Choctaws, Chickasaws and Creeks, there are other tribes of pagan and savage Aborigines; some in different states and territories on this side the Mississippi, and many more in the vastly extensive wilds beyond. While, therefore, the counsels and labors and funds of this Board are bestowed upon the four specified nations, and they are regarded as especially our field; there is yet ample room for the benevolent exertions of other societies. And if different societies occupy different fields, unpleasant interferences and collisions may be avoided, and all may co-operate in the great and good work, with harmony of feeling, and with the fairest prospects of success.

FOREIGN MISSION SCHOOL.—The Agency appointed at the last aniversary, for the purpose of "forming a plan for establishing and conducting a school for the education of heathen youth in this country," lost no time in attending to the important business; and it has been the cheerful endeavor of the Prudential Committee to render them every facility and aid in their power. On the 29th of October the Agency agreed upon a constitution for the proposed school,—fixed upon a plan for its establishment,—nominated a preceptor or principal,—and appointed a visiting committee, and a committee to make the necessary contracts for the purchase of land for the use of the institution. On 12th November these doings were approved and ratified by the Prudential Committee; and the official commissions were given, and the requisite appropriations were made. The Committee also authorized the publication by the Agency of a "Narrative of five youth from the Sandwich Islands," under the patronage of the Board, for the information and excitement of the Christian public.

Shortly afterwards, lands and buildings for the Institution were purchased in Cornwall, (Con.) and measures were put forward to get it into operation as soon as it could well be done.

As the Rev. Joseph Harvey, who was first elected principal of the school, was induced by a change of circumstances to decline the appointment, the Rev. Herman Daggett was afterwards duly appointed to the office: and as his engagements would not admit of his assuming the office under several months, Mr. Edwin W. Dwight was designated to take charge of the school in the intervening time. The school was commenced under the instruction of Mr. Dwight about the first of May; the number of pupils is twelve; and the accounts which your Committee have received of their deportment and progress are highly satisfactory.

As a particular account of this seminary, styled in its constitution, THE FOREIGN MISSION SCHOOL, is expected from the School Agency, it would be superfluous to go into minute details, or to dilate on the subject in the present Report.

Your Committee, however, cannot dismiss this topic without stating, that, from extensive information and various evidence, it appears, that the school is regarded, in all parts of our country, with particular favor and a very lively interest. By this Board it will ever be fostered with parental care. Designed, as it is, to fit young persons who come to this favored land, from amidst the darkness and corruptions and miseries of paganism, to be sent back to their respective nations with the blessings of civilized and christianized society; with the useful sciences and arts; with the purifying light of salvation; with the elevating hopes of immortality; the relative importance and eventual utility of this infant seminary can hardly be too highly estimated. May abundant grace, from HIM in whom all fulness dwells, make it a living fountain, whose pure and fertilizing streams shall cause many a wilderness and solitary place to be glad, and many a desert to rejoice and blossom as the rose.

NEW MISSIONARIES. Our Missionaries at Bombay, in Ceylon, and in the Cherokee nation, all express an earnest desire that more laborers may be sent out to help them in their great work. Not only, indeed, is it evidently of high importance, that the several stations already occupied should be strengthened; but other fields are opening with inviting prospects and with urgent claims, and the harvest truly is plenteous. It must therefore rejoice the hearts and excite the gratitude of all the friends of the cause to know, that new laborers are coming forward to the holy and momentous work.

On the 3d day of the present month, in pursuance of arrangements previously made by your Committee, Messrs. ALLEN GRAVES, ELISHA P. SWIFT, JOHN NICHOLS, DANIEL S. BUTTRICK, and LEVI PARSONS, were ordained in Boston, as missionaries to be employed under the direction of this Board. It was found convenient that the ordination should be in connexion with the induction of the Rev. SERENO EDWARDS DWIGHT into the pastoral office in the church in Park-street; and the sermon for both occasions was by the Rev. Lyman Beecher. The introductory prayer was offered by the Rev. Mr Taylor of New Haven, Conn. the prayer consecrating the missionaries by your Corresponding Secretary; the charge to them was delivered by the Rev. Dr. Morse, and the right hand of fellowship by the Rev. Mr. Bates of Dedham, assisted by the Rev. Messrs Codman of Dorchester, Huntington of Boston, Gile of Milton, and Storrs of Randolph; and the Rev. Mr. Homer of Newton offered the concluding prayer. These services were followed by a celebration of the Holy Supper, in which the Vice President of this Board presided; the Rev Mr. Beecher, and the Rev. Mr Payson, of Portland, were the administrators; and hundreds of grateful communicants assembled from different and distant churches, united in shewing forth the Lord's death as the propitiation for the sins of the world, and the foundation of hope to all the families of the earth. It was a day of impressive solemnity, of holy joy, and of sacred vows.

Of the missionaries thus solemnly separated to the work, Messrs. Graves and Nichols are destined for India, to strengthen our stations there, and are expected to take their departure in two or three weeks. Mr Butrick is soon to be sent to one of the Indian tribes in the southwestern part of our country Mr. Swift holds himself in readiness for the Eastern or Western service, to be sent forth as soon as certain particular contingencies will enable your Committee finally to decide on his destination. And Mr. Parsons is intended to be employed for some time, as an agent for promoting the objects of the Board at home; and afterwards to be sent forth to any field, to which Divine Providence may direct.

Besides those now named, there are two others, who hold themselves engaged and ready for the service. About nine months ago a letter was received by the Corresponding Secretary from the Rev. Ard Hoyt, then pastor of a church in Wikesbarre, Pennsylvania, in which he expressed himself as follows: "With diffidence and trembling I write to you on a subject, which for some months past has pressed on my mind with great weight, viz. offering myself and family to go on a mission to some of the heathen tribes on our frontiers. Attending to your plan for evangelizing these tribes, I thought I could see it perfectly practicable; and was led to believe that a divine blessing would attend the undertaking, if American Christians would enter into the spirit of this plan, and prosecute it upon that large scale, and with that benevolence and perseverance, which the magnitude of the work calls for. My mind was expanded, my heart was enlarged, and imagination painted these now savage tribes, 'English in their language, civilized in their manners, and Christian in their religion.' I then said, Who will go?—and for my life could not help replying in the language of the prophet, 'Here am I; send me.' Since that time waking or sleeping, my mind has been on this subject more than any other, and frequently to the exclusion of all other care and thought."—"After repeatedly seeking divine direction, I have concluded, dear sir, to write to you, and through you to the Prudential Committee, if you should see cause to lay the subject before them." "I am now forty-six years old "—"We have three children, (one son and two daughters) who are the hopeful subjects of renewing grace, and who had manifested strong desires to be sent to the heathen, before there was any thought of my going. The youngest of the three has passed her eighteenth year. The son is now a member of Princeton College in the junior class. There is also a young man twenty-five years old, of approved talents and piety, who has been for sometime a member of my family, studying under the patronage of a benevolent society, for the express purpose of being prepared to go to the heathen. Should my family be accepted, he will be pleased to go with us."

This interesting communication demanded attention, and what was deemed a suitable course of proceeding was suggested. Mr. Hoyt submitted his case to ecclesiastical advisement; was regularly dismissed from his pastoral charge; and, by the same ministers, who were present at his dismission, was very affectionately and amply recommended to the Prudential Committee as "a regular and respectable minister of the Gospel, highly esteemed for his talents, prudence, and piety, and eminently qualified for usefulness in the contemplated mission." By the same ministers, also, Mr. William Chamberlain, the young man mentioned by Mr. Hoyt, as a member of his family, was recommended, "as a suitable character to be employed in an Indian Mission;—as a discreet, pious, zealous, and promising young man;" and a highly satisfactory testimonial was given in favor of the whole family.

There are known to your Committee five or six young men, now in a course of preparation for the ministry, who hold themselves devoted to the service of Christ among the heathen, and intend ere long to offer themselves in form to the patronage of this Board.

In no instance have the Committee *sought* for missionaries, or used solicitation or persuasion with an individual to engage in the service. All who have been received under the patronage of the Board, have offered themselves, and not till their course of preparatory studies for the ministry was completed, or nearly completed; constrained, as they have thought, by the influences of divine grace, and esteeming it the highest privilege to be employed in making known the way of life to the perishing heathen. Nor have they been received, until the Committee have obtained satisfactory evidence of their essential qualifications.

FUNDS. The Board was apprised at the last anniversary, that its extended plans could not be carried into effect without greatly augmented expenditures. To secure the necessary funds required early and earnest attention. Agreeably to the recommendation of the Board, the Rev. Mr. Cornelius has been continued by the Committee, as an Agent; and his well directed diligence and zeal, his fidelity and success, entitle him to the thanks of all who love the Lord Jesus and his cause, and call for most grateful acknowledgments to the God of all grace. Other Agents have been employed, among whom our missionaries, the Rev. Mr. Hoyt in Pennsylvania, Mr. Swift in New Jersey and New York, Mr. Nichols in New Hampshire, and Mr. Parsons in Vermont,—and besides them, the Rev. Nathan Perkins in Hampshire and the adjoining counties, the Rev. Samuel J. Mills in Maryland and Virginia, and Mr. Robert C. Robbins in the southern states, have rendered very essential services. Other agents have yielded occasional assistance, in the places where they respectively reside.

Within the past year donations have been received from *forty-seven* Foreign Mission Societies, *one hundred and sixteen* other Societies, under different names, principally, however, denominated *Cent* Societies, and *one hundred and thirty-six associations* for the education of heathen children and youth; making about *three hundred* in the whole. Of these societies *eighty-one* consist of males only, *one hundred and seventy-three* of females only, *twenty* of persons of both sexes; the remaining *twenty-five* not being distinguished, (whether composed of males or females, or of persons of both sexes,) in their communications to the Treasurer.

Though many of these Societies remit but small sums, they exhibit most pleasing evidence that a multitude of hands are already employed in this work of the Lord; and they furnish a rational prospect, that donations may be greatly increased, if the knowledge of the Christian public advances, and the zeal and activity of the friends of missions are augmented. As auxiliary societies are multiplied, as new fields for missionary exertion are opened; as new and urgent calls are made upon Christian benevolence, the Committee feel the necessity of a more constant intercourse with the various patrons of the Board, than has hitherto subsisted. Such an intercourse, by means of the press, is easily practicable, if the functionaries of the Board can command the time requisite for it.

The donations to the Board, during the year past, have somewhat exceeded *twenty-seven thousand dollars.*

To the numerous friends of this Board, in the different parts of our country, associated and unassociated, male and female, who, by their liberal benefactions, their active exertions, or their efficient influence, have aided its general design, or its particular objects, every member will concur with the Committee in feeling and expressing the liveliest gratitude. The true friends of missions are one body, having one common object, one common interest. There are many members, but they are all necessary. If this Board is necessary, its various auxiliary associations are also necessary; and so too are the individuals, even to the widow of two mites, who contribute to its funds, and labor and pray for its success. This sentiment should be deeply and mutually felt. It should be felt and acknowledged that the small contribution of the humblest friend of the cause is as really a service to it,—as really, though not in the

21

same degree, **necessary** to its advancement, as the munificent donation of its most opulent benefactor, or the arduous labors of its most important functionary. With this sentiment, it is devoutly to be wished that the whole Christian community may be inspired.

Though in the course of the last year many new associations have been formed, and many new contributors have come forward, and the amount of contributions and donations has been more than double that of any former year; yet there is need, most urgent need of increased activity, of more enlarged liberality, of greatly multiplied numbers, of vastly augmented funds If the income of the Board has increased, so also has the expenditure. Our expenses the last year for missionaries, schools, and translations at Bombay and Ceylon, amount to almost eleven thousand dollars; those for the various purposes of the Cherokee establishment, to almost two thousand and six hundred; those for the foreign mission school at Cornwall, to about five thousand; and those of various contingencies to about seventeen hundred: making a total of somewhat more than twenty thousand dollars. This augmented expenditure, considering the objects to which it has been applied, will be matter of devout joy and thankfulness to all, who, with singleness of heart, seek the enlargement of the Redeemer's kingdom and the best interests of mankind. It has been applied for the support of eight preachers of the Gospel to the heathen,—for the employment of as many teachers of schools in heathen lands,—for the instruction directly of four or five hundred youth and children, heathen and Jewish,* for the founding of establishments, designed for the unlimited benefit of heathen nations, and for the translation into various heathen languages, and the dispersion among millions of heathen people, of the lively oracles, given from heaven, to turn them from their vanities unto the living God, and to raise them from their wretchedness to immortal glory.

Must not the expenditure of the ensuing year be much greater? Is it not desirable that it should be?

It is calculated, indeed, that the foreign mission school and the Cherokee establishment will henceforth do much for their own maintenance, though they will still require, from year to year, very considerable aid But to the eight missionaries, already dependent on the Board for support, six or seven more are now to be added; other establishments, similar to that in the Cherokee nation, are to be founded, other schools are to be established in India, and in the printing and distributing of the Scriptures and other books advances must be made, attended with proportionably increased expense.

In this prospective view there is nothing to appal or to dismay, but every thing to animate and to incite. The work must advance; and the means will be supplied. The cause is God's; the silver and the gold are his; and the hearts and the hands of men are in his power. His word of promise also is ample and sure. Yet the plan of his sovereign wisdom connects with his all powerful grace the otherwise inefficient exertions of men, and makes it the high duty and privilege of his friends, in their various places and relations, to unite their hearts with his, and to be active co-workers with Him.

---

* While this sheet was partly in type, intelligence was received from Bombay, which authorises us to say *seven* or *eight* hundred, instead of *four* or *five* hundred.

Here then is ample warrant, encouragement, and scope for both associated and individual effort for the advancement of the best of objects; for the exertion of that sacred influence which peculiarly belongs to the ministers of Christ; for the exercise of that female love to the Savior and his cause, which so often displays itself as his brightest image on earth, and of which so many precious memorials are borne upon his heart; and for the activity and liberality of all, who would wish to have it appear in the final, revealing day, that they have done something for the spread of his great salvation. And your Committee are persuaded that, when the Christian public shall be made acquainted with what has been done, and given distinctly to understand, that augmented funds are urgently needed, for the support of missions and schools already established, for the establishment of others, and for carrying forward the interesting work of translating, printing and distributing the Word of Life, an animated activity and liberality will be displayed.

If, during the last year, a year of uncommon and almost unexampled scarcity and embarrassment in our country at large, our more than doubled expenditure was met with more than doubled receipts; what may not be reasonably expected for the ensuing year, now that the Lord has opened the windows of heaven, and poured out a blessing upon the land extensively, so that there is scarcely room enough to receive it? Will not this exuberance of divine goodness flow, through the grateful recipients, to thousands and millions who are famishing for the bread of life?

Will the Christian people of this favored country compel us to cease our operations, or to abridge our plans? Will they say to us, 'Recall the missionaries, who are already gone forth; stop those who are going. Let the work of translating, printing, and distributing the Scriptures proceed no further. Shut up those schools, and send those hundreds of children to remain in the ignorance and to follow the ways of their parents Let the heathen take care of themselves and of their own. If the Savior will have them for his inheritance, he will take possession of them when he pleases. It is no concern of ours' Will they say this?

Trusting in God, this Board may, and must "GO FORWARD." We have the high commission of the ascending Redeemer. We have the commandment of the everlasting God. OUR OBJECT IS SECOND TO NONE UNDER HEAVEN. *"For after that, in the wisdom of God, the world by wisdom knew not God, it pleased God,* BY THE FOOLISHNESS OF PREACHING, *to save them that believe"* The translation and dispersion of the Scriptures, and schools for the instruction of the young, are parts, and necessary parts, of the great design. But it must never be forgotten, or overlooked, that the command is, to *"preach the Gospel to every creature,"* and that the *preaching* of the word, however foolish it may seem to men, is the grand mean appointed by the wisdom of God for the saving conversion of the nations.

It is therefore matter of devout gratulation, that the missionary spirit is continually rising and spreading. And though this Board is not limited to any geographical division of our country, or to any denomination of Christians; yet it will gratefully hail other societies, formed for the same general object; welcome them to a share in this great work of beneficence; and reciprocate with them every affectionate and friendly office. The field is wide enough for all. Let all, who will, come forward to the work. We cordially bid them God speed.

The true missionary spirit, is the spirit of love;—of that charity which seeketh not her own—which envieth not; and it is not the least among the blessed effects to be expected from the diffusion of this spirit, that in so far as it prevails, it will break down the barriers of party, destroy invidious distinctions, and unite the hearts and hands of Christians in one glorious design, the spread of "THE COMMON SALVATION." The prophetic word is sure. When the earth is to be "filled with the knowledge of Jehovah as the waters cover the sea;" then "Ephraim shall not envy Judah, and Judah shall not vex Ephraim." Happy day!—Blessed consummation! Heaven will look down with delight; and united Zion in all her dwellings shall hear the majestic voice, "Arise, shine, for thy light is come, and the glory of the LORD is risen upon thee.—And the gentiles shall come to thy light, and kings to the brightness of thy rising. Lift up thine eyes round about and see: all they gather themselves together; they come to thee thy sons shall come from far, and thy daughters shall be nursed at thy side. Then shalt thou see, and flow together, and thine heart shall fear and be enlarged; because the abundance of the sea shall be converted unto thee, the forces of the gentiles shall come unto thee."

EXTRACTS FROM THE REPORT OF THE AGENTS OF THE FOREIGN MISSION SCHOOL.

[The Report from which the following extracts are made, was prepared by the visiting Committee of the school, soon after the semi-annual visitation, which was on the first Wednesday of September. The agents met early in October, 1816; and soon after fixed upon a place for the establishment of the school,—and subsequently proceeded to appoint a principal, as is stated in the Report of the Prudential Committee. As the instruction of the youths in practical agriculture is an important object of the establishment, the agents appointed Deacon HENRY HART of Goshen, to superintend this branch of business.

It is very natural for the public, and especially for the patrons of the institution, to expect a particular account of the character of the youths, who are patronized. So far as respects the young men themselves, it would perhaps be as well if nothing were published concerning them; but, it is to be hoped, that their instructors will guard them against being elated with the favorable opinion, which may be formed of them, by fallible men, and will press upon them the duty of humbling themselves before God, examining their hearts as in his presence, and possessing such a character as he will approve.

After stating at large the facts, which have been briefly adverted to, the Report proceeds as follows.]

"The contracting committee, having received authority from the Prudential Committee of the Board, proceeded to purchase in Cornwall two dwelling houses: one for a boarding house, two stories high, newly finished throughout, and painted red; for which, and five and a half acres of good arable land adjoining, and eighty acres of timber land one mile distant, they gave two thousand dollars. The other house is for the Principal, and is two stories high, has two stacks of chimnies, was covered and painted white on the outside, for which and three quarters of an acre of land adjoining they gave six hundred dollars. The house has since been finished inside, which cost six hundred and twenty-five dollars more.

"The people of Cornwall gave, in consideration of the school being established there, a convenient academy, 40 feet by 20, with three apartments, which is near the abovementioned houses. They also gave thirteen acres of wood land, a part within a half a mile, and the remainder within a mile of the academy. And they also subscribed in money and articles of clothing a considerable sum. The whole amount of donations from Cornwall is judged to be somewhere from eleven to thirteen hundred dollars. Deeds of the abovementioned property have been taken by the contracting committee in behalf of the Board, and having been duly acknowledged and recorded, are now in possession of said committee*

"About the 1st of May last, the buildings having been prepared, the school commenced its operations at Cornwall under the care of Mr Dwight.

"Soon after the commencement of the school in Cornwall, the Committee received an application from two young men of our own nation to be admitted into the school, for the purpose of being educated for missionary labors among the heathen. Their desire is to give themselves up to the Board to be educated and disposed of, as to their field and station of future labors, just as the Board shall see fit to direct. The name of one is SAMUEL RUGGLES, of Brookfield, (Con.) The name of the other, JAMES ELY, a native of Lyme, (Con.) They are both of age to act for themselves. Ruggles has been a member of Morris Academy at South-Farms, under the instruction of the Rev. William R. Weeks, and is highly spoken of by his instructor. He has gained a good knowledge of Latin, and been through several books of the Greek Testament. Ely has been a member of Bacon Academy, Colchester, (Con.) He is well recommended, and has been through the most of Virgil. They are members in good standing of the churches in their native towns. They are both destitute of property.

"The committee hesitated, at first, about their admission, but viewing the hand of Providence in this application, and recollecting the principles of the Missionary Seminary at Gosport, (Eng.) they deemed it their duty to give the young men a trial, until the pleasure of the Board could be known. The committee wished, also, to acquaint themselves more fully with the particular character and promise of these young men. They have consequently been in the school most of the summer; and the committee can now freely express their decided approbation of these young men, and cheerfully recommend them to the patronage of the Board. They appear to be pious and discreet, and to possess respectable talents. They possess, in a high degree, a missionary spirit, and have, we think, some peculiar qualifications to be useful as missionaries. Their desire for the missionary life appears to be not a transient emotion of youth, but a deliberate choice, and a settled principle. And we believe, from all that we can observe, that full confidence may be placed in their firmness and perseverance. They have had their attention and desires, from the first, turned to the Sandwich Islands, though they are willing to abide the direction of their patrons. It is not their expectation that they shall be sent to college, nor do they aspire to the rank of teachers or leaders. They expect to obtain such knowledge of the sciences and of theology, as they can in the seminary, and then be schoolmasters, catechists, or teachers, as the Board shall direct. Ely is a cooper by trade, which we think an additional recommendation.†

"These young men have been extremely useful in the school. Their

---

* The Legislature of Connecticut passed an act last May, empowering the Board to hold real estate to a certain extent.

† The reader will bear it in mind, that the introduction of the mechanical arts among savages holds a prominent place in every wise plan for their civilization.

example and influence among the other youths has been very salutary. Having gained the entire confidence of the foreign boys, they keep them from desiring other company, and maintain a kind of influence, which greatly assists the instructor, and promotes the harmony of the school. They are also fast catching the language of the youths, with whom they associate, and will soon be able to converse in the language of Owhyhee. On the whole, the committee cannot but express the hope that they shall be permitted to retain these young men as members of the school.

"Besides these two young men, the school now consists of ten members. Five of these are the youths from the Sandwich Islands; viz. *Obookiah, Hopoo, Tamoree, Tennooe and Honoree.* Concerning these an account is already before the public. The committee have it to say, that their conduct, since they have been in the school, is satisfactory. *Obookiah* has for several years been a professor of the religion of Jesus; and we are happy to say, that his conduct and conversation have been such as become the Gospel. He appears to grow in grace, and more and more to evince the reality of his new birth. He has been studying Latin chiefly the last summer, and has made as good proficiency as youths of our own country ordinarily do. *Hopoo,* having for about two years entertained a hope in Christ, has been the past summer admitted to the first church in Cornwall, and received the ordinance of baptism. He shines uncommonly bright as a Christian; has the zeal of an apostle, and ardently longs for the time, when it shall be thought his duty to return to his countrymen with the message of Jesus. His friends who know his feelings, have no doubt that Hopoo would burn at the stake for the honor of Christ. *Tennooe* and *Honoree* have given satisfactory evidence of having passed from death unto life; and should their example continue to correspond with this judgment, they will probably soon be admitted to confess Christ before men. Tennooe and Hopoo are about in the same advance of study, they have been attending to English grammar and arithmetic the past summer. Honoree has been employed in reading and spelling, together with exercise of the pen.

[An account is next given of *Tamoree,* who, soon after he joined the school, was less submissive to authority, and less patient of restraint, than was desirable. The committee say, however, that he has "conducted himself the past summer much to their satisfaction," and that "he has been obedient and respectful." The account concerning him concludes thus.]

"He has uncommon talents and activity, and by the grace of God, will be eminently useful. Considering the interest which the Christian public feel in him, and the many prayers which daily ascend for his conversion, we are cheered with the hope, that he is a chosen vessel of God to bear his name among the heathen.

"*John Johnson* is a native of Calcutta. His mother is a Jewess of the race of Black Jews. His father is the son of an English gentleman by the name of Johnson, and a Hindoo woman, whom he married in India. He is a merchant in Calcutta, and put his son on board a British vessel to send him to England for the purpose of receiving an education. On her passage the vessel was captured by an American privateer, and ordered to New York; but on her way thither she was retaken by a British frigate and carried into Halifax. Here she was refitted, and sent on her voyage to England. But she fell in with an American frigate, and was taken and sent into New York. From this place Johnson and the crew were put on board a cartel, and ordered to England as prisoners of war. But touching at Grenada, in the West Indies, Johnson took the yellow fever. His case being considered hopeless, and the cartel about to sail, the captain, fearing the infection, and knowing Johnson to be a friendless stranger, ordered him to be wrapped in a blanket, and laid on the beach to die. Here he was found by a gentleman of the island, who, with his lady, was taking an evening walk on the beach. The gentleman, learning his situation, ordered his servants to take Johnson to his house. Here by seasonable aid and nursing he soon recovered, and was then left to go whither he pleased. Not finding a ready passage to England, he went on board an American vessel, and came directly to Derby, (Ct.) From this place he went to live with the Rev. Nathaniel G. Huntington of Woodbridge; and when the Foreign Mission School was opened, he was sent on to the committee and admitted a member. Johnson is a Mohammedan by habit, and when he first joined the school was very bigoted, usually saying his prayers to the prophet four times a day. But his attachment to this way has evidently much declined. He now begins to doubt the divine mission of Mohammed; and is willing to hear him called an impostor. He manifests a great reverence for the Scriptures, and a great desire to read them, which he is just beginning to do. His progress has as yet been moderate, and his talents are not of the most lively cast. Yet he is diligent and studious. And considering the remarkable leadings of Providence by which he has been placed under our care, we cannot but hope he is designed to be an instrument of good in some station. Johnson speaks the Arabic and Hebrew languages with ease, and is, we think, an important acquisition on this account. He knows Dr. Carey, and has heard him preach: and says the Doctor passes by his father's door every Sabbath in going to church.

"*John Windall* is, according to his own account, a native of the province of Bengal, born about 30 miles from Calcutta. He early entered on board a vessel, and has since followed the seas in vessels of different nations. When the late war commenced he was thrown out of employ, being in this country; and on this account found it necessary to apply himself to labor for a subsistence. He came from New York to the western part of Connecticut, and was finally taken up by the Rev. D. A. Clark of Southbury, and after a short residence with him he came into the hands of the agents.

"Windall is steady and free from vicious habits, though not religious. He is anxious to learn, and persevering in his exertions, though his talents are of the moderate cast and his progress slow. He began with his letters and is now able to read sentences in the Bible.

"*George Sandwich* is a native of the Sandwich Islands, and came to America when very young. Since his arrival in this country, till the last spring, he has lived principally in Enfield, (Mass.) When he was received to the school last spring, he scarcely knew the alphabet, and had, by his own account, lived in a thoughtless manner. Soon after he joined the school, he became apparently deeply impressed with the concerns of his soul. His concern continued to increase until, to use his own expression, "all the sins he ever committed came and stood before him." He has since manifested new views and feelings, and gives very comforting evidence of a change of heart He is naturally of a very amiable friendly disposition, and has acquired habits of industry and economy. His talents are good, and his improvement very encouraging. The committee consider him one of the most promising members of the school.

"*William Kummoolah* is a native of the Sandwich Islands. He came with Capt. Robert Edes to Charlestown, (Mass.) last year. He is a youth of about 17 years. He can speak but little of our language yet, and is gradually learning to read and spell. To use the language of his instructor; "William is a lovely boy He is remarkably amiable and affectionate He has, during the past summer, evidently been the subject of religious exercises of some kind; though from ignorance of our language he is unable to give an account of them. He has derived great advantage from his serious companions, who could converse and pray with him in his own tongue."

"*Simon Annance* is from one of the Indian tribes in Canada. He has been taken into the school on trial, and has so lately entered that the Committee have not had an opportunity to form any settled opinion concerning him; neither have they any thing very interesting to state. If he should be continued in the school, we hope hereafter to give a more detailed account of him.

"Other students might have been admitted, but the state of the school and of our accommodations would not permit As soon as we can complete our establishment, and the Principal arrives, we hope to be able to receive a considerable addition to our present number. We can have students, as fast as we can accommodate them and support them. Several are now waiting for permission to join the school

"The semi-annual examination of the school took place before the visiting committee, on the first Wednesday of September instant, at nine o'clock, A M. It was an interesting occasion. Several of the neighboring clergy and a number of ladies, who have taken an interest in these youths, attended. The students acquitted themselves to the satisfaction of all present. Their accuracy in grammar and arithmetic, and the handsome specimens of their penmanship, which were exhibited, were particularly remarkable. In spelling they found the greatest difficulty.

"In the afternoon, an interesting discourse, adapted to the occasion, was delivered in the meeting house by the Rev. Mr. Prentice, from Matt. xiii. 16, 17. After the sermon, the Committee attended in the academy, to hear the register of behavior for the term, and to distribute two premiums to the highest on the register. On examination, it appeared that the first premium belonged to *Tamoree*, and the second to *Hopoo*. It ought, however, to be stated, that Obookiah, and the two American youths, not being present at the beginning of the term, no account was opened with them.

"The students, after a short recess, will spend the vacation in preparing wood for winter

"As to the expenses of the school, they have necessarily been greater at the outset, than will hereafter be the case Many articles of furniture and implements of husbandry and articles of bedding have been necessary, which we shall not have to furnish every year. The school was set up at a time when provisions were universally scarce and high. And many repairs and conveniences about the buildings were found necessary, which have swelled the bill of expenses.

"The expenses we hope will diminish as we are enabled to take advantage of circumstances. The young men in the school all labored, in their turn, a part of the time. They have cultivated four acres of corn, which is promising; and about three acres of potatoes; and secured some hay. The committee hope to be able to extend the farming business next season, so that each student will, by laboring two days in a week, nearly earn his food. Arrangements are making in many neighboring towns, among benevolent females, to supply clothing for the school; and we think a competent supply will in this way be shortly afforded. The committee have to acknowledge particular obligations for liberal aid in this way from benevolent females in New Haven, Litchfield, Goshen, South-Farms, Cornwall, East-Guilford, North-Guilford, Hadlyme, and Stockbridge, (Mass.)

[After making several inquiries, with respect to the domestic affairs of the school, and suggesting, whether it would not be best to have some of the youths study physic and surgery, (the professors of the medical institution at New Haven offering to permit them to attend lectures gratis,) the committee conclude as follows.]

"The committee cannot conclude this report without expressing the satisfaction they feel in this institution, and the growing interest taken in it by the Christian public in this region. The plan of the school meets with universal approbation; and the conduct of the students has been so regular and respectable as to gain the confidence and affection, not only of the people of Cornwall, but of all the surrounding towns. Hitherto the Lord hath helped us. His hand has been conspicuous in every stage of the institution. And when we look forward, the most encouraging prospects are presented. We hope ere long to see this small stream become a river, which shall make glad the city of our God. We long to see the dear youth under our care departing to set up the standard of Jesus in the land of their nativity. We long to see them on the way to their kindred after the flesh, laden with the richest blessing that man ever received; bearing the most joyful message man ever heard. May God hasten the time when the Board will see the way open to establish a mission in the Sandwich Islands.

"The late glorious events at the Society Isles, particularly at Otaheite and Eimeo, make our hearts burn with desire and expectation of witnessing the same triumphs of the cross at Owhyhee and Woahoo. From all accounts we receive, this field is already white to the harvest. Oh may the laborers, whom God is raising up, soon be prepared to thrust in their sickles and reap.

"The committee pray that the Board may enjoy the presence of God in their present meeting, and that the blessing of many ready to perish may come upon them.

"Signed by order,   JAMES MORRIS, *Chairman.*"
"*Cornwall, (Ct.) Sept.* 2, 1817.

PECUNIARY ACCOUNTS.

The American Board of Commissioners for Foreign Missions, in account current with Jeremiah Evarts, their Treasurer, Dr.

To cash paid from Sept. 1, 1816, to August 31, 1817, in conformity to orders of the Board, and of the Prudential Committee, from No. 150 to No. 210, both inclusive, $20,461 39

Losses by counterfeit and altered bills, and by bad or deficient coin, remitted donations during the year,   23 32

Balance carried to the credit of the Board in new account, Sept. 1, 1817,   53,841 61

$74,326 32

Contra Cr.

By balance brought to the credit of the Board in new account, Sept. 1, 1816, as appears by the Auditor's certificate of Sept. 4, 1816, $44,277 69

By cash received in donations, as published particularly in the Panoplist, between Sept. 1, 1816, and Aug. 31, 1817, $27,225 66

By cash received as interest of money and income of stock, during the year past; viz. on account of the Norris Legacy, $2,251 75

On other funds,   553 29—2,805 04

By gain on a small bill of exchange on London,   2 93

By the avails of the Narrative of Five Youths sold,   15 00—17 93—30,048 63

$74,326 32

MINUTES

NINTH ANNUAL MEETING.

———

The ninth annual meeting of the American Board of Commissioners for Foreign Missions, was held in the Philosophical Chamber of Yale College, Sept. 10th and 11th, 1818. Present,

Rev. Joseph Lyman, D. D.
Rev. Samuel Spring, D. D.
Rev. Seth Payson, D. D.
Hon. Stephen Van Rensselaer,
Hon. John Hooker,
Rev. Jedidiah Morse, D. D.
Rev. Calvin Chapin, D. D.
Rev. Jesse Appleton, D. D.
Rev. Alexander Proudfit, D. D.
Rev. Eliphalet Nott, D. D.
Rev. Samuel Worcester, D. D.
Rev. Henry Davis, D. D.
Rev. Jeremiah Day, L. L. D. and
Jeremiah Evarts, Esq.

The meeting was opened with prayer by the Rev. Dr. Appleton; and, on the following day, by the Rev. Dr. Lyman.

The accounts of the Treasurer were exhibited, as examined and certified by the Auditor, and accepted.

The Report of the Prudential Committee, was read, and accepted.

At 3 o'clock, P. M. on Thursday, the 10th, a sermon was delivered, according to previous appointment, by the Rev. Dr. Spring, at the first church, from Acts viii. 30, 31.

Resolved, That the Recording Secretary, Mr. Evarts, and Dr. Morse, present the thanks of this Board to the Rev. Dr. Spring for his sermon delivered by appointment of the Board, and that they request a copy for publication.

A report was communicated from the visiting committee of the Mission School among the Cherokees. Sundry other documents on the subject of that school were also exhibited.

The Hon. William Reed, of Marblehead, (Mass.) the Rev. Zephaniah S. Moore, D. D. President of Williams College, the Hon. Charles Marsh, of Woodstock, (Vt) and Col. John Lincklaen, of Cazenovia, (N. Y.) were unanimously elected members of the Board.

Resolved, That this Board cherish a very affectionate and grateful sense of the faithful, zealous, and highly important services of the Rev. Elias Cornelius as an Agent of the Board, for a length of time, and for various purposes; and that the Corresponding Secretary communicate to him this cordial testimonial

The officers of the Board are as follows; viz.

The Hon. JOHN TREADWELL, Esq. *President.*

Rev. SAMUEL SPRING, D. D. *Vice President.*

Rev. Dr. SPRING,
Rev. Dr WORCESTER,
Rev. Dr. MORSE,   } *Prudential Committee.*
Mr. EVARTS, and
Mr. REED,

Rev. Dr. WORCESTER, *Corresponding Secretary.*

Rev. Dr. CHAPIN, *Recording Secretary.*

JEREMIAH EVARTS, Esq. *Treasurer,* and

Mr. ASHUR ADAMS, *Auditor.*

A memorial was communicated from the executive committee of the Agency for the Foreign Mission School, on the subject of sending an agent to the Sandwich Islands, to prepare the way for establishing a mission upon those Islands, and was referred to the Prudential Committee.

Resolved, That the next annual meeting of the Board shall be in Boston, Mass. on the third Wednesday of September, 1819, at ten o'clock, A. M.

A committee having been appointed at the last meeting of the Board to devise means for an effectual discharge of the duties of the Corresponding Secretary; and said Committee having proposed such measures as they deemed proper, and referred the same to the Prudential Committee, the last named Committee made a Report to the Board, which was accepted.

Resolved, That the Prudential Committee be directed to express the thanks of this Board to all societies, congregations, churches, and individuals who have contributed, within the year past, to the benevolent objects, for which the Board was incorporated.

Resolved, That it shall be the duty of the Prudential Committee to compile and publish a report, including their report for the last year; the report from the Agency for the Foreign Mission School, an abstract of the Treasurer's accounts; a detail of donations; extracts from minutes of the present session; and such other information as they shall judge expedient.

The Rev Dr. Payson having been chosen to preach the next annual sermon, the Rev. Dr. Nott was chosen to preach in case of his failure.

The Recording Secretary was directed to present the thanks of the Board to the President and Fellows of Yale College, for the use of the Philosophical Chamber; to those persons, whose hospitality had been experienced by the members, during the session; and to the choirs of singers for their acceptable services in the public religious exercises.

On the evening of the 11th, extracts from the Report of the Prudential Committee were read in public to a respectable audience.

REPORT.

BRETHREN,—By the lapse of each brief year, we are brought perceptibly nearer to those bright and gladdening scenes, to which, with sure direction, all things are tending. Attuned to millennial strains, the prophetic lyre has cheered long ages of darkness, and waked the children of Zion, in successive generations, to hope, and prayer, and joyous anticipation. The hopes were not fallacious; the prayers have been heard on high; the anticipations are beginning to be realized with augmenting joy. God has arisen to have mercy on Zion; for the time to favor her, yea, the set time is come. Her children are at length aroused to action; and as they advance, the opening and brightening prospects inspire them with fresh and increasing animation. Blessed are our eyes, for they see; and our ears, for they hear. Thanks be unto HIM, who, hath the times and the seasons in his own hand, that ours is a day so auspicious that to us the high privilege is granted of bearing a part in the arduous, glorious work of such a day; and that we are not without assurance that our labor has not been, and will not be, in vain.

In what is now to be submitted, in the way of annual Report, your Committee will observe the method which they have heretofore adopted: passing in review, first, our establishments abroad in their order, and then our operations and objects of attention at home.

BOMBAY.—At our last anniversary the Rev. John Nichols and the Rev. Allen Graves, who, together with others, had then recently been set apart by solemn consecration, and received the right hand of fellowship that they should go unto the heathen, were mentioned as being "destined for India to strengthen our stations there," and soon to take their departure. Arrangements were accordingly made for the purpose with all convenient despatch; and on the 5th of October, they with their wives, and Miss Philomela Thurston, who, with the express approbation of your Committee, was sacredly affianced to the Rev. Mr. Newell, embarked at Charlestown, on board the ship Saco for Bombay. During the scenes of preparation and departure,—in their various conversations and attentions, in receiving the instructions, counsels and exhortations of the Committee; and in taking final leave of their country and friends, they severally manifested a spirit of love and of a sound mind,—of enlightened self-renunciation, devotion to Christ, confidence in his all-sufficiency, and desire to make known his salvation among the heathen, which gave a highly satisfactory promise of fidelity and usefulness. And with many prayers and tears, they were affectionately and fervently commended to God and to the word of his grace.

It is the pleasurable office of gratitude to record, that the Hon. William Gray, in a very obliging manner, declined receiving any remuneration for the excellent accommodations, and abundant supply of substantial provisions, afforded to the missionaries for their passage in his ship. And in furnishing them with various articles for their convenience, health, and comfort, benevolent individuals in Charlestown and Boston, shewed a liberality and love to the cause very gratifying to be remembered.

Wafted, for the most part, by favorable winds, and under the guardian care of Him, who rules the raging of the sea, the Saco, arrived at Bombay on the 23d of February. Excepting Mrs. Nichols, whose sufferings from sea sickness appear to have been unusual in degree, and still more so in duration, the missionaries, while crossing the wide waters, enjoyed a good measure of health. And united in fervent affection,—favored, at the proper seasons with the privileges of prayer and preaching,—and engaged daily in studies and exercises, according to rules early adopted, for the improvement of their own minds and hearts, and for the benefit of the mariners,—they passed the greater part of their time on board not unpleasantly, and, it is hoped, not unprofitably.

By the brethren and sisters at Bombay they were welcomed, with affectionate tenderness and grateful joy. "The same day," say these brethren in a letter to the Corresponding Secretary, "one of us waited on the governor with your letter to him. He received it, and shortly after in a personal interview, spoke of it, and also of our mission, in expressions of his accustomed liberality and kindness. The second day after this interview, one of us again waited on his excellency, with the brethren Nichols and Graves. They were kindly received by his excellency, who said that he had that morning written to the Court of Directors in favor of their settlement here."

In a joint communication of March 28th, Messrs. Nichols and Graves express their grateful sense of their obligations to divine goodness, in the following terms. "While reviewing the catalogue of mercies we have experienced, since we left our native land, we are constrained to make a renewed consecration of ourselves to our covenant God· we are bound to take the cup of salvation and call upon his name. Whether we remember the kindness of our Christian friends in America; the unremitting assiduity of the Prudential Committee in providing for our comfort while on the ocean; the measure of health which most of our number have enjoyed; or our favorable reception at this place; we have equal occasion for gratitude and praise. Were the inquiry to be made, "Lacked ye any thing?" —we would reply—"Nothing."

In the instructions given them by your Committee, Mr. Nichols was directed to settle at Bombay, provided the door should be opened to him there; and Mr. Graves to proceed thence to Ceylon; unless, in the concurrent judgment of the brethren at Bombay, "particular circumstances should render it expedient for him to abide with them." As soon as convenient after their arrival, the question of their location was deliberately considered; and it was determined with entire unanimity, and upon grounds satisfactory to your Committee, that it was expedient for both of them to remain in connection with the mission at Bombay one of them to occupy a station at Mahim, on the northern part of the island of Bombay, and the other at Tanna, on the island of Salsette.

With the same unanimity the station at Mahim was assigned to Mr. Graves; and from that place under date of March 27th, Mr. Graves writes· "Our separation would not be so far that we could not occasionally consult and assist each other. They had already two schools at Mahim, and two or three in its vicinity, so distant that it was tedious to superintend them; and they judged it as easy for me to attain the language here as in Bombay, having intercourse only with natives. Accordingly, myself and wife removed to this place on the 7th inst. We are about six miles from the brethren, and seven or eight from the fort of Bombay; and, owing to the difficulty and expense of any mode of conveyance, and the danger of walking so far in this climate, neither of us can frequently meet with the brethren in their religious exercises, so that we spend most of our Sabbaths with ourselves alone, attending religious exercises at the usual time. We are truly happy in our condition. The place contains nineteen thousand souls; the immediate vicinity is also populous; and it is but about half a mile across to a thick population on Salsette. You see then, dear Sir, that we need nothing but faithfulness and the divine blessing to make us useful. For these we trust our Christian friends will ever pray in our behalf.—Mrs. Graves is attempting to instruct in English a number of Portuguese and Hindoo boys in our Verandah."

On the 11th of March, Mr. Nichols visited Tanna, in company with Mr. Newell; and was courteously received by the magistrate, Mr. Babington, who remarked to him, that there was on the island a very wide field for usefulness." The island of Salsette, formerly separated from the northern part of the island of Bombay by a narrow strait, but now connected with it by a causeway, contains a population of about sixty thousand,—Hindoos, Parsees, Jews and Portuguese, but chiefly Hindoos, —in a deplorably abject and wretched condition. Tanna is the chief town; is distant from the mission house at Bombay about 25 miles; and commands the passage, (about a furlong broad,) from the island to the neighboring continent, where the principal language, both of Bombay and Salsette is common to a population of about nine millions. Mr. Nichols appears to have been pleased with the place, as a missionary station; and calculated on fixing his residence there, after spending a few months in studying the language with the brethren at Bombay.

"The occupying of these two stations," say the previously settled brethren, "we consider a great and promising advancement of our mission. It will give a much wider range to our operations, and enable us, almost immediately, to carry our schooling system to a much greater extent, and also the dissemination of the various productions of our press; and, in a little time, with a divine blessing, it will extend the preaching of the gospel to a great population, who are almost beyond the reach of the establishment at Bombay. We feel highly grateful and joyful that these two places are, under such encouraging circumstances, occupied by the missionaries of the Board; and we cannot but believe that the event will be equally joyous to all the members of the Board. We would render unfeigned thanksgiving and praise to our most blessed God, who has dealt so mercifully with us, and who has shewn so many tokens of favor to this mission."

On the 26th of March, the marriage of Mr. Newell to Miss Thurston was solemnized; and of the accessions to the mission the brethren speak in terms of high and grateful satisfaction. "Sixteen months ago," they say, "the mission consisted of but two persons. Now there are twelve, including two infant children. Surely God has greatly enlarged us; and we would bless his holy name forever"

In the course of the last autumn Mr. and Mrs. Bardwell were visited with heavy affliction; first in the death of their infant son, and then, about two months afterwards, in the severe and very dangerous sickness of Mr.

Bardwell himself. But the Lord was gracious; and the life of his greatly beloved servant was precious in his sight. Blessed be his holy name.

Beside these painful domestic visitations, from the 20th of May, 1817, the latest date reported at our last anniversary, to the 6th of April of the present year, the latest date to be reported at this time, the mission sustained no special adversity, but was constantly advancing in its operations, with encouraging prosperity. Of the system of its operations, the principal parts are preaching, printing, and dispersing portions of the Scriptures and other books and tracts, and the instruction of children in schools.

Their manner of preaching was reported the last year with considerable particularity. It continues much the same. It is not to congregations, regularly convened for the purpose at set times and places: but "Wisdom crieth without; she uttereth her voice in the streets. She crieth in the chief place of concourse; in the openings of the gates; by the way, in the places of the paths; at the coming in at the doors, in the city she uttereth her words." Every day our indefatigable missionaries are engaged in this, which they justly consider as the first and highest part of their work; addressing themselves, as they find opportunity, to individuals, to families, to assemblages, small and large, on various occasions, and at different places—especially on sacred occasions and at the temples of dumb idols; calling upon the deluded votaries to turn from these vanities unto the living God, and pointing them to the fountain opened for sin, and for all uncleanness."

Before the arrival of Mr. Graves, now stationed at Mahim, Mr. Newell spent several weeks at that place, "where he preached the Gospel to many who never heard it before" And besides preaching to the natives in the language of the country, the brethren have statedly, during the year, preached in English, at the mission house on the Sabbath, and at the Fort on Thursday evening.

With ardent hope, they look forward to the time when, by the free will offerings of Christians dwelling at home in their ceiled houses, and enjoying the fulness of blessings with which the God of all grace has so richly endowed his American Zion, they will be enabled to erect a house for his name, for his stated worship, and for the public exhibition of his great salvation, among the heathen with whom they sojourn, and when, in that land of darkness and of the shadow of death; He will find a habitation, where He will delight to appear in his glory, to bless the provisions of his house, and to fill the famishing—perishing poor with bread.

In the Report of last year, it was stated that, with almost unexampled diligence, and pains, and perseverance, they had gotten their printing press into operation, and printed fifteen hundred copies of a Scripture tract, of eight pages octavo, in the Mahratta language. They have since printed a large edition of the Gospel of Matthew, of the Acts of the Apostles, and of another tract consisting of select portions of Scripture; all of which are translations made by themselves into the same language They had also at their last date, commenced the printing of a book, which they had prepared for their schools. Specimens of their work have been sent home, and have been pronounced by competent judges here to be in a good style of execution.

"The translation and printing of the Scriptures entire," they say, "we calculate to continue until the whole shall be completed, should we live so long; but in the mean time, we intend to prepare and print, in a series of tracts or numbers, an abridgement of the Bible in the regular order of events. The first number, embracing the history of the period from the creation to the flood, is now ready for the press, and will be printed soon. The whole work will make a volume of 200 or 300 pages octavo. They have engaged besides, to print an edition of the Gospel of Matthew, for the Bombay Bible Society.

Before they commenced printing themselves, they had procured 5000 copies of a tract in the Guzerattee language to be printed for them. "The greater part of these," they say, "have been distributed. The two Mahratta tracts, printed by us, are very nearly exhausted, and several hundred copies of the Gospel of Matthew have also been distributed."

On the subject of schools, your Committee cannot do better than to give at large the statement made by Messrs. Hall, Newell, and Bardwell in their joint letter of 6th April.

"Since we last wrote," say they, "the number of schools has been increased to eleven. Four of them are on the opposite end of the island, where it can hardly be said there was before any such thing as schooling among the natives. Consequently we found less readiness in the people to avail themselves of the advantages of schooling for their children. This circumstance only rendered it the more desirable that schools should be established among them, and we were much encouraged to find that, in less than two months, about one hundred boys were collected in these four schools with the prospect of an increased number.

"The whole number of boys attending all the schools, we estimate at six hundred. Many more are attached to the schools and attend more or less. Probably twice the number mentioned actually belong to the schools; making in the course of a year *twelve hundred*, Jewish, Mahommetan, but chiefly heathen boys, instructed in the arts of reading, writing, and arithmetic; and what is much more, educated too, in some good degree, in the knowledge of the holy Scriptures, and the way of salvation through Jesus Christ. Here is a measure of success far exceeding our most flattering anticipations. It animates our hearts, and we cannot but believe, that it will be not only satisfactory, but highly animating to our Christian friends at home, by whose noble liberality these schools are patronized and supported.

"In these schools, we seem to see a thousand *Hindoo* hands at work, from year to year, in undermining the fabric of Hindoo idolatry. We desire to repeat our expression of gratitude, first to our most merciful God, who has so exceedingly blessed us and caused our work to prosper; —and also to our dear friends at home, by whose pious liberality, so many of the rising generation in India are blessed, not only with the rudiments of common learning, but also with the light of the Gospel. And we wish to assure our friends that it is our determination to continue and extend the plan of schooling, as far as their liberality and the blessing of God on our own exertions, will enable us. The accession of two fellow-laborers, occupying the new and very important stations of Mahim and Tanna, will afford new and great facilities for multiplying the number

23

of schools, and for superintending them, in that manner, which will render them most subservient to the great object of diffusing useful learning and Christian knowledge in this benighted land."

In regard to taking heathen children to be brought up as Christians, or to be educated in the mission family, your Committee have not the means of reporting so fully as they could wish. As it is a part of the general system, in which not a few of the friends of the cause have taken a particular and lively interest, the Committee have felt in regard to it, a very wakeful solicitude, lest, by any means, the benevolent feelings and hopes of individuals and societies should in any respect, be disappointed. If, however, circumstances be duly considered, it will not be thought strange if little, in this part, has yet been done. It is only about two years since contributions or donations for this particular object began to be received at the treasury; and but little more than a year, since the first remittances for it could have been received in India. The domestic state of the missionaries was then such, as not to admit of their immediately taking many children into the family, and some time would of course be required for selecting and obtaining suitable objects of the charity. But the mission has since been enlarged by accessions of persons of both sexes: their advantages for taking children are of course increased; and no doubt should be entertained, that, in due time, a good account will be rendered in regard to this object, in which the missionaries themselves have expressed a very deep interest.

It would be the highest joy of the Committee, could they communicate to their brethren of this Board and of the Christian community intelligence of signal success at Bombay, in the conversion of many from darkness unto light, and from the power of Satan unto God. This joy they have not yet. In regard to success in this respect, our beloved and devoted missionaries express themselves in the following moving terms. "We can now say that for years, we have preached the Gospel to the heathen. But we are constrained to take up the bitter lamentation of the prophet—"Who hath believed our report, and to whom hath the arm of the Lord been revealed." We know of no one who has been brought to the faith of the Gospel under our preaching. This severely tries, but does not discourage, us. We implore, and, oh! may all our dear Christian friends at home, daily implore, divine grace, that we may faithfully labor and not faint; remembering the blessed promise, that he that goeth forth with weeping, bearing precious seed, shall doubtless return with joy, bringing his sheaves with him. Though we now see no visible tokens of converting grace, yet we cannot but indulge the pleasing hope, that out of the great number, who have so repeatedly heard from our lips the glad tidings of the Gospel, the hearts of some have been touched, and that the unseen operations of divine truth and grace are now preparing them to turn from death unto life."

Feelings and views like these cannot be cherished and strengthened too assiduously or devoutly, by missionaries themselves, and all who love the holy and glorious cause of missions. It would show a deplorable defect of faith, it would be an impious affront to the God of the Gospel and of all its promises and grace and power, to be discouraged because the desired success is not immediately seen. The husbandman is not discouraged, because he does not see his fields white for the harvest, as soon as he begins to clear his grounds, to plough, or to sow. The merchant is not discouraged, because his coffers or his warehouses are not filled with the avails of his enterprise, as soon as the preparations for the voyage are commenced, or his ship gets out to sea. How often, even in this land, where the darkness and corruptions, and long established mummeries and superstitions of the most debasing and besotting idolatries are not first to be cleared away, do faithful and devoted ministers of Christ labor among their people a much longer time, than the missionaries have been laboring at Bombay, with very little, if any, visible success? How long did the missionaries from Europe labor at Tranquebar, and how long in Bengal, before their hearts were cheered with any considerable fruits? Who should be discouraged, after what has been witnessed in Eimeo and Otaheite?—A nation born in a day, after twenty years of missionary labors and sufferings, under circumstances of the darkest and most cheerless aspect.

Success, in the actual conversion of the heathen, cannot indeed be too earnestly desired; and when granted, is encouraging, and animating, and to be acknowledged with the most devout thankfulness. Success, however, is not the rule of duty, nor the test of expediency. *It is the commandment of the* EVERLASTING GOD, *that his word should be made known among all nations—that the Gospel should be preached unto every creature.* The question is, Has this commandment been fulfilled? Have we done, or are we doing, in obedience to it, all that belongs to us—*all that we can?* It ill becomes Christians, especially at this late day, to fold their hands, and prudently wait to see the success of missions, before they lend their aid to the work. What if all were to assume this attitude? The last trumpet would sound, before the work would begin! As little does it become those, who are engaged in this cause, to be discouraged—still less those, who are standing idle in regard to it, to justify their negligence—on account of any supposed failure or slowness of success. It is *ours*, in humble and cheerful obedience to the command, to do what we can for the publication of the Gospel, it is *God's* to determine the effect. If the desired success be delayed, it is a reason for the prayer—'Lord increase our faith—our diligence—our willingness to make exertions and sacrifices,'—no reason for the abatement of our zeal.

At Bombay, by means of Christian efforts and liberalities in this country, the Gospel has already been published to thousands, to whom it was unknown and a system of operations is advancing for its eventual *publication to thousands and millions more.* Let all who have a part in this work, rejoice in what has been done; look well to what they have yet to do; and trust the event with HIM to whom it belongs.

CEYLON.—In the Report of the last year an account was given of the commencement of our Ceylon mission, reaching to the close of the year 1816: little more than nine months from the arrival of the missionaries at Colombo, and about three months from their arrival at Jaffna. The present Report will bring down the history to February of the present year, embracing a period of about fourteen months.

The plan settled by the missionaries was to form two divisions, occupying separate stations, but to act in concert and manage their general concerns as composing one mission. In pursuance of this plan, it was agreed, that Messrs. Warren and Poor should be stationed at Tillipally, and Messrs. Richards and Meigs at Batticotta. At the commencement of the period, now proposed for review, Messrs. Warren and Poor had resided at Tillipally, making beginnings in their work, about ten weeks; but Messrs. Richards and Meigs remained at Jaffnapatam, as the house assigned to them at Batticotta was not yet in a state to be occupied.

It will be gratefully recollected, that, by favor of the government of the island, the brethren were allowed to take possession, for the purposes of the mission, of the ancient churches, mansion houses and glebes of the two parishes, which they had chosen for their stations. To put the buildings, in a state of repair fit for use was their first care, and a work of considerable time. In a joint letter of Sept. 1st, they say, "The brethren at Batticotta have been employed most of the year, in repairing their dwelling house. As the building is large, as it had gone much to decay, they have been under the necessity of occupying more time, and of expending a larger sum of money to render it comfortable, than the brethren at Tillipally. The buildings at both our stations, when completed, will be very valuable." Of the expenses of the repairs the missionaries have duly rendered their accounts: and the amount, though considerable, yet weighs very lightly against the highly important advantages of possessing the buildings. The mansion houses are sufficient for their families; the churches afford ample accommodations for their religious assemblies, and partly for their schools; and the produce of their lands will be of no small convenience and value to the mission.

But the liberality of the government has not been limited to the buildings and lands in Tillipally and Batticotta; it has granted to our mission, since its establishment, similar buildings and lands in six other parishes in the vicinity. Upon these also our missionaries have bestowed some care. They have besides procured the building of a school at Mallagum, and another at Panditeripo; the former chiefly by subscriptions of the native inhabitants; the latter in great part by the grateful liberality of an individual. A son of a native was brought to Tillipally, in a state of mental derangement, for medical aid. "On his recovery," say the brethren, "the father understanding that we intended to establish a school at Panditeripo, generously offered to furnish timber, and a piece of ground, near the old church building, for a school house, and to superintend the building of it. He is now interesting himself much to engage boys for the school." In another communication, they say, "The brethren at Tillipally have been at some expense in preparing suitable houses for schools in four of the parishes near them; and as it is our intention to establish schools in all the parishes around us, as fast as it lies in our power, we shall be under the necessity of constantly expending small sums of money for this purpose, at some places more, and in others less, according to the size and quality of the buildings which may be prepared. At some places we propose to build small houses in the native style, at others partially to repair either the dwelling house or the church, when either of them remains in a suitable state to make it an object to preserve them."

It is thus, that these diligent missionaries have seen fit to provide for important and extended operations, and no remarks can be necessary to make it evident, that the preparations which they have made, and the advantages which they have secured, must be highly conducive to the great objects of the mission. While engaged, however, in these preparations, they have redeemed time for other purposes.

Immediately after their settlement at Tillipally, Messrs. Warren and Poor established a school at that place, for the instruction of children and youth, both in English and in Tamul. Shortly afterwards they established another, at Mallagum; and they proceeded, as fast as circumstances would permit, to make arrangements for similar establishments at Milette and Oodooville.

"The school at Tillipally," say the brethren, in a letter of 27th Dec. "is in a flourishing state Sixteen boys are able to read, with a good degree of facility, the Tamul and English Testaments; and as many more who are younger are making good progress in both languages. The boys in the school are instructed in the principles of the Christian religion, as fully as if they were the children of Christian parents. Most of them have committed to memory two or three catechisms in Tamul, and large portions of the Scriptures. They are now engaged in transcribing on olas the book of Genesis. This exercise is particularly important, as the Tamul Old Testament is now out of print: and it is very desirable, that the absurd notions of this people respecting the creation, the fall of man, and the commencement of idolatry, should be corrected. On the Sabbath, immediately after the morning service, the boys rehearse a part of what they have committed to memory, and are questioned respecting their knowledge of Christianity."

For their other schools they found it difficult to procure good instructors. Some, whom they engaged, proved incompetent or unfaithful, and were dismissed from the employment. On account of this and other difficulties incident to the newness of their situation, they judged it advisable to contract their plan, until they should be possessed of advantages for extending it to a compass and with an effect, more proportionate to their wishes.

The situation of Messrs. Richards and Meigs did not admit of their engaging so soon in establishing schools. It was not until June, that they found it convenient to fix their residence, together at Batticotta; and even then, they were still encumbered with the repairs of their buildings. But though they could not establish a regular school, a considerable number of boys and young men received instruction in English constantly at their house; and in the latter part of September, a Tamul school was established by them at Batticotta, which commenced and proceeded with encourgaging auspices.

The missionaries have a high sense of the importance of taking native youths completely under their own care and direction; as this would withdraw them from the pernicious influences of their heathen parents and connections, and place them in the most hopeful way of improvement, and for being qualified for usefulness. "Upon inquiry," they say, "we are well assured, that many active boys may be found whose parents will gladly put them wholly under our care, if we will support them. The brethren at Tillipally, have been solicited by parents to *take their sons* to support, and employ them as they wish. They have given much attention to the subject of supporting boys; and have concluded, that with twelve Spanish dollars a year they can, with the present exchange of Spanish dollars on this island, and the present price of rice, their principal food, support a boy under 20 years of age, provided they can have 30 or 40 to eat together. The Rev. Christian David of Jaffnapatam, has a school on this plan, supported by government; and there is one attached to the Tranquebar mission. The good effect which must result from the establishment of schools on such a plan are so obvious, that the brethren at Tillipally have determined to embrace the present favorable opportunity of taking 10 or 12 of their most promising boys, who are anxious to put themselves under their constant care, and keep them in a building which they have erected in their garden, for the accommodation of the school. By this means, they will be able to keep the boys from the influence of heathen society, and regularly employed in useful studies. The great importance of establishing schools on this plan appears still more obvious, when we consider the great need there is of well qualified native teachers, and the superiority they will possess, in many important respects, over foreigners:—particularly, if God should, as we would most devoutly pray, prepare them by his grace. Should the Board approve of this plan, they will give us all the assistance in their power for the support of promising boys, at each station: many of whom, without our support, cannot receive an education, but who, with the small pittance they require, may be made, by the grace of God, distinguished blessings to multitudes of these heathens, now sitting in the region and shadow of death. If proper teachers could now be found, schools might now be established and superintended by us, in many parishes.—Are there not many pious individuals in our native land, who will most cheerfully contribute for the support of one or more boys? We feel persuaded that the benevolent Christian public will not suffer an object so intimately connected with the success of our mission among these heathen people, to fail for want of support. We cannot surely be disappointed in the belief, that the pious zeal and liberal charities of our sisters in the churches, so often manifested on similar occasions, will be called forth for the support of this object, and little associations will be formed, to rescue from the tyranny of Satan these unhappy youths, and bring them to the light of the gospel of the *Prince of Peace.* Their charities and their prayers will, we trust, ere long, cause many, who are now growing up in all the usual superstitions of idolatry, to *rise up and call them blessed.*"

This forcible appeal has already touched many a heart; and in answer to it, "pious zeal and liberal charities" *have* been displayed, and "associations for the support of this object"—*have* been formed. And your Committee are persuaded, that a design which promises so much for the advancement of the general cause, will be liberally and effectually patronized, by this Board, and by the Christian public. The experiments made, and the facts communicated by the missionaries, afford ample encouragements for a steady and vigorous prosecution of the plan of establishing schools and furnishing instruction, for the heathen children and youth in the district of Jaffna, as fast and to as great an extent, as the means at disposal and a due regard to the various objects of our several establishments will permit.

Earnestly engaged as the missionaries have been for the instruction of the young in schools and in their families, they have not been unmindful of the paramount importance of *preaching the gospel*. At Tillipally and in the neighboring parishes, Messrs. Warren and Poor have preached statedly on the Sabbath, and on other days, as they have had opportunity; as have also Messrs. Richards and Meigs at Jaffnapatam, while resident there, and at Batticotta, and in the vicinity, since their removal to their station. Their preaching has, of course, been for the most part through the medium of interpreters; but in October, just a year after settling at Tillipally, Mr. Poor commenced preaching in Tamul, the language chiefly spoken in the northern part of Ceylon. The numbers of their hearers have been considerable, and at the latest dates were increasing. Many have been constant and earnest in their attention; and some, it is hoped, have received abiding impressions, both from the public and private instructions given them."

Messrs. Warren and Poor have entered in their journal, March 21, eighteen months ago, an interesting record. "The case," they say, "of Supyen, a young Malabar from Jaffnapatam, of about nineteen years of age, has become very interesting to us. He is the eldest son, the favorite of his parents, who have high expectations respecting him. His father, who is a man of considerable property, placed Supyen under our care about three months ago, to be instructed in the English language. He committed him to us in a very formal manner, and said, that Supyen was no longer his son but ours. A few days before, Supyen had visited us. He told us that in consequence of reading a few chapters in the Bible, which he received from a native Christian, he thought that the heathen religion was wrong, and he earnestly desired to become acquainted with Christianity. We had much interesting conversation with him, as his mind was awakened to a very serious inquiry. He said he would request his father to permit him to come to school to learn English, though his principal object would be to learn the Christian religion. His conduct, since he has been with us, has been uniformly good. His modest deportment and earnest desire to receive instruction, have induced us to encourage him to be much with us. We rejoice in the belief that he has felt in some degree the power of divine truth on his heart. A few weeks ago when D. Bast, Esq. was with us on a visit, Supyen took us aside, and told him in Tamul, as he (Supyen) understands but little English, that he had something to communicate to us. He was considerably agitated, and manifested a deep interest in what he was about to say. He said he had been examining the Christian religion; and being convinced it was true, he wished to receive it. He learned from the New Testament, that no one could become a true disciple of Christ, unless he forsook father and mother, &c., and he wished us to know, that he was willing to leave all for Christ. When we explained to him the meaning of those passages, and told him it was even his duty to continue with his parents, unless they endeavored to prevent his serving Christ, his mind was somewhat relieved. As his parents were heathens, he appeared to think that he must leave them without reference to the treatment he might receive from them. Perhaps, however, he foresaw the storm which has since arisen."

On the 20th of April, the father of this interesting youth, hearing that he had become a Christian, repaired to Tillipally, and with fair pretences, took him from the mission family. Scarcely were they out of sight of the missionaries, when Supyen was stripped, degraded, and treated with great abuse. At home, no persuasions or threats, no blandishments or severities were spared, to induce him to renounce Christianity. About a month after he was taken from the mission house, "his former companions gave a feast, which he was obliged to attend. He was solicited by the company to make an offering to one of the gods on the occasion, and was compelled to accept the appointment. He went into the apartment of the temple, where the idol was, and was left alone to perform the ceremony. He immediately stripped the idol of his ornaments, and kneeled down and prayed to the living God. When his companions, looking through the curtain, saw him in prayer, they were afraid, and went and informed his father. Supyen was carried home and punished with severity. He told his father that "Christ warned his disciples to expect such treatment." Three or four weeks afterwards, "rudely seized by his father and relations, his feet were pinned fast in the stocks, his hands and arms closely bound with cords, and he was severely whipped." His father then brought his Christian books, and burned them before him; and compelled him to write a letter of recantation, which was sent to the missionaries. "He was kept bound in the stocks for several days, and received but very little to eat."

Still, however, he remained firm in his adherence to Christianity, which his parents and friends perceiving, after all other means had been employed in vain to shake him from his steadfastness, he was sent, about the middle of September, to Candy, in the interior of the island, where, it was supposed, he would be beyond the reach of Christian influence. There he stayed about six weeks, conversed freely on religion with some of the head men, promised at their request to send them the Cingalese New Testament, and returned to his father's house without any signs of apostasy. His sufferings after his return were extreme, until his father, in the fore part of January, resolved on taking him to the coast, that he might live with some of his heathen relations there, where, again, he could have no intercourse with Christians. Having proceeded to the place from which they were to sail, just as they were about to embark, Supyen had the courage to remonstrate. "You have done many things," said he to his father, "to turn me from the Christian religion—but to no purpose You sent me to Candy, but I returned a Christian. If you now carry me to the coast, I shall return a Christian. For as I am a Christian in heart, I shall always be one."—The father abandoned his purpose. Supyen was sent back to Jaffnapatam; not to go to his father's house, but to beg among the natives, till his father should return from the coast with a husband for his sister; and was told, that as soon as his sister should be married, "he might go wherever he could find support." He was afterwards seen by Mr. Poor, and though desirous of going with him to Tillipally, was advised to remain at Jaffnapatam until his father's return.

No later information has been received of this young Malabarian confessor, of whom it may be devoutly hoped, that he is designed by sovereign grace to be an ornament to the Christian cause, a blessing to his bewildered countrymen, and a crown of missionary rejoicing in the day of the Lord Jesus.

Other individuals are mentioned, (of whom one has been employed as a schoolmaster, another as a teacher of the missionaries themselves in Tamul, and another as an interpreter,) whose minds appear to have received deep convictions of divine truth. And not a few of the natives, brahmins, headmen, and others, have been excited to inquiry, and have expressed doubts respecting their own religion. If the inquiry occur, why effects of this kind should appear, so much sooner at Jaffna, than at Bombay; it may be proper to recollect, that in Jaffna rays of divine light, long ago scattered there by missionaries, have pierced, and in a measure, dissipated the thick mists of heathenism, and laid the minds of the people more open to instruction and conviction. Especially should it be considered and devoutly acknowledged, that He, with whom is the residue of the Spirit, is a wise and holy sovereign, who giveth not account of any of his matters."

The medical knowledge of Messrs. Warren and Richards gave early promise of great advantages to the mission, and important benefits to the surrounding population. On this subject the brethren, under date of June 1st, write as follows: "Our attention since our arrival here has been much called to the sick around us. Many flocked to our doors as soon as they were informed that we had the means of assisting them. We have reason to believe, that God will bless our attention to them for their spiritual, as well as temporal good. It affords us an opportunity of commending the *great Physician* to many from different parts of the district, whom otherwise we should probably never see, and at a time best calculated to leave a good impression on their minds. Our morning prayers are attended by many, who come for medical aid; at which time we take occasion to preach to them Jesus. We find, however, that an attention to their wants subjects us to considerable expense. Many of the objects are wasting with hunger, as well as disease; and some have no place in their sickness to shelter them from the weather. These circumstances induced the brethren at Tillipally to solicit assistance from their friends here. Through the active benevolence of the Rev. J. D. Glenie, chaplain of this district, and J. N. Mooyart, Esq. magistrate of Jaffna, they have collected enough to put up a building for a hospital, and to furnish it with some accommodation for the sick poor. The Rev. Mr. Glenie gave the timber for the building, and circulated himself a subscription. Mr. Mooyart contributed very generously for the object. Several of the civil and military gentlemen have contributed toward the institution. There is at present a small monthly subscription raised to support the hospital; but it is inadequate and uncertain. The contributors belong either to the civil or military list, and their continuance here is wholly uncertain. The Rev. Mr. Glenie was removed four weeks since to Point De Galle. His departure we very much regret. He is a decided friend of missionaries, and feels deeply interested for the moral improvement of this heathen people. Mr. Mooyart, whom we have mentioned before in our letters, is a valuable friend to us. He is an active, zealous Christian."

He who came from heaven—from the bosom of everlasting love,—to seek and to save that which was lost, *himself*, while intent on this great work of preaching the gospel, *took our infirmities, and bare our sicknesses*. His disciples, and especially his ministers, should possess and display the same compassionate spirit. And it cannot but afford a high

24

satisfaction and cause of thankfulness to this Board, and to the friends of missions and of mankind in this country, if by any means of theirs, the miseries of their fellow beings in India, have been, or shall be relieved.

But how frail is man, and how liable to disappointment or to interruption, are even the most benevolent human purposes! Physicians have their own infirmities and sicknesses to bear, and are themselves objects of Christian sympathy. At the latest dates, Messrs. Warren and Richards were both suspended from their labors, and languishing with disease. It will be recollected, that Mr. Warren, after his ordination, and before leaving this country, was taken with bleeding at his lungs:—with symptoms, which awakened no little concern for the event. It was, however, the opinion of physicians, that he could not do better for his health or life than to go to India. The voyage proved beneficial, and the climate of Ceylon propitious: and for about sixteen months after his arrival there, he was able to be constantly and entirely engaged in the business and cares of the mission, and his prospect for established health was fair. But on the 13th of August, a year ago, to the great affliction of all the members of the mission, and of many others, his malady returned. Noticing his case in their journal ten days afterward, the brethren say, "Our friend, J. N. Mooyart, Esq. who visited us this morning, generously offered us the use of his house, which is furnished with every convenience, and advised that brother Warren should be removed to Jaffnapatam. Brother Warren's peace of mind, and resignation to the divine will, are to us a cause for gratitude, and a ground of encouragement to all missionaries, to confide in the promise of their Lord and master, *Lo, I am with you always*"

At the house of Mr. Mooyart, to whom the missionaries and this Board are under great obligations for his multiplied benefits, Mr. Warren experienced all the solace and relief, which the most affectionate kindness and assiduous attention could afford. After some weeks however, it was judged advisable, that he should be removed to the southern part of the island, to avoid the effects of the approaching rains; and accordingly on the 9th of October he left Jaffna for Colombo.

In a letter of December 27, Messrs. Meigs and Poor say, "We have also informed you of the ill health of brother Richards; that for more than a year past he has been unable to study, in consequence of weak eyes, and that for several months, he has been in a debilitated state. We must now inform you, that his symptoms have become alarming; and we have many fears respecting his recovery. His lungs are affected, and his whole system much reduced. After due deliberation, we have thought it expedient that he should go to Colombo by water, and that, unless some special reasons should prevent, he and brother Warren should thence proceed for Bombay. Brother Richards left Jaffna for Colombo on the 13th inst. leaving sister Richards and son at Batticotta.

"The advice of physicians here, and the experience we have had on the subject, particularly in the case of brother Warren and sister Poor on our passage from America, and recovery of brother Bardwell's weak eyes, on his passage to Bombay, are considerations which unite in directing to a voyage, as the most probable means of restoring them to health."

At Colombo the two invalid brethren contracted for a passage to Bombay, and expected to embark about the middle of January. But on the

27th February, the latest date from Ceylon, Mr. Poor writes: "We have this day received a letter from Colombo, informing us that both our brethren there are more unwell. Sister Richards set out for Colombo on Tuesday last."

In their letter of the 27th December, the brethren Meigs and Poor, in their trying situations, express their feelings in the following affecting terms: "By the removal of our two brethren, in such circumstances, we feel that our strength is greatly reduced. Whether we regard them as beloved companions, and fellow laborers in the mission, or as *Physicians* whose services, our families, situated as they are at a distance from the European settlements, greatly need, we cannot but regard their removal as a great affliction. But our minds are more deeply affected when we consider its influence upon the state of the mission. Just at the time when we had nearly completed the necessary repairs for living comfortably among the heathen, and in some degree prepared ourselves for engaging with undivided attention to the appropriate duties of the mission with pleasing prospects of success, we are deprived of half our strength.

"The same reasons which induced the Prudential Committee to send us hither, the additional ones contained in several of our letters, and now the reasons arising from the importance of supporting an establishment already commenced, unite in rendering it most desirable that more missionaries should be sent out without delay."

These communications will be received by this Board, as they have been by the Committee, with affectionate sympathy and deep concern. By all the members of the Board, and by the many thousands who take part with them in this great cause, prayer will be offered without ceasing to the Father of our Lord Jesus Christ, that, with all the riches of his mercy, he will be present with the beloved missionaries in the day of trial—with the sick, and with those on whom consequently redoubled labors, and cares are devolved—affording to them respectively, all needed help and support and consolation; and that all their afflictions may redound to their sanctification and joy, and to the furtherance of his glorious Gospel among the heathen. Missionaries—faithful, devoted missionaries, are his servants, engaged in his work, and holden at his disposal. He loves them, and the cause for which they are sent forth to labor, infinitely better than do any of their patrons or friends on earth. He commands them to go, and teach all the nations; and assures them of his presence, and of a glorious reward; but he does not promise them exemption from sickness or from death. The field, in which they are to labor, and to die, is the field of unfading glory; and by the same high mandate, which shall call them to rest from their labors, others will be summoned to fill their places.

Our mission to Ceylon has been marked with signal tokens of the divine favor; and notwithstanding the cloud on which our eyes have been fixed, its general state and prospects are highly encouraging. The climate, for a tropical one, is uncommonly salubrious; the living is cheaper than in almost any other part of India; the glebes and buildings in so many pleasant and populous parishes, assigned by the government to the mission, are acquisitions of great importance; a translation of the Scriptures has already been made into the language of the people; and in various respects the facilities for communicating to them the knowledge of the Gospel, and spreading it extensively, are such as are seldom found in heathen lands. And it is the purpose of your Committee, trusting in God, to use all diligence in strengthening the mission, and all care to prevent a failure of its hopes.

AMERICAN ABORIGINES.—It was on the 13th of January, 1817, that the Rev. Mr. Kingsbury arrived at Chickamaugah in the Cherokee nation, and commenced preparations for an establishment there. On the 7th of the following March, he was joined by Messrs. Hall and Williams with their wives. Before the annual meeting of this Board in September, they had erected, four small log buildings, made considerable advances in preparations for other and larger buildings; taken into their family, and under their instruction, twenty-six native children and youth; and done not a little, for the time, towards procuring crops of various productions, and stocking the plantation with domestic animals.

In the Report of the last year, the Committee communicated their design of sending other missionaries and teachers to the Cherokees, and other Indian nations, as soon, and as fast, as Providence should open the way, and supply the means. This design, which was explicitly approved by the Board, has not been forgotten.

Agreeably to arrangements made by the Committee, the Rev. Daniel S. Butrick embarked at Boston on the 13th of November, for Savannah; and on the 17th of the same month, the Rev. Ard Hoyt, with his family, embarked at Philadelphia, for the same port. On the 27th, under the kind care of their Divine Master, they all safely arrived at Savannah; where they were received by the Rev. Dr Kollock and other friends to the cause, with demonstrations of affectionate courtesy, hospitality, and generosity, which they have acknowledged with expressions of lively gratitude. From Savannah they proceeded with as little delay as possible, by the way of Augusta and Athens, to the Indian country, and on the 3d of January, having experienced much kindness and some affecting expressions of interest, from the Cherokees on their way, they reached the mission house at Chickamaugah.

Their feelings on the occasion, were expressed in the following terms. "With satisfaction inexpressible, with joy unspeakable, we are now permitted to erect our Ebenezer in this place, and date Chickamaugah. The Lord has been trying us with mercies ever since we left Savannah. We have met with no disaster; we have not been hindered in our journey for a single hour by the sickness of any one of our numerous family; we have never felt the heart of a stranger: nor do I know that any one of the family has had a gloomy hour. You will certainly join with us in praising our covenant God for his kind protecting providence, for his abundant mercy and grace.—We must leave you to judge of our feelings, —to meet our dear brethren here, find all well, and join with them and their Cherokee congregation in the public worship of God. Our hearts are united; our spirits are refreshed; and we trust in God, that in all our labors, he will cause us to be of one heart and one mind."

Early in December, the Rev. William Chamberlin left Wilkesbarre, Pennsylvania, the late residence of Mr. Hoyt, and proceeded to Pittsburg; where, agreeably to appointment, he met the Rev. Elisha P. Swift, in concert with whom he was to act as an agent for promoting the objects of the Board in the western states. After having visited many of the principal places in Ohio, Kentucky, and Tennessee, experienced many kindnesses, and made very considerable collections for the mission, he arrived at Chickamaugah on the 10th of March.

Of the missionaries, thus assembled at the Cherokee station, it was the design of your Committee that such a disposition should be made, as would best serve the purposes of that establishment, and promote the object of a similar establishment, in the Choctaw nation. Advices to this effect were duly communicated; and on the 18th of March the brethren wrote as follows. "Your suggestions and instructions relative to designating the persons, who should go to the Choctaws, immediately engaged our prayerful attention. After repeatedly committing the case to God, and renewedly devoting ourselves to him in the work before us, it was given, unanimously, as our opinion, that brother Kingsbury and brother and sister Williams, will be the most suitable persons to select for this service, and that it will not be expedient to send any more from this establishment at present. The remainder of us, we think, may be more usefully employed here, and that it may be best to make a distribution of our labors somewhat in the following manner; viz. Brother Hoyt to take the fatherly and pastoral care of the institution and of the church; brother Hall to continue in his present station; brother Chamberlin to take charge of the school and superintend the labor and other exercises of the boys while out of school; and brother Butrick to pay special attention to the Cherokee language and act as an evangelist. We wish, also, as far as practicable, to give brother Chamberlin some time to attend to the Cherokee language. This distribution of our labors we cheerfully submit to the Prudential Committee to be confirmed or altered, as they, in their wisdom, shall see fit."

These dispositions were perfectly in agreement with the views of the Committee, and were accordingly ratified.

In the latter part of autumn and beginning of winter, it was found, to the deep concern of your Committee, that the health of the Treasurer was seriously impaired. It was the opinion of his physicians, that relaxation from business, and a visit to the south, would be the best means for his recovery, and were of essential importance. In this afflictive emergency, it was his wish, not less than that of his colleagues of the Committee, that the time of his absence from home should not be lost to the cause most dear to his heart. And it was thought, that the important objects of the Board might be greatly promoted by his acting at the south under a commission as a general agent; and especially by his visiting in his tour our Cherokee establishment. Accordingly, a special arrangement was made for securing the treasury, and conducting the business of that department; and, on the 20th of January, he took passage for Savannah. After spending about three months in Georgia and South Carolina, visiting the principal places in those states, and doing as much as the state of his health would permit, in the business of his agency; he proceeded, by the usual route from Augusta, through the Indian country to Chickamaugah, where he arrived on the 8th of May.

About ten days after his arrival, having had opportunity to make himself thoroughly acquainted with the establishment in its various departments and operations, he addressed to the Corresponding Secretary a letter, containing a very ample and interesting account of its state and concerns. Of this account the Committee think it right to avail themselves largely, under the present head of this Report.

First, however, and this they are sure of the full and affectionate concurrence of the Board, they would devoutly record their grateful acknowledgments to the all-gracious Disposer, for the Treasurer's safe return, with recruited health, and for the important services, which he has been enabled to render to the best of causes.

"As Chickamaugah," says the Treasurer, "comprehends a considerable district, extending up and down the creek of that name, and including an Indian village near the Tennessee, it has been thought best by the missionaries, Mr. Cornelius, and myself, that the missionary station should receive a new name and since I commenced this letter, we have given it the name of Brainerd, in affectionate remembrance of that able, devoted and successful missionary. The mission house is situated about 50 rods south-west of the creek, and two miles north-east of the Georgia and Tennessee road. It fronts the south-east, has the dining hall and kitchen in the rear, and several log cabins on each wing for the accommodation of the children and some of the missionaries There are several other log buildings for store rooms, corn houses, and stables. The school house is 30 rods to the south-west; and is sufficiently large to accommodate 100 scholars on the Lancasterian plan, and to answer for a place of public worship on the Sabbath. The cultivated land of the mission farm lies in several fields, principally in front of the buildings, and amounts to 45 acres The creek here pursues a north-westwardly direction, but below takes a northwardly course to the Tennessee, which is distant 15 miles, following the creek, though only 6 miles at the nearest place. The brow of the Lookout mountain, immediately under which the Tennessee passes, is about 7 miles distant in a due west course. The creek is navigable for boats to the mission house. At the landing place is what is called a fish trap, formed by a partial dam. It was rebuilt the last year and is of great benefit to the establishment Should it prove as valuable in future seasons, as in the two last, it will be worth more than $500, the sum which the Board paid for the improvements of the place The fish are caught as they pass down the stream in the night. No preparation is necessary to catch them. On the first morning after my arrival, about forty fish were taken, the aggregate weight of which could not have been less than 150 pounds. When the water is high, none are taken, but, except at such times, they are caught at all seasons of the year. Once this spring 150 were taken at a time, and the next morning 120. the largest weighed 30 pounds, and a considerable proportion from 5 to 10 pounds Most of them are fat and good; some excellent, either fresh or salted. The mission house and other buildings stand on a gentle eminence and present an agreeable appearance. The mission house, school house, dining hall and kitchen, are built of hewn logs, having the insterstices filled with mortar. The first mentioned of these buildings has two rooms on the lower floor, with an open hall between them. The upper story has two lodging rooms; but when finished will have four. The principal expense of the buildings is defrayed by government.

Since the Treasurer left Brainerd, the mill, which has been to the brethren an object of earnest desire and attention, and cost them much labor and trouble, has been gotten into operation; and promises to be of great utility, not only to the mission, but to the nation extensively.

"It was on Friday evening," the Treasurer proceeds to say, "the 8th inst. (May) just at sun set, that I alighted at the mission house. The path which leads to it from the main road, passes through an open wood, which is extremely beautiful at this season of the year. The mild radiance of the setting sun, the unbroken solitude of the wilderness, the pleasantness of the forest with all its springing and blossoming vegetation, the object of my journey, and the nature and design of the institution I was about to visit, conspired to render the scene solemn and interesting, and to fill the mind with tender emotions.

"Early in the evening the children of the school, being informed that one of their northern friends, whom they had been expecting, had arrived, eagerly assembled in the hall, and were drawn up in ranks and particularly introduced. They are neither shy nor forward in their manners. To a stranger they appear not less interesting than other children of the same age. but if he considers their circumstances and prospects, incomparably more so

"At evening prayers, I was forcibly struck with the stillness, order, and decorum of the children, and with the solemnity of the family worship. A portion of Scripture was read with Scott's practical observations, a hymn was sung, in which a large portion of the children united; and Mr. Hoyt led the devotions of the numerous family. If all the members of the Board could hear the prayers, which are daily offered in their behalf at this station, (and I presume at all others under their superintendence;) and if all patrons and contributors could hear the thanks, which are returned to God for their liberality; and especially if they could see a large circle of children, lately rescued from heathenism, kneeling with apparent seriousness and engaging in the solemnities of Christian worship, one of them already a hopeful convert, and others thoughtful and inquiring;—if all these things could be seen, one may safely predict, that the exertions and sacrifices of the friends of missions would be increased fourfold. These things are not less real, however, because they cannot be seen by every friend to the cause.

"The mission family, when assembled for prayers, consists of the missionaries and their wives, Mr. Hoyt's children, the Cherokee children, occasional visitors, the hired men, and the kitchen domestics. All these make a goodly number. The missionaries lead at family prayers in rotation. The children are called together by the house bell; at the close of the evening prayers they are wished a good night, which they reciprocate; and soon afterwards the horn is blown, as a signal for them to retire to rest.

"Half an hour before sunrise the horn is blown as a signal to rise; and just as the sun appears above the horizon the family assemble in the hall for morning worship. After prayers the children proceed to their different employments The boys, as they come from the hall, file off to the right, and form in a straight line; the girls to the left, to a log cabin assigned for their accommodation. The boys are immediately joined by Mr. Chamberlin, their instructor, who has the charge of them from the blowing of the horn in the morning, till it is blown at nine in the evening. During the whole of this time he is with them, except the interval at noon; and then they are under his superintendence.   They join the rank with great alertness in the morning, as tickets are given to those who are most distinguished for quickness and punctuality; and the fine of a ticket is imposed upon any one who shall be culpably dilatory.   These tickets, which are given as rewards on other occasions also, answer the purpose of a circulating medium among the boys, as they are redeemed with little books, or such articles as the holders need.   As soon as the rank is form-ed, the boys are despatched to the various employments assigned them. Those employments which are of a permanent nature, are assigned by the week, so that there is a change of labor.   Occasional services are per-formed by a detachment for the occasion.   Some are sent to dress the fish, when they are taken; some to assist in milking the cows; some to hoe in the garden; some to pound the corn, &c.   Some of the boys are too small to do any thing; but, after all the abovementioned services are provided for, Mr. Chamberlin has commonly about ten active lads to take with him to the field.   On one morning since my arrival, they plant-ed an acre of corn before breakfast; on another they planted six or seven bushels of potatoes, the hills being prepared; and these are fair specimens of their morning labor.   When breakfast is ready, the various family is called together by the horn.   Two long tables are supplied with wholesome and palatable, though plain food.   One of Mr. Hoyt's daugh-ters sits at the head of each table; Mr. Hoyt and Mr. Kingsbury at the other end; and the other missionaries, where it is most convenient.   The boys sit at one table, the girls occasional visitors, and hired men at the other.   They take their seats at table as they enter the room, and when all, or nearly all, are seated, a blessing is pronounced.   Till the bless-ing is concluded, not one touches his knife and fork, or plate; nor is the slightest impatience discovered, as is common among children in civil-ized society.   The most entire stillness and decorum prevail, while a blessing is asked and thanks returned, as well as at family prayers.   The behavior of the children while eating is very decent; and they are less noisy, than any equal number of young persons whom I ever saw to-gether.   The stillness arises in part no doubt, from the fact, that many of them do not speak English readily, and are therefore rather bashful about speaking at all, either in English, or their own tongue.   Some cannot speak a word of our language on their first arrival.   After breakfast there is another period of labor, which lasts till nearly nine, when the school commences.   The morning labor is about equally divided by breakfast, and amounts to about two hours and a half.   To this is to be added an hour's labor in the evening.   The only time the boys have for play is a little while before dinner, and again at dusk.   They labor as cheerfully, and as effectually, as any company of boys I ever saw.   They handle axes and hoes with great dexterity.

"I have been more particular on this subject, as it has often been said, that the children of Indians cannot be taught to work.

"Each detachment of boys has a leader, even when no more than two are employed upon a service.   When all are convened, they meet at the sound of the whistle.

"The school is opened by reading a portion of Scripture, singing a hymn and prayer; and closed by prayer and singing. It is conducted upon the Lancasterian plan, a plan not only excellent in itself, but peculiarly suited to catch the attention of Indian children. The principal exercises are reading, writing on sand, slates, and paper, spelling and arithmetic. None have yet commenced the study of grammar. Of the writing I hope to shew you specimens. Fifteen read in the Bible. They have attended school from eight to twelve months, and more than half began with the alphabet. This class would be considered as reading and spelling pretty well for children of the same age (from ten to fifteen) in one of our common schools at the north; and I think such a fact indicates uncommon assiduity on the part of their instructors. Eleven others, all of whom began with the alphabet, can read intelligibly in easy lessons. Eighteen have commenced writing on paper. There are now in the school forty-seven Cherokee children, Mr. Hoyt's two youngest sons, and two other white boys. The two latter will stay a short time, and were admitted from peculiar circumstances. These numbers have been just ascertained by Mr. Kingsbury, for the purpose of making out his report to the Secretary at War. Fourteen are full blooded Cherokees; the remainder of different degrees of Indian blood.

"When the girls are out of school, they are under the charge of Mr. Hoyt's second daughter, now Mrs Chamberlin. They are all (sixteen in number) lodged in one log cabin which has a chamber. Here all their domestic industry is carried on. Two spin, two card, and the rest sew and knit. They wash, mend, and often make their own clothes, and assist in mending the clothes of the boys. Mrs. C. prays with them every evening; and they unite in singing a hymn. When engaged in their work, they are often overheard singing. Mrs. C. says, that the girls are remarkably good tempered. They have few disagreements among themselves; and three or four of them have never been out of humor in the least. The boys also are represented as mild and gentle in their tempers; and as much less apt to quarrel than an equal number of white boys. From my own observation, I can state, that there is much less noise and disturbance about the house, than is common with half the same number of children among ourselves. It is said to be a general characteristic of the Cherokees, that they are mild, and not apt to quarrel, unless inflamed by whiskey.

"A Sabbath school, for the instruction of blacks, has been kept up since last summer. The improvement which a number of them have made, is truly wonderful. A man of thirty years, who only knew the alphabet when the school commenced, can now read a chapter, or a psalm, very decently. A boy of fifteen, who did not know a single letter, can now read very well in the Testament. Several others have begun to read the Bible. The greater part come six miles, or more, to meeting; some fifteen or twenty on foot; and none less than two miles and a half. The number has varied from 10 to 25. Mr. Hall has paid particular attention to this school. The season for instructing these people is at the close of public worship. Several of them are under serious impressions; and all pay the strictest attention to religious services. They sing a hymn before the school is dismissed, and a prayer is offered by the instructor."

25

Your Committee have deemed it important, that at every missionary station a church should be duly organized, as soon as circumstances permit, for the regular administration of Christian ordinances and Christian discipline. This has been particularly recommended, in the instructions given to the missionaries. In a joint letter of the brethren at the Cherokee station, they say—"On the last Sabbath in September, a church was organized in this place, and we solemnly renewed our covenant with God and with each other. We should have done this at an earlier period, but hearing that brother Cornelius was on his way to this country, we were anxious that he should be present on this interesting occasion. At present our church consists of only the missionary brethren and sisters; but we hope soon to be able to number some, who have recently been brought into the kingdom of the Redeemer."

The ground of the hope here expressed may appear from what is further stated in the same letter. "We are now able to tell you what the Lord is doing among us for the glory of his name. And though it be but the day of small things, we know that it will rejoice your hearts, as it has done ours, when you hear, that the Lord Jesus is bringing into his kingdom some of the sons and daughters of the western forests. For some time past we have had the satisfaction to witness a pleasing change in the conduct of some of our neighbors, who on the Sabbath attended our religious worship. Two white men, in our neighborhood, who had been profane and immoral, became sober and serious. One Cherokee woman, who had a tolerably good education, and who is married to a white man, appeared to be under very serious impressions. Such was the state of things, when brother Cornelius arrived at our station. His conversation and preaching excited an increased attention, both among the Cherokees and white people around us. Our assembly on the Sabbath was increased. The last Sabbath that he preached, which was the first Sabbath in November, a very solemn impression was made on the minds of several. One white man, one Cherokee man, the woman above mentioned, and a Cherokee girl who was attending our school, were much affected. The Cherokee man is a half breed, by the name of Charles Reece, and speaks our language tolerably well. He was one of the three intrepid Cherokees, who at the battle of the Horse-shoe, swam the river in the face of the enemy and brought off their canoes in triumph. It was interesting to see this undaunted warrior bowing before the influence of the gospel. After the public exercises, Mr. Cornelius conversed with him. He sunk upon his feet, as if deprived of strength, said he knew not what to say. He felt as he never did before. This man has repeatedly visited us since, and says it is his fixed determination to be a disciple of Jesus Christ, and that it is his great desire to know and do the will of God."

The animating hopes inspired by these encouraging circumstances have not been disappointed. The Treasurer, in his letter says, "You have been informed of the admission of five native converts, and one white man to the little church, which the Lord has planted here. On the first Sabbath in this month, Mr. Hoyt's youngest daughter, who had, as was hoped, experienced a saving change since the family arrived at this place, was admitted to communion. At the same time a black woman was also admitted. The second Sabbath after my arrival, a colored man was added to the church; so that it now contains nine persons, whom, as we trust, the Lord has called, within a few months past, to be heirs of his kingdom.

"The general deportment of all who have joined the mission church, is such as to afford increasing evidence, that they are what they profess to be, the disciples of Christ. Though God alone can search the heart, and we must expect mistakes and disappointments, in our judgment of Christian character, it is no more than gratitude to the Giver of all good, to acknowledge his kind interposition in behalf of any, who were recently in a state of total ignorance of Him, and of the salvation which he has revealed."

With a view to strengthen public confidence extensively, and in various respects to promote the interests of the institution, your Committee have adjudged it advisable that there should be a Visiting Committee of this Cherokee school, composed of characters of established respectability, and not too far distant from the station. The gentlemen designated for this purpose, are Col. R. J. Meigs, agent of the government in the Cherokee nation, Rev. Isaac Anderson, Maryville, Blount county, (Ten.) Col. Daniel Campbell and Col. Francis A. Ramsay, Knox county, and Rev. Matthew Donald and Daniel Rawlings, Esq. Rhea county. In the commission given them, they "are requested to make an annual visitation of the school, for the purpose of examining its general state and management, its expenditures and improvements; and making a report to be exhibited to the Board, to the United States government, and to the public." Their first visitation was in the last of May, a few days after the Treasurer left the station; and their Report, which will be communicated to this Board, is at all points in perfect agreement with his account of the establishment. In regard to the state of the church and the gracious influences with which the Father of lights has been pleased to bless the institution, the Report is as interesting and affecting, as it is explicit and full.

"Your Committee," they say, "tarried at the missionary station, until after the Sabbath, that we might have an opportunity of observing the moral and religious influence, which this institution has had on the scholars, and neighborhood. On the Lord's day, the sacrament of the supper was administered. A congregation of more than 100 collected, of Cherokees, Africans, and some whites. During divine service the people were composed, very attentive, and many of them solemn, and some tender. Five of the natives joined in the communion, one of them a young female, aged about 18, a member of the school, the others live in the neighborhood. Two blacks also joined, one of them a freed man, the other a female slave. We conversed particularly with most of them on their knowledge of the gospel, and their experimental acquaintance with religion. We were truly pleased with the scriptural and feeling account they gave, of Christ formed in them the hope of glory. We had similar conversation with several others, who had not yet been united with the church, but who gave good evidence of a saving change of heart, particularly with two Indians and two white men, connected with Indian families. These four would readily be admitted into the church, where less caution was necessary, than in an infant church in a heathen land. One of these was a very old Indian woman who could not speak

English, but could understand what was said to her, and had to answer us by an interpreter. She lamented that she had not heard the word of God when young; but said, that since she had heard it, she had tried to do good. Her knowledge of divine subjects was really surprising. She was much affected during divine service. One, who had joined the church said, that he had been made to see himself so vile a sinner, that when walking about in deep distress, he felt that he was not worthy to walk upon the earth. All, with whom we conversed, expressed a deep sense of their sinfulness and guilt, and of their need of a Savior." After relating here several particulars, respecting the female member of the school and of the church, mentioned before as being eighteen years of age, and of whom a more detailed and very interesting account is given by the Treasurer, the Report proceeds to say; "When she first came to the school, we were informed she was proud and haughty, and loaded with ear-rings and trinkets. She is now modest and amiable; has stripped off the greatest part of her ornaments, and consecrated them to the Board of Foreign Missions, as did another of the natives since she joined the church. This young female is now an active member of a praying society of females. Would not many mothers in Israel blush before the example and zeal of this girl? Is not the Lord raising her up and qualifying her for a missionary? For this work she has an ardent zeal.

"There are some others under religious impressions, with whom we had no opportunity of conversation. Numbers of the congregation came ten, fifteen, and even twenty miles to be at church. We were told that when taking a walk morning or evening, little girls, from eight to twelve years of age may be heard praying in secret places; and we observed several of them very serious, and attentive to divine things.

"From what we have seen in this school and neighborhood, we are convinced, that the direct way to civilize a heathen people, is to Christianize them.

"Surely the Lord is in this place, the work is *his;* and it is marvellous in our eyes. Will not Christians be encouraged to pray for its prosperity? Will they not cheerfully support it by their liberality? To meet one of these souls in heaven rescued from eternal gloom by the instrumentality of Christian exertion, oh what an unspeakable joy! The Lord may rescue them speedily; the present appearances are encouraging."

Still more recent intelligence of the same refreshing, animating kind has been received. Under date of July 25, within about six weeks of the present time, the brethren write, "Next Sabbath we expect to admit to the church two people of color, who give satisfactory evidence, that, within a few months past, they have been converted to God. We have also hopes for two Cherokee women; one of them the wife of the man of whom the mission place was bought. She is perhaps as universally respected and beloved, as any woman of the nation. She has been a constant attendant on the means of grace, since the commencement of this mission."

In a communication of a date a few days earlier, they say; "The general state of the church has been prosperous; the new converts, for aught that appears, have walked steadfastly and uprightly in the ways of truth; and so far as we know, the church has favor with all the people."—"Our children have been more obedient, faithful, and industrious than could have been expected. We believe the natives are well satisfied, as to the manner in which the school is conducted, and the general treatment of their children. We hear no complaint."—"Our school of blacks continues to prosper. The colored man, who has been received into the church, is a very dear brother, and promises great usefulness to the other people of color. His heart is fixed, and much engaged to instruct them all he can."

"The season of the year has been ordered very favorably in this part of the country. We have about seven acres of rye and oats, which we are now gathering in, more than thirty acres of corn, about three acres of Irish and two of sweet potatoes; and a small patch of cotton. All these look well, excepting the cotton."

Eighteen months ago, at the place now called Brainerd, and consecrated to the Savior of men, Mr. Kingsbury was a solitary stranger in the midst of a wide wilderness—(there not being a single individual, within many miles of him, who knew the Lord Jesus,)—and, like his Divine Master, not having where to lay his head. Now, there are commodious buildings of various descriptions—large and fruitful fields—herds and flocks not inconsiderable in numbers—a school, consisting of about sixty children and youth, collected from the surrounding forests, comfortably lodged and fed, instructed for the present world and for the world to come, and about twenty of them already able to read well in the Bible;—and a church established on the foundation of the apostles and prophets, and to which, within six months have been added ten or twelve, who before were strangers and foreigners, having no God in the world!—The people who were sitting in darkness now see a great light. The land, which for long and dreary ages lay in the shadow of death, is now cheered with exhibitions of heavenly glory, and made vocal with the songs of the redeemed.

"Such are the riches of divine goodness. "When the poor and needy seek water, and there is none, and their tongue faileth for thirst, Jehovah will hear them, the God of Israel will not forsake them. He will open rivers in high places, and fountains in the midst of the vallies: he will make the wilderness a pool of water, and the dry land springs of water. He will plant in the wilderness the cedar, and the shittah tree, and the myrtle, and the oil tree; and set in the desert the fir tree, and the pine tree, and the box tree together: that they may see, and know, and consider, and understand together, that the hand of the Lord hath done this, and the Holy One of Israel hath created it."

The facts now reported have the weight and conclusiveness of a thousand arguments in proof of three important points; viz. that it is not a vain thing to attempt the conversion of the *Indians;* that they may be brought to the knowledge of Christ, before they are advanced in civilization; and that the plan of instructing them in English is feasible and eligible.

It is a truth, worthy to be repeated, until it reach the mind and heart of every friend of God and men in these Christian states, that, in proportion to time and means employed, no missions to the heathen, since the apostolic age, have been more successful, than those to the American aborigines.

Nor has the success, in manifest conversions to God, and in fruits meet for repentance, been delayed until the plastic hand of civilization had prepared the way. In the days of Elliot, of the Mayhews, and of Brainerd, and now in our own day, rude children of nature and of the forest—men and women and young persons of both sexes—have had their understandings enlightened and their hearts opened to receive the gospel, and have become humble and exemplary followers of the Lord Jesus. The facts are as encouraging as they are incontrovertible. They are encouraging, in regard not only to the spiritual interests of the untutored tribes, but also to the melioration of their temporal condition What so efficacious for subduing the ferocious spirit, and restraining the roving inclinations of the savage, as the renovating grace of the gospel? What like this to engage the mind of the noblest objects, and to generate and animate the desire for general improvement? It was by means of the *gospel* that the nations of Europe were civilized; and by means of the gospel may the tribes of the American wilderness be civilized.

The gospel prompts to general education. But tedious would be the process and slow the advances of education in the vernacular languages of those natives, whose minds are altogether unlettered, and their languages unwritten. Most auspiciously it is found, that the obstacles which have been supposed to lie in the way of teaching them in *English*, are rather imaginary than real. They are willing to be taught, are desirous of being taught, and of having their children taught, in English; and experiments at our establishment have proved, that Indian children, eight years old and upwards, may be taken from the wigwams, and in one year be brought forward to read with a good degree of correctness and facility in the English Bible. In the mean time, they are making proportionate proficiency in speaking and understanding the language, and in various branches of improvement.

The necessity, then, of making translations of the Scriptures, and of elementary books, into the vernacular languages, is superseded, and the labor and time and expense of doing it are saved. If indeed Bibles and other books were already at hand in those languages, it would be extremely questionable, whether any considerable use should be made of them. The Indians, old or young, would derive no benefit from them, *until taught to read.* But the young may as well be taught in English books as in Indian; and the old would no sooner learn to read in Indian than in English; and when once taught in English, they are brought into a new world, and the treasures of knowledge, and the arts of civilized life, are laid open to them.

Fully persuaded of the soundness and efficacy of the system, now brought into operation, and animated by its success in the Cherokee nation, your Committee have been earnest in the desire of imparting the benefits of it to other tribes.

CHOCTAWS.—The Rev. Mr. Cornelius, whose zealous and able services as an agent of this Board continue to entitle him to very grateful notice, agreeably to his instructions visited, in the course of the last autumn, not only the Cherokees, but also the Chickasaws and Choctaws; and he saw a large council of Creeks within the Cherokee limits. Every where he was kindly received, and found dispositions highly favorable to the objects of the mission. The Creeks wished for time to consider; but the Chickasaws and Choctaws shewed not only a readiness, but an ardent desire, to have establishments, such as that at Brainerd, commenced among them.—The United States government, also, has engaged to afford the same patronage and aid to establishments for the benefit of each of these nations, as for the Cherokees.

Being satisfied that there was an open door, your Committee resolved on commencing an establishment in the Choctaw nation without loss of time. This is the largest nation of the four, consisting of about twenty thousand souls. They have a fine country, are possessed of considerable wealth, and have strong tendencies toward a civilized state The government agent, Col. M'Kee, takes a lively interest in their welfare, and is disposed to exert his great influence in favor of our design.

The Rev. Mr. Kingsbury's acquaintance with the native character, his high standing in the esteem and confidence of both red men and white, and the experience, which he had in commencing and advancing the establishment at Brainerd, combined to render it, in the view of the Committee, highly important, that the superintendence of the Choctaw mission should be committed to him. He consented to the proposal with his wonted alacrity; and, in pursuance of arrangements made for the purpose, he and Mr. Williams and his wife left Brainerd about the first of June, and arrived at Yalo Busha, in the Choctaw nation, in about four weeks.

The mutual attachments subsisting between these beloved persons, and the rest of the mission family, including the Cherokee youth and children, were of the strongest, most endearing, and most sacred kind; and the scenes of parting were marked with a tenderness, and a fervor of Christian feeling, not easy to be described, nor soon to be forgotten.

About the middle of June, Mr. Peter Kanouse, and Mr. John G. Kanouse and his wife, from Rockaway, N. J., and Mr. Moses Jewell and his wife, from Chenango County, N. Y., embarked at New-York, having been designated as assistants in the Choctaw mission. They arrived at New-Orleans, on the 24th of July, where they received from several persons distinguished marks of kindness and Christian attention; and on the 28th took the steamboat for Natchez. Of a later date no intelligence has been received from them; but the hope is entertained, that by the kind providence of God they have been carried safely to the place of their destination;* where they would be welcomed by Messrs. Kingsbury and Williams, with great joy and thanksgiving, and engage, it is believed, with most cheerful self-devotement, in the concerns of the establishment.

The seat of this mission is about 400 miles south-westerly, from Brainerd, and near the Yalo Busha creek; about 30 miles above its junction, with the Yazoo. It is in a fine country, in a situation supposed to be salubrious; and by the Yalo Busha, the Yazoo, and the Mississippi, will have a water communication with Natchez and New Orleans.

The first care of Messrs. Kingsbury and Williams, was to select a suitable spot, and make arrangements for erecting the necessary buildings. In this work they were assured of every assistance which the agent, Col. M'Kee, could afford them; but many difficulties were to be encoun-

---

* They arrived in comfortable health, but worn with fatigue, on the 29th of August

tered, and for want of good laborers, the work for some time must proceed slowly.

At the latest date, July 30th, Mr. Kingsbury writes, "The half breeds and natives, who understand our object, appear highly gratified, and treat us with much kindness; though there are not wanting those, who look up on all white people, who come into the country, with a jealous eye."—"The prospect in this nation is, on the whole, favorable; but there are some circumstances which at times bear down our spirits, and sink our hopes. One is the immoral and impious lives of multitudes of whites, who are either passing through the Choctaw country, or residing in it. Another is the prevalence of intemperance in drinking. This vice has of late increased to a most alarming degree.—But our dependence is not on our own strength. Trusting to that, we must despair of success. But the Lord Jesus has all power in heaven and in earth; and has promised to be with his disciples, even unto the end of the world. Through Him we can do all things. And it gives us some satisfaction to state, that, notwithstanding the moral stupidity and licentiousness of both whites and Indians, preaching is better attended, than we had any reason to expect."

May the same grace, which has been so signally displayed at Brainerd, be not less signally displayed at Elliot,† and He, who has made of one blood all nations, mercifully shew himself the God, not of the Cherokees only, but also of the Choctaws.

FOREIGN MISSION SCHOOL.—This interesting Seminary appears to be rising in favor with God ·and man. The present number of pupils is twenty; six from the Sandwich Islands; two from the Society Islands; one from the island of Timor, a Chinese in language; one from Bengal; one from Malaya; six American Aborigines, of different tribes; and three sons of our own country. Of the whole number, eight are church members, of whom four are from the Sandwich Islands; and several others shew marks of different degrees of religious seriousness. The Rev. Mr. Daggett, the Principal, in an official communication just received, says, "The scholars appear to maintain a great deal of harmony in their intercourse with each other, have been very punctual and attentive at all seasons of devotion and religious instruction, and their general deportment as well as their application to study, has been very satisfactory."

Amid the gracious smiles of Heaven, with which the Seminary has been favored, and which claims the most grateful acknowledgments; it has experienced, in the course of the year, a deeply affecting frown, which calls for profound submission. On the 17th of February, Henry Obookiah, the eldest and most extensively known of the members, from the Sandwich Islands, was taken from the midst of his companions, from the affections and hopes of his patrons and friends, and from all terrestrial scenes. His sickness was a fever, which he bore with exemplary patience, with cheerful resignation, and with an elevated and animating hope of a better life. He died as the Christian would wish to die. His divine master knew well, whether to send him back to Owhyhee, to publish

* The name given to the place of the Choctaw Mission, in honor of him, who has been called "the Apostle of the Indians."

salvation to his perishing countrymen, or to call him to higher scenes, in another world; and equally well does He know how to make his death redound to the good of his surviving school-fellows and friends, and to the furtherance of the great cause, to which he was so ardently devoted.

NEW MISSIONARIES.—The abundant grace of the Lord Jesus continues to be displayed in bringing forward young men of devoted hearts, and furnished minds, to bear his name to the distant heathen. Messrs. Pliny Fisk, Levi Spaulding, and Miron Winslow, now closing their studies at Andover, and Messrs. Cephas Washburn, and Alfred Finney, regular licentiates for the ministry, have offered themselves to be employed under the patronage and direction of this Board, severally with ample testimonials. And not a smaller number, now in a course of preparation, have made known their settled purpose of offering themselves in due time.

FUNDS.—The donations to the Board, within the year past, have amounted to more than *thirty-two thousand dollars*, and the other sources of income to about *three thousand*. Though the receipts have surpassed those of the preceding year about *five thousand dollars*, they have fallen short of the expenditures, which amounted to more than *thirty-six thousand*.

The number of auxiliary associations, under different names, which bring their collections to the treasury of the Board, is about *five hundred*.

From year to year, as the plans and operations of the Board are extended, and its establishments and laborers are multiplied, the expenditures are, of course, and of necessity, proportionably increased; and as the work proceeds, it must continue to be so. On this account, however, there is no cause of discouragement. Hitherto the liberalities of the Christian community have answered, in a measure, the demands for them; and there is good ground for the confidence, that they will yet be more and more abundant.

It is as certain as any mathematical demonstration, that the Christian world is amply able to supply the means for evangelizing the many millions of the heathen. The duty is clear and imperious. JESUS CHRIST IS LORD OF ALL. The silver and the gold are HIS;—the world with all its fulness is HIS: and his high command, that his Gospel should be preached to every creature, puts in most sacred requisition the necessary means for the purpose. No man can be justified in withholding his due proportion; no one is impoverished, or will be impoverished, by complying with the requisition in its utmost extent, every one who obeys it with a true and cheerful heart, will receive manifold more in this present world, and in the world to come, life everlasting.

To many, indeed, the spirit of this new era, as was that of our Savior's ministry, may be like new wine to old bottles.—if occasionally infused into them, it may soon be gone. But in others it will remain; and the numbers of those, in whom it will be preserved, and be like a springing well, will be continually and rapidly increasing. Views and feelings and habits, suited to the advancing and brightening era, will grow, be propagated, and prevail. Christians will learn what is meant by not living to themselves; for what other and higher purposes, than merely a temporal support for themselves and families, and a hoarded provision for those who are to come after them, the bounties of Providence are bestowed upon them; and in what ways, and by what means, not limiting their beneficence to the narrow circles of their immediate connexions or communities, they may do good unto all men. *"Their merchandise and their hire shall be holiness to the Lord, it shall not be treasured, nor laid up."* They will not give grudgingly nor sparingly; they will not wait to be solicited, but will come forward with their *freewill offerings*, with singleness and gladness of heart, and fill the treasury of the Lord to overflowing. The cause is worthy. The treasures of heaven have been freely given for it; and the treasures of the earth will not always be withheld —There is every reason for animated confidence, and increased exertion; but the confidence must take hold on the all-sufficiency of Zion's Redeemer and King, and the exertion must be made in his strength, and with humble and prayerful waiting on his will.

In behalf of the Prudential Committee,
New-Haven, Sept. 10, 1818.   S. WORCESTER, *Clerk.*

FOREIGN MISSION SCHOOL.

The annual report of the agents of this promising establishment, signed by the chairman of the executive committee, JAMES MORRIS, *Esq.* and brought down to September, has lately been forwarded to the Prudential Committee. We lay it before our readers in the form of an abridgement, using the language of the report, wherever it can conveniently be done.

THE instruction of the school continued under the superintendence of Mr. Edwin W. Dwight, till last May. On the second of that month, at the annual meeting of the agents, the Rev. Herman Dagget was inducted into office as the principal of the school. The Committee have the pleasure of stating, that Mr. Dwight, while discharging the duties of principal, had the progress of the pupils near his heart; both with respect to their advancement in science, and their proficiency in religious knowledge and piety. It appeared, on the public examination, that the scholars had made satisfactory improvement, in the several branches of learning, in which they had been taught by him, and under his direction.

At the commencement of this report, the committee cannot refrain from noticing the death of Henry Obookiah, which took place on the 17th of February. Our loss in his removal was, we trust, his unspeakable gain. He adorned the Christian character, and his influence in the school was salutary and commanding. An account of his last sickness and death, together with some memoirs of his life, will soon appear before the public.

Samuel Ruggles, and *James Ely,* still continue members of the school. They are both young men of piety and promise. Their deportment and example are such as become the high profession they have made. Their progress in study is honorable to themselves; and they continue to hold themselves devoted to the missionary cause. The former has been employed, during a part of the time, in visiting sundry towns, both in this and the neighboring states, to solicit donations for the school, in which he has been greatly successful. He obtained many useful articles, both of clothing and bedding, besides books and money. The conduct of these two young men has been such as to increase the high anticipations of their future usefulness.

[The committee next mention a youth of our own country, who, as it is thought inexpedient that he should continue at the school, need not here be brought before the public.]

The seventeen youths, who were born pagans, are six Sandwich Islanders, two natives of India, a Chinese, two Society Islanders, and six of the Aborigines of our own country. Four natives of the Sandwich Islands are now professors of religion. *Thomas Hopoo* was mentioned in the last report as having been admitted to the church He continues to give good evidence of piety, and burns with an ardent desire to carry the glad tidings of salvation to his perishing brethren at Owhyhee. His countrymen, *William Tennooe, John Honooree,* and *George Sandwich,* having, for a considerable time, given satisfactory evidence of faith in Christ, made a public profession of that faith the first Sabbath in September, were baptised, and admitted to the church in Cornwall. *Tennooe* is persevering in his studies, writes a good hand, and displays a happy talent in composition. *Honooree* retains his native language in a high degree; but does not speak English with ease and clearness. He has a turn for the mechanical arts, possesses considerable vigor of intellect, is discreet and stable, and sets an example worthy of imitation. *Sandwich* is industrious, makes good improvement, and adorns the Christian character.

George Tamoree has seasons of religious impressions, is of an ardent temperament, makes good proficiency in his studies, and improves in his general deportment. The remaining Owhyhean, William *Kummo-oo-lah*, is a pleasant, agreeable youth, learns English well, and is now hopefully pious.

John Windall's progress in learning has been slow. His powers of mind are small; and it has been deemed inexpedient to continue him longer in the school. The committee have placed him under the care of a farmer, who will give him religious instruction, and allow him a compensation for his labor.

John Johnson was dismissed from the school last February, for improper conduct. He has probably gone on board a vessel to revisit his native country.

Simon Annance has made reasonable proficiency in his studies; has been respectful and obedient, but has, on some occasions, been rather averse to labor.

Wong Arce, a Chinese, was taken into the school for a season; but was dismissed for misconduct.

Adin Gibbs, one of our Aborigines, was born in Pennsylvania, is a descendant of the Delaware tribe, speaks the English language fluently, and impressively, makes laudable progress in study, is a professor of religion, and highly adorns the character of a Christian. He is exemplary in all his conduct; and his character procures him influence among his fellow students. He was religious before he joined the school, which was in April last.

George Timor, a native of the island of Timor in the Indian sea, came to this country from Batavia. He lived a while in Philadelphia as a servant; and was sent to the school by a worthy clergyman of that city. He is mild and inoffensive; but not having sufficient powers of mind to make advances in study, he has been placed under the care of a religious farmer, that, while he earns his living, he may learn the simple truths of the gospel.

Stephen Poo-po-hee, a native of one of the Society Islands, has lived with Pomare, and was in the battle which took place on the Sabbath between the Christian party and the idolaters, and which ended in the defeat of the latter. *Poo-po-hee* has no parents living; came to this country only to see it; and joined the school in April last, soon after he landed on our shores. Since that time he has been thoughtful and serious, and the committee are not without hope, that he has become truly pious, and is a chosen vessel to carry the gospel to some islanders of the Pacific.

Charles Papa-yoo is a companion of *Poo-po-hee,* came to New York in the same ship, and joined the school at the same time. He is a native of Otaheite. His talents are promising; but he, like many other young persons, is thoughtless in regard to religion. Both these Society Islanders are about twenty years of age. They and the Sandwich Islanders are well formed, fine looking young men.

Joseph Bontang Snow, a native Malay, was stolen from Malacca, when four or five years old, carried to Batavia, and thence to Canton. He was held as a slave, and offered for sale to a Chinese merchant; but he begged himself off. His master then disposed of him to Mr. Samuel Snow, of Providence, (R. I.) who was then a commercial agent of the United States at Canton, and who brought this Malay with him, on returning to this country. *Botang* learnt the Chinese language, while resident at Canton, and retains it still. He speaks English intelligibly. At Providence he became serious, and hopefully renewed in heart; was baptised on a profession of his faith, and admitted to a church there. He joined the school last spring; and his conduct has been unexceptionable. From his appearance it is supposed he is about thirty years of age.

Three Cherokee youths, and a Choctaw, from 14 to 17 years of age, were brought to the school by Mr. Cornelius in August. The names of the Cherokees are, *Leonard Hicks, Elias Boudinot,* and *Thomas Basil;* the two latter being named after gentlemen, who have the welfare of our Indians much at heart. The first is a son of Mr. Hicks, who is a Cherokee of more influence than any other in the tribe, and has been, for five years, a professor of religion, and a member of the Moravian church at Spring-place. The name of the Choctaw is *M'Kee Folsom.* His father is a white man; his mother a full-blooded native.

Arnold Krygsman, a Malay boy of 12 years old, has just been received into the school. He was born at Padang, on the south side of Sumatra; his mother a native Sumatran, his father a Dutchman. Both parents being dead, he was sent to this country for his education, by an elder brother, and committed to the care of a captain, who brought him to Newburyport last April.

It ought to be acknowledged with gratitude, that the smiles of Providence have remarkably attended the school. It numbers eight professors of religion: and two or three others, who are hopefully pious. Its pupils have literally come from the east and the west, the north and the south, from different climates, and remote continents and islands, to have the darkness of Paganism dispelled, and the light of the gospel communicated, in this benevolent institution. Many prayers are continually offered for the youths here assembled, that their souls may be saved, and they may carry salvation to multitudes of their brethren.

Little more than two years ago, the idea of this school was suggested by an individual to two of his friends. They united in prayer for divine direction. The subject was proposed to the Board, whose committee we are now addressing, and the subsequent history of the design need not here be repeated.

The report concludes with appropriate reflections, and an honorable testimony to the Rev. Mr. Daggett, as peculiarly qualified to preside over such a school, and to impress religious truth upon the expanding minds of these interesting youths.

VISIT OF THE PRUDENTIAL COMMITTEE TO THE FOREIGN MISSION SCHOOL.

After the meeting of the Board in September, the Prudential Committee made an official visit to the school, for the purpose of viewing the houses and land which had been purchased, and becoming more fully acquainted with the minute interests of the establishment. Though it was in vacation, the greater part of the scholars were present. After an examination into the state of the school, a short exhibition was made of the improvement which the pupils had made in public speaking. *M'Kee Folsom* delivered a short declamation in Choctaw; *Elias Boudinot* in Cherokee; *Poo-po-hee* in Otaheitan; *Honooree* in Owhyhean; one of the American youth in Chinese, as he had learned it from *Botang*, *Gibbs*, *Hopoo*, and others in English. These declamations, excepting the English ones, were composed by the youths themselves; we do not mean, that they were all written; but they were connected speeches, prepared for exhibition. The declamation of *Honooree* was a part of a colloquy which had been composed for the public examination in May. He delivered it with surprising force and animation. As he came to the part, which affected his feelings most, the excessive agitation of his countenance and his whole frame, and the unparalleled rapidity and vehemence of his utterance, were so much beyond our standard of animated delivery, as to be rather painful to the audience. The English pieces, except that of *Hopoo*, were extracts from the noblest parts of Robert Hall's, and of Dr Dwight's sermons. It was interesting to hear these grand compositions uttered by tawny youths, but lately rescued from the forests, and the islands inhabited only by heathens. They were generally delivered with great propriety. The piece spoken by *Hopoo* was composed by himself, as a farewell address to the scholars, in contemplation of the separation, which would take place, should he first visit the land of his fathers, to bear the message of salvation. The performance was highly creditable to his talents, and many parts of it were suited deeply to affect a considerate mind. Towards the close he alluded to the death of Oboo-kiah, and of his friend and benefactor, Mr. Mills, in the tenderest manner. The whole exhibition, and the prospects of the school were calculated to warm the benevolent heart, and to prompt to activity and diligence in the great work of sending the gospel to the heathen.

PECUNIARY ACCOUNTS OF THE BOARD.

The American Board of Commissioners for Foreign Missions, in account current with Jeremiah Evarts, their Treasurer, Dr.

To cash paid from Sept. 1, 1817, to August 31, 1818, in conformity to orders of the Board, and of the Prudential Committee, from No. 211 to No. 295, both inclusive, $36,310 16

Losses by counterfeit and worthless bills, received in donations during the year,   -   -   -   -   -   -   -   -   -   -   36 09

Balance carried to the credit of the Board, in new account, Sept 1, 1818,   52,923 08

$89,269 33

Contra Cr.

By balance brought to the credit of the Board, in new account, Sept 1, 1817, $53,841 61

By cash received in donations, as published particularly in the Panoplist, between Sept. 1, 1817, and August 31, 1818,   -   - $32,392 53

Interest of money and income of stock,   -   -   2,761 55

A note given by a missionary to refund what had been advanced to him, his ill health preventing him from going forth to the heathen,   100 00

Avails of the sale of books, published by the Board, principally the "Conversion of the World."   -   -   -   -   173 64-----35,427 72

$89,269 33

MINUTES

OF THE

TENTH ANNUAL MEETING.

———

The tenth annual meeting of the American Board of Commissioners for Foreign Missions, was held in the council chamber of the state house, in Boston, Sept. 15th, 16th, and 17th, 1819. The following members were present; viz.

> Rev. Joseph Lyman, D. D.
> His Honor William Phillips, Esq.
> Rev. Jedidiah Morse, D. D.
> Rev. Calvin Chapin, D. D.
> Rev. Zephaniah S. Moore, D. D.
> Rev. Jeremiah Day, LL. D
> Jeremiah Evarts, Esq.
> Hon. John Treadwell, LL. D.
> Gen. Henry Sewall,
> Hon. Charles Marsh,
> Hon. William Reed,
> Rev. Samuel Worcester, D. D.
> Rev. Henry Davis, D. D.

The session was opened with prayer by the Rev Dr. Lyman, and on the following days by the Rev. Dr. Morse, and the Rev. Dr. Chapin.

The annual accounts of the Treasurer were exhibited, as examined and certified by the Auditor, and accepted.

The Prudential Committee made their annual Report, which took up the greater part of the first day, and which was accepted.

The report of the Executive Committee of the Foreign Mission School, was read and accepted.

The Rev. Leonard Woons, D. D , Professor in the Theological Seminary at Andover, (Mass.) the Hon. John Cotton Smith, of Sharon, Con. Divie Bethune, Esq. of the city of New York, and Elias Boudinot Caldwell, Esq. of Washington, District of Columbia, were unanimously elected members of the Board.

After the annual organization of the Board, the officers were as follows:

The Hon. JOHN TREADWELL, LL. D. *President.*
Rev. JOSEPH LYMAN, D. D. *Vice President.*
Rev. JEDIDIAH MORSE, D. D.
Hon WILLIAM REED,
Rev. LEONARD WOODS, D. D. } *Prudential Committee.*
Rev SAMUEL WORCESTER, D. D.
JEREMIAH. EVARTS, Esq.
Rev Dr. WORCESTER, *Corresponding Secretary.*
Rev. CALVIN CHAPIN, *Recording Secretary.*
JEREMIAH EVARTS, Esq. *Treasurer,* and
ASHUR ADAMS, Esq. *Auditor.*

The Rev. Dr. Lyman preached the annual Sermon, at the Old South Church, on the afternoon of Thursday, the 16th, from Isaiah lviii, 12. *And they that shall be of thee shall build the old waste places: thou shalt raise up the foundations of many generations; and thou shalt be called,* THE REPAIRER OF THE BREACH, THE RESTORER OF PATHS TO DWELL IN.

His Honor Lieut. Gov. Phillips, and the Rev. Drs. Worcester and Morse, were requested to present the thanks of the Board to the preacher for his Sermon, and to ask a copy for the press.

JOHN TALLMADGE, Esq. was unanimously elected a member of the Agency for the Foreign Mission School.

In the course of the session the following resolutions were adopted.

Resolved, That individuals, clergymen and laymen, residing in different, and especially in distant, parts of the United States, and in other lands, be now, and, as shall be deemed advisable, hereafter, elected by ballot, to be connected with this Board as Corresponding Members; who, though it be no part of their official duty to attend its meetings, or to take part in its votes or resolutions, yet, when occasionally present, may assist in its deliberations, and, by communicating information, and in various other ways, enlighten its course, facilitate its operations, and promote its objects.

In pursuance of the foregoing resolution, the following persons were unanimously elected by ballot to be corresponding members; viz.

The Rev. FRANCIS HERON, Pittsburgh, Pen. the Rev. JAMES CULBERTSON, Zanesville, and the Rev ROBERT G. WILSON, D. D. Chillicothe, Ohio; the Rev. JAMES BLYTHE, D. D. Lexington, and the Rev. DANIEL C BANKS, Louisville, Kentucky; the Rev WILLIAM HILL, D. D. Winchester, and the Rev. Dr. BAXTER, Lexington, Va.; the Rev. CHARLES COFFIN, D. D. President of Greenville College, and Dr. JOSEPH C. STRONG, Knoxville, Tennessee; Col. R. J. MEIGS, agent of government in the Cherokee nation; Col. JOHN M'KEE, agent of government in the Choctaw nation; SAMUEL POSTLETHWAITE, Esq. Natchez, Miss.; the Rev. SYLVESTER LARNED, New Orleans, Lou.; Rev. HENRY KOLLOCK, D. D. Savannah, the Rev. MOSES WADDEL, D. D President of the University of Georgia, JOHN BOLTON, Esq. Savannah, JOHN WHITEHEAD, Esq. Waynesboro', and the Hon. JOHN ELLIOT, Sunbury, Georgia; the Rev. BENJAMIN M.

PALMER, D. D. Charleston, and Dr. EDWARD D. SMITH,* Professor in the College, South Carolina; and Gen. CALVIN JONES, Raleigh, N. C.

Abroad the following persons were elected; viz. WILLIAM WILBERFORCE, Esq. CHARLES GRANT, Esq., the Rev. JOSIAH PRATT, and the Rev GEORGE BURDER, London; the Rev. JOHN CAMPBELL, D. D., the Hon. KINCAID MACKENZIE, and the Rev. RALPH WARDLAW, D. D., Scotland; Mr. FREDERIC LEO, Paris; the Rev. Mr. JOWETT, Malta; the Rev. Archdeacon TWISLETON, Ceylon; the Rev. WILLIAM CAREY, D. D., and the Rev. THOMAS T. THOMASON, Calcutta; and the Rev. ROBERT MORRISON, D. D., China.

The manner, in which the Corresponding Members are to be informed of their election, was submitted to the Prudential Committee.

Resolved, That this Board, is deeply impressed with the holy devotedness, zeal, fidelity, labors and excellence of character, of their late beloved missionary, the Rev. EDWARD WARREN; that his memory is precious; and that the Prudential Committee be authorized and directed to erect a suitable monumental stone over his grave, at the Cape of Good Hope.

Resolved, That the Board will ever exercise an affectionate and provident care for the widows and children of such missionaries, as shall have deceased in its service; and the Prudential Committee are authorized, and it will be their duty, to make such provisions in these cases, as will be consistent with the principles of the missionary cause, and adapted to the circumstances of the respective missionary stations.

Resolved, That the Board gratefully acknowledge the liberal and increasing patronage of the Christian public extensively afforded to this institution, its measures, and objects; and that the Prudential Committee be directed to express the thanks of the Board to all societies, churches, congregations, and individuals, from whom donations and contributions have been received.

Various interesting subjects were referred to the Prudential Committee, and to the future deliberations of the Board.

[The details of business, which annually demand the attention of the Board, in relation to funds, the duties of officers, &c. &c. and the appointment and report of various committees, would not be particularly interesting to the public. The important objects and plans of the Board are brought to view in the Report of the Prudential Committee.]

Resolutions of thanks were unanimously adopted, and ordered to be presented to the Committee of the Old South Church, for the use of that house of worship for the public religious services of this annual meeting;

To the choir of singers, for their attendance and aid on this occasion;

To his Honor, the Lieut. Governor of Massachusetts, for his kindness and politeness in procuring the use of the council-chamber for the use of the Board during the present session; and

To those individuals and families in Boston, whose hospitality has been experienced by the members.

The Prudential Committee were directed to compile and publish a Report, comprising the various annual documents.

---

* This gentleman died quite lately, on a visit to St. Louis, Missouri, greatly lamented by all who knew him.

The next annual meeting was appointed to be held at Hartford, Con. on the third Wednesday of September, 1820, at 10 o'clock, A. M. The Rev. Dr. Nott having been appointed to preach on that occasion, the Rev Dr. Proudfit was appointed to preach in case of his failure.

The meeting was concluded with prayer by the Rev. Dr. Worcester.

REPORT.

BRETHREN,—The year is quickly gone; and in the kind providence of HIM, who has crowned it with his mercies, we are returned to this Board of sweet and high counsel, to review the past, and to consult for the future.—But not all are here. The revered friend of man and of God;— who had borne a conspicuous part in the cares and toils of his country's deliverance and elevation,—and, with still more ardent devotion engaged in the great design of raising up the world to virtue and to glory,—the Hon. JEDIDIAH HUNTINGTON—*is not here.*—The venerated champion of the cross,—whose highest joys were its holy triumphs,—whose conceptions were among the first in the teeming deliberations, from which this Board, with all its plans and enterprises, sprung,—who, in each succeeding year, has been the second of its officers, and a prime counsellor of its measures,—and whose fidelity to his many and weighty trusts was an example to his compeers and a light to the world,—the Rev Dr. SPRING —*is not here.*—Their course is finished;—their work is done;—their trials are ended; and our Master and Lord, supremely wise and good, has called them to rest from their labors, in the mansions which he had prepared for them. The places that have known them will know them no more. We have mingled our tears with many at their tombs; we have embalmed the memory of the one and of the other in our hearts; and we now record their names in the assured persuasion, that they have long since been enrolled for everlasting remembrance on high.

But the time demands, that they who weep be as though they wept not. *Our* work is not done. We have still to be followers of them, who through faith and patience inherit the promises. The removal of laborers, one after another, is no intimation that the design is to be relinquished; or the work suspended. He, whose design it is, still lives, and still reigns on the holy hill of Zion, for its accomplishment; and is continually giving increased emphasis to the mandate, *Go ye, therefore, and teach all nations;*—and to the assurance, *Lo, I am with you alway.*

The missions, concerning which report is now to be made, are seven: BOMBAY, CEYLON, PALESTINE, CHEROKEE, CHOCTAW, ARKANSAS, and SANDWICH: the first, only six years ago, dubiously struggling for a place, and even for existence; the last, just on the eve of embarkation; and the whole extending from east to west, more than two thirds around this globe, which, as the dearly purchased domain of the Son of God, Christian benevolence desires completely to encircle, and to fill with the light of his salvation

BOMBAY.—This mission, the first child of the Board, can never be mentioned by your Committee, without emotions, which the heart wishes always to feel, and recollections, on which it dwells with ever refreshing gratitude and delight. It has lost nothing of its title to be regarded with the liveliest affection, confidence, and hope.

The mission now comprises three stations. The first, which is also the principal seat of the mission, is in the great native town of Bombay; and is still held by Messrs. Hall, Newell, and Bardwell. At Mahim, about six miles distant, on the northern part of the same island, is the station of Mr. Graves,—in the midst of about twenty thousand heathen people, dwelling compactly around him, and near to a still greater number on the neighboring island of Salsette. Mr. Nichols has his station at Tanna, the chief town of Salsette, distant from the first station about twenty-five miles, and separated only by a very narrow strait from a dense and wide spread population on the continent. These stations are regarded as eminently eligible, combining many and great facilities, and advantages for extensive operations.

About a year ago, Mr. Nichols was visited with a severe bilious illness, by which he was brought near to death. "My physician, my friends, and myself," he says, "for several days anticipated the rapid approach of that hour, when my soul would be summoned hence. But the Almighty Physician appeared to save. The chastisements of his rod were mingled with the sweetest tokens of his love.—He made all my bed in sickness. —I cannot think of the goodness of God, and the unremitting attention of Dr. Taylor, and my beloved friends about me, but tears of gratitude fill my eyes." His speedy recovery is mentioned by the other brethren, and will be regarded by this Board, as a particular mercy, to be recorded with devout thankfulness. It is, however, only a touching instance amid an ample display of Divine goodness. In the general health of its members,—in its internal harmony, in the favor it has obtained with the rulers, and with the people, European and native,—in the free course afforded to its operations,—and above all, in its lively steadfastness in the work of faith, and labor of love, and patience of hope,—the Lord has marked this mission with distinguished kindness.

Since the dates reported the last year, a wide expansion has been given to the sphere of its operations. At first, the labors of the brethren were limited to the town of Bombay. After the arrival of Messrs. Nichols and Graves, by occupying the stations of Mahim and Tanna, they brought the whole island of Bombay and Salsette also, within their range. Nor is this all. By the late war in India, the Mahratta states and territories, on the side of the peninsula or continent adjacent to Bombay, and to a great extent, were subjected to the British dominion. This event, as it rendered those countries more easily and safely accessible, gave a new spring to hope and to enterprise.

In October last, Mr. Newell made an excursion to Caranja, an island near Bombay, "containing about ten thousand inhabitants, mostly Hindoos." There "he preached to numbers of the people, and distributed a hundred books."

In the same month, Mr. Hall passed over to the continent, and visited Choule, a place upon the coast, about thirty miles south of Bombay. "Here, in a small compass," he says, "are six or eight towns, belonging to the English; and in these towns there may be thirty thousand inhabitants; who, with the exception of about two hundred Roman Catholics, fifty families of Jews, and a few Mussulmans, are all Hindoos." He visited most of the towns and villages in the district, "preached to, and conversed with, large numbers of the people, and distributed about two hundred books. Not only were the books kindly received; but, before he left the district, the people thronged around him, at different places, eagerly desirous of obtaining them. This afforded him very favorable opportunities for preaching to them, which he as gladly embraced. When his stock of books was gone, pressed by their importunities, he promised to send them more; and in fulfilment of the promise, after his return to Bombay, he sent them, by the hand of a schoolmaster, about four hundred.

In the forepart of November, Mr. Newell made a visit to Bankote, about sixty miles south of Bombay, of which he gives the following account.

"I staid at Bankote eleven days; and from thence visited the principal towns in that vicinity, and held conferences with the people in all the places to which I went. I read, also, in all those places, some of our tracts, which contain a general view of the gospel, in a small compass; and distributed among the people copies of the Gospel of Matthew, and of the Acts, and of all the different tracts which we have published. I found the people attentive and inquisitive. When I visited the same people a second time, I generally found they had a number of inquiries to make about what they had heard before.—The town of Bankote, with its dependent villages, contains about 1700 inhabitants. I distributed in this place, of the Gospel of Matthew 50 copies, of the Acts 30, and 200 Tracts. I had the satisfaction of finding, that I could communicate with the people on the continent as readily, as with the people on this island, and that the people and the language are precisely the same there as here."

In December, Mr. Hall made another excursion; visited Cullian and Basseen, two large towns on the continent, the former about forty miles north east, and the latter about thirty miles north of Bombay; imparted instruction to many people; and distributed more than five hundred books.

"Our experience of this mode of laboring," say the brethren, "has led us to estimate more highly the importance of itinerating extensively, for the double purpose of preaching and distributing the Scriptures and tracts. And we indulge the pleasing hope, that He, who has helped us thus far, will enable us to go on, extending our instructions and distributions farther and farther; and we would rest assured, that our labor will not be in vain in the Lord."

It is their constant, daily practice to go about among the heathen, preaching more or less publicly, as opportunities offer; and distributing books to such as seem willing and able to read them. "It will, no doubt," they say, "be grateful to the feelings of the Board to reflect, that five of their missionaries, in the same region, and the same language, are now daily and actively engaged in the use of means, both direct and indirect, for the conversion of the heathen."

Among the indirect means here referred to, are the translating and printing of the Scriptures in successive portions, and the preparing and printing also of other books and tracts.

Mention was made in the Report of the last year, of their having printed in large editions, the Gospel of Matthew, the Acts of the Apostles, and two tracts, consisting chiefly of select portions of Scripture. They have since printed two editions, a thousand copies each, of a tract composed by them, and entitled, *The Way to Heaven;* the first *Number* in a series of *Scripture History;* the *Gospel of Matthew,* for the Bombay Bible Society; *Christ's sermon on the mount,* partly for the Bible Society, and partly for their own distribution; a *Reading Book* for schools; and a book entitled, *An easy and expeditious Method of acquiring a Knowledge of the English language; designed for the benefit of those Natives, who wish to study the English Language and the Sciences.* And at the last dates, they were expecting soon to print the book of Genesis, and several other tracts; and an edition of the Way to Heaven, in the Guzerattee language.

"The demand for books," they say, "has been greatly increased. A large number have been distributed; and some of them have been sent to a considerable distance on the continent. A few copies of the Reading Book for Schools, were sent, some months since, to a large town about twenty miles to the east of Bankote; and were so highly approved, that they were immediately introduced into the principal schools there, and a farther supply was requested through a European gentleman residing there. The supply desired has since been forwarded. A number of Gospels and copies of the Acts, and tracts, have been distributed in the same place, through the same gentleman. He also remarked, concerning a copy of Matthew and the Acts, bound together, that an officiating Brahmin of the principal temple in that place, asked for it; and it was given on condition, that it should be publicly deposited in the temple for the use of all that might wish to read it. On this condition, it was received; and the gentleman had ascertained that it was accordingly deposited and actually read."

The two thousand copies of *The Way to Heaven,* which they printed in two editions, were quickly distributed; and another edition was wanted.

These statements shew, in a strong light, the diligence of the missionaries, and the utility of their printing establishment. Hitherto indeed, they have received little remuneration for the expenses and labors of the press. They have done some printing however, for the Bombay Bible Society; which directly served the general cause, and at the same time brought something to the funds of the mission; and they entertain the hope, that from their book, *"designed for the Benefit of those Natives who wish to study the English Language and the Sciences,"* the mission will derive no inconsiderable emolument. Copies of the book have been sent home. It is an octavo of 168 pages; and, in the judgment of your Committee, is highly creditable to the mission. But it is chiefly by supplying the missionaries with copies of the Scriptures and other books and tracts for their schools, and for liberal and extensive distribution, that their press will be an engine of incalculable utility.

The schools of this mission, as reported at our last anniversary, were eleven. The number has since increased to *twenty-five.* The total number of pupils in these schools is not stated in any of the communications received, but we may fairly estimate those who attend constantly at nearly a hundred Jewish, and more than twelve hundred heathen children; besides a nearly equal number, in the course of a year, whose attendance is inconstant. The system is extending, the field is widening, the number of schools and of pupils is increasing; and the hearts of the missionaries are expanding with benevolent desire and with animating hope.

"For various reasons" they say, "we thought it desirable to establish schools on the continent. Schools being established in the large towns there, the superintendence of them must open to us an extensive intercourse with the people, and afford new and important facilities for diffusing Christian knowledge in other ways, in addition to what would be taught in the schools.

"With respect to Choule the circumstances were very favorable. At the time brother Hall visited this place, it was said there was not a single school in operation. The people, understanding that we had it in contemplation to establish charity schools, favored the object, and several persons requested to be employed as teachers. The Jew, who has been employed as teacher of the Jewish school in Bombay, was from Choule, and was willing to return and teach a school there. We found him to be a well qualified and faithful schoolmaster. Accordingly, about the middle of the month, he was sent to Choule, with directions to open one school in the large town of Rawadunda, and to employ one man to teach another school in a neighboring village. The first school was expected to embrace the Jewish children, and more or less children of other descriptions. Forty large boys have already joined this school, 30 of whom are Jews, and the number is increasing. The other school has 25 boys, and the number is also increasing. In the compass of five or six miles there are other populous villages, where schools are equally needed, and where, as we are informed, there are boys in readiness for *four* more schools.

"We some time since concluded to establish at least one school on the island of Caranja, which was visited some time since by brother Newell, but it has not yet been commenced. We hope that before long, we shall see flourishing schools both here and at Choule. But we should much more rejoice to see a missionary at each of those stations, to give greater effect to the schools, and teach the risen as well as the rising generation the words of eternal life. Each would have an ample field, equal to his utmost exertions; and we cannot forbear to raise our supplicating voice in behalf of these still neglected, perishing thousands, and to entreat that ere long they may be furnished with spiritual teachers, to guide them in the right ways of the Lord.

"The large towns of Cullian and Basseen, visited by brother Hall, present additional openings for the establishment of schools; and so do other towns less distant from Bombay. We cannot speak with precision as to the extent to which schools might be carried, but we are sure that they might be very greatly extended; and we feel very desirous that this should be done. Yes, we more than ever desire it, for our further experience and observation have only served the more deeply to convince us of the eminent importance of such schools, and of their powerful agency in the diffusion of Christian knowledge."

In this connection, the brethren make a statement respecting the expense of their schooling system, from which it appears, that, on an average, the teaching of a hundred boys costs the mission about eleven dollars a month, and is not likely to cost it more. Taking twelve hundred, as the total number of pupils in their twenty-five schools, the total expense for a year amounts to about fifteen hundred and eighty dollars.

The brethren proceed in the following very interesting and impressive recital and appeal.

"As a thing of course, the children are taught reading, writing, and arithmetic in their own language. Special pains are taken to bring them forward in reading, an exercise greatly undervalued and very little encouraged in their own schools. Besides, as the schools are chiefly designed for the *poor*, who do not think themselves able to provide instruction for their children, by means of them large numbers are instructed in the art of reading, &c. who otherwise would never be able to read, and consequently in no capacity to be benefited by the perusal of the Scriptures if given to them.

"To increase the proportion of people in a community who are furnished with the art of reading, writing, and arithmetic, is to raise that community in the scale of intellectual being: and as charity schools for the education of the poor and destitute obviously effect this, they certainly claim the approbation and patronage of every friend of humanity. But this is by no means the chief motive. It will be remembered, that these schools are filled with heathen children, who, in a few years, are, in no small degree, to give a character to the community, to which they belong. In these schools, these heathen youth, in addition to the ordinary branches of learning, are taught the fundamental principles of Christianity. Instead of heathen fables, the very first thing put into their hands to read is the pure word of God, which is able to make them wise unto salvation through faith in Jesus Christ. Such portions are selected for them, as are best calculated to store their minds with divine knowledge. The most important moral precepts are enforced upon their hearts. They commit to memory the decalogue and form of prayer.

"Thus are these heathen children daily employed. Is not this simple statement enough? Will—can—the disciples of Jesus—can the friends of mankind, withhold their silver and gold, so long as there is a call for another such school among the heathen? If more argument were necessary, much more might be said. But we must forbear to amplify. We would only add, that this method of schooling has far exceeded our most sanguine expectations. We find no obstacle to the multiplying of our schools; and none in our way of teaching in them whatever we please. If we only had time, we might visit and catechise each school every day; and in some respects, we are under as great advantages, for imparting a religious education to these heathen children, as though they were brought up in our families. We are therefore earnest in pleading for these schools, that they may not only continue to be supported, but that they may be greatly extended.

"At the same time, would we desire to acknowledge, with most unfeigned gratitude, that liberal patronage, which the Christian public in our native land have hitherto extended to the various objects of our mission, and which we hope never to forfeit."

These views of the beloved missionaries are animating, and these sentiments impulsive. They will be deeply felt, not only by this Board, but by the Christian community extensively, and the liberal patronage so earnestly solicited, will not be withheld

It would have been gratifying to your Committee, had they been able to report a proportionate success in the design of educating children in the missionary families. But in respect to this part of the general plan, the missionaries at Bombay have not yet been so happy as to have their hopes realized; and they express concern, lest the expectations of their patrons and friends at home should not soon be fulfilled. At the latest dates, they had not more than three or four native children under their special domestic care; nor were they certain, that even these would be found eligible as beneficiaries of the sacred and particularly interesting charities, to be applied to the education of heathen children as Christians, and with specified and select names. The most assured confidence, however, may be cherished, that what can be done will be done, for carrying the design into effect; and preventing a disappointment which, both the missionaries and your Committee would most deeply regret.

In the mean time, monies, specially given for this object, will be held in sacred trust; and will not, without the direction or consent of the donors, be otherwise applied. It will be at the option, however, of societies and individuals by whom these donations have been made, to direct their application, as to them shall seem most desirable. Some monies, originally intended for this specific application at Bombay, have already, by direction of the donors, been transferred, for the same purpose to Ceylon, where children can be obtained with less difficulty, and supported at less expense. And your Committee beg to commend it to generous consideration, that only twice the sum requisite for educating a heathen child in a missionary family at Bombay, would be sufficient for the support of a school there of forty or fifty heathen children; and to the establishment of schools to any extent, for which funds shall be supplied, no obstacle is likely to be found.

In two years the schools of this mission have increased in number from four to twenty-five; and the pupils in an equal ratio. Let the present number in these schools be taken at a thousand;—let the increase henceforward be only at the rate of doubling in five years;—and let five years be allowed, as the average term of the continuance of the same pupils at the schools;—and, in twenty-five years from this time, *thirty-one thousand* heathen children will have been instructed, and issued from the schools,—and at the close of this period the number of schools will be 640, and the number of pupils in them 32,000.

Considering the wide extent of the field now opened, and the continually increasing facilities and advantages afforded, these estimates will be regarded as quite moderate. But even these supply a basis for expanded hope, and open prospects on which the benevolent mind will delight to dwell.

Slender as the probability may be, that adult Hindoos, and especially such as are advanced in years, will be turned from their vanities unto the living God; it surely is in no degree improbable, that Hindoo children, brought early under a course of Christian instruction, taught and accustomed daily to read the Holy Scriptures, and impressed with the precepts and doctrines and counsels and exhortations of the gospel—will learn to see, to despise, and to abhor the hideous absurdity, deformity, sottishness, and impurity of the Hindoo system; will become advocates for the religion of Christ; and, by the grace of God accompanying the means of his own appointment, many of them be made devoted and exemplary disciples.—Thirty thousand children, not only themselves instructed, but carrying the Bible into as many, or nearly as many, heathen families, and reading it to their parents, and brothers and sisters, and connections, and acquaintances, will do much, even in their early years, for diffusing the light of divine truth. When attained to riper age, their activity, their influence, and their impressions upon the mass of population, with which they are intermixed, will be proportionably increased. Not a few of them may become not only heads of families, but teachers of schools,—and teachers too, possessed of much better qualifications than can now be obtained. And some of them may be catechists, and preachers,—regularly engaged, and efficient helpers in the missionary work.

Meanwhile, the other parts of the system will be advancing. The missionaries, in their circuits, will preach the gospel directly to many thousands of heathen people, and distribute the Scriptures and other books and tracts, and cause them to be distributed, throughout cities and districts and provinces, containing millions.

But the system is not to cease its operations in twenty-five years. It will then have gathered strength, augmented its resources, and multiplied its facilities and advantages, for extended and more effective operations.

CEYLON.—At the last anniversary, our hearts were afflicted with mournful anticipations, respecting two of the brethren of this mission. Those anticipations were but too sure.

The Report, then made, left Messrs. Warren and Richards, the last of February, 1818, at Colombo, where they had been for several weeks, retired from their labors, and in quest of health, dubious as to the issue. There every attention, with generous hospitality and Christian kindness could prompt, was bestowed upon them; and various expedients were proposed for their benefit; until at length, in the latter part of April, they embarked for the Cape of Good Hope. Of this measure, Messrs. Meigs and Poor, in a joint letter, written about a month afterwards, give the following particular and satisfactory account.

"As sending our brethren to the Cape, was a measure necessarily attended with considerable expense, we deem it important to state to you definitely the reasons of our conduct; and, in doing this, it will be necessary to give a concise history of the business. The last attack which brother Warren experienced of bleeding from his lungs, was so severe and reduced him so low, that we greatly feared he would never be able to be removed from Colombo. We had strong desires, that, if possible, he might be removed to this place, and spend his last days with his missionary brethren and sisters. But, for a long time, it appeared to those about him, that, on account of the great weakness and irritability of his lungs, it would be highly imprudent to attempt to remove him.

"In the forepart of March, brother Richards, who had been at Colombo for some time, found an opportunity of engaging a passage in a small vessel, that was going the circuit of the island; and in this he first came to Jaffna, where he arrived on the 15th of the same month. While brother Richards remained here, a letter arrived at Colombo, enclosing a certificate from the two principal physicians at that place, who attended brother Warren, very strongly recommending, that he should take a passage to the Cape of Good Hope: and, on account of the need he would have of a physician, and the great benefit, which brother Richards would,

28

in all probability, experience by the voyage, it was thought best that he should accompany brother Warren.

"When the subject came before us at our meeting, we had many doubts, as to the propriety of the measure.—After much deliberation and prayer, however, we came to the following conclusion:—That it was expedient for brother Richards to return immediately to Colombo, and not to prosecute his voyage round the island. If, after his arrival at that place, all things appeared favorable for their going, they had our permission to go. We also concluded, that brother Richards must be the judge, whether all things were favorable or not, after knowing our opinion and feelings on the subject. We had, however, but faint expectations that our brethren would go. We thought it hardly probable, that a good opportunity would be presented, as vessels would not come to Colombo, after the middle of May. We feared that brother Warren's health would be such as to render it inadmissible to attempt to remove him to the vessel. We did not know, that our funds would be sufficient to meet the expense, without very much curtailing our missionary operations here. All these difficulties were in the providence of God to be removed, before they could go, as it will appear in the sequel that they were.

"Soon after brother Richards' arrival at Colombo, the weather there became suddenly cooler, and brother Warren's health was evidently much benefitted by the change. The physicians had before given their opinion, that he ought to be removed to a cooler climate, that he might recover strength. They now urged this as an additional reason why he should go to the Cape, in preference to any part of India.

"The venerable Archdeacon Twisleton was so kind, as to offer to write to the governor, then in Candy, to request, that a free passage might be granted to our brethren on board one of the government transports, which was expected shortly from the coast, and would then sail immediately to the Cape. The request was very generously complied with by his excellency, governor Brownrigg. Our brethren, however, were to find their own provisions for the voyage. We are informed, that brother Richards spent much time in conversation with brother Warren, on the subject, and particularly with his physicians. He found brother Warren very desirous to go. He entertained a strong persuasion, that a voyage to the Cape and back again, would be the means, under God, of restoring him to a comfortable degree of health; and he had a strong desire to live that he might do something for the heathen. His physicians, also, concurred in the same opinion, respecting the probable benefit to be experienced from the voyage. In conversation with brother Richards they stated distinctly, that, in their opinion, there was a great degree of probability, that the voyage would be the means of so far restoring brother Warren to health, that he might be useful in the mission for some years, although they did not think he would ever again be able to preach. After this opinion was given, brother Richards said, that he felt it to be his duty to advise brother Warren to go. All the circumstances appeared to him favorable. The opportunity was a very good one. The expense would not be very great: and brother Warren's health was so much better, that it was thought proper to attempt to remove him to the vessel.

"On the return of the two transports, they were offered their choice of the one, in which they would sail. After brother Richards and brother

Chater had been on board of both, they chose the Regalia   Every thing
on board was found convenient for the voyage.   The captain was a very
agreeable and obliging man, and the ship, in which they were to sail,
almost empty.   As the rules of the ship would not permit them to furnish
their own provisions, the captain agreed to furnish them with every thing
necessary, for thirty-five pounds each, which was considered at Colombo
to be very reasonable.

"On Saturday, April 25th, they attempted to remove brother Warren
to the ship, and succeeded beyond their expectations.   When he arrived
at the wharf, however, he had symptoms of bleeding from the lungs; but
soon after he was put on board, these symptoms subsided; and before
brother Chater left them in the evening, brother Warren was quite comfortable.   At eight o'clock the next morning, the transports set sail with
a fair wind, and proceeded on their voyage "

For the greater part of their voyage, as appears by a letter written by
Mr Richards, after their arrival at the Cape, the weather was very favorable; and the health of both the brethren, particularly of Mr. Warren,
was so much recruited, as to afford hope of its being in a good measure
restored.   These propitious circumstances continued, until they came in
sight of land, and expected to be in port at the Cape in about two days.
The scene was changed.   They encountered heavy gales,—were driven
out to sea,—and for a fortnight were tossed upon the waves in cold and
boisterous weather.   They landed at Simon's Bay in the forepart of July,
and were conveyed thence to Cape Town, on the 14th of the same
month   Both of them had taken severe cold, and their health was much
depressed.

They were received at Cape Town with distinguished kindness, and
particularly in the Rev. George Thom, missionary there from the London
Missionary Society, they found a friend and a brother, who, by his assiduous attentions, conferred great obligations upon them and upon their
patrons and friends.   Your Committee feel a satisfaction of no ordinary
kind in recording the following passages of a letter to the Corresponding
Secretary, written by Mr. Thom, at the instance of the brethren, four
days after their arrival.

"I cannot describe to you the pain I have felt on seeing these dear
brethren—pain, indeed, of a different kind from what some of us have
of late been called to experience in Africa.   Though worn down by disease, particularly Mr. Warren,—yet the heart is on the right object.   "If
I am so ill," says Mr. Warren, "that it would be a great risk to undertake another voyage, then let me die in the blessed work."   Mr. Richards seems to afford some hope of recovery; but the three medical gentlemen, who have met to consider their case, say they can hold out but
little hope of the recovery of Mr. Warren.   Both are in a consumption.

"We have provided them a lodging at the most reasonable rate, and I
shall do my utmost in their behalf.   Permission has been granted by the
colonial Government for their residence; and several of our pious friends
express great sympathy on their account.

"The trials, to which your Board have been called, have been uncommon, but not so great as others: and the painful trial in the present instance of two holy and prudent brethren, being driven by disease from
the sphere of their missionary labors, will, no doubt, be deeply felt; and,

if it should please our Lord and Master to remove them from his church on earth, great will be the affliction. One thing gives me infinite delight, to behold the dear brethren entirely resigned to the will of their heavenly Father, and with comfortable views of their interest in his love

"The Rev. archdeacon Twistleton of Colombo, says, in his letter of introduction to me, 'The American missionaries, Messrs. Richards and Warren, I recommend to your brotherly love. Men of more amiable manners and purer piety I never saw! to these qualities may be added others, amongst which are gratitude, discretion, and benevolence. May it please the Eternal God to restore them to health and renewed exertion in his service.' For this testimony the Board will give God praise."

This devout assurance Mr. Thom might well express. Such a testimony from archdeacon Twistleton, so well known to this Board, and to the Christian community in this country, for his many acts of favor to our beloved missionaries, and to the general cause of missions, cannot fail to excite gratitude to the adorable Fountain of all good.

In about three weeks after the date of Mr. Thom's letter, on the 11th of August, Mr. Warren rested from his labors and sufferings.

The missionary course of this lamented servant of the Lord Jesus, short as it pleased Sovereign Goodness it should be, was marked with celestial radiance. His brethren, who were associated with him in the scenes of his toils and trials, bear united and most affectionate testimony to his eminent and uniform devotedness to the holy cause,—his ardent, yet benign and well directed zeal,—his alacrity and diligence in labors, —his patience and cheerful equanimity in sufferings,—his wisdom in counsel and prudence in action,—his kindness of disposition, his heavenly mindedness, and his general excellence of character. During his lengthened illness, his exemplary resignation, his sweet serenity of mind, and his heavenly conversation were in a high degree edifying, and inspiring. His last days and closing scene, as described by his afflicted friend and companion, Mr. Richards, were such, as this Board and all the friends of the cause would wish those of every missionary to be·—marked with a lively and steadfast confidence in the Lord Jesus,—solaced with a sacred and cheering enjoyment of the divine presence and love,—and brightened with visions, not fantastic, of the glories of immortality.

His flesh rests in hope at no great distance from that of Mrs. Newell; his spirit, we cannot doubt, is with hers, and with those of the apostles and prophets, and all the multitude of the redeemed, before the throne of God and the Lamb.—To the Father of mercies, and God of all grace, everlasting thanks are due, for such examples of living and dying,—such seals to the missionary cause.

Mr. Richards, after burying his friend, remained at the Cape, with no very material alterations in his case, until the 25th of November, when, not finding an opportunity for a direct return to Ceylon, he embarked for Madras,—hoping that, in no long time, he might thence get back to his wife and his brethren at the seat of the mission. His letters, written at the time, breathe a spirit eminently Christian.

"On the whole," he says, "I think the opportunity a very good one. The Lord is always exceedingly kind to me, and I desire to be thankful, and to make mention of his unspeakable mercy. Though he has been trying me with afflictions ever since I landed in Ceylon, he has tried me more with mercies. I think I can truly say, I find it good to be afflicted."—"I do not expect to recover from this sickness; but think it possible that I may live many months. I have a desire to return to Ceylon, that I may die on missionary ground, and in the bosom of my friends.—As I draw nearer the grave, my hope of salvation through the atonement of Christ becomes stronger, and my views of heaven become more and more pleasant."

The latest letters from Ceylon make mention, that intelligence had just been received of Mr. Richards' arrival at Madras, in much the same state of health, as when he left the Cape.*—He is in the hand of his Divine Master, the sovereign and gracious, and all-sufficient Lord of missions. Living or dying he is safe; and the cause, to which his heart has been so evidently devoted, will be advanced.

Our Ceylon mission, thus afflicted and weakened, has been regarded with deep sympathy and concern. The purpose of your Committee, as expressed at the last annual meeting, to use all diligence in strengthening the mission, and all care to prevent a failure of its hopes, has not been dormant.

Immediately after the meeting, the resolution was decisively taken to send more missionaries to Ceylon; and Messrs, Miron Winslow, Levi Spaulding and Henry Woodward, were appointed for the service.

On the 4th of November, at the Tabernacle Church in Salem, the individuals now named, and Mr. Pliny Fisk, were publicly set apart for the service of God in the Gospel of his Son among the heathen, by solemn ordination. In impressive tokens of the divine presence;—in a deep felt interest in the holy cause;—in a lively and exalted participation in the appropriate services; in union of sentiment and feeling, and fellowship in the breaking of bread,—the occasion was equal to any, which your Committee had ever the privilege to witness.

The hope was entertained, that the three brethren designated for Ceylon, might be embarked in a few weeks after their ordination, and preparations for the purpose were actively put forward. No opportunity, however, was offered for conveyance to the field of their labors, until after the lapse of the winter and spring.

The delay was irksome; but Providence had a kind intention. Just in season to go at the time finally fixed upon, yet not without the necessity of great despatch in preparation, John Scudder, M. D. a young physician of good professional reputation and practice in the city of New-York, and of well established Christian character, after having long deliberated on the subject, came to the determination to make a sacrifice of his worldly prospects, and of all that could attach him to his native country, for the benefit of the heathen, and the glory of Christ. Being apprised of the expected departure of the three waiting missionaries, he made a solemn offer of himself, his wife and child, to be sent with them to Ceylon.

Dr. Scudder had for several years entertained serious thoughts of the ministry; had addicted himself to theological reading and study; and been accustomed to take a part in social religious exercises. It would, therefore, accord with his feelings and desires, to prosecute sacred studies,

---

* Since this Report was made, a letter has been received from Bombay, which mentions the arrival of Mr. R. at the seat of the mission in Ceylon.

enjoying the aid of the brethren with whom he might be associated, during his passage and after his arrival, until it should be deemed proper for him to receive ordination; and, in the mean time, and ever afterwards, to hold his medical science and skill sacredly devoted, and to be employed as opportunity should be afforded, for the benevolent purposes of the mission.

Desirable as it was, that the deeply deplored breach, made by the removal of Mr. Warren from the mission, from its hospital, and from the miserable multitudes to whom his medical practice promised to open the most hopeful access for the Gospel, should be supplied; your Committee could not but regard the offer of Dr. Scudder, as signally providential. His testimonials were ample and satisfactory; and he was gratefully accepted.

On the 8th of June, the three ordained missionaries, and the beloved physician, with their wives, having previously received the instructions, and the affectionate counsels and exhortations of the Committee, embarked at Boston, on board the brig Indus, bound to Calcutta, but engaged provisionally to touch at Ceylon. It was a scene of sacred and melting tenderness; and while the parting hymn was sung, and the valedictory prayer was offered,—devoutly commending them to the grace of God for the holy and arduous service to which they were devoted,— a numerous assemblage of friends and spectators attested the deep sympathy and interest, with which their hearts were affected, by many tears. It may be hoped, that the fervent desires of many hearts are in gracious remembrance with Him, who rules the elements; and that within three or four weeks from this time, a scene scarcely less tender,—a scene not of parting but of meeting,—will be enjoyed in Ceylon.

The circumstances and operations of the mission at Ceylon are considerably different from those at Bombay. As there has been extant for many years a good translation of the Scriptures into the Tamul or Malabarian, the common language of the northern part of Ceylon, where the mission is established; our missionaries there have no occasion to employ themselves in making a translation,—an arduous work which occupies no inconsiderable portion of the time and laborious attention of our Bombay mission. Nor have they yet at Ceylon got the printing establishment into operation. They have a press and types, both Tamul and English,—and apparatus and paper; and in no long time, it is hoped, will have a sufficiency of hands for commencing the printing of the Scriptures and other books and tracts. An edition of the Tamul Scriptures is greatly needed; as are also other books for their schools, for distribution, and the various purposes of the mission.

The labors of this mission have consisted chiefly, hitherto, in preaching to the people, establishing and superintending schools, and instructing children in the family; with the necessary preparations for these important departments of labor.

At the three stations of the Bombay Mission, the brethren are in the midst of large cities, comprising in all not less than two hundred thousand souls; and throughout which they preach and distribute books and tracts to the people in the streets, at their houses and temples, and different places of resort, as opportunities are afforded,—but without the satisfaction and advantage of stated places and regular assemblies. The

Ceylon mission is in a country of villages, where the people, though not thinly scattered, are yet very differently situated from those in crowded cities In general, they are less deeply immersed in the darkness and corruptions of paganism, and have more activity of intellect, more knowledge, and more disposition to listen and inquire, than the mass of the Hindoos of Bombay.

Besides Tillipally and Batticotta, the two stations of the mission, the brethren have six other large parishes under their particular care Mallagum, Milettee, and Panditeripo, belonging to the Tillipally station; and Changane, Oodooville, and Manepy, belonging to the station of Batticotta.

In these parishes, as formerly reported, there are ancient church buildings and glebes, which our missionaries have been permitted to occupy, and which, after considerable expense in repairs, are of great advantage to the mission.   And within these parishes chiefly, though not solely, the brethren have bestowed their labors and attentions; making their circuits from week to week, for preaching, visiting the schools, and the various purposes of the mission.

For a considerable time, they could of course preach to the native people only by interpreters; but now, for more than a year, both Mr. Poor and Mr. Meigs have been able to preach in the language of the country.

The instruction of children, however, has been with them, from the beginning, an object of very earnest attention. They early took the resolution to establish schools in all the parishes under their care, the superintendence of which should be assigned in divisions to the several brethren of the mission; and to extend the system to as great an amplitude, as they should find themselves able.   But their operations have been retarded by the afflictive dispensations towards Messrs. Warren and Richards.

In a joint letter, bearing date May 24, 1818, Messrs. Meigs and Poor say:

"Our schools, for reasons which we have before mentioned, are not so numerous as we hoped they would be before this time. But still we are making advances in this good work. The school at Tillipally is in a flourishing state, and consists of forty boys. Twelve of these brother Poor has taken from their parents, and they are supported at the expense of the mission They are making very good progress, both in Tamul and English. The school at Panditeripo, between three and four miles west of Tillipally, established and superintended by Mr. Poor, consists of 36 boys.   The school at Batticotta consists at present of 40 boys, since we wrote last, it has been, for a time, much less than that. Many boys will attend the school for one, two, or three months, and then be taken away by their parents for various reasons; but principally, because they need them to labor. This is indeed a trial, but one which we must expect to meet often, till these people have learned the value of an education.

"About the middle of April, brother Meigs opened a school in another part of Batticotta, where he goes to preach every Sabbath afternoon, which already consists of 30 fine boys, and is almost every day increasing. He has now also opened a school in Changane, the next parish north of Batticotta. This school has been opened a fortnight, and consists of upwards of 30 boys. The whole number of boys, in the schools superintended by brother Meigs, is 100; those of brother Poor 76; in all 176 boys."

Only six months after this, in his journal of November, Mr. Poor states·

"Near our house is a heathen school, which has been taught many years by a man now considerably advanced in age. He has in his school about thirty boys, the children of stout heathens, who would not send them to this place. I have lately several times visited the school, and become acquainted with the master and boys. This evening, the master came to make proposals for putting the school under my superintendence. I agreed to give him four rix dollars a month, on condition, that he should instruct thirty boys, and that I should have the direction of their studies. He is doubtless influenced to do this by the hope of obtaining one dollar a month; and the parents consent to it, on condition that they shall make him no compensation for his services. These boys have proceeded further in their studies, than those who have hitherto been received into my schools. This is the eighth school connected with this station. As these schools are in six different parishes, it would be impossible for me properly to superintend them, had I not the assistance of Maleappa, who is at Mallagum, and of my interpreter. At this time, my schools are well attended. The whole number of boys in the eight schools is nearly four hundred."

These statements shew a rapid and very animating increase. The total number of pupils under the care of Mr. Meigs at this time, is not in any of the communications so definitely given. In September, however, two months earlier, he had five schools—four in Batticotta and one at Changane; and was intending soon to establish others in Manepy and Oodooville.

It may be pretty safely estimated, that at the close of the year 1818, the period to which the present Report brings down the history of the mission, the total number of pupils in the schools belonging to the two stations, was about seven hundred.

Highly gratifying, also, is the success in obtaining children to be held under the special care of the missionaries, and brought up in the nurture and admonition of the Lord, in their families. In Mr. Poor's there were, at the last dates, twenty-four native boys; to whom, or the most of whom, select names were given, denoting them as the beneficiaries, respectively, of particular societies or individuals in this country; and of whom, as to their minds, their behavior, and their improvement, very pleasing accounts are given. The number in Mr. Meigs's family is not stated; but would seem, from facts and circumstances incidentally mentioned, to be considerable, and fast increasing.

In this place, the following brief extracts from the journals and letters of Messrs. Meigs and Poor, may be interesting to the Board, as they will shew, in varied lights, the state and labors, the spirit and prospects of the mission.

In the journal of the Batticotta station, Mr. Meigs writes·

"Sabbath, June 8, 1818. The number of our boys is fast increasing on the Sabbath. To-day 106 were present, besides 30 other persons."

"June 29. A pleasant Sabbath. One hundred and thirty boys were present, besides a goodly number of men."

"Aug. 26. After much delay, and many difficulties, have this day commenced boarding heathen boys, in the cook house, which I have erected for them. I commenced with five boys. This is an important day in the history of this mission.—the commencement, I hope, of much good to these poor heathen boys. It will, however, greatly increase our cares. We expect to meet many trials in pursuing this object.

"One of my neighbors, who is a strong heathen, whose boy attends the day school, says frequently in a triumphant tone, 'When you can persuade four boys of good caste from Batticotta, to come and live with you, I will then give you my boy,' meaning to assert strongly, the great improbability, if not impossibility, of my getting them. I have two, however, from Batticotta already, besides the one abovementioned, whose relatives by threats prevented him from coming. The triumph of this man, I trust, will be short."

"Sept. 5 A number more of boys have applied to be received into the school and supported. When I am not previously acquainted with the boys, I take them a few days upon trial, before I make a final agreement with their parents. It is highly gratifying to Christian feelings, to witness the change that is made in the appearance of these boys, in a few days. We give them a plain cloth, of a yard and a half or two yards in length, according to their size, to cover them. We give them plain food, as much as they need. This change in their circumstances not only surprisingly alters the appearance of the boys, but also increases the vigor of their minds and bodies.

"It has always been principally to the poor, that the gospel is preached. So it is among this people. It is from this class that we must look for boys to be supported and educated in our families. The rich are usually unwilling to give us their sons; and even if they were willing, we should not think it expedient to take them; for they commonly give us much trouble by their complaints about their food and clothing. We greatly prefer poor boys on this account; and even orphans, when we can obtain them. Many, who are brought here, are destitute of one or both their parents; and on this account, as also on account of their poverty, are objects of charity.

"Sept. 23. Christian David came out to Batticotta to spend the day with us and preach to the people. In the morning, I collected the boys from my four schools in Batticotta. Two of these have been but recently opened, and contain but few boys There were present, however, from these four schools, 120 boys. Other people assembled, which made the number 200. Our large room was well filled. The Changane school was not called here, as we had made an appointment to go to that place and preach in the school-house After service was ended at Batticotta, we accordingly went thither, and held public worship. The school at Changane consisted of 77 boys, of whom 60 were present. In all, we had 115 hearers. The people had covered the floor of the school-house with mats, and placed chairs for us to sit in, covered with white cloth We then visited a family of Roman Catholics in the neighborhood, and partook of some refreshment in the native style, and returned home well pleased with our excursion."

29

A daughter of Christian David, who is about 15 years of age, is living with us for the purpose of making further progress in English studies. She is a very amiable young woman.

"*Oct.* 3. Have commenced a new plan with my schoolmasters, which is, to assemble them all on Saturday afternoon, to hear a report of their schools, and to communicate to them religious instruction. They had before been accustomed to come on Sabbath evening. But as some of them live at a considerable distance, this is often found inconvenient. It is very important, that those who are employed to teach others, should themselves be instructed.—

"12th. Yesterday attended the communion at Tillipally: preached in Tamul to 300 people, and baptized the infant son of brother Poor. It was a very interesting day.

"19. The Rev. Messrs. Squance, Gogerly, Knight, and Christian David, came here to spend the day. Mr. David preached to a good audience of the natives.

"25th. It is pleasant to witness the change which is gradually effected, in some instances, in the minds of the natives. Their prejudices, we may expect, will by degrees wear away. The man mentioned above, who boasted that we should never be able to get four boys of good caste from Batticotta to eat with us, is an instance to illustrate this remark. Though a very strong heathen, and violently opposed to the truth, yet he spends the greatest part of his time at our house. His son is a lovely boy, and the father is often in the school and very diligent in teaching him. He is almost always present at our morning worship in Tamul, and has not been absent from meeting on the Sabbath for a long time, and always gives good attention. Yet when conversed with on the subject of religion, he shews a very strong attachment to his own superstitions; though he will admit, that much we tell him of the Christian religion is good and true. For some days past, he has permitted his son to stay here through the night, and sleep with my boys. The lad usually goes also to the cook house with the others, when they take their meals, though he does not eat with them. To-day the man told Mrs. Meigs, that we had succeeded in getting more than four boys, and asked her if she did not want his son? She told him, no; for she expected we should be able to take as many *poor* boys, as we had money to support. He then told her, that she might have his son, if she wanted him,—that he might stay here and sleep with the other boys, and learn such things as we wished him to learn; only, as he lived so near us, it was better for the boy to take his meals at home. I should not be surprised, if, in a few days, he should propose to have his son eat with the other boys."

The next are notices by Mr. Poor, in the journal of Tillipally.

"June 11th. Visited the school at Milette for the first time. Found thirty-three boys present, five of whom were able to read on the olla. Most of the others are learning the Tamul alphabet. The head man of the parish, and several others, parents of the school boys, were present, to whom I explained the object of my coming into the country, and prayed with them. Their curiosity was considerably excited, because I spoke to them in Tamul. Though I spoke with a stammering tongue, more attention appears to have been excited to what I said, than when I speak by an interpreter.

"July 1. Our weekly prayer meetings on Wednesday evenings have become more interesting of late, in consequence of my having requested all the schoolmasters connected with this station to attend, that they may give to me, and to each other, some account of their schools, and receive instructions and directions from me.

"July 6. I have this day finished two school houses, which I have been building on the church land at Mallagum. One is for a school, which was commenced a few weeks ago, and the other is for Franciscus Maleappa to live in. We regard Maleappa, agreeably to his own and his father's wishes, as one permanently connected with our mission, and consider ourselves obliged to give him a competent support, so long as his conduct is worthy of his station. At present, he receives 30 rix dollars* per month. As he dresses in the European style, his expenses are much greater, than they would have been, if he had retained his native dress.

"That the Committee may have a correct idea of every branch of our mission, it is necessary to give some further account of Maleappa. He is a native of Malabar, about 20 years of age, the son of a native preacher, supported by government at Negombo. He was one or two years in the government school at Jaffnapatam, under the care of the Rev. C. David. He attended the school taught by us, during the six months we were at Colombo. Since brother Warren and I came to Tillipally, he has served us as an interpreter, and pursued his studies with reference to his becoming a catechist. He has a facility in speaking to the people on those topics, both in the Christian and heathen religion, which are most important to be insisted on; and he appears to take a delight in so doing.

"Sept. 9. To excite among the people attention to the school, I have this day held a public examination of the boys in the church. The effect appears to have been good, both on the parents and children.

"Nov. 20. Eight girls usually attend our female school during the week, and on the Sabbath about a dozen girls attend and recite the catechism. About the same number of women attend the church."

In their joint letter of May 24th of the last year, the brethren say,

"We are highly gratified with your liberality and that of the Christian public, in regard to schools. The expense of native schools is a mere trifle. For the erection of a suitable building, in the first place, we must pay about 16 dollars; this will answer very well to preach in to the people, when there is no better building. Such teachers as the country affords, who only teach Tamul, may be obtained for $1,50 per month. To those who have sufficient education to teach English as well as Tamul, we must give from 4 to 8 dollars a month.

"The expense of supporting boys in our families, is also very small. We think we may safely say, that with proper economy, a boy from 6 to 12 or 14 years of age, may be fed and clothed in the native style, for one Spanish dollar a month, or twelve dollars a year. Older boys will require a little more, principally because their dress must be a little more expensive. The dress of the native children, and even of the men generally, is of the most simple kind. It consists merely of a piece of plain India cotton, of one yard in width, and two or two and a half in

---

* Equal to about eight Spanish dollars.

length, wound round the person. From the statement which we have made respecting the education and support of children, you will see that we have here an opportunity of doing great good at a comparatively small expense. We have no doubt, that many benevolent individuals, of both sexes, will be found in our native land, who will rejoice in the opportunity of contributing the small sum of 12 dollars annually, if by that means they may rescue a heathen youth, of promising talents, from the miserable condition of idolaters, and place him in a missionary family, where he will possess many of the advantages of being educated, which are enjoyed in a Christian land. In what manner can they dispose of this sum to better advantage? In what fund can they vest it where it will yield greater profit? What pure and exalted pleasure will it afford them, in the day of judgment, to meet some of these heathen children, emancipated from their miserable condition, and made happy forever, through their liberality. Surely the object is great enough to warrant the sacrifice necessary to obtain it. Any individual or society, contributing this sum for the support of a boy, may select a name for him. We regret exceedingly, that we cannot educate female children, as well as male. If we inquire of the natives, why they do not teach their girls to read, their only reply is, 'We have no such custom in our country.' "

To the extracts now given, your Committee will add only the following, from the latest joint letter, bearing date Oct. 16, 1818.

After several particular acknowledgments of donations from societies and individuals, for the education of children in their families, the brethren proceed to say,—

"You, Dear Sir, and the other members of the Board, doubtless participate in our feelings of gratitude towards those, who are disposed to assist the cause, in a manner so suited to our wants, and so directly calculated to strengthen and encourage us in our work. It can hardly be conceived, by persons in our native country, how great is the difference between the boys, generally, in this heathen land, and those whom we have taken, and upon whom we expend one dollar per month. Their manners, dress, mode of living, as well as the state of their minds, are essentially benefitted. Verily the blessing of them, who are ready to perish, will come upon those, who, with a right spirit, give but a mere trifle for the support of heathen boys.

"We have often expressed to you our conviction, that the most effectual means that can be used, for extending and perpetuating a knowledge of Christianity among the heathen, is, that of training up native preachers, who may go forth properly qualified to preach to their countrymen. It is with reference to this, that the object of taking children into our families appears to be of primary importance; and presents powerful motives to us, for using special exertions with those whom we have taken.

"We have before mentioned Franciscus Melcappa, a native of the country, who for a year and a half served the brethren at Tillipally as an interpreter. About four months ago he was stationed at Mallagum, an adjoining parish, on the south of Tillipally. He there instructs a few boys in English, attends to the moral instruction of the Tamul school established in that parish, reads to the people on the Sabbath, and assists in superintending two other schools in that vicinity. We indulge a hope, that he will be of considerable service to our mission.

"We trust, Dear Sir, we understand something of the nature of those feelings, which dictated the closing injunction of your last letter to us 'Forget not that your great concern is to preach the Gospel.' Could we attend to this duty with apostolic zeal, we should act agreeably to our convictions of duty. We wish to have more deeply impressed upon our minds, the truth, that *it hath pleased God by the foolishness of preaching, to save them that believe.*

"It is our practice to preach twice on the Sabbath; once in the morning at our station, and in the evening at some places in our parish. We occasionally preach in other parishes, where our schools are established. Two evenings in the week we give religious instruction to such as are inclined to attend at our houses. During the week we converse more or less with the people, as our other avocations will permit."

These extracts afford ample evidence, that the brethren of this mission have been laborious in their work, and much reason to hope that their zealous labors will not be in vain in the Lord. When joined by those, who are now on their passage, the mission will be strengthened, its schools may be multiplied, and its operations extended.

Supyen, the interesting youth noticed at some length in the Report of the last year, was, at the time of the latest dates, upon the coast of the neighboring peninsula, still suffering from persecution, but apparently steadfast in the faith. Of Maleappa it may reasonably be hoped, that he will not only prove himself to have been made a partaker of the grace of the Gospel, but also be a helper to the mission and a blessing to the heathen. Mention is made, in the letters and journals, of one or two others, hopefully turned from darkness unto light; and of a prevailing conviction on the minds of not a few, that their idolatrous system is vanity and a lie.

PALESTINE.—As this mission is intended for the same great quarter of the globe, in which the two already reported are established, it seemed proper to introduce it in immediate connexion with them: though in chronological order this is not its place.

If the countries of Southern Asia are highly interesting to Christian benevolence, and have strong claims upon Christian commiseration, on account of the hundreds of millions of human beings immersed in the deepest corruption and wretchedness; the countries of Western Asia, though less populous, are in other respects not less interesting, nor do they present less powerful claims. These were the scenes of those great transactions and events, which involved the destinies of mankind of all ages and all nations, for time and eternity; the creation of the progenitors of our race—the beginnings of the sciences and arts, and of civil and political institutions—the fatal transgression, which "brought death into the world and all our woe"—the successive revelations of Heaven, with all their attestations, their light and their blessings—the incarnation, labors and agonies of the Son of God, for the recovery of *that which was lost*—and the first exhibition of that mighty and gracious power, which is to bow the world to his sceptre, and fill the mansions of immortality with his people. They have since been the scenes of direful changes; and the monuments of all their glory have long lain buried in dismal ruins. —But the word of Jehovah abideth forever, and that word gives promise of other changes there—changes to be followed by a radiance of glory, which shall enlighten all lands.

In Palestine, Syria, the Provinces of Asia Minor, Armenia, Georgia and Persia, though Mohammedan countries, there are many thousands of Jews, and many thousands of Christians, at least in name. But the whole mingled population is in a state of deplorable ignorance and degradation,—destitute of the means of divine knowledge, and bewildered with vain imaginations and strong delusions.

It is to be hoped, however, that among the Christians there, of various denominations, some might be found, who are alive in Christ Jesus; and who, were proper means employed for their excitement, improvement, and help, might be roused from their slumbers, become active in doing good, and shine as lights in those darkened regions. It is indeed to be hoped, that no small part of those, who bear the Christian name, would willingly and gladly receive the Bible into their houses, and do something towards imparting the heavenly treasure, as opportunities should be afforded, to the Jews, Mohammedans, and Pagans; and, dispersed as they are, among the different nations, they might do much; at least might afford many and important facilities and advantages for carrying into effect the expanding desires of benevolence.

To the Jews we and all Christians are indebted, under Divine Providence, for the Oracles of God, and all the blessings by which we are distinguished from heathen nations. Long have they been an awful monument to the world of the sovereignty of God, under the tremendous curse so terribly imprecated, when the blood of the Lord of life and glory was demanded. But their dereliction is not to be perpetual. *They are beloved for the fathers' sakes; and there shall come a Deliverer out of Zion, and shall turn away ungodliness from Jacob.*

It is not to be forgotten, however, that it is *through our* MERCY,—by means of the benevolent prayers, and sacrifices and labors of Christians for their restoration,—*that they are to obtain mercy.* And the time seems to have arrived for his mercy to be displayed, and for these means to be employed, in a manner and with an earnestness, suitable to the momentous object. The dispositions recently manifested by the Jews extensively, and the success, which has attended the late attempts, which have been made for gaining their attention to Christianity, together with the more general movements and aspects of the age,—are indications not to be disregarded.

By these, and other kindred considerations, your Committee have long had their mind and heart drawn towards Western Asia, and particularly towards the land of ancient promise, and of present hope. The lights afforded them, for surveying the field, have not been neglected; the circumstances favorable and unfavorable to the contemplated enterprise have been attentively considered; and ten months ago the resolution was taken to send a mission to PALESTINE, as soon as the requisite preparation could conveniently be made.

The Rev. LEVI PARSONS and the Rev. PLINY FISK have been designated for this mission. For several months after their designation they were employed as agents of the Board in different parts of the Union; and being known as missionaries, under appointment for Jerusalem, they excited, in the Christian community extensively a lively interest, which has been marked with distinguished liberality. Lately they have been engaged in particular preparations for the mission, in the expectation of embarking for the Levant before winter

The design is, that they shall go first to Smyrna; and there remain for a longer or shorter time, as circumstances shall render advisable, for the purpose of acquiring more perfectly the requisite languages, and obtaining such information, of various kinds, as will be of importance in their subsequent course. Thence, they are to proceed to Palestine, and there fix their station at Jerusalem, if found practicable and eligible; if not, at such other place, within or without the limits of Judea, as Providence shall indicate.

This whole Board will unite with their Committee, in commending this mission most fervently to the grace of God.

CHEROKEES.—The system of this mission,—its principles, its structure, its operations, and its first results, were so fully exhibited, at our last anniversary, that it cannot be necessary to enter largely into details in the present Report. During the year, the system has been advancing without any noticeable adversity, or abatement of success.

The SCHOOL has been gradually increasing; and, at the end of July, consisted of eighty three children;—fifty males, and thirty three females. Their residence at the mission house appears to have been more constant, than during the preceding year; their behavior not less satisfactory, nor their progress in learning less encouraging.

Some who were taken from the school, and little expected there again, have been returned. Among these are Catharine Brown, and a boy, who had been named Jeremiah Evarts.

In November, the father of Catharine, having resolved to migrate to the Arkansas, and not to be overcome by intreaties and tears, firmly required her to leave the school for the purpose of going with the family. Though to her, as she said "it was more bitter than death," yet she dutifully obeyed, and went home to her father's house. There, as the migration was deferred, she remained about four months; and then to the great joy of herself, and of the mission family, her father brought her back. "She can assign," say the brethren, "no external cause for this change in her father's mind concerning her, but ascribes it to the special providence of God, and in answer to fervent believing prayer. The time for their departure drew near, and she felt that it would not be for the best that she should go; and that God could change the minds of her parents, and make them willing to leave her. That their minds might be thus changed was the subject of her prayer. She had a confidence, particularly one evening, that the Lord would grant her request; and she rose from her knees, with a degree of assurance, that she should be sent back to Brainerd. Returning to the house, and entering the room, where her father and mother were sitting by themselves, he addressed her to the following effect—"We know you feel very bad about leaving the missionaries, and going with us to the Arkansas. We have been talking about it; we pity you; and have concluded that you may go back."

Your Committee feel no ordinary pleasure in recording this signal instance of condescending mercy, for grateful remembrance, and as an earnest, not to be lightly regarded, of good to the beloved individual, and to the favored mission.

In their journal, July 20th, the brethren say: "Three days ago the father of the fine full blooded boy whom we called Jeremiah Evarts, came with Jeremiah and a younger son It is now about ten months since he took Jeremiah home, on a visit, expecting to return him in six weeks.— He remained with us until this morning; saying little, but attentively observing all that was done. This morning he told us, that he wished to leave his two sons with us until they were well learned, and should only want them to go home on a visit once a year: adding that he had been brought up in ignorance himself, and once thought that, as he had but little time to live, he would spend it in idleness, drinking, frolicking, &c.; but finding this to be a bad way, he had left it, and gone to work, which he found a much better way to live. He did not wish his sons to be brought up in the way he had been, and to do as he had done. He was now too old to go to school himself; but he thought, if his sons were instructed, they might teach, and he would be glad to learn from them."

For reasons, which are too obvious to need particular statement, since the number of children has become so great, it has been deemed advisable to separate the females from the males, and to assign to them a house and school by themselves Accordingly, a temporary building has been provided for them, until a better house, soon to be erected, shall be finished, and a separate school for them has been established.

Besides attending every day, during the appointed hours, to their studies in the schools, the pupils, male and female, have constantly their regular hours and allotments of labor, and of various exercises and attentions for their general improvement; and, in all, they acquit themselves in a manner highly satisfactory. Besides the interesting female, who has become so well known to this Board and to the Christian community, other individuals are distinguished, and some of them scarcely less than Catharine, for their amiable dispositions, their excellent faculties, their rapid progress, and their praise-worthy deportment. Altogether, they are a lovely band of youth and children, whom the committee, with heartfelt interest and pleasure, can commend to the affections, the charities, the prayers, and benedictions of this Board and of the Christian public, as having strong claims to kind and liberal patronage, and affording high promise of usefulness among their own people

At the mission-house, the preaching of the gospel, the administration of Christian ordinances, and various exercises and means for religious instruction and improvement, appear to have been continued with life and regularity, and with encouraging success.

Upon the little church, planted in that wilderness, the Spirit of glory and of God still evidently rests. The record in the journal of the mission, for the last day of January, is an interesting memorial.

"Previous to the administration of the Lord's supper, brother Reece offered for baptism an infant and three other children, who till lately have lived with their mother, a woman not now considered as his wife; he having parted from her and left the children with her, before his conversion. When separations of this kind take place, which are frequent among this people, the mother is considered as having the sole right to the children; but, if she please, she can relinquish this right to their father. Since this brother has found the Savior, he has been very desirous of recovering his children, that he may train them up in the way in which they should go. A part of them he obtained, and offered them in baptism some time since. Two of the three oldest offered in baptism at this time, he has lately obtained from their mother; and taken into his family as his own. The oldest of them, the mother will not yet consent to deliver up entirely, but she has agreed, that this daughter shall be educated in the mission-family and school. We therefore thought she might be admitted to baptism.

"With these four children, we also baptized Lydia Lowry, aged about sixteen. She has been in the school about twelve months, and became a hopeful subject of divine grace last summer. For several months, she has been under particular instruction as a candidate for baptism. Her whole deportment, since the apparent change, has been such as to give increasing evidence that it is real and saving. She will now be considered as a candidate for full communion, in all the ordinances and privileges of the church of God.

"A Cherokee woman supposed to be about 70 years of age, (the same mentioned in the Report of the visiting committee last June, as a hopeful convert,) this day put herself under our care, for special instruction, as a candidate for the ordinance of baptism.

"The wilderness and solitary place is glad for them, and the desert blossoms as the rose. Oh how precious are the privileges we enjoy here in this wilderness. We would not change our place and our employment for any thing, short of that eternal rest, which God has prepared for those that love him.

"After baptism was administered to the above-mentioned persons, the professed followers of Christ, consisting of black, red, and white, surrounded the table of our common Lord, and found "a feast of fat things." This day completes twelve months since the first new converts were added to this church; and it now contains 11 adult members and 24 baptized children, beside the mission-family. The Lord hath done great things for us, whereof we are glad."

In June, the aged Cherokee woman above-mentioned, was admitted to full communion, and two female members of the school, one aged 16 and the other 15, were examined and received as candidates for baptism.

In a joint letter, the brethren say; "All, who have been admitted to church privileges, give increasing evidence that their hopes are well founded." They also say;

"There has been so much uniformity in our Sabbath day congregations at Brainerd, for some time past, that we have nothing new worthy of particular notice. They still continue much the same. While there is reason to hope that some are edified every Sabbath, there is reason to fear, that others are hardening more and more. They attend with decency; hear as if they assented to all as true; and yet remain, like many thoughtless hearers in old congregations, unawakened and unconcerned. But, through the power of divine grace, some appear to hear in a different manner. We hope for several, who have not yet publicly professed Christ, that they do indeed receive the truth in love.

"A slave, belonging to one of the old religious men, as their adherents call them, says he should be willing to travel twice as far as at present, for the privilege of such meetings; though he now has to walk ten miles over a very rough and high mountain, and to return the same day.   This man and his wife, of whom also we have some hopes, appear much grieved, that their master is about to remove with them to the Arkansas; because they think they shall no more hear preaching.   He was greatly rejoiced to-day when we told him it was possible, that God would send missionaries there."

Instances are mentioned of persons occasionally coming from a great distance to hear preaching at the mission-house.   Among these one may be noted.   In a tour made by Mr. Hoyt in December, he preached at the house of Catharine Brown's father, and an aged Cherokee woman present was much affected.   In May, this woman came from a distance of 120 miles, "to hear, as she expressed it, more about the Savior."   "It appears," say the brethren, "that soon after her first impression, she sent for Catharine, (who was then at home,) to read and explain the Bible to her, and to pray with her; and before Catharine came away, she told her, she intended to come hither for further instruction; as soon as she could "

Besides the exercises at the mission house, the missionaries, and particularly Mr. Butrick, and Mr. Chamberlin, have made frequent and distant excursions to different parts of the nation, for the purpose of visiting and conversing with the people in their families, and preaching as they should find opportunity.   They appear to have been always, and in all places, kindly and gratefully received; and in many instances have been urgently intreated to repeat their visits.

In several places, also, a strong desire has been expressed to have stated preaching, and the missionaries constantly with them.   In compliance with this desire, in the neighborhood of Mr. Hicks, about 20 miles from Brainerd, regular appointments have been, for most of the year, made and fulfilled, as often as once in a fortnight or three weeks.   The number of hearers has been very considerable; and their attention highly encouraging.   And in other places, where appointments for preaching have been made, appearances have been pleasing and hopeful.

The expenses of our Cherokee establishment have not been light.   A great part, indeed, of the expenses for buildings and for farming and other utensils, has been reimbursed by the government.   But to supply provisions for the mission family, consisting of four missionaries with their wives and children, and eighty children of the natives, besides hired laborers, cannot cost little; and the contingencies of such an establishment must unavoidably be considerable.

The produce of the farm the last year, owing partly to the dryness of the season, and partly to the depredations of unruly and wild animals, was less than had been anticipated, and was consumed in a few months.   And, owing to various causes, some of them transient, and others permanent, great difficulties and some heavy disappointments have been experienced, in obtaining supplies from the white settlements in Tennessee, the nearest in which contracts for supplies have been made, being 60 or 80 miles distant from Brainerd.   A single disappointment the last winter, in the failure of a contract for corn, occasioned partly by the state of the river, was a detriment to the mission of several hundred dollars.

Your Committee have from the first regarded the cultivation of the farm, as an object of high importance. It is important for the purpose of exercising the native boys of the institution in agricultural labors; and of shewing to them and to the nation a sample of a farm under good husbandry, and yielding its products in variety and plenty. And it is important for the purpose of supplying, in the surest and cheapest manner, the principal provisions for the maintenance of the establishment. This last consideration has been urged upon our attention by the facts and circumstances just referred to.

It became, therefore, an object of earnest desire to obtain a man of suitable qualifications, for the skilful and vigorous management of a farm, intended to be enlarged to an ample extent. And it would not fail to be regarded as a particular favor in Providence, that just as the exigence came to be deeply felt, the desire was answered.

About four months ago, Mr. Abijah Conger of Rockaway, N. J. made a sacred offer of himself for the service. In his letter, making the offer, he says, "My wife is a native of Bridgehampton, Long Island We were married in the year 1803; and begun to keep house in the spring of 1804 with nothing but our hands. God has prospered us greatly in the good things of this world, and I hope we both have a treasure laid up in heaven for us. I have a large property here; and had any body told me, two years ago, that I would leave it, and go into the wilderness, I should have thought them beside themselves; as some of my neighbors and friends now do me. But while reading last winter of the difficulty the establishment had to get mechanics &c., the thought struck me, that I ought to go to their assistance. I tried every way to get it out of my mind, but to no purpose, till my sleep left me. I then made my wife acquainted with it; and she said, 'Go and I will go with you.'—I have concluded to offer myself to the Board, to go to Brainerd, and act in the sphere, which the Board shall think me most capable to fill,—provided it is for the furtherance of the Redeemer's Kingdom. My business for fifteen years back has been to manage a large family, consisting of fifteen to more than twenty persons,—most of them grown persons;—besides several families living on my land, that came directly under my care.— My own family consists of seven persons, myself and wife, and five children, two boys and three girls; all remarkably healthy, and well educated according to their age, the oldest fourteen, the youngest two years old,— all trained to industry when out of school."

Mr. Conger is himself about 36 years old,—a Christian of good report; by trade a carpenter, but accustomed to turn his hand to various kinds of business, as carpentry, cabinet-making, coopering, blacksmithing, and farming; all which he has had upon a large scale under his direction. "He has been," says his minister, the Rev. Mr. King, "for ten years past one of the most industrious, and persevering, men in the business of the world, that I ever knew." For six years in his youth, he was a schoolmaster; and for the two last years has been a principal teacher in a Sabbath school.

When the determination of Mr. Conger came to be known, others of kindred spirit connected with him in business, and some of them by family alliance, and whose minds had for some time before been employed on the subject, came to a similar resolution. Messrs John Vail, a farmer, —John Talmage a blacksmith, and John Mott, a carpenter, but all of them more or less, like Mr. Conger, accustomed to different kinds of business,—offered themselves, with very satisfactory recommendations; and were accordingly accepted for the service. Mr. Vail has a family of five children; Mr. Talmage and Mr. Mott are young men recently married.

These four devoted men, have given themselves to the service, on the same principle with the missionaries and assistants now at the stations,—as an engagement for life; consecrating themselves, their faculties, and their earnings, to the sacred and benevolent object of christianizing and civilizing the Aborigines; and expecting no earthly compensation but a comfortable maintenance. Their children, when they come of age, are of course to be held as free in regard to any engagement for the service, as any other persons.

Preparations have been made with all convenient despatch; and the company, well supplied with various mechanical tools, and such household articles as are suitable to take with them,—started from Rockaway, as it is supposed, on Monday of the last week,* travelling with wagons, and expecting to reach Brainerd about the first of November.

The hope is entertained, and with a degree of confidence, that in a short time, by the exercise of husbandry, and the various mechanical trades, in which they are skilled, they will supply the establishment with the principal provisions, requisite for its support, and thus save this Board a heavy expense.

The establishment at Brainerd is regarded by your Committee as a Primary Institution, to serve as a centre of operations for evangelizing and civilizing the Cherokee nation;—to be enlarged and advanced, as means shall be afforded, and as shall be found to be advisable; and to have branches connected with it, in the form of Local Schools, in different parts of the Cherokee country. The local schools, being established in places of densest population, may be attended by children living at home; and a farm, of larger or smaller extent, may yield to it the means of support.

For one school of this kind, a place has been selected, and preparations are now in forwardness. It will be 50 or 60 miles southeasterly from Brainerd, and under the immediate care of Mr. Hall, one of the first assistants of the mission.

This school is established at the earnest desire and solicitation of the natives residing in that neighborhood. Similar solicitations have been made for schools, in other places. And it is a fact of special importance, that a disposition favorable to the general design, and even an ardent desire for schools, is prevailing throughout the nation. Some evidence of this fact will be interesting to the Board.

About the first of November, ten months ago, a council of the nation was held, at which Mr. Hoyt was present. He was received with marked kindness and attention. On the evening before the council was opened, he had a free and lengthened conversation with the aged king and the chiefs, and found them in a most pleasant disposition.

"The king and chiefs," he says, "expressed great satisfaction in the

---

* About the time they were to start Mr. Vail's family was heavily visited with sickness, which detained them until the 27th of the month.

school, and many thanks to those who are engaged for the instruction of their children and people. The king observed, 'It was evidence of great love to be willing to teach and feed so many children without pay· and he did not doubt it would be greatly to the benefit of the nation; for though bad men could do more mischief when learned, the good would be much more useful; and he knew we taught the children to be good, and hoped many of them would follow our instructions.' "

The next day, when the council was in session, Mr. Hoyt was admitted to an audience, and made a talk to them; stating the intentions and objects of the mission, and expressing the feelings and desires of the missionaries, and of their patrons and friends.

"I was heard," he says, "with the most fixed attention; and have reason to believe, from the starting tear on every side, that the warm feelings of brother Hicks imparted an affecting pathos to the interpretation, which was given sentence by sentence as I spoke. I continued my discourse much longer than was at first intended; being encouraged to do so from my own feelings, and the appearance of the audience.

"When I had taken my seat, a few words passed between the king and his chiefs, in their own language; after which the king said, they thanked me for the good talk I had given them, and were all well pleased with the whole of it. They knew as he had told me the evening before, that nothing but a desire to do good, could induce us to instruct and feed so many children without pay. It was further observed, that they must now attend to the business of great national importance; and as soon as that was finished, they would attend to what I had said about other schools, and communicate freely according to my requests. I then observed, that I must leave them and return to the school; but, if agreeable, I would first take the king by the hand, in token of our mutual love and friendship, and of the mutual love and friendship that subsisted between his people and all concerned in the mission. The king most cordially gave his hand, as a token and seal of this, while I implored the divine blessing upon him and his people. This being done, the chiefs all rose from their seats, came up to me, one by one, and each gave his hand, in a most affectionate manner. This closing scene was to me truly impressive, and I think will not be forgotten.

"Brother Hicks left the council, and accompanied me a short distance on the way. While by ourselves, he assured me, there was no dissimulation in what I had seen: that all were highly pleased, and he thought much good would result from the interview."

On the first of January, the king and one of the principal chiefs from the southern part of the nation, visited the school at Brainerd.

"On winter evenings," say the brethren, "our children are collected in one room, where they are exercised in spelling, answering questions, singing, &c. When the old king saw the children assembled this evening, he was greatly delighted, and shook hands with them most affectionately. He appeared much pleased during the first exercises, (though he does not understand English:) but when they began the singing, he could not refrain from tears; though evidently endeavoring to repress his feelings as if ashamed to weep. The furrows of his war-worn cheeks were plentifully watered, and his handkerchief was almost constantly applied to dry them. He spoke to the children affectionately, as did also the accompanying chief.

"2nd. The king and chief, visited the school. After the children had passed through their various exercises, the king addressed them, in a grave, affectionate manner. The chief then arose, and spoke, as it appeared to us, in a most eloquent and persuasive manner for some time. By his gestures we supposed he was talking to the children about getting an education—then dispersing through the nation—doing great good through life, and then meeting together above, to receive a reward The children listened with great attention, and most of them were considerably affected. From them we afterwards learned that our conjectures, respecting the subjects of the discourse, were correct, that the chief told them the missionaries must be good men, or they would not be willing to do so much for them without pay: that we knew more than the Indians did: and they must listen to our instructions, keep steady at the school, and be obedient, until they had learned all that we wished them to learn; and that, when they went away from the school, they must remember and follow the good way they had learned here;—if they did so, they would do much good to their people while they lived, and when they died they would go above and be happy.

"After the chief had concluded, the king again addressed the children a few minutes, and requested that they might all come round and shake hands with him,—which they did. Both the king and chief expressed their warmest thanks for the good we were doing to their nation; said they should think much of us and of the school, and would tell their people every where, that it was very good to send their children here, where they could learn good things, &c.

"In February, a letter was sent to the missionaries, said to have been written, at the request and in behalf of all the people of the district called Battle Creek, down the Tennessee, about forty miles from Brainerd,—earnestly entreating, that a schoolmaster might come and teach their children."

This Board have been apprised, that it was the intention of the United States government, to procure an extended exchange of lands, and to remove the Cherokees and other Indian nations and tribes, residing on this side the Mississippi, over into the wilderness of the Arkansas, and of the Missouri. The Cherokees, being urgently pressed with proposals, in pursuance of this intention, were in great consternation and distress, and a delegation of twelve of their principal men, with the well known and excellent chief, Charles R. Hicks, at the head, were appointed by the council of the nation, to go to the city of Washington on the subject. Communications, relating to the business, were made to your Committee; and a desire was signified, that one of the Committee or an agent of the Board, might be present with the delegation. The Committee could not but feel, that it was a crisis of great moment; and the Corresponding Secretary was deputed to Washington. Accordingly, about the middle of February, he met the Cherokee delegation there.

A principal argument, employed on the part of the Cherokees, was:—That their removal from their country, where they had begun to cultivate the land, and made considerable advances in civilizing arts; and where a system of instruction for their general improvement had commenced with the fairest prospects of success;—into a boundless wilderness, where every thing would invite and impel them to revert to the hunting, and wandering, and savage life,—would frustrate the desires of the better part of the nation, and destroy the hopes of their benevolent friends; and, in effect, doom them to extermination; that the desire for civilization had become prevalent among them, and their capability of improvement, and of being elevated to the rank and to the enjoyments of civilized people, had been decisively evinced by the success, which had attended the attempts for their instruction. The argument appears to have had weight with the government; and the delegation, instead of finding themselves obliged, as their fears had led them to anticipate, to sign a virtual surrender of their country, had the high satisfaction to put their signatures to a treaty of a very different kind.

This treaty, after a cession of lands by the Cherokees, in consideration of a portion of the nation having migrated to the Arkansas, and had lands assigned to them there, secures to them the remainder of their country in perpetuity. And of the ceded lands, an appropriation is made of about a hundred thousand acres, for a perpetual school fund, to be applied, under the direction of the President of the United States, to the instruction of the Cherokees on this side of the Mississippi.

This, the Committee are persuaded, will be regarded by the Board, and by all, who wish well to the American aborigines, as a signally auspicious event. It is auspicious, as it shows on the part of the government, not only a favorable disposition towards the Indians, but also a conviction that they can be, and must be, civilized; and a settled and generous purpose to patronize and aid the benevolent work. It is auspicious, as it provides funds which eventually will not be small, for promoting the design. And it is auspicious in the influence, which it has, and which it will have, upon the Cherokees and other Indian nations, and upon the American community. It marks, indeed, a new and propitious era.

The Cherokee delegates and the nation, were filled with joy and gratitude. In the journal of the mission, April 12th, the brethren record.

"This day, brother Hicks, having a few days since returned from the seat of government, made us a visit This brother, as might be expected, is much engaged for the instruction of his people. While an entire exchange of country was thought of, as a measure they might be pressed to adopt, his spirit was often greatly borne down with discouragement; but since they have succeeded in having part of their country guaranteed to them anew, and so many Christian people are engaged for their instruction, that hope, which was almost expiring, is raised to confident expectation. His heart is overflowing with joy, gratitude, and praise to God, whom he is ever ready to acknowledge as the *Giver of every good and perfect gift.*

"May 11th. By appointment of the brethren, father Hoyt attended the national talk and council. This talk was for the purpose of making known to the people what the delegates had done at Washington, &c. The success of this delegation has raised the hopes of the nation. They feel, more than ever, anxious to make improvement; and are convinced that the instruction of their children is very important for this end. The missionary is received and treated as an old tried friend.

"Dr. Worcester's parting address to the delegates, when at Washington, was read in open council, and interpreted as read. All appeared much pleased with the address.   As the way of their improvement was pointed out, and the blessings that would follow described, all seemed to say, "We will follow this advice, and shall experience this good."—They want mechanics and schoolmasters, and wish to have them come from one of the two societies, which have already begun to help them: as they say, they are acquainted with them, and can trust the men whom they will send."

In* this connection, another circumstance recorded in the Journal, May 27th, will be regarded with interest:—

"The President, accompanied by general Gaines and lady, stopped to visit the school. We had expected the President would call, as he passed, but supposed we should hear of his approach, in time to make a little preparation, and to meet and escort him in; but so silent was his approach, that we had no information that he had left Georgia, till he was announced as at the door.   In thus taking us by surprise, he had an opportunity of seeing us in our every day dress, and observing how the concerns of the family and school were managed, when we were alone; and perhaps it was best on the whole, that he should have this view of us.   If we had endeavored to appear a little better than usual, we might only have made it worse.

"He looked at the buildings and farms, visited the school, and asked questions in the most unaffected and familiar manner; and was pleased to express his approbation of the plan of instruction, particularly as the children were taken into the family, taught to work, &c.   He thought this the best, and perhaps the only way, to civilize and christianize the Indians; and assured us he was well pleased with the conduct and improvement of the children.

"We had just put up, and were about finishing, a log cabin for the use of the girls.   He said that such buildings were not good enough, and advised that we put another kind of building in place of this;—that we make it a good two story house, with brick or stone chimneys, glass windows, &c., and that it be done at the public expense.   He also observed, that after this was done, it might, perhaps, be thought best to build another of the same description for the boys, but we could do this first.   Giving us a letter directed to the Agent, he observed, 'I have written to him to pay the balance of your account, for what you have expended on these buildings, and also to defray the expense of the house, you are now about to build.   Make a good house, having due regard to economy.'"

Your Committee have no ordinary satisfaction in recording this visit, in which the dignified condescension, the generous philanthropy and the paternal character of the President of the United States, appear in so amiable and interesting a light   It has excited, and will excite, most grateful feelings, not only in this Board, but in this Christian community extensively.

Hitherto the Lord has continued to smile on this favored mission.   Its prosperity has been great. and its prospects are cheering.   Every encouragement is afforded to prosecute the design, with humble and grateful reliance on that Almighty aid, which has been so graciously granted.

CHOCTAWS.—A year ago this mission was just commencing. As then reported, the Rev. Mr. Kingsbury and Mr. Williams and wife, having taken an affecting leave of Brainerd, had recently arrived in the Choctaw nation, and selected the site for their station, and Mr. Peter Kanouse, and Messrs. John G. Kanouse and Moses Jewell with their wives, from New Jersey and New York, were on their way to join the mission.

"About the 15th of August," says Mr. Kingsbury, "we felled the first tree on the ground, which we considered as henceforth consecrated to the cause of Zion's King, and from which we hope to diffuse among this wretched people the benign influences of civilization and Christianity. The place was entirely new, and covered with lofty trees; but the ancient mounds, which here and there appeared, showed, that it had been once the habitation of men."

This consecrated spot has since been named Elliot, in affectionate memorial of the venerable "*Apostle of the American Indians.*"

In three or four days after the felling of the first tree, their first house of logs was raised.

"The weather," say the brethren, "was excessively hot and our prospects discouraging. The timber for the buildings necessary for the establishment was still growing; and the forest was waving over the ground, which we wished to cultivate. The men, whom we expected to undertake the buildings, declined the contract. The season was so far advanced, that we had little hope of immediate assistance from the north; and we had a poor prospect of help from this country. We had also been informed, that we could obtain supplies by water at any season of the year; but now found there would be no opportunity before winter. We were almost destitute of mechanical tools and implements of husbandry, and of many other important articles; having brought only a few of the most necessary ones in our wagon through the wilderness. But in this hour of difficulty, we remembered that the Lord had been our helper; and our hope was not in vain that He would again bring us relief."

On the day after the brethren, in the midst of their difficulties and discouragements, had raised the log of their first little cottage, they were cheered with a report, that three or four men were at Natchez, coming to their assistance; and in ten days afterwards, on the 29th of Aug. the assistants from New Jersey and New York arrived at the station "in safety, though much worn down by fatigue."

"Thus" say the brethren, "were our hearts made glad in a way we hardly presumed to hope for. The kind providence of God, in preserving the lives of our dear brethren and sisters, and granting them so great a degree of health, during so long and fatiguing a journey, through a burning and sickly clime, called forth our warmest gratitude."

The arrival of these assistants, and particularly of the females, was subsequently seen to be a reason for more especial gratitude, than was at first apprehended; as in about a week afterwards, Mrs. Williams, before the only female at the station, was seized with a severe fever, by which she was brought near to death.

Mr. Peter Kanouse, whose health for some time before leaving New Jersey had been feeble, and who suffered much in the passage by water to New Orleans, soon after reaching the station found his health declining; and, becoming in a short time persuaded, that he should not be able to render assistance in the arduous labors of the mission, on the 5th of October, with many painful regrets, left Elliot and returned to his family.

In November, Miss Sarah B. Varnum, and Miss Judith Chase, under the particular care of your Committee, and with a respectable company of passengers, were embarked at Salem, for the purpose of joining the mission. They were met at New Orleans by Mr. Kingsbury, whose marriage to Miss Varnum was there solemnized; and by whom they were conducted thence to the station, where they arrived on the first of February. About a fortnight before, Mr. Aries V. Williams, an approved brother of him who went with Mr. Kingsbury from Brainerd, arrived there as an assistant.

Thus increased and strengthened, the mission was filled with grateful joy.

"We have our trials," says Mr. Kingsbury, in a letter at the time, "but they seem only such as are calculated to keep us humble, and teach us our dependence. And we have so many mercies, that we think no people are so highly favored as ourselves."

Among the trials alluded to, were sickness with which, in greater or less degrees, several members of the mission family of both sexes had been visited; various disappointments and difficulties in regard to procuring provisions and necessary help; and many inconveniences, privations, and hardships, unavoidable in the commencement of such an establishment so far in the wilderness.

Meanwhile, however, the work was advancing. And in a letter bearing date April 12, only about eight months from the felling of the first tree, the brethren say;

"So far as health and strength would permit, we have lost no time in getting forward the necessary preparations for our school; and we have much occasion for thankfulness, that we have been able to accomplish so much.

"We have erected seven log dwelling houses; two 22 feet by 20 each; two 22 by 18; one 20 by 16; one 18 by 15; and one 16 by 12. For five of these, the logs are hewed on two sides; and the roofs project in back and front about eight feet, and are supported by posts in the form of piazzas. These are very useful in this climate. We have erected, besides, a mill house 36 feet by 30; a stable, 20 by 14; a store house 20 by 16; and two other out buildings. All these buildings except one, are completed. The mill is on a simple construction, is turned by one or two horses, and grinds well. We have a part of our timber hewed for the school house, dining room, and kitchen: and have had sawed, by hand, about 9,000 feet of cypress and poplar boards, for floors, doors, &c.

"On the plantation, we have cleared, and fitted for the plough, about 35 acres of good land, which is inclosed with a substantial fence. A part of this was covered with heavy timber; and the chopping, burning and rolling of logs, has cost us much hard labor. In this we have been much assisted by Choctaws, whom we have hired. Several of them have worked faithfully. We have also inclosed a garden, and yards for cattle; and have set out a few peach, apply, quince, and plumb trees. Considerable labor has been spent, also, in cutting roads in different directions;

and in constructing several small bridges, which were found necessary in order to transport articles with a wagon. And it may be noticed, that we have had many of our tools, and much of our wooden furniture, to make.

"We wish we could say, that as much has been done to enlighten and save the souls of these perishing people, as to make preparations for the instruction of their children. But alas! as yet we have been able to accomplish but little towards this most important object.—It is impossible for us to express our feelings on this subject. The expectation of this people has been, that all our efforts would be directed towards the commencement of a school, and indeed it could not be supposed, that they would feel a particular desire for gospel instruction. But with respect to a school, they have ever manifested a great anxiety; and their expectations have greatly exceeded our ability to meet them.

"We have preaching, however, every Sabbath at our house, at which a number of half-breeds, and white people, and negroes attend; and occasionally several of the natives. Two or three appear seriously disposed."

On the last Sabbath in March, after solemn preparation, by fasting and prayer, a church was organized at the mission house; and the dying love of the Lord Jesus was commemorated, in the Holy Supper.

"We trust, say the brethren, the Lord was with us. A number of our neighbors came at an early hour to witness the transactions.—The season was interesting. We were in the midst of a wilderness, which had never, till lately, resounded with the accents of Gospel mercy. The emblems of the great sacrifice for sinners had never before been exhibited here." "At present our little church consists of only the ten missionary brethren and sisters; yet by faith we look forward to the time, when some of these dear people will be gathered into the fold."

As yet they were not prepared to commence the school. A school house, and some other buildings, were wanted; and their hands were not sufficient for the erection of them. The Choctaw people, however, not aware of the preparations, which were requisite, or of the difficulties to be surmounted, became impatient and urgent, and about the middle of April eight promising children were brought from a distance of 160 miles, to be placed at the school; the parents having been informed, that the mission was in readiness to receive them. It was a trying case. To turn the children away, would not only be a great disappointment to the parents, but make an unfavorable impression upon the nation; and to receive them under circumstances then existing, was a matter of extreme difficulty, and no small risk, especially, as, if they were received, others also must be taken. After prayerful deliberation, as the parents seemed willing to have their children disposed of, as circumstances would render necessary, if they might only be left, the brethren decided in favor of receiving them. "We felt it to be our duty," they say, "to keep the children, and open our school; believing that the Lord would continue to provide."

Accordingly, on the 19th of April, the school was commenced with ten Choctaw children.

The next morning after the opening of the school, Mr. Kingsbury was seized with a severe illness; which, at first, was a bilious fever; but, after two or three weeks, changed to a regular intermittent, which continued with variations, into June. During this period, from April to June, all the members of the mission, male and female, were visited with sickness, in a greater or less degree, and some of them were not slightly ill.

Referring to their sicknesses, the brethren say.

"We cannot impute these repeated afflictions to any particular unfavorableness of our situation. That we should be affected by the great change of climate was to be expected, especially considering our many exposures. Nor was the change of climate greater than the change of diet: both must have had considerable effect on our health."

Their labors, their hardships, their exposures were great;—and their privations, owing to the newness of their situation, their distance from white settlements, and the unusual scarcity of bread stuffs the last winter, in that country, were also great. But the Lord was gracious. The lives of them all were precious in his sight; and health has been restored to the mission.

In April, Dr. William W. Pride, a young physician, of Cambridge, New York,—and Mr. Isaac Fisk of Holden, Mass. a blacksmith and farmer, in the prime of life, and of more than ordinary thrift and prospects in the world,—having devoted themselves to the service, and been accepted upon ample testimonials, set out for the Choctaw station. They travelled by land; visited Brainerd in their way, where for particular purposes they staid two or three weeks; and arrived at Elliot in good health on the first of August.

Something of the disposition of the Choctaw people towards the mission, appears from recitals already made. Other particulars will shew it in a still stronger light.—Soon after the brethren arrived in the nation, the king, Puk-sha-nub-bee, gave for the school, $200 to be paid annually from the annuity received by his part of the nation, from the U. S. In the fore part of August, a council of the nation was held, at which Mr. Kingsbury, by particular invitation, was present. Under date of Aug. 12, Mr. Kingsbury writes:—

"For some time I was apprehensive, that nothing decisive would be done for schools. Yesterday, by the consent and approbation of the Agent, I gave them a short talk. It was well received. To-day the subject of the school was taken up in the council. It was proposed, that individuals who felt interested for the school, should give cows and calves, and money, as they felt able and disposed. A subscription was opened on the spot; and eighty five cows and calves, and $500 to be paid annually, and $700 as a donation to the establishment, or annually while their children are at school, were subscribed.

"The cows and calves, it was expressly stated, were a free gift, whether the individuals send children or not. The money generally was considered as a partial compensation for board of children, either now at school, or to be sent hereafter, except $500 from their annuity.

"It is, however, to be understood, that great allowance must be made for failures in collecting, and it will also be attended with considerable expense. But I cannot doubt, that the establishment will realize a substantial benefit from the result."

These facts speak much, and are in accordance with the general disposition manifested by the nation.

In his letter last referred to, Mr. Kingsbury says. "Our school at present consists of 29 promising children. Many more are anxious to come, but we are unable to obtain provisions for them at present. And in his talk, delivered to the council about the same time, he said to them: "Brothers, we have twenty of your children in our school, who are learning very well. When dry corn comes plenty, about the first of October, we will take 20 or 30 more. We wish to do all for your children that we can."·

To meet and secure these favorable dispositions, is a matter of great importance. The effect of disappointing them might be incalculably detrimental. The brethren of the mission have done what they could: and they have done much. Feeble handed, as they have been; weakened and afflicted with sickness; subjected to inconveniences; encompassed with difficulties; struggling on in weariness and painfulness, it is wonderful, that in so short a time, they have brought the establishment to its present state. They need help, and must have help.

More than five years ago, Mr. Alfred Wright, while a student in the Theological Seminary at Andover, after serious and prayerful deliberation, came to the resolution to devote himself to the missionary work among the heathen, should Providence open to him the way; but a failure of health has hindered him. After a residence, however, in North Carolina for two or three years, in a climate favorable to his constitution, he found his health so far restored, as to encourage him to commence preaching; and for several months past he has been employed in missionary labors to good acceptance, in South Carolina. With the return of health, his desire to go to the heathen has gained strength and animation.

Having offered himself to the service, under the patronage of this Board, with satisfactory testimonials, he is now under appointment to the Choctaw mission. A request has been sent on for him to be ordained at Charleston, (S. C.) and it is hoped, that he will join the mission before winter.

Several young men, teachers and mechanics, have offered themselves, and been accepted, for the service among the Aborigines; some of whom are intended for the Choctaw nation. And the Committee cannot doubt, that it will be the pleasure of the Board, that the help and means, requisite for the work there, should be supplied, with as little delay as possible.

The appearances are of a nature not to be mistaken, that in the Choctaw nation, as well as in the Cherokee, *the fields are white already to the harvest;* and to inspire the hope, and the confidence in the Lord of the harvest, *that he that reapeth will receive wages and gather fruit unto life eternal.*

ARKANSAS.—About twenty-two months ago, proposals were made, in behalf of the Board, to that portion of the Cherokee nation that have migrated to the Arkansas, for the establishment of a mission and schools among them. The proposals were favorably received, and a strong desire was expressed by the Arkansas chiefs, that their people might be favored with means of instruction, similar to those afforded to their brethren on this side of the Mississippi. These proposals were solemnly repeated in May 1818, and were received with gratitude. About ten months ago, a conference was held with them, by the Rev. M. Peck, from the Baptist Board of Foreign Missions, and the Rev. Mr. Ficklin from the Kentucky Mission Society, with reference to establishments contemplated by their respective societies. They too were answered with kindness, but were given to understand, that their proposals could not be accepted, until more should be known respecting our intentions. At the instance of the chiefs, and with a highly creditable liberality and Christian spirit, a correspondence was opened by them on the subject; which resulted in a talk, sent to the chiefs by Mr. Peck, in the latter part of last winter, of the following purport.

"BROTHERS,—I have heard from your brothers in the north, who have a mission among the Cherokees on the other side of the Mississippi. They remember you with great love, and have not forgotten the promise to send you teachers. They have appointed a good man, who will visit you soon, and afterwards other good men, who will instruct you and your children, and seek your welfare.—I will do all in my power to promote the good work."

"And may the Great Spirit breathe upon the Chief and head men, and upon all the Cherokees on the Arkansas, both small and great—disperse all the clouds, and cause the true light to shine upon them, that they may be happpy here and after death."

The person here referred to, as having been appointed to visit them soon, was the Rev. Alfred Finney, who was mentioned in the Report of the last year. He was designated for the Arkansas in November, with the intention, that he should go out early in the spring, explore the country, make arrangements preparatory to the contemplated establishment, and be joined by others, as soon as should be deemed advisable. But particular circumstances occasioned delay.

Mr. Finney and his wife are now with the company from Rockaway, mentioned under the head of the Cherokee mission, as being bound to Brainerd. At Brainerd, he is to be joined by the Rev. Cephas Washburn, mentioned also in the last year's Report; who has been employed for the last nine months in Georgia, and has received instructions to leave Georgia, in season to reach Brainerd about the first of November.

From Brainerd, Messrs. Washburn and Finney are to proceed to Elliot; and there leave their wives with the Choctaw mission, until they shall have visited the Arkansas and made such preparations, as shall render the residence there of females, belonging to the mission, safe and proper. The mission is projected on the same general plan with those already established; and is intended to be put forward with all convenient despatch.

The Chickasaws, whose country lies partly between the Cherokees and the Choctaws, have been for a considerable time expecting and desiring a mission to them; and it has been declared to be the pleasure of the Board, that means of instruction should be extended them, similar to those afforded to their neighbors. It has not yet been found convenient to commence an establishment among them; but the design is entertained with much earnestness, and will be put in execution with as little delay as possible.

This business of civilizing and christianizing the Indian tribes, is becoming extremely urgent. The national government is convinced,—the people throughout the States are convinced,—the Indians themselves, the better informed of them at least, are convinced,—that they must become civilized, and that soon,—or soon become extinct. The alternative is absolute. It should be felt as such by every heart. Not a few, it is to be feared, in different parts of the country, really desire the extermination of these original possessors of the soil; and, of course, will favor no designs for their improvement. A larger number either think their civilization impracticable, or else think little, and care little, about it. But the benevolent part of the community is waking up to the object,—the government favors it;—the Indians shew a disposition respecting it, such as has been manifested by them in no former period—a desire tending to deep anxiety;—divine Providence is opening the way to it, with unexpected facilities and advantages;—and the divine Spirit has given to it his decisive sanction, and an assurance of his readiness to accompany the proper means with his Almighty aid.

The time for the work is come. If it be neglected, the object is lost. Baleful circumstances will arise;—scenes of strife and of destruction will ensue, and the Indians will melt away and perish. But they will not perish, before it shall have been made clear to the world, that they might have been preserved, and raised up to the enjoyment of the privileges and blessings of Christian civilization. If they perish—if they become extinct—their blood will be upon this nation.

The responsibility is not a light one —Nor is it, though feasible, a small work. It will require much attention, much wisdom, much labor, much expense. This Board must not be weary in well doing; the friends of religion and of humanity throughout the nation must be excited; all hearts and all hands must be engaged for one mighty effort.

SANDWICH ISLANDS.—It is well known to the Board, and to the Christian community extensively, that there are several youths from the Sandwich Islands under special patronage and instruction in this Christian land. It was, indeed, the desire for their instruction,—that they might not only enjoy the blessings of Christianity themselves, but also be instrumental in communicating them to their friends and countrymen,—that gave birth to our Foreign Mission School. And the expectation has been fondly cherished by many thousands, that as soon as suitably qualified, these youths would be sent back to their native islands, and that missionaries of our own country would be also sent, with a view to the introduction and establishment of the gospel there, with all its civilizing and saving influences.

Obookiah, whose heart was filled with the holy design, in whom a particular interest was extensively felt, and on whom no ordinary hopes were placed,—is not to return to Owhyhee.—God had provided some better thing for him.—But though dead, he yet speaketh; and in a tone, and with an emphasis, not to be unheeded. His Memoirs,—like those of the still dearly remembered Mrs. Newell,—are pleading the cause, which was dearest to his heart, with powerful effect.

His mantle too is with his brethren. Three of them, giving satisfactory evidence of piety, of well established Christian principles and habits, of promising abilities for usefulness, and of a sincere and ardent desire of being employed in the great work of evangelizing their countrymen, are thought to be so far advanced in knowledge, and other qualifications, as to render it advisable to gratify their desire, as soon as convenient. And a fourth, the son of Tamoree, one of the kings of the islands, is impatient of delay: and though not like the others, exhibiting evidence of a truly religious character, yet possessing vigorous faculties, having made good proficiency in his studies, and being impressed with a conviction of the importance of Christianity to himself and to his countrymen, the hope is entertained, that he will be a friend to the mission, and a blessing to his nation.

Of the sons and daughters of our Zion, several appear to have had their hearts prepared by divine grace for this arduous mission to the isles afar off. Mr. Daniel Chamberlain, of Brookfield, Mass., a substantial farmer in the prime of life, with a rising family, and in the midst of prosperity, has given up all that would hold him to his country, to his home, or to his earthly pursuits, and willingly offered himself and his family for the service. Dr. Thomas Holman, a young physician of Cooperstown, N. Y.—Mr. Samuel Ruggles of Brookfield, Con., a member of the Foreign Mission School from its commencement; Mr. Elisha Loomis, of Middlesex, N. Y., by trade a printer, and for some time past a student at the same school; and Mr. Samuel Whitney of Branford, Con., a member of Yale College, and also possessed of mechanical skill;—have, in like manner, devoted themselves, desiring to be enrolled for the mission, and to be employed in such parts of the work, as they are best qualified respectively to execute.

Mr. Hiram Bingham, of Bennington, Vt., and Mr. Asa Thurston of Fitchburg, Mass., approved men, whose preparatory studies in the Theological Seminary at Andover are just closed—yet of mature age, and somewhat acquainted with mechanical arts—are designated, as principals of the mission, and their ordination is appointed to be at Goshen in Connecticut, on the last Wednesday of the present month.

A passage to the Sandwich Islands is engaged for these missionaries and assistants, with their wives and the four islanders, on board the brig Thaddeus, bound from this port to the Northern Pacific Ocean, and expected to sail in about a month from this time. It is intended, that the mission shall be amply furnished; and an assurance is felt that it will be attended with the hopes and desires, and prayers of many thousands.— The Society Islands have proclaimed JEHOVAH for their God; and the Sandwich Isles *are waiting for his law.*

FOREIGN MISSION SCHOOL.—This seminary, so strong in the affections, and so dear to the hearts of Christians, is in a highly gratifying course of advancement.

The present number of pupils is thirty-two. Of this number nine are from distant heathen countries—six from the Sandwich Islands, one from Otaheite, one a Chinese from Malacca, one from Sumatra;—seventeen are aboriginal Americans—seven Cherokees, two Choctaws, two Oneidas, two from the Stockbridge tribe, one from Pennsylvania, and one from Canada;—and six are young persons of our own country, preparing for the missionary service.

Seven of the youths from heathen lands, have publicly professed their faith in the Redeemer, and been admitted to the sealing ordinances of the Everlasting Covenant; and their conduct has been such in general, as to adorn the doctrine of God our Savior, and to give an example very salutary in its influence on the school.' Besides these, several others indulge the hope, that they have passed from death unto life; and others still are impressed with serious convictions of the truth and importance of Christianity.

At the late examination, the Executive Committee of the school took particular note of the pupils individually, as to their behavior and their progress; and their Report is such as to inspire confidence and hope.

"It is exceedingly animating, say that Committee, to see what improvements have already been made by all these Cherokee and Choctaw youths. It is but a little time, since they were in regions of heathen darkness; and but for the interference of Christian beneficence, they had lived and died strangers to the privileges and blessings, which the Gospel tenders to a lost world. It would seem that no person, who should examine the youths at the Foreign Mission School, together with the successful efforts, at the missionary stations of Brainerd and Elliot, could doubt the utility of persevering exertions, to civilize and christianize the Aboriginal Americans."

The Executive Committee proceed to say,—

It has been deemed expedient, that the members of the school should be taught the various branches of husbandry. They have accordingly labored in rotation, under the superintendence of the steward. Their attention the past season has been turned particularly to horticulture.—Most of the various kinds of vegetables for culinary use have been raised in the garden this season —The pupils have been able to perform the requisite labor in the early and latter part of each day, without encroaching upon the regular hours of study.

"Mr. Daggett has found it necessary to employ an assistant through the year, and the Executive Committee have engaged the same person, Mr. John H. Prentice, as an assistant in the school for the ensuing year."

The Committee would notice with gratitude the liberality of Christians in various parts of our country, in support of the institution. Donations have been received for this purpose from many individuals—from female benevolent societies, and from associations of males. The donations have been in money, in various articles of clothing and bedding, in books, and many other things of utility to the institution.

"The expenses of the establishment are necessarily considerable: and increase of course in proportion to the admissions to the school. The Committee cherish the belief, that the exertions and charities of the Christian community will be commensurate with the increasing expenses. Without their continued beneficence, the dear youth at the school must be abandoned—sent back to the region whence they came, and left to wander through life amid the glooms of pagan darkness. May He, whose are the silver and the gold, impress it indelibly on the mind of every Christian, that IT IS MORE BLESSED TO GIVE THAN TO RECEIVE."

In the conclusion of their Report, the Executive Committee pay a very handsome, and it is believed, a very just, tribute of grateful commendation to ' the distinguished excellence of the Rev. Mr. Dagget, the Principal of the school,—who appears to be eminently qualified to preside over such an institution—is universally respected and beloved by his pupils—and labors in season and out of season to promote their best welfare."

FUNDS—The donations to the Board within the year past have been about *thirty-four thousand dollars*, and other sources of income have amounted to *three thousand*. Thus there has been a small advance in the receipts, notwithstanding the pecuniary embarrassments of our country The expenditures of the Board, within the same period, have somewhat surpassed *forty thousand dollars*, which is about *three thousand* more' than the receipts. The sum immediately needed, particularly for the Palestine and Sandwich Islands missions, is much greater than the balance on hand, after deducting from that balance the permanent fund, and those legacies, which though not expressly 'assigned to that fund, it seems desirable to keep as a last resort. But the Committee do not hesitate to confide in that Christian liberality, which has been hitherto displayed.

Donations have been received from more than *five hundred* associations, of various names, some formed for the general objects of the Board, and others for specific objects. Many of these associations are new; but it must be stated also, that many others, previously existing, have not made remittances within the time above-mentioned. From a considerable proportion of these, however, aid may still be expected. Others have united with larger auxiliary associations in their vicinity Contributions made at the monthly concert have been received from *ninety-four* churches, of which *fifty-nine* made their first remittances during the year past. It is confidently believed, that this source of income will be greatly increased. Nine Masonic Lodges have made donations for the distribution of the Scriptures: eight of them for the first time within the limits embraced by this Report.

CONCLUSION —To the Auxiliary Societies and various Associations, formed and acting on the principle of giving permanent aid to the Board; —and to many thousands of individuals, associated and unassociated, who regularly make their weekly, monthly, or yearly offerings,—very grateful acknowledgments are due, for their continued, and, in many instances, increased liberality. They, under Providence, are the support and strength of the Board. Grateful acknowledgments are also due to the churches, congregations, and individuals, from whom occasional contributions, and not a few of them in a high degree liberal, have been received.—And your Committee have a lively and elevated pleasure in saying, that in these acknowledgments our brethren and sisters of the south,—and especially of Georgia and South Carolina, are entitled to a distinguished share. Societies and individuals there have shewn a liberality, which it is to be hoped will provoke many in other states and sections of our country to generous emulation.

It is in the spirit and agreeable to the principles and plan of this Board, which neither in name, in constitution, in system, nor in feeling, is sectional, sectarian, or exclusive, to engage and unite American Christians, in concurrence with the Christians of other countries, in the great work of enlightening the dark places of the earth, and bringing the world under the benign sceptre of its Redeemer and rightful Sovereign. And the multiplying and strengthening of the ties of Christian affection, and the expanding and invigorating of the spirit of Christian fellowship, which must be the effect of union in such a design, must be delightful to every well informed Christian mind, and well pleasing to HIM, whose commandment it is—*that his disciples should love one another.*

The Board has now under its direction, and dependent upon its funds, twenty three MISSIONARIES, and as many ASSISTANTS in the different parts of the work,—sacredly devoted to the service for life;—with thirty five FEMALE HELPERS of like spirit. In its mission families and schools it has from two to three thousand heathen children and youth under Christian instruction; of whom from two to three hundred are also chiefly supported from its funds.—The numbers are continually increasing; the operations are extending, and the necessary expenditures are multiplying and augmenting. If our nation—if American Christians—have been long under the guilt of *robbing God;* most favorable opportunities are now afforded to them, and most powerful motives are presented,—if not for cancelling their irredeemable arrears,—yet for *bringing their tithes, as they are constantly falling due, into his store house,* with punctuality, and in full amount; and making their *free will offerings* with largeness and gladness of heart. It should be the devout prayer and endeavor of every lover of his country, of every friend to the best interests of mankind, that the guilt be not accumulated and aggravated, by neglect of the opportunities and disregard of the motives.

The command, never to be forgotten is—GO YE INTO ALL THE WORLD, AND PREACH THE GOSPEL TO EVERY CREATURE. By Christians and Christian ministers the command must be fulfilled.—THE GOSPEL MUST BE SENT—AND PREACHED—TO EVERY NATION AND FAMILY ON EARTH. This is the duty of Christians:—to render it effectual to the conversion of every nation and family—is not required of them. Let them obediently do *what is required;* and humbly wait on Him, with whom is the residue of the Spirit, to command the blessing. *He will not be slack concerning his promise, as some men count slackness.*

By the Prudential Committee,

S. WORCESTER, *Clerk.*

Boston, Sept. 15, 1819.

PECUNIARY ACCOUNTS OF THE BOARD.

The American Board of Commissioners for Foreign Missions, in account current with Jeremiah Evarts, their Treasurer, Dr.

To cash paid from Sept. 1, 1818, to August 31, 1819, in conformity to orders of the Board, and of the Prudential Committee, from No. 296 to No. 434, both inclusive; viz. as classed summarily under the following heads·

Salaries, translations, schools, and other necessary expenses of the mission at Bombay,	$5,498 10	
Outfits, passages, salaries, printing, schools, and other necessary expenses of the mission at Ceylon,	11,209 79	16,707 89
Outfits, travelling expenses, schools, labor, provisions, and various necessary supplies of the Cherokee mission,	6,956 93	
Do. do of the Choctaw mission,	2,985 45	9,942 38
Foreign Mission School at Cornwall, Con.		4,926 40

Carried forward, $31,576 67

Brought forward,		$31,576 67
Preparatory expenses of the Arkansas mission, - -	609 47	
Do. do. of the Sandwich Islands mission, - -	- 132 50	
Do. do. of the Palestine mission, - - -	160 00——901 97	
Miscellaneous expenses of the Board, embracing all charges, not so conveniently classed under the foregoing heads, and having reference to all the objects of the Board, - - - - -		7,738 61
Correction of a mistake, occasioned by the same sum having been communicated in two different ways, - - - - -		30 00
Losses by counterfeit and worthless bills, - - -		90 00
		$40,337 25
Balance carried to the credit of the Board, in new account, Sept. 1, 1819,		50,136 46
		$90,473 71

Contra Cr.

By cash brought to the credit of the Board in new account, as the balance, Sept. 1, 1818, - - - - - - -	-	$52,923 08
By cash received in donations, from Sept. 1, 1818, to August 31, 1819, both inclusive viz. as published particularly in the Panoplist,		34,166 68
Interest of money and income of stock, - - -	2,369 63	
From the government of the United States for the support of Indian youths at the Foreign Mission School, - -	400 00	
Half the travelling expenses of the four first youths, who joined the school from the Cherokee and Choctaw nations, refunded by the government of the United States, -	238 00——638 00	
Refunded by the Rev. Dr Worcester, the balance of $150 advanced to him to defray the expenses of his journey to Washington,	16 32	
Avails of books sold, principally "the Conversion of the World,"	316 25	
Received in uncurrent bills, &c. from the mission treasury at Brainerd,	41 25	
Premium on Boston money, &c. - - - -	2 50——3,383 95	
		$90,473 71

Since the annual meeting, it has been ascertained, that the donation of $200 06, acknowledged as having been received from Liberty county, Georgia, was designed for the American Education Society. The mistake was made in the letter announcing the donation; and has been corrected by paying over the money. Of course, the donations for the year were $200 06 less than above stated.

MINUTES

ELEVENTH ANNUAL MEETING.

———

THE eleventh annual meeting of the American Board of Commissioners for Foreign Missions, was held in Hartford, Conn. at the house of Henry Hudson, Esq. on the 20th and 21st of Sept. 1820:—Present

> Hon. JOHN TREADWELL, LL. D.
> Rev. JOSEPH LYMAN, D. D.
> Hon. STEPHEN VAN RENSSELAER,
> Rev. JEDIDIAH MORSE, D. D.
> Hon. JOHN C. SMITH, LL. D.
> Hon. JOHN HOOKER, Esq.
> Rev. CALVIN CHAPIN, D. D.
> Rev. ALEXANDER PROUDFIT, D. D.
> Rev. ZEPHANIAH S. MOORE, D. D.
> Rev. JEREMIAH DAY, LL. D. D. D.
> Rev. ELIPHALET NOTT, D. D.
> Rev. JAMES RICHARDS, D. D.
> Rev. SAMUEL WORCESTER, D. D. and
> JEREMIAH EVARTS, Esq.

The session was opened with prayer by the Rev. Dr. Lyman, and on the following day by the Rev. Dr. Morse.

Minutes of the last annual meeting were read.

Letters were communicated from sundry members expressing regret, that they were unable to attend this session of the Board.

The accounts of the Treasurer were exhibited, as certified by the Auditor, and were accepted and approved.

The report of the Prudential Committee was read, accepted and approved.

On Wednesday evening, at 7 o'clock, attended public worship, when a sermon was delivered by the Rev. Dr. Nott, from Mark xvi, 15; *Go ye into all the world, and preach the Gospel to every creature.*

The report of the Agents of the Foreign Mission School was communicated, accepted, and approved.

Gen. Van Rensselaer and Drs. Worcester and Proudfit, were appointed a committee to present the thanks of this Board to the Rev. Dr. Nott for his sermon delivered before them, and to request a copy for the press.

The following gentlemen were chosen officers for the ensuing year; viz.

The Hon. JOHN TREADWELL, LL. D. *President.*
Rev. JOSEPH LYMAN, D D *Vice President.*
Rev. JEDIDIAH MORSE, D. D.
Hon WILLIAM REED,
Rev. LEONARD WOODS, D. D.   } *Prudential Committee.*
Rev. SAMUEL WORCESTER, D. D.
JEREMIAH. EVARTS, Esq.
Rev. SAMUEL WORCESTER, D D. *Corresponding Secretary.*
Rev. CALVIN CHAPIN, D. D. *Recording Secretary.*
JEREMIAH EVARTS, Esq. *Treasurer,* and
ASHUR ADAMS, Esq. *Auditor.*

Governor Smith, Mr. Hooker, and President Day, having been appointed a committee to consider the subject of a periodical publication, which shall belong to the Board, reported, Whereupon

Resolved, That it is expedient, that a periodical publication, such as is described in "Proposals for continuing by subscription the Missionary Herald," should be established at the expense of the Board, and that the Prudential Committee be requested to carry this vote into execution.

In the course of the annual meeting it was resolved,

That the next annual meeting of this Board be holden in Springfield, (Mass.) on the third Wednesday of Sept. 1821, at 10 o'clock, A. M. and that the Hon. John Hooker, and the Rev. Samuel Osgood be a committee of arrangements for that meeting.

That this Board is gratefully impressed with the liberal and increasing patronage of the Christian public extensively afforded to this institution, its measures, and objects; and that the Prudential Committee be directed to express the thanks of this Board to all societies, churches, congregations and individuals, from whom donations have been received.

That the thanks of the Board be presented to Henry Hudson, Esq. for the accommodation and hospitality, with which he has provided for the meeting; to other individuals and families, whose kindness and hospitality have been experienced by the members; and to the choir of singers, in the Brick Church, for their services.

That it shall be the duty of the Prudential Committee to compile and publish a report, including their report for the last year; the report from the Agents of the Foreign Mission School; a statement of the Treasurer's accounts; such a detail of donations as may be found useful; extracts from the minutes of the present session; and such other information as they shall judge expedient.

The Rev. Dr. Proudfit having been appointed to preach at the next meeting, the Rev. Dr. Morse was appointed to preach in case of his failure.

The meeting was closed with prayer by the Rev. Dr. Proudfit.

REPORT.

BRETHREN,—It is after the labors of ten years, that, by the favor of our Master and Lord, we are assembled to-day in this bower of Zion, to review the operations and mark the results; to erect our memorials, to refresh our spirits, and to gather strength and counsel for the prosecution of our work. The various recollections and endless associations of the occasion—running back to the past and forward to the future—mingle themselves with whatever is dear to our best affections and interesting to our best hopes; and open to us a lively and extended participation in the holy fellowship, *that gathers together in one all things, which are in heaven, and which are on earth.*

Of the eight individuals, who at first composed this Board, *three*—of the thirty-seven, who have been enrolled as chartered members, *six*—have been advanced, as we humbly trust, nearer to the central glory of the same Divine Fellowship. The former three, DWIGHT, HUNTINGTON, and SPRING—loved and revered names—have been in preceding years affectionately recorded. The other three, LANGDON, APPLETON, and PAYSON—names also revered and loved, and worthy of like affectionate record, have, in quick succession, been removed from us since our last anniversary. They rest from these labors; but have not ceased to have an interest in them. They are labors for eternity; and the results, we may humbly assure ourselves, are for joy and grateful celebration, in the highest of the heavenly places.

It seems most suitable to the design of the present Report to observe, in the view to be submitted, the *chronological order* of the several missions.

BOMBAY MISSION.—As this is not only the first mission of this Board, but the first mission ever sent from this Christian country to any foreign heathen land, or portion of the unevangelized world, it cannot but be regarded by all, who wish well to the best interests of mankind, with peculiar interest. The circumstances of its origin and early history are too deeply impressed on the minds of those, who were immediately concerned in them, ever to be forgotten.

For a year and a half the Prudential Committee had been looking with anxious earnestness for an opportunity and means for sending forth the young men, whose solemn dedication of themselves to the service of Christ among the heathen had, under the wise ordering of Providence, given rise to the deliberations, which issued in the formation of this Board. It was in the days of that mighty and dreadful conflict, which shook the pillars of the world, and filled all hearts with dismay and all minds with perplexity. Our vessels were not permitted to go from our ports, and no way was open to any part of the pagan world. All then was gloomy suspense, and the prospect seemed to be growing still darker, when, on a sudden, intelligence was communicated of a vessel preparing, under special permission, to sail for Calcutta. It was on the 27th of January, 1812, that the Prudential Committee met at Newburyport, to consider and act upon the question of sending the missionaries; and the Harmony was appointed to sail from Philadelphia, on the 10th of February. The missionaries had not been ordained; their outfits were not ready, and very little money had yet come into the treasury. It was an hour of intensely serious deliberation. It seemed to be the will of Him, whose servants they were, that the missionaries should be sent; and, with reliance on his aid, the decision was taken to send them. It was not a vain reliance. The necessary arrangements were made; the requisite means were supplied, and, by the whole scene of the preparation and departure of this first American mission, an impulse was given to the missionary spirit, to which, under Providence, are in no small measure to be attributed its subsequent diffusion, activity and productiveness.

The destination of the mission was not fixed; but, with such instructions to the missionaries, as were deemed proper, was referred to the determination of Providence. Providence, ever wise and ever good, enveloped itself for not a short season in darkness; and put the faith and patience of the missionaries, and their patrons and friends, to severe trial; and it was not until the former part of the year 1814, about two years from leaving this country, that, after repeated repulses and various adversities, the mission was quietly settled at Bombay.

Many months before this time, Messrs. Judson and Rice had separated themselves from the mission; and Mrs. Newell had been taken from it, —that every where she might plead for the cause with irresistible eloquence. And about a year and a half after, Mr. Nott, enfeebled by disease, came to the determination to return with his wife to his native land.

Only Mr. Hall and Mr. Newell now remained:—and this was only five years ago. "In point of numbers," said they in a letter at the time, "we two missionaries are to the people of Bombay—to say nothing of the millions in sight of Bombay—what two ministers would be to the whole population of Connecticut, were the people of that state all heathens, and the two ministers far removed from all ministerial intercourse and Christian counsel." Not only were they the only missionaries then at Bombay, or on all the hither side of India, but, so far as appears, Roman Catholics excepted, they were the first ministers of Christ, who had ever preached the gospel in the native language of Bombay, and the extensive provinces adjacent, containing a more numerous population than the whole of the United States

In the knowledge and use of this strange and difficult language, the two missionaries, at the time now referred to, had but just attained to such proficiency, as to begin to speak and preach in it to the people. Of course, they were but just prepared to commence their system of operations; having as yet no permanent school, no printing press, no Bibles or tracts for distribution.

In the Report, made at our last anniversary, the narrative of this mission was brought down to the latter part of the preceding May. Your Committee regret to state, that they are now able to bring it down only to the fore part of January, about seven months later, and for this the materials are comparatively scanty.

While our merchants were trading at Bombay, communications from the missionaries were frequent and copious; but since that trade has ceased, no conveyance is afforded, but what is circuitous and precarious, and the communications are infrequent

The entire period, then, of the active operations of the Bombay mission, now under general review, is only a period of about four years and a half; viz. from the summer of 1815, when Mr. Nott left the mission, and the two who remained were just prepared to begin to act, to the beginning of 1820.

Your Committee are the more particular in respect to these dates, and this period of action, as it is apprehended, that they have not been sufficiently adverted to by the community, or perhaps by the members of this Board. It seems a great while—especially to minds more ardent than considerate—since the first missionaries sailed for India. It is scarcely remembered, that, from the time of their sailing, nearly two years elapsed before they were quietly settled at Bombay; or that then very little could be done, until they had acquired a knowledge of the language of the country Hence it has happened, that the harvest has been looked for, before the seed could be sown, or even the ground broken up.

Of the state and progress, the plans and operations of this mission, ample statements and details have been given in preceding reports. For the present occasion only a succinct recapitulation is designed.

At the very time that Mr Nott was embarking at Bombay, for his return, Mr. Bardwell, with four of his brethren, who were intended for Ceylon, was ordained for the mission; and he arrived at Bombay on the 1st of November, 1816. About sixteen months after, viz. on the 23d of February, 1818, Mr. Nichols and Mr. Graves with their wives, and Miss Philomela Thurston, now Mrs. Newell, arrived. Thus strengthened, the mission, so far as is known to your Committee, has since continued without diminution; consisting of five missionaries with their wives; holding its primary seat in the great native town of Bombay, and occupying a station at Mahim, distant about six miles on the northern part of the same island, and another distant about 25 miles, at Tannah, on the island of Salsette, of which it is the chief town.

PREACHING THE GOSPEL, as they have opportunity, to the untold multitudes around them, of whose corruption, darkness, and wretchedness no adequate conception can be formed in this land,—is a principal and daily work of the missionaries. In the prosecution of it, they not only visit the temples and places of resort in the city; but make circuits of less or greater extent, upon the islands, and in the provinces of the continent. In the course of a year, many thousands thus hear from them something concerning the true God and eternal life.

"Our daily custom"—they say in their latest joint letter, dated in January—"our daily custom of addressing the people, wherever we find them, we consider our most important business. In this branch of our labor we find some of our highest pleasures, as well as our chief trials.

"The brethren in Bombay have hired a large room for a school, and have made some use of it for the stated instruction of the people on the Sabbath. Attendance at present is rather encouraging, and those, who assemble are in general as silent and attentive as could be expected. We would hope, that the divine blessing will enable us to continue these exercises, and will make them ultimately profitable to many.

"During the past seven months, we have taken the following tours for the promotion of our object. Brother Hall visited Panwell, and the vicinity, across on the coast. Brother Bardwell went to Bancote, and several adjacent towns, with some others nearer Bombay. Brethren Nichols and Graves went northward to Cullian and Bhewndy with several small places between them and Basseen. In all the towns we distributed many copies of the tracts and portions of Scripture, which we have printed. All these tours were very pleasant and refreshing to us. But we were called to mourn over many thousands living in spiritual darkness and death, while we could only give to some of them a hasty outline of the way of salvation. There are several important towns, where, if a missionary were permitted to settle, he might enjoy a more promising station than some of us now occupy. We would hope soon to welcome brethren, who will supply at least some of these places."

Of their tours for preaching some idea may be formed from the following extracts.

In the journal of his tour to Panwell, Mr. Hall says:

"About seven o'clock in the morning, Dec. 14, we landed at Panwell, which is about 12 or 15 miles east of Bombay.

"16. I went out among the people three times, which occupied nearly the whole of the day. I found opportunities for communicating religious instruction to a very considerable number of people. In some places, I spoke to 30, 40, 50 or 60 in one company. In another place, there were no more than three or four. I distributed a few books during the day. At first, when the people were told I had religious books to *give*, they could not believe it; but seemed deterred from receiving them, through fear they should have to pay for them sooner or later. The idea of a gratuitous distribution of books among them, was what they probably never before heard or thought of. But when they were convinced, that nothing would ever be received of them for the book, and that they were *religious* books, they seemed to be in no fear of receiving them. And the fact of their being *religious* books, was mentioned among themselves more than once, in my hearing, as a reason why they should be received. I soon perceived, however, that only a small part of the people could read, and that I was not likely to dispose of a large number of books, unless I were in effect to throw them away.

"The first person, who asked me for the books, was a Jew of respectable appearance. I gave him Genesis and John, bound together, and a tract. Of this man I learned something of the state of the Jews in this place.

"I reached the further village, called by the natives Tukkeer, between eleven and twelve o'clock. It was an hour of the day, in which many of the people were engaged in their respective labors, and therefore less favorable for their assembling to hear me. I walked through the village and saw no convenient opportunity for commencing my labors. After walking about until I began to be weary, and almost discouraged, I turned aside to a border of the village, where a few boys were at play, and a few adults standing near them under the grateful shade of a large tamarind tree. I came to them, and asked them if they would listen to what I had to communicate to them. They readily complied, and I took my seat and desired them to sit down around me, and also to invite the other villagers, who were disengaged, to come and hear. About thirty persons were soon assembled, and to them I read and discoursed on the great things of the gospel, for about an hour. They seemed very attentive: no one contradicted; and I thought their appearance manifested, that their consciences testified to the truth of God's word, which they heard. I gave books to a few among them, who could read, and they were received with apparent gratitude.

"A little detached from the town, and in the rear of a large Hindoo temple, was a little hamlet containing about 15 huts. Hearing the sound of music among these poor cottages, I bent my course thither, and found nearly the whole village, men, women, and children, 60 or 70 in all, assembled in one house, stowed together as thick as possible, and engaged in their ceremonies. The occasion was this. A woman was ill of a fever, though to appearance she was by no means severely ill Her poor heathen neighbors, in their sympathy and compassion, were assembled to relieve the sick woman from her illness by their incantations and nameless extravagances The woman was seated nearly in the middle of the assembly. Before her, some white marks were fancifully drawn upon the ground, (the common flooring of their poor houses,) flowers, parched rice, &c. were scattered about, and incense was burning. A number of the people, men and women, nearest to the sick person, were writhing and forcing themselves into the most wild, unnatural and painful attitudes, sometimes blowing ashes into each other's faces, beating themselves, and striking their foreheads violently on the ground. The design of the whole seemed to be to move their god, from a view of what they were voluntarily suffering, to extend relief to the sick person; and this seemed to be accompanied by a kind of challenge, that if their god would not grant their request, they would·torture themselves to death. For now and then they would exclaim to their god, "Hear us, or we will die: why should we live, if thou wilt not hear us." The noise of several drums, beating at the same time in the house, made it a scene of much confusion, which is generally the case, when any ceremonies of idolatry are performed. The scene excited in my mind an unusual degree of tenderness and pity for these my deluded fellow mortals, and I resolved that, before I left them, I would instruct their ignorant minds in the knowledge of the true God. After waiting awhile, they, in a great measure, intermitted their devotions; and I addressed myself to them, and desired, that they would hear what I had to say. They very readily complied, and soon all were still in the house. I asked them, why they thus tortured themselves! Should your child, said I, come and ask any thing of you when it stood in need, would any one, who is a parent, be pleased to see his child put itself in pain and anguish, in order to induce the parent to give the thing requested? "No, no," was the reply, from several of the company. I told them, that God was their kind and tender parent; that he did not take pleasure in seeing any of his creatures inflict pain upon themselves; and that he was able and ready to hear and grant the prayers of all, who come to him humble and penitent. I enlarged upon the character of God; endeavored to convince them of their great sin in rejecting him, and worshipping idols and beasts and men; and told them, how their offended Maker would be reconciled to them through his crucified Son, if they would repent, believe, forsake their idols, and obey the truth.

"They were very attentive, and some of them were somewhat affected with what they heard. One called aloud and said, *I was a God;* from which I took occasion to reprove her, and to speak further to them on the character of the true God, whom alone they must worship, if they would escape everlasting wo and obtain eternal happiness. Some said, "Let us lay aside our ceremonies;" and I have reason to think they did so I exhorted them to think, from day to day, of what I had told them, for it was God's message of love and mercy to them. They said they would. I then left them highly grateful for the attentive hearing, which they gave God's word.

"It was about midday, when I hastened towards the village of Tamboor, which lies on the road to Cullian, and is about three miles distant from Panwell. On my way I fell in with two travellers; one an inhabitant of Cullian, to whom I gave tracts, and who promised to have them read in the circle of his relations and friends. To both of my fellow travellers, I endeavored to point out the only way to heaven.

"When I reached the village of Tamboor, I inquired for the Pattell, that is, the head man of the village. Being directed to him, he received me in a very friendly manner, and, on my proposing it, most of the people, who were disengaged, amounting to about 60, were almost *immediately* assembled: for the houses of this little hamlet, though more than 20 in number, are, as I should judge, all within the limits of an acre of ground.

"I spent nearly an hour in preaching to this little assembly. The people were very attentive. None contradicted or objected; but all seemed to approve; and they promised to remember and regard what they had heard. They told me, that there were three persons belonging to the village who could read, but that they had all gone abroad. I left books for them, which the people promised to have read. It seemed a matter of some surprise to these villagers, to see *a white man* travelling about on foot, in the character of a religious teacher. They seemed, however, to be highly gratified with my visit to them; and, on my departure, they gave me many compliments and good wishes, and insisted on my acceptance of one of their villagers, to guide me in the best foot path to the next village.

The next place I arrived at can hardly be called a village, as it contained only five huts. I sat down by the way side, under the shade of a large tree, and addressed myself, for a short time, to eight or ten persons. On taking my leave of this little audience, I was again, in the same friendly manner as before, furnished with a guide to the next village, called Adda. There I called on the Pattell as at Tamboor, was received in the same friendly manner, and within a few minutes after I reached the place, I was seated in the midst of not less than 70 Hindoos. I discoursed to them about three quarters of an hour. They were very attentive; and their whole appearance was very interesting and encouraging to my feelings. At the conclusion of my discourse, I addressed them, as I had previously addressed several other like assemblies, nearly in these terms; "My friends, I have come to you in the name of God your Maker. I have come with a message from Him to you. I have delivered his message to you. You have heard it. It is *his* word, and not mine. I never saw you before, and I know not that I shall ever see you again until the day of judgment.—Such a day is coming, when the one only true God will assemble all men before him, and judge and reward all men according to their works. Then I must give an account to God of the manner, in which I have this day delivered his holy message to you, and you also must give an account to God of the manner in which you have received, and shall have treated his gracious message of saving love. He is now looking into our hearts, observes all our actions, and knows all things. Oh prepare for that awful day. Fear and worship and serve the true God, your Maker, and your Judge. Repent and forsake your sins. Believe in Jesus Christ; obey his gospel. No more worship your vain idols, which are an abomination to God. Let this sink into your hearts. Regard it, and it surely shall be well with you in life—well with you in death—well with you in judgment—well with you in eternity."

"The idea of being called to judgment seemed considerably to affect them. Several spoke out aloud, "We will no more worship idols, we will worship only the one true God, as you have told us" They asked when I should come to them again, and expressed many strong wishes, that I should soon make them another visit. I was told, that not one person belonging to the village could read There was present a young man from Panwell, who acted in the capacity of a writer in the village, who could read. I gave him books, which he promised to read to the people. This village, like each of the others which I visited to-day, did not, as I was informed, contain a single bramhun. Wherever we find the people removed from the bramhuns, they seem more accessible and more attentive; and the prospect of winning souls to Christ seems the greatest.

"Leaving the village of Adda, I returned to Panwell, having made a circuit, as nearly as I could judge, of seven or eight miles, the greater part of which was performed in the hottest hours of the day I was extremely fatigued; but know not, that I ever spent a day more agreeably to my feelings and wishes."

The next are passages from the Journal of Mr. Nichols at Tannah.

"*September* 20. Brother Graves and myself have determined on a tour of 10 or 12 days, Providence permitting, though it will be attended with much fatigue and danger, on account of the season.

"30. Have just returned from our tour. Went to Cullian by water, and passed an uncomfortable night on board the boat Visited the school, and found many things in it to correct. Brother G. addressed many people, and encountered one angry bramhun. We tarried two days in that place. Went to Bhewndy, seven miles from Cullian, where we distributed many books, and our whole stock was soon nearly exhausted. None, that we know of, had been distributed in the place before. A detachment of the native army under European officers were cantoned there We were treated with much attention by the officers. It is impossible for one, who has always lived in our free country, to conceive with what strictness all white people are here noticed by the police and the army. We cannot set our foot on the continent without a formal passport.

"Left Bhewndy on the 24th and proceeded about 3 miles to a village on our way to Basseen. After addressing the villagers, we retired to rest in an open *veranda*. The Hindoos have neither chairs, tables, nor beds Of course, whoever travels among them must sit on the ground, eat on the ground, and sleep on the ground. Our journeying from village to village was through deep mud, long grass, and water sometimes up to the middle. To wear shoes and stockings was out of the question, though our feet suffered much from the stones and gravel. With bare feet we travelled over a region inhabited by tygers, and were in continual danger from serpents which might be concealed in the long grass. On the evening of the 25th we arrived at a village, where we spent a Sabbath of rest. Sabbath evening, before we had retired to rest, while reclining on a mat in an open *veranda*, I was roused by a serpent crawling over my feet;

and, before I could speak, it was under the feet of brother G. Through mercy we were not bitten. The serpent was killed before the door. We doubt not that it was poisonous, though not of the most venomous kind. There is a species of serpent very common here, whose bite causes death in 5 or 10 minutes, and for which the natives know of no remedy. Just as we had crossed the river at Cullian, we came near treading on a horned viper. From the above mentioned place, we embarked in a large canoe for Basseen, finding it so exceedingly uncomfortable to proceed further by land. Arrived at Basseen after a tedious day on the water. We are much affected with the divine goodness, which has preserved us so well, when so much exposed.

"We were both delighted with the fine order in which we found the school at Bassen. There is a greater number of expert readers and writers in this school than in any one, which I have seen in this country. The days we spent at this place being holidays, the people gave little attention to the Gospel. However, brother G. addressed two or three large companies. We gave away the remainder of our books.

"The institutions of idolatry are very flourishing at this place. Satan has laughed to scorn that kind of Christianity which was set up with so much pomp by the Portuguese, and fortified his own kingdom with double strength. Returning to Tannah in a boat with several passengers, brother G. spoke largely on the gospel plan of salvation; but the whole of it was declared to be a hard saying, which Hindoos never could nor would hear.

"On the whole, our tour has been interesting, but hazardous. Many have heard what they never heard before, but God alone can make his own word effectual. During our absence, divine goodness has been richly extended to our dear companions, and our little ones, as well as to ourselves."

A brief passage or two, from the Journal of Mr. Graves at Mahim, will close these extracts.

"*Sabbath*, 5. Met with several Jews. Had much conversation with them respecting the time of the Messiah's coming, and the claims of Jesus to the Messiahship. They were neither prepared nor inclined to contradict my reasoning. The misery of their state is their extreme ignorance and carelessness respecting the Messiah. One of them, however, said, that some of his people regarded the late dreadful earthquakes as betokening the near approach of the Messiah. He had also inquired of a certain Jew, who informed him, that when the world ended then the Messiah would come. I told them he would indeed come a second time ere long to judge the world, and it became them to prepare to meet him.

"*Sept.* 30. Returned from Tannah from which place I had travelled with brother Nichols, having spent nine days in a tour to Cullian and Basseen. At Cullian and Bhewndy from 20 to 100, or 150 and 200 attended our addresses, and we were interrupted very little while attempting to publish the words of life. From Cullian by Bhewndy we travelled about 20 miles on foot. We invited the people in the several villages, through which we passed, to come together and hear the way of salvation. And they commonly collected in numbers proportioned to the size of the village, and heard with a silent attention, or made such inquiries as were generally quite appropriate. They behaved also with much propriety while, as we parted from them, they were commended to the mercy of God in Christ Jesus by prayer.

"There being much rain and very deep water, through which we were obliged to pass on foot, we judged it advisable to go the remainder of our way to Basseen by a boat. In the latter place also we had many interesting opportunities of addressing the people, and in all the places distributed a number of tracts. While on our way we had favorable and pleasant seasons of attempting to publish the gospel to the boatmen and passengers. As we spent one night on board with 25 or 30 men, they all decently attended, while the protection and blessing of God were requested through the name of Jesus."

THE TRANSLATING OF THE SCRIPTURES, early engaged the attention of Messrs. Hall and Newell. That the Scriptures in the vernacular language of the people would be of essential importance to the great object of the mission, must be evident to every mind. To the missionaries it was most palpable. And scarcely less palpable were the evils of a bad translation, in its effects upon the minds of the people, in the embarrassment it would occasion to missionaries, and in the waste and loss of time and money.

"It would seem," they say, in a paper upon the general subject, of which mention was made in the Report of 1816,—"It would seem to be a self evident principle, that no person can translate correctly into any language, which he does not understand as well, or nearly as well, as his mother tongue; and it seems to be no less evident, that no person can understand a foreign language as well, or nearly as well, as his mother tongue, without residing at least a number of years in the country where that language is vernacular, and conversing habitually with all kinds of people who speak the language.

"The language of books, in every country, is rather above the ready comprehension of the common people. But in the east, where instruction is limited to the few, while the pride of learning leads those who possess it to affect, in their language and compositions, a style of studied superiority, the language of books becomes nearly as unintelligible to the common people, as Latin is to the unlearned in Europe and America. Now those translators, who have never been in the countries, where the languages, into which they translate, are vernacular, must have acquired their knowledge of the languages principally from books; and their translations, of course, will be in the book style, and not in the popular dialect. Hence such translations, it would seem, can be of little if any use to the great body of the people, for whom they are designed."

This is sensibly said; and it might have been added, that, for a good translation, not only is a lengthened residence among the people necessary; and a free intercourse with them; but also the practice of preaching to them, expounding to them the Scriptures and conversing with them familiarly on divine subjects. And it has become a well known fact, that some of the translations of the present age, hastily made without these advantages, have proved unintelligible and useless to the people, for whose benefit they were intended.

Under these impressions, in a letter which accompanied the paper just cited, the missionaries say;

"We consider it our duty, if God should spare our lives long enough, to attempt a translation of the Bible, in the Mahratta language, which is vernacular here, and is spoken by many millions of people on this side of India. And if we, with the aid of others, who, we hope, will shortly come to our assistance, are enabled, in the course of our lives, to make a good translation of the sacred volume, into this, one language, in addition to preaching the Gospel daily to the heathen, (which we consider the principal business of a missionary,) we shall think that we have not labored in vain, nor spent our strength for nought."

Such were the feelings and views with which, about five years ago, they commenced the arduous and responsible undertaking; and in accordance with them is the manner, in which, as your Committee believe, the work has been prosecuted.

At first they took care, that portions of the Scriptures, which they had translated, should be perused in manuscript, by learned and by unlearned natives, and then ascertained how these portions were understood. As soon as they got their printing press into operation, they began to print select passages, and to distribute them among the people, and use them in their schools. In this practice they have ever since continued; and the advantages it must have afforded them for revising and correcting, and making their translation in all respects what it ought to be, will be obvious to every mind.

More than a year ago, they had translated the whole of the New Testament and a considerable part of the Old; and they are by this time prepared for printing and distributing the Scriptures in part, or in whole, as soon and as fast as means for defraying the expense shall be afforded to them, and a due attention to the other departments of their general work will admit. They have labored in this department with indefatigable diligence.

Besides the great work of translating the Scriptures, they have composed, compiled, and translated several tracts and school books, and some of them such as must have cost no inconsiderable time and labor.

Another part of their work, in which they have shewn the same exemplary industry, is PRINTING. As soon almost as they entered upon active operations, they began to feel the want of a printing press. Not only were they without Bibles, tracts, and school books, for the various purposes of the mission, but there were none to be obtained. There was not even a press with the Nagree type, the proper character for the native language, within a thousand miles of them. Measures were accordingly taken for a printing establishment. With a view to it, Mr Bardwell acquired some knowledge of the printing business before he was sent out; and about the time of his arrival, a press, with a fount of Nagree types, which had been engaged, was received from Calcutta. No time was lost in putting it into operation, and early in March, 1817, they finished the printing of fifteen hundred copies of a Scripture Tract of eight pages, executed almost entirely with their own hands.

In their first attempt, they had many and great difficulties to overcome, but they have since proceeded in this part of their work with facility and despatch. At the date of their last joint communication, in the fore part of January last, they had printed, besides the tract now mentioned, the *Gospel of Matthew*, the *Acts of the Apostles*, and *two Tracts*, consisting chiefly of *select portions of Scripture*, all in large editions; three editions, 1000 copies each, of a Tract composed by themselves, entitled *The way to Heaven;* another Tract entitled *The Compassion of Christ towards sinful man;* the *First Number* of a work, which they have begun, giving a succinct view of *Scripture History; the Book of Genesis;* the *Gospel of John;* a *Catechism,* designed especially for the use of schools; a *Reading Book,* also for the schools, *An easy and expeditious method of acquiring a knowledge of the English Language, designed for the benefit of those Natives who wish to study English and the Sciences;* another School Book, and were preparing to print the Epistles of James, Peter, John, and Jude. Besides these for the mission, they had printed an edition of the *Gospel of Matthew* for the Bombay Bible Society; and *Christ's Sermon on the Mount,* partly for that Society, and partly for the mission. Thus much, amidst all their other labors, they had accomplished with their press, in little more than two years.

THE EDUCATION OF NATIVE CHILDREN is an object, on which these missionaries have bestowed very earnest and laborious attention. Their first free school was commenced in the summer of 1815, and in our last annual Report the number of their schools was stated to be twenty-five, and the total of pupils was estimated, from communications which had then been received, at nearly a hundred Jewish, and more than twelve hundred heathen children. In their joint letter, thirteen months ago, the account is more exact, and the total number enrolled in their schools, as regular pupils, is given at 1,019. Besides these, there are large numbers of inconstant and less regular attendants. What additions have been made to the number of the schools or of the pupils, in the last thirteen months, your Committee have not yet the means of reporting In their last joint letter the missionaries say, "Applications for new schools are very frequent." But their funds were not sufficient to answer either the necessities of the people, or their own benevolent desires. But the field is wide and the harvest is most plenteous; and this Board and the Christian community may be assured, that if sufficient funds are afforded to those faithful and energetic laborers, few as they are, within less than five years to come they will number in their schools ten thousand pupils.

"In all the schools," they say, "those who can read, are daily employed in reading or committing to memory some portions of the Scriptures or tracts which we have printed." "We occasionally pray in the schools, and instruct them with our own lips." In various respects indeed, their schools afford them very important advantages for the benevolent purposes of the mission. In them they have access, at all times, to many young and susceptible minds, under circumstances eminently favorable for deep and salutary impression; through them, they find, also, the best avenues to the minds and hearts of the parents and connexions of the pupils, and by means of them, they have great facilities, in their visiting and preaching circuits, for distributing the Scriptures, or portions of the Scriptures, and their different tracts, with the fairest hope of their being attentively read.

The extreme difficulty of obtaining children to be educated in their families, was stated and explained in the Report of the last year. "The natives," they say, "have not forgotten the violence practised on them and their religion by the Portuguese; and their jealousies are ever

34

awake. Indeed, it is matter of astonishment to us, that we have been permitted to proceed so quietly with our schools and our daily instruction."

Mr. Hall, however, has taken into his family, and under his own special care and instruction, two African children; and Mr. Bardwell two Portuguese children. They were miserable outcasts; objects of compassion, as really as the Hindoo children, and as suitable for charitable and Christian education. And of such as these, many, it is supposed, might be obtained.

It is also particularly gratifying to state, that at Salsette the difficulty of obtaining Hindoo children for family instruction, is found to be not so insuperable as at Bombay. As soon as they were comfortably settled, and tolerably acquainted with the native language, Mr. and Mrs. Nichols "resolved on using every effort to establish a school in their house."—In his Journal, May 17, 1819, Mr. Nichols says.

"Our family school of Hindoo boys is increasing· it is to us a most interesting charge; they spend almost the whole day with us, and are made apparently happy by our familiarity. We instruct these dear boys in the most familiar manner, in the leading truths of Christianity. Several of them can repeat the commandments from memory, and also a hymn. We have taught the boys to sing this hymn; and I doubt not our beloved patrons and friends would be delighted to hear their sweet voices accompanying ours, as a part of our morning service. Abraham a Jew, and Peteya a Hindoo, on account of their even temper and pleasant disposition, have become as dear to us as our own child. They were the first, that came to us. Daoojee, another Hindoo, and Balajee, a Jew, are boys of as fine talents, as we ever met with in America. Bha-oo, another Hindoo boy, whom we loved on account of his open manners and friendly disposition, has been taken from us by his uncle, lest we should make him a Christian."

In a letter, dated Feb. 12, 1820, Mr. N. says further, "Our family school of Hindoo and black Jewish boys affords us much satisfaction. We have nine under our care. We are endeavoring, in the tenderest manner possible, to detach them from the idolatry and wickedness of their fathers. Their improvement is very laudable"

It is still the great trial of these devoted laborious servants of the Lord, to spend their strength in a field, on which there is scarcely rain or dew from on high; and where the harvest, from the seed which they sow, is hardly to be expected before they are called to rest from their ·labors. But the seed must be sown, or there will never be a harvest. To sow is the work, the duty, and the privilege of·men; to give the increase, and the joy of harvest, is the work, the prerogative, and the glory of God.

Your Committee, however, have the satisfaction gratefully to announce one hopeful and interesting convert by the instrumentality of this mission.

In a letter of March 1819, Mr. Newell writes thus:—

"I have had, for some days past, a Nicodemus to instruct, Mohammed Kadin, of Hydrabad.* He came about a month ago to receive, as he

* This city is in the province of Golconda, nearly due east of Bombay

says, Christian baptism. He is a Mussulman of high rank, and came down with a train of 20 men. He has sent them all back, and lives here in retirement, and does not wish to be known. He has been with me every day for more than a week past, but desires the object of our conferences to be kept a secret for the present. He has stated to me his object in conversation, and has put into my hands a paper in Hindoostanee, which is certainly a very curious and interesting one."

In a letter about two months after, Mr. Newell says further:

"In March last, I mentioned to you a Mussulman inquirer from Hydrabad, and promised to give you a more particular account of him by the next opportunity. He is still in Bombay and has been with me, and has eaten at my house the most of the time, since the date of my last letter to you. He states, that his sole object in coming from Hydrabad to this place, (a distance of more than 400 miles,) was to gain further instruction in the Christian religion, and to receive baptism. He says that he is of a very respectable family, and of high standing in his own country; and his personal appearance, and comparatively extensive information, agree perfectly well with his own account of himself. I put into his hands Mr. Martyn's Hindoostanee translation of the New Testament, and of the common Prayer Book, and pointed him to such places, as I thought would be most useful to him. I have repeatedly read and explained to him, the third chapter of the Gospel of John. He assents to the necessity of a spiritual change, but does not profess to have any experimental knowledge of it, and seems to be more inquisitive about the forms and the history of Christianity, than about its spiritual and practical part. I once asked him whether he now read the Koran, and worshipped in the Musjd.* He replied that he had not done either, for a long time. I asked him, what he now thought of his former religion.—He said he thought it was right for him to live as a Mussulman, while he continued in that faith; but that, becoming a Christian, it was no longer right for him to live as a Mussulman. This is a specimen of the state of his mind, as to religious knowledge."

In their joint letter of January last, the brethren write;

"On the 25th of September last, the Mussulman Kadin Yar Khan was baptized. We indulge the hope, that he is truly born of God: if so, may the glory be given to whom alone it is due. We have employed him some as a Hindoostanee teacher; and as opportunity presents, he recommends, both by argument and example, the religion of Jesus to others. He was very willing to change his name and his dress, and to cut off his beard. But as such a change appeared inexpedient to us, he is not distinguished, in these respects, from a Mussulman."

A little later is this brief notice from Mr Nichols:

"Our new convert is now with us. His walk and his conversation are truly encouraging."

In the close of their last joint letter the missionaries thus express the state of their feelings.

"As messengers of the Lord Jesus Christ, from the Board, and the churches, we assure them, that we are not at all disheartened; but live in the pleasing anticipation that God will ultimately bless our poor labors

---

* Mosque or temple.

to the salvation of many souls, and we hope the reception of one is but a token of an approaching harvest to be gathered in. Surely the word of God will not return void, and we would never slacken our hands in the dispensation of it. And oh, may we have more faith and zeal and patience, that we may be so blessed as to gather fruit unto eternal life."

MISSION IN THE ISLAND OF CEYLON.—On behalf of Messrs. Winslow, Spaulding, Woodward, and Scudder, mentioned in the report of the last year, as having embarked on the 8th of the preceding June, there is reason for great thankfulness to the Supreme Disposer. The vessel was not indeed in season to touch at Ceylon, and leave the missionaries there, as it was hoped she might, on her way to Calcutta; but at the latter place, the port of her destination, she arrived, all on board being well, about the middle of October. "Though our passage," they say in their first letter, "has been longer than we hoped it would be, it has been much more pleasant than we anticipated. On the whole, our sea has been smooth, our accommodations good, and our long passage the journey of a day."

Their time, during the passage, as there is good reason to believe, was not spent in vain.

"Soon after we began to recover from sickness," they say, "we agreed, in addition to our morning and evening devotions, and public worship for the Sabbath, to meet on Tuesday for improvement in singing; on Wednesday evening for a public conference in the cabin; on Friday for prayer and free remarks on experimental religion, or any impropriety seen in the conduct of each other; and on Saturday for reading the public journal and for prayer. We have also observed the monthly concert. In the course of our voyage, we have set apart two days, as seasons of fasting and prayer, and two for seasons of thanksgiving. Other meetings for prayer have been frequent.

"Our labors among the seamen have been considerable. The particulars you will find in our public journal. We only remark here, that we are not left to mourn that we have labored in vain, but are called to rejoice, that the pleasure of the Lord has prospered in our hands.

"Of Capt. Wills we have reason to speak with much gratitude. He is a Christian brother dear to us. From him we have had many favors, to render our situation agreeable and our passage pleasant. We shall ever remember him with affection. The other officers have been obliging. The seamen have treated us with great respect, and listened to our instructions with much attention."

In a subsequent letter, written just as they were leaving Calcutta, nearly a month after the first, they say:—

"All the seamen on board were impressed, and we did hope that every one had become the subject of renewing grace. After our arrival at Calcutta, some to our grief, did not maintain a consistent Christian character, and though with the exception of one, who left the vessel in a singular manner, and perhaps two more, who appear to a considerable degree hardened, the remainder shew signs of repentance, we are constrained to stand in doubt of some. We hope, indeed, that a removal from the incitements of a wicked city, and being again at sea, when there will be opportunity for serious reflection, will bring all to remember whence they have fallen, and to repent. This we are encouraged to hope, from the manner in which they parted from us last evening, all being very much affected, and sorrowing that they should see our faces no more. But we commit them to the protection of him who is able to keep them from falling.

By the particular and full account given by the missionaries in their letters and journal, and most amply confirmed by the testimony of the highly and justly beloved and respected captain, and of the officers and men generally, it is placed beyond doubt, that the abundant and faithful instructions and warnings given to the seamen, were efficacious in an extraordinary measure. The seriousness, which began with a few, became general; and for a considerable time before their arrival, the impression upon the whole company was most solemn and most profound. From all that is known since the return of the vessel, it is most fully believed, that the Lord, in very deed, was with the missionaries, and that few instances are on record, in which the power of his grace was more manifest, or those within its influence in greater proportion evidently reformed, and hopefully renewed for immortality and glory.

Of what befel these favored brethren at Calcutta, your Committee cannot give a better account, than is given by themselves, in the letter from which the last quotation was made.

"On our arrival at Calcutta, we thought it best to accept a kind invitation from Capt. Wills, to take a part of his house. We can never say too much concerning the kindness of this dear man; nor mention the many little attentions, which contributed to render our passage pleasant. During our stay of three weeks at Calcutta, he not only provided rooms for us, and kept us all at his table free of expense, but in various ways contributed, in articles of necessity and convenience for our mission, not less than two hundred dollars; beside many nameless expenses, incurred for our comfort while we were with him. By his exertions, likewise, and those of Mr. Ceyder, an American resident in Calcutta, whom we would mention with gratitude, more than a hundred dollars were raised for us from other American friends. Mr. Newton too, whose name is probably familiar to you, partly by his means, became so much interested for us, as not only to take the trouble of providing for us a passage to Ceylon, but in connection with a few other friends of missions, to contribute five hundred dollars towards the expense. This benevolent gentleman, with Mrs. Newton, a native of Pittsfield, Mass., who likewise shewed us much kindness, is about to return to Boston.

"At Calcutta, though in a land of strangers, we found ourselves surrounded by friends. The evening after our arrival, we met most of the Baptist brethren, of whom there are now six in Calcutta, (the younger brethren, who were at Serampore, having separated from Drs. Carey and Marshman, and established themselves in Calcutta,) all the brethren from the London Society, of whom there are four, and Mr. Schmidt, from the Church Missionary Society. We enjoyed with them a precious season of prayer, and Christian intercourse. The first hymn was given out by Mr. Townley, of the London Society:—"*Kindred in Christ for his dear sake,—a hearty welcome here receive.*" This, we believe, expresses the real feelings of those, whom we met. They are precious men, and are doing a good work in Calcutta. Their moral influence is already felt, and an important change is effected; especially as to the treatment of missionaries. This was seen in our polite reception at the police office, and in the generosity at the custom house, where all our baggage, together with the boxes of medicine, books, &c. belonging to the Board, were passed, both in landing and re-shipping, free of duty, and even of inspection.

"But it was not designed that we should leave Calcutta without trials. We had been there but five days, when brother Scudder was called to part with his dear little daughter. She died of an illness of three days. The next day, sister Winslow was taken sick, and brought near the grave. The woman of color was also very sick, and sister Woodward was brought so low, that her life was almost despaired of, and we were obliged to leave her and her husband behind. After her recovery they will take the earliest opportunity of a passage to Ceylon.

"We are now on board the Dick, of London, Capt. Harrison, a pleasant ship, with good accommodations; and are to be landed either at Trincomalee, or Colombo, as we please."

It was a painful circumstance to Mr. and Mrs. Woodward, to be left behind; and before the Dick had got far down the river, Mrs. Woodward felt herself so much better, that, after advising with her physician, they made arrangements for attempting to overtake the ship. But just at the time, their infant was seized with severe illness, and the attempt was relinquished. In the fore part of December, they embarked in a brig, bound, as was the Dick, to Trincomalee, and Colombo.

The only communication, which has been received from these young brethren, since their leaving Calcutta, is contained in a letter from Messrs. Winslow and Spaulding, dated Colombo, Feb. 2d.

"We took passage," they say, "for Ceylon, Nov. 10th, in a good ship, the Dick of London, and had only to regret the detention of brother Woodward by the sickness of his wife. We left him however, with the assurance, that though in a land of strangers, he was surrounded by sympathizing friends, and under the care of a kind Providence.

"Our passage was long, but pleasant. By the kindness of our captain, we were permitted not only to preach on the Sabbath, but to hold meetings every evening with the seamen. They generally gave good attention. some appeared seriously impressed; and we left the ship with the hope, that two at least were under deep convictions. We made the island of Ceylon, 19 days after embarking, and 12 from the time of leaving the river; but it was three days more before we could gain the harbor of Trincomalee, being carried beyond it at night by a very strong current, which exposed us to some danger from the rocks on the coast. At Trincomalee we were very kindly received by the Wesleyan brethren, Messrs. Carver and Stead, who did every thing in their power to assist us

"We hoped to find some method of direct conveyance from this port to Jaffna; but as the monsoon rendered it impossible to go by water, there was none except through an almost trackless jungle of 130 miles, in the course of which were several rivers to be forded. The journey we concluded to attempt; but on endeavoring to procure palankeens and coolies, we found they could not be obtained for so many travellers. Our passage was paid at Colombo, and the prospect was, that we could find a more ready conveyance there, than from any other port on the island. Brother Scudder, however, as his labors seemed to be peculiarly needed at Jaffna, on account of the ill health of our brethren there, concluded to attempt the journey by land. With some difficulty the means of conveyance were found; and we left Trincomalee after a stay of three days, while our dear brother and sister were preparing to go through the wilderness.

"On our way to Colombo we touched at Galle, a very pleasant port on the southern extremity of the island, and were detained several days. During this time, we were most hospitably entertained, in the family of a Mr. McKenney, a Wesleyan missionary; and our hearts were cheered by a sight of the good work, which he and his colleagues are there carrying on. The schools, which form the glory of the Wesleyan missions here, are at this station very flourishing, and afford an interesting spectacle.

"We finally reached Colombo, Dec. 20th, rejoicing to see this capital of the country, which is to be our future home. The Rev. Mr. Chater, who is well known as the very kind and hospitable friend of our brethren, immediately invited us to his house, till we could make arrangements for proceeding to Jaffna."

After mentioning here some circumstances, which unavoidably lengthened their stay at Colombo, and stating, that they were to go thence to Jaffna in company with that very valuable friend of our mission, J. N. Mooyart, Esq. they proceed to say;—

"We are now to start to-morrow. The delay we have regretted, though our situation has been rendered as pleasant as it could be, by the kindness of those around us, especially of Mr. and Mrs. Chater, to whom we are deeply indebted, and to the Wesleyan brethren at this station. The other friends of our mission, who reside at this place, have treated us with attention and kindness.

"We had the pleasure of meeting most of the missionaries on the island: the Wesleyans holding their annual conference here, and the church missionaries being met on the business of their mission. There were yesterday at our table fifteen missionaries; such a thing as probably never was seen at Colombo before. The church missionaries are regularly with us in the same family. They are most valuable men."—

"Since coming here, we have received many communications from the brethren at Jaffna. They are still afflicted with sickness. Brother Richards is better than it was expected he ever would be, but far from having any prospect of final recovery. Brothers Poor and Meigs are both nearly laid aside by sickness; though they were both better at the date of our last accounts. Brother and sister Scudder arrived in safety to their assistance after a long and dangerous journey. He seems to have entered with spirit into the work. You will have learned before this, that the brethren have already seen some fruit of their labor—in the apparent conversion of several among the natives."

"We have to-day heard of the safe arrival of our brother and sister Woodward at Trincomalee. The Lord has afflicted them, since we parted, by the removal of their little son. From brother and sister Scudder we heard three days ago, that she had become the mother of a fine little girl; and to-day we have the sad intelligence of its death. We long to see and sympathize with the afflicted parents."

In a postscript, bearing date Dec. 23d, the brethren in Jaffna express their feelings as follows:—

"As cold water to a thirsty soul, so is good news from a far country. On the first Monday in the month, (a joyful day to missionaries,) we went to Nellore, to unite with our missionary brethren in the observance of the monthly prayer meeting. On our arrival at the mission house in that place, we found a letter containing the joyful intelligence, that four American missionaries and their wives, destined to Ceylon, had arrived at Calcutta. In regard to some of the important petitions which we were about to offer at the prayer meeting, we could testify to the truth of God's gracious promise, 'And it shall come to pass, that before they call I will answer, and while they are yet speaking, I will hear.' The contents of the preceding letter will give you a better idea of our feelings on this occasion, than any particular description of them. You can readily imagine, in some degree, what effect this intelligence must have had upon our minds, as we entered upon the pleasing solemnities of the day.

"In the midst of our services, yea 'while we were yet speaking,' we were interrupted by the receipt of a letter from a kind Wesleyan brother at Trincomalee, informing us that three of our brethren and sisters had arrived at that place, and that he was making arrangements for some of them to come to Jaffna by land. This information gave a fresh impulse to our feelings, which were already highly excited. Our missionary brethren present were partakers of our joy, and could unite in rendering thanksgiving to God, both on our account, and on account of the missionary cause in this district.

"Though it was the intention of our brethren to come from Trincomalee to Jaffna by land, they found it to be impracticable. Proper conveyances could be obtained only for two persons.

"Brother and sister Scudder arrived at Tillipally the 17th instant, to our great joy and comfort. They were the bearers of large packages of letters, which made us quite ashamed of the suspicions we had indulged, that our American friends had forgotten us. We are sorry to say, that a number of letters, referred to in those we have now received, have not reached us; and we fear they are lost. We hope our friends will consider, that the possibility of some of their letters being lost, is no small reason, which should induce them to write to us *more frequently.*"

A private letter dated in Feb. states, that Dr. Scudder arrived at the station on the 17th of Dec. Mr. Woodward early in January, and Messrs. Winslow and Spaulding just before the date of the letter.

It is gratifying to your Committee to state, that in all the places visited by Messrs. Winslow and Spaulding, at Trincomalee, at Galle, and at Colombo, they found an unanimous sentiment of high and affectionate esteem and admiration of our missionaries in Jaffna, as most laborious, and faithful, and devoted men; and, which cannot be stated without strong and mingled feelings, a general and deep impression, that by their increasing efforts, their constant self-denial, their readiness to spend, and be spent, in the service, they were fast wearing themselves out;—and that it would be much for the honor of American Christians to afford them a more liberal patronage and more ample aid.

It will be recollected that, (as was mentioned in the Report of 1818,) soon after our missionaries in Ceylon first entered upon their work, they felt and expressed a strong desire to be furnished, as speedily as possible, with a printing establishment, and means for putting it into vigorous operation The reasons for such a measure appeared to be solid and urgent, and your Committee charged themselves with the care of answering the request. It was hoped, that a printer would go out with the missionaries, who went a year ago, but that hope was disappointed. A printing press, however, a donation from a most liberal friend to this Board, and to its objects, having been previously sent by the way of Calcutta, a fount of types for English printing, and a supply of paper were added. Types for the Tamul, the native language of the principal population of that part of Ceylon, and of the neighboring districts of the continent, have been obtained from Calcutta. And your Committee have since had the satisfaction to send out a printer.

Mr. James Garrett, a young man belonging to Utica, N. Y. offered himself for the service, with very ample testimonials, as to his abilities and disposition and habits—his moral and Christian character—and his qualifications for taking charge of a printing establishment; and while he was in Boston, waiting for his passage, he established himself in the affectionate confidence of the Committee. On the 6th of April, he embarked in a vessel bound to Pondicherry. From that place, it is but a short distance to the seat of the mission, at which, it is hoped, he has ere this time arrived.

It was on the 2d of March, 1816, that Messrs. Richards, Meigs, and Poor, with their wives, and the dearly remembered Mr Warren, arrived at Colombo in Ceylon, and it was not until the first of the following October, now four years ago, that they had all reached Jaffna, the northern district of the island, where the mission was to be established.

Mr. Warren's course was short and bright, and its termination full of immortality. The life of Mr. Richards, so precious in the estimation of all the friends of mission's, it has pleased a gracious Providence to lengthen out, beyond our utmost hopes, and to render, in no small degree, consolatory and helpful to his brethren, under the pressure of multiplied labors and cares and afflictions. It was about sixteen months ago, that Mr. Poor began to be affected with pectoral weakness, and with slight raising of blood. For a considerable time, he was unable to attend to his accustomed labors, and there were serious apprehensions, that he was soon to follow Mr. Warren But the latest accounts give reason for hope. Of the impaired health of Mr Meigs, our first intelligence was what is contained in the extract just given of the letter from Colombo.

In a second postscript, dated Jan. 10, 1820, the brethren at the station write:—

"The afflicting hand of our God is still upon us. We are grieved, that we have occasion to say, that about a month ago brother Meigs was visited with a heavy cold and cough. About a week since his complaints became somewhat alarming. He has had a severe affection of the lungs. But from his present state, we have good reason to hope, that the seasonable and energetic means, which have been used, will be made effectual to his restoration to health The health of brethren Richards and Poor is the same, as it has been for months past. If there be any alteration, we think it is for the better. We have much reason for thanksgiving that brother Scudder arrived at the time he did."

As the Lord has been gracious, so prayer will continue to be made without ceasing, that he will still be gracious, and spare lives so inestimably valuable.

If all, who have lately been sent out, have duly arrived, and no breach has been made, of which intelligence has not been received, our Ceylon mission now consists of six ordained missionaries, a physician preparing also for ordination, their wives, and a printer. It occupies two principal stations, Tillipally and Batticotta, and has specially assigned to it six large parishes, with ancient buildings and lands, devoted to religious use, and containing a dense pagan population It is advantageously situated for communication with the different parts of the island, and with a populous province of Southern India, and for extensive and efficient operations· and it has enjoyed, in no slight degree, the confidence of the people and of the government.

Here, of course, as well as at Bombay, the missionaries are under the necessity of devoting labor and time to the acquisition of a language, having very little affinity with any language, with which they were previously acquainted. But it was not necessary for them to undertake the *translating of the Scriptures;* as a good translation into the native Tamul had long before been made.

IN PREACHING the missionaries have been constant and laborious; and their advantages for collecting regular congregations, or assemblies of hearers, are much better than are enjoyed by their brethren at Bombay, though they do not, in the course of a year, address by any means so great a multitude of immortal beings.

During the three years, from the time of their arrival to the 13th of Nov. last, the date of our latest accounts direct from the mission, they, afflicted and weakened as they were, had established fifteen schools; nine in connexion with Tillipally, and six with Batticotta. The total number of regular pupils was reckoned about 700, at the last date.

Besides these common free schools, there is at each station, a boarding school, consisting of youths, taken under the especial and parental care of the missionaries, supported by the bounty of benevolent societies and individuals in this country, and bearing names selected by the respective donors. Of these there were, at the time now specified, 48 males and nine females.

The accounts of the schools generally, and of the boarding schools in particular, are exceedingly interesting and encouraging. In all the schools, with the common branches of instruction, Scripture tracts are read and the principles of Christianity are taught. The pupils in general make good progress in their studies.

In the last letter, after various statements and remarks on the general subject, the missionaries proceed to say

"On the whole, respecting our boarding schools we have much pleasure, after two years of experience, in assuring the Prudential Committee, that our warmest expectations have thus far been fully realized; that we now experience important advantages, which we did not anticipate; that we do not realize those difficulties and impediments to improvement, which we expected would arise from the circumstance of our taking the children of idolaters; but, on the contrary, *we do not see how we should materially alter our plan of instruction, or our course of conduct, in case the same number of children, belonging to Christian parents, should be committed to our care.* Judging from what we already experience, and what we may with confidence anticipate, we consider our boarding schools as holding the second place in the system of means, which are to be used for the conversion of this people;—as second only to the stated preaching of the gospel. You, dear sir, can readily estimate the probable advantages to the cause of Christianity from the Christian education of 50 youths, on heathen ground, in circumstances which almost entirely free them from the baneful influence of idolatry. Our boarding schools are giving shape to all the other schools connected with our station. The progress which our boys have made, has become a powerful stimulus to many, who attend our day schools. Several boys of the first families around us, whose parents would not permit them to eat on land occupied by Christians, spend most of their time, day and night, upon our premises, that they may enjoy equal advantages, and make equal progress with our boarders.

"We are very desirous, that this subject should be distinctly before the American churches. We wish them to know and attentively to consider, the peculiar advantages, with which the state of this people furnishes them for the exercise of their charity.

"In the first place, this is a very poor people. To their poverty we are greatly indebted for the success we have had, in obtaining boarding schools, and for the influence we have among the people, by which many have been brought within the sound of the gospel. We therefore confidently believe, that their poverty will, in the providence of God, be made the occasion of many of them receiving the unsearchable riches of divine grace.

"Probably in no part of the heathen world, can children be supported and educated in a decent, comfortable mode of living, so cheap as in this district. We repeat now with confidence, what we ventured to conjecture three years ago; viz. that twelve dollars are sufficient for the annual support of boys from six to fifteen years of age. Though we labored a long time without success, to obtain boys to be educated, such is the change that has taken place in the minds of the people, that as many children could now easily be obtained, as we can find means and accommodations to support.

"Considering the rank and influence, which females ought to hold in every society, and the well known state of degradation in which they are held in this, as well as in every idolatrous country, your mind, and the minds of the Christian public, will at once be deeply impressed with the importance and utility of *Female Charity Boarding Schools.* The obstacles to such we have found to be very great. Sometimes we have thought them to be insuperable. But we are now greatly encouraged on the subject, by our present success and future prospects.

"The facility of supporting children here, forms one of the strong claims, which this people have upon the charity of the American public. Within a short time, we have had five or six pressing requests to establish free schools in the neighboring villages, where yet there are none. The monthly expense of such schools, after suitable buildings are prepared, is from $1,50 to $2. We have now 15 such schools, and they might easily be greatly multiplied. Applications have also been made from other parishes, that missionaries would come and establish themselves among the people, as we have done at Tillipally and Batticotta. And we may say generally, that our influence and missionary operations, which were at first feared and dreaded, are now welcomed by many, and sought after by some.

"We have now more health and strength, than in months past. We have, in some degree, got through with the pressure and expense of building, and the drudgery of learning a new language. We might therefore, superintend a few more schools, take more children, and in other respects enlarge our missionary plans. But we dare not further hazard the consequences of involving the mission in debt. We look to America with great anxiety for adequate supplies. We wish to tell you more distinctly how much our hearts are pained within us, on witnessing the forlorn state of many children around us. More than 20, principally orphans, many of whom appear to be in a starving condition, have appeared at our doors, intreating, oftentimes with tears, that we would receive them to our boarding school; but whom we have been compelled to reject, for the want of means to support them. Thus, these miserable objects are cast back again upon the world, some probably to perish in the streets; others to drag out a long and miserable existence in poverty; and all to live in the darkness of idolatry till they go down to the regions of death. It is an awfully interesting inquiry with us, to know in whose skirts the blood of these souls will be found."

These impressive and affecting representations will not have been made in vain. As, since the writing of this letter, the mission has received a large augmentation, it will be able to take under its care a proportionably large number of general schools, and of youths in their families or boarding schools.

Not only have these missionaries been thus encouraged by the facilities given to their operations, and the general success which has attended them; but they have also been favored with more special tokens of the divine presence and manifestations of divine grace. Mention has been made, in preceding reports, of several individuals, who appeared to be subjects of abiding religious impressions. Of two, Supyen and Franciscus Maleappa, more particular accounts have been given. With respect to Supyen no later intelligence has been received Maleappa, who had been a valuable helper at Tillipally, and was afterwards, in connection with that station, placed as a schoolmaster and catechist at Mallagum,—who was strongly attached to the mission, and was expected to abide as a permanent assistant, felt it to be his duty, about sixteen months ago, to leave the mission for the purpose of accompanying his aged and infirm father to Colombo; and his return was considered as uncertain.

Very interesting accounts have since been given of other individuals.

"Since the date of our last letter," say the missionaries in their letter of November 13th, "we have received to our communion Gabriel Tissera and Nicholas Paramanundu, who have served us in the mission as interpreters. They appear to us to give decisive evidence of saving conversion, and to manifest a becoming zeal for the honor of Christ, and for the salvation of the heathen. By their being thus closely united with us, at this time, we feel much strengthened and encouraged in our work. They are now valuable assistants to us, and we have reason to believe, that they will render important service to our mission, and become lasting blessings to the heathen.

"At each of our stations are several persons, who give pleasing evidences of faith in Christ, and will probably ere long, be admitted to our church. Two of the persons, here referred to, are members of our boarding schools We notice also, with much pleasure, that there is an unusual degree of seriousness upon the minds of several other boys, who are under our instruction. We feel that we are, at this time, in a special manner, called upon by the providence of God towards us, to humble ourselves before him, on account of our past deficiencies in his service, and to redouble our diligence in the use of the means of grace, that we may be prepared to experience, what we would ever consider the greatest of all blessings; viz. a special outpouring of the Holy Spirit. We do hope, that the American churches, especially on the first Monday in the month, unite their supplications with ours for such manifestations of divine grace among this heathen people."

In a letter ten days later, Mr. Meigs says:

"Inclosed I send you a letter from Gabriel Tissera, of whose character and qualifications to assist in our mission, you will by this time have considerable knowledge.

"He is a young man of distinguished promise. Since he has become hopefully pious, we regard him with new and increased attachment; and think his connection with our mission of very great importance. He possesses talents of a superior order, and an ardent thirst for knowledge; and, so far as we can judge, possesses sincere piety. He is now well qualified to act as a catechist among the people; and, at no very distant period, he will probably be well qualified for ordination. He shows a strong desire to be permanently connected with our mission; and we are certainly no less desirous of such an event. He manifests a fervent love for the souls of this miserable people; and I have strong faith to believe that he will be made, by the blessing of God, an instrument in the conversion of many souls. Indeed his labors have already been attended with the divine blessing."

The letter here referred to has been given to the public, and has probably been read by the members of the Board. It speaks much for the praise of divine grace, and much for hope respecting this interesting young man and his future usefulness.

MISSION TO PALESTINE.—At the delivery of our last annual Report, the Rev. Messrs. Parsons and Fisk were in expectation of embarking, by the first convenient opportunity, for Asia Minor, with a view to their ultimate residence as missionaries in the Holy Land, or some neighboring region. A very favorable opportunity soon after presented itself, and active preparations were made to embrace it. The missionaries arranged their affairs, visited their near relatives and friends, took leave of many circles of Christians with whom they were acquainted, and arrived at Boston, ready for departure, about the close of October. The short interval which elapsed, previously to their sailing, was employed in a manner most gratifying to the friends of the cause in which they were engaged, and most auspicious to the mission.

On Lord's day, Oct 31st, at the return of the communion in the Old South church, the two missionaries, and the members of Park Street church, with several clergymen, were present by invitation. While surrounding the table of the Lord, the exhortations, the prayers, and the numberless associations, were calculated to increase that zeal and self-denial, which are peculiarly necessary to the prosecution of this divine work. In the afternoon of the same day, Mr. Parsons preached in Park Street church, from Hosea iii, 4, 5, on the *Dereliction and Restoration of the Jews;* and, in the evening, Mr. Fisk delivered a farewell discourse, from Acts xx, 22, on the *Holy Land as a field for missionary enterprise.* On this occasion, the Old South church was excessively crowded, and a highly respectable audience testified their interest in the subject, by the profoundest attention, and a liberal contribution. The Instructions of the Prudential Committee were then delivered in public. They relate principally to topics, which belong especially to the contemplated mission; and, as they have been printed, and extensively circulated, your Committee need only refer the Board to them.

On Monday evening, the united monthly concert for prayer was held at Park Street church. As the collections at this meeting, for the preceding twelve months, had been made expressly for the Palestine mission, it was peculiarly grateful to join with the first missionaries, in prayer and exhortation, just before their departure.

Having been detained a few days by head winds, and thus allowed a convenient season to take leave of their brethren, they embarked on board the ship Sally Ann, Wednesday morning, Nov. 3rd, and soon bade adieu to the shores of their native country. It was a part of the plan, that, as the ship was about to touch at Malta, they should seek acquaintance with the Rev. Mr. Jowett, Dr. Naudi, and others, with a view to cultivate a brotherly intercourse, and to obtain useful information. They entered the harbor of Malta, after a favorable passage, on the 23rd of December Though the rigid quarantine laws of that island would not permit them to land, they had the happiness to meet Mr. Jowett and Dr. Naudi, at the Lazaretto, and to be introduced to the Rev. Mr Wilson, a missionary, and Mr. Jones, who had been American consul at Tripoli, where he had resided seven years. From these gentlemen they received much valuable information, and proofs of the kindest and most benevolent interest in their mission. They were favored, also, with letters of introduction to persons of intelligence and influence, at Smyrna and Scio. Mr. Jowett was at the pains to draw up a paper of *hints,* for the use of our missionaries; and has shown his love to the cause, and his hearty and zealous cooperation with all faithful laborers, by an excellent letter addressed to the Corresponding Secretary of the Board. This laborious missionary, whose travels in Egypt and Western Asia have been read with eagerness by the Christian world, not only received Messrs. Parsons and Fisk kindly, but, in common with his associates, was at personal inconvenience and expense to meet them almost daily, while they remained in the harbor. This generous attention had the most cheering effect on the minds of those, to whom it was shown, and will make a grateful impression on the hearts of American Christians.

On the 9th of January the ship pursued her voyage, and in six days entered the harbor of Smyrna The missionaries were received with cordiality by all the gentlemen, to whom they had letters of introduction; particularly, by the Rev. Charles Williamson, chaplain to the British consulate, Mr. Lee and the Messrs. Perkinses, eminent merchants in that city.

During the voyage, religious services were regularly attended on board, according to the arrangement and at the request of Capt. Edes, from whom the missionaries received many acts of kindness on their passage, and after their arrival. They labored with assiduity for the spiritual good of the ship's company, and were encouraged to hope, that their exertions were not without some good effect They appear to have been deeply impressed with the moral wants of seamen, and to have ardently desired the salvation of all, who sailed with them.

At Smyrna they found the most satisfactory evidence, that the shores of the Mediterranean present many extensive fields of missionary labor. By the aid of Christians in more favored parts of the world, missionaries may carry the Scriptures and religious tracts into every town and village throughout those benighted regions There are many professed Christians, to whom immediate access can be gained, and who would receive religious books with gladness. Christian missionaries may reside in any part of Turkey, so far as appears, without the least apprehension of interference from the government. Numerous and powerful inducements urge to send forth laborers into this part of the harvest.

The acquisition of the Modern Greek, and other languages spoken in Asia Minor, principally occupied the time of Messrs. Parsons and Fisk. They found opportunity, however, to collect useful information with respect to the condition of the people in neighboring regions, and the various means which could be used, for the promotion of religion. They distributed the Scriptures to various classes of persons, and gave occasional instruction to individuals, who fell into their private society. At the close of a journal, which they sent to this country on the 10th of March, they announce the intention of spending the summer at Scio, (the Chios of the New Testament,) an island 70 miles from Smyrna. Their expectation was, that they should possess superior advantages for acquiring the Modern Greek, under Professor Bambas, the principal instructor of the college there, to whom they had letters from Mr. Jowett, and other gentlemen of high respectability.

On the first monday in February, the Rev. Mr. Williamson united with the missionaries in the monthly concert of prayer. This was probably the commencement in Turkey of a holy celebration, which will, at some future day, be observed in every village of that populous and extensive empire. The gentleman just named addressed to the Secretary an interesting and affectionate letter, from which it will be suitable to lay before the Board the following extracts.

Smyrna, Feb. 1820.

"REV. AND DEAR SIR,—Although our friends, the missionaries, have acquainted you with their safe arrival in Smyrna, yet I would wish to join in the annunciation of the fact."

"I would first greet you and every member of the American Board of Commissioners for Foreign Missions. Accept of my most cordial salutations, and Christian congratulations, on the happy commencement of an enterprise, which must, in due time, terminate in the completest success —in the conversion of the heathen and reformation of the Christian world. Every attention has been, and shall be paid to Messrs. Parsons and Fisk, and to all their successors, who will come as the messengers of the Lord, as far as my abilities and influence will possibly avail."

"Within the last fifty years, literature is beginning to peep out among the Greeks from her hiding places in Turkey. Some of the best informed are acquainted with the history of the Reformation, and will grant that Luther was a great man, sent for the benefit of the human race, though they are far at present from desiring a like reformation. Luther and those other reformers, who did not condemn and sweep away episcopal superintendence, are respected by a few of the Greeks, though the majority will have nothing to do with reformation, and know nothing about it. Besides the Christians all around the shores of the Mediterranean, those of Egypt, Abyssinia, Arabia, Syria, Persia, Asia Minor, Russia, and Turkey in Europe, of whatever denomination they may be, all have their own episcopal magistrates in ecclesiastical affairs; and each party has fixed laws for clergy and laity, of which the violation of the most trifling these ignorant people consider as more heinous, than of the most important law of the state.

"The sale and distribution of the Holy Scriptures and religious tracts, have been hitherto the only missionary operations carried on in this country. A missionary visiting the different towns must endeavor, not only to make the acquaintance, but to gain the confidence of the leading men and priests of the Greeks. With the assistance of his new friends, the missionary may be able to distribute many copies of the everlasting Word, in a language intelligible to the people, a blessing of which those regions have been deprived for some hundreds of years. Next to the countenance of the Greeks, religious tracts, compiled from the first fathers of the Christian church, will be of the greatest service to missionaries The Greeks highly esteem and venerate the ancient martyrs. Their writings are looked upon as oracles; but they are very scarce, and unintelligible to the people, as they stand in ancient Greek. In case of opposition, which sometimes happens, and of a deadly indifference, which generally prevails, tracts will be of the greatest utility in bringing forward the fathers to allay opposition, and to recommend the duty of perusing the Scriptures, as well as to awaken a spirit of piety, and of inquiry after Gospel truth "

"Two other important parts of missionary labor remain to be entered upon. The first is Education;—the other a translation, not of the Scriptures, for that is accomplished, but of all other good religious books and tracts. The printing of a religious monthly publication in Modern Greek, not offending the institutions of the country, is of primary importance, and would be, in the hands of prudent conductors, of incalculable service. The extensive fields of education are not, to foreign Protestant missionaries, so easily and completely accessible, as the rich and most abundant streams of a fount of types, which would ere long, silently water every portion of the field sowed with the word of God; and, with the divine blessing, would render luxuriant and plentiful the Christian harvest."

The writer proceeds to offer several suggestions, in regard to the best methods of extending the knowledge of Christianity in the Turkish empire. He dwells on the vast good, which could probably be effected by a printing establishment, with Greek, Turkish, and French types, (the latter comprehending the general European alphabet,) at Smyrna; and another at Jerusalem, with Greek, Syriac, and Arabic characters. In the most unqualified manner he sanctions the opinion, which the Committee formed originally, that 'Smyrna is by far the best situation in the Levant for a permanent missionary establishment, on the eastern shores of the Mediterranean, having a frequent communication with all the parts of the Ottoman empire, and that it is the best place in those regions for learning Greek, Turkish, Italian, and French, and for the security and liberty, which foreigners and Christians enjoy.' The advantages of an extensive printing establishment may be conceived, when it is stated, that though the Greeks are very fond of reading, there is not a single newspaper, or other periodical publication, in all the Turkish dominions. There is little reason to doubt, that the shores of the Mediterranean afford many of the best openings to Christian enterprise; and it surely is not too much to anticipate, that the churches of this country will delight to send back to those central parts of the earth, the inestimable blessings, which were derived from thence, but which have, in the righteous visitations of Providence, been so long banished from the countries, where they were first enjoyed.

MISSION AMONG THE CHEROKEES.—With this mission not only the Board, but the Christian community extensively, have become familiarly acquainted. It is near, seemingly even in the midst of us; has intercourse with all parts of the country; is established in the affections and confidence of all, who wish well to the long neglected natives of the wilderness; and, from various causes, has engaged general attention, and inspired elevated hope. May it please the Father of Lights, that it may continue to be worthy of all these kind regards, and never disappoint its patrons and friends.

The company consisting of Messrs. Abijah Conger, John Vail, and John Talmage, with their families, designed, for the Cherokee mission; and the Rev. Alfred Finney, with his wife, and Miss Minerva Washburn, an unmarried female assistant, for the Arkansas mission; described in the Report of last year, as having then, as was supposed, just set out from Rockaway, N. J., arrived at Brainerd, on the 10th of November.

Their setting out was delayed by a heavy visitation of Providence. An epidemic prevailed at Rockaway, by which the families of Mr. Vail and Mr. Talmage were visited severely. Two sons of Mr Vail were buried in one grave; and another, after the company had been detained about three weeks, the bereaved parents were constrained to leave behind, as too feeble to bear the journey. The affliction was deeply felt by them all, but appears to have been made, by divine grace, a means of promoting in them the feelings, suitable for all Christians, and especially for those who are devoted to the missionary work.

They left their houses and their kindred and friends, with tender cheerfulness; went on their way rejoicing; and from Rockaway to Brainerd, a distance of more than nine hundred miles, had a prosperous journey, of only about six weeks. On their arrival, the hearts of the brethren and sisters of the mission, burdened as they had been with continually increasing labors and cares, were filled with gladness and thankfulness. "It is a time," say they in the journal—"It is a time of great rejoicing at Brainerd. We feel, that the Lord has heard our prayers for help; and it is now our duty to render praise. Oh that we could be sufficiently thankful to our gracious Savior, for the abundant mercies, which we have experienced, and the sweet consolations now afforded us."

On the 3d of January 1818, the Rev. Ard Hoyt with his family, and the Rev. Daniel S. Butrick, arrived at the station; and the Rev. William Chamberlin on the 10th of the ensuing March.

About the last of May of the same year, Mr. Kingsbury, with Mr. and Mrs. Williams, left this mission, for the purpose of commencing an establishment in the Choctaw nation: and your Committee regret to state, that about four months ago, Mr. Talmage, from some feelings of discontentment, retired from the mission.

It will be grateful to the Board, here to be refreshed with a quotation from a letter of the Rev. Cyrus Kingsbury, 30th June, 1817

"I arrived at this place," (the place now called Brainerd,) "on the 13th of January. The weather for some time after was extremely cold for this climate, and I felt the want of comfortable lodgings, having only a skin spread upon the floor, and a thin covering of blankets; but my health was kindly preserved. Immediately on my arrival, I commenced making preparations to cultivate the land, and to open the school upon the plan proposed. On the 7th of March I had the great satisfaction of welcoming the arrival of brethren Hall and Williams, with their wives. A kind Providence preserved them through many dangers, and brought them to their destined place in safety. Since their arrival, we have all, when health would permit, been employed from Monday morning till Saturday night, either in hard labor, or on journies for the mission. We have had to provide for a numerous family, and to make preparations for supplying the wants of a still more numerous one. In such a situation we felt it to be our indispensable duty, to labor, as far as health and strength would permit, that we might not be chargeable.

"Soon after our arrival in the nation, we opened our doors to receive children into our family to teach them the rudiments of the English language, the principles of the Christian religion, and the industry and arts of civilized life. The present number is twenty-six, of different ages, from four to eighteen years."

Such were the beginnings of our Cherokee mission three years and some months ago. During the first year, Mr. Kingsbury and his two assistants, Messrs. Hall and Williams, with their wives, were the only members of the mission, bearing with exemplary fortitude and cheerfulness, the privations, fatigues, and discouragements of untried and arduous situation and enterprise.

There remains of the mission, Mr. Hoyt, superintendent, with his wife and children, four of whom are very useful assistants; Mr. Conger, with his wife and children, and an apprentice, George Halsey, about twenty years old, and a devoted helper of excellent promise; Mr. Vail with his family, Mr. Butrick, Mr. Hall with his family, and Mr. Chamberlin with his family.

Mr. Milo Hoyt, who served with his father in the work, as a true son, has lately been married to an amiable and distinguished native convert, Lydia Lowry. And as, by this marriage, he has become entitled to all the privileges of a native Cherokee, he thinks, that by occupying a situation near the establishment, or in an eligible place for a local school, he can well support himself, and render as much service to the mission, as if he were under the immediate direction of the Board.

The general plans and operations of the mission are all known to the Board and to the community. Of the state and appearance, particularly of the establishment at Brainerd, as found in December, a detailed and authentic account is given in the Report of the Visiting Committee, the greater part of which it is deemed fitting to quote in this place:

"Since the date," (say the Committee) of the last Report, (which was in June 1818,) "there have been considerable improvements made. Four cabins have been built for the accommodation of the pupils, besides a large cabin house in which the girls are taught. There is also the frame of a barn raised, and covered, which will be commodious and useful when finished. The whole farm is inclosed by excellent fences, and about thirteen acres of fresh land have been cleared; eight of which, we are informed, have been done by the labor of boys in the school, in the morning and evening. The last season the land was cultivated as follows; six acres in wheat, five in rye, and thirty in Indian corn, besides potatoes, turnips, and a large garden.

"The live stock belonging to the station, was reported as being pretty numerous; and what they saw was in good condition. There are ten horses, seventy horned cattle, thirty sheep, and hogs of all sizes about one hundred and fifty. There belongs to the mission some other property, as a cart, three wagons, a yoke of oxen, farming utensils, &c.

"Since your Committee last visited this station the school has been divided, and the girls and boys are now taught in separate houses. The Rev. William Chamberlin teaches the boys, and directs them when out of school. Miss Sarah Hoyt teaches the girls, and directs their employment, when out of school. The number of boys in the school is 42, the number of the girls is 25. A few more are, as we are informed, entered in each school, who are now absent, some on visits to their parents, and some on account of sickness, and for fear of it. The pupils are under the age of fifteen, except two males, who may be twenty or upwards, and two females, who may be about eighteen or nineteen. A great many of them have entered since our last visit, and some of them have been here but a short time. The great majority are making very pleasing progress, both in their studies, and in learning to speak the English language.

"The order and good conduct of these children in school, at the table, and in the church, are truly exemplary. Their cheerfulness in yielding obedience to all that is required of them, either in or out of school, is rarely exceeded by the best governed children among ourselves.

"The facility with which they learn to write, has often been remarked: the specimens, which we have seen of the writing of the present scholars, confirm the fact. Their progress in spelling and reading, is encouraging, considering the difficulty they have to encounter, in speaking and pronouncing our language. Many of them have committed to memory a part of the Assembly's Catechism, and some chapters of the New Testament, which they repeated with ease.

"An excellence in the management of this missionary station is, that the pupils are not only taught reading, writing, and arithmetic, with the principles and worship inculcated in the word of God; but they are instructed in the most useful arts of civilized life. The boys learn the use of the hoe and the axe; while the girls learn the use of the spinning wheel and the needle. The instructress of the girls informed us, that since the 16th of March last, the girls had made eighty garments, such as shirts, pantaloons, &c., without including smaller articles; that they had pieced thirteen bedquilts, and quilted nine. We examined a part of the work, and it appeared to be well done.

"Your Committee, on their first visit, were not more affected by any thing relating to the whole mission, than by the infant church, here planted in the wilderness. We are happy to find, that it has increased, by the addition of such as we hope shall be saved. Four of the natives, and two blacks, have made a public profession of religion, since our last visit. We have also seen or heard of five or six, who were under strong impressions from the Spirit of God; some of whom give evidence of being the hopeful subjects of a saving change of heart All, with whom we have met, converse with great freedom, concerning their lost and helpless state, as sinners, their views and feelings respecting the Savior, and with an artless simplicity not easily to be described.

"Among the various circumstances, that must interest the feelings of any Christian friend of man, who may visit this station, a short detail of one or two will not be unacceptable to the Board. Last Christmas a young man, called John Arch, who had been born and bred in the mountains near the confines of South Carolina, happened to be at Knoxville, where he met with Mr. Hall, who informed him that there was a school in the nation. As soon as he went home, he took his gun, and wandered off in search of the place, which we hope has proved to him the house of God and the gate of heaven. After travelling one hundred and fifty miles, he arrived at the missionary station; told the missionaries he had come to attend school; and offered them his gun, his only property, for clothes. His appearance was so wild and forbidding; that the missionaries said they hesitated to receive him, inasmuch as he was upwards of 20 years of age. He would not be put off They took him upon trial In a short time, he discovered a thoughtful concern about his soul, and now gives the most satisfactory evidence of a gracious change of heart. His thirst for knowledge is great. He has learned to read and write well; though he has not been more than ten months at school. Sometime after he became serious, he was accused of doing an improper act; he was conscious of innocence, and could not well brook the false charge. That evening he was missing; and the next morning the conclusion was, that he had gone off. But about nine o'clock he came in. Upon being questioned respecting his absence, he gave the following account. 'I felt angry, and knew that it was wicked; but I could not suppress it; and I went to seek the Savior, that he might reconcile my heart.' It appeared, that he had been praying, and wrestling with God all night. He says he often feels strongly inclined to tell the Indians about God and the Savior; but he knows so little, he thinks it would not please God. He desires to obtain an education that he may preach.

"Are not the wilderness and the solitary place beginning to be glad, and the desert to rejoice and blossom as the rose? Here the ransomed of the Lord are returning and coming to Zion with songs, *literally with songs* and everlasting joy. They have obtained joy and gladness, and sorrow and sighing have fled away. It is enough to warm a heart of ice, and dissolve a heart of stone, to see and hear from these late savages of the forest, the evidence of all conquering grace on their hearts. Has not the Board, has not the Christian public, already received an ample reward for all the toil and expense, to which they have submitted even if another immortal being should not be gathered into the fold of the great Shepherd and Bishop of souls.

"On the whole, your Committee are more and more convinced of the practicability of civilizing and christianizing this long neglected people. They are capable of every noble feeling of our nature to a high degree: of the warmest affection, tenderness, and gratitude. The children are sprightly and sagacious, and on many subjects discover an excellent judgment.

"The sacrament of the Lord's supper was administered the day after we arrived, it being the Sabbath. The congregation contained more than one hundred; they behaved with great decorum: Father Hoyt presented the little Osage captive, whom he has adopted, for baptism. He was called *John Osage Ross*."

This witness unquestionably is true, and should be recorded for the praise of divine grace.

At the time of the first Report referred to by the Visiting Committee, the buildings of the establishment were described by the Treasurer upon the spot, only a few days before, as follows:

"The mission house is situated about 50 rods southwest of the creek Chickamaugah. It fronts the southeast; has the dining hall and kitchen in the rear; and several log cabins in each wing, for the accommodation of the children and some of the missionaries. There are several other log buildings for store rooms, corn houses and stables. The school house is thirty rods to the southwest, and is sufficiently large to accommodate 100 scholars on the Lancasterian plan, and to answer for a place of public worship on the Sabbath."

"There have since been built," say the Committee, "four cabins for the accommodation of the pupils, and a large cabin-house in which the girls are taught." Also, "the frame of a barn is raised and covered." And since the Committee were there, besides finishing the barn, they have erected a house for Mr. Conger's family, and a warehouse about six miles distant, on the banks of the Tennessee, for the purpose of receiving corn and other articles conveyed for them upon that river, and a saw-mill is in forwardness with some other buildings.

To the farm, of which about sixty acres were in a state for cultivation, when the Visiting Committee were there, large additions and improvements have been made, and are making. The design, indeed, is entered upon with spirit, to raise from the farm, as soon and as fast as possible, a large and increasing proportion of the corn, and other productions of the soil, necessary for the establishment.

The number of scholars in the two schools at Brainerd has not been definitively stated in any recent communication; but the general representation has been, that the schools are full, and in a highly satisfactory state.

The gracious influences from on high, which have been so signally the glory of this mission, appear to be still continued. The young man John Arch, of whom so interesting an account is given by the Visiting Committee, has since been received to the church. Another hopeful convert also has been received, David Brown, a brother of Catharine. To your Committee, and to many others, who have seen him, he appears to be a youth of great promise. He is now in our school at Cornwall.

The whole number, gathered from the wilderness into this mission church, and thus made fellow citizens with the saints, and of the household of God, including four or five black persons, is about *twenty*. A considerable number more; some at Brainerd, and some at other places in the nation, where our missionaries have bestowed attention, are made subjects of deep religious impressions; and several of them hopefully of renovating grace.

At Springplace also—and it is with high and heartfelt pleasure, that your Committee report and record the fact—at Springplace, where the Rev. John Gambold, the venerable Moravian missionary, with the excellent helper, his wife, has been for years laboring for the good of the Cherokees, with the spirit of humility, devotion and perseverance, by which the Union of Brethren has been long and eminently distinguished,—the power of divine grace has lately been manifested; and three or four persons of consideration and influence, in that part of the nation, have come as believers to the ordinances of Christ; and others give serious attention to divine instruction.

In the Report of the last year, the design was submitted of establishing at eligible places, in different parts of the nation, *local schools*, in connexion with the primary establishment at Brainerd; and it was stated, that for one school of this kind a place had been selected, and preparations were in forwardness. This station, called Talony, was assigned to Mr. Moody Hall, who, in the infancy of the mission, bore, with the Rev. Mr. Kingsbury, and Mr. Williams, the burden and heat of the day. A house for his family, and a school house have been erected; and the school was opened on the ninth of May. In a letter, dated June 30th, Mr. Hall says:

"About twenty entered the school the first week; and it has gradually increased to fifty. These, however, do not all attend constantly. A number probably entered from curiosity, not intending to learn. There are about thirty-five who regularly attend, and undoubtedly will continue their attendance, if the schools is judiciously managed. The school I think very promising, and the natives generally appear highly satisfied."

"You will doubtless expect to hear some particulars relative to the general management of the school. It is always opened and closed by reading a portion of Scripture, singing and prayer; and these exercises are often preceded by such remarks as most sensibly strike my mind. A number of the neighbors are generally present at the evening exercises. Three hours are spent in the fore part of the day, and three in the latter part, in teaching, Saturdays excepted. I require all the scholars to attend meetings on the Sabbath, when they are specially taught the principles of our holy religion. Their progress in general is good, fully equal to my expectations, considering their advantages.

"We have three orphan boys in our family; and we have engaged to take one or two more. I presume, if our circumstances would admit of it, and we had liberty, 15 or 20 boys and girls, who are real objects of charity, might be obtained immediately. Those we have give us great satisfaction and are truly dear to us.

"Since the school house has been in a situation to be occupied, meetings have been constantly held in it, and from 75 to 100 have attended.

"My labors are great, and constantly increasing. There is enough at this place on the Sabbath, for two or three active servants of the Lord to do. I have generally taught a Sabbath school for the blacks, and occasionally several adult Cherokees have been instructed on that day. I spend half an hour, both before and after meeting, with the children of the school."

This school at Talony was established in compliance with the earnest solicitations of the principal men of that village and the vicinity: solicitations, not less earnest, have been made from other considerable places in the nation, and particularly from the neighborhood of Fort Armstrong in the south, near the Creeks, and distant from Brainerd about 60 miles; and from Creek Path on the west side of the nation, about 100 miles distant.

Early in December such representations were made to the missionaries, of the dispositions and desires of the people near Fort Armstrong, as engaged very serious attention. These representations were afterwards repeated, and it was deemed advisable, that Mr. Chamberlin should make a visit to the place. On his return, the following account was entered in the Journal.

"March 24. This evening brother Chamberlain returned from Fort Armstrong. In his opinion, it is a very favorable and important time to establish a local school there.

"In an interview with the principal chief of that district, brother C. inquired if the people wanted a school. He answered by the interpreter, that they did not merely *want* a school, but that they wanted one VERY MUCH. He said, they would be very glad of a large school, like that at Brainerd, and proposed a place for it on the Coosa river, where he said supplies of all kinds might be brought by water. On being told, we were not able to give them such a school,—at least for the present,—but could only furnish a teacher for such children as could board at home, he said they would be very thankful for such a school. that he had a small cabin, situated precisely where they wanted the school, which he would give us for the use of the teacher; and that himself and neighbors would build the school house.

"So far as could be ascertained, the chief spoke the mind of the whole district. All were agreed that it would be best to have the school at the place named by the chief, which is on the Chatooga Creek, about six or eight miles from Fort Armstrong, and brother C. gave encouragement to send a teacher in a few days. He also understood, that the Path-killer intended to ask for such a school, in his neighborhood. This aged warrior and king, is telling his people, wherever he goes, that schools are very good for them, and they must keep their children at school until their teachers say they have learned enough; which, he tells them, will require at least four years. This venerable old man, who is now so much engaged for the instruction of his people, we understand, has never himself had the least instruction in a school."

On hearing this statement, it was resolved, that Mr. Milo Hoyt should go to Chatooga and commence a school without delay. Accordingly he left Brainerd for the purpose, on the 3d of April, taking with him his wife and younger brother Darius. In a letter dated June 9th, the Superintendent writes:

"The number of scholars has been small,—seldom or never more than 17 or 18 at a time. Still we have great hope that it will increase, and much good be done. There are many things, which render it desirable to maintain our position there, even should the number of children continue to be small. That section of the country appears to be in greater darkness than almost any other part of the nation, if we except, perhaps, the mountains towards Carolina. It is in the neighborhood of the Creeks, has considerable intercourse with them, and is remote from any settlement of whites. Several natives of influence reside there, who are very anxious to have the people instructed."

In the latter part of January, David and Catharine Brown went from Brainerd to Creek Path to visit their father, then sick. In the Journal, March 4, is the following passage:

"Sister Catharine and her brother David returned. Their father, whom they went to visit on account of his ill health, has so far recovered, as to be able to come up with them. Catharine says David seized his Bible as soon as he reached home, and began to read and interpret to his father and mother and other members of the family, exhorting them all to attend to it as the word of God; to repent of their sins, which he told them were many and very great; to believe on the Lord Jesus Christ and become his followers, &c. By his father's consent he maintained the worship of God in the family, morning and evening, and at table. He conversed freely with their friends and neighbors, and was not ashamed to own himself a Christian, or afraid to warn others to flee from the wrath to come. Several, in that neighborhood, appear serious, and disposed to inquire after the way of truth and life."

Mr. Brown, the father, brought a letter, signed by himself, and others, and in terms as follows.

"We, the headmen, chiefs of Creek Path town, Cherokee nation, have this day assembled ourselves together for the purpose of devising some plan for the education of our children. We daily witness the good effects arising from education, and therefore are extremely anxious to have a school in our neighborhood, as the distance from this part of the nation to Chickamaugah is so great, as not to suit our convenience. We therefore solicit your aid in carrying our plan into execution. We can raise twenty or perhaps twenty-five children. You will please write us immediately on the recept of this. Given under our hands, this 16th February, 1820."

It was resolved, that Mr. Butrick should go to Creek Path. On the 11th March he left Brainerd, taking John Arch with him: and on the 8th of April he wrote a letter to his brethren, in which he gives the following account:

When we left Brainerd, we lost our path, travelled till sometime after dark, and came to the road near Little Meat's. We stopped, and were greatly refreshed by the kindness of our dear Cherokee friends. We left that place early on Sabbath morning, and went to brother Hicks's. The congregation there was not large.

"On Monday we travelled to Mr. Pardue's; visited Path killer on the way; Tuesday to Mr. Burn's; got a recruit of provisions. Wednesday, to a large hickory blown down by the wind, where we had a very comfortable lodging. Thence to Mr. Scott's;—Friday to a large white oak log in the woods, between Shoat's and Cox's; Saturday to captain J. Brown's. We told him our business, and he informed others. Sabbath, we came to his father's, where we were kindly received; but it being late in the day we had no meeting. Monday capt. J. Brown came;—told me he had seen the chiefs;—that they were glad we had come, and wished me to accompany him the next day—select a place for the school house—and meet them at an appointed place. On Tuesday I went with captain J. Brown, but referred it to him to say, where the house should stand. He selected a place. We met the chiefs, and I told my errand. They told me they would do as I had stated, and appointed the next Friday to begin the house. On Friday they assembled, old men and children. They cut the timber and put up the house, making the inside 22 by 17. Saturday, they made the boards without a saw; covered the roof; put up most of the chimney; cut out the door, split part of the puncheons for the floor; put in the steps; and hewed down the house inside I think the house is nearly or quite as high as that at Brainerd. We appointed a meeting on the next day.

"Sabbath we met—perhaps thirty Cherokees, and a number of black and white people.

"On Monday, Tuesday and Wednesday, a less number worked on the house, made a good floor, door, hearth, and back; finished laying up the chimney; chinked the floor; made benches, &c.; Thursday we began school, having eight scholars the first three days.

"On the Sabbath, we attended meeting. Perhaps 60 or 70 Cherokees attended. I began a Sunday school for the blacks, with 10 or 15 scholars. Monday about 20 scholars came: since that we have had this week about 27, in all upwards of 30 different scholars. Old Mr Gunter told me to-day, he expected to send 10 in a month from this time. Last night the people had a talk; Path Killer advised them to be attentive to our instruction, and to give their children into our care; telling them, that they must continue their children with us at least four years, in order to profit them.

"This morning they desired me to meet them at the store. I went; saw Path Killer. I cannot but love him.

"The people here from the oldest to the youngest, appear anxious to receive instruction, and some appear really inquiring after the truth. All the people, whom we see, receive us as their nearest friends.

"I have written this letter in the singular, as if no one were with me; but our dear brother John has done much more than I have. He has not only done all that I have by interpreting, but has done much himself."

Speaking of the progress, which the children have made in these few days, Mr. Butrick says. "About fourteen who knew none of their letters, have learned them, and read in syllables of two letters, and some in three."

The above appears to have been written on Saturday. Sabbath evening he adds: "To-day we have had a large collection of people for this country, about 100 Cherokees and blacks."

Referring to this station, the Rev. Mr. Hoyt, June 9th, says:

"The first school being well filled with scholars to overflowing, they requested another. Catharine, by our approbation, offered to teach a school of females, if they would prepare a house. The news was received with enthusiastic joy. In four days a great number collected to build the house—with surprising despatch they finished one of the same dimensions as the former, and within a few rods of it, and immediately sent a messenger for Catharine. She left us the last of May, with the expectation of commencing a school immediately on her arrival at Creek Path. Religious instruction appears also to be eagerly sought by all the people in that district. *Hopes are entertained of the saving conversion of several; and brother Butrick has written for our advice respecting the immediate formation of a church there.*"

These statements and representations shew at once the spirit and operations of the mission, the dispositions of the Cherokee chiefs and people, and the kindness of God our Savior; and, in these several respects, were deemed by your Committee, too interesting to be tedious, though particular, and in some instances minute.

From the whole, it will be seen, that the "field is indeed white already to harvest; and he that reapeth receiveth wages, and gathereth fruit unto life eternal." Compared, however, with the plenteousness of the harvest the laborers are yet few; and their hearts and their hands are filled and burdened. Both Mr. Butrick and Mr. Milo Hoyt engaged in the new schools, under the pressure of urgent circumstances; and as soon as they can be relieved by others, who shall go to the help of the mission, they will be otherwise employed.

The purpose of Mr. Hoyt has already been mentioned. Mr. Butrick has for a considerable time, been giving what attention he could to the acquisition of the language, with a view to his being chiefly employed in visiting families and neighborhoods, and preaching, without needing an interpreter, in the different parts of the nation. This has, from the first, been regarded as an important part of the general plan of operations; and its importance is continually more and more strongly perceived and felt. With all his other avocations, his proficiency in the language is such, that he converses and discourses in it with considerable facility; and, with the assistance of David Brown, he has composed a Cherokee Spelling Book, which has been printed for the use of the mission.

In the schools of the mission, there are now more than 200 pupils. In other places, schools are wanted. Indeed, throughout the nation there is a general and strong impression in favor of having their children instructed in the learning and arts of civilized life, and were sufficient means supplied, the greater part of the children, of suitable age, might at once be brought under a system of instruction.

A disposition favorable to preaching, is also prevailing. As appears from what has now been cited, wherever the missionaries go, they find a welcome reception, and people readily come together to hear them. At several places, also, besides the places of the schools, they have regular opportunities for preaching. In their Journal, Dec 5th, they say:

"Brother Butrick, who went out yesterday to attend an appointment, ten miles south of us, returned this evening. Preaching at that place is once in four weeks, and brother Reece generally attends as interpreter. The attention of the people in that neighborhood is not abated. Last evening four came to the place of meeting on foot, a distance of ten miles, five of which they walked after dark, fording one large creek. It being too dark to see any thing, that was not white, one went before, feeling out the path with his feet, and the others followed in succession, by each observing the blanket of his conductor.

"Brother C. is absent to preach at brother Hicks's. It is our intention to have but one appointment abroad on each Sabbath; but in consequence of one appointment being postponed, to attend the sacrament here, we had two this day."

In the great and beneficent design of bringing the Cherokees into the pale of christianized society, the Rev. Mr. Gambold is an inestimable worker. Spring Place, where he resides, is only about 35 miles distant from Brainerd; and from the commencement of our mission there has been, between him and our missionaries, the most perfect good understanding, and affectionate intercourse and fellowship. In the Brainerd Journal, November 9, 1819, is a passage, which well deserves a place in this Report

"The Rev. Abraham Steiner, of the Society of United Brethren in the southern states, made us a friendly visit. He brought an affectionate letter to us from the directors of that society. They desire, that no sectarian differences may be known among the heathen, and propose a reciprocal communion and fellowship between their church and ours among this people, and a mutual intercourse of members, if any should so alter their residence, as to render such a change convenient and expedient. They also desire, that no children dismissed for bad conduct from one school may be received by the other, except by request from the directors of the school from which they are dismissed.

"We replied that these proposals were agreeable to the desires of our directors, so far as we were acquainted with them, and were in perfect accordance with our wishes. Mr. Steiner has, for a number of years, been warmly engaged for the christianization of this tribe.

"In 1799 he was sent out by the directors of that society, to ask permission to establish a school in that nation. He pressed the subject with great zeal in the national council, backed by the officers of government, but was utterly refused.

"In 1800 he came out again, renewed his application, and was again refused; but, before the close of the council two influential chiefs agreed to patronise the school, independently of the national council, and offered a place near the residence of one of them, on land which he had cleared. The other chiefs did not after this press their opposition; and shortly after the mission at Spring place was commenced, which has continued without suspension, though at times with great difficulty, ever since.

"Mr. Steiner says, that no wagon road had ever been cut, or a wagon entered the nation, till sometime after this. The chief on whose land the mission was established, built the first wagon, for which he was severely censured by the council, and forbidden the use of such a vehicle. But he did not regard their mandate. The objection was; 'If you have a wagon, there must be wagon roads;—and if wagon roads the whites will be in amongst us.' Mr. Steiner has been absent from the nation 16 years. The improvement since that time, has been, he says, most delightful and astonishing."

The sentiments of these proposals are worthy of the respected society, from which they emanate; and perfectly accordant with them are the views and feelings, which, from the first, your Committee have been studious to cherish in their own minds, to inspire in the breasts of the missionaries, to infuse into the proceedings of this and our other missions, and to cultivate and promote in all their intercourse and transactions with other societies and connections. And the representations here given of the altered state and disposition of the Cherokees must strike every mind with great force, and press home to every heart most powerful motives to seek their good.

MISSION TO THE CHOCTAWS.—"The Rev. Mr Kingsbury's acquaintance with the native character, his high standing in the esteem and confidence of both red men and white,—and the experience, which he had in commencing and advancing the establishment at Brainerd, combined to render it, in the view of the Committee, highly important that the superintendence of the Choctaw mission should be committed to him." Such was the statement made in the Report, two years ago, at the commencement of this mission; and your Committee think it right now to say, that the confidence thus expressed has been fully justified, and the anticipations thus made public have even been surpassed, in what has been realized.

The place now called Elliot, the primary seat of this mission, is within the chartered limits of the state of Mississippi,—on the Yalo Busha creek, about 30 miles above its junction with the Yazoo; 400 miles W. S. W. from Brainerd,—70 miles west of the Chickasaw Agency,—100 north of the Choctaw Agency, and 145 from the Walnut Hills, which last mentioned place is a little below the entrance of the Yazoo into the Mississippi, and about 130 miles above Natchez.

It was on the 27th of June, 1818, that Mr. Kingsbury, and Mr. and Mrs. Williams, arrived at this place from Brainerd. The place was then an entire wilderness; and after various hindrances, and necessary arrangements, the first tree was felled, upon the spot selected for the establishment, on the 15th of August. On the 16th of the same month, their first log house was erected, for the lodgment of the family. On the 29th, Mr. Peter Kanouse and his brother John G. Kanouse and his wife, from Rockaway, N. J., and Mr. Moses Jewell and wife, from Chenango Co. N. Y., arrived at the station, as assistants. About the middle of the next January, Mr. A. V. Williams, from Saratoga Co N. Y. a brother of the first assistant, joined the mission. On the 1st of the ensuing February, Miss Sarah B. Varnum, now Mrs. Kingsbury, from Dracut, Mass., and Miss Judith Chase, now Mrs. Williams, from Cornish, N. H., were gratefully welcomed to the mission family. Six months after, on the 1st of August, the mission was further cheered and strengthened, by the arrival of Dr. William W. Pride, a young and devoted physician, from Cambridge, N. Y., and Mr. Isaac Fisk, a highly approved blacksmith and farmer, from Holden, Mass. On the 1st of July last, Mr. Anson

Dyer and Mr. Zechariah Howes, agriculturists and schoolmasters, in the prime of life, reached the station, from Ashfield, Mass. Their companions on the journey, Mr. Joel Wood, of like qualifications, and his wife, sister of the Messrs. Williams, from Salisbury, N. Y., were left some distance behind, on account of sickness; and it is not known how long they have been detained.

The Rev. Alfred Wright, who was mentioned in the Report of the last year, as being designated for this mission, and then expected to proceed to the station from South Carolina before winter, owing to circumstances not to be controlled, found it necessary to defer going until spring; and, having returned to visit his friends in New England, he set out from Colombia, Con. June 1st, with instructions, for purposes of agency, to proceed leisurely and somewhat circuitously, to Elliot. He was at Marietta, in Ohio, about the middle of August.

On Wednesday of the last week, Messrs. John Smith, Calvin Cushman, and Elijah Bardwell, with their wives and children, substantial farmers, and two of them accustomed to school keeping, aged from 35 to 40, of Goshen, Mass. and Mr. William Hooper, of Berwick, Me. a young man, a tanner and shoemaker, and well qualified also to act as a schoolmaster and catechist,—set out with four wagons from Goshen, for this same mission.

Mr. Peter Kanouse, on account of ill health, as mentioned in the last report, left the station about five weeks after his arrival, and returned to New Jersey. And the last of August, a year ago, his brother, Mr. John G. Kanouse, who did not consider himself engaged, like the rest, for life, —returned also, with his wife, from the mission.

Only a week after, on the sixth of September, the mission was still farther diminished and deeply afflicted, by the decease of the younger Mr. Williams. His disease was distressing and rapid, but his mind was steadfast and serene, and his death peaceful and consolatory. In the journal the following very affectionate and honorable memorial is recorded:

"Brother A. V. Williams had cheerfully devoted himself to the cause of Christ among the heathen. Having set his face to the work, he cheerfully endured the burdens and hardships which fell to his lot. While on a dying bed, he was asked if he regretted that he had come to this distant land to labor for the cause of Christ. "Oh no," he replied with emphasis, "I only regret that I have done no more for him." Through his whole sickness he was calm and resigned.

"To his deeply afflicted wife, and to his brothers and sisters in the mission, he said; "Let your light shine—live above the world—be fervent in spirit." To Mrs. P. the Choctaw woman, who we hope has savingly embraced the Gospel, he said, as she entered the room," Can I not call you a dear sister in Christ? Jesus is my friend; I hope he will be yours."

"It may truly be said of him, that he was waiting the coming of his Lord. And, at times, he would say, "oh my dear Savior, what wait I for? why dost thou so long delay thy coming." Thus, with a lively hope, he resigned himself to the arms of his Savior, and, we trust, has gone to receive the reward of those, who continue faithful unto the end. His memory will long be precious to us, and long shall we bewail the loss we have sustained. May the Lord of the harvest raise up others, of a similar spirit, to come and occupy the place, vacant by his death."

This beloved and lamented youth, was hardly nineteen years old, when with uncommon maturity of mind, and strength of modest, fervent, and active piety, he entered the service; saying, in a letter written at the time, "I have a desire to do all the good I can I feel willing to be spent in the service of my God " His revered and respected father could say,—and did say,—in answer to inquiries with respect to his feelings on the subject: "I would hereby, and do hereby, give my most cordial and hearty approbation to his joining in the missionary cause. My children are near and dear to me. But I trust I feel as though I received them from God, and have given them back to him in the holy ordinance of baptism; and I am willing to devote them to him for the service of the poor heathen, if they can be of any service. Had I a hundred sons and daughters, I should not think the sacrifice too great to devote them, for the salvation of one poor heathen. A better life than the life of man has been laid down for them. Shall I withhold a son, or a daughter, if God calls them, and they can be of any service? God forbid. Take them, therefore, dear Savior; take them, my Lord and my God Oh take them, ye servants of the most high God, ye agents for God, in behalf of the suffering, benighted pagans; send them wheresoever your wisdom and prudence shall dictate "

Happy son! Happy father! And not the less happy for what the Lord, in his sovereign wisdom, has seen fit to do in this early removal. Nor by such a death will the cause eventually suffer.

There are now belonging to the mission, already in the field and on their way to it, thirteen men and nine women.

In their joint letter, June 12th, the brethren say,

"In reviewing the scenes, through which the Lord has led us, we see much to excite our humility, our gratitude, and our unshaken confidence in him whose cause we are laboring to build up.

"The hand of the Lord was laid heavily up onus last winter. Thirty-six of our family were sick at one time Two or three cases only were considered as dangerous But, in the midst of judgment the Lord remembered mercy. By the close of March, general health was restored, which, considering the number of our family, has been enjoyed to an unusual degree ever since. There have been, however, among the laborers and children many distressing cases of sore eyes."

At Elliot they have cleared fifty or sixty acres of excellent land for cultivation, a good proportion of it bottom land of inexhaustible fertility. Several acres of the land were cleared by the native boys of the school, under the direction of their immediate instructor, Mr. Williams. In their Journal, the last of December, the brethren give this general account of the produce of the preceding season:

"Our plantation was entirely a wilderness; but it has yielded us a rich harvest. Besides several hundred bushels of corn and potatoes, we have gathered about 30 bushels of peas and 12 or 15 of white beans These last contribute not less to health than comfort. We have no doubt that the feeble health of our family the last winter was occasioned by a deficiency of vegetable diet. We would recommend this subject, particularly to the consideration of missionaries going into the western country, and refer them to a very able and excellent Report, made to the Secretary of War, by the Surgeon General of the Army of the United States, respecting the component parts of the soldier's rations. The subject applies, in all its force, to missionaries in uncivilized countries."

The buildings for the establishment are eight commodious log cabins occupied as dwelling houses, a dining room and kitchen contiguous, fifty-two feet by twenty, and with a piazza on each side; a school house thirty-six feet by twenty four, of hewn logs and finished on the Lancasterian plan; a mill-house thirty-six by thirty; a commodious blacksmith's shop and joiner's shop; a lumber house and granary; a stable, and three or four out-houses.

There are belonging to the mission more than two hundred neat cattle, including calves,—teams of oxen and horses, wagons, carts, ploughs, and other implements of husbandry, suitable for a large plantation;—mechanical tools for various arts; and all the varied apparatus for the accommodation of a family consisting of a hundred persons.

In the school, there are seventy or eighty children and youths, male and female.

"They are of different ages," says Mr. Kingsbury in his report to the government, "from six years to nineteen and twenty; and of various complexions, from full blooded Choctaws to those who are apparently descended from white parents.

"In addition to the common rudiments of education, the boys are acquiring a practical knowledge of agriculture, in its various branches; and the girls, while out of school, are employed under the direction of the female missionaries, in different parts of domestic labor. We have also a full blooded Choctaw lad, learning the blacksmith's trade, and another, now in the school, wishes to engage in the same employment, so soon as there is opportunity. All the children are placed entirely under our control; and the most entire satisfaction is expressed, as to the manner in which they are treated.

"The school is taught on the Lancasterian plan, and the progress of the children has exceeded our most sanguine expectations. There have been instances of lads 14 or 16 years old, entirely ignorant of our language, who have learned the alphabet in three days; and on the fourth could read and pronounce syllables. We have never seen an equal number of children, in any school, who appeared more promising. Since they commenced, their attention has been constant. No one has left the school, or has manifested a wish to leave it.

"The moral and religious instruction which we have communicated to the adults, has been very limited, for want of interpreters. A considerable number of those, who could understand, and some others, have attended public worship. And it is evident, that a favorable impression has been made on the minds of some, and the state of morals, in a small degree, improved. Our hope is, from the habits which may be formed by the young, and the principles which we may instil into their minds."

In this connexion, two or three paragraphs, from the journal of the mission, will open some interesting views.

"Nov. 18. A caravan of 17 half breeds, besides a number of women and children, arrived and encamped near the mission. Their intention is to form a settlement near the Yazoo, above its junction with the Yalo-

Busha, and about 15 or 20 miles north of this place. There are yet no settlements in that part of the country. They have with them about thirty horses, nearly half of them packed with provisions, kettles, farming tools, &c. It is interesting to see these people removing into the wilderness, for the purpose of engaging in agricultural pursuits. They stopped to get their tools repaired at our smith's shop. The Indians say that they do not know what they should do, if brother Fisk should go away. In the evening had an exhibition of the school, at which all our visitors were present. The children sung several hymns, and an opportunity was seized to make such remarks to the children and those present, as were fitted to be useful. The spacious school room hung round with Lancasterian lessons, was well lighted up, which, with the order and decorum of the scholars, and the melody of their voices, produced the most pleasing emotions, and led us for a moment to forget that we were in a heathen land. A recollection of the contrast between the present condition of these children and what it was six months ago, called forth our liveliest gratitude to Him, who caused the light to shine out of darkness, and who is now, through the instrumentality of the Gospel, causing the wilderness and solitary place to bud and blossom as the rose. One of our Indian visitors observed, that he should not be tired of sitting there all night.

"*Dec.* 7. Brother K. preached three times during his absence, on a visit to the Lower Towns. The audiences were small, but generally attentive. The people, every where appeared anxious to have their children instructed. Some, who were well informed, said there were a thousand children in the nation ready to come to school, if they could be received; and that many of their parents would contribute towards their support. During this journey brother K. met with the chief of the Chickasawhay town, one of the most distant parts of the nation. He was on his way to Elliot, with a little boy of mixed blood, belonging to his town, whom he wished to place in the school. In answer to some remarks designed to shew the importance of the Indians becoming civilized and industrious, he replied, that his part of the nation had been in great ignorance; that it was not till lately, that they had received any good advice on these subjects; but that now he should use his exertions to have them change their mode of living.

"*Dec.* 18. There are thirteen girls belonging to the school. These are divided into two companies, each of which alternately assist, while out of school, in the dining room and kitchen. They perform their duties with despatch and neatness which are truly pleasing. The two companies are emulous to excel. Some idea of the labor in our kitchen may be formed from the following schedule of articles which are cooked in one week, and which may be considered a fair specimen of every week's work. Five hundred pounds of beef, 14 bushels of potatoes, 40 large loaves of bread or puddings to make up the deficiency, 200 gallons of *tomfulah*, 60 gallons of weak coffee, 3 pecks of beans and peas, besides other small articles. One company of the girls, when out of school and not engaged in the kitchen, assists in washing for the family; in sewing, knitting, spinning, &c. Friends of Indian civilization have great reason for being encouraged by their improvement.

"*March* 26. Brother Kingsbury preached at Capt. Folsom's. Had much conversation with him.   He said the leading men among the Choctaws, by their acquaintance with religious people, had discovered that they were friendly to the red people, and wished to do them good.   He said, that the good book, the Bible, had taught good white people thus to love all mankind.   Many of the Choctaws wished to know what was in this good book, which produced such good effects; but they were very ignorant on the subject, and it would require great pains and patience to instruct them.   He thought the way was prepared for them to open their ears to those, who would come to teach them."

From the first the Choctaws,—the chiefs especially, have manifested toward the mission the most friendly dispositions.   They have done more than merely to give their consent to the establishment, and allow their children to be instructed; of the sincerity and ardor of their desire for the instruction of their children and improvement of their nation, they have given substantial and unexampled proofs.

"It has been our endeavor," says Mr Kingsbury, "to impress on the minds of this nation the advantages of instruction, and the propriety of their contributing towards the education of their own children.   We are decidedly of opinion, that in every point of view, it is important that they should learn to help themselves.   By commencing on a liberal and extensive scale for their improvement, we have drawn forth a spirit of liberality, as unexpected as it is encouraging."

In the Report of the last year, it was stated, that soon after the missionaries arrived in the nation, the king Puck-sha-nub-bee gave for the school $200 to be paid annually from the annuity by his part of the nation, from the U. S., and that at a council of the nation in the fore part of August, after an address made to them by Mr. Kingsbury, a subscription was opened upon the spot; and 85 cows and calves and $500 dollars to be paid annually, and $700 as a donation to the establishment, were subscribed.   Your Committee have now the gratification to report other and greater donations.

"At a treaty holden in 1816, the Choctaws sold a tract of country for which they are to receive of the U. S. $6,000 annually, in cash, for 17 years.   The nation is divided into three districts, called the Upper, the Lower, and the six Towns.   At a council, holden on the 4th Sept. by what are called the Lower Towns, including the northeast part of the nation, between the public road and the Tombigby river, it was voted unanimously, that the sum of $2,000, their proportion of the $6,000 above mentioned, be appropriated to the support of a school in their own district, under the patronage of the American Board.   They also sent a letter to the chief of the Upper towns, in which Elliot is situated, requesting them to appropriate their proportion, an equal sum, to the support of this school."

From another district the following communications have been received.

"Resolved in council, this 21st March 1820, held for Mingo Pushamatahaw's district in the Choctaw nation, That the balance of the annuity due to the said district from the United States, for the purchase of land in the year of our Lord 1816, made by Gen. Coffee, Col. McKee, and John Rhea, Esq., of two thousand dollars per annum, shall be appropriated in the following manner, viz.   One thousand dollars for the erection and continuance of a blacksmith's shop, with iron and the necessary utensils for conducting the same for the best accommodation of the Indians; and one thousand dollars to be applied to the use of a school to be established as soon as practicable. The said amount to be paid by the United States Agent in the nation, to the above establishment quarter yearly.

Signed,   PUSHAMATAHAW, *in behalf of the council.*"

Choctaw trading house, March 21st, 1820.

"REV. CYRUS KINGSBURY,—Dear sir,—It was with much pleasure I can inform you, that we have this day resolved in council to appropriate one half of our annuity due to us from the United States, for this district, of one thousand dollars for the use and benefit of a school to be established in our district, as soon as practicable, and we particularly wish you to take charge of it for us, as we are much pleased with your exertions already made for the benefit of a part of our nation.

"Please to present our thanks to our Father the President of the United States, and also to your *friends*, for their thoughtfulness of us, and tell them we hope, the day is not far distant, when we shall take our place among the enlightened States of this happy land. Very respectfully your obedient servant.

PUSHAMATAHAW, *Chief of one District of the Choctaw Nation.*"

In a letter to Mr. Kingsbury accompanying these documents, Eden Brashears, Esq. acting agent in the absence of Col. McKee, says:

"You will see by the enclosed copy how Pushamatahaw's district have disposed of their annuity—and when making that disposition they requested me to furnish you a copy of the same, and further, to request you to take the care and arrangement of the blacksmith's shop, by sending on to the north, and engaging a suitable blacksmith to conduct said shop; one that may have a small family would be preferred, and a good mechanic, as it is their intention to put some of their own people to learn the trade. The site for the school establishment is also left to your own selection, after taking a view of the district, which they wish you to do, so soon as it may suit your convenience; and further hope that your friends (as they term them) and our government, will hold out a helping hand to them, so as to enable them soon to have a school in that district, as they consider themselves much behind the other districts in civilization, and think, on many occasions, that they have been neglected by their white friends."

Mr. Kingsbury, in a letter 5th of May, says, "It is probable that an alteration will be made, so that the $2,000 dollars annuity will go to the establishment, leaving the particular application of it to our own discretion, with the understanding that there shall be a blacksmith's shop connected with it on the plan of the one at Elliot."

In the beginning of June, this national bounty was completed, by a like formal donation, on the part of the district in which Elliot is situated, of that part of the annuity, $2,000 for that establishment. And on the occasion the following Letter was addressed to the Corresponding Secretary.

Elliot, June 1820.

"BROTHER,—This is the first time we have visited this school in our nation since it was established here. We think the school is in a very flourishing condition and all things going on well.

"Brother, our hearts are made glad to see our children improving so fast. We are pleased to see our boys go into the woods with their axes and into the field with their hoes, under the care of their teacher, to learn to work, that they may know how to clear and cultivate our land; for we cannot expect to live any longer by hunting.—Our game is gone;—and the missionaries tell us, the Good Spirit points out to us now this new and better way to get our meat, and provide bread and clothes for ourselves, women, and children. And we are very glad to see our daughters learning to cook, and to make and mend clothes, and do all such things as the white women do.

"Brother, we have never until now, had the pleasure of becoming acquainted with the good people here, except Mr. Kingsbury, whom we had seen before. Now we see and believe, that all the missionary brothers and sisters at Elliot, are our friends, and wish to teach us and our children good things, which we have not known before.

"Brother, we wish to express to all our good white brothers at the north, who have sent good missionaries and teachers here, our sincere and hearty thanks for their great kindness in so doing. We are well pleased in every respect with the school, and with our good white brothers and sisters of the mission family; and we are satisfied and well pleased with the manner, in which our children are treated by them.

"Brother, we had never been sensible of the great expense, at which our white brethren have been, in establishing this school, until yesterday, when we had a talk, and our white brethren gave us the information. And we feel now more deeply our obligations to all our kind benefactors, for the love which they have shown the red people in this distant land. It is likewise cause of great joy to us, that our good father the President of the United States, has stretched out his helping hand to his red children for their good. We feel very thankful for his favor in appropriating so much money for our school, encouraging and helping on the missionaries in their work.

"Brother, we wish to repeat to all our white friends every where, that we are very thankful for all your favors, and all the good you have done to us your poor ignorant red brethren,—and we hope you will still remember us.—We are yet in a very destitute situation. We have one good school, in which 70 of our children, are, by your great kindness, placed and now receiving instruction. But brother, we would with boldness tell you our wants. We have more than 1,000 children in our nation, who are now waiting and looking up to our white brothers for the means of instruction. Our nation is open for more missionaries, and our hearts are ready to receive them.

"We know that it must be at a great expense that you send out and support missions among us; and we feel it our duty to assist and to do all we can for ourselves. We have lately appropriated 2,000 dollars of our annuity from each of the three districts in our nation, for the benefit of the mission school, making in the whole $6,000 a year for 16 years to come. We are your friends and brothers,

PUCK-SHA-NUB-BEE, *his* X *mark,*
MUSH-UL-LA-TUB-BEE, *his* X *mark.*"

These donations and communications speak for themselves; and they speak with an emphasis that should arrest every mind—with a pathos that should touch every heart in this Christian land. They betoken an influence from the All-powerful Spirit that originally caused the light to shine out of darkness. The movement presses upon the mission with the force of a mighty rushing wind. The missionaries have found it impossible, and your Committee have found it impossible, to proceed as fast as it would impel them. They have felt it however to be their duty—as they have found it to be a matter of necessity—to do what they could, towards answering the desires of the Choctaws, and preventing a disastrous disappointment or impatience.

The call for an establishment in the Lower Towns, the district which set the noble example of giving their annuity for the purpose, could not be resisted. Early in the winter it was resolved, that a beginning should be made as soon as possible. "It was agreed by the brethren," says Mr. Kingsbury, "that I should select the site, have a house erected and preparations made, for raising a crop. After making all possible arrangements for the mission at Elliot, I left there on the 10th of February for the purpose of commencing the contemplated establishment.

"*Feb.* 19. Reached Major Pitchlynn's, one of the public interpreters. He is a white man, has a Choctaw family, and large possessions.

"*Feb.* 20. Preached at Major Pitchlynn's. Several were present, among whom, were two or three captains. Conversed with them through the public interpreter. They expressed great thankfulness that good white people had come to teach them They had seen many white people, but did not know till lately, that there were any such men as preachers.

"*Feb.* 21. Went in company with Captain Folsom and Major Pitchlynn to select a site for the new establishment. Found many good places, but at all of them some things were wanting. It was difficult to determine which combined the most advantages. Felt a responsibility on my mind which I cannot express. My heart was lifted up in fervent supplication, that the Lord would direct to that place, where he would delight to record his name, and to erect monuments to his glory.

"*Feb.* 22 Expected to have returned to Major Pitchlynn's last night, but the distance was too great. Endeavored to reach the house of a native, but was unable to cross a large creek, which in consequence of the late rains, overflowed its banks. Stopped in the woods without food or fire, and having collected some dry grass for a bed, and commended ourselves to the protection and guidance of our heavenly Father, enjoyed a good night's rest.

"*Feb.* 23. After mature and prayerful deliberation, resolved to establish the school on the borders of an extensive prairie on the south side of Ook-tib-be-ha creek, about 12 miles above its junction with the Tombigby. This creek is the boundary line between the Choctaw and Chickasaw nations. As no one of the sisters could at present be spared from Elliot, I hired a young man and his wife from the settlements in Alabama for ten months.

"Came with three laborers upon the ground, which is henceforth to be consecrated to the service of God. The particular site selected for the buildings was the very spot on which we had slept the night before in our grass bed. It is a pleasing eminence overlooking towards the south a prairie of several miles in circumference. The part of this immediately contiguous is of exhaustless fertility,—requiring only a very little labor to prepare it for the plough. On the right is a small creek, which will furnish water for stock and on the left is the Ook-tib-be-ha navigable in high water for keel boats, which at particular times may come within a quarter of a mile of the establishment. May the Lord God of Israel bless us, cause his face to shine upon us and prosper the labor of our hands."

After sustaining almost incredible labors and hardships, with surprising fortitude and alacrity, Mr. Kingsbury makes in his journal, March 23d, this affecting record.

"Removed into our new house. It was a day of rejoicing. We had lived in a smoky wet camp four weeks. May the Lord vouchsafe his presence, and make this house a Bethel, and fill our hearts with gratitude and praise.

"March 25. Having made arrangements for a garden and cornfield, set out on my return to Elliot." He arrived at Elliot in health on the 29th, and the grateful note was made in the mission journal, "The Lord has been gracious to him and those with him, in preserving their health amidst their exposure to cold, wet, and fatigue."

In their letter 12th June, speaking of these beginnings at Ook-tib-be-ha, the brethren say:

"A convenient house has been completed, a garden and yards for cattle prepared; and it is expected that 20 or 25 acres of corn and potatoes will be cultivated. It is highly important that a number of additional buildings should be erected in the course of the next fall and winter, and large preparations made for raising provisions. This will enable us to open a school in the autumn of 1821, without great embarrassment, and we think with less expense than has been incurred at the other establishments. If these preparations should be made with suitable activity, we think the natives will wait with patience."

The brethren say further—"The Prudential Committee have also been informed that the Six Towns have made an earnest request, that the American Board would establish a school and a blacksmith's shop in their district.

"The work to be accomplished is a great one: The natives view it as a great one, and one which cannot be done without ample means. They do not consider their appropriations as adequate to the object, or as capable of being employed to advantage without further aid. They have made the appropriations in full confidence, that the good people of the United States will grant them such further aid, as will complete the establishment at Elliot, and place the other two on a similar foundation. Should the plan of operations here commenced be followed up for a short time, further aid may be expected from the natives. Judging from their friendly disposition, from the great interest they take in education, and from what they have already done, we think it a reasonable conclusion, that, at no very distant period the Choctaws will provide in a great measure for the support of their own schools. But should the impulse they have received be suffered to subside, should the appropriations they have made remain unproductive, for want of such additional aid as would put them in operation, their hopes would be disappointed; their school would languish, and the labor of years and the expense of thousands would be necessary to raise them to the same pitch of benevolent exertion."

ARKANSAW MISSION.—Of the particular reasons which induced to this mission, a brief statement was submitted in the Report of the last year. And it was then also stated that the Rev. Alfred Finney and the Rev. Cephas Washburn, were designated for the mission, and were under directions to proceed—the former from Vermont, and the latter from Georgia—to Brainerd, and thence together to Elliot. There they were to leave their wives, until they had visited the place for their establishment in the Arkansaw country, and made some inceptive arrangements and prepared some accommodation for their families.

Conformably to the directions they proceeded with their wives to Brainerd in October and November.

"Our feelings on entering the [Cherokee] nation," says Mr. Washburn, "and beholding the natives of the same country to which we were going as heralds of mercy, are better conceived than described. Suffice it to say, we have never seen any strangers towards whom we felt our hearts so powerfully drawn in affection. When we beheld them in their ignorance, and thought of the worth of their souls, we felt that no service was too great to be performed, no sacrifice too dear to be made, no trials too severe to be endured for their salvation. Our meeting with the dear brethren and sisters of the Brainerd mission, was grateful to our hearts. They gave us a most cordial welcome, and their Christian society was truly refreshing. Never have we found a family to which, in so short a time, we have formed so strong an attachment. When introduced to the dear Cherokee brethren and sisters, we could only say, "this is the Lord's doing." Surely, if the Christian community could see and converse with these children of the forest, now lambs of the Redeemer's fold, they would consider this fruit of missionary labors more than a double equivalent for the expense of establishing and supporting missions among the heathen. By faith, I trust, we were enabled to look on the school as a fountain, from whence streams of salvation should finally flow to every part of the nation."

They left Brainerd on the 30th of November, and after almost incredible difficulties and dangers, from filled swamps and creeks, from wet and cold, and hunger and unsheltered lodging, they arrived at Elliot on the 3d of January. In a letter of the 12th of the same month they say:

"Notwithstanding our journey has been long and toilsome, and our exposures and privations many, through the wilderness, our Father in Heaven has indeed manifested himself a faithful and covenant keeping God through all our wearisome pilgrimage. We have lain on the ground repeatedly, wet and cold with rain and snow; we have waded creeks and swamps, and mire; we have travelled the wilderness, some part of it a trackless way among people of barbarous tongues; yet in all our trials He has supported us; in all our difficulties and wants He has aided and relieved us; in all our dangers and exposures He has preserved us, our wives and our little ones. May we feel our obligations to our merciful preserver and benefactor, and may we receive his continual goodness as an excitement to future trust in Him, and to active obedience in his service."

As the season was not favorable for travelling in the country, they tarried at Elliot, helping the missionaries there until the fore part of February, when they made an attempt to proceed to the Arkansaw, of which an account is given in a joint letter, March 8th.

"From what was stated in a letter of February 1st, you doubtless expected our next communication from the Arkansaw; at least this was our expectation when we last wrote you. But Providence, which ever orders wisely, has caused in this respect a severe disappointment, which has greatly tried the feelings of our hearts. Some account of our fruitless attempt to get to the Arkansaw will explain our meaning."

Their attempt in a word was frustrated, by the rise and overflowing of the Mississippi which rendered it impracticable to get to the Arkansaw by land, and extremely difficult and dangerous, if at all practicable by water. They explain the circumstances very fully and satisfactorily; and proceed to say:

"All the circumstances as presented to our minds induced the belief, that our object would in no degree be forwarded by a visit to Arkansaw, were it possible to accomplish it at that time. We were hence led to the conclusion, though reluctantly and tardily, that duty, if not necessity, required our return to Elliot. In pursuance of this conclusion we retraced the steps we had taken and arrived here 29th ult.

"What good will result from this part of our seemingly fruitless wandering, is at present unknown. Our visit to the Walnut Hills, was however very seasonable to the temporal concerns of this mission; as we found on our arrival there a considerable part of the supplies, forwarded from Boston and elsewhere, in a condition soon to be destroyed. We put them all into a safe condition till they can be brought up the Yazoo, which will be probably soon. While at the Hills we had opportunity to preach several times, from which may result spiritual good to some there, who, though willing to hear, are destitute of a saving knowledge of the gospel.

"Our return also was seasonable to the spiritual interest of this mission; as brother Kingsbury is absent and expected to be for some time, on the Tombigby, making arrangements for a new establishment for the benefit of the nation. In the mean time, nothing is done for the furtherance of the particular object of our mission Had it not been for some unforeseen and unexpected delays at and soon after the commencement of our enterprise, we might have reached, in human view, the Arkansaw in the month of December, according to the expectation of the Prudential Committee. But the delays and hindrances were entirely providential, beyond the control of those concerned in them.

"While our own particular enterprise is calling us here, anxiety and suspense are constant attendants. What the Lord intends by retarding our progress and disappointing the expectations of the Prudential Committee in us, is yet to be unfolded. We fear that our faith and courage will fail, and that the confidence placed in us, and the patience of the Prudential Committee and of the Christian public will be exhausted, before we shall be established in the field of our future labors. We hope we have an interest in your prayers, if not for ourselves, yet for the influence our conduct may have upon the precious cause of Christ."

By these disappointments, and delays the intended commencement of the establishment in the spring was prevented; but the countervailing advantages are not of small consideration. Besides the very timely help afforded to the mission at Brainerd and Elliot, Messrs. Washburn and Finney, by their residence at those stations, had opportunity for acquiring knowledge and experience of prime and substantial importance. After their return from the Walnut Hills, they remained at Elliot, taking part in the work there, until it was supposed the state of the rivers would admit of their proceeding to their destined station. Since their departure from Elliot, no intelligence has been received from them

Mr. Jacob Hitchcock of Brimfield, Mass., and Mr. James Orr of Groton, Tompkins Co. N. Y., young unmarried men, who had offered themselves for the service, with expressions of readiness and desire to devote themselves unreservedly for life, with all that they possessed, and whose testimonials, as to their qualifications for assisting in the schools and in the agricultural and mechanical branches of the general work, were highly satisfactory,—were designated for the Arkansaw establishment. Conformably to their instructions, they proceeded to Pittsburg, at which place they arrived the last of April,—and there in company with their brethren destined for the Choctaw mission, took passage upon the river,—hoping to meet Messrs. Finney and Washburn at the post of Arkansaw, and with them thence to proceed to the proposed seat of the mission.

Your Committee can only express the hope, that, under the protection and guidance of Providence, the several members of this mission have safely reached the field of their future labors, and that they all experience in equal measure the gracious blessing which has so signally attended their brethren at Brainerd and at Elliot. Other devoted individuals are holding themselves in readiness to go forth to their assistance as soon as it shall be deemed advisable to be sent.

MISSION TO THE SANDWICH ISLANDS.—For several years past, the eyes of the Christian community have been fixed upon Owhyhee, and the neighboring islands, as an inviting field for missionary labor. Attention was first drawn to this most delightful cluster in the northern Pacific, by the fact, that some of the natives, providentially cast upon our shores, were receiving the advantages of a liberal and Christian education, and had apparently become the subjects of that spiritual change, which alone could fit them to be useful to their countrymen in the highest sense. The hope, that they might return to their native islands, accompanied by faithful missionaries, and bearing the offers of mercy to ignorant and perishing multitudes, was greatly strengthened by the wonderful displays of divine grace in the islands of the Southern Pacific. The lamented Obookiah was anxiously looking for the day, when he should embark on this voyage of benevolence and of Christian enterprise. Though it seemed good to the Lord of missions, that this young servant should not be employed, as had been desired by himself and others, but should be called to the enjoyments of a better world, divine wisdom had prepared, as we trust, other agents to aid in accomplishing the same blessed design.

The period arrived, soon after the last annual meeting, for sending forth a mission, which had been thus contemplated; and which had excited the liveliest interest, and the most pleasing anticipations. The passage having been engaged, and other preparatory arrangements made, the mission family assembled in Boston, on the 12th of October. It consisted of twenty-two persons, and presented a most interesting collection, rarely if ever surpassed on a similar occasion. The Rev. Messrs Bingham and Thurston had been ordained as ministers of the Gospel. Mr. Daniel Chamberlain, of Brookfield, Mass., a farmer in the prime of life, who, by his own industry and good management, was placed in very eligible worldly circumstances; Dr. Thomas Holman, who had just finished his education for the practice of medicine; Mr. Samuel Whitney, a student in Yale College, capable of being employed as a catechist, schoolmaster, or mechanic; Mr. Samuel Ruggles, a catechist and schoolmaster; and Mr. Elisha Loomis, a printer, having previously offered themselves for this service and been accepted, went forth desirous of carrying the arts of civilized communities, as well as the blessings of the Gospel. Mr. Chamberlain had been the head of a family for 13 or 14 years, and took with him a discreet and pious wife and five promising children. The other persons who have been named, had formed recent matrimonial connexions, and obtained, as helpers in the work, well educated females, of the fairest character for piety and virtue. To this goodly company were added Thomas Hopoo, William Tennooe, and John Honooree, natives of the Sandwich Islands, who had been educated at the Foreign Mission School, instructed in the doctrines and duties of Christianity, and made partakers, as was charitably hoped, of spiritual and everlasting blessings. They burned with the desire of imparting divine truth to their brethren according to the flesh. All the adults here mentioned were formed into a church of Christ, with very impressive solemnities, and were committed to the pastoral care of the two ordained missionaries. This infant church, soon after its organization, celebrated the Redeemer's sacrifice, and invited to its communion all who love our Lord Jesus Christ in sincerity. The season was refreshing and delightful. Numerous friends of Christ and of missions pledged themselves to each other, and to the departing family, never to forget them when removed to another hemisphere, to pray for them with affectionate importunity, and to contribute for the supply of their temporal wants, and for the general success and prosperity of the mission. The instructions of the Prudential Committee were delivered in the presence of a great assembly, and amid many tokens, that the cause of Christ among the heathen was taking a new and stronger hold upon the affections of his followers.

On Saturday, Oct. 23d, the mission family embarked on board the brig Thaddeus, Captain Andrew Blanchard. Previously to their taking a final adieu of their friends and their country, they stopped on a spacious wharf, and there, surrounded by a multitude of Christian brethren, were commended to the favor of God by prayer, and united in a parting hymn. The vessel soon weighed anchor, and sailed a few miles into the lower harbor, whence, on the following day, she put to sea. After she had been 50 days on the voyage, and had passed the equator, the missionaries had an opportunity to write hasty letters to the Committee, and to enclose copious journals to their friends. They had all been well, with the exception of a somewhat uncommon share in sea-sickness, and were united and happy among themselves, cheered with anticipations of usefulness among the heathen, and employed, as they had opportunity, in communicating religious knowledge to the ship's company, and improving the Christian character of each other, with a particular view to the duties, which would devolve upon them in their arduous undertaking.

What trials await these beloved brethren and sisters it is impossible for man to foresee; nor ought we to be anxious. Trials of some kind undoubtedly they, as well as all other missionaries, must expect. That they may not be elated by prosperity, nor disheartened by adversity, but may lead humble, prayerful, laborious lives, feeling their dependence upon God, and gratefully acknowledging every token of his favor, will be the unfeigned petition at the throne of grace, frequently offered by their numerous personal friends scattered widely through our country, and by all the friends of missions, to whom their design and destination shall be known.

It is proper to mention here, with expressions of gratitude to the Supreme Disposer, the astonishing change, which took place at the Sandwich Islands, just at the time the missionaries were embarking at Boston. To the surprise of all, who had been acquainted with those islands, the government and the people unanimously, or nearly so, determined to abandon their idols, and to commit them with all the monuments of idolatry to the flames. This was done at Owhyhee, then at Woahoo, and then at Atooi, with no dissent, much less opposition, except that, in the former of these islands, a chief of secondary influence stood aloof from the whole proceeding, and preserved an idol, which had been presented to him by Tamahamaha. The accounts, given by eye-witnesses, are perfectly explicit and harmonious, as to these facts. Tamoree, king of Atooi, expressed himself as being exceedingly desirous that missionaries should come and teach the people to read and write, as had been done in the Society Islands. This he did in conversation with American sea-captains, and wrote a letter, to the same effect, by the vessel which brought this intelligence, addressed to his son at Cornwall This son, though not attached to the mission, sailed with the missionaries, and professed a desire to befriend them, and to promote the cause of truth among his countrymen. It is hoped, that he was received by his father in health and peace, several months before the abovementioned letter, the principal object of which was to solicit his return, arrived in this country.

The principal means, which Providence used to bring about this surprising result, was the continually repeated rumor of what had been done in the Society Islands, and the continually repeated assurance of our sea-captains and sailors, that the whole system of idolatry was foolish and stupid. Thus has a nation been induced to renounce its gods by the influence of Christian missionaries, who reside at the distance of nearly 3,000 miles across the ocean. Thus, while the Gospel is becoming the power of God and the wisdom of God, to many in the islands of the Southern Pacific, the distant rumor of these blessed results has made the idolaters of the Northern Pacific ashamed of their mummeries, and consigned to the flames the high places of cruelty, the altars, and the idols together.

FOREIGN MISSION SCHOOL —This consecrated Seminary was instituted in the autumn of 1816, and opened in the beginning of May 1817. There belong to it a commodious edifice for the school, a good mansion house, with a barn, and other out-buildings, and a garden for the Principal;—a house, barn,*&c., with a few acres of good tillage land for the Steward and commons.—all situated sufficiently near to each other and to the Congregational meeting-house, in the south parish of Cornwall, Con. —and eighty acres of excellent wood land, about a mile and a half distant.

The object of the school as set forth in the constitution, is—"*The education in our own country of heathen youths, in such manner, as, with subsequent professional instruction will qualify them to become useful Missionaries, Physicians, Surgeons, School Masters, or interpreters; and to communicate to the heathen nations such knowledge in agriculture and the arts, as may prove the means of promoting Christianity and civilization.*" As these youths are designed for a higher education, than is expected to be obtained at our mission schools in heathen countries, it is deemed of no small importance, that they be only such as are of suitable age, of docile dispositions, and of promising talents.

In the constitution there is a provision, that youths of our own country, of acknowledged piety, may be admitted to the school, at their own expense, and at the discretion of the Agents.

In the first year of the school twelve youths were admitted—ten from heathen lands and two natives of Connecticut. Of these, Henry Obookiah, John Honooree, Thomas Hopoo, and William Tennooe, had before been objects of Christian liberality, and for some time under Christian instruction. The raised hopes, founded, under Providence, on the unquestioned piety, the distinguished talents, and the excellent character of Obookiah, terminated in his triumphant departure from these earthly scenes, before the first year of the school had expired. Of his three companions, Honooree, Hopoo, and Tennooe, Mr. Ruggles, one of the two Connecticut youths, and George Tamoree, particular mention has just been made under the head of the Sandwich Island mission.——Of the other six, admitted the first year, James Ely, the other Connecticut youth, and George Sandwich and William Kummoo-olah from the Sandwich Islands, are still members of the school; one has been dismissed for misbehavior, one for incapacity, and the other is absent.

From year to year, since the first, youths of different nations have been admitted, two or three of whom, after longer or shorter trial, have been dismissed. Care, however, has been taken, that those, who have been dismissed, should be placed in good families, where they might still have the benefit of Christian instruction.

The present number of pupils is twenty-nine; four from the Sandwich Islands—one from Otaheite—one from the Marquesas—one Malay—eight Cherokees—two Choctaws—three of the Stockbridge Tribe—two Oneidas —one Tuscarora—two Caughnewagas—one Indian youth from Pennsylvania, and three youths of our own country.

Under the instruction of the able and highly respected Principal, the Rev. Mr. Daggett, and his very capable and faithful Assistant, Mr. Prentice, the improvement of the pupils, in general, has been increasing and satisfactory, and in not a few instances uncommonly good. Besides being taught in various branches of learning, and made practically acquainted with the useful arts of civilized life; they are instructed constantly and with especial care in the doctrines and duties of Christianity. Nor has this instruction been communicated in vain. Of the thirty-one heathen youths—including, with the twenty-six now at school, the deceased Oboo-kiah, and the four, who have gone with the mission to their native Islands—seventeen are thought to have given evidence of a living faith in the Gospel; and several others are very seriously thoughtful on religious concerns. The Lord, in his sovereign goodness, has made it strikingly manifest, that his face is toward this favored Seminary, and that his blessing rests upon it. May it be eminently instrumental in making known the glory of his name in many lands, and of bringing multitudes of different nations and tongues, to unite in songs of everlasting joy and praise.

EXPENDITURES AND RECEIPTS —Since the last Annual Meeting, your Committee have sent forth to different fields 23 men and 13 women: 10 men and 7 women to the Sandwich Islands—1 man to Ceylon—2 men to Western Asia—8 men and 6 women to the Choctaw nation—and 2 men to the Cherokees of the Arkansas. Of the men, five are ordained missionaries—one is a physician, one is a printer, and the rest, besides being skilled in husbandry and various mechanical arts, are men of vigorous and well informed minds, in sound bodies, inured to labor, and of approved civil and Christian character; 4 are men in middle life with well governed and well educated families,—the rest, young men, 8 of whom are married; the most of them have been exercised in the instruction of schools, and all of them are deemed well qualified to take part in the arduous, benevolent, and sacred work of evangelizing and civilizing pagan and uncultured people.

The fitting out of missionaries, and getting them to the fields of labor, must be attended with not inconsiderable expense. Many things are to be done in the preparations, requiring various attentions, and journeyings, and labors, and occasioning numberless contingent expenses. Many articles are comprised in the necessary outfits and provision, for the individuals, and families, and establishments. And conveyances by water or by land are expensive.

The total expense of the Sandwich mission, paid from the Treasury, besides much which was given by liberal individuals in various articles not included in the Treasurer's account, was somewhat more than $10,000. Of this sum $224 were paid for the travelling expenses of the members of the mission,—$275 for transportation of baggage to Boston,—$2,500 for passage to the Islands,—almost $2,000 for stores for the use of the missionaries on their passage and after their arrival,—almost $1,000 for family furniture, clothing, and mechanical and agricultural implements,—$775 for printing press and apparatus,—and $866 for mathematical, philosophical, and surgical instruments.

To persons not conversant with these matters, these items and the total amount might appear extravagant. And yet in proportion to the magnitude of the mission the expenditure was small. It would appear so on comparison with the cost of English missions.

If it costs less to fit out and convey men to our stations in the wilderness of our own country, it does not, however, cost less to get an establishment there into operation, or in its early stages to maintain it. And during the year, the missionaries already in the field were to be provided for, and the establishments already in operation to be supported as well as new men to be sent out and new establishments to be commenced.

Within the year the Treasury has disbursed for the Bombay mission, $7,221—for the Ceylon, $7,135—for the Cherokee, $9,967—for the Choctaw, $10,414—for the Arkansas, $1,150—for the Palestine, $2,348 —for the Foreign Mission School, $3,350—and for all the objects and purposes of the Board, $57,420.

It was not to be expected—especially if the distressing scarcity, or stagnation of the circulating medium were considered,—that there would be in the year an advance, upon the receipts of preceding years, equal or proportionate to the large additions made to our missions, or the consequent augmentation of expense. It is not indeed according to the general course of things, that in the management of extensive and progressive concerns, public or private—incurring large expenditures, and depending upon many contingencies—the receipts in each year should be very exactly or nearly proportionate to the disbursements. In one year the disbursements will come short of the receipts,—in other years they will go beyond them; even in concerns conducted upon the soundest principles, and with the greatest success. It has been so with the concerns of this Board. In some former years there was a surplus of income which was kept in reserve, to be used in succeeding years, as the exigencies or interests of the Institution should require.

The donations, contributions, and benefactions, from societies, churches, congregations, and individuals, received at the treasury, within the year ending with the last month, amounted to $36,500; and the income from the permanent fund, and other sources, to $2,600, making in the total sum $39,000. This, as will be seen, come shorts of the total amount of expenditures by $18,000.—For the supply of the deficiency, it has been found necessary to draw upon the disposable funds of the Board, accumulated from preceding years.

Though these receipts are not equal to the disbursements, yet your Committee have the high gratification to state,—and they would do it with a grateful sense of the liberality of individuals and of the Christian public, and with devout thankfulness to the God of all grace,—that the donations exceeded those of any preceding year by $2,600. This deserves more especial notice on account of the scarcity or stagnation, before alluded to. Allowing for the embarrassment and distress, arising from this cause, and felt in all parts of the country, and by all classes of the community—it were moderate to consider $36,000, given in this last year, as being equal to $50,000 in times as they were in preceding years. And in this ratio, it may be right, in point of justice, and gratitude, and encouragement, and confidence,—to estimate the increase of liberality in the community towards the objects of the Board.

And it is deemed proper, and of some importance to be noted, that this increase of liberality, is not to be attributed to extraordinary efforts in the way of solicitation or excitement. Efforts of that kind were even less abundant and less expensive than in former years. Little, indeed, was done, excepting by an Address of the Committee to the Auxiliaries and patrons, and benefactors, and friends of the Board; and a considerable number of brief local agencies in connexion with it. Of the manner in which this address was every where received and answered, the Committee would find it impossible adequately to express their grateful sense. It afforded a proof, inestimably valuable, of the affectionate, and stable, and liberal confidence and attachment of the Christian community towards the Board, and its great object.

Besides the donations in money, numerous contributions have been made in various articles for the mission.   These are not included in the Treasurer's account; and the amount of value cannot be ascertained.   It is not, however, inconsiderable.   For the Sandwich mission a noble spirit of liberality was displayed; particularly in the places and vicinities where the missionaries had resided; and in Boston, Salem, and some of the neighboring towns, of whose cheering liberality every mission has participated.   And for the Cherokee and Choctaw missions, a spirit not less noble has been very extensively manifested, and continually increasing and spreading.   From more than a hundred different places in the north and in the south—boxes of clothing, of almost every kind suitable for the children of the schools—and some for the missionaries and their families —have been prepared and sent forward.   Of about a fifth part of them, the value was estimated and marked by the donors; and the amount is about $1,140.   This taken as a general average, would give the amount of the whole at $5,700.   This sum, added to the $36,500 in money would make a total of $42,200.

The articles of clothing are chiefly the fruits of female benevolence;— that rich and perennial source, whose streams give life and beauty to Zion, and shall make the wilderness glad, and the desert to rejoice and blossom as the rose.

"We ought to be very grateful to God," says the Brainerd Journal, "for putting it into the hearts of his children, to send from the most remote parts of the United States, these seasonable supplies—to cover these naked children of the forest, and in that way to evince the power and excellency of his Gospel, which he has commanded to be preached to every creature."

To these donations from the Christian community, ought surely to be added, and with a strong note of grateful admiration, the unprecedented donations of the Choctaws.

That poor, pagan, and lost people of the wilderness have, within a year, pledged the annual sum of $6,000, to be received by them from the government, during the whole time it shall be paid, that is, for 16 or 17 years to come, in aid of the operations of this Board, for the instruction of themselves and their children in Christianity and civilization.

It should be observed, however, that as the Choctaw donations do not come into our treasury, they do not afford to the Board all the strength and facilities and advantages, that would be afforded by the same amount in the state of our ordinary funds.   No part of these donations was at disposal for supplying the insufficiency of the receipts of the year from the customary sources, not even in regard to the Choctaw mission, the expenses of which exceeded those of either of the other missions.   Still, for the purposes of that mission it is a substantial endowment, and will, from year to year, relieve the general funds, and facilitate and strengthen the general operations.

"The establishment at Elliot," say the missionaries there, "is not yet complete. Houses for the accommodation of the mission families are needed; as are a barn and two or three small buildings. A hundred more acres of land ought to be opened and cultivated. When this is done, and the young stock grown so as to supply the family in a considerable degree, which will be in the course of two or three years, we think the $2,000 a year, appropriated by the natives, in connexion with the donations of provisions and clothing, which may be expected from the states, will go very far towards supporting the establishment. But to complete the buildings, open sufficient land, and provide for the support of the family until other means can be brought into operation, considerable money will be required.

"The appropriations made by the natives, for the two other establishments, though they will do much towards supporting them when put into operation, will be wholly inadequate to laying the foundation. Unless there are means, in the first instance, for procuring a large stock, and bringing under cultivation an extensive plantation, the expenses of provisions would be so great, that it is doubtful whether it would long be supported."

The Board have been made acquainted heretofore, with the patronage afforded to our Indian missions by the general government, with a view, expressly, to the instruction of the Indians in the arts of civilized life. At the commencement, assurance was given by the Executive that for each establishment the expenses of erecting a school house and a dwelling-house should be defrayed from the public funds, and that a specified number of certain kinds of implements and utensils for husbandry and domestic manufacture should be furnished. "The limited appropriations for the Indian Department," said the Secretary of War at the time, "will for the present preclude the executive government from extending a more liberal patronage to the Board, in their laudable efforts for the accomplishment of objects so very desirable." Agreeably, however, to a hope then expressed by the secretary, Congress has passed a law for the appropriation of $10,000 a year, to be applied under the direction of the President to the instruction of the Indian Tribes. Of this sum, $1,000 is "for the present allowed to our establishment at Brainerd, and $1,000 to that at Elliot." "When," says the secretary, "the department is in possession of the necessary information [respecting the several establishments commenced by this Board and other societies] a more full and complete distribution will be made, agreeably to prescribed regulations."

The favorable disposition manifested by the government, and with increasing strength and benignity, towards the great object of civilizing the Aborigines, is to be most gratefully recognized and highly valued. not only on account of the direct pecuniary aid afforded: but more especially for the security which it gives to the Aborigines themselves, to those who are engaged in this labor of benevolence on their behalf, and to the whole Christian community, respecting them. An opposite disposition or policy would be of dark and disastrous aspect.

For these Indian establishments, however, and for our more distant missions, money, much money will yet be required. It is not to be dissembled, that to maintain the several missions, and establishments now under the direction of the Board, in the vigorous operation which should be desired, will cost scarcely less in each successive year, than the amount of the last year's disbursements. And yet the field is wide, and yet more missions are urgently needed and demanded. Thanks to the all-bounteous Sovereign of the world, the Christian community in this favored land are abundantly able to supply the requisite funds, not only for the missions already sent out, but for the support of many more. Nor is there any reason to doubt that the same DIVINE INFLUENCE, which has so wonderfully raised and diffused the spirit of benevolence, during these first ten years, will raise it still higher, and diffuse it more widely.

In these ten years there has been paid from the treasury of the Board the total sum of $201,600.—For the mission to the East—Bombay and Ceylon—just about $100,000—for the mission to the American Aborigines $51,000—for the mission to the Sandwich Islands, $10,470—for the Palestine mission, $2,350—for the Foreign Mission School $17,340, and for various subordinate and contingent objects and purposes $20,000.

In the same period the treasury has received the total sum of about $235,000. Of this amount something more than $220,000 were given by benevolent individuals, males and females, associated and unassociated, in donations and bequests for the general and particular objects of the Board, and the remaining sum of about $15,000 were the proceeds of monies invested, books sold, &c. Besides the monies paid into the treasury, many liberalities have been bestowed in various articles, in different ways, and to no inconsiderable aggregate. But the amount, whatever should be the estimate, is to be added to the regularly accounted for expenditures, as well as to the regularly entered receipts.

Of the sum expended much has necessarily been consumed, yet not a little remains for important and durable use.

In the ten years there have been received under the patronage and direction of the Board, as missionaries and assistants, 62 men and 48 women—in all 110 Of this number three—Mrs. Harriet Newell, the Rev. Edward Warren, and Mr. A. V. Williams,—have been called to their reward: ten, six men and four women, have left the service,—three on change of sentiment—five on account of impaired health, and two from discontentment,—and nine are yet at home, waiting with desire to be sent forth to their work Eighty-eight—49 men and 39 women—are now either in the fields respectively assigned to them, or on their way to them:—25 in the East,—2 in Western Asia,—17 in the Sandwich Islands,—and 44 in the countries of the American Aborigines. Upon the same funds, and engaged in the same cause, are the Rev. Principal of the Foreign Mission School and his worthy assistant.

Of the men now under the patronage and direction of the Board, TWENTY-SIX ARE ORDAINED MINISTERS OF THE GOSPEL, educated, the most of them, in Literary and Theological Seminaries of the first order in our country; two are especially designed for ordination; and the rest are approved men for the various departments of the general work, as catechists, school-masters, agriculturists and mechanics All of them, the Principal and assistant of the Foreign Mission School excepted, have given themselves devotedly for life to this arduous and holy service, and the most of them, with the same spirit of devotion and sacred disinterestedness, have given also all their possessions, which, in not a few instances, were of very considerable amount. Of the women mention, proportionably commendatory, might be made.

At home is the Foreign Mission School, designed for the *thorough education* of promising youths from different heathen lands;—an institution firmly established in the hearts of Christians, in a highly prosperous state, and blest most signally with heavenly influences. Abroad belonging to our several missions are more than 50 free schools, in which there can scarcely be fewer, probably there are now more, than 3,000 children, Hindoo, Tamul, Jewish, Cherokee, and Choctaw, under Christian instruction; not less than 300 of whom are boarding or family pupils, lodged, and fed, and educated, as under the especial care of the missionaries.

NINETY PERSONS with qualifications for the different parts of the work, from rudimental instructions in the primary branches of knowledge and arts of civilized life, to the highest and holiest administrations of the gospel—not only ready for the service, but actually for the most part in the distant fields at their allotted stations—disposed in order and furnished —engaged in their various labors, and some of them having for a considerable time borne the burden and heat of the day:—and more than fifty schools, established in different regions of darkness, and containing under Christian instruction three thousand children of families and nations long ignorant of God, and never blest with the news of the Savior—Could we mention nothing more, the *two hundred thousand dollars* expended in ten years, should not be accounted as lost. But something more may be mentioned.

"It is estimated," says Mr. Kingsbury, "that the establishment at Elliot has cost upwards of $12,000, exclusive of all the labor done gratuitously by the missionaries. But it ought to be distinctly kept in mind, that the greater part of this money has not been consumed. It has been vested in various property, some of which is of the most productive kind, and which may be considered as a permanent fund for the support of the mission. There are now belonging to the establishment at Elliot, more than 200 neat cattle. There are also teams of oxen and horses, wagons, carts, ploughs, and other implements of husbandry, suitable for a large plantation. More that fifty acres of land are cleared and under cultivation. Upwards of twenty buildings, including a blacksmith's shop, mill, and joiner's shop, have been erected. Mechanical tools for various branches;—lessons, books, and stationary for the school, have been provided; and all the varied apparatus prepared for the accommodation of a family consisting of one hundred."

Similar statements and estimates might be made respecting the establishments at Brainerd, on the Tombigby, and at Talony.—The missions over the sea are upon a different plan. But at Bombay we have a printing establishment, comprising two presses, founts of English and Nagree types, with the requisite apparatus; and various accommodations and articles of durable utility for the various purposes of the mission. Our Ceylon mission, besides the very valuable glebes and edifices secured to it, has also a printing press with founts of English and Tamul types, a hospital, and several school houses; and a proportional provision of what is necessary for a permanent mission. A large part of what was sent out with the Sandwich Islands mission, was not for immediate consumption, but for durable use. The lands, buildings, &c., of our school at Cornwall—what may be denominated permanent property, were estimated at more than $5,000. The libraries, and the surgical instruments,

40

belonging to our several establishments, would, altogether, be of considerable value.

The two hundred thousand dollars then is not all consumed—has not all vanished away By means of it a preparation for action of no inconsiderable extent has been brought forward.   And in the general view of this preparation, besides what has now been mentioned, whatever has been acquired of knowledge, of experience, and skill, in directing and executing this great work, where every thing was new, and every thing was to be learned,—and whatever systematic and permanent arrangements have been made for continued and extended operations, at home and abroad, —should doubtless be included.

GENERAL RESULTS.—Of effects and fruits actually produced, it is yet time to expect but little, and to say but little.

The translation of the Scriptures, however, into one of the principal languages of India—ready to be given to ten millions of people, as soon and as fast as means for the printing and distributing shall be afforded,— the actual printing and distributing among that pagan population of large editions of select portions of the Scriptures, and scriptural catechisms and tracts;—the teaching of several thousands of heathen children—including those who have attended, as well as those who are now attending the schools, so that they are able to read the Bible, and other useful books, and have some knowledge of the truths and precepts of the Gospel;—the preaching of the Gospel to many thousands of heathen people of different ages, ranks and conditions, thus sowing the *incorruptible seed*, in a widely extended field, where, under the genial influences of heaven, it may in due time take root and spring up, and where undoubtedly it will not have been sown in vain;—and the turning of more than fifty heathen persons hopefully, from darkness unto light, and from the power of Satan unto God, for their own salvation with eternal glory, and for the communication, through their instrumentality, of the blessings of Christianity to many of their respective kindred and nations:—These effects and fruits, which to pass over unnoticed in this general review, would be an ungrateful omission, and the value of which is not to be estimated by thousands, or hundreds of thousands, or millions, of money.

Ten years ago the Aborigines of our country were regarded by this great community, with the exception of here and there an individual, as an utterly intractable race, never to be brought within the pale of civilized society, but doomed by unalterable destiny, to melt away and become extinct; and a spirit of vengeance and of extermination was breathed out against them in many parts of our land.   Not a few, even of the generally well disposed and well informed friends of missions, held the projected mission to those outcasts of the wilderness a hopeless enterprise.   Now the whole nation is moved by a very different spirit.   From the highest places of the national government down to the humblest conditions of society, all classes are inspired with good will towards the Indians.   The desire to serve rather than to destroy them is every where testified; and to evangelize and civilize them is regarded as no infeasible or very difficult work.   The method seems plain and easy.—If by favor of Providence this Board has been leadingly instrumental in effecting this auspicious, change,—if the system of instruction which it has put into operation in the Cherokee and Choctaw nations has conciliated the favor and secured the confidence of the Indian chiefs and tribes extensively, and also of the rulers and people of our nation,—has commended itself as a model for other societies coming forward to take part in the general work,—and has produced examples of Indian improvement, which have engaged the attention of all classes of the community and awaked in them a lively interest in the great design;—the Board has not existed in vain, nor labored in vain.

To the good effects produced in our own country, while the great object has been to do good to heathen nations, further attention seems to be due.

The spirit, the genuine spirit of missions, is the true spirit of the Gospel. It is love to God and love to men; the *charity which seeketh not her own, and is full of mercy and of good fruits;* benevolence in its purest, loveliest, and highest character. It is the same mind, that was in the Redeemer of men, when he came to seek and to save that which was lost;—the spring of living, active, never-to-be-restrained desire for the promotion of the great design for which he endured the cross, and for which he sits as King on the holy hill of Zion. When this spirit is produced or advanced in an individual, or a community, in the same measure is pure and undefiled religion, in that individual or community, produced or advanced.— If then this spirit has been promoted, good has been done.

The matter of fact is manifest. The Christian community has been waked from its slumbers. An influence more vivifying than the breath of spring has been diffused through the land. The minds and hearts of many, of different classes and denominations, have been opened and expanded, to perceive and to feel the common brotherhood of all nations and of all human beings, as *made of one blood,* and REDEEMED BY ONE BLOOD. The reasonableness of the injunction, *to do good unto all men as we have opportunity, and the commandment of the everlasting God that the Gospel should be made known to all nations, and preached to every creature,*—have come to be practically acknowledged. Societies for various charitable and religious objects have rapidly risen into existence and action; and benefactions for these objects—contributions in churches and congregations and meetings for prayer, and individual subscriptions, donations and bequests—have become so common, that we are ready to forget how little of them was known only a few years ago.

In as far as this Board has been instrumental in producing these effects; by its several missions to heathen nations—by the cheerful sacrifices and labors of its devoted missionaries—by its disclosures of the ignorance, corruption and wretchedness of the dark places of the earth—by its successive agencies in different parts of the country, the communications it has made of intelligence with motives and excitements to benevolent exertions, and its various operations at home and abroad,—its endeavors and influences have conduced to the benefit of many. Especially has it been so, if by them the monthly concert of prayer, which is connected in a particular manner with missions to the heathen, has been promoted and extended,—and if these extensively united prayers and alms have gone up with acceptance before God, and in answer to them, in any measure, he has granted those plenteous effusions of his Spirit with which our churches and the various classes of the community have been so signally blest.

Had the object been, chiefly or solely, the advancement of religion in our own land, in what other way could two hundred thousand dollars have been better laid out. The support of FORTY ministers of the gospel at home, during the ten years, as settled pastors or domestic missionaries would have cost probably little more than the sum specified. But had this same money been used for the support, during the term, of forty settled pastors or domestic missionaries—two to each of the several States and Territories of the Union—is there good reason to believe that more would have been done for the general interests of religion in our country, than has actually been effected by means of this institution for Foreign Missions?—more to impress a deep and widely extended conviction of the infinite importance of the Gospel—more to counteract the selfishness and worldliness and sordidness of feeling and practice every where so prevalent—more to illustrate the nature, to display the excellence, and to raise the standard of Christian charity—more to bring the members of the community acquainted with the great concerns of the Redeemer's kingdom, or to a livelier interest in them—more to give enlargement and elevation to their views and affections, and to make them know how much more blessed it is to give than to receive—more to promote good will among themselves and towards all men, and to do good unto all as they have opportunity—more to beautify our Zion, to make her walls salvation and her gates praise,—and cause her so to rise and shine, as that the Gentiles shall come to her light, and kings to the brightness of her rising?

It is the spirit of missions—the spirit which burns with quenchless desire *to teach all* nations and to preach the Gospel to every creature—that has produced in Christendom the mighty movement, and the diversified and multiplied exertions of benevolence, by which the present age is so signally marked. Until the first missions of this new era were sent forth to the distant heathen, Christendom was asleep, while the world was perishing—was dreaming of temporal changes, disastrous or prosperous, while darkness covered the earth and gross darkness the people. Aroused from their slumbers by the efforts of those great Christian enterprises, the friends of God and of men were amazed at the ignorance, corruption and wretchedness every where to be seen—not only afar off, but near and all around them. Their eyes affected their hearts. The liberal set themselves to devise liberal things; and Bible Societies, Tract Societies, Education Societies, sprung up in quick succession: and a system of beneficent action has been advancing with surprising and animating rapidity. The spirit of missions—of missions to the heathen—is the main-spring of the whole.

Under the impression of this general review, the directors and patrons and friends of missions will humbly adore the goodness of God, and be animated to continued and increased efforts for communicating his saving health to millions ready to perish.

For this great object, this Board, under the divine favor, possess advantages, which cannot be too highly prized. Its constitution is eminently adapted to vigorous action, and extended enterprise, under responsibilities, affording the best possible security to public and individual confidence. It is limited to no section of the country,—to no denomination of Christians. Its members, chartered and corresponding, and its patrons, auxilaries and agents are in all the States of the Union, and of nearly all the considerable religious communions In its form and spirit—its arrangements and provisions—its whole design and system of action—it is a NATIONAL INSTITUTION. And hitherto the Lord has given it favor in all parts of the land; and made it instrumental in uniting many thousands of benevolent minds from the north to the south, in one common and glorious cause.—To Him everlasting thanks are due.—The advantages which he has granted are a sacred trust of immense importance—never to be abused—never to be neglected.

To auxiliaries, agents, and benefactors, fresh occasion is afforded for heartfelt thanks; for their steady attachment, their generous confidence, their continued and in many instances increased activity and liberality; for their prompt assistance in pressing emergencies, and their many pledges of substantial and permanent support to the cause.

The particular objects of the Board are such in variety and interest as to meet the feelings of every benevolent heart. Upon our own borders we present to this Christian community, long neglected tribes of uncivilized fellow beings, earnestly raising the imploring cry,—"Send us more of these good missionaries and teachers; help us to learn husbandry and the mechanic arts, and household manufactures and economy—teach our children to read, and write, and work—instruct us from the good book what the great and good Spirit would have us to do." And there too we present hundreds of children from the wigwams of the forest, now under the care of devoted missionaries and assistants, male and female, and dependent on Christian charity for food and lodging, for clothing and instruction, and thousands more, not less needy of these benefits, yet remaining still in all the ignorance and nakedness and wretchedness of the forest life. Far off in the Western Ocean; yet not beyond the reach of Christian beneficence—we shew a nation of Islanders, giving the fairest promise of becoming, in no long time, by the blessings of God upon such means as American Christians have it amply in their power to afford, a civilized and christianized, a wealthy and virtuous and happy people. From these we turn to the far distant East, and point to millions and millions of human beings in the lowest state of debasement, for whom there is no remedy, but that quick and powerful Word, which is spirit and life, and that Blood, which cleanseth from the foulest and deepest pollutions. That Word, translated into their own language by our indefatigable missionaries, is ready to be dispersed among these millions, as soon as the liberalities of the friends of mankind in this country shall supply funds sufficient for the printing and distribution; and to that Blood the missionaries already sent and to be sent, will direct them, if adequate support be continued. And there, to the thousands of heathen children already in our mission schools, multiplied thousands might speedily be added, were the requisite funds and help afforded. And to the land, whence the light of immortality first shone upon the darkened nations, we solicit the attention of all, who rejoice in this light; and invite them, not to the bloody achievements of maddened crusades, but to enterprises of glory, with the weapons which are mighty through God to the pulling down of strong holds, casting down imaginations and every high thing, which exalteth itself against the knowledge of God. And besides support for the missionaries who are gone thither, and those who are ardently desiring to go, we earnestly ask for funds for a printing establishment at such places as shall be found most eligible, by means of which the mission may be enabled to communicate extensively the light of divine truth, and thus prepare the way of the Lord, who will ere long appear in his glory, in the places, where he has been crucified.

These objects demand attention, and are making an appeal to Christian benevolence, of intense pathos Far off, geographically, as some of them are, yet morally and for the purposes of charity, they are near. The liberal in this country may do good and communicate to the ignorant and the miserable in India, for their immortal welfare, with as little inconvenience to themselves, as they can give bread to the needy at their doors. This is known and felt by many; and by the charities which they are in the course of dispensing to the needy and the perishing in the remotest lands and islands of the sea, as well as in their own immediate neighborhoods, they are continually expanding their existence, enlarging their spheres of usefulness, and multiplying their objects of interest, their sources of enjoyment, and their ties of delightful union with all on earth and all in heaven.

In these sacred charities many more would bear a part, were they acquainted at all, or better acquainted, with the objects. Taking the amount of donations the last year at $40,000, and assume a dollar as an average donation, and the number of donors will stand at 40,000. If we assume as the average donation fifty cents, the number of donors will be 80,000. But were there not more than forty thousand—more than eighty thousand—more than five hundred thousand in this Christian nation of ten millions, who would willingly and gladly contribute from fifty cents to fifty or five hundred dollars each towards some or all of the designated objects—were these objects only presented to them in such manner as to engage their attention? This is a consideration of immense importance to be impressed upon all the members, and agents, and auxiliaries, and friends of the Board and of the cause. Does an individual, who is in the practice of contributing, wish to do something for increasing the general amount of contributions? Let that individual look around him for one, or two, or more, who might be induced to contribute, and take care to use the best means for the purpose, and an increase not temporary only, but permanent, will be secured. In this way, the annual amount of contributions might be vastly augmented without any increase of the donations of the present regular subscribers or contributors.

In this view the diffusion of missionary intelligence will be seen to be of primary importance. It is hence the purpose of the Committee, with the approval of the Board, to make the Missionary Herald the property entirely of the institution, to give to it increased energy and interest, and to spare no pains in extending its circulation. And in this design, and in the general work of enlightening, improving and exciting all classes of the community, they hope for the active aid of every friend to the cause

CONCLUSION.—The cause is the noblest on earth—the work the greatest —the sure results the most durable and glorious. No person on earth is in a condition too high to take part in this work—none in a condition too low. Help from all, according to the ability afforded them, is urgently needed.

The tone of this Report is not that of despondency. Not a feeling of despondency should have place in any mind. Yet with all the prosperity, which has attended this institution and its attempts, and with all the cheering auspices, on this day so gratefully to be noticed; it is not to be forgotten, that for supplying the deficiency of the last year's receipts, the disposable funds from the surplus receipts of preceding years, have been nearly exhausted. Should the receipts in equal, or indeed in any considerable degree, fall short of the expenditures necessary for maintaining the establishments, for the support of which the most sacred pledges have been given; from what source, or in what way, is the deficiency to be supplied, or the cause to be saved from a serious depression? It were an unwarranted confidence, that he, whose cause it is, will maintain it, without the willing, the continued, the increased efforts, benefactions, and sacrifices of his friends. What he has been willing to do, and what sacrifice to make, is manifest to the universe, and he will take care that what they are willing to do, and what sacrifices to make, shall also be made manifest. And what your Committee deemed it right to say, in their address of last March, they deem it right now, with permission, emphatically to repeat—

"The question is to be decided, and it may be decided soon—whether there is in this country Christian benevolence enough—sufficiently undivided, unobstructed, and unrestrained—sufficiently resembling the charity which descended from heaven—to bear any proportionable part in the great work of evangelizing the heathen."

Can there be a doubt what the decision will be? Can it be apprehended, for a moment, that this great Christian community—so rich, in blessings temporal and spiritual, so deeply indebted to the Author of these blessings,—will determine, in his face, and in the face of the universe, that they will do no more for the recovery of their fellow beings, for whom, as well as for themselves, he died? that the devoted missionaries, who have gone forth in obedience to his call and command shall be left unsupported —that the schools for raising up an enlightened and improved generation shall be discontinued or diminished—that the heathen, rather than make for them any further exertions or sacrifices, shall perish in their ignorance and corruptions? After such an issue, who in our land could look up toward heaven? Rather than such an issue should come, who in our land, that hopes in the mercy of God our Savior, would not merely give a few cents, or a few dollars a year, but make a cheerful devotement of all that he has? This sentiment will be felt. Not a few feel it already. And when it shall have fired the hearts of American Christians, as it may be reasonably hoped it ere long will, there will be no lack of funds for the maintenance and enlargement of the missions and establishments already commenced, and for many more which the necessities of the heathen affectingly demand. Then shall glory dwell in our land, and bless with its enlightening and healing emanations, the most dismal abodes of men.

By the Prudential Committee,

Sept. 21, 1820.   S. WORCESTER, *Secretary.*

PECUNIARY ACCOUNTS OF THE BOARD.

The American Board of Commissioners for Foreign Missions, in account current with Jeremiah Evarts, their Treasurer, Dr.

To cash paid from Sept. 1, 1819, to August 31, 1820, in conformity to orders of the Board, and of the Prudential Committee, from No. 435 to No. 576, both inclusive, viz. as classed summarily under the following heads. viz.

FOR THE MISSION IN BOMBAY AND THE VICINITY.

Salaries of the missionaries, rent, and other general expenses of the mission, - - - - - - - - -	$3,811 17	
To support free schools, for the instruction of heathen and Jewish children; and to support heathen children in the families of the missionaries, in case promising children can be obtained, - -	2,387 96	
For the translation and publication of the Scriptures in the languages of the heathen, - - - - - - -	1,022 09	7,221 22

FOR THE MISSION IN THE ISLAND OF CEYLON.

Salaries of the missionaries, rent, repairs, and other general expenses of the mission, - - - - - - -	4,616 05	
To support free schools for the instruction of heathen children; and to support heathen children in boarding schools, under the immediate superintendence of the missionaries, - - - -	1,253 67	
For printing school books, portions of Scripture, &c., for the use of the schools, and for distribution, - - - - -	648 01	
Expense of sending out Mr. Garrett. viz.		
For his passage to the Coromandel coast, - - 200 00		
Advanced for his ulterior expenses and his services, - 300 00		
Board while in Boston, stores, medicines, &c., for the voyage, 107 52—607 52		7,135 25

FOR THE PALESTINE MISSION.

Residue of outfits of the missionaries, - - - -	728 88	
Preparatory expenses for the mission, medicines, &c. - -	81 85	
Passage to Smyrna, - - - - - - -	400 00	
Advanced for salaries and other general expenses of the mission, -	800 00	
Books, &c , for the mission library, - - - -	204 50	
To commence the establishment of the Bible Society in Palestine, or elsewhere in that region, the don. of an individual for this purpose,	133 33	2,348 56

CHEROKEE MISSION.

Remitted from the Treasury, for the general expenses of the mission,	5,214 81	
Drafts of the missionaries paid at Boston, - - - -	4,140 00	
Donations made at Brainerd, - - - - -	479 50	
Articles purchased for the use of the school, - - -	133 03	9,967 34

CHOCTAW MISSION.

Remitted from the Treasury for the general expenses of the mission	4,122 66	
Drafts of the missionaries paid at Boston, - - -	3,200 00	
Donations received at Elliot, - - - - -	187 93	
Outfits and travelling expenses of the missionaries and assistants,	1,469 09	
Various articles purchased at Boston for the mission, and shipped to New Orleans, comprising clothing, bedding, groceries, hardware, farming utensils, &c. &c - - - - -	1,278 81	
Provisions purchased at Marietta, Ohio for the use of the mission,	155 31	10,413 80

ARKANSAS MISSION.

Remitted from the Treasury for the general expenses of the mission,	945 19	
Donations received by the missionaries on their way, - -	204 65	1,149 84

INDIAN MISSIONS GENERALLY

Services and travelling expenses of agents employed to collect donations,	229 83	
Transportation and purchase of articles, - - - -	21 84	251 67

MISSION TO THE SANDWICH ISLANDS.

Outfits of missionaries and assistants, - - - -	1,821 55	

Carried forward,

	Brought forward,	$1,321 55	$38,487 63
Travelling expenses of the missionaries,		224 20	
Other preparatory expenses		85 87	
Transportation of articles to Boston for embarkation,		274 67	
Passage to the Islands,		2,250 00	
Stores for use on the voyage,		1,657 42	
Cash advanced to the missionaries,		500 00	
Stores for use after arrival,		315 87	
Frame of a house, boards, shingles, glass, nails, &c., for completing it, and the charge of storing and putting it on board,		548 06	
Clothing and materials for clothing,		523 74	
Furniture and mechanical implements,		421 35	
Printing press, types and other apparatus,		426 44	
Books, maps, globes, mathematical and philosophical instruments,		819 08	
Surgical instruments and medicines,		396 18	
Services rendered in receiving and putting the various articles on board,		18 00	
Boxes, barrels, bags, kegs, &c. &c. to contain the articles,		36 87	
Premium on Spanish dollars,		10 00	10,329 30

FOREIGN MISSION SCHOOL.

Cash remitted from the Treasury for the general expenses of the school,		3,132 65	
Cash received at the school in donations,		182 76	
Trav. expenses of the Marquesas boys and others, and various contingencies,	35 30		3,350 71

GENERAL CONTINGENCIES.

Trav. exp. of the Mem. of the Board in attend. the ann. meeting	287 50		
Other expenses of the meeting,	21 34	308 84	
Trav. expenses of the Sec. and Treasurer on the business of the Board,		169 39	
Expense of meetings of the Prudential Committee,		62 83	
Services of agents employed to collect general funds,	104 00		
Travelling expenses of do.	157 06	261 06	
Printing, viz. Copies of the Missionary Herald, distributed by the Board to Auxiliary Societies, sent to missionary stations, and to distinguished patrons and benefactors and friends of the missionary cause,	915 50		
Tenth Annual Report and Dr. Lyman's Sermon,	312 40		
Mr. Humphrey's Sermon, Instructions of the Prudential Committee, Messrs. Fisk and Parson's Sermon, Address of the Prudential Committee and other miscellaneous printing,	330 20	1,558 10	
Salary of the Corresponding Secretary,		500 00	
Expenses in Cor. Sec. department; viz. clerkhire, postage, and stationary,		181 90	
Salary of the Treasurer for the year preceding,		600 00	
Reimbursement of monies actually expended by the Treasurer in the discharge of his office, on account of the Board, principally for clerkhire, as ascertained by a committee appointed by the Board,		750 00	
Paid by the Treasurer for postage,	129 64		
Printed and other stationary, depository and furniture,	61 30		
Transcribing and copying,	19 58		
Freight & transp. & directing Mis. Herald, Rep. & Sermons,	107 43	317 95	
Counterfeit bank notes,		28 75	
Discount on bank notes, some of which were much depreciated,		155 32	
Advanced to the Rev. M. Winslow, to enable him to publish his history of missions from the avails of which this advance is to be refunded,		275 60	
Periodical works for the mission stations,—some articles of printing app. expense of meeting at the O. S. Church, charges of a lawsuit, &c.		83 50	5,253 24

			$57,420 93
Refunded to the American Education Society a sum which had been paid to the Board by mistake.			200 06
Carried to the credit of the Board in new account, Sept. 1, 1820,			33,049 98
			$90,670 97

The Board Cr.

By balance brought to new account, Sept. 1,1819,		$50,136 46
By cash received in donations within the year past, as published in the Missionary Herald, and in the appendix to this Report,		36,582 64
From Government, for educating Indian youths, at Cornwall,		400 00
Avails of publications, and gain on exchange,		197 27
Interest of money and stocks, deducting interest paid		2,154 60
Extra expense, paid for landing the missionaries at Ceylon, refunded,		1,200 00
		$90,670 97

Lightning Source UK Ltd.
Milton Keynes UK
UKHW031029100620
364712UK00003B/54

GCSE
Law

GCSE Law

Law

JACQUELINE MARTIN

Hodder & Stoughton

A MEMBER OF THE HODDER HEADLINE GROUP

Orders: please contact Bookpoint Ltd, 39 Milton Park, Abingdon,
Oxon OX14 4TD. Telephone: (44) 01235 400414,
Fax: (44) 01235 400454. Lines are open from 9.00 - 6.00,
Monday to Saturday, with a 24 hour message answering service.
Email address: orders@bookpoint.co.uk

British Library Cataloguing in Publication Data
Martin, Jacqueline
  GCSE Law
  I. Title
  344.2

ISBN 0 340 60009 8

First published 1995
Updated 1999
Impression number   13 12 11 10 9 8 7
Year   2004 2003 2002 2001 2000

Copyright © 1995 Jacqueline Martin

Typeset by Wearset, Boldon, Tyne and Wear.
Printed in Great Britain for Hodder & Stoughton Educational,
a division of Hodder Headline Plc, 338 Euston Road,
London NW1 3BH by J. W. Arrowsmith Ltd., Bristol.

Contents

CONTENTS

Preface

The idea for this format of law textbook came from many years of teaching students of different ability levels and different ages. Although it is aimed primarily at the Southern Examining Group's syllabus for GCSE the addition of extra material, particularly on employment law and welfare benefits, should make it suitable for other introductory courses. Within the Southern Examining Group's syllabus, the style of the book makes it suitable for students taking the foundation tier examination, while the coverage and development of topics makes it equally suitable for students taking the higher tier examination.

The order of topics bears in mind the fact that students at this level are unlikely to have any prior knowledge of the subject. The introductory chapter pays particular attention to the differences between civil and criminal law. The sources of law are dealt with after the court structure, jurisdiction and personnel, since it seemed sensible to start with the criminal courts which are, at least vaguely, familiar to most students from media coverage.

The vocabulary is relatively straightforward, but specialised legal vocabulary is introduced as necessary. Summary tables and flow charts are used throughout the book in order to provide additional help for students. There are suggested activities, some truly 'active', such as carrying out a survey or finding out information, others using source material as the basis for an exercise. Simple problem situations are given at the end of many of the substantive law sections for students to practise applying the law.

In the preparation of this book I have been grateful for the help and criticisms of my colleagues, in particular Mary Gibbins, who read the major part of the script at the draft stage with an eye to correcting both legal and grammatical errors. I would also like to thank the students on the Legal Secretarial course who were enthusiastic guinea pigs for many of the suggested activities and sections on applying the law!

This latest reprint has given me a chance to update key sections of the book and to include extra examination questions at the end. The text now includes the changes (April 1999) to the civil justice system under the Woolf Report; some of the implications of the Access to Justice Bill 1998; references to the Crime and Disorder Act 1998 and the Human Rights Act 1998 and the renumbering of the Articles in the Treaty of Rome. So far as the changes to terminology in the civil courts are concerned, the chapter on the civil courts uses the new words (claimant, claim form etc.). However, in the chapters on contract and tort, where cases are explained the word plaintiff is retained as this is the word used in the law reports of the day. The law is now stated as I believe it to be at 1 June 1999.

Acknowledgements

The author and publisher would like to thank the following for permission to reproduce material in this volume:

the Southern Examining Group for the following questions: Chapter 1 – Summer 1993, Paper 1, Chapter 2 – Summer, 1993, Paper 1, Chapter 3 – Specimen Paper for 1990, Chapter 4 – Sample Paper for 1996, Foundation Tier, Chapter 7 – Summer 1993, Paper 1 and Summer 1994, Paper 1, Chapter 8 – Summer 1992, Paper 1, Chapter 9 – Sample Paper for 1996, Higher Tier, Chapter 11 – Summer 1992, Paper 2 and Sample Paper for 1996, Higher Tier, Chapter 13 – Sample Paper for 1996, Higher Tier, Summer 1994, Paper 2 and Summer 1992, Paper 2, Chapter 14 – Sample Paper for 1996, Foundation Tier, Chapter 15 – Summer 1993, Paper 2 and Sample Paper for 1996, Foundation Tier, Chapter 16 – Summer 1992, Chapter 17 – Sample Paper for 1996, Foundation Tier, Chapter 18 – Sample Paper for 1996, Higher Tier, Chapter 19 – Summer 1992, Paper 1, Question 7 – Higher Tier 1998, Question 5 – Foundation Tier 1997, Question 7 – Higher Tier 1997, Question 8 – Foundation Tier 1998, and finally, for the list of suitable titles given for coursework. Any answers or hints on answers are the sole responsibility of the author and have not been provided or approved by SEG. The Northern Examinations and Assessment Board for the following questions: Chapter 10 – Summer 1992, Chapter 16 – Summer 1992, Chapter 17 – Summer 1990, Question B(4) – Tier H 1998; the Associated Examining Board for the following question: Chapter 14 – Summer 1993, Paper 2; the Lord Chancellor's Department; *The Times*; David Pannick, QC; Paula Davies; *The Independent*; Associated Newspapers Ltd; *The Guardian*; the *Sevenoaks Chronicle*; Sweet & Maxwell Ltd; Butterworth Heinemann; Butterworths; the Legal Aid Board; the National Association of Citizens Advice Bureaux; the Equal Opportunities Commission; the National Council for Civil Liberties; the BBC; Littlewoods Pools Ltd; A.L. South, Solicitors; The Artwork Company Limited; PA Photos; and Bridge Travel Service.

Introducing law 1

Gambler jailed

Murder charge

Killer given life term!

Headlines like these often provide the main source of information about law for the ordinary person, together, of course, with TV programmes such as *The Bill* or *Crimewatch*. People do not usually stop to think about law; it just exists. So the first question to ask is:

1.1 What is law?

It is difficult to give a short simple answer to this question. There is no generally agreed definition, though many legal writers have attempted to define law. For example an English legal writer, Sir John Salmond, defined law as 'the body of principles recognised and applied by the state in the administration of justice'.

A simpler definition is that law is a set of rules. Many organisations, however, have rules and there are also rules of morality. So what makes law different from these? Rules become law when they are recognised by the majority of people in a country and given government backing to enforce them in the country as a whole; in other words, 'recognised and applied by the state'. A rule in an organisation is a private matter and is not in force

throughout the community. A moral rule is a matter for people's consciences; it will not be enforced by the government. In this country there is a complicated legal system to make sure that laws are obeyed; that is a system concerned with the 'administration of justice'.

1.2 Why do we have law?

There are people who believe that there should be no laws at all. These people are called anarchists, but it is difficult to imagine how any society would operate without at least some rules. What if there were no law against stealing; or assault; or murder? What do you think society would be like? It has been said that without law man's life would be 'brutish, nasty and short'. These are very obvious examples of why we have law, but there are many other examples. Try imagining what traffic conditions would be like if there were no law about which side of the road you should drive on ... or ... if everyone could ignore traffic lights! Most people will agree that this would lead to traffic chaos, numerous accidents and injuries. Even in other less extreme examples the need for law can be clearly seen. When items are bought and sold, there must be rules as to what should happen if the item is faulty. When two people marry, some rules are necessary, for example, should there be a minimum age at which they can marry? If they divorce, how should their property be divided? In the world of business, laws on a number of points are needed. How do you form a company and what are the rules about contracts and employment?

All these show that a modern society needs laws and the more complex society becomes the more laws it will need. If you lived alone on a desert island it would not be necessary to have any laws.

A C T I V I T Y

Make a list of areas of life in which you think it is necessary to have laws and compare your list with other people's.

In some cases it does not matter what the rule is, as long as there is a law. The side of the road on which we drive is not important. What is important is that all traffic drives on the same side. In the United Kingdom traffic drives on the left side of the road. In many other countries, traffic drives on the right side of the road. Other countries may also have different laws in areas such as marriage and divorce. The age at which a person can marry varies from country to country; in some countries it is permissible to have more than one wife; rules about divorce vary. Laws about drinking alcohol also vary; there are different ages at which one is allowed to buy a drink and in some countries alcohol is completely forbidden. So why do laws vary like this?

1.3 Law and morality

In many areas of law there is an overlap between law and morality, that is, the law says the behaviour involved is not allowed and most people would also view it as being 'wrong', even if there were no law against it.

All major crimes come into this category; murder, robbery, rape, burglary are clear examples. However law and morality are not the same. Some actions may be regarded as morally wrong by sections of the community even though the law does not forbid them.

Do you think this could be said about the following?

- abortion
- homosexuality
- telling lies

Other acts are legally 'wrong' but it is unlikely that anyone would say they are morally 'wrong'. Do you think this is true of the following?

- driving at 35 m.p.h. where there is a speed limit of 30 m.p.h.
- smoking a cigarette in a 'no smoking' compartment of a train
- making a copy of a videotape which is protected by copyright

Even when morality is not involved there are laws where there is an element of 'fairness'. Much of what we call consumer protection law is based on this. If you buy an item that turns out to be faulty, for example, a Walkman that will not play tapes, it seems 'fair' that you should be able to return the Walkman to the shop and that the shop should give you back your money.

The main problem, both with morality and fairness, is that people and societies have different views of what is right and what is fair. This is one of the reasons why laws are different in different countries. It is also one of the reasons for changes in the law within our country. Ideas are likely to change from one generation to another.

A C T I V I T Y

Ask other people their views on the two lists above.

1.4 Changes in the law

English law has changed many times in the past and is likely to continue to change in the future.

The law changes as a result of many things.

1 *Government policy.* This can have a large effect on the types of changes made, particularly in areas such as taxation and social welfare. Different political parties have different ideas and often in the past a change of government has led to quite major changes in the law. Each year between 60 and 70 Acts of Parliament are passed creating new law.

2 *Changing values in society.* As a result of changing ideas the law sometimes changes, though quite often it is criticised for not changing quickly enough. Many laws have been passed that show people's changing ideas: the legalising of abortion; rules about sexual discrimination; rules about racial discrimination; even the age at which one can legally marry. In England and Wales before 1929 technically there was no minimum age for marrying. It was possible to marry at any age, although in order to give a valid and binding consent to the marriage a boy had to be 14 years old, but a girl needed only to be 12 years old. If the parties were under that age, they could marry, but had the right when they reached 14 (boys) or 12 (girls) to decide if they wanted the marriage to count.

Do you think that people today would accept a law that allowed a 12-year-old girl to marry?

3 *Pressure groups.* Linked to the changing values in society are the increasing number of pressure groups that campaign for particular laws to be changed. An example of a law being changed as a result of pressure was seen in 1994 when Parliament voted to change the age of consent for homosexuals from 21 to 18. A number of pressure groups had campaigned for this change in the law.

4 *Technological progress.* New inventions are likely to lead to new laws. A clear example of this was the development of traffic laws following the invention of the motor car. A more modern example was the passing of the Data Protection Act 1984 to control the keeping and disclosing of information on computers.

5 *Law reform bodies.* In 1965 the Law Commission was set up by Parliament to review the law and recommend reforms on a regular basis. The Commission makes a report to Parliament each year and some of its suggestions are used to change and improve existing laws. There are also other law reform bodies such as the Criminal Law Revision Committee, which have the responsibility of producing ideas for law reform in specific areas of the law. One of the reports of the Criminal Law Revision Committee led to Parliament passing the Theft Act 1968 which simplified the law on theft and related offences. In addition the Government sometimes sets up a committee or a commission, often chaired by a judge, to investigate one particular area of law and recommend changes. An example of this was the Runciman Commission which reported on the criminal justice system in 1993. Some of its suggestions were introduced into the law by the Criminal Justice and Public Order Act 1994.

6 *Membership of the European Union.* As a result of our membership England has had to introduce new laws to bring us into line with European law in some areas, especially those connected with trade and work. For example this influence has resulted in new laws against sex discrimination at work and greater protection for consumers under the Consumer Protection Act 1987.

These are only some of the forces that lead to changes in the law, because change is a complex process. It is important to realise that law does not stand still; it is continually altering as a result of many things.

1.5 Divisions of law

From the references already made to various laws, it is obvious that there are many different types of law. Law can be divided up in several ways.

International and national law

First there is an important distinction between international law, which governs disputes occurring between nations, and national (municipal) law, which is concerned only with the rules of one country – in our case England and Wales. Scotland has its own municipal law. That is why there have already been references to England in this book, rather than Great Britain.

Public and private law

The second main division is between public and private law; public law involves the State or Government in some way while private law (often called civil law) is concerned only with disputes between private individuals or businesses. If you have bought a Walkman which does not work you would probably wish to claim your money back from the shop where you bought it; this type of dispute would come under private law since it concerns only you and the shop.

Both public law and private law can be further divided. Public law may be divided into:

a *constitutional law* dealing with the method of government, for example laws setting out who has the right to vote at a general election;

b *administrative law* which governs how public bodies such as local councils should operate;

c *criminal law* which states what behaviour is forbidden at risk of punishment; it involves the state as one party and one or more individuals as the other party accused of a particular crime. The headlines at the beginning of this chapter all involved criminal law.

Private (civil) law has many branches. Look at the following situations, all of which are covered by different areas of civil law:

- John is behind with the hire-purchase payments on his car – contract
- Imran is injured through faulty machinery at work – tort
- Sheila and Henry decide their marriage has broken down – family law
- Jane wants to start a new company – company law
- David claims he has been unfairly dismissed from work – employment law
- William has died and not left his son any money – inheritance law

These are just a few examples of civil law. It covers a wide variety of situations.

Figure 1.1 summarises the different divisions of law.

1.6 The distinction between civil and criminal law

For our purposes the distinction between civil and criminal law is the most important division in law. It is important to know whether a case is

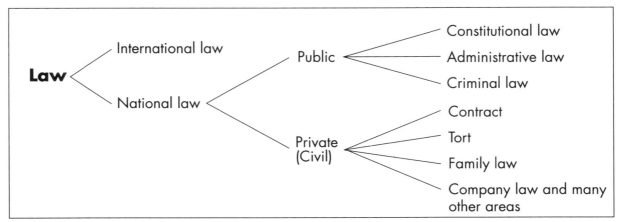

Figure 1.1   Summary of the divisions of law

civil or criminal as it affects how the case is started, who starts it, in which court it will be heard and what powers are available to the judge.

A C T I V I T Y

Look at the newspaper extracts, Sources A, B and C. You should notice that there are some points in common.

Source A

Two guilty of murdering policeman

A man and a youth were found guilty last night of murdering a police sergeant who was stabbed and beaten while dealing with an incident on a housing estate.

Paul Weddle, aged 26, was jailed for life, and Philip English, aged 16, will be detained at Her Majesty's Pleasure.

The jury at Teesside Crown Court returned guilty verdicts after deliberating for three hours. In Mr. Weddle's case the decision was unanimous, while there was a 10–2 majority to convict Mr. English.

(Source: The Guardian, 18 February 1994.)

Source B

Man jailed for six months

A man involved in trying to steal an £8,000 Shogun from a Sevenoaks car park has been jailed for six months.

Walter Wilson, 34, of Clynton Way, Ashford, was sentenced at Maidstone Crown Court on Friday.

Co-defendant, Frederick Collins, 22, of Barnhurst Cottage, Bethersden, was ordered to do 100 hours community service.

Both denied the attempted theft but were convicted by a jury.

(Source: Sevenoaks Chronicle, 26 November 1992.)

Source C

Taxi spree costs rugby star £2,000

The Welsh international rugby player Scott Gibbs was fined £2,160 yesterday for driving off in a taxi from a cab company's offices after a drinking session.

Gibbs, 23, of Pencoed, Mid Glamorgan, who is due to leave for New Zealand with the British

Lions, took the vehicle with two other players. At Bridgend Magistrates' Court he admitted taking a vehicle without consent, driving without insurance and drink-driving. He was banned for two years.

(Source: The Times, 7 May 1993.)

These are all criminal cases where the State has accused someone of a crime and the purpose of the trial is to decide if the accused is guilty or not guilty. If the accused admits his or her guilt or is found guilty, the court can deal with him or her in a number of ways, but often there is an element of punishment involved. The criminal law has developed to protect the community. A wide variety of actions are forbidden by the State and if one of these laws is broken a penalty or punishment can be imposed. The main types of crimes are offences against the person, offences against property, offences against public order and driving offences.

Look at the articles again and answer the following questions:

1 In which courts were the cases heard?
2 In Sources A and B who made the decision to convict the defendants?
3 What different punishments were used?

Now look at the next two articles, Sources D and E. They are also about cases in court, but there are important differences between them and those described in the previous articles.

Source D

Designer pays for 'paddy field'

A couple won £20,000 in damages after their spectacular water and rock garden, designed by an award-winning gardener, turned out to be more of 'a cross between a paddy field and a moat'.

John and Joan Hoban paid Dougie Knight, 52, winner of a Chelsea Flower Show award, £25,000 to transform their one-acre garden in Ormskirk, Lancashire.

Making the award at Liverpool County Court, Judge Lynch said: 'The garden falls below the usual high standard of the defendant.

'The water runs down what looks like a set of roof tiles and would not score many points in a competition. We are talking about a very expensive garden. You don't get an inadequate garden for £25,000. You should get one of quality.'

(Source: The Times, 28 April 1993.)

Source E

Widow wins £900,000 damages

The widow and daughter of a businessman who died after a hospital failed to diagnose his malaria in time were awarded £900,000 damages by the High Court yesterday.

Peter Smyth, an executive for Tourism International, died in February 1991 at Charing Cross Hospital in London. He had been discharged then readmitted after having collapsed.

Riverside Health Authority admitted liability and agreed to pay damages to Nicola Smyth, 38, of Nairobi, Kenya, including £10,000 for her two-year-old daughter, Emma.

(Source: The Times, 5 May 1993.)

These are civil cases. In Source D, there was an agreement to create a garden, in other words a contract, and the dispute occurred because it was not done properly. This is a private dispute between the owners of the garden and the man they paid to make the garden. The purpose of this trial is to decide whether the work was worth the money they paid for it. In Source E a widow claimed that her husband died because doctors at a hospital failed to find out what was wrong with him, when they should have been able to do so. This is what the law calls a tort or civil wrong. Again it is a private dispute; in this case between the widow and the hospital employing the doctors, and the widow is claiming money as compensation for the loss of her husband. Instead of using the word guilty, the article mentions liability. This may appear to mean almost the same thing, but in law there is an important difference. The word guilty is usually only used in criminal cases, whereas the word liability is used for civil cases. This is because the main purpose of the civil law is to investigate disputes between parties and

decide if one of them should pay compensation to the other. There is no idea of punishment involved. The court is trying to put the people back into the position they would have been in, if the contract had been properly carried out or the tort not committed. In most cases the only way the court can do this is by ordering one party to pay money to the other, though there are other remedies available in some circumstances.

Read Sources D and E again and answer the following questions:

4 In which courts were these cases heard? Are they different from the courts mentioned in Sources A, B and C?

5 In both cases money was awarded to the winning party; what is the word used in the articles for this award?

Figure 1.2 on p. 7 gives a summary of some of the most important differences between civil and criminal law.

The name of the case will usually tell you if the case is criminal or civil. In the examples at the bottom of Figure 1.2 'R.' stands for Rex (which means King) or Regina (which means Queen), showing that the case has been started by the State. Some criminal cases will be started by the Director of Public Prosecutions and this is always written as DPP in a case name. In each of the examples the small 'v.' between the names means versus or against. In the civil cases the surname of the person starting the case is given first, then the surname of the person he is suing (taking the case against). If a company is involved in a case, then the company's name is used. The legal term for the person starting the case is the *claimant*.

The burden of proof

Another important difference between civil and criminal cases is what is called the burden of proof or the standard to which the case has to be proved. In criminal cases this standard is a high one, *beyond reasonable doubt*, since a conviction could result in the defendant going to prison for a long time. In civil cases the standard is lower, *on balance of probabilities*. This is because the judge has to decide for one party or the other and so he gives judgment for the party he thinks is most probably right.

Figure 1.2 Differences between civil and criminal law

	Criminal	Civil
Purpose of the law	To maintain law and order; to protect society	To uphold the individual's rights
Purpose of the trial	To decide if the defendant is guilty	To decide if there is a breach of those rights
Person starting the case	The State, usually through the police and Crown Prosecution Service	The individual whose rights have been affected
Legal name for that person	Prosecutor	Claimant (previously plaintiff)
Courts used to hear cases	Magistrates' Court OR Crown Court	County Court OR High Court
Person/persons making the decision	Magistrates OR Jury	Judge Very rarely a jury
Decision	Guilty or not guilty	Liable or not liable
Powers of the court	Prison, fine, probation, discharge, community service order and others (see Chapter 12)	Award of damages, injunction, special remedies (see Chapters 13 and 15)
Name of the case	R. v. Smith DPP v. Smith	Jones v. Smith XYZ Company Ltd v. Smith

1.7 Double liability

Sometimes one action can be in breach of two types of law. This gives rise to what is known as double liability; that means that two separate court cases may take place. Double liability can occur wherever there is a crime and, in the course of that crime, an individual's rights are affected. The most common occurrence of this is where there is a road traffic offence (involving criminal law) and someone is injured as a result so that he or she wants to claim damages (under the civil law called *tort*).

Let us take an imaginary example. Mr Brown drives through a red traffic light and crashes into Mrs Green's car, damaging her car and injuring her.

First, Mr Brown has committed a crime by going through the red light. This is the criminal case and will be started by the police and then taken over by the Crown Prosecution Service. Mr Brown will be summonsed to appear at the Magistrates' Court. If he disputes the case by claiming the lights were green, the magistrates will hear evidence and decide if he is guilty or not guilty. If they decide he is guilty, they have the powers to order him to pay a fine, put penalty points on his driving licence or even disqualify him from driving. In other words they are punishing him for his bad driving.

Secondly, Mrs Green will want to claim compensation, both to pay the cost of repairing her car and for her injuries. This means she will have to start another case against Mr Brown in the County Court to make her claim. This is the civil case. The judge will have to decide if Mr Brown was negligent and caused her injuries. If he decides this is so, then he will award damages to Mrs Green. This will be money to pay for the repairs to her car and another sum of money as compensation for her injuries.

So the one act of driving through red lights by Mr Brown means that he has two cases taken against him in two different courts. This is why it is called double liability.

Examination question

A crime is an offence against the State, punishable by the State. Civil matters, such as contract and tort, arise between individuals. Occasionally, one incident can give rise to both civil and criminal proceedings.

In **each** of the following situations, explain what particular area or areas of law are involved, and whether the situation will give rise to civil proceedings, criminal proceedings or both.

a   Angus removes a car without permission and drives to the next town. Whilst in the process of abandoning the vehicle in a car park, he carelessly damages Belinda's car. *(4 marks)*

b   Colin, who teaches at a local school, overhears one of his pupils, Dulgit, tell her boyfriend, Ibrahim, that Colin is a hopeless teacher and does not know his subject.
(4 marks)

c   Frank is climbing through the downstairs window of a house hoping to find something to steal. He then hears a dog bark. Fearing he will be disturbed, he decides to leave.
(4 marks)

Total: 12 marks

SEG 1993

The legal system: criminal courts (1) magistrates

2.1 Classification of offences

In England and Wales there are two types of court which deal with criminal cases: the Magistrates' Court and the Crown Court. To understand the way cases are allocated to these courts it is necessary to understand how crimes are classified. This is done by dividing crimes into minor crimes, middle-range crimes and serious crimes and making different arrangements for each group. In legal terms these three categories of crime are called:

- summary offences (minor crimes)
- offences triable either way (middle-range crimes)
- indictable offences (serious crimes)

The differences between these three categories of crime are summarised in Figure 2.1.

Summary offences

Summary offences are offences that can be tried only in a Magistrates' Court and are the least serious crimes. There are many different offences in this category, including nearly all driving offences. Other examples are taking a vehicle without consent, minor assaults and being found drunk in a public place.

In recent years there has been a downgrading of some offences which were previously triable either way, so that they have become summary offences which can be tried only at the Magistrates' Court. Driving whilst disqualified and driving whilst over the limit of alcohol are now summary offences. Under the Criminal Justice Act 1988, taking and driving away a vehicle was also made a summary offence, although in 1992

Figure 2.1 The three categories of offence

Category of offence	Place of trial	Examples of offences
Summary	Magistrates' Court	Driving without insurance Taking a vehicle without consent Common assault
Triable either way	Magistrates' Court OR Crown Court	Theft Assault causing actual bodily harm Obtaining property by deception
Indictable	Crown Court	Murder Manslaughter Rape Robbery

pressure on the Government caused the creation of a new offence of aggravated vehicle-taking which is considered more serious and so belongs in the triable either way category.

Offences triable either way

These are offences that can be tried either in the Magistrates' Court or in the Crown Court. They are the middle range of crimes and include theft, obtaining property by deception and assault causing actual bodily harm.

Mode of trial

At the moment in any case where the defendant is charged with a triable either way offence, the defendant is first asked whether he pleads guilty or not guilty. This is called 'plea before venue'. If the defendant indicates that he intends to plead guilty, he loses his right to insist that the case go to the Crown Court. The magistrates will listen to any points that the prosecution and the defence want to make about where the case should be heard and then the magistrates decide where the sentencing procedure should be held. If they think that it is a suitable case for them to deal with they will decide the sentence. If they feel the case is too serious for them to deal with they will send it to the Crown Court.

Not guilty plea

Where a defendant indicates that he intends to plead not guilty, he has the right to elect trial by jury at the Crown Court or he can choose to be tried by the magistrates in the Magistrates' Court. However, even if the defendant chooses the Magistrates' Court, the magistrates can decide to send the case to the Crown Court for trial if they think that it is too serious for them to try.

Effectively this means that the case goes to the Crown Court if **either** the magistrates **or** the defendant thinks it should. It can only be tried in the Magistrates' Court if **both** the magistrates and the defendant agree to that course of action.

Indictable offences

These are offences that can be tried only at the Crown Court by a judge and jury. They are the more serious offences and include murder, manslaughter, rape and robbery. These offences are called indictable (pronounced in-dight-able) offences because they are tried on indictment (pronounced in-dight-ment), that is, the document on which the charges are written down.

2.2 Magistrates' Courts

These are local courts; almost all towns have one and big cities have several. There are over 700 courts throughout England and Wales. Each court deals only with cases that are connected with its area, in other words there is a geographical limit on its jurisdiction. Even so such courts have a large workload, mostly involving criminal cases, though they also hear some civil cases. The main functions of the magistrates are:

1 To try certain offences and decide if the defendant is guilty or not guilty. Where the defendant pleads guilty or is found guilty in these cases the magistrates then decide what the sentence (punishment) should be. The cases they can try are all summary only offences, the first category in Figure 2.1, and any triable either way offences where the magistrates are prepared to hear the case and the defendant agrees. These combined make up over 98 per cent of all criminal trials, so the hearing of these cases is a very important function of Magistrates' Courts.

2 To deal with preliminary matters in cases that are going to be tried at the Crown Court. Whenever a defendant is charged with an offence the first hearing of the case is at the Magistrates' Court. In fact, if the police are not prepared to allow the defendant bail (let him out) after charging him, the defendant must be brought in front of a magistrate as soon as possible for the magistrate to decide whether the defendant can be granted bail (*see* Chapter 10 for more details on bail). Another preliminary point for the magistrates to deal with is the decision on where a triable either way offence should be tried.

3 Matters connected with criminal cases, such as

issuing a warrant for the arrest of a defendant who fails to come to court or issuing a warrant allowing the police to search a building.

4 Youth court proceedings to hear cases where those aged 10–17 inclusive are charged with crimes. This court sits in private and is less formal than adult courts. The magistrates who hear these cases are specially trained.

5 Finally there is the civil jurisdiction, which strictly speaking belongs in Chapter 4, but a brief list is included here to illustrate the wide variety of work done in a Magistrates' Court. The civil work includes:

a licensing pubs and restaurants to sell alcohol;

b granting licences under the betting and gaming legislation;

c enforcing council tax demands and debts owed to the gas, electricity and water authorities;

d family cases including orders for protection against violence and maintenance orders (NB: Magistrates' Courts cannot grant a divorce);

e affiliation orders, that is, deciding the paternity of a child when this is disputed;

f proceedings concerning children under the Children Act 1989.

For family cases and for cases under the Children Act there is a special family proceedings bench and this involves magistrates who have had extra training. Family and child cases are held in private.

A C T I V I T Y

Find reports in newspapers of proceedings in Magistrates' Courts.

2.3 Magistrates

Considering the amount and range of work that magistrates are required to deal with it is, perhaps, surprising to realise that apart from about 80 or so qualified magistrates, all the people who sit to hear cases in the Magistrates' Courts are ordinary, non-legally qualified people. Both qualified and non-qualified magistrates deal with all the different sorts of cases listed above. Qualified magistrates are called stipendiary magistrates and are paid and full-time. Non-qualified magistrates are called lay magistrates and they are not paid (except for expenses) and only sit as magistrates part-time.

Stipendiary magistrates

Stipendiary magistrates are legally qualified in that they must have practised as a barrister or solicitor for at least seven years before being appointed. Stipendiaries sit to hear cases in London and other big cities such as Birmingham and Manchester. They sit alone and have the same powers as a bench of lay magistrates. They are appointed by the Queen on the recommendation of the Lord Chancellor and they hold office during Her Majesty's pleasure. This means that they can only be dismissed by the Queen on the recommendation of the Lord Chancellor. They normally retire at 70 but can be authorised by the Lord Chancellor to stay on until the age of 72.

Lay magistrates

Another name for lay magistrates is lay justices or Justices of the Peace (JP) and as already stated they are not legally qualified. The only requirements are that a lay magistrate must be between 21 and 60 years old on appointment and must live within 15 miles of the area for which they are commissioned. They are appointed to one commission area only. Outside London a commission area means a county (metropolitan or non-metropolitan), whereas in London there are six commission areas. Lay magistrates sit part-time, for a minimum of 26 sessions a year and the only payment they receive for this is for their travel expenses and meals. Since they are not qualified they do not usually make decisions on their own but sit as a bench. This means that there must be at least two magistrates sitting together and normally there will be a panel of three. A single lay magistrate has very limited powers, though they can do such things as issue warrants for arrest. There are approximately 30,000 lay magistrates, with about 2,000 being appointed each year. They are appointed by the Lord Chancellor, or in Lancashire by the Chancellor of the Duchy of Lancaster, on behalf of the Queen. The Lord

Chancellor relies on recommendations made to him by local advisory committees. Lay justices cannot sit to hear cases after they become 70 years old, but the Lord Chancellor can place their names on the supplemental list, as he can with magistrates who retire earlier because of ill-health. This means that although they no longer sit in court to hear cases, they retain the title Justice of the Peace. The Lord Chancellor can also completely remove a magistrate for good cause, if he decides that person is no longer suitable to be a magistrate. Some of the reasons for such removal have been criticised, e.g. removal for transvestite behaviour, or for taking part in a CND demonstration, but the usual reason for removal is a criminal conviction. About 10 magistrates are removed from office each year.

History

The office of Justice of the Peace is very old, dating back to the twelfth century at least. In 1195 Richard I appointed 'keepers of the peace'. By the mid-fourteenth century the judicial side of their position had developed and by 1361 the title Justice of the Peace was being used. Over the years they were given many administrative duties, such as responsibility for highways, weights and measures and the poor law. In the nineteenth century elected local authorities took over most of these duties, though some odd remnants remain, and this is why, for example, licensing is part of their duties. Up until 1906 a person had to own or rent property above a certain value to be eligible to become a lay justice. Women have only been eligible since 1919.

Appointment

As so many magistrates are appointed each year the Lord Chancellor has to have advice on who to choose. For this he relies on local advisory committees. Until January 1993 the committees' membership was secret, but since that date all the members' names must be available to the public. The committees mainly consist of existing or retired JPs, often under the chairmanship of the Lord Lieutenant of the county. The Lord Chancellor intends that committees should have a maximum of 12 members, including non-JPs. Names are put forward to the committees by

groups such as local political parties, trade unions and chambers of commerce. In addition committees can advertise for individuals to put themselves forward for consideration. In general the candidates are members of good standing in their local community. People with criminal convictions are not usually eligible (minor motoring offences do not disqualify people), undischarged bankrupts are not eligible, nor are members of the armed forces or the police. The intention is to create a panel that is representative of all sections of society. In 1966 the then Lord Chancellor, Lord Gardiner, issued a directive to advisory committees telling them to bear in mind people's political allegiance in order to get a balance. This said:

The Lord Chancellor cannot disregard political affiliations in making appointments, not because the politics of an individual are a qualification or a disqualification for appointment, but because it is important that justices should be drawn from all sections of the community and should represent all shades of opinion.

This object would not be attained if appointments were made in too large a degree from supporters of any one political party. It is the aim of the Lord Chancellor to preserve a proper balance by the appointment of suitable persons from the main political parties, and, if they can be found, from persons who are independent of any political party.

For these reasons the Lord Chancellor wishes advisory committees to have regard to the political affiliations of the persons whom they recommend for appointment.

Composition of the bench today

There is still a feeling that magistrates are 'middle-class, middle-aged and middle-minded'. Women are fairly well represented; they make up 47 per cent of lay magistrates. However ethnic minorities are under represented, though over the past four or five years more have been appointed (making up 6 per cent of appointments per year). The middle classes are still dominant, though the position has improved. Since magistrates must sit for at least 26 sessions per year, it is difficult to attract members of the working classes to become magistrates. Although employers are obliged to give time off for such public duties, pay and promotion chances may be affected if an employee has to take so much time off work.

Training

New magistrates are given about 40 hours of training spread over one year. Training consists of:

- observing court proceedings
- attending workshops and lectures
- visiting prisons and other penal institutions

The training is not intended to make magistrates proficient in law, but to give them understanding of their duties. Since about 90 per cent of defendants appearing in the Magistrates' Court plead guilty, a major part of training is aimed at sentencing and all magistrates are issued with a Handbook' and a guide to sentencing. Magistrates also have to attend refresher courses and there are weekend courses for this purpose. Magistrates on the youth panel or on the family proceedings panel receive extra training for these duties.

The clerk

Every bench of lay magistrates is assisted by a clerk. The senior clerk in each court has to be a barrister or solicitor of at least five years' standing. His duty is to guide the magistrates on questions of law, practice and procedure. He is not meant to assist in the decision making and should not normally retire with the magistrates, when they leave the court at the end of a case to consider their verdict.

Disadvantages

This system of using unqualified local people as magistrates has been criticised. The following is a list of possible criticisms.

1 Lay justices are middle-class, middle-aged and middle-minded.
2 There is inadequate compensation for loss of earnings, thus discouraging 'workers' from applying to become magistrates.
3 The training is inadequate, although this has improved.

4 Lay justices are prosecution minded, pro-police and more likely than a jury to believe police officers, partly due to their class background and partly because they are likely to see the same police officers giving evidence often. The conviction rate (80 per cent) is higher than in the Crown Court (55 per cent).

5 Since lay magistrates are not qualified, they rely too heavily on their clerk.
6 There is inconsistency in sentencing and in granting bail. There are big variations from one court to another, even in the same area.
7 There is too wide and heavy a workload for amateurs. This is particularly so with the increasing crime rate, the increasing number of offences made summary only and the move to prevent some defendants electing jury trial. The family court's workload has also increased and become more complicated.

Advantages

However, there are many good points to the system of lay magistrates.

1 The system involves members of the community and provides a wider cross-section than would be possible if only professional judges were used. In particular there are relatively high percentages of women (47 per

cent of lay justices and 22 per cent of stipendiaries). Also, despite the lack of magistrates from ethnic minorities, the figures are far better than for judges.

2 Lay magistrates have local knowledge because they live in or near the area in which they sit as magistrates.

3 Improved training, together with the availability of a legally trained clerk, means the system is not as amateur as it used to be.

4 It is cheaper to have magistrates than to have a hearing in the Crown Court, both for the defendant and for the Government.

5 Cases are dealt with more quickly in Magistrates' Courts than at the Crown Court, but even so there may be a delay of several months.

6 There are few successful appeals which suggests that the system is working satisfactorily.

Other points which make the system acceptable are the limits on sentencing power, six months' imprisonment and £5,000 fine, and the fact that for offences triable either way the defendant has a choice of court. Also magistrates sit at the Crown Court to hear appeals, thus having contact with professional judges and learning more about the system.

A C T I V I T Y

Read the following newspaper extracts and then answer the questions below.

Source A

Most magistrates in England and Wales are supporters of the Conservative party despite the Lord Chancellor's aim that local courts should reflect the political make-up of their community. Figures showing political sympathies of magistrates were provided by the Lord Chancellor's Department at the request of Stephen Byers, the Labour MP for Wallsend and chairman of Labour's home affairs committee.

The study shows that in St. Helens, Lancashire, where Labour took 60 per cent of the votes cast in the general election, more than half the magistrates are Conservative

supporters. Only 26 per cent support Labour. Mr Byers called for an urgent radical overhaul of selection procedures. The role of the magistrate should be 'demystified', he said, and people should be told they do not need legal skills. He also urged more extensive advertising of vacancies. 'A small ad in the public notices section of a local newspaper is not enough.' Paid time off should be given by employers (this is discretionary) and a national recruitment drive, which goes to factory shop floors, should be launched like the recent government campaign for more school governors, he said.

'If you want to restore public confidence in the legal system you need to have a more representative bench and take positive steps to achieve it.'

The Lord Chancellor's Department said yesterday that the aim was always to try to ensure that a bench reflected the community it served. Advisory committees 'made great efforts' to this end, but their efforts were governed by the people who actually put themselves forward.

The department's spokesman said Lord Mackay had repeatedly exhorted people from all walks of life to put themselves forward and in discussion with representatives from industry he had sought to persuade employers to give paid time off. In a recession, employers were not always happy to do this.

(*Source: The Times*, 9 December 1992.)

Source B

The public image of justices, however, remains that of the middle-aged, middle-class do-gooder who has nothing better to do than sit in judgment on others. That the image is far from the reality seems to make little difference.

In more than 15 years on the bench, I have yet to see a behatted lady or a blimpish colonel. Colleagues range from teachers and doctors to builders and shop-floor workers. There are academics and social workers. Yet there are still too many like me who are middle-aged and middle-class who can find time, not only for court sittings, but also for intensive training, compulsory since 1966, and the necessary committee work.

Getting time off work is the main problem. Men between 35 and 45 are thin on the ground but these are the people whose companies look at them sideways if they want time off for such voluntary work. A Post Office worker I knew had to give up part of his holidays to fulfil the 26 days a year compulsory for justices in inner London.

(*Source:* Adapted from an article by Paula Davies in *The Times*, 7 July 1992.)

1 **To what political party do most magistrates belong?**
2 **Why does Mr Byers object to this?**
3 **How does he suggest recruiting a wider range of people?**
4 **What age group is likely to be under represented? Why is this so?**
5 **Do you think it is important to have a representative cross-section of society sitting in Magistrates' Courts? Give reasons for your answer.**

2.4 Procedure in the Magistrates' Court

Starting a case

Many cases will start by a summons being issued against the defendant, informing him of the charge against him and giving him a date to attend at the court. Summonses are often sent by post to the defendant, particularly for driving offences. For other offences the defendant may have been arrested by the police and charged. If the offence is not serious, the police will release the defendant on bail, giving him a date on which he must attend court or be in breach of his bail. Where the police are not prepared to grant bail, the defendant will be brought to the court as soon as possible after the police have charged him, usually within 24 hours.

In court

At the first hearing it is unusual for a case to be fully heard, although this is possible provided the defendant pleads guilty and either he does not want legal representation or there is a duty solicitor available. For most driving offences there is a special procedure to allow a defendant who wishes to plead guilty to do this by post, so that he need not attend court. Where the defendant is pleading not guilty the case will be adjourned to another day so that the prosecution can arrange for witnesses to attend court. There are increasingly lengthy delays on adjournments and defendants who plead not guilty may wait months for their trial. When a case is adjourned the most important point at this stage for the defendant is whether he is going to be remanded on bail or in custody. If the prosecution object to bail, the magistrates have to make the decision after hearing arguments from both the prosecution and the defence. (*See* Chapter 10 for further information on bail.)

Conducting the case

Most cases are now conducted by the Crown Prosecution Service (CPS) using their own in-house lawyers, though it is possible for private prosecutions to be brought. For example some shoplifting cases are brought by the shop involved, with the shop instructing its own lawyer. Defendants can be represented by a barrister or a solicitor, as both professions have the right of audience in Magistrates' Courts; this means that both have the right to stand up in court to represent people. (*See* Chapter 6 for further information on the legal profession.) Defendants do not have to have a lawyer and many defendants are unrepresented. In such a situation, the clerk of the court helps the defendant with the court procedure, for example, telling him when he can ask questions.

Procedure for summary offences

At the start of any case the clerk of the court will check the defendant's name and address and then ask whether he pleads guilty or not guilty. (Remember that summary offences have to be tried at the Magistrates' Court.) Over 90 per cent of defendants plead guilty and the following is a short summary of the normal procedure in such cases. Figure 2.2 on p. 16 provides a flow charge of the proceedings in the Magistrates' Court.

Guilty plea

1 The court will be given a resumé of the facts by the CPS prosecutor.
2 The defendant is asked if he agrees with those facts (if he does not the magistrates may have to hold an enquiry as to the facts).
3 The defendant's past record of convictions, if any, is given to the court.
4 Information about the defendant's financial position is given to the magistrates. This is very important for deciding the amount of any fine.
5 Any relevant reports are given to the court; for example there may be a pre-sentence report prepared by a probation officer or a medical report.
6 The defendant or his lawyer can then explain anything he wants to about the reasons for committing the crime or his personal circumstances. This is called making a speech in mitigation.
7 The magistrates decide the sentence.

Not guilty plea

When a defendant pleads not guilty the case, naturally, is longer and more complicated since both sides will want to call witnesses. As the prosecution have to prove the charge, they always start the procedure, usually making a short speech explaining to the magistrates what the case is about and how they hope to prove it. Then the prosecution calls their witnesses and asks them questions about what they saw or heard. This is called the examination in chief. The defence are allowed to cross-examine these witnesses in order to try to show that their evidence is not reliable. Once all the prosecution witnesses have given evidence, then the defence calls its witnesses, including the defendant if he wishes to give evidence. The procedure follows the same pattern as for prosecution witnesses, this time with the defence asking the questions in chief and the prosecution cross-examining afterwards. When all the evidence has been given the defence will make a speech to the magistrates, trying to persuade them that the case has not been proved 'beyond reasonable doubt', pointing out the weaknesses in the prosecution evidence. Further speeches are not allowed unless there is a point of law to be argued. The magistrates then decide whether the defendant is guilty or not guilty. If

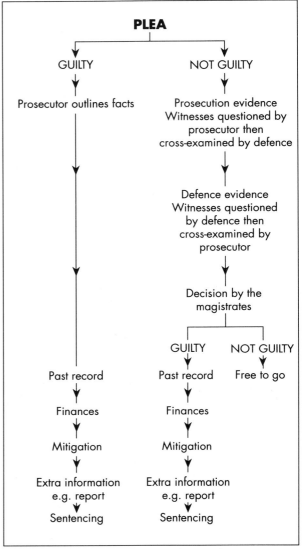

Figure 2.2   Flow chart of proceedings in the Magistrates' Court

they convict, they hear about his past record, if any, and may also look at reports about the defendant. The defence can make a speech in mitigation, then the magistrates will decide on the sentence.

Offences triable either way

The first part of the procedure for these offences is to decide where the case will be tried, as described in the first section of this chapter. If the case is going to be tried in the Magistrates' Court, then it proceeds in the same way as for a summary offence. However, at the end of the case, instead of sentencing the defendant the magistrates have the right under section 38 of the Magistrates' Court Act 1980 to commit (send) him to the Crown Court for sentence. This will only happen when the magistrates think their sentencing powers are insufficient because of the seriousness of the offence. The sentence will then be decided at the Crown Court by a judge and two magistrates.

If the case is going to be tried in the Crown Court then it is transferred from the Magistrates' Court to the Crown Court, where it will be tried by a judge and jury.

2.5 Sending cases to the Crown Court

If the case is to be tried at the Crown Court (whether because it is indictable and only triable there or because it is triable either way and the Crown Court has been chosen), the case will start at the Magistrates' Court. The magistrates will make a decision about whether the defendant can be released on bail while waiting for his trial at the Crown Court.

After the first hearing cases involving indictable offences will be transferred to the Crown Court (Crime and Disorder Act 1998 s.51) and all issues will be dealt with there. For triable either way offences the case will have to go through committal proceedings in the Magistrates' Court to see if there is enough evidence for the case to be tried at the Crown Court.

Committal proceedings are preliminary hearings of the case and are intended to establish whether there is a *prima facie* case against the defendant. A *prima facie* case means that there is sufficient evidence on a 'first look' to justify trial by jury. Originally this was done by getting all the prosecution witnesses to give evidence at a preliminary hearing at the Magistrates' Court. From 1967 onwards the majority of committal proceedings became 'paper' proceedings with the magistrates not being required to check the evidence if the defence agreed that they did not need to. Oral evidence was given in only a very small number of cases.

Although there were only a small number of old-style committals, they took up a lot of time in the Magistrates' Courts compared to the paper committals. So under the Criminal Procedure and Investigations Act 1996 oral committal proceedings were abolished. No witnesses can now be called at committal proceedings. Instead the prosecution put forward written statements by witnesses. The actual procedure will then take place in one of two ways:

1 *Committals with consideration of the evidence.* Here the magistrates must read all the witness statements, consider all the evidence and listen to the arguments put forward by the lawyers. The magistrates will then decide if there is a *prima facie* case against the accused. If they decide that there is, they will commit (send) the case to the Crown Court for a full trial to be held there. If the magistrates decide that there is not enough evidence to justify a trial, they must dismiss the case against the defendant. However, this is not the same as being found not guilty of the charge. This is important as it means that if the police later discover more evidence against the defendant, they can recharge him and start proceedings again.

2 *Committals without consideration of the evidence.* Under this procedure the magistrates do not look at the evidence at all. If the defendant is legally represented and he and his lawyers agree to this 'quick' procedure, the prosecution lawyer just hands in the papers with all the prosecution evidence. The magistrates then complete the formalities of the committal and send the case for trial at the Crown Court.

2.6 Future of offences triable either way

There have been suggestions that the defendant should no longer have the right to elect trial by jury at all, but that the decision as to where the trial should take place could be made either by the prosecution or by the magistrates' clerk. The reason for these proposals is the fact that 70 per cent of defendants who elect to be tried at the Crown Court plead guilty to the charges against them when they get to the Crown Court and most of these defendants are then given sentences that could have been imposed on them at the Magistrates' Court. This shows that there was no need for these cases to go to the Crown Court. In May 1999, the Home Secretary, Jack Straw, announced that he wants to change the law so that defendants charged with triable either way offences such as theft will not be able to choose jury trial. However, civil liberty organisations argue that a conviction for theft, however small, can destroy a person's reputation and therefore the defendant's right to choose trial by jury must be kept. Jack Straw pointed out that nine out of every ten defendants who elect to be tried by the jury already have convictions, so that the question of reputation in most cases is not relevant

2.7 Appeals from decisions of the Magistrates' Court

Where a criminal case has been tried in the Magistrates' Court there are two separate methods of appealing:
• to the Crown Court

• to the Queen's Bench Divisional Court

Figure 2.3 (below) presents these routes in the form of a diagram.

To the Crown Court

Appeal to the Crown Court is the usual appeal route and is available only to the defendant. If the defendant pleaded guilty in the Magistrates' Court he can only appeal against sentence. If the defendant pleaded not guilty in the Magistrates' Court he can appeal against conviction or sentence or both. An appeal to the Crown Court is as of right; this means the defendant does not need leave or permission to make such an appeal. The prosecution do not have the right to appeal to the Crown Court. The appeal takes the form of a complete re-hearing, by a judge sitting with two magistrates. They have a variety of powers:

1 On an appeal against sentence the Crown Court can decrease the sentence or substitute a different type of sentence, e.g. put the defendant on probation instead of imposing a prison sentence, or increase this sentence up to the magistrates' maximum for the offence. There is no further appeal.
2 On an appeal against conviction the Crown Court can confirm, vary or reverse the

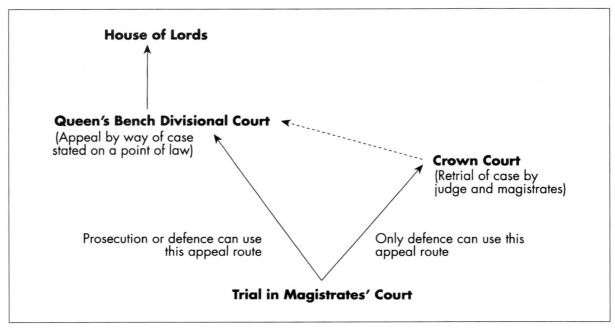

Figure 2.3 Appeal routes from a decision by the Magistrates' Court

decision. In other words the court can agree with the original verdict of guilty or can find the defendant guilty of a less serious offence or can decide he was not guilty at all. There is a further appeal, on a point of law only, to the Queen's Bench Divisional Court.

To the Queen's Bench Divisional Court

Both prosecution and defence can appeal to this court on a point of law by way of case stated. Case stated means that the magistrates are asked to set out the facts of the case and their decision, so that the case is decided on documents and arguments on law. No witnesses are called. The appeal will be heard by a panel of two or three High Court judges. Only an appeal against conviction (by the defendant) or an appeal against an acquittal (by the prosecution) can use this appeal route. An appeal against sentence must go to the Crown Court. The Divisional Court may confirm, vary or reverse the decision or remit (send back) the case to the Magistrates' Court with its opinion.

From the decision of the Queen's Bench Divisional Court there is the possibility of appealing to the House of Lords. This is so whether the case reached the Divisional Court via the Crown Court or direct from the Magistrates' Court. Appeals to the House of Lords are very rare. There can be an appeal to the House of Lords only if:

a the Divisional Court has certified that the case involves a point of law of general public importance; and

b the Divisional Court or the House of Lords has given leave to appeal because the point is one which ought to be considered by the House of Lords.

APPLYING THE LAW

1 John has been charged with theft.
   Explain to him where the case could be tried.
2 Sylvia has been charged with manslaughter.

Explain what the role of the magistrates will be in her case.

3 Edward has been found guilty of driving without insurance. He wishes to appeal against this decision.
   Advise him of the possible appeals available to him.

Examination question

Study the extract below and then answer all parts of the question which follows.

> A magistrates court is presided over by at least two and not more than seven Justices of the Peace (lay magistrates). In England and Wales there are about 27,000 lay magistrates and about 50 stipendiary magistrates.
>
> Stipendiary magistrates are full-time paid magistrates. They have to be barristers or solicitors of at least seven years standing.
>
> Justices of the Peace are appointed by the Lord Chancellor on the advice of local committees. They can also be removed by the Lord Chancellor and must retire at 70.
>
> A single magistrate may sit alone:
>
> i   in minor cases involving very small fines or periods of imprisonment, **or**
> ii when conducting a preliminary hearing, **or**
> iii when conducting a remand hearing, **or**
> iv when appointed as a stipendiary magistrate.
>
> Every magistrates court has a Justices' clerk, who is paid, usually legally qualified, and helps the magistrates on matters of law and procedure. Although magistrates may preside only in the magistrates courts in the area of their commission, they may also sit in any Crown Court when required.

(*Source:* Adapted from W J Brown, *GCSE Law*, Sweet & Maxwell.)

a Explain why stipendiary magistrates sit alone but lay magistrates usually sit in benches of three.   (*4 marks*) *b* For what sorts of cases would a magistrate conduct a preliminary hearing?

What is the purpose of such a hearing?

(6 marks)

c The purpose of a remand hearing is to decide, usually because of an adjournment, whether or not the accused can be released until his trial.

i What is the correct legal term for releasing the accused whilst awaiting trial? *(1 mark)*

ii What is the correct legal term for refusing to release the accused before trial? *(1 mark)*

iii What factors will be taken into account when the question of remand is being decided? *(6 marks)*

d Until quite recently the identities of the people who sat on selection committees for new magistrates were kept secret. This is no longer the case.

How do you think this more open system of appointment will affect the type of person appointed to be a magistrate? *(6 marks)*

e Under what circumstances may magistrates sit with the judge in the Crown Court? *(2 marks)*

f The vast majority of magistrates are not legally qualified. Just like juries, they play a key role in the criminal justice system.

i What are the advantages **and** disadvantages of using lay people as magistrates as opposed to stipendiary magistrates?

ii What reforms would you like to see which would improve the way in which lay magistrates carry out their duties? Give reasons for your answer. *(14 marks)*

Total: 40 marks

SEG 1993

The legal system: criminal courts (2) the Crown Court

3.1 The Crown Court

Under the Courts Act 1971 the Crown Court was set up to replace the previous system of Assizes and Quarter Sessions which was out of date and unable to cope with the growing number of criminal cases. The Crown Court hears all indictable criminal cases as well as those triable either way that are sent for trial at the Crown Court by magistrates. In 1997 the total number of cases tried at the Crown Court was about 90,000. The court sits in some 90 towns and cities throughout England and Wales and has three different types of judges dealing with the cases: High Court judges, Circuit judges and part-time judges called Recorders. The biggest centres, known as first tier and second tier courts, can try any crime as High Court judges sit to hear the most serious cases.

The other centres, known as third tier courts, cannot try very serious crimes, such as treason, murder, manslaughter and rape because they are not staffed by High Court judges. These courts have only Circuit judges and Recorders. Figure 3.1 shows the different types of Crown Court.

3.2 Trial on indictment

At the Crown Court it is said that the defendant is tried on indictment. An indictment is the document setting out the charges against the defendant; if he is accused of committing only one crime, the indictment will contain only that charge or count. If the defendant is accused of committing several crimes then the indictment will list each one. Figure 3.2 on p. 22 shows a sample indictment.

Figure 3.1 Types of Crown Court

Court	Location	Judges	Types of cases
First tier	Main towns and cities, e.g. London, Bristol, Leeds, Liverpool	High Court judges Circuit judges Recorders	All indictable offences Any triable either way offence There is also a division of the High Court sitting at these centres to hear civil cases
Second tier	Main towns, e.g. Reading, Northampton	High Court judges Circuit judges Recorders	All indictable offences Any triable either way offences
Third tier	Other towns, e.g. Derby, Hull, Taunton	Circuit judges Recorders	Most indictable offences but not treason, rape, murder, manslaughter Any triable either way offences

---

BARCHESTER CROWN COURT

The Queen v. Anthony Absolute
charged as follows:

STATEMENT OF OFFENCE
Theft contrary to section 1(1) of the Theft Act 1968

PARTICULARS OF OFFENCE
Anthony Absolute on the 2nd day of March 1995 stole a gold watch
belonging to Donald Duck.

Figure 3.2   Sample indictment

Procedure

At the start of a trial the indictment is read out to the defendant and he is asked whether he pleads guilty or not guilty to each charge. If a defendant pleads guilty a jury will not be used, but a judge will hear information about both the crime and the defendant and will decide on the sentence.

When a defendant pleads not guilty a jury of 12 is sworn in and a full trial takes place. The procedure is similar to that in the Magistrates' Court. The prosecution call their evidence first as it is for the prosecution to prove the charge against the defendant. All prosecution witnesses can be cross-examined by the defence. If the prosecution do not have sufficient evidence the defence will ask the judge to rule that there is insufficient evidence for the case to go to the jury. About one in three of all trials at the Crown Court are stopped by the judge for this reason at the end of the prosecution case and the judge directs the jury to acquit the defendant. Where there is enough prosecution evidence the case continues and the defence can produce any evidence they wish to. The defendant can give evidence, but does not have to do so, although if he does not the judge may comment on that fact in his summing up. Any witnesses called by the defence, including the defendant, can be cross-examined by the prosecution. After all the evidence is given, first the prosecution and then the defence make a speech to the jury pointing out the strengths of their respective cases. Finally the judge sums up the whole case to the jury, explains any relevant points of law to

them and tells them that they must only convict the defendant if they are sure beyond reasonable doubt that he committed the offence. The jury then decide the verdict and if that verdict is guilty the judge decides the sentence.

A trial at the Crown Court normally takes longer than one at the Magistrates' Court because there are usually more witnesses and because the presence of a jury tends to slow down the whole procedure. In particular there are more speeches during the case as it is necessary to explain to the jury what the prosecution and defence are trying to prove. The other main difference between trials in the two courts is that a defendant at the Crown Court will nearly always have a lawyer to represent him, whereas many defendants at the Magistrates' Court will not be represented. Only barristers or solicitors with a special certificate of advocacy can represent the prosecution and defence at the Crown Court. The main differences between trials in the Crown Court and the Magistrates' Court are set out in Figure 3.3 on the page opposite.

3.3 The jury system

In the Crown Court when a defendant pleads not guilty a jury is then sworn in to hear the case and decide whether he is guilty or not guilty. Since less than 3 per cent of criminal cases are tried in the Crown Court and in these about three-quarters of defendants plead guilty, it can be seen that a jury is used in less than 1 per cent of all criminal trials.

Figure 3.3 Differences between trials in the Crown Court and trials in the Magistrates' Court

	Crown Court	Magistrates' Court
People trying case	Judge and jury of 12	1 Stipendiary magistrate or 3 Lay magistrates
Person deciding sentence	Judge	As above
Sentence available	Maximum for offence up to life imprisonment	Maximum 6 months' and £5,000 fine
Representation	Prosecution and defence almost always represented by a lawyer	Local CPS lawyer for prosecution Defence often not represented
Type of lawyer	Barrister or Solicitor with advocacy certificate	Barrister or Solicitor

Jury qualifications

To be eligible for jury service a person must:

- be aged between 18 and 70
- be registered to vote on the electoral register and
- have lived in the United Kingdom, Channel Islands or Isle of Man for at least five years since reaching the age of 13

These qualifications are set out in the Juries Act 1974, as amended by the Criminal Justice Act 1988. However some people, who qualify under the criteria above, are still not allowed to serve on a jury, because they are disqualified or ineligible for some other reason.

Disqualification

Some criminal convictions will disqualify you from serving on a jury, the length of time of the disqualification depending on the sentence given. The full list is given in Box A on the section of a jury summons shown on p. 24.

In addition, the Criminal Justice and Public Order Act 1994 has disqualified those on bail from sitting as jurors.

Ineligibility

Those who are ineligible include:

- people suffering from certain mental illnesses (*see* Box B)
- people whose occupations are concerned with the administration of justice or who have been so employed within the last 10 years; this is a wide group as it includes judges, court clerks, barristers, solicitors and police (*see* Box C for full list)
- priests, monks and nuns (see box D)

Excusable as of right

Apart from these groups there are also people who have the right to refuse to do jury service; they are 'excusable as of right'. This group includes:

- Members of Parliament
- those serving in the armed forces
- doctors, nurses and pharmacists (*see* Box E for full list)
- anyone aged 65 to 70
- anyone who has done jury service within the last two years

Selection of a jury

Each Crown Court has an official who is responsible for sending out summonses calling people for jury service. This official will have all the electoral registers for the area and he will select names

The following two pages show an extract from a jury summons explaining the rules about jury service (© Crown Copyright)

Rules about jury service

Some people cannot be jurors by law. These people are **not qualified** for jury service.
Other people may, by law, **have the right to be excused** from jury service.

Are you qualified for jury service?

Warning
You may have to pay a fine if you serve on a jury knowing that you are not qualified for jury service.

You are qualified for jury service if

you will be at least 18 years old
and under 70 years old
on the day you start your jury service

and your name is on the Register of Electors for Parliamentary or Local Government elections

and you have lived in
the United Kingdom
or the Channel Islands
or the Isle of Man
for a period of at least 5 years
since you were 13 years old.

But you are not qualified for jury service if
you are someone listed in
Box A
or Box B
or Box C (on page 3)
or Box D (on page 3).

Do you have the right to be excused from jury service?

The law gives some people the right to be excused from jury service if they want to be excused.
You may ask the jury summoning officer to excuse you from jury service if

you are more than 65 years old

or you have been on jury service during the past 2 years. **This does not apply if you were a juror at a coroner's court.**

or you have been a juror and the court excused you for a period that has not yet ended.

or you are someone listed in Box E (on page 3).

Please turn to page 4>

Box A   Convictions

You are not qualified for jury service

■ if you have **ever been** sentenced

to imprisonment for life

or to imprisonment, or youth custody, for 5 years or more

or to be detained during Her Majesty's Pleasure or during the pleasure of the Secretary of State for Northern Ireland.

■ if you have in the **last 10 years**

served any part of a sentence of imprisonment, youth custody or detention

or received a suspended sentence of imprisonment or an order for detention

or been subject to a community service order.

■ if you have in the **past 5 years** been placed on probation.

This list relates to sentences passed in the United Kingdom, the Channel Islands or the Isle of Man.

Box B   Mental disorders

You are not qualified for jury service

■ if you suffer, or have suffered, from a mental disorder and, because of that condition,

you are resident in a hospital or other similar institution

or you regularly attend for treatment by a medical practitioner

■ if you are in guardianship under section 37 of the Mental Health Act 1983

■ if a judge has decided that you are not capable of managing and administering your property or affairs because of mental disorder.

If you are in any doubt whether this list applies to you, please talk to your doctor or ask someone to explain it to you.

Box C   The Judiciary and other people concerned with the Administration of Justice

The Judiciary

You are not qualified for jury service if you are, or ever have been

- a judge
- a stipendiary magistrate
- a justice of the peace
- the Chairman or President; the Vice-Chairman or Vice-President; the registrar or assistant registrar of any tribunal.

Others concerned with the Administration of Justice

You are not qualified for jury service if you have been, **at any time within the last 10 years**

- an authorised advocate, or authorised litigator
- a barrister, a barrister's clerk or assistant
- a solicitor or articled clerk
- a legal executive employed by solicitors
- a Public Notary
- a member of the staff of the Director of Public Prosecutions
- an officer employed under the Lord Chancellor and concerned with the day to day administration of the legal system
- an officer, or member of the staff, of any court whose work is concerned with the day to day administration of the court
- a coroner, deputy coroner or assistant coroner
- a justices' clerk, deputy clerk or assistant clerk
- one of the Active Elder Brethren of the Corporation of Trinity House of Deptford Strond
- a shorthand writer in any court
- a court security officer
- a governor, chaplain, medical officer or other officer of a penal establishment
- a member of the board of visitors of a penal establishment
- a prisoner custody officer
- the warden, or a member of the staff, of a probation home, probation hostel or bail hostel
- a probation officer or someone appointed to help them
- a member of a Parole Board, or of a local review committee
- a member of any police force (this includes a person on central service, a special constable, or anyone with the powers and privileges of a constable)
- a member of a police authority or of any body with responsibility for appointing members of a constabulary
- an Inspector or Assistant Inspector of Constabulary
- a civilian employed for police purposes or a member of the metropolitan civil staffs
- someone employed in a forensic science laboratory

Box D   The Clergy

You are not qualified for jury service if you are

- in holy orders
- a regular minister of any religious denomination
- a vowed member of any religious order living in a monastery, convent or other religious community.

Box E   People who have the right to be excused

You have the right to be excused if you are one of the following people

Parliament

- a Peer or Peeress who is entitled to receive a writ of summons to attend the House of Lords
- a Member of the House of Commons
- an Officer of the House of Lords
- an Officer of the House of Commons

European Assembly

A representative to the assembly of the European Communities.

Medical and other professions

- a dentist
- a nurse
- a medical practitioner
- a veterinary surgeon or a veterinary practitioner
- a midwife
- a pharmaceutical chemist

if you are practising the profession and you are registered, enrolled or certificated under the law which relates to your profession.

The Forces

You may be excused if you are a full-time member of

- the army, navy or air force
- the Queen Alexandra's Royal Naval Nursing Service
- any Voluntary Aid Detachment serving with the Royal Navy

and your commanding officer certifies to the jury summoning officer that your absence would be 'prejudicial to the efficiency of the service'.

from these in a random manner. In some areas a computer is used to select people's names, in other areas the court official will look at the registers and choose names at random. Once the names have been chosen, those people are sent a jury summons telling them to come to the Crown Court on a certain date. The normal length of jury service is two weeks, though jurors are warned that some trials may last longer. More people than are needed are summonsed as the court official will not know who is disqualified, ineligible or excusable as of right. If someone is within one of these categories he or she has to declare it and anyone who is disqualified can be fined up to £5,000 for failing to declare that disqualification.

Discretionary excusals

There will also be other people who do not want to do jury service and they have to explain their reasons in writing to the court. If they have a sufficiently good reason, they will be excused from doing jury service on that occasion, but may have to do it in the future. Good reasons include being too ill to go to court, business appointments, having a holiday booked or even having an examination to take. This sort of excusal is called a discretionary excusal, since it is up to the court to decide whether that person should be excused or not. If a person is not excused he must attend court on the date given on the summons or risk being fined for failing to do so. The maximum fine for non-attendance is £1,000.

A C T I V I T Y

Decide which of the following could sit on a jury:

- a 17-year-old college student
- a 68-year-old pensioner
- a parish priest
- a member of Parliament
- a 23-year-old woman fined for shoplifting a month ago
- a 24-year-old man who was placed on probation for shoplifting two years ago
- a solicitor
- a chemist
- a veterinary surgeon

- a probation officer
- a mother with a three-month-old baby

At court

In most Crown Courts there will be several courtrooms, each with a different case going on. Whenever a new trial starts, the first thing that happens is that the defendant is asked whether he pleads guilty or not guilty. If the plea is not guilty then jurors who are not doing another case, but waiting to be used, will come to that courtroom. The court clerk will have a list of their names and if there are more than 12 waiting, the clerk will choose 12 to form the jury. This part of the selection process is done in public in the courtroom, with the clerk reading out the names of those chosen.

Do YOU THINK I OUGHT TO CHALLENGE THAT JUROR ON THE END?

Challenging

As the 12 jurors come into the jury box it is possible that some of them may be challenged by either the prosecution or the defence. This is only done if there is a reason why the juror should not sit on the jury, for example because they are disqualified or because they know the defendant. It is also possible to challenge the whole jury on the basis that it has not been selected properly, but such a challenge is very rare. The prosecution has one further right, the right to put a juror on standby. This means that the juror's name is put at the end of the list of available jurors and he or she will only become a juror in that particular trial if there are not 12 others.

If there are not sufficient jurors to hear all the cases going on at the court, there is a special power to select anyone who is qualified to be a juror from the local streets or offices. This type of juror is called a *talesman*. It is very unusual to use this power, but it was used in London at Middlesex Crown Court in January 1992, when about half the jury panel failed to attend court after the New Year holiday.

Trial

The role of the jury is to listen to the evidence and decide whether the accused is guilty or not guilty. During the trial jurors may make notes of any points they wish and will be given copies of any documentary evidence or photographs. The judge decides any necessary points of law during the trial and at the end of the trial he explains any legal matters that the jury need to know to reach their verdict. If any member of the jury wishes to ask a question, he or she can write it down and a court official, called an usher, will hand the question to the judge. All trials start with 12 jurors, but if the case is a long one it is possible that one or more members of the jury may become ill or even die. When this happens the law allows the judge to let the trial continue with a reduced number of jurors, provided the number does not fall below 9.

Verdict

In order to make their decision the jury leave the court and go to a private room to discuss the case. No-one else is allowed to hear their discussions, nor are members of the jury allowed to tell anyone about these. If a juror does disclose what happened, he is guilty of contempt of court and may be fined or even sent to prison. When the jury first retire to consider their verdict, the judge tells them they must try to come to a decision on which they all agree. This is called a unanimous decision. However, if after long discussion the jury cannot agree, the judge will ask them to return to the courtroom and then tell them they may reach a majority decision. This will not happen until the jury has spent at least two hours trying to come to a unanimous decision. When a majority verdict is allowed, at least 10 jurors must

agree, so that the vote could be 11–1 or 10–2 for either guilty or not guilty. Where the jury has fallen below 11, then at least 9 jurors must agree. Once the jury have decided, they return to court and the clerk asks what that verdict is. The spokesman for the jury, who is known as the foreman or forewoman, must give the verdict and say whether it was a unanimous verdict or a majority one. When it is a majority verdict of guilty, the foreman/woman must also state how many jurors agreed. If the verdict is guilty, the judge then has to decide what sentence to give the defendant; if the verdict is not guilty the defendant is acquitted and can never be charged with that crime again.

A C T I V I T Y

Visit a Crown Court.

3.4 Advantages and disadvantages of jury trial

Lay participation

The most important advantage is that ordinary people are involved in the decision. The idea is that a defendant is tried by his peers, that is, his equals and that there should be a cross-section of society involved. However research has shown that juries are not always a true cross-section. Certain groups of people are not fully represented, these include young people aged 18 and 19, women and ethnic minorities. The main reason for such under-representation is the use of the electoral register in the selection process. Young people and those from ethnic minorities are less likely than other groups to register to vote. The Runciman Commission on the criminal justice system has proposed that in some cases if random selection does not produce a multiracial jury, then such a jury should be deliberately chosen.

Another cause of under-representation is the number of discretionary excusals allowed. In the London area as many as a third of all those summonsed to do jury service may be excused. Again this affects some types of people more than others. Mothers with young children find it difficult to arrange child care and will often ask to be excused.

Public confidence

Most people feel that the jury is an important element in the administration of justice. Juries are not biased; the fact that there are 12 jurors will help cancel out any individual biases. The jury has no direct interest in the case; they do not know any of those involved. The jury should not be pressurised by the judge. In *R.* v. *McKenna* (1960) the defendant's conviction was quashed on appeal because the judge at the trial threatened the jury that if they did not return a verdict within another 10 minutes, they would be locked up all night. This means that the jury can acquit a defendant even though the judge disagrees with that verdict and even if the judge has told the jury that the defendant legally has no defence. As a result a jury can refuse to operate a law they feel is unjust. This happened in the case of Clive Ponting in 1985, when Ponting was charged with an offence against section 2 of the Official Secrets Act 1911 because he leaked information to an MP about the sinking of a ship, the *Belgrano*, in the Falklands War. Later, mainly as a result of the Ponting case, Parliament reformed the law. In another case two defendants, Patrick Pottle and Michael Randle admitted helping a spy (George Blake) escape from prison 25 years earlier, but were found not guilty by the jury. The jury probably felt that the prosecution had taken too long (25 years) to bring the men to trial!

It is examples like this that caused one famous judge, Lord Devlin, to say that the jury is 'the lamp that shows that freedom lives'. On the opposite side of the argument, it could be said that verdicts against the evidence, known as perverse verdicts, show that the jury system is unsatisfactory. Why should a defendant who admits breaking the law be found not guilty.

Ability to understand trial

One of the main arguments against the use of juries is that some jurors find court procedure confusing and are unable to understand the evidence even in a straightforward case. To help jurors a booklet is sent out with the jury summons explaining in simple language what is likely to happen at court and some courts show a short video to jurors when they first arrive at court, again explaining where the different people in the case will be sitting and the general procedure of the court.

Since it is illegal to interview jurors about their decision, it is not possible to know whether they did understand the case or not. To try to research this area, there have been studies using shadow juries. These are people chosen in exactly the same way as the real jury, who listen to the whole case, discuss it and come to a verdict, but because they are not the real jury their verdict does not count. The important thing about shadow juries is that their discussions can be filmed and they can be questioned about their findings. This type of research shows that usually the jury get the main facts right, but that they may miss some of the fine distinctions.

There have been proposals to stop using juries in long complicated fraud trials, since this type of trial is particularly difficult for an ordinary person to understand.

Other disadvantages

Some jurors dislike doing jury service or become bored and may rush the decision.

There is a risk that members of the jury will be bribed or threatened by the defendant's friends. Majority verdicts were introduced in order to make this more difficult, as at least three jurors will have to be 'nobbled' to affect the decision.

The lower age limit of 18 is too young; it could be said that a person of this age has not got enough experience of life to make such important decisions.

Media coverage can cause jurors to form a biased view of the case. This occurred in a murder case involving two sisters in 1993. Some newspapers published a still picture from a video sequence which gave a false impression of what was happening. After the jury convicted the defendants, the trial judge gave leave to appeal because of the possible influence the media coverage might have had on the decision and the Court of Appeal quashed the convictions.

A C T I V I T Y

Read the following passages and answer the questions at the end giving reasons for your answers.

Source A

The use of the jury in English law stretches far into history. However, it was only by the beginning of the nineteenth century that it was settled that jurors should not have personal knowledge of the accused; until the eighteenth century the juror's function was invariably to assist the judge with an intimate assessment of the defendant's character, good or bad. In R. v. Gough (1993) the question for the Court of Appeal and the House of Lords was whether there was a real risk of bias where a juror was the next door neighbour of the defendant's brother.

Source B

Lord Denning has argued that some jurors are not up to the task, and commenting on the 1988 incident when some jurors were intimidated at a trial in Leeds Crown Court, he remarked: 'You may get girls or lads of 18 serving on a jury who may be an easy prey to bribery or intimidation.'

Source C

Louis Blom-Cooper has argued that juries' acquittals ought to be appealed against, for instance, over the acquittal of Patrick Pottle and Michael Randle for having organised the escape of the spy, George Blake, from jail some twenty-five years previously.

(All sources are from Paul Denham, *Law: A Modern Introduction*, Hodder & Stoughton, 1994.)

1 **Do you consider it is important for the jury to be free from bias?**
2 **Should jurors be told about any previous convictions of the defendant?**
3 **The present age range for jurors is 18 to 70: do you think this is satisfactory?**
4 **Are 18-year-olds more likely to be intimidated or bribed than older people?**
5 **Should it be possible to appeal against an acquittal?**
6 **What reforms to the jury system would you suggest?**

3.5 Alternatives to the jury

Single judge

In Northern Ireland the decision is made by one judge without a jury. This method of trial is used because of the extra risk of violence to jurors and possible bias. Other countries also use this method. It is probably the cheapest and most efficient way of conducting a trial, but since it removes a long tradition of public participation it is not likely to be acceptable in England and Wales.

A panel of judges

This is the method of trial in some continental countries. It is expensive and would mean that several hundred new judges would have to be found. There is also the same criticism that it does away with public participation and is unlikely to be a popular option.

A judge and two lay assessors

This is probably the most acceptable alternative to jury trial, as it would eliminate the slowness and cost of using a jury, whilst retaining public involvement. The two lay assessors could be chosen in much the same way as jurors. The decision would be made jointly by the judge and the lay assessors, thus avoiding problems of lack of understanding. The main objection is that there would not be such a wide cross-section of society as in the present system.

A judge and a mini-jury

Another option is to reduce the size of the jury to six or seven jurors. This would only help by halving the number of jurors needed, so saving some cost, but most of the present disadvantages would remain.

3.6 Appeals following a trial in the Crown Court

As in any criminal case it is important that there should be a right to appeal against a conviction, to protect the defendant from errors that might occur during the trial. All appeals go to the Court of Appeal (Criminal Division). The defendant has the following rights to appeal:

1 *Against conviction.* Under the Criminal Appeal Act 1995 the defendant must show that the conviction was 'unsafe'. This could be, for example, because the trial judge explained the law wrongly to the jury or because there is now some new evidence which casts doubt on the defendant's guilt.
2 *Against sentence.* Here the defendant is arguing that the sentence he was given was too severe.

In all cases the appeal must be started within six weeks of the conviction or sentence. As leave to appeal is needed this means that either the original trial judge or a judge in the Court of Appeal must give permission for the appeal to go ahead. This permission is difficult to obtain. If the case is heard by the Court of Appeal, that court can allow an appeal against a conviction (and quash the conviction), or substitute an alternative conviction for a less serious offence; this means a defendant could be found guilty of manslaughter instead of murder. The court can also allow an appeal against sentence and reduce the sentence. There is also the power to order a retrial, but this is very rarely done.

Prosecution rights

The prosecution can appeal:

1 *Against an acquittal.* This can only be done if the jury or witnesses at the original trial were 'nobbled'. In other cases there is no right to appeal against an acquittal, as the jury's verdict is final, but the Attorney-General can refer a point of law under section 36 of the Criminal Justice Act 1972 to the Court of Appeal (Criminal Division). The decision does not affect the acquittal but creates a new precedent on the law for future cases.
2 *Against a lenient sentence.* The Attorney-General can appeal against an unduly lenient sentence under section 36 of the Criminal Justice Act 1988. This power has been used in a number of cases, for example in 1993 when the judge ordered a 15-year-old boy who was convicted of raping a 13-year-old girl to pay her £500 in compensation and did not impose a

custodial sentence on him, the Court of Appeal changed the sentence to two years' detention in a Young Offenders' Institution.

Further appeal to the House of Lords

Both the prosecution and the defence have the right to appeal from the decision of the Court of Appeal (Criminal Division) only if:

a the Court of Appeal certifies that the case involves a point of law of general public importance; and
b either the Court of Appeal or the House of Lords gives leave to appeal.

An appeal to the House of Lords must involve a point of law; this means that there cannot be an appeal about the sentence. The Court of Appeal's decision on the sentence is the final one.

Figure 3.4 summarises the route for appeals following a trial on indictment at the Crown Court.

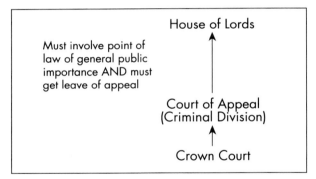

Figure 3.4 Appeals following a trial on indictment in the Crown Court

European Court

Any case that involves a point of European law can be referred to the European Court by either the Court of Appeal or the House of Lords for a ruling on that point of law. The English court then decides the case by applying the law to it. (*See* Chapter 9 for further information on European law.)

3.7 Problems with appeals

In 1993 the Runciman Commission reported, among other things, on the problems of miscarriages of justice. This report followed a number of cases where defendants had been convicted by a jury, failed to get the verdict changed on appeal and served several years in jail before it was established that the original evidence was faulty. Between 1988 and 1993 the Government paid out a total of £3.4 million in compensation to 70 people who had been wrongly convicted. These cases showed that the appeal system was not working for such people. The main problems with the appeal system are:

1 It is difficult to get leave to appeal to the Court of Appeal.
2 The Court of Appeal is reluctant to allow new evidence to be given.
3 There is the belief that as the jury saw all the original witnesses, the jury's verdict must be correct.

Criminal Cases Review Commission

The Home Secretary had power to refer suspected miscarriages of justice to the Court of Appeal. This was done in several cases in the early 1990s, including the Birmingham Six who were wrongly convicted of terrorist offences. However, it was felt that the Home Secretary was not independent enough and many cases were not properly investigated. After the recommendation of the Runciman Commission, the government set up the Criminal Cases Review Commission to take over consideration of suspected miscarriages of justice in 1997. There are fourteen commissioners and about 65 support staff. They consider cases and decide if there is need for a fuller investigation. A major criticism is that the Commission has not been given power to carry out its own investigations, but must appoint someone else, often a police officer. Since many miscarriages of justice were because of inadequate (or even corrupt) police work, this does not seem satisfactory.

Examination question

Study the newspaper article below and then answer **all** parts of the question which follows.

JURY DEFIES JUDGE ON KILLING VERDICT

An Old Bailey jury yesterday refused to obey a judge's order to find a man guilty of the manslaughter of his older brother.

In defiant exchanges with Mr Justice Farquarson, jurors told him: 'Every one of us is saying he is not guilty. However long you make us stay here, it is still not guilty.'

The jurors wanted to free William 'Leo' Jennings, 23, of Shepherds Bush, West London, who had been tried for murder but changed his plea to admit manslaughter.

After sending the jury out three times to reconsider, the judge discharged the jury from giving any verdict. He treated the case as a guilty plea and gave Jennings a two-year suspended sentence.

(*Source:* the *Independent*, 14 November 1987.)

a The article is about a case which took place at the Old Bailey. This court can also be called the Central Criminal Court and is part of the Crown Court system in England and Wales.

Explain how the Crown Court fits into the hierarchy of criminal courts and what type of criminal cases are dealt with by this level of court. (*6 marks*)

b In this case a dispute took place between the judge and the jury.
  i Explain the role of the judge and a jury in a Crown Court trial. (*8 marks*)
  ii Explain why there was a dispute in this case. (*4 marks*)

c The judge was told by the jurors in this case, 'Every one of us is saying he is not guilty'. This would be referred to as a unanimous verdict by a jury.

Do you think it is important to have a unanimous verdict following a criminal trial? Give your reasons. (*6 marks*)

d We are told that 'the judge discharged the jury from giving any verdict'. Why do you think he did so in this case? (*4 marks*)

e Do you think that the jury system is a good system of trying people accused of crimes? Are there any better alternatives? Explain your answer. (*12 marks*)

Total: *40 marks*

SEG 1990

4 *The legal system: civil courts*

4.1 Civil claims

As we saw in Chapter 1, civil law is quite separate from criminal law and has its own courts and procedure. It involves individuals or companies who wish to make a claim because their rights have been affected in some way. Common examples of the sorts of cases that could go to a civil court are:

a a television rental company claiming for money not paid on a TV renting agreement;

b a claim for the cost of repairing damage caused to a car because of the other person's negligent driving;

c a family claiming compensation for being put in sub-standard accommodation on a holiday package they paid for in this country;

d a landlord claiming for unpaid rent and for an order that the tenant leave the property;

e a workman claiming for injuries he suffered at work because of faulty machinery.

In civil cases most people will try to come to an agreement rather than start court proceedings. Court cases cost money. To start a case, even without consulting a solicitor, means paying a court fee; using a solicitor costs more and there is never any guarantee that you will win your case, nor even that, if you do win, the other party will have enough money to pay the claim and your costs. If the case is complicated it could last years and cost hundreds of thousands of pounds. In most cases it is sensible to write to the other person, making it clear what is being claimed and the reasons for the claim. It is only when the other person disputes the claim or will not reply at all, that court proceedings should be considered. Even then it is usual to write a final letter stating that unless the claim is paid in full within seven days, a court case will be started. This type of letter is known as a *letter before action*. An example of a letter before action is included in the leaflet 'What is a small claim?', an extract of which is shown opposite.

If, after all this, the other person still refuses to meet the claim, then the person making the claim has to decide whether he or she is prepared to go to court or whether to just 'write it off' and forget all about it. Many individuals who have good claims decide that the time, effort and cost involved will be too much. Companies are more likely to take action, particularly large companies that have their own legal department.

4.2 Starting a court case

The first decision is which court to use. The two courts that deal with civil cases are the County Court and the High Court. The amount claimed is usually the deciding factor in where to start a case, but the seriousness and difficulty of the case will also be considered. Most civil cases can be started in either court, but claims for less than £15,000 must be started in the County Court, and defamation actions can only be started in the High Court. Most civil cases can be started in either court, but claims for less than £15,000 must be started in the County Court. Also cases of personal injuries where the claim for compensation for those injuries is less than £50,000 must be started in the

Crystal
Mark

Clarity
approved by
Plain English Campaign

What should I do before I start a claim?

- Think carefully about starting a claim. You may be wasting your time and money if the person you are claiming from does not have the money to pay.

- Write to the person who owes you the money. Say how much they owe and what it is for. Include a warning that you will start a claim through the court if it is not paid; sometimes they will pay up and you will not have to go to court.

```
2 Spring Gardens
Anytown
AO6 3BX

                                    10 March 1991

Dear Mr Plummer

You repaired my central heating boiler on 6
January. I rang you on 7 January and again on
10 January to tell you that it was still not
working properly.

You promised to call and put it right but you
did not. I had to get someone else to come and
repair it on 26 January which cost £57 + VAT.

I asked you on 2 February to pay me this money
because it was work you should have done.

You have not paid it.

If I do not get the money in the next 7 days I
will have to start a claim in the county court.

Yours sincerely

E Sprogett

Mrs E Sprogett
```

Extract from the leaflet, 'What is a Small Claim?'
(© Crown Copyright)

County Court. In nearly all civil cases the person making the claim is called the claimant and the other party is the defendant.

The claimant will start the case and this is done by filling out certain documents, taking them to the court and paying the court's fee. The procedure in the two courts is slightly different.

There are almost 300 County Courts in England and Wales. There is either a court or a court office in most towns so that access for starting a case is easy. Unless the claim involves land, for example a landlord claiming for arrears of rent and to evict the tenant, the claimant can choose to start the case in the most convenient County Court, usually the one nearest to his home or work. If land is involved the case must be started in the County Court for the district in which the land is situated.

The High Court is based in London, but also sits in 26 towns and cities throughout the country.

A C T I V I T Y

Find out your nearest County Court.

Figure 4.1 Summary of civil court jurisdiction in contract and tort actions

Value of claim	Court in which case will usually be tried
Under £5,000	County Court small claims procedure
£5,000 up to £25,000	County Court
£25,000 to £50,000	Either County Court or High Court
£50,000 and above	High Court

Allocating cases

Since April 1999 all cases are allocated to one of three tracks. These are:

- small claims for cases involving less than £5,000
- fast-track for cases between £5,000 and £15,000
- multi-track for cases where the claim is for more than £15,000 or where the case is very complex

Small claims and fast-track cases are always heard in the County Court but multi-track cases can be dealt with in either the County Court or the High Court as shown in Figure 4.1 above.

4.3 Small claims

Since small claims are for amounts under £5,000, it is important that there should be a comparatively cheap and simple way of resolving them. The full County Court procedure is too expensive for many individuals to use. As a result in 1973 the Lord Chancellor introduced an arbitration scheme within the County Court for small claims. Originally it was only used for claims up to £75, but inflation and the success of the scheme have led to the limit being increased to £5,000.

The small claims court is often referred to as a do-it-yourself court. This is because people are encouraged to take action themselves and not use lawyers. To help people there are leaflets on how to sue and defend cases without a solicitor, which are available from County Court offices or Citizens Advice Bureaux. The first stage is to get a claim form from the court, fill it in and take or send it to the court and pay the court fee. The court then sends the claim by post to the defendant. The cost of issuing a claim form depends on the size of the claim, but the minimum cost is £20 for claims of up to £200 rising to £100 for a claim of £5,000. One of the leaflets explains how to fill in a claim form for most ordinary cases. The important points are to make it clear who is claiming, how much is claimed and why the claim is being made. Again the leaflets show how this should be done.

When the defendant receives the claim form he may admit the claim and pay the full amount to the claimant. If this occurs the case ends at this point, since the claimant has achieved what he wanted. Where the defendant disputes the claim he should reply to the court within 14 days explaining that he wants to defend the action and file a document called a defence at the court setting out why he disputes the claim. A copy of this is then sent to the claimant and the case will eventually be tried by a District Judge. In some cases the defendant will not bother to reply at all to the claim and in such cases the claimant can apply for judgment, that is, the claimant will automatically win the case.

At court

If the case is defended it is heard by a District Judge in private. The District Judge can use any suitable method of procedure at the hearing. As a result the matter is usually dealt with in a relatively informal way without the strict rules of evidence and procedure that are used in County

The following two pages show a Claim Form (© Crown Copyright)

Claim Form

In the

Claim No.

Claimant

SEAL

Defendant(s)

Brief details of claim

Value

Defendant's name and address

	£
Amount claimed	
Court fee	
Solicitor's costs	
Total amount	
Issue date	

The court office at

is open between 10 am and 4 pm Monday to Friday. When corresponding with the court, please address forms or letters to the Court Manager and quote the claim number.

N1 Claim form (CPR Part 7) (4.99)   *Printed on behalf of The Court Service*

You have 21 days from the date of the postmark to reply to this summons

(A limited company served at its registered office has 16 days to reply.)

If you do nothing	**Judgment may be entered against you without further notice.**
If you dispute the claim	Complete the white defence form (N9B) and return it to the court office. The notes on the form explain what you should do.
If you want to make a claim against the plaintiff (counterclaim)	Complete boxes 5 and 6 on the white defence form (N9B) and return the form to the court office. The notes at box 5 explain what you should do.
If you admit all of the claim and you are asking for time to pay	Fill in the blue admission form (N9A). The notes on the form explain what you should do and where you should send the completed form.
If you admit all of the claim and you wish to pay now	**Take or send the money to the person named at box (2) on the front of the summons.** If there is no address in box (2), send the money to the address in box (1). Read How to Pay below.
If you admit only part of the claim	Fill in the white defence form (N9B) saying how much you admit, then **either:** Pay the amount admitted as explained in the box above; **or** Fill in the blue admission form (N9A) if you need time to pay

Interest on Judgments

If judgment is entered against you and is for more than £5000, the plaintiff may be entitled to interest on the total amount.

Registration of Judgments

If the summons results in a judgment against you, your name and address may be entered in the Register of County Court Judgments. **This may make it difficult for you to get credit.** A leaflet giving further information can be obtained from the court.

Further Advice

You can get help to complete the reply forms and information about court procedures at any county court office or citizens' advice bureau. The address and telephone number of your local court is listed under " Courts" in the phone book. When corresponding with the court, please address forms or letters to the Chief Clerk. Always quote the whole of the case number which appears at the top right corner on the front of this form; the court is unable to trace your case without it.

How to pay	To be completed on the court copy only
• **PAYMENT(S) MUST BE MADE** to the person named at the address for payment quoting their reference and the court case number.	Served on
• **DO NOT bring or send payments to the court. THEY WILL NOT BE ACCEPTED.**	By posting on
• You should allow **at least 4** days for your payments to reach the plaintiff or his representative.	
• Make sure that you keep records and can account for all payments made. Proof may be required if there is any disagreement. It is not safe to send cash unless you use registered post.	Officer
• A leaflet giving further advice about payment can be obtained from the court.	Marked "gone away" on
• If you need more information you should contact the plaintiff or his representative.	

Court cases involving larger claims. The District Judge should make sure that he discovers all the relevant facts; he is expected to be more 'inquisitorial' than judges in other courts. This means that he takes an active part in the proceedings, asking questions and helping both parties to put their cases. Either party may have a lawyer to represent him or her, but this is discouraged by the fact that the winning party cannot claim back the cost of using a lawyer from the other party, but will have to pay his own legal expenses. Instead of having a lawyer, the claimant or defendant may have a 'lay representative', that is, a non-legally qualified person, with him or her at the hearing to help put the case.

Approximately 105,000 cases each year are dealt with by the small claims procedure and research has shown that it is used by many small businesses and large companies as well as by private individuals.

Problems with small claims

The first problem with small claims is that some people are not aware of the procedure and are afraid of 'going to court'. The process is still quite complicated to use for someone who has no legal knowledge. Legal aid is not available, so if the other side has a lawyer a poor person may be at a disadvantage. The system is meant to be quick, but there can still be delays. Although the intention is that the case should only go to court once, there may be several hearings because one of the parties is not ready; for example, they have not brought all their evidence to court. Since the court only sits during the working day, this can cause problems as the plaintiff and defendant may have to take time off work.

Despite these problems, the Civil Justice Review in 1986 found that two-thirds of people using the procedure were very satisfied with it.

The biggest problem lies in enforcing the judgment after the case, in other words collecting the money from the losing party. It is left up to the claimant to do this and can require payment of more court costs to send the bailiff to take possession of goods belonging to the claimant. Even this does not guarantee that the full amount of money will be obtained.

4.4 County Court

Jurisdiction

County Courts can try almost all civil actions, though as we have already seen, complicated claims and claims over £50,000 are more likely to be tried in the High Court. As well as actions involving contracts and torts, the court can hear family cases, including any proceedings under the Children Act 1989 and proceedings to exclude a partner from the family home because of domestic violence. Some County Courts can also grant divorces and deal with all the related matters such as maintenance and property disputes. All County Courts can deal with disputes over mortgages, partnerships and trusts up to a value of £30,000. There is also the power to decide disputes over inheritance where the value of the estate left by the deceased is less than £30,000. Some courts also have bankruptcy jurisdiction, so that orders can be made about individuals or companies who are insolvent. Including small claims, about four million cases are started each year in the County Court. The vast majority are settled without an actual trial.

Limits on jurisdiction

Although theoretically the County Court can hear any case involving a contract or a tort, the following types of case are considered as being best dealt with in the High Court:

a   cases involving claims because of a fatal accident;
b   cases involving claims through professional negligence;
c   cases where there is an allegation of fraud;
d   defamation cases;
e   malicious prosecution cases;
f   false imprisonment cases.

This does not mean that the County Court can never try such cases, but it is unusual for such cases to be heard in the County Court.

Personnel

Cases are usually heard by a Circuit Judge sitting on his own. It is possible for there to be a jury of eight people to hear certain categories of case, but the use of a jury in the County Court is extremely rare, since the types of cases which can have a jury are normally tried in the High Court. They are c, d, e and f in the list in the previous paragraph.

The Woolf Report (1996) criticized the courts as being too slow and too expensive. Lord Woolf recommended a fast track system for claims of £3,000 to £10,000 to deal with cases more quickly and that there should be a set maximum figure for legal costs in such cases.

4.5 High Court

The High Court sits in London and in 26 towns and cities throughout England and Wales. It has the power to hear any civil case. In order to help with administration and to provide specialist judges for the different types of law involved in cases the High Court is divided into three divisions. These are the Queen's Bench Division, the Chancery Division and the Family Division and each hears different types of case.

Queen's Bench Division

The main work of this division is to hear cases involving breach of contract (*see* Chapter 13) and cases based on claims under the law of tort (*see* Chapter 15). There is no upper limit on the amount which can be claimed, The Division also has specialist judges to decide commercial cases and admiralty cases. Commercial cases cover such areas as insurance and banking. The judges in the Commercial Court will have practised in this area of law before they became judges. The court also uses procedures that are different from those used by the rest of the Queen's Bench Division. It can be considered another form of arbitration, since strict rules of evidence are not used, witnesses are not often questioned in court and more evidence is presented on paper. The Admiralty Court hears cases involving shipping and covers claims for damage caused by a collision at sea or as a result of a defect in a ship. It also decides disputes over salvage rights when a ship has sunk or been stranded. The judge in the Admiralty Court will often sit with two lay assessors, who are experts on questions of seamanship and navigation.

Civil juries in the Queen's Bench Division

In the ordinary courts of the Queen's Bench Division cases are usually heard by a judge alone, but in about 1 per cent of cases a civil jury of 12 people will sit with the judge to decide the case. (The Commercial Court and the Admiralty Court do not use juries.) The Supreme Court Act 1981, section 69, provides that there is a right to jury trial only in four types of case: fraud, defamation, malicious prosecution and false imprisonment. In other cases it is possible to apply to the court for a jury to hear the case, but the court will only allow a jury to be used in exceptional circumstances. If the claim is for damages for personal injuries, the court is very unlikely to allow a jury to hear the case. The main reason for this is that civil juries, as well as deciding which party has won the case, also decide the amount of damages that will be awarded. These amounts are unpredictable and will vary enormously from one jury to another. Where the whole purpose of the case is to compensate the claimant for injuries suffered, it is unfair that one claimant may be given a very much larger sum than another plaintiff who has suffered identical injuries. The Court of Appeal in *Ward* v. *James* (1966) said that because uniformity and predictability were so important in such cases a jury should not normally be used.

Civil juries are used most often in defamation cases, but even in these cases the amount of damages awarded has been criticised. In 1992 Jason Donovan was awarded £200,000 after an article suggested that he was a homosexual, while William Roach (the *Coronation Street* actor) was awarded £50,000 because the *Sun* newspaper described him as 'self-satisfied, smug and boring'. One of the highest awards was £1.5m to Lord Aldington in 1989. The Court of Appeal now has power under section 8 of the Courts and Legal Services Act 1990 to reduce (or increase) the amount of damages if it is shown that no reasonable jury could reasonably have awarded the original sum. The first time this power was used was in 1992 in a case brought by a Member of Parliament, Teresa Gorman. The jury awarded her £150,000 damages, but the Court of Appeal reduced the amount to £50,000 saying that the original sum was excessive and unreasonable.

Chancery Division

The jurisdiction of the Chancery Division includes claims and matters arising from:

- sale or exchange of land
- mortgages
- trusts
- bankruptcy
- partnerships
- disputed wills
- company law
- patents, trade marks or copyright

Cases are heard by a single judge. Juries are not used in the Chancery Division.

Family Division

As the name suggests the work undertaken by this division is connected to family disputes. It can deal with any case involving marriage from declaring that a marriage is valid to dealing with divorce. The court can also hear all the related matters such as maintenance and property disputes and make decisions about residence and welfare of any children involved. The court has jurisdiction over adoption and any matters under the Children Act 1989. The court can also make orders to protect spouses or partners from violence under the Domestic Violence and Matrimonial Proceedings Act 1976.

Cases are heard by a single judge and although juries were once used to decide defended divorce cases, juries are not now used in the Family Division.

Woolf Reforms

In 1996 an enquiry into the civil courts led by Lord Woolf reported that there were many problems with taking civil cases to court. The main problems were:

- delay (often several years)
- cost (often more than the amount claimed)
- complexity

Lord Woolf proposed several reforms which were aimed at making civil cases quicker, cheaper and easier. These reforms were brought into force in April 1999. The most important points were:

- small claims limit raised to £5,000.

- a fast-track for claims of £5,000 to £15,000. The aim is that these cases should be heard within 30 weeks and that costs should be kept to a reasonable level.
- a multi-track for cases over £15,000 or complex cases.
- new simpler procedures: for example, cases in the County Court and the High Court are started in the same way. The person starting a case is now called the claimant instead of plaintiff and Latin phrases have been replaced with English words.
- judges to be case managers setting timetables and making sure that parties do not delay the case.

A C T I V I T Y

Advise the people in the following situations:

1 Samantha wishes to start an action for defamation against her local newspaper. Advise her as to which court she should use and explain to her who tries defamation cases.
2 Frank has bought a laptop computer, costing £600. The computer has never worked properly and he wants to claim back its cost. Advise him as to which type of court will hear this case and explain the likely court procedure to him.
3 Nigel, who lives in Southampton, is injured in a car accident in Birmingham. Nigel claims that the accident was the fault of the other driver, Jason, who lives in Ipswich. Nigel wants to claim £20,000 in damages. Advise Nigel as to which court he can use to start the case.

4.6 Divisional Courts

As well as its ordinary court, each of the three divisions of the High Court has what is called a Divisional Court. For these special courts two or three judges from that division will sit to hear certain applications and some appeals.

Queen's Bench Divisional Court

The Queen's Bench Divisional Court is the most important Divisional Court and has special supervisory powers which are used to check whether public authorities, government departments, government ministers, inferior courts, such as County Courts and Magistrates' Courts, and tribunals are exceeding their powers. This type of proceeding is known as judicial review. Judicial review proceedings were even brought against the Lord Chancellor in 1993, when the Law Society challenged his right to make certain changes in the Legal Aid scheme. The challenge was not successful as the Queen's Bench Divisional Court in that case decided that the Lord Chancellor was acting within his powers. When the court finds that there is a breach of power it has three orders that it can make. These are:

a   *certiorari* which has the effect of quashing the decision which is being challenged;

b   *prohibition* which prevents an inferior court or tribunal from continuing to hear a case; and

c   *mandamus* which is a command to perform a public legal duty.

The Queen's Bench Divisional Court has two other important functions. The first is to hear appeals on a point of law from criminal cases tried in the Magistrates' Court, as already shown in Chapter 2. The second is to hear applications for a *writ of habeas corpus* (literally meaning, have the body) from anyone who claims he or she is being unlawfully detained. This is an important way of protecting the right to liberty and has existed since Magna Carta.

Chancery Divisional Court

The Chancery Divisional Court deals with only a small number of cases, the main ones being appeals from decisions made by Tax Commissioners on the payment of tax and appeals from decisions of the County Court on insolvency orders.

Family Divisional Court

The main function of the Family Divisional Court is to hear appeals from decisions of magistrates regarding family matters and orders affecting children.

4.7 Appeals from the County Court and the High Court

The normal appeal route for decisions made by the County Court or any of the three divisions of the High Court is to the Court of Appeal (Civil Division). For small claims cases, however, there is no right of appeal. The decision by the District Judge is usually final. Cases involving more than $5,000 can appeal but all cases must get leave (permission) to appeal from the Court of Appeal. An appeal in the Court of Appeal is heard by three judges known as Lords Justices of Appeal. From their decision there is the possibility of another appeal to the House of Lords, but only if leave is given for the appeal by either the Court of Appeal or the House of Lords itself. There is also a special appeal route from the High Court straight to the House of Lords, missing out the Court of Appeal. This type of appeal is known as a 'leapfrog' appeal, but can only be made on a point of law of general public importance where either the Court of Appeal is already bound by a previous decision or the case involves interpretation of legislation (that is, a question of what the words in an Act of Parliament mean). There are only four or five 'leapfrog' appeals each year. These routes are shown in diagram form in Figure 4.2.

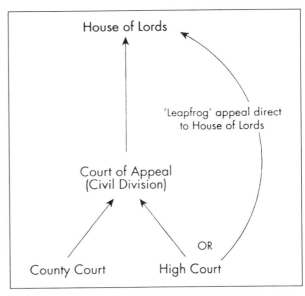

Figure 4.2   Diagram of the civil appeal routes

European Court

A point of European law can be referred to the European Court under Article 177 (234) of the Treaty of Rome by any civil court. The European Court will decide the point of law and then send the case back to the original court to apply that law and make the actual decision in the case. The European Court is dealt with more fully in Chapter 9.

4.8 Coroner's Court

The Coroner's Court is separate from the mainstream of courts. Its chief function is to inquire into violent or unnatural deaths, deaths in prison and sudden deaths where there is no obvious cause. The coroner can hold an inquest if the death occurred in his area or if the body is in his area even though the death occurred somewhere else. This was decided in the case of *R. v. West Yorkshire Coroner (ex parte Smith)* (1982) where an English nurse had died abroad but her body had been brought back to England. Her father, who was not satisfied with the investigations into the death carried out abroad, asked the coroner to hold an inquest. The coroner refused to do so, so the father sought an order for mandamus from the Queen's Bench Divisional Court (*see* 4.7 above) to make the coroner hold an inquest and the Divisional Court held that the coroner was obliged to hold an inquest. A jury of between seven and eleven people must be called to decide the cause of death if the death occurred in prison or police custody or as a result of injuries caused by police action, for example when making an arrest. A jury must also be used where the death is the result of an alleged breach of health and safety regulations. In other cases a jury may be used but the coroner can decide to hear the case on his own without a jury.

The second function of the court is to decide whether old items that have been dug up are 'treasure' under the Treasure Act 1996. Objects more than 300 years old which contain at least 10 per cent gold or silver are treasure; also coins over 300 years old, provided one of the coins contains gold or silver. A single coin is not treasure, even if it is a gold coin. Any item found with the object or the coins is also considered to be treasure.

Treasure belongs to the Crown, not the finder, though the finder is usually paid a substantial reward if he reports his finding promptly.

Coroners

To be appointed as a coroner a person must have been qualified as a barrister, solicitor or doctor for at least five years.

4.9 The Judicial Committee of the Privy Council

This court is also separate from the rest of the court structure. It hears an odd mix of cases. One of its most important functions is to hear appeals from some Commonwealth countries. Originally all final appeals from the Commonwealth used to be heard here, but as countries became independent some opted out of the system and have their own appeal courts. Countries which have kept this route as their final appeal court include the Bahamas, Barbados, Bermuda, Fiji, Jamaica and New Zealand.

The other functions of the Judicial Committee of the Privy Council are:

a to hear appeals against being struck off by a ruling professional body and so prevented from practising as a doctor, dentist, optician, physiotherapist or other similar profession;

b to hear appeals on some matters connected with the church from the ecclesiastic courts;

c to decide whether any member of the House of Commons is disqualified from being an MP.

The judges are the Lord Chancellor, the Law Lords and other members of the Privy Council who hold or have held high judicial office in the United Kingdom or a Commonwealth country. The Judicial Committee does not hear many cases. In 1996 there was a total of 85, of which 12 were from Jamaica and 16 from New Zealand but its decisions are regarded as important and can affect later decisions in English cases.

Examination question

Study the extract below and then answer **all** parts of the question which follows.

> The county courts were set up in 1846 to provide a system of cheap and speedy local civil justice. At the moment there are about 260 county courts in England and Wales in which approximately three-quarters of all civil cases start.
>
> For a civil case to be heard in the county court, it must fall within the court's authority or 'jurisdiction'. Jurisdiction depends on the locality of the court, on the type of claim and also on the amount claimed by the plaintiff, the person who brings the case to court.
>
> Each court has a District Judge responsible for the administration and day-to-day running of the court. Also, the District Judge has a judicial role, in that he may hear claims for less than £1,000 by referring the action or 'case' to an arbitrator, a role normally performed by the District Judge himself.
>
> People bringing or defending an action in the county court can seek legal advice, either through the Green Form scheme or from any other source available to them. Legal aid is also available for actions before the full county court, where the case is heard by a circuit judge. But legal aid is not available for a hearing in front of an arbitrator.

a Explain what is meant by the phrase in the second paragraph, 'Jurisdiction depends on the locality of the court . . .'. *(2 marks)*

b i Identify **two** different types of case which the county court has the jurisdiction to hear.

    ii Identify **two** different types of case which the county court cannot hear. *(4 marks)*

c Give **four** of the stages through which a plaintiff has to go before an action can be brought in the county court, or through the Small Claims. *(4 marks)*

d Describe **two** ways in which an arbitration hearing through the Small Claims is different from a full judicial hearing in the County Court. *(4 marks)*

e Briefly explain **one** problem of arbitration that a full judicial hearing does not have. *(2 marks)*

f Explain the difference between legal aid and legal advice. *(4 marks)*

g Identify **two** sources of legal advice, other than the Green Form Scheme. *(2 marks)*

h Describe the two tests a person will have to pass in order to receive civil Legal Aid. *(4 marks)*

i The current system of civil legal aid is considered by some to have faults in it. Identify and explain **two** reasons for this opinion. *(4 marks)*

Total: 30 marks

SEG Sample Paper for 1996 Foundation Tier

Settling disputes outside the court structure

5

There are methods of resolving disputes outside the court structure and this chapter looks at these. Figure 5.1 provides a summary of methods of dispute resolution.

5.1 Tribunals

During the second half of the twentieth century a number of social and welfare rights have been established. These include payments for people who are suffering from a disability, payments for those injured as a result of their work, payments for people who are made redundant from their job, the right not to be discriminated against because of one's sex or race and the right not to be unfairly dismissed from work. These are only a few examples; there are many more. In order to protect these rights it is necessary to have either a court or another place to which one can apply if there are any problems. Since the courts were already very busy, the Government set up separate tribunals to deal with this type of claim.

Many tribunals are administrative tribunals which resolve disputes between private individuals and a government department. These include the Immigration Appeal Tribunal to which immigrants who are refused the right to settle in this country can apply; the Mental Health Review Tribunal which decides if the detention of a mentally ill person in a hospital is justified; and social security appeal tribunals which handle appeals against refusal to grant various benefit payments. Other tribunals specialise in disputes arising from employment; these are called industrial tribunals. Altogether there are over 2,000 different tribunals and they hear many more cases than the civil courts.

Composition

Since the various tribunals have been set up over a number of years in a bits and pieces way, they do not all operate in the same way. However, the majority will have a panel of three people sitting to decide the case. The chairman will usually be legally qualified, and in the case of industrial tribunals must be so qualified. The other two members will have some experience or specialist knowledge in the particular subject matter of the tribunal. For instance in any tribunal where there is a question involving health, the two lay (non-

Figure 5.1 Methods of dispute resolution

Negotiation	Parties themselves
Mediation	Parties plus neutral third party
Arbitration	Parties agree to let third person make a binding decision
Litigation	Parties go to court and a judge decides the case

lawyer) members will be doctors; in industrial tribunals one will be from an employers' organisation and the other from an employees' organisation, often a trades union.

The procedure for each tribunal varies, with many using no formal rules of evidence or procedure. The industrial tribunals are the most formal and their procedure is very similar to that of a court; the social security appeals tribunals are less formal. In all tribunals individuals are encouraged to bring their own case and not to use lawyers. Indeed, apart from the Mental Health Review Tribunal, the Lands Tribunal and the Employment Appeal Tribunal, legal aid is not available, so that anyone wishing to be represented by a lawyer will have to pay his or her own legal costs. The decision of most tribunals is final, that means there is no appeal available. Again there are some exceptions, the most important being the industrial tribunals which have a complicated appeal route, going first to the Employment Appeal Tribunal and then to the Court of Appeal (Civil Division).

5.2 Advantages and disadvantages of tribunals

There are many advantages to using this system of tribunals instead of the courts.

1 It is cheaper since there are no expensive court or lawyers' fees to pay as most applicants represent themselves. In industrial tribunals people are more likely to be represented by a lawyer than at social security tribunals.
2 The proceedings are less formal than a court, making it easier for ordinary people to start proceedings and conduct their own case.
3 Each tribunal specialises in one type of case so that they become expert in that area. In addition the two lay members will have their own specialist knowledge of the subject.
4 Cases are dealt with more quickly than in the courts.

However the system also has some drawbacks.

1 Applicants who are unrepresented are less likely to win their case. Statistics in the early 1990s showed that in industrial tribunals the success rate for those with lawyers was 49 per

cent, while for those without lawyers the rate was only 28 per cent. One of the main problems in tribunals is that although the individual will not be represented, the employer or government department on the other side is likely to have its own lawyer. Legal aid is not available.
2 Although the procedure is comparatively informal, many people still find it confusing and intimidating. The fact that each tribunal is likely to have its own methods adds to this confusion.
3 The specialist knowledge of tribunals may make an applicant feel at a disadvantage since he will not share that knowledge.
4 Tribunals do not always operate quickly. Reports by the Council on Tribunals have highlighted delays. It is normal for employment cases to take a year or more to be heard and if the case goes to appeal there will probably be another two years to wait. One case actually took nine years from start to finish. (*See Darnell* v. *United Kingdom* (1993), p. 219.)

5.3 Control of tribunals

Since tribunals operate outside the court system a special council was set up in 1958 to review the constitution and the working of tribunals. This is the Council on Tribunals and it hears complaints about tribunals and publishes an annual report. It can only make suggestions for reform as it has no power to alter any decisions made by any tribunal. The other problem is that it is very small, with a limited number of staff, and it cannot deal with the growing number of tribunals and cases. The Council also has very little power; it can only report on problems and make recommendations for the future; it does not have the right to overrule any decision by a tribunal.

It is, however, as already noted, possible to appeal from the decisions of some tribunals. Most employment cases can appeal first to the Employment Appeals Tribunal and from there to the Court of Appeal. In these cases the courts can control the workings of the tribunals and correct any errors they may have made.

Apart from an actual appeal the courts have some control over tribunals with the process of judicial review. These proceedings are brought in the Queen's Bench Divisional Court (*see* Chapter 4) but the Divisional Court will only overturn the tribunal's decision for one of the following reasons:

1 The tribunal has acted *ultra vires*, that is, it has done something it has no power to do.
2 The decision was clearly wrong in law.
3 The decision was against the rules of natural justice. The rules of natural justice include the point that no person is allowed to act as a judge in a case in which he has an interest and that both sides must be given the chance to put their case.

Finally there is an Ombudsman to whom dissatisfied parties can complain.

THIS IS OUR LATEST FORM OF MEDIATION.

5.4 ADR and mediation

We will now look at methods of resolving disputes which are quite independent of the legal system. Remember that in civil cases it is one of the parties involved who decides whether or not to start a court case. People do not want to start a case unnecessarily and will usually try to settle the problem in another way where possible.

ADR means Alternative Dispute Resolution and is becoming popular among big companies as a cheap and quick way of sorting out a dispute. ADR takes a number of different forms but the common factor is that the parties are encouraged to come to a satisfactory settlement themselves, instead of allowing another person (a judge or arbitrator) to make a decision. Negotiation is one form of ADR. In this the parties try to reach an agreement themselves, often by each party being prepared to give up part of his or her claim. Another method is mediation in which a neutral party will intervene to try to encourage the parties to settle the dispute.

In 1991 the *Centre for Dispute Resolution* was set up in London and many important companies have become members, including ICI and Sony and almost all the big London law firms. The Centre does not make a judgment, instead the aim is to act as a mediator and help the parties reach a settlement. The Centre offers a variety of ways of resolving a dispute. One method is to have a 'mini-trial' with a panel of three reaching a decision. The unusual part of this procedure is that only one of the panel will be independent and neutral, the others will be one executive from each of the companies involved. The panel will hear a short presentation of each side's case and the two executives will then, with the neutral advisor's help, try to find a solution that satisfies them both. The solution is likely to be based more on commercial realism than on pure law and it may contain certain agreements about future business, a matter on which the court could not make any decision. Apart from saving time and money this sort of procedure avoids the 'head-on' conflict that can occur in court and makes it easier for the companies to continue doing business with each other.

Examples of disputes which have been settled through the Centre include a £5 million claim involving insurance negligence, a £1 million construction claim over electrical and mechanical installations and a £20 million dispute over breach of contract between manufacturing firms. All these disputes were resolved in one or two days of mediation, saving estimated court costs of several thousands of pounds.

5.5 Arbitration

Going to arbitration means that the parties voluntarily agree to have their dispute judged by another person privately, not in court, and agree to accept his or her decision. The agreement to go to arbitration is generally made in writing at the time the parties made their original contract. At this time, of course, there would have been no dispute, but the agreement would be aimed at any possible future disputes. This type of arbitration agreement is known as a *Scott* v. *Avery* clause, being named after a case in 1855. Many organisations automatically include arbitration clauses in any contracts made; in particular arbitration clauses are commonly found in car insurance contracts and contracts for package holidays. The example below is from a holiday brochure.

8: In the event that you have a dispute with us which we cannot amicably resolve if you so wish the dispute may be referred to Arbitration under a special scheme which though devised by arrangement with ABTA is administered quite independently by the Chartered Institute of Arbitrators. The scheme (details of which ABTA will supply on request) provides for a simple and inexpensive method of arbitration on documents alone with restricted liability on the customer in respect of costs. The scheme does not apply to claims for an amount greater than £1,500 per person. There is also a limit of £7,500 per booking form. It does not apply to claims which are solely or mainly in respect of physical injury or illness or the consequences of such injury or illness.

A C T I V I T Y

Try to find an arbitration clause in a contract.

Apart from making an arbitration agreement at this early stage, it is also possible to agree to go to arbitration after a dispute arises. When people agree to use arbitration the courts will normally refuse to allow them to take proceedings in court instead of going to arbitration. This rule is in the Arbitration Act 1996. The one exception to this is if the dispute involves consumer rights and the claim is for less than £1,000. In this case the con-sumer can decide to use the small claims arbitration scheme in the County Court instead of a private arbitration scheme. Arbitration is popular with businesses and is used by both big and small companies. International companies often use what is called the London Court of Arbitration to resolve their disputes. There is also the Institute of Arbitrators which provides arbitrators for major disputes. About 10,000 arbitrations take place in London each year. Apart from these major disputes, arbitration is also used as a way of resolving disputes between businesses and customers in a variety of services and industries. This is sometimes referred to as domestic arbitration since it is the industries themselves that have set up the arbitration schemes. The difference between arbitration and mediation is that in arbitration a decision is made by the arbitrator and both parties are then bound by that decision, whereas in mediation the parties are helped to come to an agreement by a neutral third party. The parties can accept or reject the mediator's suggestions for resolving the dispute.

The arbitrator

An arbitrator can be anyone whom the parties agree should decide their case. He or she may be a lawyer who specialises in the type of law involved in the dispute or may be a non-lawyer who is a technical expert in the area involved. This second type of arbitrator is often used where the dispute is over the quality of goods or work done. An example would be an engineer being asked to make a decision in a case about faulty machinery. The agreement to go to arbitration will generally name the arbitrator or provide a method for choosing him. Commercial contracts often say that the president of the appropriate trade organisation shall appoint the arbitrator. If the parties want to use arbitration but cannot agree on how to choose an arbitrator, they can ask the High Court to appoint one for them.

The award

The decision of the arbitrator is called an award. This award is usually final, that means neither party can appeal from it. The award can be enforced in the same way as a judgment of the court.

5.6 Advantages and disadvantages of arbitration

There are many advantages to using arbitration instead of going to court:

1 The parties can make their own rules as to how the arbitration should be conducted. This means they can choose a formal hearing with witnesses giving evidence on oath in a similar way to a court hearing or they can agree to a more informal hearing. They may even agree that all the evidence will be put in as documents and have a 'paper' arbitration with no witnesses.

2 The time and place of the hearing can be arranged to suit the parties. Where suitable the hearing may be in the evening or at a weekend so as not to interfere with business.

3 The whole case will take place in private, so that business disputes are not made public. If a case goes to court the hearing is almost always open to the public.

4 The case will be finished more quickly than in the courts.

5 Questions of quality are decided by an expert, rather than a judge. This can also save time since the parties will not have to waste time explaining technical points.

6 It is much cheaper than going to court. Some estimates suggest that a court case costs 10 times more than an arbitration hearing. This is particularly true if the parties agree that they will not use lawyers at the hearing.

As with all schemes, however, there are some disadvantages:

1 Arbitration is not always cheap. If the parties use a professional arbitrator from an organisation such as the London Institute of Arbitrators, the charge for such an arbitrator could be £1,000 per day. In addition, if the parties use top barristers to present their cases at the hearing, the costs may well be the same as going to court.

2 An individual with a dispute against a big business may feel at a disadvantage. Legal aid is not available for arbitration hearings, although it may be if the same dispute were heard in court, so the individual will either have to do without a lawyer or pay his own costs. In some instances he may find that he has to go to arbitration since there was an arbitration clause in the original contract. Many organisations, such as package holiday firms and insurance companies, include such a clause in their standard contracts and consumers may have to accept that arbitration clause if they wish to go ahead with the contract.

3 The fact that there is no general right of appeal can be a disadvantage.

4 If a point of law is involved then it may be more suitable for a judge to make the decision than an arbitrator.

Arbitration is being increasingly criticised as being almost as costly and time-consuming as going to court and many companies now prefer to use ADR.

6 The legal profession

In England and Wales there are two types of lawyers, barristers and solicitors. Most countries do not have such a definite division amongst lawyers; a person will qualify as a lawyer though it will be possible after qualifying to specialise in one particular area of law. We have this system in this country for doctors; all those wanting to become a doctor will take the same general qualifications and will be able to practise as a doctor, but anyone wanting to be a specialist will have to do further training in their specialist subject. In the English legal system this idea of a common start to training which will qualify you as a lawyer able to practise general law does not exist. Although 75 per cent of entrants start by taking a law degree, this does not allow you to practise as either a barrister or a solicitor. After taking the degree it is necessary to decide which branch of the profession you want to qualify in, before going on to the next stage of training. In 1994 the Lord Chancellor's advisory committee on legal education recommended that, instead of having separate training for barristers and solicitors at this stage, the two branches of the profession should have joint training.

6.1 Solicitors

There are about 66,000 solicitors practising in England and Wales and they are controlled by their own professional body called the Law Society. To become a solicitor it is usual to have a law degree and then to take a one-year Legal Practice Course. This is followed by a two-year training period, previously called articles, where the trainee solicitor works in a firm of solicitors or for an organisation such as the Crown Prosecution Service or local or central government. During this two-year period he will be paid, though not at the same rate as a fully qualified solicitor, and will do his own work supervised by a qualified solicitor. He will also have to complete a Professional Skills Course, which gives training in interviewing clients and witnesses, negotiating, advocacy and business management including dealing with accounts. Finally the trainee will be admitted as a solicitor by the Law Society and his name will be added to the list or roll of solicitors. Those who have a degree in another subject must take an extra year's course on law, called the Common Professional Examination, before going on to take the Legal Practice Course. There is also a possible entry route which does not involve taking a degree first, but this is only available to mature students and it takes longer to qualify by this route. The three routes to becoming a solicitor are shown in Figure 6.1 on the opposite page.

The main criticisms of the training process are that, first, many people with good degrees cannot get a place on the Legal Practice Course; secondly, students have to pay the fees for this course and also support themselves during the year it lasts. This problem has occurred because most Local Authorities refuse to give a grant for the Legal Practice Course if the student has already had a grant to do a degree. The result of this is that students from poor families cannot afford to take the course and are therefore pre-

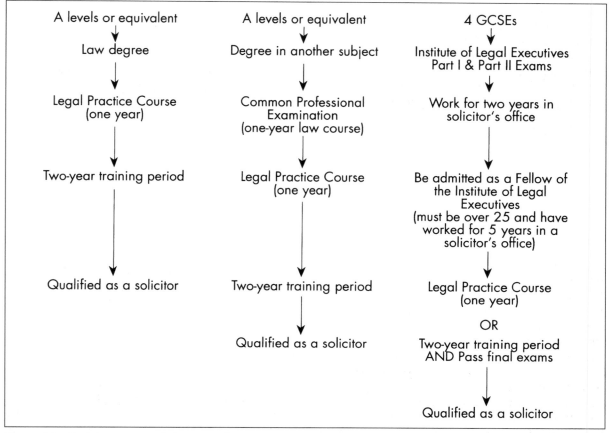

Figure 6.1   Training routes to become a solicitor

vented from becoming solicitors. Many students from lower- and middle-income backgrounds take out bank loans and by the time they qualify, they may owe thousands of pounds. In order to overcome this problem some universities have started offering a four-year course combining a law degree and a practical course which allows the student to receive a grant for the four-year period. The University of Northumberland was the first to offer this course in 1993, so that the first students to use this route qualified in 1997. The third criticism is that even after passing the Legal Practice Course students are not qualified as solicitors but must find a training place with a firm of solicitors or other suitable organisation. Not all students will be able to find training places and may be prevented from qualifying as solicitors as a result. In 1993 it was estimated that there were 6,000 applicants and only 3,000 training places available.

Solicitors' work

The majority of those qualifying as a solicitor work in private practice in a solicitor's firm, but there are other careers available and some newly qualified solicitors may go to work in the Crown Prosecution Service or become advisors in local government or 'in-house' solicitors for commercial or industrial firms.

Private solicitor's firms vary enormously from small 'high-street' practices in towns throughout England and Wales to the very large firms in London. The number of solicitors working in each type of practice will also vary from the 'one-man band', known as a sole practitioner, to hundreds of solicitors. One of the largest firms in the early 1990s had over 200 partners and over a thousand assistant solicitors. The work of these firms is equally varied. A small high street firm will be a general practice advising clients on a wide variety of topics, such as consumer problems, housing problems, business matters and family problems. A solicitor working in such a practice will spend some of his time interviewing clients in his office and dealing with paperwork, possibly drafting a contract or drawing up a will or dealing with documents for the sale of houses or other property or preparing papers for court. He may also, if he wishes, act for some of his clients in court. Standing up in court to put a client's case is known as advocacy and some solicitors will spend much of their time in court while others may prefer to concentrate on office work. In most firms of solicitors there is an element of specialisation. The firm itself may only deal with a certain type of work, for example some firms will only deal with civil matters and not take any criminal cases. Within the firm solicitors are likely to specialise so that, for example, one solicitor may deal solely with property matters while another concentrates on matrimonial work. The bigger the firm of solicitors the more the individual solicitors

will specialise. Some of the big city firms will deal mainly with company work and solicitors working for them are likely to do highly specialised work.

Prior to 1987 solicitors had a monopoly over conveyancing work, that is, dealing with the legal side of transferring property in house sales. However under the Administration of Justice Act 1985 other people were allowed to become licensed conveyancers and under the Courts and Legal Services Act 1990 this right was extended to banks and building societies. As a result solicitors became more competitive and reduced their fees, but even so they lost a large proportion of conveyancing work and this led to a demand for wider rights of advocacy.

Solicitors may do advocacy work in the Magistrates' Courts and in the County Courts but have very limited rights to appear in the Crown Court and High Court. Normally a solicitor can only act as an advocate in the Crown Court on an appeal or a committal for sentence from the

A solicitor's office

Magistrates' Court and then only if he had been the advocate in the original case. High Court appearances are usually limited to making statements in cases that have been settled. If a solicitor wishes to specialise in advocacy and have an unlimited right to appear as an advocate in all courts he must get a certificate in advocacy. Such a certificate will only be granted if the solicitor has already acted as an advocate in the Magistrates' Court and the County Court, taken a short training course and passed examinations about court work. Solicitors were given the right to apply for these certificates under the Courts and Legal Services Act 1990 and the first certificates were granted in 1994.

A solicitor deals directly with clients and enters into a contract with them. This means that if the client does not pay the solicitor can sue for his fees. It also means that clients can sue the solicitor either for breach of contract or for negligence.

Complaints against solicitors

As already mentioned the Law Society controls solicitors and its Disciplinary Tribunal may 'strike off' any solicitor found guilty of serious professional misconduct such as fraudulent use of clients' money. There was also the Solicitors' Complaints Bureau, which was set up in 1986 following a High Court decision that Glanville Davies, a solicitor and a member of the Law Society's Council, had overcharged a client by £131,000. The Law Society struck off Glanville Davies after the court decision and realised that it needed a more independent complaints procedure. The number of complaints made to the Bureau rose steadily to over 25,000 a year. Most complaints were about delay or overcharging. However, the Solicitors' Complaints Bureau itself came under attack for its own delays and inefficiency in dealing with complaints. A survey by the Law Society in 1995 found that in a sample of 2,246 complainants, two out of every three were dissatisfied with the outcome of their complaint. As a result of these findings, and also in response to criticism by the Legal Services Ombudsman, the Law Society abolished the Solicitors' Complaints Bureau and in its place set up the Office for the Supervision of Solicitors. However, this new 'watchdog' is still funded by the Law Society, so that the criticism of lack of an independent complaints body is still valid.

The Courts and Legal Services Act 1990 created the post of Legal Services Ombudsman to whom complainants who are not satisfied with the Office for Supervision of Solicitors' decision can go. In 1997 the Ombudsman received 1332 complaints about solicitors and in a third of these cases he decided that the complaint was justified. Most of the complaints are about cost, delay or the failure to keep clients informed as to what is happening in their case. The Legal Services Ombudsman also receives complaints about barristers and licensed conveyancers.

Apart from making a complaint about a solicitor, a client can sue the solicitor for breach of contract or for negligence. This happened in the case of *Griffiths* v. *Dawson* (1993) where the plaintiff's solicitors had failed to make the correct application in divorce proceedings against her husband. As a result the plaintiff lost out financially and the solicitors were ordered to pay her £21,000 in compensation for their error. Other people affected by the solicitor's negligence may also be able to sue in certain circumstances. An example of this was the case of *White* v. *Jones* (1995) where a father wanted to make a will leaving both his daughters £9,000. He wrote to his solicitors instructing them to draw up a will to include this. The solicitors received this letter on 17 July 1986 but had not drawn up the will when the father died on 14 September 1986. As a result the daughters did not inherit any money and they successfully sued the solicitor for the lost £9,000.

6.2 Barristers

There are about 9,000 barristers in independent practice in England and Wales and they are controlled by their own professional body called the General Council of the Bar. To become a barrister it is usual to start by obtaining a law degree; those with a degree in another subject will have to do a one-year course on law and pass the Common Professional Examination. In order to go on to the next stage of training it is necessary to join an Inn of Court and be accepted on the Bar's Vocational Training Course which lasts one academic year. It has become increasingly difficult to obtain a place on this Training Course and the method of selecting students has been criticised. Prior to 1994 it was necessary to have at least a 2(I) pass at degree level. In 1994 the procedure was changed; the grades obtained at A level became more important and critical reasoning tests were introduced. One result of the changes was that students with first class degrees were being refused places and there were many successful appeals against the refusal of a place. The Vocational Training Course concentrates on practical skills, particularly advocacy, and students learn to draft legal documents and present cases in court. As with solicitors there is a financial problem for students doing the Vocational Course since Local Education Authorities rarely give a grant for this stage of training. Joining an Inn of Court and attending there to dine or for weekend courses is compulsory but students may choose which of the four Inns – Lincoln's Inn, the Inner Temple, the Middle Temple and Gray's Inn – they wish to join.

Pupillage

Once the student has passed the Vocational Course and dined the correct number of times he will be called to the Bar by his Inn of Court. He is then a barrister but will not be allowed to practise in court until he has completed the first six months of the next stage of his training which is called pupillage. Being a pupil barrister means studying under an experienced barrister, reading his work, practising writing advices and opinions on points of law, drafting other legal documents and going to court with the pupil master to observe cases. The total length of pupillage is one year and this can be served with the same pupil master or as two periods of six months with different pupil masters. During this period the trainee barrister must also take part in a programme of continuing education organised by the

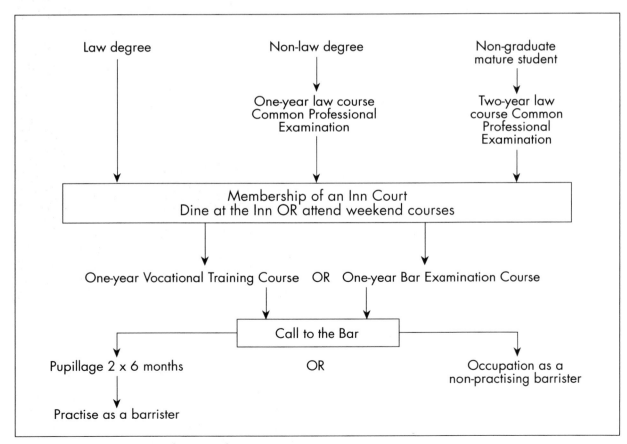

Figure 6.2 Training routes to become a barrister

Bar Council. In order to help people with this stage of training the Bar has introduced a scheme to provide a minimum level of funding for all pupils.

It is possible for mature non-graduates to read for the Bar, but they must first do a two-year Law Course before going on to take the Vocational Course. There is also an alternative one-year course to the Vocational Course for those who want to qualify as barristers but not practise at the Bar. The various training routes are shown in Figure 6.2 on p. 52.

Barristers' work

Barristers practising at the Bar are self-employed, but usually join a set of chambers (offices) consisting of a small number of barristers (often about 20) and support staff of whom the most important is the clerk. The clerk is effectively the business manager and is in charge of administration and acts as an agent for his barristers. Solicitors who want a barrister to act for them in a case will ring up the clerk to arrange it. When a solicitor sends work to a barrister it is known as briefing a barrister and the papers that the barrister receives are called a brief. Accountants and similar professionals can brief a barrister directly but all other clients must go through a solicitor. Appearing in court on behalf of clients is the main part of most barristers' work. Barristers have the right to appear in any court in England and Wales and, until the Courts and Legal Services Act 1990, they were the only lawyers allowed full 'rights of audience' (to appear) in the Crown Court, High Court, Court of Appeal and House of Lords. When a barrister appears in court, his instructing solicitor or someone from the solicitor's firm will also be present at court, sitting behind the barrister to provide any necessary information and to take notes. Barristers also do paperwork, mainly giving advice and opinions about the law or drafting documents for use in court. Indeed, some barristers who specialise in certain areas of law, such as company law, tax law, planning and housing law will rarely, if ever, appear in court.

Queen's Counsel

Some senior barristers will become Queen's Counsel and be able to use the initials QC after their names. A barrister must have been qualified for at least 10 years before he applies to the Lord Chancellor to become a Queen's Counsel and only those who are recognised as being the best barristers are appointed. There is criticism that not enough women or candidates from ethnic minority groups are chosen; out of about 900 Queen's Counsel fewer than 80 are women. Becoming a QC is also known as 'taking silk'. This is because QCs (or silks) wear a different gown in court from that worn by junior barristers (all barristers who are not QCs are junior barristers regardless of their age!) and this gown is traditionally made of silk. As a QC the barrister will be able to charge more and will undertake more complicated cases. Often a QC will have a junior barrister to work with them on cases.

A group of barristers in front of the Royal Courts of Justice

Complaints against barristers

A barrister does not enter into a contract with his client and so cannot sue if his fees are not paid. Similarly the client cannot sue for breach of contract, nor can the client sue for professional negligence for any work done in court. This was decided in *Rondel* v. *Worsley* (1969) and is based on the idea that a barrister's first duty is to the court and he must be 'free to do his duty fearlessly and independently'. There is also the fact that in almost all cases in court there are two parties and one of those parties will win the case while the other will lose and be dissatisfied with the result, so that after every decision there would be the risk of further litigation. Barristers can, however, be sued for negligent advice. This was decided in *Saif Ali* v. *Sydney Mitchell and Co.* (1978), where a barrister gave the wrong advice about who to sue, with the result that the plaintiff was too late to start court proceedings against the right person.

Barristers can be disciplined by the Senate of the Inns of Court if they fail to maintain the standards set out in their Code of Conduct. Amongst other things this code forbids them to discriminate against clients on the grounds of race, ethnic origin, sex, religion or political beliefs. Barristers can be ordered to pay up to £2,000 for poor work. In extreme cases a barrister can be disbarred and prevented from practising.

6.3 Fusion of the legal profession

The division of the legal profession into barristers and solicitors has frequently been criticised. In 1979 the Benson Commission into Legal Services considered the arguments for and against fusing the profession into one common profession and recommended that the division should remain. The Courts and Legal Services Act 1990 has to some extent eroded the differences between barristers and solicitors, especially in giving solicitors the right to become advocates in the higher courts and to become High Court judges. Supporters of fusion (that is, having one combined profession) feel that the Act did not go far enough. However the two professions remain separate and, as already noted, have different education and roles.

Advantages of fusion

1 The main advantage of fusion is that costs would be reduced since the client would only have to employ one lawyer. A person taking a case to court will have a solicitor and a barrister. Also, in major cases, a second barrister, often a QC will be briefed.

A famous quote by Michael Zander says that 'To have one taxi meter running is less expensive than to have two or three.'

2 There would be less duplication of work. When a barrister is briefed the solicitor will send him copies of all the documents in the case, together with statements from witnesses and an explanation of what has occurred. This involves repetition of work which would not be necessary if the same person could handle the case from beginning to end.

3 There would be more continuity. The client would deal with the same lawyer throughout the case instead of having his case transferred to a barrister whom he does not know. In criminal cases in the Crown Court research has shown that the majority of defendants do not meet their barrister until the day the trial starts.

4 Students would not have to decide on which profession to enter at such an early stage. All students would qualify as lawyers. Those who wished to become advocates would then go on to specialist training.

This idea has been recommended by the Lord Chancellor's advisory committee on legal education.

Disadvantages of fusion

1 Solicitors working in small firms would no longer have independent experts whom they could ask for opinions and advice on complicated points of law. Under the present system solicitors working anywhere in the country can go to a barrister for expert advice. This means that a solicitor in Cornwall or Northumbria can provide his clients with a full range of legal advice, which he could not do if there were no independent experts available. Under a fused system all lawyers would be working for their own firm and this would lead to two problems; first, it would be difficult to identify specialists and secondly, one firm of lawyers is not likely to go to a rival firm to ask advice.

2 The specialist skills of advocacy might be lost if more lawyers did court work. Although there would be compulsory training in advocacy

under fusion, at present top barristers appear in court almost every day and this regular work is likely to improve their skills. In a unified profession there is more likelihood of having lawyers who only occasionally do court work and who, as a result, will be less skilful.

3 At present barristers are obliged to accept the first case offered to them in their field of work, provided they are not already briefed to appear in court on that day. This is known as the 'cab rank' principle. It is important because it makes sure that anyone can get representation, even if their case is unpopular or not likely to succeed. This principle does not apply to solicitors and would be difficult to operate in a unified profession.

4 A barrister is more detached from the case and so will be more objective. There is also the point that 'two heads are better than one'.

5 Finally, those against fusion argue that the savings in cost to the client will be very small since solicitors' overheads are much greater than those of barristers. Also only a small amount of extra work will be saved as the same number of witnesses will have to be interviewed, the same documents will have to be prepared and the case will last the same length of time in court. It is probable that there would still be specialisation within the firm of lawyers so that one lawyer would deal with all the preliminary stages and then hand the case over to another lawyer to do the court work.

6.4 Legal executives

Apart from solicitors and barristers, there are also legal executives who work in solicitors' firms. To become a legal executive it is necessary to pass the Part I and Part II examinations of the Institute of Legal Executives and to have worked in a firm of solicitors or an organisation such as the Crown Prosecution Service for at least five years. Legal executives will often deal with the more straightforward cases themselves, for example, preparing simple wills or leases. They also have some limited rights to appear in court, mainly making applications in the County Court where the case is not defended. The partners in the firm of solicitors for whom the legal executive works are responsible for his or her work.

A C T I V I T Y

Read the following passage and then answer the questions below.

Support for fusion has come from a variety of quarters, including, for example, the Trades Union Congress. In its evidence to the Royal Commission on Legal Services (the Benson Commission) the Congress argued that fusion would enable firms to provide efficient and cheaper services; it was of the opinion that specialisms would be best maintained and enhanced within a united legal profession. Certainly, with the recent trend towards mergers amongst solicitors' firms, so individual solicitors will increasingly concentrate on specialist areas.

And the question has also been raised as to how far solicitors should be able to form partnerships with other professions such as accountants. Since 1988 the Law Society has permitted solicitors to form arrangements with building societies, estate agents and housing developers for the introduction of new work, but solicitors are still prohibited from participating in 'all-in' conveyancing packages. A direct relationship between the client and the solicitor has to continue.

(*Source:* Adapted from Paul Denham, *Law: a Modern Introduction,* Hodder & Stoughton, 1994.)

1 Why did the Trades Union Congress support fusion of the legal profession?
2 Do you agree that the two legal professions should be fused? Give reasons for your answer.
3 Are solicitors allowed to form partnerships with other professions?
4 What would be the advantages in having several professions working together in the same partnership?

6.5 Judges

Judges as a group are also called the judiciary. There are many different levels of judge although the main division is into inferior and superior judges. This may sound an odd way of referring to judges but it reflects the different levels of court in which they sit. Inferior judges include:

- stipendiary magistrates
- district judges
- recorders
- circuit judges

Superior judges are:

- the puisne judges who sit in the High Court
- the Lords Justices of Appeal in the Court of Appeal
- the Law Lords in the House of Lords

To become a judge at any level it is necessary to be either a barrister or a solicitor. The Courts and Legal Services Act 1990 made changes basing qualifications on certificates of advocacy and rights of audience in the courts. In other words, a barrister or solicitor must have been qualified to be an advocate in the court to which he is appointed as a judge. The Courts and Legal Services Act also introduced a type of career structure for judges, with the possibility of being promoted from a lower judicial office to the next one up on the ladder. Prior to the Act it was very rare for a judge to be promoted from one court to a higher court except from the High Court to the Court of Appeal and it was impossible for solicitors to progress further than a circuit judgeship. No matter how good a judge a solicitor was he could not be appointed as a High Court judge; this was clearly wrong as the best judges should be able to be promoted. The first High Court judge to come from solicitor circuit judges was Sir Michael Sachs, who was appointed in 1993.

Stipendiary magistrates

The qualification for this position is to have practised for at least seven years as a barrister or a solicitor. The appointment is made by the Queen on the Lord Chancellor's recommendation. They work in Magistrates' Courts in cities, the majority being in London. There can be a maximum of 100 and in 1999 there were about 90, of whom about 20 per cent were women.

District judges

To become a district judge it is necessary to have been a solicitor for at least seven years. They are appointed by the Lord Chancellor and work in the County Court, that is, doing civil work, hearing small claims cases and others up to a limit of £5,000. They also have responsibility for the administration of the court.

Recorders

A recorder must have practised as a barrister or a solicitor for at least 10 years and it is usual to be a deputy recorder before being appointed. They are part-time judges, usually sitting for one month a year and continuing to work as a barrister or a solicitor for the rest of the time. The appointment is for three years and their work is normally in the Crown Court, although they can also be asked to sit to hear cases in the County Court.

Circuit judges

To become a circuit judge it is necessary to have practised as a barrister for 10 years **or** to have held a certificate of advocacy in the Crown Court for 10 years **or** to have been a recorder for three years. This allows solicitors to become circuit judges and they make up about 10 per cent of all circuit judges. The Courts and Legal Services Act 1990 also allows for promotion after being a district judge, stipendiary magistrate or chairman of an industrial tribunal for at least three years. These proposals widen the pool for appointments considerably and should lead to a better cross-section amongst the judges. There has been much criticism that recorders and circuit judges tend to be male and white. At the beginning of 1999 there were only 36 women out of 558 Circuit judges. Circuit judges sit in both the Crown Court and the County Court and so hear both civil and criminal cases.

High Court judges (puisne judges)

Until the Courts and Legal Services Act 1990 all High Court judges were chosen from the Bar. The qualification was 10 years' practice as a barrister. Now it is also possible for a circuit judge to be promoted to the High Court bench after at least two years as a circuit judge. This should widen the pool for judicial appointments as it breaks the Bar's monopoly. As already noted, the first solicitor was appointed to the High Court in 1993. Although there have been a small number of women judges in the Family Division or its predecessor, the Probate, Divorce and Admiralty Division for a number of years, it was not until 1992 that the first female appointment to the Queen's Bench Division was made and 1993 when the first woman judge in the Chancery Division was appointed. In 1999 there were just eight women out of more than 90 High Court judges and no judge from any ethnic minority.

The appointment of High Court judges is made by the Queen on the advice of the Lord Chancellor.

Each division of the High Court has its own head or chief judge. In the Chancery Division this is the Lord Chancellor, but as he is too busy to sit there is a Vice Chancellor. In the Queen's Bench Division the Lord Chief Justice is the head and in the Family Division there is a President.

Lords Justices of Appeal

These sit in the Court of Appeal, together with the Lord Chief Justice, who is the head of the Criminal Division of the court, and the Master of the Rolls who is the head of the Civil Division of the court. The qualifications for these judges are that they must either be a practising barrister or have held a High Court certificate in advocacy for at least 10 years **or** be an existing High Court judge. This last is the more usual route and almost all Lords Justices of Appeal will have previously been a High Court judge. As solicitors can now be High Court judges it means that it will be possible for a solicitor to become a judge in the Court of Appeal but to date (1999) no solicitors have been appointed. They are appointed by the Queen, after having been nominated by the Prime Minister, though presumably he/she first consults the Lord Chancellor. There has only been one woman judge (Lady Butler-Sloss).

Lords of Appeal in Ordinary

These are also known as the Law Lords, and with the Lord Chancellor they form the Judicial Committee of the House of Lords. To be a Law

Lord it is necessary to have held high judicial office in England and Wales, Scotland or Northern Ireland for at least two years or to have been a barrister or the equivalent for 15 years. The appointment is made by the Queen, though the Law Lords are nominated by the Prime Minister, again presumably after consulting the Lord Chancellor. Law Lords are made life peers and are entitled to sit in the House of Lords and take part in the law-making process. At the time of writing (1999), there has never been a woman appointed as a Law Lord.

Background of judges

A survey in 1999 of 692 judges by Labour Research found that 69% of judges had been to public school and 64% to Oxford or Cambridge University. The average age of the judiciary was 60. As well as the low numbers of women, the survey also found that ethnic minority judges made up less than one per cent of the total.

Criticisms

The method of appointing judges has been subject to criticism, though some of the problems have been resolved by the Courts and Legal Services Act 1990 which, as already stated, has made solicitors eligible for appointment and provided a career structure with promotion possibilities. There are three main criticisms:

1 *The Lord Chancellor has too much power.* This can lead to criticisms of political bias, since the Lord Chancellor is himself appointed by the Prime Minister and changes with the Government. It is suggested that a Judicial Appointments Commission should be responsible for selection.

2 *Secrecy of the present system.* At the moment the system relies on word of mouth and the confidential opinion of existing judges and senior members of the Bar.

Since April 1995 vacancies for circuit judges and district judges have been advertised and shortlisted applicants will face formal interviews with a panel which includes a serving judge, an official from the Lord Chancellor's Department and a lay person. The interview panel will put their view to the Lord

Chancellor, but he will keep the right to make the final decision. However, High Court appointments still depend on the Lord Chancellor inviting people to become judges.

3 There are not enough *women judges* or judges from *ethnic minorities*.

Retirement

All judges appointed since 1995 have to retire at 70 years of age. This age was introduced by the Judicial Pensions and Retirement Act 1993. Judges appointed before that date can continue in office until the age of 75. Before 1959 there was no retirement age and some judges sat until they were 90!

Dismissal

Superior judges have security in their positions, in that they cannot be dismissed by the Government or the Lord Chancellor. This right originated in the Act of Settlement 1701, which allowed them to hold office whilst of good behaviour. The same provision is now contained in the Supreme Court Act 1981 for High Court judges and Lords Justices of Appeal and the Appellate Jurisdiction Act 1876 for the Law Lords. Although they hold office during good behaviour, there is power to remove a judge who misbehaves. This can only be done by the Queen if requested to do so by means of an address presented to her by both Houses of Parliament. The only exception is the Lord Chancellor who is a member of the Government and can be dismissed by the Prime Minister at any time and in any event will cease to be Lord Chancellor if a general election should lead to a change of party in government.

Since 1701 no English judge has been removed from office under the provisions, though an Irish judge (Sir Jonah Barrington) was removed in 1830 when he misappropriated £700 from court funds and fled to France!

Inferior judges are not so secure in their positions as the Lord Chancellor has the power to dismiss them on the grounds of incapacity or misbehaviour (Courts Act 1971, s. 17(4)). However in practice the Lord Chancellor has only used this power once, in 1983 when a circuit judge (Bruce Campbell) was convicted of evading customs duty on cigarettes and whisky.

6.6 Doctrine of the separation of powers and judicial independence

The theory of the separation of powers was first put forward by Montesquieu in the eighteenth century. The theory is that, in order to safeguard the liberty of the citizen, the three primary functions of the State must be exercised by separate and independent bodies. This means that each arm of the State keeps a check on the others.

These functions are:

- legislative – making laws
- executive – administering the law
- judicial – enforcing the law

Some countries, in particular the United States of America, have written constitutions which clearly set out that there should be separation of the powers. In the United Kingdom, although we have no written constitution, our government is still based on the idea that the three organs are more or less separate.

Our system is:

- legislative – Parliament
- executive – the Cabinet
- judicial – an independent judiciary

There is some overlap since members of the Cabinet are also members of Parliament, but the Lord Chancellor is the only person to be involved in all three areas. (*See* 6.7 for further information on the Lord Chancellor.)

It is thought to be important that the judiciary is independent. Judges are independent in the following ways:

1 *Independent of Parliament.*

   a judges cannot be members of the House of Commons, with the exception of recorders who are only part-time judges;

   b judges can, however, sit in the House of Lords. The Law Lords are life peers and can take part in debates during the legislative function, **but** by convention they do not take part in very political debates;

   c by convention a judge cannot be personally criticised by Parliament. The law can be criticised but not the judge.

2 *Independent of the executive.*

  a superior judges are in a particularly strong position as they cannot be removed from office by the Lord Chancellor or the Prime Minister or even on the decision of the entire Cabinet. Only the Queen can remove them and then only after receiving a petition from both Houses of Parliament;

  b however inferior judges can be removed by the Lord Chancellor.

3 *Independent financially.* Judicial salaries are paid from the consolidated fund. This secures their payment even if Parliament does not meet. It also means that the salaries do not have to be authorised by an annual vote, unlike the civil service. However judges are not protected from changes made by statute as to the terms upon which they hold office. This was shown in 1993 when Parliament passed the Judicial Pensions and Retirement Act which changed the retirement age for judges and the length of time they had to serve in order to get a full pension.

4 *Independent from politics.* This is true only in the sense that they cannot be Members of Parliament. This is one of the areas of greatest criticism. Judges are accused of being too conservative and too pro-establishment. Various decisions made by the House of Lords appear to support this idea. For example there have been some anti-trade union decisions, one of which was in *Rookes* v. *Barnard* (1964). This decision so displeased the governing Labour party that it introduced the Trade Disputes Act 1965 to overrule it. Another case was the GCHQ decision in 1984, where the Law Lords upheld a minister's decision to withdraw the right to trade union membership without consultation, on the grounds of national security.

5 *Independent from pressure.*

  a immunity from suit – this means that they cannot be sued for actions or decisions made in the course of their judicial duties. The fact that no-one can sue a judge because of his decision was confirmed in the case of *Sirros* v. *Moore* (1975), where Lord Denning felt that the principle ought to apply to all judges to make sure 'that they may be free in thought and independent in judgment'. The rule applies to any decision that is within their powers **and** to any decision outside their powers provided they acted in good faith. The Courts and Legal Services Act 1990 extended this immunity to magistrates;

  b security of tenure of office means that judges cannot be pressured into making decisions favourable to the Government. They know that the Government cannot dismiss them just because it does not approve of a decision.

Judges are **not** independent in the following ways:

1 *As to appointment.* There are political overtones in appointments. The Prime Minister chooses the Lord Chancellor, who can be described as the linchpin of our judicial system. Often the Lord Chancellor has been very active in politics before his appointment, though this was not true of the last holder of the office, Lord Mackay of Clashfern.
There is also the fact that the Prime Minister nominates the most senior judges. These are:

- the Law Lords
- the Lords Justices of Appeal
- the Lord Chief Justice
- the Master of the Rolls
- the President of the Family Division

The remaining members of the judiciary are nominated by the Lord Chancellor.

2 *As to social background.* Judges tend to come from the same type of background, especially the judges in the High Court and above. Many of these will have been to a public school and then to either Oxford or Cambridge University. One judge, Lord Justice Scrutton, wrote about how difficult it was to be impartial: 'This is rather difficult to obtain in any system. I am not speaking of conscious partiality, but the habits you are trained in, the people with whom you mix lead to your having a certain class of ideas of such a nature that when you deal with other ideas you do not give as sound and accurate judgments as you would wish.' In November 1993 it was announced that judges would receive training in racial awareness.

6.7 The Lord Chancellor

Lord Irvine, Lord Chancellor

The Lord Chancellor is appointed by the Prime Minister and remains in office until either there is a general election or the Prime Minister decides to replace him. In this way it is clear that the appointment is a political one.

The role of the Lord Chancellor is very important and wide-ranging. He is:

a a member of the Cabinet;

b Speaker of the House of Lords;

c the key figure in the appointment of judges and magistrates;

d head of the Chancery Division and he can sit as a judge there;

e a judge in the House of Lords;

f responsible for overseeing the legal aid schemes;

g responsible for the work of the Council on Tribunals;

h responsible for the work of the Law Commission;

i responsible for certain administrative bodies such as the Land Registry and the Public Trustee Office.

As already noted earlier he is the one person who is involved with each of the three elements of government: legislature, executive and judiciary. In order to assist him with his wide range of duties he has a staff of over a thousand people working in the Lord Chancellor's Department.

6.8 The Attorney-General

The Attorney-General is a member of Parliament and the Government, but he is not a member of the Cabinet. He is chosen by the Prime Minister and is usually a barrister. He is one of the Law Officers of the Government, the other being his deputy the Solicitor-General, and his main function is to advise the Government on any necessary legal points. As he is a barrister he will sometimes personally prosecute in an important criminal case, for example, treason. For some offences the Attorney-General's consent is necessary before a prosecution can be started. Such offences include corruption, possessing explosive substances and hijacking. He also has the right to refer criminal cases to the Court of Appeal for a point of law to be considered and he can appeal against a sentence he considers to be too lenient.

The Attorney-General appoints the Director of Public Prosecutions.

6.9 The Director of Public Prosecutions

The position of the Director of Public Prosecutions (DPP) was established as long ago as 1879, but the duties are now set out in the Prosecution of Offences Act 1985. This Act created the Crown Prosecution Service and made the DPP head of that service. The DPP has the power to take over the prosecution of any criminal case. The DPP also has a duty to advise the police on points of law, when asked by them to do so. The first woman DPP (Mrs Barbara Mills) was appointed in 1992. The DPP has to make a yearly report to the Attorney-General on the work of the Crown Prosecution Service and the DPP's department.

6.10 The Crown Prosecution Service

Before 1986 the police were responsible for bringing almost all prosecutions before the courts. This meant that different methods and standards applied in the different police areas and led to more people being prosecuted in some areas than in other areas. In order to get a uniform system throughout the country the Crown Prosecution Service (CPS) was created and started work in 1986. Crown Prosecutors can be either barristers or solicitors and there is also a large support staff. Initially the Service could not recruit enough lawyers and this caused some inefficiency, but by 1993 the Service was virtually up to full strength.

Once the police have charged a person with a crime the papers go to the Crown Prosecution Service and they take over the conduct of the case. The police criticise the Service for dropping too many of the charges or reducing the charge originally made by the police to a less serious one. In 1993–4 the Crown Prosecution Service discontinued nearly 200,000 cases started by the police. The DPP defended the decision to discontinue so many cases, pointing out that in many there was insufficient evidence to prove the case, while in others it was not in the public interest to continue (for example the defendant had already been convicted and was in prison for another crime). Crown Prosecutors will appear in the Magistrates' Courts to conduct cases, but they do not have rights of audience in the Crown Court. This means that they have to brief another barrister to appear in court on the case. The CPS is trying to get this rule changed, so that qualified lawyers working for the CPS have the same rights of audience as lawyers in private practice. The CPS feels that the present system causes unnecessary costs and delays; using their own 'in-house' lawyers would be more efficient.

7 *Legal aid and advice*

Since the law is complicated, it is clear that most people will need advice on any legal problem they may have. A large part of the work of solicitors is advising individuals and companies on various aspects of law. For the ordinary person there are three main difficulties in getting advice from a solicitor. The first is lack of knowledge. Many people do not know where their nearest solicitor is located or if they do know this they do not know which solicitor specialises in the type of law needed in their case. The second problem is that often people have a fear of dealing with lawyers; they feel intimidated. The final problem is one of cost. Solicitors charge from about £80 per hour for advice from a local solicitor in a small town to over £300 per hour for advice from a top firm of solicitors in London. In order to help people on low incomes there are several schemes which provide advice free.

7.1 Citizens Advice Bureaux

The Citizens Advice Bureaux (CAB) were first set up in 1938 and today there are about 700 throughout the country so that most towns will have a bureau. They issue general advice to anyone on a variety of points including legal matters, but the staff are not usually legally qualified. They can also provide a list of local solicitors and information on which ones do legal aid work. The bureaux have schemes under which they can refer people to certain solicitors who are prepared to offer a short interview at a very low cost or even free and some have an arrangement where local solicitors take it in turn to attend once a week or fortnight at the Citizens Advice Bureau to give advice to people.

The Benson Commission in 1979 emphasised the importance of Citizens Advice Bureaux as a first tier legal advice service as they are local and easily accessible. Benson recommended they should be staffed by 'para-legals', that is non-lawyers who have had some legal training, and given more government funding. This has not happened. Most bureaux rely on volunteers for staffing although Local Authority grants do pay for some training, and many CAB volunteers have built up very considerable expertise in welfare law.

A C T I V I T Y

Find out where your nearest Citizens Advice Bureau is situated.

7.2 Law centres

The first law centre opened in 1970 in North Kensington and its aim was to provide an easily accessible service, which was not intimidating and to which local people could turn for guidance as they would to their family doctor, or as someone who could afford it would turn to his family solicitor. The Legal Advice and Assistance Act 1972 provided for the establishment of further local law centres to offer free legal advice in areas where there are few solicitors. The intention was to provide a community or neighbourhood service in poorer areas, especially inner city areas. Law centres are staffed by full-time paid lawyers. The main problem has been the funding of such centres; central government provides some money, as do charities, but the centres are largely dependent on Local Authorities for funding. This has led to a patchy service. In 1994 there were only 53 centres and the number was declining because of problems over funding. The areas of work most commonly done by law centres include matters concerning housing (for example, tenants' rights), social security and other welfare rights, employment problems, planning and environmental issues and women's rights. In most of these areas legal aid is not available. Law centres will advise and represent people both in court and before tribunals.

7.3 Specialist organisations

For some problems it may be possible to get advice from a related organisation; in particular trade unions will help their members in work-related matters, while organisations such as the Automobile Association will help their members in motoring cases. There are also such schemes as the Bar's Free Representation Unit under which barristers will represent people in court free of charge.

7.4 Legal aid and related schemes

A government funded legal aid scheme to help those who cannot afford a lawyer has existed since 1949. However, under the Access to Justice Bill 1999 the system will be changed with a Community Legal Fund replacing legal aid. But at the moment most of the provisions are contained in the Legal Aid Act 1988. The purpose of the Act, as set out in section 1, is: 'to establish a framework for the provision ... of advice, assistance and representation which is publicly funded with a view to helping persons who might otherwise be unable to obtain advice, assistance or representation on account of their means'.

There are four main schemes set out in the 1988 Act. These are:

a an advice scheme called the Green Form Scheme;
b assistance by way of representation (ABWOR);
c legal aid for civil cases;
d legal aid for criminal cases.

These schemes, together with two other schemes that are available to people in criminal cases, are summarised in Figure 7.1 (p. 64).

For all the schemes it is necessary for the applicant to be below certain financial limits. The limits for each scheme are different but in all legal aid cases two figures are considered to decide if the applicant is eligible or not. These figures are the disposable income and the disposable capital. Disposable income is the amount left out of a person's income after deducting tax, National Insurance payments, rent or mortgage payments, council tax, pension contributions, union dues and other work expenses. Disposable capital is the assets owned by a person, such as money in a bank account or building society, stocks, shares or other investments and property, but not including their house.

7.5 Green form scheme

This scheme allows solicitors to do up to two hours' worth of work (three in matrimonial cases) for people on low incomes. The scheme is means tested and free for those below Income Support level. It enables the solicitor to give advice and to assist by, for example, writing letters. People can use the Green Form scheme to get advice on both civil and criminal matters. Since the 1988 Act the scheme has no longer been available for such areas as advice on conveyancing and drawing up wills, except for people over 70 years old or people who are handicapped.

Figure 7.1 Summary of legal aid and advice schemes

Green form scheme	Advice only – covers most civil and criminal cases, but NOT wills or conveyancing
ABWOR	Representation in court for civil cases in the Magistrates' Court and the Mental Health Review Tribunal and some other matters
Civil legal aid	Full representation – available for most cases in the County or High Court and Appeal Courts. NOT available for defamation, small claims or undefended divorces
Advice at police station	Available for anyone arrested and held at a police station
Duty Solicitor	Advice available for defendants in criminal cases at the Magistrates' Court
Criminal legal aid	Full representation for a defendant on a criminal charge

The main criticism of the scheme is that it is (in 1999) only available to single people with a disposable income of below £83 per week, provided they do not have disposable capital of more than £1,000. The allowances for people with dependants increase according to the number of dependants. Until 1993 the scheme was available to people on higher incomes, provided they paid a contribution towards the cost. This meant that someone receiving Invalidity Benefit used to be able to receive advice on payment of a contribution of about £12. Under the present income levels such a person is above the qualifying limit and cannot get advice at all through the Green Form scheme. They would have to see a solicitor privately at a cost of £150 or more for the two hours of advice. Prior to 1993 the scheme was a widely used service with about 1.5 million interviews being given per year under it. The Government admitted that the changes in eligibility cut the percentage of households which qualified for the scheme from 48 per cent to 21 per cent and the Law Society estimated that about 11.5 million people lost access to free or cheap advice as a result.

7.6 Assistance by way of representation

In order to give representation in court for some cases not covered by legal aid the Green Form scheme of advice was extended to give 'assistance by way of representation' (ABWOR). Under section 8 of the Legal Aid Act 1988 this is avail-

able for most civil proceedings in the Magistrates' Court, especially family cases; some criminal matters such as where the police apply for a warrant of further detention; and proceedings before Mental Health Review Tribunals.

The financial qualifying limits are more generous than for the Green Form scheme so that more people are eligible to use ABWOR. The limits are usually increased each year in line with inflation. In 1999–2000 any person whose disposable income was less than £75 per week did not have to pay towards their representation. Those whose disposable income was between £75 and £178 per week had to pay a contribution towards their legal costs. The further above the bottom limit of £75 per week the more the person would have to pay as a contribution. The maximum disposable capital allowed was £3,000.

7.7 Legal aid in civil cases

A legal aid order allows a solicitor to do all the necessary work in a case for his client including appearing in court or, where suitable, instructing a barrister to appear on behalf of the client.

The civil scheme is now run by the Legal Aid Board, but under the Access to Justice Bill, a new Legal Services Commission will take over in the future. Civil legal aid is available in most civil cases. But it is NOT available for:

a small claims;

b defamation cases;

c undefended divorce cases;

d most tribunal hearings (though it is available for the Employment Appeal Tribunal, the Lands Tribunal and Mental Health Review Tribunals are covered by ABWOR).

Eligibility

There is a means test and a merits test. On the **merits**, the client must show that he has reasonable grounds for taking or defending proceedings (s. 15(2), Legal Aid Act 1988). This means he must have a suitable cause of action and a reasonable chance of winning the case. A person can be refused legal aid if the Board think that although he would win his case he would gain only a trivial advantage from the proceedings. The application for legal aid goes to a local committee to consider the merits.

The **means** are assessed by the Department of Social Security at the moment, though there are provisions in the Act for the Legal Aid Board to take over this task if and when the Lord Chancellor decides that it should. The disposable income and the disposable capital are considered and there is a 'cut-off' point where the income and capital are considered too high for the person to qualify for legal aid. If a person's income and capital are below minimum figures laid down by the Lord Chancellor then that person will qualify to receive legal aid free; if the income and capital are above those minimum figures but below set maximums, legal aid will be granted on payment of a contribution; if either the income or the capital is above the set maximums then legal aid will not be granted.

For 1999–2000 the figures were:

	Disposable income	Disposable capital
Minimum amount	£2,680 p.a.	£3,000
Maximum amount	£7,940 p.a.	£6,750

The upper level is higher for people making a claim for personal injury, and pensioners on low levels of income will have some of their capital disregarded when calculations are made.

If the person qualifies, an offer of legal aid is made to him and he must accept it before a legal aid certificate is issued. If he has to pay a contribution, the amount of the contribution is now 1/36

of any excess over the minimum level and this has to be paid monthly for the life of the case.

The statutory charge

At the end of a case a person who has been successfully legally aided will be asked to pay any shortfall in costs out of his damages (Legal Aid Act 1988, s. 16). This is called the clawback and can mean that a claimant gains very little by bringing the case.

Criticisms

There are many criticisms of the legal aid system.

1 *The financial limits on the means test are too low.* Only the very poor now qualify for legal aid and this does not conform with the original idea of a legal aid scheme.

2 *The rates of pay are too low.* The rates are fixed by the Government and are well below the fees charged by private solicitors. This means that many solicitors refuse to do legal aid work as the rates do not even cover their overheads. The problem has increased in the last 10 years. For example in 1991 the Law Society cited one case where a woman wanting an injunction for domestic violence was turned away by 26 firms of solicitors in South London.

3 The fact that legal aid is not available at all for most tribunal cases can put an individual at a severe disadvantage as often such cases are against an employer or a government department which will employ a lawyer to represent their side.

Legal Aid

Conditional fees

Because most people are not eligible for legal aid, lawyers are now allowed to offer what is called a 'no-win, no-fee' service. This means that the lawyer will set a price for the case which will be paid only if the case is won. In some cases a small amount will be paid at the start and then an increased amount if the case is won. In other cases the agreement may be that nothing at all will be paid if the case is lost.

At the beginning, conditional fees were only allowed in cases where the claim was for personal injuries. However, the Access to Justice Bill, which is likely to become law in late 1999, allows conditional fees to be used in almost any case. The main exception where they are not allowed is family cases.

There are two main problems with conditional fees. The first is that, although the person taking the case knows how much his or her own lawyer is going to charge, they may still have to pay the costs of the other side if they lose the case and this could be a much larger amount. To help with this problem it is possible to insure against losing the case. The second problem is that people with a difficult case are unlikely to find a lawyer who is prepared to take the case on a 'no-win, no-fee' basis. This affects people with cases such as claiming for injuries because of medical negligence, where the success rate is low and the cost of getting expert evidence is high.

7.8 Legal aid in criminal cases

As with civil legal aid, a legal aid order will entitle the client to full representation throughout all phases of a case. This means that a solicitor can not only advise and do all the work in preparation for a trial, he can also appear in court to act for the defendant or, where appropriate, brief a barrister to represent the defendant.

Under the 1988 Legal Aid Act there are provisions for the Legal Aid Board to take over the administration of criminal legal aid but at the moment the courts administer it. Once a person has been charged with a criminal offence he can apply to the Magistrates' Court where his case will be dealt with, either for the trial or for the preliminary stages prior to the case being sent to the Crown Court for trial. He has to fill in a form explaining what he has been charged with and any special reasons why he should get legal aid as well as giving details of his income and capital. The application is dealt with by the clerk of the court who looks at the merits and also at the defendant's financial position.

Merits test

The basic test is whether it is in the interests of justice for the defendant to be given legal aid. Under section 21 of the Legal Aid Act a defendant **must** be given aid if:

a the charge is murder; or
b the prosecution is appealing to the House of Lords.

For other cases the Lord Chancellor has issued guidance on what is meant by 'the interests of justice'. There are five categories of factors to be considered by the clerk. These are:

1 Is the defendant likely to lose his liberty or his job or is there a risk of serious damage to his reputation?
2 Does the case involve a substantial point of law?
3 Is the defendant able to understand the proceedings and state his own case? If the defendant cannot speak English or is deaf, he should be granted legal aid.
4 Is it necessary to trace and interview witnesses or does the case involve the need for expert cross-examination of a witness?
5 Is representation desirable in the interests of another person, for example a child witness in a sex abuse case?

These are only guidelines and other factors may be considered. If there is any doubt as to whether legal aid should be granted then that doubt should be resolved in the defendant's favour (Legal Aid Act 1988 s. 21(7)). The decision on the merits is left to the clerk, with the result that some courts grant legal aid more readily than other courts. In the early 1980s the refusal rates for cases which were tried in Magistrates' Courts varied from 4 per cent to 40 per cent. In the early 1990s the position was much the same, as research by

Young and McNair showed. They put in the same six applications for legal aid to different courts and in each court two clerks considered the applications, so that there were twelve identical cases dealt with by each court. One court granted legal aid in ten out of the twelve cases, while two courts granted legal aid in only five cases. It is clearly wrong that the chances of someone being granted legal aid should be so variable. Their report, 'In the interests of Justice', was published in 1992 by the Legal Aid Board.

Financial limits

Criminal legal aid will be granted free if the defendant's disposable income is less than £51 per week and the disposable capital is less than £3,000 (1999–2000 figures). Above these figures, legal aid will be granted only if the defendant pays a contribution. The contribution is £1 for every £3 or part of £3 by which the disposable income exceeds £51. This amount must be paid each week for as long as the case lasts. In addition any excess capital will also be payable. Prior to 1993 the disposable income limits were much greater (£65 per week in 1992) and critics argue that the present levels of contribution are too high.

Apart from legal aid in criminal cases there are two special schemes designed to give free advice to people in criminal cases. These are:

- advice and assistance for persons in police stations
- the provision of a duty solicitor at Magistrates' Courts

7.9 Advice and assistance for persons in police stations

This scheme was set up under the Police and Criminal Evidence Act 1984. Local solicitors operate a rota scheme so that theoretically there is a solicitor on duty in a 24-hour service to give advice to anyone who is being held at a police station. There is no means test or merits test and the service is free. Suspects do not have to use the scheme. They may choose instead to pay their own solicitor to attend the police station and advise them. Research by Sanders and others in 1989 showed that only about 20 per cent of those

held in the 10 police stations surveyed received legal advice under the Duty Solicitor scheme and often that advice was given over the telephone.

7.10 Duty solicitor at the Magistrates' court

Originally the provision of a duty solicitor at the Magistrates' Court was a voluntary service, but it became statutory in 1982 and is now covered by the Legal Aid Act 1988. Local solicitors take it in turn to attend when the Magistrates' Court is sitting in order to give advice to any person appearing there who is not represented. There is no means test or merits test and the defendant is not required to pay any contribution. The duty solicitor is, however, limited in what he may do. He can give advice in most cases but can only appear in court to:

a   apply for bail;
b   appear for a client who is at risk of going to prison for non-payment of a fine or breach of any other order;
c   finish a case where the defendant is in custody, usually when the defendant is pleading guilty.

The solicitor will also help people to apply for legal aid if they qualify for it.

Examination questions

1 Legal aid is available for both civil and criminal cases. It is available for most civil actions though it is not generally available for undefended divorce and defamation or in tribunals. The applicant must also qualify financially.

In criminal cases there are also financial limitations and, in addition, the court must consider that it is in the interests of justice that legal aid be granted.

In each of the following situations, explain whether or not legal aid would be granted, giving reasons for your answer.

a   Samantha was involved in a car accident caused by Terry. As a result of this she

was sacked from her job and is still unemployed. She wishes to take action against both Terry and her ex-employer.
(4 marks)

b Una, who has a low paid, part-time delivery job, has been charged with a minor motoring offence before her local Magistrates' Court. The offence carries three penalty points and Una already has 10 penalty points on her licence. (Drivers can be disqualified when they reach 12 penalty points on their licence.)
(4 marks)

SEG 1993

2 Study the extract below and then answer **all** parts of the question which follows.

CUTS TO HIT LEGAL AID

The Lord Chancellor yesterday refused to retreat on his policy of cutting back on legal aid spending and solicitors' fees. The Law Society national conference in Birmingham listened in silence and gave Lord Mackay only hesitant applause for a speech in which he announced:

Tougher means tests for people seeking legal aid,
Greater efforts to settle divorce disputes out of court,
Standard fees in magistrates courts this year, with a later extension to Crown Courts, and
No-win, no-fee arrangements to be allowed soon.

Access

Lord Mackay warned the conference: 'Legal aid cannot continue to take an ever-increasing share of public expenditure. It must be more affordable – and it must be better targeted towards those whose need is greatest and areas where it is most cost-effective.

'Expenditure on legal aid is now £1.1 billion a year gross – more than double what it was a mere four years ago. If the trend continues, it will be near £2 billion by the middle of the decade. In 1991–2, when inflation was around 4 per cent, legal aid rates went up by 7 per cent. Every extra pound for legal aid means a pound less for the NHS, for schools, for social security or for the infrastructure of the economy.

'Giving reasonable access to justice while controlling costs would involve a radical rethink which might be uncomfortable for some solicitors. I do wonder whether certain aspects of the eligibility regime are quite right. For the most part it is right, even though it can produce odd results, as when the Press reports that someone who by most people's standards would be considered rich has been awarded legal aid. I am concerned, however, that the approach towards means testing legal aid is out of step with that adopted for other means-tested benefits.'

On divorce cases, the Lord Chancellor said: 'I would like wider use of mediation, which avoids some of the disputes now settled through matrimonial legal aid. There should be incentives to reach agreement.'

Budget

A Law Society spokesman said the proposals would reduce drastically the number of firms handling legal aid work and he added: 'It raises the question whether the public would have general free access to legal advice when they need it most.' Standard fees would mean contractual changes as dramatic as those recently introduced for Health Service doctors.

Shadow Home Secretary Tony Blair said: 'Any attempt to slash the legal aid budget would be disastrous for the many ordinary citizens to whom access to the courts would be denied.'

(*Source:* Adapted from *The Mail on Sunday*, October 25, 1992.)

a i Explain the difference between legal advice and legal aid. *(4 marks)*
ii Name **four** places where legal advice can be obtained. *(4 marks)*
b i Name the Lord Chancellor who made the speech. *(1 mark)*
ii The Lord Chancellor commented on a number of different things.

Explain what he meant by

1 a 'means test'; *(3 marks)*

2 'no-win, no-fee arrangements';

(3 marks)

3 'mediation' in divorce cases. *(3 marks)*

c **i** What is the Law Society? *(2 marks)*

ii Why do you think the Law Society national conference was not too happy with the Lord Chancellor's proposals?

(4 marks)

d In 1979, 70 per cent of the population qualified for the various Legal services funded by the Government. By 1989, that percentage had dropped to 50 per cent with a further drop to 37 per cent by 1992.

i Assuming the Lord Chancellor's proposals were implemented, what would be the likely effect on this percentage figure?

ii Who would be the likely winners and losers under these proposals?

Give reasons for your answers. *(8 marks)*

e Assuming the resources could be made available, what changes would you like to see introduced which would improve the current systems of Government funded legal aid and advice? *(8 marks)*

Total: 40 marks

SEG 1994

8 *Sources of law (1)*

So far in this book we have been looking at the system which exists for enforcing the law. We must now consider how the law is made. Where do we get our law from? The answer is a number of different places or sources. This is why lawyers use the phrase 'sources of law'. It refers to the different roots from which English law comes.

8.1 Common Law

The origins of our law today can be traced back to the Norman conquest in 1066. In order to keep control of the conquered land it was necessary that the King should control, among other things, the law. So William the Conqueror set up the Curia Regis (or King's Court) and appointed his own judges. These judges applied the laws that the Norman Kings made but, if there was no King's law, they used the laws or rules and customs that already existed in the country. The judges used to travel from London to all the areas of the country under the King's control in order to decide major disputes, usually those between the nobles of the time. In the reign of Henry II (1154–89) these tours of the country became more regular and the King divided up the country into 'circuits' or areas for the judges to visit. As the judges went to different areas of the country they found that some places had different local laws or customs from other places. Over a long period of time the judges, on their return to London, would discuss the different customs they had discovered and decide to use the best customs as laws throughout the country. This meant that the laws became common to all parts of the land. From this we get the phrase 'common law'. Common law also means that the law has come into being as a result of the judges' decisions. It is unwritten law in the sense that neither Parliament nor any other law-making body has written down that part of the law. Some very important areas of our law today are part of the common law; for example the crime of murder is defined by the common law, by the judges' decisions in several cases. Parliament has never defined murder, although it has passed an Act of Parliament stating the sentence for murder.

8.2 Judicial precedent

It is clear from the previous section that decisions by the judges are very important in English law. Judicial precedent refers to decisions by judges which create laws for later judges to follow. This source of law can also be called case law.

When a judge decides a case he makes a speech at the end of the case explaining what his decision is. This speech is called a judgment. In the County Court or High Court each case is heard by a single judge and so there is just one judgment. In the appeal courts (the Divisional Courts, the Court of Appeal and the House of Lords) there will be at least two judges and there can be up to seven judges in the House of Lords; as a result there may be speeches (judgments) from more than one judge. In each judgment the judge will give a summary of the facts of the case and explain the principle of law he is using to come to his decision. He may sometimes discuss what the law would have been if the facts had been different. These are called hypothetical situations. The important part of each judgment is the principle of law the judge is using to come to his decision. This is known as the *ratio decidendi*. These words are Latin and mean 'the reason for deciding'. The ratio decidendi is the part of the judgment that creates law (or a precedent) for future judges to follow. All the rest of the judgment is called *obiter dicta*. This means 'other things said'. The obiter dicta does not create binding law, although judges in subsequent cases may look at it and use it if they wish.

Precedent is based on another Latin phrase, *stare decisis*. This literally means 'stand by the decision' and expresses the idea that once a decision has been made in one case on a point of law, it is fair and just to keep to that decision in later cases. Most countries have the same basic rule about this, but the English legal system follows precedent more rigidly than other countries. This has not always been so. Up to the middle of the nineteenth century, judges had a flexible approach to precedent; they would usually follow past decisions, but did not feel obliged to do so. This meant that some judges even refused to follow decisions by the House of Lords if they believed that the decision was incorrect.

In the second half of the nineteenth century precedent became much more rigid. There were two main reasons for this. First, in 1873–5 the civil court system was reorganised by the Judicature Acts, so that there was a clear hierarchy, that is, each court had a definite place in the court structure. The system that was created is virtually the same as that in use today, with the House of Lords being the final court of appeal. The second factor was the creation in 1865 of the Incorporated Council of Law Reporting which meant that there were accurate reports of cases and judgments. Prior to the creation of this Council, reports of cases had been made by private individuals and often these law reports were too brief and not very accurate. These two facts led to a more rigid approach to precedent so that lower courts in the hierarchy are bound by the courts above them and the appeal courts are usually bound by their own past decisions. This is basically the doctrine of precedent as it applies today.

8.3 Hierarchy of the courts

The position of the court in the hierarchy is important. The more senior the court the more likely its decision will create a binding precedent, that is a precedent the other courts must follow. Figure 8.1 shows the hierarchy.

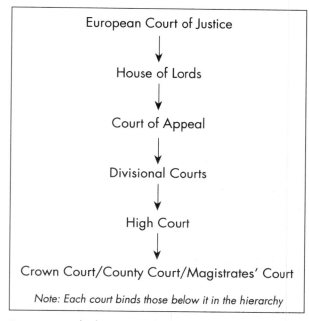

European Court of Justice

↓

House of Lords

↓

Court of Appeal

↓

Divisional Courts

↓

High Court

↓

Crown Court/County Court/Magistrates' Court

Note: Each court binds those below it in the hierarchy

Figure 8.1   The hierarchy of the courts

There are special rules about whether the appellate courts, that is, courts which hear appeals, are bound by their own past decisions. It is therefore necessary to consider each appellate court in turn.

European Court of Justice

On points of European law the decisions of the European Court of Justice are binding on all English courts. However this court is not bound by its own past decisions.

House of Lords

The House of Lords is the most senior court in England and Wales. Any decisions by the House of Lords must be followed by all other courts. However the House of Lords does not now have to follow its own previous decisions. This has not always been the position. At the end of the nineteenth century in a case called *London Street Tramways Co. Ltd.* v. *London County Council* (1898) the House of Lords decided that it would always follow its own past decisions. The reason for this was that the judges of the time felt that certainty in the law was very important. They argued that if they could decide cases in different ways it would be difficult for people to know what the law was and this could lead to more cases coming to court because the law was uncertain. Although this rule created certainty, judges realised that it also meant the law could not change to meet changing social conditions. Eventually in 1966 the Lord Chancellor issued a Practice Statement on behalf of himself and the other Law Lords which said:

Their Lordships regard the use of precedent as an indispensable foundation upon which to decide what is the law and its application to individual cases. It provides at least some degree of certainty upon which individuals can rely in the conduct of their affairs, as well as a basis for orderly development of legal rules.

Their Lordships nevertheless recognise that too rigid adherence to precedent may lead to injustice in a particular case and also unduly restrict the proper development of the law. They propose, therefore, to modify their present practice and, while treating former decisions of this House as normally binding, to depart from a previous decision when it appears right to do so . . .

This makes it clear that the House of Lords will normally follow its own past decisions, but it gives the judges flexibility so that they can refuse to follow a previous decision when 'it appears right to do so'. However, the House of Lords has been reluctant to use this flexibility because most Law Lords still feel that certainty is important in the law. The Practice Statement was used in *Herrington* v. *British Railways Board* (1972) to change the law in respect of the duty of care owed by the occupier of land to children who trespassed on the land. The previous decision had been made in 1929 when it was held that the occupier would only be liable for injuries suffered by the child if the occupier had caused those injuries deliberately or recklessly. In *Herrington* the Law Lords held that social and physical conditions had changed since 1929 and an occupier had

to take some care to protect child trespassers from coming to harm.

The House of Lords feels that it is especially important to have certainty in the criminal law but even here it has used the Practice Statement to overrule a past decision. The first criminal case in which this occurred was *R.* v. *Shivpuri* (1986) which involved the law of attempting to commit a crime.

Court of Appeal (Civil Division)

The Court of Appeal has to follow decisions by the European Court of Justice and the House of Lords. It is also bound to follow its own past decisions. This was decided by the Court of Appeal in *Young* v. *Bristol Aeroplane Co. Ltd.* (1944) where it held that it would be bound by its own past decisions with three exceptions. These exceptions are:

1 Where two previous decisions of the Court of Appeal conflict, the court may decide which to follow and which to reject.
2 Where there is a House of Lords decision which conflicts with a Court of Appeal decision, the court must follow the House of Lords decision and reject its own past decision.
3 Where a decision has been made *per incuriam*, that means, a decision made carelessly or by mistake, for example, not realising there was an Act of Parliament which affected the case.

These exceptions do not give any real flexibility to the Court of Appeal and in the 1970s Lord Denning, who was then head of the Civil Division of the Court of Appeal, felt that it should have the same flexibility as the House of Lords. Lord Denning's attempts to win this extra freedom for the Court of Appeal were ended when the House of Lords held in *Davis* v. *Johnson* (1978) that the rule in *Young* v. *Bristol Aeroplane Co. Ltd.* was still the law and the Court of Appeal must follow its own past decisions unless the case came within one of the three exceptions. There are two main reasons why this rule should continue. The first reason is that the Court of Appeal hears many more cases than the House of Lords and if it were able to override its own past decisions, the law would become very uncertain. Imagine a lawyer trying to advise a client as to what decision the court might come to in his case if the Court of Appeal was not bound by its own past decisions. The lawyer might have to say 'If the court follows the decision they made last week, you will win your case. But there was a similar case a month ago in which the court came to a different decision; if the court follows that decision you will lose your case.' The second reason for the Court of Appeal being bound by its own past decisions is that it is not the final court of appeal. In most cases there is a possibility of an appeal to the House of Lords who can correct any mistakes made by the Court of Appeal.

Court of Appeal (Criminal Division)

The Criminal Division of the Court of Appeal has a little more freedom than the Civil Division because criminal cases often involve the risk that the defendant will have to serve a lengthy prison sentence. This means that the Criminal Division,

as well as using the three exceptions allowed in *Young*'s case, will also refuse to follow a previous decision where it feels that the law was misapplied or misunderstood.

Divisional Courts

Divisional Courts operate the same rules as the Court of Appeal, so they are bound by their own past decisions unless the case comes within one of the three exceptions in *Young*'s case or it involves the liberty of the subject. They must, of course, follow decisions of the European Court, House of Lords and Court of Appeal.

High Court

The High Court has to follow decisions made by all the courts above but it is not bound by its own past decisions.

Figure 8.2 shows which courts' decisions bind other courts.

Figure 8.2 The courts and precedent

Court	Courts bound by it	Courts it must follow
European Court	All courts	None
House of Lords	All English courts	European Court
Court of Appeal	Divisional Courts High Court Crown Court County Court Magistrates' Court	European Court House of Lords
Divisional Courts	High Court Crown Court County Court Magistrates' Court	European Court House of Lords Court of Appeal
High Court	County Court Magistrates' Court	European Court House of Lords Court of Appeal Divisional Courts
Crown Court County Court Magistrates' Court	None	European Court House of Lords Court of Appeal Divisional Courts High Court

8.4 Precedent in operation

Binding precedent

When a case involves a point of law, the lawyers for both parties will research past cases in the Law Reports to try and find decisions that will help their client win the case. If there is a previous case on similar facts, the judge will consider that case and if the decision is by a court above him in the hierarchy, he must follow it. This is known as a *binding precedent*. So a precedent or past decision is binding only if the court making the decision is at the right level in the hierarchy and the facts of the second case are sufficiently similar.

If the point of law has never been decided before, the decision the judge comes to will form a new precedent for subsequent cases. This is known as an *original precedent* and again it will depend on the court's position in the hierarchy as to whether that precedent will be binding or not. An example of a new decision being made can be seen in *R.* v. *R.* (1991), which was a case about whether in law a husband could be guilty of raping his wife. The case started at Leicester Crown Court where the judge was asked to make a ruling on this point. The judge, a High Court judge, ruled that if a wife did not consent to sexual intercourse, her husband could be guilty of rape. Following this ruling the defendant appealed to the Court of Appeal (Criminal Division) on the ground that the judge had got the law wrong. The judges in the Court of Appeal agreed with the original judge and so their decision made an original precedent which would bind the Crown Court in any future cases but did not bind the House of Lords. The defendant appealed again, this time to the House of Lords, which also agreed that the act of 'marital rape' was a crime. This decision in the House of Lords made a binding precedent which all courts have to follow.

Persuasive precedent

Sometimes there is a past decision on a point of law but it does not have to be followed in a later case. However, the judge may still consider it and if he thinks that it was a correct decision he can decide to follow it. In this instance he has been persuaded by the previous decision and so it is called a *persuasive precedent*.

Persuasive precedents can result from a number of different situations.

1 Where the court that made the previous decision is lower in the hierarchy. This happened in *R.* v. *R.* (*see* previous paragraph) when the House of Lords agreed with the Court of Appeal.
2 When the court is not part of the English hierarchy of courts. This most often occurs with decisions made by the Judicial Committee of the Privy Council (*see* p. 41). Since the judges of the Privy Council are highly respected, the Court of Appeal or House of Lords may decide to follow their decisions.
3 Where the statement on law in the previous case was not the reason for deciding but was obiter dicta. This happened in deciding when duress (being forced to commit a crime) could be a defence for someone charged with murder. In *R.* v. *Howe* (1987), the House of Lords ruled that duress could not be a defence to the crime of murder; this was the ratio decidendi of the case. The judges in their judgment also commented that duress would not be a defence for someone charged with attempted murder. This comment was obiter dicta, that is, it was not the reason for deciding the case of *Howe*. When in 1991 a case occurred in which a defendant charged with attempted murder tried to argue that he could use the defence of duress, the Court of Appeal considered the obiter dicta statement in *Howe* and were 'persuaded' to follow it.
4 Where the statement made on the law is by a dissenting judge. When there are three or more judges deciding a case the decision can be by a majority, for example, two to one. The decision of the majority forms a binding precedent but the judge who disagrees with the majority is entitled to give his own view of the law and this is called a dissenting judgment. In later cases it is possible that judges may decide they prefer the dissenting judgment and are persuaded to follow it.

Overruling

This is the term used where a later court decides that the law in a previous case was wrongly decided. This occurred in the case of *Herrington*, which we have already looked at (*see* p. 72). Here the House of Lords decided to overrule the old decision made in 1929.

Reversing

This occurs on an appeal when a higher court rules that the lower court made the wrong decision in the same case. So a decision by the Court of Appeal could be reversed if the losing party successfully appealed against the Court of Appeal's decision to the House of Lords.

Distinguishing

This is a method used by judges to avoid following what would otherwise be a binding precedent. The judge will point out some difference in the facts between the previous precedent and the present case he is trying. That is, he draws a distinction between the two cases. As a result he can say that he need not follow the previous decision because it was based on a different set of facts.

8.5 Advantages and disadvantages of judicial precedent

As with all systems there are both advantages and disadvantages to the system of precedent as it is operated in the courts of England and Wales.

Advantages

1 *Certainty*. The strict hierarchy of the courts means that it is often possible to state with certainty what the courts' decision will be on a given set of facts. In particular this makes it easier for people to organise their businesses and make contracts. They know what the effect of a particular term in a contract will be. It also makes it easier for lawyers to advise their clients on what to do and what the law is. As a result fewer cases will need to go to court for a decision.
2 *Flexibility*. Although there is certainty, there is also room for the law to grow and change with changing conditions. In this the House of Lords' Practice Statement is very important, since it allows this flexibility. Distinguishing

gives flexibility too, as judges can use it to avoid following past decisions which they feel are not suitable to the present case.
3 *Precision*. Since there are about half a million reported cases, there is a vast amount of detail in the law. It would be difficult to write as much detail into a code of law.
4 *Examples*. All decisions are based on true facts and so the law is illustrated by real cases. Having real examples makes it easier to understand the law and to apply it to future cases.

Disadvantages

For each of the above advantages it is possible to argue that there is a corresponding disadvantage.

1 *Rigidity*. It is claimed that our system is too rigid. The law is not merely certain, it is too difficult to change. Critics argue that the House of Lords is too unwilling to use its power in the Practice Statement to overrule old decisions even when judges in the House of Lords themselves agree the old law is wrong.
2 *Illogical distinctions*. When distinguishing is used to avoid a previous decision, there is the risk that the judge may distinguish the two cases on a very small point that is difficult to justify.
3 *Bulk and complexity*. Having such a large number of cases to illustrate the law makes it too complex. Lawyers will have difficulty in finding all the relevant past cases, although a computer data base called LEXIS has made this easier. Where there are several different decisions on the same point of law, the law may be very complicated.

Apart from these disadvantages there is another problem in the system of precedent. This is the problem of finding the ratio decidendi in a judgment. Some judgments are several pages long and the judges do not always separate the relevant and irrelevant points clearly. The problem becomes worse if, in an appeal court, more than one judge gives a judgment in a case. In one instance the judges in the Court of Appeal said they were unable to discover the ratio decidendi in a previous case decided by the House of Lords! Despite all the problems of precedent it is generally agreed that there must be some form of following past decisions. If there were no consistency in decision making, the law would become chaotic.

ACTIVITY

Read the following passage and answer the questions below.

The Practice Statement is one of great importance, although it should not be supposed that there will frequently be cases in which the House thinks it right not to follow their own precedent. An example of a case in which the House might think it right to depart from a precedent is where they consider that the earlier decision was influenced by the existence of conditions which no longer prevail, and that in modern conditions the law ought to be different.

(*Source:* Adapted from an explanatory note issued with the *Practice Statement.*)

1 **To which 'House' does this passage refer?**
2 **Why is the Practice Statement of great importance?**
3 **Do you agree with the statement that 'in modern conditions the law ought to be different'? Give examples to support your answer.**
4 **How can the Practice Statement help to keep the law up to date?**

8.6 Law reports

As already mentioned, to operate a system of judicial precedent there must be full and accurate written reports of cases and judgments. In England there has been some form of Law Reports since the thirteenth century. However the early reports were brief and not always accurate.

The earliest reports (from about 1275 to 1535) were called Year Books. These were short reports of medieval cases, usually written in French. They are rarely cited (referred to) in court today.

From 1535 to 1865 cases were reported by individuals, who made a business out of selling the reports to lawyers. The detail and accuracy of the reports varied from reporter to reporter, but many of them are still used today. In 1865 the Incorporated Council of Law Reporting was set up and reports made since then are recognised as being accurate with the judgments being word for word reports of what the judge said. Two of the main series of reports today are the All England Law Reports and the Weekly Law Reports. In addition some newspapers, especially *The Times*, give shortened reports of important cases.

On pp. 78–9 there is a copy of the Law Report in the case of *Re S* (1992). Look at that report.

At the top of the page is the name of the series of Law Reports publishing the case. Immediately after the name of the case at (a) there is stated the name of the court hearing the case, the judge and the date of the hearing. At (b) in italic print is what is called the headnote. This is a brief version of the facts and law involved written by the barrister reporting the case. This is not part of the judgment, only a quick method of discovering the key points in the case. At (c) and (d) there is a summary of the facts, followed at (e) by what the court decided. The judgment itself starts at the bottom of the first page. On the second page at (f) the judge points out that there is no English authority which is directly in point. This shows that he does not think he is bound by any previous precedent. He then goes on to say there is some American authority; this would only be persuasive precedent. This is an unusually short law report, but it illustrates the way law reports are set out.

Examination question

Study the extract below and then answer **all** parts of the question which follows.

> Their Lordships regard the use of precedent as a vital foundation upon which to decide what is the law and how to apply it to individual cases. It provides at least some degree of certainty upon which individuals can rely in the conduct of their affairs, as well as a basis for the orderly development of legal rules.

Their Lordships nevertheless recognise that keeping too rigidly to precedent may lead to injustice in a particular case, and may also unduly restrict the proper development of the law.

They propose therefore to change their present practice. Whilst still treating their former decisions as normally binding, they propose to depart from a previous decision when it appears right to do so.

In this connection, they will bear in mind the special need for certainty as to the criminal law.

(Source: Adapted from *The Lord Chancellor's Practice Statement,* 1966.)

a　Name
　　i　the Court **and**
　　ii　the judges
　　to which the Practice Statement applies.
　　　　　　　　　　　　　　　(2 marks)
b　The Practice Statement makes a number of references to the doctrine of precedent.

Explain how the system of binding precedent operates through the hierarchy of courts in England and Wales.　　*(8 marks)*

c　A precedent can be either binding or persuasive. Explain and illustrate the difference between these two different types of precedent.　　　　　　　*(6 marks)*

d　Explain why the Lord Chancellor saw the 'special need for certainty in the criminal law'. Do you think he was right?　*(6 marks)*

e　Explain why 'keeping too rigidly to precedent' could be seen as a disadvantage of the doctrine of precedent.　　*(6 marks)*

f　Taking into account
　　i　any other advantages or disadvantages of precedent, **and**
　　ii　the change introduced by the 1966 Practice Statement,
　　explain whether or not you consider precedent to be a good system.　*(12 marks)*

Total: 40 marks

SEG 1992

The following two pages show the Law Report in the case of Re S a

Re S (adult: refusal of medical treatment)

FAMILY DIVISION
SIR STEPHEN BROWN P
12 OCTOBER 1992

b   *Medical treatment – Adult patient – Consent to treatment – Right to refuse consent – Refusal on religious grounds – Discretion of court to authorise emergency operation – Health authority seeking authority to carry out emergency Caesarian section operation on pregnant woman – Operation in vital interests of patient and unborn child – Patient objecting to operation on religious grounds – Whether court should exercise inherent jurisdiction to authorise operation.*

c

A health authority applied for a declaration to authorise the surgeons and staff of a hospital under the authority's control to carry out an emergency Caesarian section operation upon a 30-year-old woman patient who had been admitted to hospital with ruptured membranes and in spontaneous labour with her third pregnancy and who had continued in labour since then. She was six days overdue
d   beyond the expected date of birth and had refused, on religious grounds, to submit herself to such an operation. The surgeon in charge of the patient was emphatic in his evidence that the operation was the only means of saving the patient's life and that her baby could not be born alive if the operation was not carried out.

e

Held – The court would exercise its inherent jurisdiction to authorise the surgeons and staff of a hospital to carry out an emergency Caesarian section operation upon a patient contrary to her beliefs if the operation was vital to protect the life of the unborn child. Accordingly, a declaration would be granted that such an operation and any necessary consequential treatment which the
f   hospital and its staff proposed to perform on the patient was in the vital interests of the patient and her unborn child and could be lawfully performed despite the patient's refusal to give her consent to the operation (see p 672 c d and g, post).

Notes
For consent to medical treatment, see 30 *Halsbury's Laws* (4th edn reissue) para 39,
g   and for cases on the subject, see 33 *Digest* (Reissue) 273, 2242–2246.

Cases referred to in judgment
AC, Re (1990) 573 A 2d 1235, DC Ct of Apps (en banc).
T (adult: refusal of medical treatment), Re [1992] 4 All ER 649, CA.

h

Application
A health authority applied for a declaration to authorise the surgeons and staff of a hospital under the health authority's control to carry out an emergency Caesarian operation on a patient, Mrs S. The facts are set out in the judgment.

j   *Huw Lloyd* (instructed by *Beachcroft Stanleys*) for the health authority.
James Munby QC (instructed by the *Official Solicitor*) as amicus curiae.

SIR STEPHEN BROWN P. This is an application by a health authority for a declaration to authorise the surgeons and staff of a hospital to carry out an emergency Caesarian operation upon a patient, who I shall refer to as 'Mrs S'.

Mrs S is 30 years of age. She is in labour with her third pregnancy. She was admitted to a hospital last Saturday with ruptured membranes and in spontaneous *a* labour. She has continued in labour since. She is already six days overdue beyond the expected date of birth, which was 6 October, and she has now refused, on religious grounds, to submit herself to a Caesarian section operation. She is supported in this by her husband. They are described as 'born-again Christians' and are clearly quite sincere in their beliefs.

I have heard the evidence of P, a Fellow of the Royal College of Surgeons who *b* is in charge of this patient at the hospital. He has given, succinctly and graphically, a description of the condition of this patient. Her situation is desperately serious, as is also the situation of the as yet unborn child. The child is in what is described as a position of 'transverse lie', with the elbow projecting through the cervix and the head being on the right side. There is the gravest risk of a rupture of the uterus if the section is not carried out and the natural labour process is permitted *c* to continue. The evidence of P is that we are concerned with 'minutes rather than hours' and that it is a 'life and death' situation. He has done his best, as have other surgeons and doctors at the hospital, to persuade the mother that the only means of saving her life, and also I emphasise the life of her unborn child, is to carry out a Caesarian section operation. P is emphatic. He says it is absolutely the case that *d* the baby cannot be born alive if a Caesarian operation is not carried out. He has described the medical condition. I am not going to go into it in detail because of the pressure of time.

I have been assisted by Mr Munby QC appearing for the Official Solicitor as amicus curiae. The Official Solicitor answered the call of the court within minutes and, although this application only came to the notice of the court officials at 1.30 *e* pm, it has come on for hearing just before 2 o'clock and now at 2.18 pm I propose to make the declaration which is sought. I do so in the knowledge that the fundamental question appears to have been left open by Lord Donaldson MR in *Re T (adult: refusal of medical treatment)* [1992] 4 All ER 649, heard earlier this year in the Court of Appeal, and in the knowledge that there is no English authority which is directly in point. There is, however, some American authority which *f* suggests that if this case were being heard in the American courts the answer would be likely to be in favour of granting a declaration in these circumstances: see *Re AC* (1990) 573 A 2d 1235 at 1240, 1246–1248, 1252.

I do not propose to say more at this stage, except that I wholly accept the evidence of P as to the desperate nature of this situation, and that I grant the *g* declaration as sought.

Declaration that a Caesarian section and any necessary consequential treatment which the hospital and its staff proposed to perform on the patient was in the vital interests of the patient and her unborn child and could be lawfully performed despite the patient's refusal to give her consent. No order as to costs. *h*

Bebe Chua   Barrister.

9 Sources of law (2)

In today's world there is often the need for new laws to be made. The method of judicial precedent described in Chapter 8 is clearly not suitable for major law making. So today most law is made by Parliament or government departments. Any law made by these is called, in general terms, legislation. Law passed by Parliament is also known as statute law or Acts of Parliament. Law made by government ministers and their departments is called delegated legislation.

9.1 Acts of Parliament

Parliament consists of the House of Commons and the House of Lords. The House of Commons has 650 Members of Parliament (MP), who are elected by the public. The country is divided into areas called constituencies and each constituency elects one MP. The House of Lords consists of people who have inherited a peerage, those who have been made life peers (often former MPs), the senior bishops of the Church of England and the senior judges (the Law Lords). When the House of Lords sits as a court, only the judges are involved. Parliament has the right to pass Acts of Parliament. An Act of Parliament is superior to all other sources of law and it cannot be challenged in the courts. If an Act of Parliament is passed which is contrary to an earlier judicial precedent, then the Act must be followed; the precedent is no longer law. Since laws made by Parliament can overrule all other laws, it is said that Parliament is supreme. This is what is meant by the phrase 'sovereignty of Parliament'. Parliament has the power to make any law it wishes and that law will override any other law.

Democracy

The reason that Parliament has this power is that it represents all the people of the United Kingdom. The Members of Parliament in the House of Commons represent the general public, while the House of Lords represents the peers and the church. Voting for MPs means that they are democratically elected and are given the power to make laws by the rest of the people. There must be a general election at least once every five years and, if the public do not approve of the way the ruling party has been governing, the electorate can vote that party out of office. In this way Parliament is accountable to the ordinary members of society.

Introducing an Act of Parliament

There are a number of stages through which an Act must go before it becomes law. Before an Act has passed through all its stages it is known as a *Bill*. There are different types of Bill:

1 *A public Bill.* This is a Bill involving matters of public policy which will affect either the whole country or a large section of it, for example the Criminal Justice and Public Order Act 1994. A public Bill is usually introduced into Parliament by the Government. It will normally have been drafted by lawyers in the civil service on instructions from the Prime Minister or another

government minister. The majority of Bills are in this category.

2 *A private member's Bill.* This is a Bill introduced by an individual Member of Parliament. Since time for private members' Bills is limited (they are usually only debated on Fridays), there is a ballot in each session of Parliament to choose which members shall have the chance to present a Bill. Twenty names are selected, although only the first six or seven MPs chosen are likely to get the chance to present their Bill. Very few private members' Bills become law, but there have been some important laws passed as a result of such Bills. Some examples are the Abortion Act 1967, the Computer Misuse Act 1990 and the Timeshare Act 1992. It is also possible for a member of the House of Lords to introduce a private member's Bill.

3 *A private Bill.* This is a Bill designed to pass a law which will only affect or benefit individual people or corporations. A private Bill does not make law for the whole country.

Passing an Act of Parliament

Most Acts start in the House of Commons, but it is possible for them to start in the House of Lords. The procedure normally requires both Houses to pass Bills before they become law. The exceptions to this are any Bills which involve taxation, which do not have to be passed by the House of Lords.

Whether the Bill starts in the Commons or the Lords it will have to go through the following stages:

1 *First Reading.* This is a formal procedure in which the name of the Bill and its main aims are read out and there is usually no discussion or debate on the Bill.

2 *Second Reading.* This is the main debate on the whole Bill. It is a debate on the main principles rather than the details. The MPs who wish to speak in the debate will try to catch the Speaker's eye, since the Speaker controls all debates in the House. At the end of the debate there will be a vote. If at any stage there is a majority vote against the Bill, then it does not go any further.

3 *Committee Stage.* At this stage the Bill is examined in detail by a committee of MPs. There are a number of committees called select committees, made up of between 20 and 50 MPs chosen so that the political parties in the House are proportionately represented. The committee's task is to go through each clause of the Bill and where it thinks necessary propose amendments or alterations. For money Bills the whole House sits as a committee instead of a select committee.

4 *Report Stage.* The committee reports back to the House with its suggested amendments and each one is voted on. The amendment will only take place if a majority of the House are in favour of it.

5 *Third Reading.* There is then a final vote on the Bill as a whole. There will be a further debate on the general principles of the Bill only if at least six MPs request it. If there is a vote in favour of the Bill it then passes to the other House where it will have to go through the same stages.

6 *House of Lords.* The power of the House of Lords is limited. When the House of Lords makes amendments to the Bill those amendments will be considered by the House of Commons before the Bill goes through to its final stage. If the House of Lords refuses to pass a Bill, the House of Commons can introduce that same Bill in the next session of Parliament and if it is passed by the Commons for a second time it can then receive the Royal Assent and become law without the agreement of the House of Lords. This procedure is set out in the Parliament Acts 1911 and 1949 and is based on the idea that the principal legislative function of the non-elected House of Lords is to revise and add to the law rather than oppose the will of the democratically elected House of Commons. There have been only four occasions when this procedure has been used to bypass the House of Lords after they voted against a Bill. The most recent Act passed by this method was the War Crimes Act 1991.

7 *Royal Assent.* The monarch has to approve the Bill and give Her Assent (agreement) to its becoming law. This stage is nowadays a formality. The last time the Royal Assent was refused was in 1707 when Queen Anne refused to consent to the Scottish Militia Bill. Once the

Royal Assent has been given the Bill becomes an Act of Parliament and normally it comes into force, that is, it becomes part of the law on the day it receives the Royal Assent. However in some Acts there is a section which either states the date in the future when the Act is to become law or it gives a government minister power to decide the date on which the Act is to become law. This can mean that some Acts passed by Parliament do not actually become law for some time. In fact the Easter Act 1928, which was intended to fix the date for Easter, has never come into force.

Figure 9.1 summarises these different stages.

Figure 9.1 Passing an Act of Parliament when a Bill starts in the House of Commons

First Reading	Formal
Second Reading	Main debate
Committee Stage	Each clause considered
Report Stage	Report back on proposed amendments
Third Reading	Final vote, there may be a debate
House of Lords	Same stages repeated May return to House of Commons if Lords make amendments
Royal Assent	Bill now becomes an Act

On the opposite page there is a reproduction of an Act of Parliament.

The name of the Act is given at the top, in this case the Cheques Act 1992. 1992 Chapter 32 means that this was the 32nd Act to be passed in 1992. There is then a short statement about the purpose of the Act. Next follows a formal statement showing that the Act has been passed by both Houses of Parliament and received the Royal Assent; this is included in all Acts. Then come the sections of the Act; this Act is unusually short as it has only four sections. Sections 1, 2 and 3 change the law on cheques by making alterations to other Acts of Parliament. The effect of these changes is to make sure that if two lines are drawn across a cheque and the person writing the cheque includes the words 'account payee' or 'a/c payee' that cheque cannot be paid into anybody else's account. This is aimed at preventing theft of cheques or fraud. The last section, section 4, has two subsections. Section 4(2) says when the Act is to come into force and in this case it is three months after the Act has received the Royal Assent.

A C T I V I T Y

Look at a cheque book and see if all the cheques have the words mentioned in the Cheques Act 1992 printed on them.

Advantages of statute law over judge-made law

Parliament is thought to be more in touch with the outside world than judges and able to react to public opinion more quickly. It is free to make law on any point it thinks necessary, whereas the judges have to wait for a suitable case to come before the courts. In this way any gaps in the law can be filled by an Act of Parliament. An Act can also cover a number of points, while a case in court will usually involve only one point of law. Finally there is the important point that the House of Commons is democratically elected and has therefore been given the right to make law by the people of this country.

Disadvantages of statute law

Although the lawyers who draft Acts try to use clear language and make the meaning of every part plain, they do not always succeed. This can then lead to court cases where the whole dispute is about the meaning of a particular section in an Act of Parliament. In fact 75 per cent of civil cases heard by the House of Lords involve statutory interpretation.

The process of passing an Act can take a considerable time and Parliament does not have enough time to deal with all the laws that are suggested. A major criticism of Parliament by lawyers is that it is not prepared to give enough time to discussion of law reform proposals put forward by the Law Commission.

ELIZABETH II
c. 32

Cheques Act 1992

1992 CHAPTER 32

An Act to amend the law relating to cheques.

[16th March 1992]

BE IT ENACTED by the Queen's most Excellent Majesty, by and with the advice and consent of the Lords Spiritual and Temporal, and Commons, in this present Parliament assembled, and by the authority of the same, as follows:—

1. After section 81 of the Bills of Exchange Act 1882 there shall be inserted the following section—

"Non-transferable cheques.

81A.—(1) Where a cheque is crossed and bears across its face the words "account payee" or "a/c payee", either with or without the word "only", the cheque shall not be transferable, but shall only be valid as between the parties thereto.

(2) A banker is not to be treated for the purposes of section 80 above as having been negligent by reason only of his failure to concern himself with any purported indorsement of a cheque which under subsection (1) above or otherwise is not transferable.".

Amendment of Bills of Exchange Act 1882: non-transferable cheques.
1882 c. 61.

2. In section 80 of the Bills of Exchange Act 1882 (protection to banker and drawer where cheque is crossed) after "crossed cheque" there shall be inserted "(including a cheque which under section 81A below or otherwise is not transferable)".

Amendment of Bills of Exchange Act 1882: protection to banker and drawer where cheque is crossed.

3. In section 4(2)(a) of the Cheques Act 1957 (protection of bankers collecting payment of cheques, etc) there shall be inserted after the word "cheques" the words "(including cheques which under section 81A(1) of the Bills of Exchange Act 1882 or otherwise are not transferable)".

Amendment of Cheques Act 1957.
1957 c. 36.

4.—(1) This Act may be cited as the Cheques Act 1992.

Citation and commencement.

(2) This Act shall come into force at the end of the period of three months beginning on the day on which this Act is passed.

PRINTED IN THE UNITED KINGDOM BY PAUL FREEMAN
Controller and Chief Executive of Her Majesty's Stationery Office
and Queen's Printer of Acts of Parliament

*The Cheques Act 1992
(© Crown Copyright)*

In order to allow extra laws to be made Parliament can delegate some of its law-making powers to other people. We will now consider this type of legislation.

9.2 Delegated legislation

The word delegate has the meaning of handing over the right to do something to others. So the phrase 'delegated legislation' means law made by some person or organisation other than Parliament, but with the authority of Parliament. Generally, Parliament lays down the framework of the law in an Act but within that Act gives the right to make more detailed law to other people. An Act doing this is called an *enabling Act*. Examples of enabling Acts include the Police and Criminal Evidence Act 1984, section 66 of which allows the relevant government minister to draw up a Code of Practice on the way an arrested person should be treated (*see* Chapter 10), and the Legal Aid Act 1988 which gave the Lord Chancellor very wide powers to alter legal aid provisions.

People with power to make delegated legislation

1 *The Queen and the Privy Council.* Under the Emergency Powers Act 1920 the Queen and the Privy Council have the right to make laws which can affect the whole country. These laws are called *Orders in Council*. This right to make law is normally only used in times of emergency, when Parliament is not sitting.

2 *Ministers and government departments.* These are given the power to make laws on various areas which are connected to their departments. For example the Lord Chancellor has powers to make rules for legal aid. Laws made by government ministers and their departments are called *statutory instruments*. These are a major source of law since over 2,000 statutory instruments are made each year.

3 *Local authorities.* A local council can make laws relating to its own area; so Kent County Council can make laws affecting Kent as a whole, while a district council such as Sevenoaks District Council can only make laws affecting its district. Such laws are called *bylaws*. Examples of bylaws are regulations about parking. Look at the pay and display noticeboards in car parks. They refer to the local bylaws on parking.

4 *Public corporations.* These include bodies such as British Rail and the British Airports Authority and they are limited to making laws within their own jurisdiction. These laws are also called bylaws and an example is the ban on smoking in the London Underground system.

A C T I V I T Y

Look for notices of local bylaws. Which council makes them?

Control over delegated legislation

Clearly with so much delegated legislation it is important that there should be some control over it. This control is exercised in two ways.

Control by Parliament

Parliament can include limitations in the enabling Act so that only certain types of law can be made under the delegated power. Some enabling Acts also contain a provision that any statutory instrument made under it must be 'laid before' Parliament, so that Parliament can consider the laws which have been made. Parliament also retains the final control of being able to revoke any statutory instrument.

Statutory instruments are subject to either an affirmative resolution, which means that Parliament must specifically approve them before they become law, or a negative resolution which means that they become law without Parliament considering them and will remain in force unless rejected by Parliament within forty days. This is known as 'the forty day rule' and applies to the majority of statutory instruments.

However, in view of the large number of statutory instruments, it was thought that more control was needed, so in 1973 a Select Committee on Statutory Instruments (usually called the Scrutiny Committee) was set up. The job of this committee is to look at all statutory instruments and decide if any of them should be brought to the attention of Parliament. The two main reasons for the Scrutiny Committee to refer a statutory instrument to Parliament are that it imposes a tax of some sort or that it is an unreasonable use of the delegated powers.

Even with this committee parliamentary checks on delegated legislation are fairly limited.

Control by the courts

The courts can consider any delegated legislation and decide if it is valid or not. This is a major difference between Acts of Parliament and delegated legislation, since the courts have no right to question an Act of Parliament.

Ultra vires

Delegated legislation can be challenged in the courts by any interested party under the doctrine of *ultra vires*. This is a Latin phrase meaning 'beyond the powers'. If a piece of delegated legislation has gone beyond the power given by Parliament, then it is not good law and will be declared void. This was seen in the case of *Attorney-General* v. *Fulham Corporation* (1921). The corporation was given power to provide wash-house facilities for the local people where they could wash their own clothes. When, instead, the corporation built a laundry where it employed people to do the work, it was held to be *ultra vires*.

When deciding how much power Parliament has given, the courts assume that unless an enabling Act expressly says so, there is no power to make unreasonable regulations, to allow sub-delegation or to interfere with the basic rights of the citizen, such as freedom of speech. An example of a bylaw being held to be unreasonable occurred in *Strickland* v. *Hayes* (1896). The bylaw prohibited the singing or reciting of any obscene song and the use of obscene language generally. The court held that the bylaw was unreasonable because it was not limited to behaviour in public places, as even using obscene language in private would be an offence under it. The courts can also decide that delegated legislation is void because the correct procedure has not been followed, as in *Aylesbury Mushrooms* (1972)

when a statutory instrument was successfully challenged because the ministry had not consulted growers as required to do before passing the law.

Advantages of delegated legislation

1 Delegated legislation creates the detailed law that Parliament does not have time to deal with. As already noted there are about 2,000 statutory instruments passed each year and Parliament would not have the time to do all this work. Some of the work is very detailed; regulations on such topics as traffic law need precise details.
2 Delegated legislation can be passed quickly in an emergency. Parliament may not be able to deal with necessary laws quickly or may not even be sitting.
3 Some laws require technical knowledge. For example, building regulations may deal with different types of building materials and the safety requirements for each. The Members of Parliament are unlikely to be expert on these matters and so it is sensible that the government department responsible should make the necessary rules. The department will have experts available to make sure that any technicalities are correctly understood.
4 Local knowledge may be needed for some regulations, such as deciding where it is necessary to have double yellow lines banning parking. This type of law is much better decided by the local council in the area concerned.
5 Delegated legislation can be amended or revoked more easily than an Act of Parliament so that if the situation alters or the law is not working properly, changes can be made to keep it up to date.

Disadvantages of delegated legislation

1 The main criticism of delegated legislation is that it takes law making away from our democratically elected MPs and allows non-elected people to make law. This is acceptable provided there is sufficient control, but as we have already seen Parliament's control is fairly limited.

2 In some areas there will be sub-delegation, this means that the power to make the law is passed on to yet another person, and so the law making is even further removed from Parliament. It is said that some of our law is made by civil servants who are not elected and who are not accountable to the public for their actions.

3 The large volume of delegated legislation makes it difficult to discover what the present law is. Since ignorance of the law is no excuse this could mean that someone could be guilty of an offence although he did not know about the law.

4 There is also a lack of publicity for delegated legislation. Most of it is made in private and some may even come into effect before being published. This is in sharp contrast with the public debates in Parliament.

A C T I V I T Y

Read the following passage and answer the questions below.

Pressure on parliamentary time, the growing technicality of legislation and the increasing anxiety of government to make life easier for itself encouraged the development early this century of statutory provisions which conferred powers on ministers to amend or repeal other Acts of Parliament. Critics called such powers 'Henry VIII clauses', after the Statute of Proclamations 1539, which entitled the King to legislate by decree.

Last year, the Hansard Society Commission published a report which expressed its concern about the use, and abuse, of Henry VIII clauses as a device to avoid effective parliamentary scrutiny of changes in the law. The commission decided that Henry VIII clauses are, of their nature, undesirable. Unless absolutely necessary, a single minister should not be given power to change the law made by Parliament as a whole.

(*Source:* Adapted from an article by David Pannick QC published in *The Times*, 1 February 1994.)

1 **What are laws made by government ministers called?**
2 **Why does Parliament hand over power to ministers to make law?**
3 **Henry VIII clauses allow ministers to change or repeal Acts of Parliament. Why do people criticise the use of such clauses?**
4 **What methods does Parliament use to control delegated legislation?**

9.3 European law

The European Economic Community, as it used to be known, was set up in 1957 by the Treaty of Rome and originally there were six member states: France, Germany, Italy, Belgium, Luxembourg and the Netherlands. The United Kingdom joined the European Economic Community on 1 January 1973 and since that date there has been another source of law in this country – European law. European law is mainly concerned with work and trade. This, however, affects many areas of law: agriculture, company law, sex discrimination and environmental law are just some of the aspects covered.

Since 1994 the Community has been called the European Union. There are four institutions involved in the running of the Union. These are:

- the Council of Ministers
- the Commission
- the European Parliament
- the European Court of Justice

The Council of Ministers

This is the Union's principal decision-making body. The government of each Member State has a seat on the Council. The foreign minister is usually a country's representative, but a government is free to send any of its ministers to Council meetings. Twice a year the heads of all member governments meet to discuss broad principles of policy.

For some particularly important decisions all the ministers must be in agreement, but other decisions can be made by a qualified majority vote. For this each country has a 'weighted' vote according to the size of its population, for example, since the size of the populations of France and the United Kingdom is similar, each country has ten votes, while Luxembourg has only two votes as it is the smallest country. In practice the Council aims at getting unanimous agreement for most proposals and the Council never imposes a decision on a Member State in a matter that member considers to be of vital national importance.

The Commission

The Commission both proposes policies for the Council of Ministers to discuss and is responsible for the administration of the Union. It has 20 Commissioners who are chosen by the agreement of all member governments. The Commissioners are obliged to act in the Union's interests and not in the interests of the country from which they come. Commissioners are appointed for a period of four years and can only be removed during this term of office by a vote of censure from the European Parliament.

Each Commissioner heads a department with special responsibilities for one area of Union policy, such as agriculture, environment or transport.

The European Parliament

The members of the European Parliament are elected directly by the citizens of each Member State. There is an election every five years. The Parliament discusses proposals made by the Commission, but unlike our Parliament, it is not the primary law-making body. Its decision may influence the Council of Ministers, although the Council can disregard such decisions if it wishes. The only real power the Parliament has is the right to reject the Council's budget proposals and the right to dismiss the Commissioners.

The European Court of Justice

This sits in Luxembourg and settles legal disputes involving Union laws. It has 15 judges and each judge is appointed for a period of six years. Judgments of the court are binding in each member country.

Different types of Union law

Treaties

The Treaty of Rome and any other Treaty signed by all the heads of government are automatically law in every member country. In the United Kingdom such Treaties are part of our law because of section 2(1) of the European Communities Act 1972, which says that 'all such rights, powers, liabilities, obligations and restrictions ... are without further enactment to be given legal effect . . .'. This means that citizens can rely on the rights given under the Treaty of Rome even if British law does not give them that same right. In *Macarthys Ltd* v. *Smith* (1981), Wendy Smith was able to claim that the company which employed her was in breach of Article 119 (new 139) of the Treaty of Rome over equal pay for men and women because she was being paid less than the man who had previously done her job. She had no rights under English statute law since the relevant Act, the Equal Pay Act 1970 (as amended by the Sex Discrimination Act 1975) only applies when the man and woman are employed at the same time.

Regulations

Regulations are laws issued by the Commission and under Article 189 (new 249) of the Treaty of Rome are 'binding in every respect and directly applicable in each Member State', so that once issued by the Commission they are automatically law in this country. This was shown in *Re Tachographs:*

THIS WAY FOR EUROPEAN LAW

TO FRANCE

EC Commission v. *United Kingdom* (1979), a case concerning a regulation which said that tachographs (mechanical recording equipment to record speed etc.) should be installed in all road vehicles used for the carriage of goods. The United Kingdom Government decided not to enforce the regulation but to allow lorry owners to choose whether they wished to install a tachograph or not. The Commission referred the matter to the European Court of Justice which held that the United Kingdom had to apply the regulation. Article 189 made it quite clear that regulations were directly applicable.

Directives

Directives are issued by the Commission, but merely direct each Member State on what the law should be, leaving each country to bring in its own law giving effect to the directive. Article 189 says 'directives shall bind any Member State to which they are addressed *as to the result to be achieved*'. When a directive is issued the Commission will set a time limit within which it must be implemented. An example is the directive on consumer liability which was issued in 1985 and required all Member States to implement it by July 1988. The United Kingdom met that requirement by passing the Consumer Protection Act 1987, which became law in March 1988. Usually in this country directives are brought in to our law by the relevant minister making a statutory instrument, though as the Consumer Protection Act illustrates, some directives are implemented in an Act of Parliament.

Although a directive does not normally become part of our law automatically in the way that a regulation does, the European Court has decided that some directives are 'directly applicable'. This means that they do become law automatically and can be relied upon by citizens in claims against the State, even though the Government has not implemented them. This happened in the case of *Marshall* v. *Southampton and South West Hampshire Area Health Authority* (1986). Helen Marshall was dismissed from her job because she was 62 years old, whereas men doing the same work did not have to retire until they were 65. A European directive issued in 1976 said that men and women should be treated equally in employment and this included reasons for dismissal.

Helen Marshall started an action for unfair dismissal and the European Court held that, since the directive was clear, it was directly applicable. This was so even though the British Government had not brought it into effect over ages of retirement. Since Helen Marshall was employed by a State organisation she could rely on the directive in her claim against them and so win her case. In 1993 in *Marshall* (No. 2) the European Court also decided that in this sort of situation the claimant should be able to recover all his loss and not merely that available in the domestic courts. This had a very important effect on tribunal awards of compensation in unfair dismissal cases, since before this decision there was a set maximum the tribunal could award. After the decision the tribunal was able to award the full amount needed to compensate applicants for the loss of their jobs.

However, when the Government has not implemented a directive, that directive does not create rights between private individuals or companies. If Helen Marshall had been working for a private company she would not have been able to rely on the Equal Treatment Directive and so would have lost her case. This appears unfair but the European Court has created another way of claiming for any loss caused because the Government has not implemented a directive. Instead of claiming against the employer it is possible, in certain circumstances, to claim compensation from the Government, since the loss has been caused by the Government's failure to act. This was decided in an Italian case, *Francovitch* v. *Italian Republic* (1991).

Decisions

Decisions can be addressed to a Member State or an individual or company and are binding only on those to whom they are addressed.

Referring cases to the European Court of Justice

If a point of European law is involved in a case, the national court can refer that point to the European Court for a preliminary ruling. This is under Article 177 (new 234) of the Treaty of Rome. Where the case is being heard by a final court of appeal (usually in this country the House of Lords) and a question of European law is raised, then that court has to send the point to the European Court for a decision. Other courts have a discretion, that is, they can choose whether to refer the case to the European Court or not. This is because their decision is not final but can be appealed against in the English courts. In deciding whether to use that discretion and refer a case, the Court of Appeal in *Bulmer* v. *Bollinger* (1974) said that several things had to be considered. These included:

1 Was a ruling by the European Court necessary to decide the case?
2 Had the point already been decided in a previous case?
3 What were the circumstances, such as the length of time it would take to get a ruling and the expense involved?
4 What were the wishes of the parties?

Courts at all levels in our legal system have referred cases to the European Court, although most referrals have been by the higher courts, for example, the case of *Macarthys* v. *Smith* was referred by the Court of Appeal.

European law and the sovereignty of Parliament

As already discussed Parliament is seen as being the supreme law-maker. The law that it makes can override any other English source of law. Does our entry into the European Union affect Parliament's supremacy? It is clear that European laws do take priority over national laws. This was decided before the United Kingdom even joined the Union in the Dutch case of *Van Gend en Loos* (1963). So far as this country is concerned it was also shown by the *Factortame case* (1991), where it was held that the Merchant Shipping Act 1988 was contrary to the Treaty of Rome in that it discriminated against ship owners on the ground of nationality. However, Parliament can still be said to be supreme, since it is only through Parliament passing the European Communities Act 1972 that European law has direct effect in this country. Parliament also retains the final right to withdraw from the Union.

Examination question

Study the extract below and then answer **all** parts of the question which follows.

Parliament is legislatively supreme and can make or repeal laws as it so chooses. Any Act passed by Parliament which is of general application is absolutely binding on all persons within Parliament's jurisdiction. However controversial a particular statute may be, a judge is bound to enforce its provisions.

Because Parliament is legislatively all-powerful, it can grant to some other person or body the power to make orders, regulations or rules which have the force of law.

Parliament cannot pass all the laws mainly because it has so much to do and so little time in which to do it. In addition it may lack the necessary expertise or local knowledge required.

It overcomes these difficulties by resorting to delegated legislation allowing for example, Ministers or Local Authorities to make laws on its behalf.

Such delegated powers have to be carefully controlled, otherwise the body to whom the powers have been delegated could abuse its power. Such control is exercised mainly by Parliament itself and also by the courts.

(*Source:* Adapted from Colin Padfield, *Law made Simple*, Butterworth-Heinemann.)

a Identify **four** stages in the passing of an Act of Parliament. (*4 marks*)
b Briefly explain the difference between a Government Bill and a Private Member's Bill, giving an example of each. (*4 marks*)
c The extract states that a judge is absolutely bound by the provision of an Act of Parliament.
   Describe **two** other sources of law that, for example, a judge in the High Court would be bound to follow. (*6 marks*)
d Comment on why, in a democracy, it is important that legislation passed by

Parliament is the supreme source of domestic law. *(6 marks)*

e Discuss some of the reasons why Parliament has 'so much to do and so little time in which to do it'. *(6 marks)*

f Name the types of delegated legislation passed by

   i Ministers **and**

   ii Local Authorities. *(2 marks)*

g Comment on how

   i Parliament and

   ii the courts

exercise control over delegated legislation. *(8 marks)*

h Critically assess **one** advantage and **one** disadvantage of delegated legislation over statute law. *(4 marks)*

Total: 40 marks

SEG Sample Paper for 1996 (Higher Tier)

Criminal law: powers of arrest 10

In order to detect and prosecute criminals it is necessary for the police to have powers to stop, search and arrest people. On the other hand it is important that police actions are controlled in order to protect citizens from harassment and pressure. To try and achieve this balance Parliament passed the Police and Criminal Evidence Act 1984. This Act, often referred to as PACE, is an effort at bringing together in one piece of legislation all the main rules. The Act also allows the Home Secretary to issue Codes of Practice on such matters as searching, detaining, questioning and identifying suspects.

10.1 Police powers to stop and search

Public places

Section 1 of PACE gives the police the right to stop and search people and vehicles in a public place. 'Public place' not only means in the street, but also includes areas like pub car parks and can even include private gardens if the officer has good reasons for believing the person does not live at that address. A police officer can only use this power if he has reasonable grounds for suspecting that the person stopped is in possession of, or the vehicle stopped contains, stolen goods or prohibited articles. Prohibited articles includes such items as offensive weapons and articles for use in connection with burglary or theft. As this power to stop and search members of the general public is quite a wide one, sections 2 and 3 of the Act add in some extra conditions as safeguards. The main ones are that the police officer must give his name and station and tell the person stopped the reason for the search. If the officer is not in uniform, he must also produce documentary evidence to show that he is a police officer. Plain clothes police have no right to stop a vehicle under PACE. During a search of a person in public, the only clothing a police officer can ask that person to remove is a coat, jacket or gloves. As soon as possible after the search, the police officer must make a written report about it.

Although PACE contains the main right to stop and search there are other Acts which also give this power in special circumstances, for instance the Misuse of Drugs Act 1971 allows the police to search for controlled drugs.

Road checks

Where it is reasonably suspected that a person who has committed a serious arrestable offence is in a particular area, section 4 of PACE gives permission for road checks to be made in that area. Such a check must be authorised by a high ranking police officer (superintendent or above). Serious arrestable offences include murder, manslaughter, rape, kidnapping and terrorist offences.

Searching premises

The police normally only have the right to enter and search premises if a Magistrate has issued a search warrant. However no warrant is needed to enter premises in order to:

a arrest any person under a warrant of arrest;
b arrest any person for an arrestable offence;
c recapture an escaped prisoner; or
d save life or prevent injury or damage.

The police can, of course, enter and search premises when the occupier of those premises gives permission.

10.2 Powers of arrest

There are certain circumstances in which not only the police, but also private citizens may arrest a person. Section 24 of PACE provides the most widely used power of arrest. This section allows arrests for 'arrestable offences'. An arrestable offence is:

a any offence for which the sentence is fixed by law (for example, murder, because it has a fixed sentence of life imprisonment);
b any offence for which the maximum sentence that could be given to an adult is at least five years. This category includes a wide range of offences, among them theft (maximum sentence 7 years), assault causing actual bodily harm (maximum sentence 5 years), rape (maximum sentence life imprisonment) and robbery (maximum sentence life imprisonment). It does not mean the offender will be sentenced to five years' imprisonment, it only means that the maximum sentence is five years or more;

c any other offence which PACE or another Act of Parliament specifically says shall be an arrestable offence even though the maximum sentence is less than five years. Examples include taking a motor vehicle without consent (s. 12 Theft Act 1968) and going equipped to steal (s. 25 Theft Act 1968).

Under section 24 any person may arrest without a warrant:

a anyone who has committed an arrestable offence; *or*
b where an arrestable offence has been committed, anyone whom he has reasonable grounds for suspecting has committed that offence.

The key factor in these two situations is that there must have been an arrestable offence committed.
There is also power for any person to arrest:

a anyone who is in the act of committing an arrestable offence; or
b anyone whom he has reasonable grounds for suspecting to be committing an arrestable offence.

Section 24 then gives police officers wider powers than ordinary citizens. A police officer can also arrest:

a where he has reasonable grounds for suspecting that an arrestable offence has been committed, anyone whom he has reasonable grounds for suspecting to be guilty of the offence.

This means that the arrest will be lawful even if it is shown later that no arrestable offence was committed. A police officer can also arrest:

b anyone who is about to commit an arrestable offence;
c anyone whom he has reasonable grounds for suspecting to be about to commit an arrestable offence.

Examples will help to explain these rules. A store detective in a shop believes he has seen Peter taking a bar of chocolate, put it in his pocket and walk past the checkout without paying for it. If Peter has taken the chocolate, then he has committed the offence of theft, which is an arrestable offence. As there has been an arrestable offence the store detective can lawfully arrest Peter. However, if the store detective was mistaken and Peter has not taken the chocolate, there is no arrestable offence and the store detective cannot lawfully arrest him. A police officer in this situation can still lawfully arrest Peter, even if there has been a mistake, provided the police officer had reasonable grounds for suspecting there had been a theft and reasonable grounds for suspecting Peter of that theft.

Where there has been no arrestable offence committed there are two important effects. First, Peter has the right to sue the store detective in the civil courts for false imprisonment but he cannot sue the police officer. Secondly, if Peter uses reasonable force to prevent the store detective from holding him he cannot be charged with assaulting the store detective. This was decided in *R. v. Self* (1992) where an off-duty police officer was wrongly suspected of theft. A store detective and a shop assistant caught hold of him and, in the struggle to get free, he kicked them. The Court of Appeal said he was within his rights to use force to try to escape as there was no lawful arrest.

Figure 10.1 sets out the rules of arrest.

Under section 25 of PACE police officers have extra powers of arrest where:

a the suspect's name and address cannot be discovered;

b there are reasonable grounds for believing that the name and address given are false;

c the arrest is reasonably believed to be necessary to prevent the suspect from causing injury to himself or others or causing damage to property; or

d the arrest is reasonably believed to be necessary to protect a child or other vulnerable person.

In all cases the police officer must inform the person arrested that he is under arrest and must tell him the reasons for his arrest, even if the reasons are obvious, as soon as is practicable.

Breach of the peace

In addition to the powers under PACE there is a common law right to arrest anyone in order to prevent a breach of the peace. Both police and private citizens have this power.

Warrants for arrest

As well as all the above powers a police officer also has the right to arrest anyone named in a

Figure 10.1 Powers of arrest

	Police can lawfully arrest	Private citizen can lawfully arrest
Arrestable offence has been committed by defendant	Yes	Yes
Arrestable offence has been committed and there are reasonable grounds for thinking defendant committed it	Yes	Yes
Arrestable offence has NOT been committed even though there are good reasons for suspicion and for suspecting defendant	Yes	No
Defendant in act of committing arrestable offence	Yes	Yes
Reasonable grounds for suspecting defendant is in act of committing an arrestable offence	Yes	Yes
Defendant about to commit an arrestable offence	Yes	No
Reasonable grounds for suspecting defendant is about to commit an arrestable offence	Yes	No

warrant of arrest issued by a magistrate or other court. A warrant will include a statement of the offence and it gives the police the power to arrest the accused and bring him before the court. If the officer does not have the warrant with him at the time of making the arrest, he must, if the accused so demands, show the warrant to him as soon as possible.

APPLYING THE LAW

In each situation state whether there has been a lawful arrest. Give reasons for your answer.

1 **Kate is arrested by a police officer after a shopper mistakenly told the officer that Kate had stolen a pair of jeans from the shop.**
2 **Harold is arrested by a store detective after the store detective saw Harold taking a purse from a woman's shopping bag.**
3 **A police officer arrests David when he sees David trying the door handles of several cars in the local car park.**

10.3 Powers of detention

Once a suspected person is arrested and taken to a police station, PACE and the Code of Practice drawn up by the Home Secretary under PACE state that the custody officer at that station must inform him of his rights. These are:

a to have someone informed of his arrest;
b to consult privately with a solicitor, and to be told that independent legal advice is available free of charge;
c to be able to consult the Code of Practice.

Where the arrest is for a serious arrestable offence, the right to a and b above may be delayed for 36 hours.

The custody officer must also keep a custody record noting all the events that occur while the arrested person remains at the police station.

PACE states that the detention of any arrested person must be 'reviewed' at set intervals. The first review must be not later than six hours after the detention and the subsequent reviews at intervals of not less than nine hours.

For most offences the police can only hold a person for a maximum of 24 hours. Then they must either charge him with an offence or release him.

For serious arrestable offences the rules are different. Here the person may be detained for up to 36 hours and then, if the police wish to detain him further, the authorisation of the magistrates must be obtained. This will involve a hearing in front of a Magistrates' Court where the detained

Figure 10.2 Time limits on detention

Time factor	
Start	The arrested person arrives at police station and the custody officer decides there is reason to detain him
6 hours	First review
15 hours and every 9 hours afterwards	Second review
24 hours	Police must charge or release arrested person unless he is being interviewed in connection with a serious arrestable offence
36 hours	Police may apply to magistrates to extend the period of detention for a serious arrestable offence
96 hours	Maximum time for holding an arrested person (except under Prevention of Terrorism Act 1989)

person has the right to be represented and to put his side of events. Magistrates may authorise the police to extend the detention for up to 96 hours in total. After this the police must either charge the suspect or release him. The only exception to these time limits is where someone is arrested under the Prevention of Terrorism Act 1989. The police may then hold that person for 48 hours and can then apply to the Home Secretary for permission to hold him for up to another five days.

Figure 10.2 on p. 94 sets out the time limits on detention.

Questioning by police may be tape recorded and a record must be kept of all interviews.

When a minor (aged under 18) or any other vulnerable person (e.g. someone who is mentally ill) is interviewed, an appropriate adult, such as a parent, must normally be present. The police must caution any suspect before interviewing them, telling them that they do not have to say anything, but also pointing out that a failure to mention something which is later used in their defence could strengthen the case against them. This is the so-called loss of the right to silence. A person being interviewed by the police can, of course, stay silent; he does not have to answer any questions. The change made by the Criminal Justice and Public Order Act 1994 means that the fact that the defendant did not tell the police about something which he might have been expected to mention, but then uses that point in his defence at court, can be considered by the court as part of the evidence.

The police may also take finger prints and non-intimate samples, such as hair or samples of saliva, from a detained person without the person's consent. If the person is not prosecuted for the offence or is later found not guilty the prints and samples must be destroyed.

10.4 Complaints against the police

PACE set up the Police Complaints Authority. Previously all complaints were investigated by the police themselves and it was felt that a more independent body was needed. Initially any complaint is investigated by a senior police officer, but serious complaints (involving death or serious injury) must be referred to the Police Complaints Authority. The Authority can also investigate other complaints. Several thousand complaints are made each year. Where a complaint is justified the complainant may be given compensation. Despite the numbers of complaints, a Home Office survey in 1991–2 found that 75 per cent of the public think the police do a good or fairly good job.

10.5 Bail

There are various stages in the process when a person may be granted bail. Bail means being allowed to be at liberty, rather than being held in custody, while awaiting the next stage in the criminal process. The first point at which an arrested person may be given bail is during the police investigation. The police may bail him with a condition that he return to the police station on a set date. The police may also give a person bail once they have charged him or her. In this instance the condition is that he or she attends court on a set date. Where the police are not willing to bail an accused, the police must arrange for the accused to appear before a Magistrates' Court as soon as possible. If, as happens in most cases, the court cannot deal with the whole case at that first hearing, the magistrates will then make the decision on whether the accused should be given bail or stay in custody until the next court hearing. If the accused is not given bail it is said that he is *remanded in custody*.

The main rules about bail are set out in the Bail Act 1976. This Act starts with the presumption that bail should be granted. However, if good reasons are shown, the magistrates may refuse to give bail. The magistrates can refuse bail if there are substantial reasons for believing that the defendant, if released on bail, would:

a fail to surrender, that is, not attend court for the next hearing;
b commit further offences;
c interfere with witnesses.

When making their decision the magistrates look at various factors. These include:

a the nature and seriousness of the offence;
b the past record of the defendant;
c his ties with the community; for example, does he live in the area?
d whether he has previously 'jumped' bail. In other words, whether he has failed to attend court when bailed to do so on a previous occasion.

If the magistrates decide not to grant bail they must give their reasons for the refusal.

The rules are different where charges of murder, attempted murder, manslaughter, rape or attempted rape are involved. The Criminal Justice Act 1988 says that in these cases magistrates who grant bail must give reasons why they have done so. However, if a defendant who is charged with one of these serious offences already has a conviction for such an offence, then bail should only be granted in exceptional circumstances.

The Criminal Justice and Public Order Act 1994 places restrictions on the granting of bail where the defendant is charged with committing an offence while already on bail for another offence.

The number of refusals to grant bail is criticised since about a quarter of those in prison are on remand awaiting trial. This is a very high percentage of our prison population. Another point is that many of those refused bail may be found not guilty or will not eventually receive a custodial sentence, but will have spent several weeks or even months in prison before their trial.

Under the Bail Act 1976 a defendant who is refused bail has a right to appeal against that decision. The appeal can be either to the Crown Court or to a judge of the Queen's Bench Division. Where bail is allowed despite objections to it, the prosecution has the right, under the Bail (Amendment) Act 1993, to appeal. This right only exists for crimes which have a maximum penalty of five years' imprisonment or more.

In any case the magistrates may impose conditions when granting bail. Such conditions can include an order that the accused must hand in his passport, an order that he live at a bail hostel or an order that he report to the police at set times. In addition it is possible to ask for a *surety*. A surety is another person who is prepared to promise that he will pay the court a certain sum of money if the defendant fails to attend court. This promise is called a 'recognisance'. No money is paid unless the accused fails to answer to his bail. This system is different from that in other countries, especially the United States of America, where the surety must pay the money into court before the defendant is released on bail, but gets the money back when the defendant attends court as required.

APPLYING THE LAW

Explain whether the defendant in each of the following situations is likely to be given bail or not.

1 **Felicity is accused of the theft of £2,000. She is married and lives locally. She has one previous conviction for theft.**

2 **William is accused of robbery. During the robbery it is alleged that he threatened the victim with a gun. He has no previous convictions.**

Examination question

Read the four extracts below relating to the **Police and Citizens' Rights**.

Use the information they contain, and any other information you may have, to help you answer the questions which follow.

Extract A

> The **Custody Officer** must make a written record of all property that a detained person has with him or her and there is a **Power to Search** for that purpose. This may be a strip search carried out by an officer of the same sex as the person detained. The police can seize and retain any property, but clothes or personal effects can only be seized if the police believe they may be used to cause injury, to damage property, to interfere with evidence, or to escape.

Extract B

> Any of us might at some stage be stopped and questioned by the police or to be asked to come along to a police station 'to help police with their enquiries . . .'. This is particularly true of young people who spend more time on the streets and in public places and who are often considered suspicious and worthy of police attention because of their

dress, appearance, the place where they live or just because they are 'hanging around'. It is therefore important that everyone and particularly young people know their rights in relation to dealings with the police.

Extract C

It is a fundamental right that we should be treated fairly and according to the law. Knowing your rights and the limit of police powers does not ensure this – you will not always be able to enforce your rights and sometimes the police will act beyond their powers. However what knowing your rights does mean is that you will have information which makes it less likely that you will be rushed or pressurised into doing anything against your better judgement. You will be in a position to make decisions on the basis of knowing what your options are – Do I have to answer these questions? Must I make a statement? Must I allow my home to be searched? Also where you are aware that the police have infringed your rights you will be in a better position to act quickly and do something about this.

(*Source* (Extracts A, B and C): 'Police Powers', a National Youth Bureau/BBC publication, 1988.)

a Look at Extract A. What do you understand by the following?
  i Custody Officer (*1 mark*)
  ii Power to Search (*2 marks*)
b Look at Extract B.
  i Explain the circumstances and powers involved when a police officer may stop and search a person in a public place. (*5 marks*)
  ii Look at Extracts C and D. How might a person receive legal advice when taken to a police station? Who might be expected to give this advice? (*4 marks*)
c George aged 22 and Tracey aged 16 were walking through a quiet area of town when approached by two police officers.
  The officers said that the pair looked like a couple wanted for questioning about a series of burglaries around the area during the last month or so.
  When George became annoyed about being 'picked on' the officers grabbed both of them and took them to the police station.
  Whilst in the police car the officers said that they would be taking fingerprints and expected to keep the couple at the police station for 'some time'.
  i What rights do George and Tracey have? (*3 marks*)
  ii What would you advise them to do if they felt they had not been properly treated? (*3 marks*)

Extract D

d   Read the following extract

Most of the police powers and corresponding rights for suspects are to be found in the
Police and Criminal Evidence Act 1984 –
known as PACE – and in the Codes of
Conduct issued by the Home Secretary
under PACE and approved by Parliament.
PACE was the product of years of discussion about police powers. It was based on
the recommendations in the Report of the
Royal Commission on Criminal Procedure
... a body which had been directed in its
terms of reference to strike a balance
between the interests of the community on
the one hand and the rights and liberties of
the individual suspect on the other. There
has now been another Royal Commission
set up in March 1991 – this time on Criminal
Justice – and some of its recommendations
along with other ideas suggested by the government, which will change defendants'
rights, are likely to be implemented in 1994.

(*Source*: Your Rights – The Liberty/NCCL Guide',
fifth edition, 1994.)

The extract talks about the law trying to 'strike a
balance' between the interests of the community
and the rights of the individual suspect.

   To what extent do you think there is a 'balance'
when it comes to the police and citizens' rights?

   What changes would you make?   (*7 marks*)

Total: 25 marks

Northern Examinations and
Assessment Board 1992

Criminal law 11

11.1 Definition of crime

In Chapter 1 we looked at the purpose of the law and compared civil law and criminal law. We said that the main aims of criminal law are to maintain law and order and to protect individuals and society. In order to do this the criminal law forbids certain types of behaviour and makes anyone who carries out that behaviour liable to punishment.

Many crimes involve conduct that injures another person or his/her property in some way; examples are rape, assault, theft and causing criminal damage. There is a victim in these crimes. Other crimes do not involve any victim; in other words nobody suffers from the crime. Examples here include failing to wear a seat belt when driving a car or failing to wear a safety helmet when riding a motor bike. In these 'crimes' it cannot be said that the law is protecting other people, although it is trying to protect the 'criminal' himself from injury. It can be argued that making such conduct 'criminal' and liable to punishment is an infringement of personal freedom. Why should the State punish a person for not wearing a seat belt when it will only be that person who suffers through not wearing it?

So to define crime as conduct which injures people or property is not accurate. Probably the simplest definition which covers all crimes is that given by Professor Glanville Williams who states:

A crime is a legal wrong that can be followed by criminal proceedings which may result in punishment.

This is wide enough to cover the fact that what is considered a crime may change as society's ideas change. This could mean that some behaviour previously regarded as criminal becomes decriminalised. Until 1994 it was a crime for men under the age of 21 to take part in homosexual acts in private. Society's view of this behaviour changed and Parliament changed the law so that such behaviour is only criminal if the parties are under the age of 18. Ideas also change so that behaviour which was previously considered acceptable is made a crime. This was seen in the Dangerous Dogs Act 1991 when it was made a crime to allow certain breeds of dog out in public without a muzzle. The Act was passed because of the public outcry over attacks by pit bull terriers which had killed and injured young children.

11.2 Classification of crimes

There are many types of crime and naturally they can be divided up into different categories. There are several ways of doing this:

1 *By the method of trying the crime.* In Chapters 2 and 3 we saw that crimes are tried in either the Magistrates' Court or the Crown Court. For this purpose crimes are divided into three types: indictable offences which are the most serious crimes and triable only in the Crown Court; offences triable either way, which are the middle range of offences and are tried either in the Crown Court or the Magistrates' Court; and summary offences which must be tried in the Magistrates' Court.

2 *By the type of crime involved.* We have

already seen that some crimes affect other people and some do not. So it is possible to divide crimes up according to whether they affect a person directly (e.g. an assault), or property (e.g. theft), or public order (e.g. being drunk in a public place) or a motoring offence (e.g. speeding).

3 *By whether the offence is an arrestable one or not.* In Chapter 10 we looked at powers of arrest and saw that in general it is only possible to arrest someone without a warrant if he or she is suspected of an arrestable offence. For other crimes the criminal proceedings are normally started by a summons being issued, that is, a document sent through the post to the defendant setting out the offence and giving the date and time of the hearing in court. Some arrestable offences are considered 'serious arrestable offences' and, as we saw in Chapter 10, the police have extra powers over detaining the suspect.

4 *By the source which created the crime.* Some crimes have been recognised as crimes in this country for hundreds of years and have been defined by cases decided by the judges. Parliament has never defined them. Such crimes are called common law crimes. The most important common law crime is murder. Other crimes are called statutory crimes because they are defined in Acts of Parliament; for example, theft, burglary and robbery are all defined in the Theft Act 1968.

11.3 Elements of a crime

In order for a person to be found guilty of a crime it is necessary for the prosecution, in the majority of crimes, to prove two elements – the *actus reus* and the *mens rea*. 'Actus reus' means the guilty act; 'mens rea' means the guilty mind or intention. There are some exceptions, called crimes of strict liability, where the actus reus alone is enough to make a person guilty without proving any element of intention. (*See* 11.4 below.)

Each crime has its own actus reus and mens rea and they are different for the different crimes. The elements of actus reus and mens rea are easier to understand if we look at actual situations.

If Jane deliberately and meaning to be dishonest, takes a purse, containing £40, from another woman's shopping bag and spends the money, she has committed theft. The actus reus of theft is appropriation of property belonging to another and in Jane's case it is the physical taking of the purse. Intending to be dishonest and to 'permanently deprive' the other woman of the purse is the mens rea. In this example both elements of the crime of theft are present.

However, if, on leaving a friend's house you pick up a jacket thinking it is your own and leave with it you have not committed theft. This is because only the actus reus, in this example the act of picking up the jacket, is present. There is no mens rea because you had no intention to be dishonest.

It is also possible for the defendant to have the mens rea for a crime but not do the actus reus. This would be the position if the defendant, intending to kill, stabbed what he thought was a sleeping victim, when, unknown to him, the victim was already dead from a heart attack. The attacker has the mens rea for murder; he intended to kill. However, the attacker has not killed the victim; the attacker has not done the actus reus; he has attempted to murder and can be charged with this, but he is not guilty of the completed crime of murder.

Actus reus

Actus reus is usually an act, as in the example above of theft, but the actus reus can sometimes be an omission. Failure to stop at a red traffic light and failure to wear a seat belt when driving are examples where the actus reus is not an act but an omission. Most crimes of omission are minor crimes created by statute, but serious crimes can be committed by a failure to do something. For example if a mother deliberately stops feeding her child, knowing that it is too young to feed itself and will die without food, that failure to feed the child can be the actus reus for a charge of murder or manslaughter.

Sometimes it is necessary for a consequence to happen as a result of the defendant's act in order for the actus reus to be complete. In the crime of an assault occasioning actual bodily harm, contrary to s. 47 of the Offences against the Person Act 1861 (*see* 11.6) the defendant must have committed an assault, but for the actus reus to be complete that assault must have 'occasioned' actual bodily harm. In other words the consequence of the assault must be an injury.

Chain of causation

Where the act has to cause a consequence for the accused to be guilty, it is necessary to show the link between the defendant's act and the consequence. In most cases there is no problem over this. In an assault occasioning actual bodily harm, the act may be a punch to the face of the victim and the injury a broken nose. In this example there is a clear link or chain of causation between the two. Problems arise where there is an intervening act contributing to that consequence. This can occur:

1 *Where the victim takes avoiding action,* for example, jumps into a river to escape an attack and drowns. This occurred in the old case of *R. v. Pitts* (1842) and the defendant was held responsible for the death.

   A similar case was *R. v. Lewis* (1970) where a wife broke her legs when she jumped from a third floor flat because she feared violence from her husband who was shouting threats and trying to break down the door to her room. The husband was convicted of causing grievous bodily harm to her.

   But the defendant is not guilty if the action taken by the victim was unreasonable or too far removed from the original attack, as, where, for example, three months after an assault the victim suffering from depression as a result of the assault commits suicide.

2 *Where another person intervenes.* If the defendant starts off a chain of events which ends with the forbidden consequence, can he be guilty if a third person has intervened and done something which leads to that consequence? This type of problem can occur in cases where there is poor medical treatment which contributes to the death. In such cases the courts are very reluctant to conclude that the intervening medical treatment broke the chain of causation. The leading case is *R. v. Smith* (1959) where a soldier was stabbed in a barrack-room brawl. His medical treatment was described by the Court of Appeal as 'thoroughly bad'. The wound had penetrated a lung and on the way to the medical centre he

was dropped twice and then given artificial respiration which aggravated the wound. There was evidence that the poor medical treatment had affected his chance of recovery by as much as 75 per cent. The Court of Appeal held the defendant's stabbing was still the cause of death and he was guilty of murder. The Lord Chief Justice, Lord Parker said:

It seems to the court that if at the time of death the original wound is still an operating cause and a substantial cause, then the death can properly be said to be the result of the wound, all be it that some other cause of death is also operating.

In *R. v. Cheshire* (1991) the victim was shot twice and his treatment included the insertion of a tube to help him breathe. This tube caused a rare complication that led to the victim's death. Even though there was evidence that the original wounds were no longer life threatening and it was the failure of medical staff to recognise and deal with the complication that had directly led to the death, the Court of Appeal held that the defendant was guilty of murder. It was his act of shooting that had caused the victim to need the treatment. The medical staff when they put the tube in were only trying to repair the harm done. The court said that it would only be in the most extraordinary or unusual case that such treatment could be said to be so independent of the acts of the accused that it could in law be regarded as the cause of the victim's death to the exclusion of the accused's acts.

The same line of reasoning was seen in *R. v. Blaue* (1975) where the victim was a Jehovah's Witness. She had been stabbed, but, because of her religion, refused a blood transfusion which would have saved her life. Blaue, her attacker was found guilty of her murder since the wound he had caused was an 'operating and substantial cause' of her death.

In *R. v. Malcherek* (1981) it was decided that switching off a life support machine did not break the chain of causation. The original injury was still an 'operating and substantial cause of death'.

Mens rea

Although the phrase mens rea means guilty mind it does not mean that the defendant has to know that what he is doing is against the law. It means that the defendant must have the level of intention required for the particular offence with which he is charged. The criminal law recognises that there are different levels of intention.

Specific intention

For most serious crimes it is necessary to show that the defendant had what the law calls specific intention. This concept of intention is difficult to define. In *R.* v. *Mohan* (1976) the judges in the Court of Appeal said that intention was: 'a decision to bring about, in so far as it lies within the accused's power, [a particular consequence], no matter whether the accused desires that consequence of his act or not'. This makes it clear that the defendant's motive or reason for doing the act is not important. The main difficulties with proving specific intention occur in cases where the crime with which the person is charged was not the defendant's main aim. However, in achieving his main aim he realised or foresaw that he would also cause or commit the crime with which he is charged. This idea is referred to as 'foresight of consequences'. An example of this situation is where a person decides to set fire to his factory so that he can claim the insurance. His main aim is the claiming of the insurance. Unfortunately, he chooses to start the fire when there are people working in the factory and some of them die because they are unable to escape the flames. Does that person have the specific intention to kill or cause serious harm to the victims of the fire?

The main rule about foresight of consequences is that it is not the same as intention, but it can be evidence of intention. To decide if there is evidence of intention in our example, the jury should ask themselves two questions: first, how probable was the consequence of the act? In other words, how likely was it that people would die or be seriously injured in the fire? Second, did the defendant foresee that consequence? Did he realise that people would die or be seriously injured? If the jury decided that it was virtually certain that people would be killed or seriously injured and that the defendant realised this, there is evidence on which the jury can find that the defendant had the specific intention for murder.

Recklessness or basic intention

For other crimes it is not necessary to prove such a high degree of intention. The law only requires proof of basic intention or what is called recklessness. Of course, if the prosecution can prove specific intent the defendant will be guilty, but they do not have to go as far as that.

Recklessness involves taking a risk. There are two levels of risk taking. The higher level is when the defendant realises that there is a risk involved, but still carries on with his conduct. The lower level is when the defendant fails to think about the possibility of there being any risk, though an ordinary careful person would realise that there was a risk involved. Let's look at a situation to explain these levels of recklessness.

A tramp, sheltering in a haystack for warmth, lights a candle. This causes the haystack to catch fire. For the higher level of recklessness, the tramp must realise that there is a risk of setting the haystack on fire, but decide to take the risk and light the candle. For the lower level of recklessness, an ordinary prudent person must realise there is an obvious risk of the haystack catching fire, but the tramp will be reckless if he fails to think about the possibility that there is such a risk.

For the mens rea of some crimes the higher level of recklessness is needed; for other crimes, mainly those charged under the Criminal Damage Act 1971, the lower level is sufficient to make the defendant guilty. The example of setting fire to the haystack only requires this lower level.

It is perhaps easier to think of the different levels of intention as the steps of a ladder. For the crimes where the lower level of recklessness is enough to prove the defendant guilty, the lowest rung on the ladder will do. Of course, the defendant is also guilty if the prosecution can prove a higher level of recklessness, but there is no need to do this. For crimes requiring the higher level of recklessness, the prosecution must prove at least the middle rung on the ladder. For crimes of specific intention only the top rung will do. The different types of *mens rea* are illustrated in this way in Figure 11.1 (opposite).

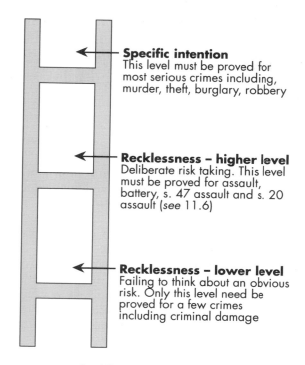

Specific intention
This level must be proved for most serious crimes including, murder, theft, burglary, robbery

Recklessness – higher level
Deliberate risk taking. This level must be proved for assault, battery, s. 47 assault and s. 20 assault (see 11.6)

Recklessness – lower level
Failing to think about an obvious risk. Only this level need be proved for a few crimes including criminal damage

Figure 11.1   The different types of mens rea

11.4 Strict liability crimes

Strict liability crimes are those where the defendant will be guilty because he did the actus reus. There is no need to prove any mens rea. An extreme example is *Winzar* v. *Chief Constable for Kent* (1983), where the police were called to remove a drunken man from the casualty department of a hospital. The police took him to their car on the road outside and then charged him with being 'found' drunk on a highway. The Court held that the offence did not require any mens rea and so the defendant was guilty. He had been drunk on a highway. Another example is *Strowger* v. *John* (1978) in which a car tax disc fell from the window on to the floor of the car after the owner had parked the car. The owner was guilty of the offence of failing to display a car tax disc. It was not necessary to show that he had deliberately left the tax disc off, he was guilty simply because it was not in the window.

Many strict liability offences are not truly criminal behaviour but are treated as offences so as to prevent potential danger to public health and safety. Causing pollution, driving a vehicle with dangerous brakes or selling contaminated food come under this heading. The offenders do not have to intend to do any of these to be guilty; the act of doing them is enough. Because such behaviour is a crime there is pressure on people to take extra care. Companies will be more careful not to cause pollution; drivers more careful in maintaining and checking their vehicles; and shops more careful about food handling and abiding by sell-by dates.

Other offences are so trivial that it would be too time consuming for the prosecutor to have to prove intention in every case; the tax disc case comes into this category.

Normally offences which can be punished by imprisonment are not strict liability offences, since it seems unfair to put people at the risk of going to prison when they had no intention of committing a crime. However, some crimes which do carry a possible penalty of imprisonment are strict liability offences. An example is *Pharmaceutical Society of Great Britain* v. *Storkwain* (1986) where there was an offence contrary to s. 58(2) of the Medicines Act 1968. This offence has a maximum penalty of three months imprisonment. The facts were that a forged prescription had been handed in to a chemist. The pharmacist dispensed the drugs because he had no reason to suspect that the prescription was a forgery. The pharmacist was then found guilty of supplying drugs without a prescription because the House of Lords held that the offence did not need mens rea. The fact that the pharmacist had made a genuine mistake about the prescription did not stop him from being guilty. The pharmacist was not sent to prison, but the fact remains that any pharmacist in this position could be at risk of going to prison.

11.5 Murder and manslaughter

This is the killing of a human being. The most serious crime is murder and the difference between it and manslaughter is in the intention of the defendant.

Murder is a common law crime, that is, it is not defined by any statute, though the punishment, life imprisonment, is now set out in a statute. The definition at common law dates back to the seventeenth century. Murder is defined as:

where a person of sound mind unlawfully kills any reasonable creature in being and under the Queen's peace with malice aforethought, either express or implied.

The *actus reus* is the unlawful killing of a person. This actus reus is the same in the crime of manslaughter. The *mens rea* of murder is 'malice aforethought, either express or implied'. It is this that distinguishes murder from manslaughter.

Actus reus – murder and manslaughter

The important elements of the actus reus in both murder and manslaughter are:

1 *The killing must be unlawful*, that is, without legal justification or excuse, such as killing in self defence.

2 *Causation must be established*, that is, it must be established that the defendant's act caused the death. The killing can be by any means, shooting, stabbing, poison etc., but it must cause the death. *See* 11.3 above for general rules on causation.

3 *The victim must be a human being when attacked.* This means that he or she must have been born; killing a foetus is not murder, though it may be another crime. However, injuring a child in the womb so that after it is born it dies of those injuries could be murder or manslaughter. This was stated in 1997 by the judges in the House of Lords in the Attorney-General's Reference (No 3 of 1994).

4 *The victim must die.* The rule used to be that the victim had to die within a year and a day of the attack. If the death occurred after this period the attacker could not be charged with murder or manslaughter. However, there were considerable criticisms of this rule as the developments in medical science, especially life support machines, meant that victims could be kept alive for longer than a year before eventually dying from their injuries. The Law Commission recommended that the rule should be abolished and this was done when Parliament passed the Law Reform (Year and a Day Rule) Act 1996. If the death occurs more than three years after the attack, then the Attorney-General must give consent for the proceedings.

5 *Under the Queen's peace.* The killing of an enemy during the conduct of war is not considered as constituting the actus reus for murder.

Mens rea – murder

Malice aforethought means that murder is a specific intent crime. *Express or implied* means that either of two intentions is sufficient. *Express malice* is the intention to kill. *Implied malice* is the intention to do grievous bodily harm. It was decided in *R. v. Vickers* (1957) that the intention to cause grievous bodily harm is sufficient to make a defendant guilty of murder if his victim dies. The facts were that Vickers in the course of stealing from a shop was found by an old lady. He struck her a number of blows which killed her. He did not use a weapon and there was no suggestion that he intended to kill her. The Court of Criminal Appeal held that there were two types of malice aforethought and either was sufficient to make the defendant guilty.

This decision was confirmed by the House of Lords in *R. v. Cunningham* (1981). The facts in this case were that Cunningham attacked his victim in a public house in Margate, repeatedly hitting him with a chair, wrongly believing him to be associating with his, Cunningham's, girlfriend. The victim died as a result of his injuries. Lord Hailsham said '*R. v. Vickers* was a correct statement of the law.'

Foresight of consequence as evidence of the specific intention for murder has been considered in several cases. The most important cases are *R. v. Moloney* (1985) and *R. v. Hancock and Shankland* (1986).

In *Moloney* a father and his stepson, who had both had a lot to drink, were having a friendly argument about the stepson's wish to leave the army. The father said the son was no good with guns and challenged him to see which one of them could load a gun the faster. The stepson won easily and his father then said that the boy would not have 'the guts' to pull the trigger. The stepson pulled the trigger and the shot killed the father. The stepson said to the police and in evidence, when he was tried for murder, that he had not intended to kill his father. He just pulled the trigger without thinking of the consequences.

The House of Lords held that foresight of consequences was not the same as intention but only evidence from which intention might be proved.

In *Hancock and Shankland* two miners wanted to frighten another miner, who refused to join a miners' strike. They pushed two lumps of concrete from a bridge on to a road in South Wales as the taxi which was taking the other miner to work was coming along. One of the lumps of concrete hit the windscreen of the taxi, killing the driver. The two defendants said that they did not want to kill or injure anyone; they only wanted to frighten the other miner. They claimed they did not realise or foresee the consequences of their action.

In both cases the defendants were convicted by the juries in their cases and appealed, first to the Court of Appeal and then to the House of Lords. In each case the House of Lords quashed the convictions for murder and substituted a verdict of manslaughter. The reason they did this was because the judge at each of the trials had given the jury the wrong direction on the law.

In *R. v. Nedrick* (1986) the Court of Appeal tried to simplify the law in this area and suggested that a jury considering foresight of consequences should ask themselves the two questions we have already looked at in 11.3; that is, (1) how probable was the consequence of the defendant's act and (2) did the defendant foresee the consequence? In a murder trial, therefore, the jury have to consider (1) how probable was it that the defendant's act would cause death or grievous bodily harm and (2) did the defendant foresee that his act would cause death or grievous bodily harm? If the defendant realised that it was virtually certain that his act would cause death or grievous bodily harm then this is evidence on which a jury can decide that the defendant had the specific intention for murder.

Special defences to murder

There are three special defences which are available only on a charge of murder and which have the effect of reducing the charge of murder to one of manslaughter. These are:

- diminished responsibility
- provocation
- suicide pact

In each case the defendant has committed the actus reus for murder, that is, unlawfully killed and has the mens rea, that is, the specific intention to kill or cause grievous bodily harm, but the law allows any one of the three defences to lessen the charge to manslaughter. This is important since a judge must send anyone found guilty of murder to prison for life, he has no discretion. For manslaughter, on the other hand, while the maximum penalty is life imprisonment, the judge can impose a lesser sentence if he thinks it suitable in the case. This means that it is possible for a defendant found guilty of manslaughter to be imprisoned for a shorter term or, in some cases, not to be sent to prison at all but instead put on probation or given any sentence the judge thinks suitable. In these cases the manslaughter is referred to as voluntary manslaughter.

Diminished responsibility

The defence of diminished responsibility is set out in section 2 of the Homicide Act 1957. This section says:

Where a person kills or is party to the killing of another, he shall not be convicted of murder if he was suffering from such abnormality of mind (whether arising from a condition of arrested or retarded development of mind or any inherent causes or induced by disease or injury) as substantially impaired his mental responsibility for his acts and omissions in doing or being a party to the killing.

The important factors are that:

1 The defendant must be suffering from an abnormality of mind. In *R. v. Byrne* (1960), where a sexual psychopath had killed a young woman, the Court of Appeal said that the phrase 'abnormality of mind' meant a 'state of mind so different from that of ordinary human beings that the reasonable man would term it abnormal'. In other words it is up to the jury to take a commonsense approach when deciding whether the defendant was suffering from an abnormality of mind.
2 The abnormality must be caused by arrested or retarded development or an internal cause or disease or injury. This covers a very wide range of problems including mental illnesses such as depression and physical illnesses that affect the mind such as brain tumours.

However, external causes such as taking drugs or alcohol are not included unless there is a disease or injury to the brain. In *R.* v. *Tandy* (1988) the defendant, who suffered from alcoholism, had killed her 11-year-old daughter. It was decided that if the alcoholism had reached a level at which the defendant's brain had been injured, the defendant could plead diminished responsibility.

3 The abnormality must 'substantially' affect the accused's mental responsibility for his acts or omissions. It has been held that 'substantially' means more than some trivial degree of impairment, but less than total impairment. It has also been said that a jury should approach the word in a commonsense way.

The defence of diminished responsibility is used successfully in about 70 to 80 cases each year.

Provocation

The defence of provocation is set out in section 3 of the Homicide Act 1957 which says:

Where on a charge of murder there is evidence on which a jury can find that the person charged was provoked (whether by things done or things said or by both together) to lose his self-control, the question whether the provocation was enough to make a reasonable man do as he did shall be left to be determined by the jury; and in determining that question the jury shall take into account everything both done and said according to the effect which, in their opinion, it would have on a reasonable man.

The section does not define what type of behaviour can be considered as provocation apart from saying that it can be 'things done or said or both together' and that it must be enough to provoke a 'reasonable man'.

Provocation covers many different situations, including discovering that one's husband or wife is having an affair with someone else; physical violence or racist remarks. It can be a single incident or a series of things; it need not be by the victim, nor need it be deliberately aimed at the accused.

The most important point is that the provocation must cause a sudden and temporary loss of self-control. If there is evidence that the accused did not lose his temper but used the situation to

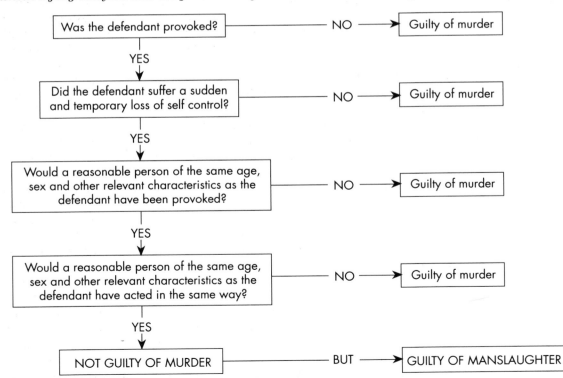

Figure 11.2 Provocation flow chart

carry out a deliberate killing, then the accused cannot use the defence of provocation.

The other important point is that it is not enough to show that the accused was provoked, the jury must also be satisfied that a 'reasonable man' would have been provoked in the same circumstances and would have acted as the accused did. The phrase 'reasonable man' means a person having the power of self-control of an ordinary person of the same age and sex as the accused. This was decided in *DPP* v. *Camplin* (1978) where the accused was a 15-year-old boy who had been sexually assaulted by an older man. When the man laughed at him the boy had hit him over the head with a heavy cooking pan and killed him. At his trial the judge had told the jury to consider how a reasonable adult would have reacted in the same circumstances, but the House of Lords held that this was the wrong test to use. The jury should have considered whether an ordinary 15-year-old boy would have been provoked and acted as the defendant did. The jury can also consider other characteristics of the accused if those characteristics are reasonably permanent and are relevant to the provocation. This means that the fact that a person has a scar on his face can be considered if the provocation is about his looks, but not if the provocation is about the person's inability to play football and has nothing to do with the scar. Characteristics such as alcoholism and drug addiction have not been allowed to provide a defence of provocation. However, the Court of Appeal in *R.* v. *Thornton* (1995) held that 'battered woman syndrome' could be a relevant characteristic. Sarah Thornton, a battered wife, had killed her husband. The evidence was that after threatening her, he had fallen asleep on the settee. She had then gone into the kitchen, got a knife, returned to the room where her husband was sleeping and stabbed him. The Court of Appeal ordered a re-trial because the jury in the original trial had not been allowed to consider the effect of 'battered woman syndrome'. The flow chart in Figure 11.2 on p. 106 shows the various tests for provocation.

Suicide pact

Under section 4 of the Homicide Act 1957 (as amended by the Suicide Act 1961), where two people agree to commit suicide and one survives, if that one has killed the other then he will be guilty of manslaughter not murder. This defence is only available if the survivor had the settled intention to die when he caused the other person's death.

Apart from these special defences to murder there are general defences available for most crimes including murder. These general defences are considered in 11.8.

Involuntary manslaughter

Involuntary manslaughter is an unlawful killing where the accused did not have the specific intention for murder. There are three possible ways in which a person may be guilty of involuntary manslaughter:

- by an act which is unlawful and dangerous
- by recklessness
- by gross negligence

An unlawful and dangerous act

The accused must do an unlawful act (e.g. a minor assault), and that act must cause the death of the victim. This will be manslaughter if the act was dangerous in the sense that a sober and reasonable person would have realised that there was a risk that the act might cause some injury, even if not serious injury. The leading case on this is *DPP* v. *Newbury and Jones* (1976) where two 15-year-old boys pushed a paving stone from a bridge on to a railway line as a train was passing. The stone killed the guard of the train. The House of Lords held that the boys were guilty of manslaughter since they had deliberately done an unlawful act, criminal damage, which was dangerous when they pushed the stone on to the railway. They did not have to realise that the act was dangerous. They were guilty because a sober and reasonable person would have realised the danger of causing some injury by that act. Any assault is an unlawful act, and if it is likely to cause some injury, the assaulter can be charged with manslaughter if the victim actually dies. An example of this is seen in *R.* v. *Mitchell* (1983). This case also illustrates the principle of *transferred malice*. Mitchell tried to push his way into a queue and when another man objected, Mitchell punched him, causing him to fall against an 89-year-old woman. The woman's leg was broken as a result and she died later from complications due to the breaking of her leg. Mitchell was found guilty of manslaughter. He had committed an unlawful act by punching the other man. That unlawful act caused the death of the elderly woman and it was dangerous in the sense that it was likely to cause some injury, though not necessarily a serious one. The fact that the unlawful act was aimed at one person but killed another did not matter; Mitchell was still guilty.

Recklessness

If there is an obvious risk that someone will be injured as a result of the defendant's conduct, it is possible that the defendant will be guilty of manslaughter, even if the conduct is otherwise lawful.

Gross negligence

Where a person owes a duty of care then if he performs that duty so negligently that someone dies, he may be guilty of manslaughter. The degree of negligence needed to make a person guilty was described in *R. v. Bateman* (1925) as negligence which 'went beyond a mere matter of compensation between subjects and showed such a disregard for life and safety of others as to amount to a crime against the state and conduct deserving of punishment'.

In *R v Adomako* (1994), the defendant was an anaesthetist who failed to notice that a tube giving the patient oxygen had become disconnected. As a result the patient died and Adomako was convicted of manslaughter. The House of Lords said that gross negligence in manslaughter cases was something for the jury to decide. The essential point was 'whether, having regard to the risk of death involved, the conduct of the defendant was so bad in all the circumstances as to amount in their judgment to a criminal act or omission.' If this was so then the defendant was guilty of manslaughter by gross negligence.

APPLYING THE LAW

In each of the following situations explain, giving reasons for your answer, whether

the person involved is guilty of murder or manslaughter.

1 **George, while driving at 60 m.p.h. through an area with a 30 m.p.h. speed limit, loses control of his car, mounts the pavement and knocks down and kills a pedestrian.**
2 **Patricia, who has a bad scar on her face, is teased by Andrew. Andrew keeps on calling her 'ugly mug'. In a temper Patricia seizes a knife and stabs Andrew, killing him.**
3 **Franklin, who is mentally retarded, hits Steven on the head with a hammer. Steven is taken to hospital and put on a life support machine. Three days later the doctors decide to switch off the life support machine and Steven dies.**

11.6 Non-fatal offences against the person

There are many different types of offences against the person. They include any assault, whether or not it causes an injury, sexual offences and even bigamy. There are too many to include them all in this book, so we shall concentrate on four main offences which involve assault. The word assault has two meanings in law; the first is the general term for physical attacks on another person; the second is a very specific meaning which we consider in the first of the offences below.

Common assault and battery

These offences are not defined in any statute but are charged under section 39 of the Criminal Justice Act 1988. This section says that they are summary offences and a person guilty of either of them shall be liable to be fined up to £5,000 or to be imprisoned for a term not exceeding six months, or to both.

There are two ways of committing the offence:

- assault
- battery

Assault

Assault is any act which intentionally or recklessly causes another to fear immediate and unlawful violence. There is no need for contact, the actus reus is committed when the defendant does any act which causes the other person to believe that unlawful force is about to be used against him. Examples include:

- threatening with a fist or a cane or any weapon
- throwing a stone or other missile
- pointing a loaded gun at someone within range

Words alone are not usually enough to constitute assault, there must be some act. Also there is no assault if it is obvious to the victim that the defendant cannot carry out his threat of violence, for example, where the defendant is in a passing train. However, if violence is possible then the fact that the defendant is on the other side of a window or door does not prevent his actions being an assault. This was shown in *Smith* v. *Chief Superintendent, Woking Police Station* (1983), where the defendant entered a private garden at night and looked through the bedroom window of the complainant. She was terrified and the Divisional Court upheld a conviction under section 4 of the Vagrancy Act 1824 which required proof that the defendant's purpose was to assault the victim.

Battery

Battery is the application, intentionally or recklessly, of unlawful force to another person. Examples include:

- punching, slapping, kicking, pushing
- hitting someone with a stick
- hitting someone with a stone or other missile
- an indirect action, such as a booby trap which hits the victim

For an offence to constitute a battery, the victim need not be aware that he is about to be struck. Many incidents include an assault and a battery. For example, the victim sees a knife drawn (assault) and is then stabbed (battery). But if the victim is hit from behind, so that the first he knows about it is when the blow lands, there is only a battery.

For both assault and battery there must be either specific intention to do the act or recklessness in the sense of deliberately taking a risk as to whether it happened; that is the higher level of recklessness considered in 11.3.

The actus reus and the mens rea must exist at the same time for the crime to be complete. In *Fagan* v. *Metropolitan Police Commissioner* (1969) the defendant drove his car on to a policeman's foot without realising it, but he then refused to move the car when the police officer told him the car was on his foot. It was held that there was sufficient overlap to make the completed crime. Mr Justice James said: 'There was an act constituting a battery which at its inception was not criminal because there was no element of intention but which became criminal from the moment the intention was formed.'

Assault occasioning actual bodily harm

Assault occasioning actual bodily harm is charged under section 47 of the Offences against the Person Act 1861 and it must be an assault or battery which causes actual bodily harm. The actus reus is that of an assault or battery plus the consequence of actual bodily harm. *Actual bodily harm* means any injury no matter how slight, a scratch or a bruise is enough. It also includes nervous shock caused by the defendant's action.

The mens rea is the same as for an assault or battery. The defendant is guilty even if he did not intend to cause an injury as the mens rea does not include any intention to cause actual bodily harm or recklessness as to whether such harm is caused. *R.* v. *Savage* (1991) makes it quite clear that the mental element is the same as for a common assault. There is no further mental state which has to be established. The offence is proved by establishing an assault and showing that it did cause actual bodily harm.

The facts in *Savage* were that the defendant on seeing her husband's girlfriend in a pub had deliberately thrown her drink over her. Savage said she did not mean to cause any injury, but in the course of the incident the glass had broken and caused a cut on the girlfriend's wrist. Savage was guilty because she had intentionally applied unlawful force in throwing the drink over the woman and a cut had been 'occasioned'.

Malicious wounding

Section 20 of the Offences against the Person Act 1861 says that:

Whosoever shall unlawfully and maliciously wound or inflict any grievous bodily harm upon another person, either with or without any weapon or instrument, shall be guilty of an offence triable either way and being convicted thereof shall be liable to imprisonment for five years.

This is known as malicious wounding. The actus reus of section 20 is that the defendant must 'wound or inflict grievous bodily harm'.

A *wound* means a cutting of the whole skin. In *R.* v. *Wood* (1830) it was held that breaking a collar bone was not wounding. Similarly in *J.J.C.* v. *Eisenhower* (1983) it was decided that the rupturing of blood vessels internally was not a wound. In this case the defendant had fired an air pistol at the victim and a pellet had struck his eye causing bleeding inside the eye but not puncturing it all. However a wound need not be a serious injury, a small cut is enough to be classed as a wound. A cut inside the mouth is classed as a wound, because it is a continuation of the external skin.

Grievous bodily harm has the meaning of 'really serious' harm, but it is not necessary to show that the injuries are either permanent or life-threatening.

The mens rea of section 20 has caused some problems since the section uses the word 'maliciously'. This does not have its everyday meaning as was decided in *R.* v. *Cunningham* (1957) where it was held that the word meant intending to do the injury or foreseeing the risk that the act might cause injury and deciding to take that risk. *R.* v. *Mowatt* (1968) followed *Cunningham* but added that it was unnecessary in section 20 cases for the defendant to have foreseen that the unlawful act might cause 'physical harm of the gravity described in the section'. Lord Diplock said: 'It is enough that he should have foreseen that some physical harm to some person, albeit of a minor character, might result.' In other words, if the defendant realised that some slight injury might be caused as a result of his act, that realisation makes him guilty under section 20.

R. v. *Parmenter* (1991) confirmed that the word 'maliciously' is a term of legal art with this special meaning. In *Parmenter* the defendant threw a baby into the air and caught it, causing grievous bodily harm. The defendant said he had done this before with slightly older children and was unaware that his actions were likely to cause harm to a young baby. It was held that he was not guilty as he did not intend to injure the child, nor did he realise there was a risk of injury to the child. Intention to cause harm to property is not enough, unless the defendant is aware that his action may also cause harm to a person. So throwing a stone at a window intending to cause damage, but being unaware that any person was near enough to be hurt, would not be sufficient to make the defendant guilty under section 20, if the stone struck and seriously injured someone.

Transferred malice

We have already seen the idea of transferring intention in the section above on manslaughter. The rule about *transferred malice* applies to all crimes including assaults. Where a defendant intends to assault one person, but actually hits another person he will still be guilty because the intention is transferred from the intended victim to the actual victim. In *R.* v. *Latimer* (1886) the defendant was held guilty of maliciously wounding R, when he struck her with a belt aimed at C with whom he had had words. The fact that he did not mean to strike R was no defence. The intention he had towards C was transferred to R.

Wounding with intent

Wounding with intent is an offence under section 18 of the Offences against the Person Act 1861. It is the most serious of the offences created by the Act. Section 18 states:

Whosoever shall unlawfully and maliciously by any means whatsoever wound or cause any grievous bodily harm to any person with intent to do some grievous bodily harm to any person, or with intent to resist or prevent the lawful apprehension or detainer of any person, shall be guilty of an offence, and being convicted thereof shall be liable to imprisonment for life.

For the actus reus the defendant must do something which causes a wound or grievous bodily harm. This is the same as for section 20, but the mens rea is the critical difference between the sections.

Section 18 is a specific intention crime. The defendant must be proved to have the intention to wound or cause grievous bodily harm **or** to resist or prevent arrest. It is this intention which makes it a much more serious offence than a section 20

crime. It is also the reason why the maximum punishment is life imprisonment.

Figure 11.3 shows a flow chart for these different assaults.

Self-defence

If a person acts in self-defence or defence of another then he may have a defence to a charge of assault or even to a charge of murder or manslaughter and will be found not guilty. The important point is that the person defending himself must use no more force than is reasonably necessary in the circumstances. So, if a person is attacked by someone with a gun then it will be reasonable to fire a gun back in self-defence. But if an attacker kicks another person in the ankle, it is unreasonable to stab that attacker. The amount of force has to be in proportion to the attack. If the attacker has stopped attacking and is walking away, then it is not self-defence if the victim runs after him and hits him. It is no longer necessary for the victim to defend himself as the attack has finished.

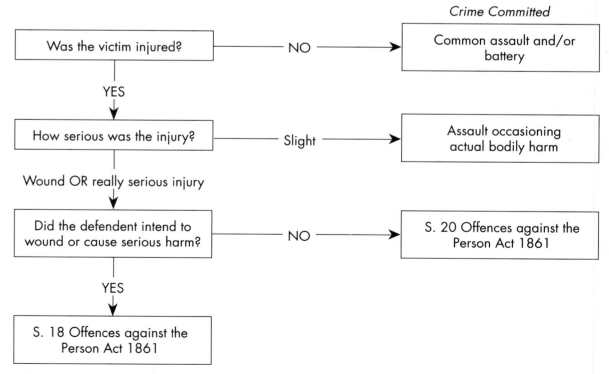

Figure 11.3   Crimes involving assaults

APPLYING THE LAW

Explain in each of the following situations what offences, if any, have been committed.

1 **Erica comes up behind Ibrahim and punches him hard in the back.**
2 **Leonard, in the course of an argument with Amy, pulls out a knife and threatens her with it.**
3 **Thomas kicks Steven, causing Steven severe bruising on his leg.**
4 **Marilyn jabs at Jane with a penknife and causes a small cut on Jane's arm.**
5 **Bruce, during a robbery, fires a gun at Anthea. The bullet hits Anthea in the chest causing injuries to her right lung.**

11.7 Offences against property

There are many offences against property and, as with assaults, it is impossible to discuss all of them in this book and only the following are included: theft, robbery, burglary, taking a car without consent, making off without payment and criminal damage.

Theft

Theft is defined in section 1 of the Theft Act 1968 as follows:

a person is guilty of theft if he dishonestly appropriates property belonging to another with the intention of permanently depriving the other of it.

The actus reus of theft is the 'appropriation of property belonging to another'. The mens rea has two parts, the thief must both be dishonest and intend to 'permanently deprive' the other person of their property.

Actus reus of theft

In order to establish the actus reus of theft there are three things that have to be proved:

• an appropriation
• of property
• belonging to another

1 *Appropriation.* Section 3 of the Theft Act says that this is 'any assumption of the rights of an owner'. This is very wide and covers a variety of different situations. Some of these are obvious, such as taking money from a handbag or a pickpocket taking a wallet from someone's pocket. Apart from these situations, there is also an appropriation where property is destroyed, because only the owner has the right to destroy any item.

Many of the cases on the meaning of appropriation involve stealing from a shop. Shoplifting is theft, but at what point can the thief be stopped and charged? All the following acts are an appropriation or 'an assumption of some of the rights of an owner'. In other words, the shoppers have treated the goods as their own.

a a shopper picks up a battery and puts it in his pocket;
b a shopper swaps price labels on two pairs of shoes, so that one pair will cost less, and takes those shoes to a sales assistant;
c a shopper puts several items in a supermarket trolley but does not pay for one item at the checkout.

Notice that in all these situations the shopper has not left the shop. This does not matter, the appropriation of the goods has already

occurred. In (a) the appropriation is at the moment the shopper puts the battery into his pocket; in (b) it is when the shopper swapped the labels; in (c) it is at the checkout. At all these points the shoppers are acting as though they are the owners of the property. In fact it is possible to say that there is an appropriation at the moment the shopper takes the item from the shelf, since at that point the shopper is getting control of the article and preventing any other shopper from taking it.

2 *Property.* The item taken must be property that can be stolen. This is obvious where the item is something like a watch or a car or any other moveable property. Coins and banknotes are also property. The main things that are not property for the purposes of the definition of theft are electricity (there is a separate offence of dishonestly using electricity) and knowledge. In *Oxford* v. *Moss* (1979) a student removed an examination paper, photocopied it and then replaced the original paper. This meant that no physical item had been permanently taken, only the knowledge of what was on the examination paper. It was decided that this was not theft, since knowledge was not 'property'. Section 4 of the Theft Act 1968 also places limits on when land and plants growing wild can be considered property that can be stolen. Land or items attached to the land can normally only be stolen by a tenant, for example, by removing a sink from a rented flat. Plants growing wild are another exception, which cannot be stolen, unless the plant is completely dug up. When flowers, fruit or leaves are picked off the plant, there is theft only if the person doing the picking intends to sell them.

3 *Belonging to another.* This again is very wide in its meaning, since it covers situations where someone else has possession or control of the item, as well as where someone else owns the property. So it is possible for the owner to be charged with stealing his own property if it was in the control of another person who had a legal right to it. This happened in *R.* v. *Turner* (1971) when a car owner took his car from a garage where it had been repaired without paying the repair bill. The garage had told him that he could not have the car back until he paid the bill and, under the civil law, the garage had the right to do this. So it was held that Turner was guilty of stealing his own car.

Mens rea of theft

The mens rea of theft has two elements which must be proved:

- dishonesty
- intention to permanently deprive

1 *Dishonesty.* The Theft Act 1968 does not define dishonesty but it does give three situations where a person's act is not be regarded as dishonest. These are set out in section 2 of the Theft Act 1968 and are:

a if he believes that he has in law the right to deprive the other person of the property;

b if he believes that the other person would consent to the appropriation if he knew of the circumstances;

c if he believes he cannot discover who the owner is by taking reasonable steps.

All these are easier to understand if we look at examples.

a an old lady keeps a football that has been kicked into her garden by a child. She believes she has a right in law to keep it. This would not be regarded as dishonest;

b a shop assistant cuts her hand at work. She takes some money from the till to buy a bandage, believing that the shop owner would consent to this if he knew of the circumstances. Again this would not be regarded as being dishonest;

c a student finds a pound coin in the street. He keeps it since he believes that he cannot find out who the owner is by taking reasonable steps. Again this would not be regarded as being dishonest. The situation might be different if the student had found a purse with money in it and the owner's initials on it, since it is much easier to trace the owner, but it is the student's belief that is important.

On the other hand section 2 says that a person can be dishonest even if he is willing to pay for the property. This means that if a person takes a CD belonging to another person, but leaves money to cover the cost of the CD, this can still be dishonest behaviour if he knows that the other person does not want to sell the CD.

Since the Theft Act 1968 does not give a definition of dishonesty, the courts have had to consider it. In *R.* v. *Ghosh* (1982) the Court of Appeal said that in proving dishonesty there was a two-stage test. First, was what the defendant had done dishonest by the ordinary standards of reasonable people? Second, did the defendant realise that what he was doing was dishonest by those standards? The defendant is acting dishonestly if the answer to both those questions is 'yes'.

2 *Intention to permanently deprive.* Theft is only proved if the person appropriating the property not only was being dishonest, but also intended to permanently deprive the other person of the property. This means that borrowing an item will not usually be considered theft. In *R.* v. *Lloyd* (1985) a film was borrowed from a cinema without permission in order to make a copy of it. The original film was then returned. This meant that the defendant was not guilty of theft as he had not intended to permanently deprive the cinema of the film. Borrowing can be considered theft if the property is kept until it has little or no value left. An example here would be 'borrowing' a week's season ticket for the train and using it for six days. The season ticket has very little value left and even if the taker then hands it back, he can be guilty of theft.

Theft can be tried either in the Magistrates' Court or in the Crown Court. It is a triable either way offence. The maximum penalty is seven years' imprisonment.

APPLYING THE LAW

Explain in each of the following situations whether a theft has occurred.

1 **On leaving a friend's house Carol takes an umbrella from a stand in the hall, believing it is her own.**

2 **Frank, intending to steal, takes a packet of bacon from the shelf in a supermarket and puts it in his pocket. He then realises that he is being watched by a store detective and puts the bacon back on the shelf.**

3 **ET comes from a planet where shop keepers are obliged to let hungry people have two items to eat free. ET is hungry and goes into Sainsway's supermarket, takes an apple and a packet of crisps and walks out without paying for them.**

Robbery

This is an offence under section 8 of the Theft Act 1968 which says that:

A person is guilty of robbery if he steals, and immediately before or at the time of doing so, and in order to do so, he uses force on any person or puts or seeks to put any person in fear of being then and there subjected to force.

So robbery is theft with force. Any force will do; pushing someone in order to snatch their handbag is enough. A threat of force is also sufficient, for example holding a knife in front of the victim. The important points are (a) that the force must be immediately before or at the time of the theft and (b) that it must be used in order to steal. In the situation where a pickpocket takes a wallet without using any force, but the victim realises what has happened, challenges the thief and the thief, in order to escape, punches the victim there is no robbery. The force was used after the theft. The pickpocket is guilty of two separate crimes: theft and battery. Another point to remember is that the force need not be used against the person whose property is stolen. In a bank robbery, the robber may point a gun at a customer in a bank in order to make the cashier hand over money. This is robbery. Robbery is an indictable offence and can only be tried at the Crown Court. The maximum penalty is life imprisonment.

Burglary

This is an offence under section 9 of the Theft Act 1968. There are several ways of committing burglary, but the common element is that the defendant must enter a building or part of a building as a trespasser. In order to have entered, it is only necessary for part of one's body to be in the building. This could occur where a thief puts his arm in through a window to steal. The word building includes not only houses, shops and factories, but also sheds and garages and even caravans and houseboats if people live in them. The words 'part of a building' are included because there are some instances where a person may have the right to be in one area of the building, but not in another part. This happens in shops. Shoppers have the right to enter the main part of the shop, but they are not allowed into store rooms or any area marked 'private – staff only'. So, if a shopper steals an item off a shelf in the main part of the shop, the correct charge is theft, but if that same shopper goes into a store room and steals, he can then be charged with burglary.

Section 9(1)(a) makes it an offence to enter any building or part of a building as a trespasser with the intention of doing any one of four things. These are:

a stealing anything in the building;
b inflicting grievous bodily harm on someone in the building;
c raping any person in the building; or
d doing unlawful damage to the building or anything in it.

Under section 9(1)(a) the burglar will be guilty the moment he enters the building if he has the intention of doing one of these four things.

Section 9(1)(b) covers situations where the defendant does not have an intent when he enters as a trespasser. This section says that a person will also be guilty of burglary if, 'having entered any building or part of a building', he steals or attempts to steal anything in the building or he inflicts or attempts to inflict grievous bodily harm on any person in the building. So to be guilty under section 9(1)(b) a defendant must do more than enter the building as a trespasser, he must steal or inflict grievous bodily harm or attempt to do one of these.

Burglary is a triable either way offence unless it involves the intention to rape or inflict grievous bodily harm. If it involves one of these serious crimes then the burglary charge must be tried at the Crown Court. The maximum penalty for burglary is 10 years' imprisonment or 14 years' for burglary of a dwelling-house.

Taking a conveyance without consent

Section 12 of the Theft Act 1968 makes it an offence to take, drive or be carried in any conveyance without the owner's consent. The word conveyance includes anything constructed for carrying people by land, water or air. So it will cover boats and aeroplanes as well as the more usual cars, motor bikes and lorries. Pedal cycles are not included, but there is a separate offence of taking a pedal cycle without consent in subsection 12(5). It is not only the original taker who is guilty under section 12, but also any driver and any passengers who know the vehicle has been taken without consent.

Taking a conveyance without consent is normally a summary offence and is tried in the Magistrates' Court with a maximum penalty of six months' imprisonment. However, there are circumstances which aggravate the taking and make it a more serious offence. These are that:

1 The vehicle is driven dangerously.
2 Due to the driving there is an accident causing injury to any person.
3 Due to the driving there is an accident causing damage to property.
4 Damage is caused to the vehicle.

Making off without payment

After the Theft Act 1968 was passed it became clear that some dishonest behaviour was not covered by that Act and so in 1978 another Theft Act was passed. Under section 3 of the Theft Act 1978 it is an offence, where the person knows that payment on the spot for goods or services is required, to dishonestly make off without having paid as required and with intent to avoid payment. This section covers situations such as running off without paying a taxi driver or leaving a restaurant without paying for a meal.

Criminal damage

Under the Criminal Damage Act 1971 it is an offence to intentionally or recklessly destroy or damage any property belonging to another. Destroying means that the property does not have to be completely destroyed, only that it is made useless for its purpose. Damage includes any damage such as scratching paint on a car or writing graffiti on walls. The defendant will be guilty if he either does this deliberately or takes a risk that property will be damaged. He does not have to realise that there is a risk of damage involved; the test is whether an ordinary careful person would realise there was a risk of damage.

11.8 General defences

When a person is charged with a crime he may admit that he has done the act involved, but claim that he has a defence. If he is successful in showing one of these defences it will mean that he is not guilty of the crime. The general defences to crime are mistake, insanity, automatism, duress and intoxication. Each of these is considered briefly below.

Mistake

Mistake is available as a defence where the defendant has made a mistake about the facts. The mistake must be such that on the facts as he believed them to be there would be no crime. An example is taking a coat mistakenly believing it to be one's own. It would also be a defence if the mistake meant that the defendant thought he was being attacked and had to defend himself. The mistake does not have to be a reasonable one, but it must be an honest mistake. In *R.* v. *Williams* (1984) the defendant thought another man was being attacked and grabbed the 'attacker'. In fact the 'attacker' was legitimately trying to arrest the other man. It was held that if Williams honestly and genuinely believed that there was an attack taking place, he had a defence to a charge of assault.

Insanity

If a defendant is proved to be insane he cannot be guilty of any crime. The verdict in such a case will be 'not guilty by reason of insanity'. The legal definition of insanity comes from the M'Naghten rules, which date from 1843. These say that a person is insane if he is suffering from a defect of reason due to disease of the mind so that either he does not know the nature and quality of his act or he does not know that he is doing wrong. It has to be stressed that this is a legal definition of insanity and not a medical one. The courts have held that a person acting in the course of an epileptic fit comes within this definition since he has a disease which affects his mind and during the fit he does not know what he is doing. A defendant may therefore be classed as legally insane, even though his illness may be a physical one such as a brain tumour.

Although the verdict is 'not guilty by reason of insanity', the judge has power to order that the defendant be sent to an appropriate hospital or make a supervision order and treatment order or give the defendant an absolute discharge. In this way the judge can make sure that, where necessary, the public is protected from danger. However where the defendant is not dangerous the judge has other methods of dealing with the defendant.

Automatism

This defence means that the defendant is not guilty of any crime since he acted like a robot because of some external cause. He was incapable of having the intention to commit any crime as he did not know what his body was doing. This could happen where a blow to the head made the defendant semi-conscious. Another situation would be where a man was being attacked by a swarm of bees. Any movements made by him to protect himself from the bees would be reflex actions. If he hit another person as a result, he would be able to use the defence of automatism.

Duress

This occurs where another person forces the defendant to commit a crime. The threat used to force the defendant to carry out the crime must be of death or serious injury to himself or his family. An example would be where a bank robber seizes one of the customers in a bank as hostage and makes that hostage drive the getaway car by pointing a gun at his head. The hostage would have the defence of duress if he were charged with assisting the robber. Another situation would be robbers holding the wife and children of a bank manager and threatening to kill them unless the bank manager opens the bank's safe and brings the money to the robbers. The bank manager would be not guilty of theft or robbery since he acted under duress.

Duress can be used as a defence to all crimes except murder and attempted murder.

Intoxication

This covers the effects of alcohol and drugs and is only a defence if it means that the defendant did not have the mens rea required for the crime. If a defendant drinks so much that he does not know what he is doing, he has a defence to any crimes which involve specific intention such as murder or theft. However, he has no defence to any crimes where recklessness is sufficient for the mens rea, since getting drunk is a reckless course of conduct. This was decided in *DPP.* v. *Majewski* (1976) where the defendant assaulted the landlord of a pub and police officers while drunk. It was held he had no defence, but was guilty of the charges.

The situation is different if the defendant does not know that he is taking alcohol or drugs. This could occur where another person slips a drug into a cup of coffee the defendant is drinking. In this instance the defendant is not being reckless and so can plead the defence of involuntary intoxication. However, if a defendant has the intention to commit the crime anyway, he will be guilty.

Children under the age of 10

It is a rule that no child under the age of 10 can be guilty of committing a crime. It is presumed that such a young child cannot have the mens rea for any crime. So, even if a child of nine years old takes an item from a shop without paying for it, that child cannot be charged with theft.

Examination questions

1 An assault is an act which causes another person to be in immediate fear of an unlawful physical attack.

Battery consists in the application of unlawful force, however slight, on another person.

Grievous bodily harm is a statutory offence under either s. 18 or s. 20 Offences Against the Person Act 1861. The s. 18 offence must be committed 'with intent' and carries a maximum of life imprisonment. The s. 20 offence is less serious, carrying a maximum sentence of five years' imprisonment. 'Grievous' is defined as 'really serious bodily harm'.

The problem

Darren, Matthew and Sally are at a football match supporting their local team. During the match, they are approached by a group of rival supporters including Simon and Wayne.

Simon throws a punch at Darren but misses, hitting Sally, who was not watching, in the back. Sally stumbles, and breaks a fingernail but is otherwise not injured.

Wayne then pushes Matthew to the ground and kicks him, breaking his jaw and two of his ribs. Darren pushes Wayne away to protect his friend. Wayne slips on the terracing, falls and bangs his head, fracturing his skull.

a Describe the offence(s) with which Simon could be charged. Give reasons for your answer. (6 marks)

b Wayne, despite his subsequent injury, is also likely to be charged with criminal offences. Discuss what these offences

might be, giving reasons for your answer.
(*4 marks*)

c **i** Discuss the criminal liability of Darren. What defence could he plead? What would be the likely outcome of his case? (*6 marks*)

ii How, if at all, would your answer be different if Wayne had died of his injury? (*2 marks*)

d The main difference between a s. 18 and a s. 20 GBH is the words 'with intent'. Do you think that difference justifies the difference in the maximum sentence between the two offences? Explain your answer. (*4 marks*)

e Apart from imprisonment, name **two** other appropriate sentences that a criminal court could impose as a result of this situation.

What are the aims of these sentences? Are these aims likely to be achieved? (*8 marks*)

Total: 30 marks

SEG 1991

2 The Theft Act 1968 contains a number of offences including theft and burglary.
Under Section 1 of the Act, theft is defined as the dishonest appropriation of property belonging to another with the intention of permanently depriving the other of it.

There are different types of burglary but the most common is when a person enters a building as a trespasser intending to steal (section 9(1)(a)) or, having entered as a trespasser, then steals or attempts to steal (section 9(1)(b)).

The problem

Bill has heard that Lady Olivia has just bought a valuable collection of miniature portraits. He enters Lady Olivia's house by breaking a window, hoping to steal the portraits because he thinks he knows where he can sell them.

When inside, he cannot find the portraits so instead he takes a collection of silverware.

He then takes a set of car keys from the hall table, enters the garage and drives away with the silverware in Lady Olivia's car. He drives about a mile to where he has left his own car, transfers the silverware and then drives home in his car, leaving Lady Olivia's car parked by the side of the road.

While transferring the silverware to his own car, Bill drops a silver cigarette box. This is later found by Alison who decides to keep it.

Later Bill is arrested and now faces a number of charges.

---

a Bill is highly likely to appear before two different courts before a decision will be reached in his case. These are the Magistrates' Court and the Crown Court.
Describe briefly the function of **each** of these two courts in Bill's case. (*2 marks*)

b **i** Discuss what offence, if any, Bill is committing as he enters Lady Olivia's house. (*4 marks*)

ii Comment on the legal significance, if any, of the fact that Bill cannot find the portraits. (*4 marks*)

c Discuss which offence Bill is likely to be charged with concerning the taking of Lady Olivia's silverware. (*4 marks*)

d If Bill were to be charged with the theft of Lady Olivia's car, discuss the likely outcome of that charge. Give reasons for your answer. (*6 marks*)

e If Alison were to be charged with theft of the cigarette box, she would probably claim that finding something is not the same as stealing it.

i Briefly comment on whether Alison is correct in her view. (*2 marks*)

ii How appropriate is the law as regards the finding of lost property? Give reasons for your answer. (*4 marks*)

f Choose any **one** of the offences illustrated in the above situation. Using that offence, explain the difference between actus reus and mens rea.
(*4 marks*)

Total: 30 marks

SEG Sample Paper for 1996 (Higher Tier)

Criminal law: sentencing 12

12.1 Principles of sentencing

When a person pleads guilty to committing a crime or is found guilty of doing it, the judge or the magistrates have to decide what sentence to impose for that crime. This is a major function as we have already seen, since 80 per cent of defendants plead guilty and of the remaining 20 per cent, many will be found guilty. There are different theories about how and why people should be punished. These are called the theories or principles of sentencing. There are two main themes on which these principles are based, the first being retribution – punishment for the sake of punishment – and the second being the utilitarian theory, meaning that the punishment must serve some useful purpose. These theories are presented in diagram form in Figure 12.1.

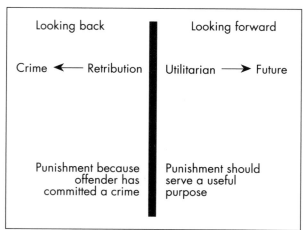

Looking back	Looking forward
Crime ← Retribution	Utilitarian → Future
Punishment because offender has committed a crime	Punishment should serve a useful purpose

Figure 12.1   Theories of punishment

Retributive theory

Under the theory of retribution we punish a man because he has done wrong and deserves punishment for his acts. This was a very popular view in the nineteenth century, for example, Kant in *The Metaphysical Elements of Justice* wrote:

Judicial punishment can never be used merely as a means to promote some other good for the criminal himself or for civil society, but instead it must in all cases be imposed on him only on the ground that he has committed a crime.

The retributive idea can be thought of as looking back to the crime and concentrating only on that. It has regained some popularity during the 1990s starting with the 1990 Government White Paper on Crime and Punishment which stated that the first objective should be denunciation of and retribution for the crime. Retribution is based on three points:

1 *Revenge.* This is an old idea and is sometimes expressed as 'an eye for an eye and a tooth for a tooth'. The most extreme example of this is the death penalty for those convicted of murder. The punishment is seen as vengeance or amends for the outraged feelings of society. However, in most western countries the death penalty is no longer used. In the United Kingdom the last hanging took place in 1961 although the death penalty was not finally abolished until 1965. In view of a series of miscarriages of justice where defendants such as the Birmingham Six and Judith Ward were wrongly convicted of murder but the errors

were not discovered until years later, it is just as well that the death penalty was abolished. However there are many people who would like to see its reintroduction, especially for serial killers.

It is also on the basis of revenge that it is possible to justify long sentences for people convicted of causing death by dangerous driving. As a result of public outcry over short sentences the government in 1993 increased the maximum sentence from five years' to ten years' imprisonment. Later that same year a sentence of seven years' detention was passed on a 17-year-old youth who had knocked down and killed a 13-year-old girl while driving a stolen car at high speed. Even that sentence was not regarded as long enough by some people and the girl's father said the youth should have got 20 years. A more imaginative approach to this idea of revenge was shown by a judge in Memphis, USA, who gave victims of burglary the right to go, accompanied by a law officer, to the homes of the burglars and take what they wanted up to the approximate value of their lost possessions.

2 *Denunciation.* It can be said that a very important aim of sentencing is to indicate both to the offender and to other people that society disapproves of the crime. It is thought that this helps to maintain respect for law and it also means that people see justice being done. Possibly this idea brought about the introduction in 1989 of the prosecution's right to appeal against an unduly lenient sentence.

3 *Proportionality or the 'just deserts' idea.* This is the idea that the defendant should only be punished to the extent that his crime deserves – no more, no less – and has led to the idea of *tariff* sentences, that is, that each crime has a set punishment. In some American states this idea of tariff sentencing means that the judge has very little discretion over sentencing. The exact number of months of imprisonment to be served is set down and the judge can only make minor variations from this. In this country the Court of Appeal has given *sentencing guidelines* for some offences which state what they consider to be the correct range of punishments. Such guidelines were given in the case of *R.* v. *Billam* (1986) where the length of imprisonment for rape

offences was set out, starting with a 'normal' tariff of five years but with longer being given where violence has been used.

Magistrates have sentencing guidelines which set out the 'entry point' for all the common crimes. Tariffs and guidelines should lead to uniformity in sentencing but there are two problems with this approach. The first is the rich man/poor man problem – should they be fined the same amount for identical crimes? Clearly an unemployed person would have difficulty in paying a fine of £1,000 while the same sum would have little effect on a millionaire. The second problem is that of unwanted side effects, such as family problems or loss of job, which can mean that the same sentence creates more of a punishment for some offenders than for others.

Utilitarian theories

There are different bases for the utilitarian idea, but they all have in common the idea that the punishment must serve some useful purpose – useful for the defendant or for society or for both. The theories look forward to what can be achieved in the future rather than back to the crime. The three most common utilitarian ideals are:

- deterrence which can be (a) individual or (b) general
- protection of society
- reformation of the offender

1 *Individual deterrence.* This aims to punish in such a way that the offender will never repeat his criminal conduct because of fear of further punishment. Prison is supposed to have this effect but in reality 65 per cent of those sent to prison re-offend within two years of release so that it does not appear to have as big a deterrent effect as one might think. Detention centres, nicknamed the 'short, sharp, shock' and dealing with 14- to 20-year-olds, were based on the same idea but proved so unsuccessful, with a reconviction rate of over 80 per cent, that they were abolished in 1988. Another penalty based on this theory is a suspended prison sentence. This means that the offender is given a prison sentence but does not go to prison unless he commits a further offence during a period of time (maximum two years) fixed by the court. Financial penalties can also have a deterrent effect.

2 *General deterrence.* The aim of this approach is to punish one (or more) offenders so severely that other potential offenders are deterred from committing similar offences. This involves punishing the individual as a means to an end. Capital punishment (the death penalty) was viewed in this way, but in America where some states have kept the death penalty while others have abolished it, there is little difference in the numbers of murders committed. Long prison sentences are also sometimes given as a warning to others who might be likely to commit the same type of offence, especially when a particular type of crime is on the increase. An example of this was the case of *R. v. Whitton* (1985), where the defendant who was involved in organised football hooliganism was given life imprisonment for riotous assembly by the judge at his trial. The judge made it clear that this was a warning to all football hooligans. However the Court of Appeal reduced the sentence to three years' imprisonment. General deterrence relies on publicity of heavy sentences so that potential offenders are aware of their probable fate. The main criticism of this theory is that it is unlikely to be effective because so many crimes are committed on the spur of the moment and offenders do not think of possible punishment.

3 *Protection of society.* The function of punishment here is to put dangerous people out of circulation. This theory was clearly visible in nineteenth-century punishments, especially capital punishment and transportation. Nowadays long prison sentences are seen as having this effect. The problem with this theory is trying to decide which defendants are so dangerous that society needs to be protected from them. The Criminal Justice Act 1991 stressed that custodial sentences should be used where the offence was of a violent or sexual nature and the public needed to be protected from the defendant. While under the Crime (Sentences) Act 1997 those who commit a second serious sexual or violent crime will normally be given life imprisonment.

4 *Reformation.* Another name for this theory is rehabilitation. It is very much a twentieth-century idea and involves looking at the individual offender's needs in terms of a sentence, as opposed to tariff sentencing. The emphasis is on the offender rather than the offence. Penalties such as probation and Community Service Orders are used and the court will be given information about the defendant's background. Reformation is considered the most important element when dealing with young offenders but can also be important for some adult offenders. The main criticism of this approach is that it leads to inconsistency in sentencing. Offenders who have committed exactly the same type of offence may be given different sentences because the court is concentrating on the offender and the possibility of reforming him.

The Criminal Justice Act 1993 stated that in considering the seriousness of the offence the court may take into account any previous convictions or any failure of the offender to respond to previous sentences. This means that a recidivist (a repeated offender) is unlikely to be thought of as suitable for a reformative sentence and will probably receive a heavier penalty than a first time offender. The court will also want to know about the offender's family background and may

PERHAPS NEXT TIME YOU'll THINK BEFORE YOU STEAL MY APPLES.

consider his work prospects too. Any medical or psychiatric problems will also be important in considering the possibility of reforming the offender, since the courts have the power to include conditions attached to a probation order aimed at helping those with such problems. To assist the court reports can be prepared by probation officers or, where suitable, by doctors. For young offenders there is a wide range of orders available which are aimed at reform and rehabilitation.

A C T I V I T Y

Carry out a survey into people's views on the death penalty.

(This could be used in coursework on sentencing.)

12.2 Custodial sentences

There are different custodial sentences available for different age groups. Young offenders can only be given custodial sentences in extreme cases and are always held in separate units from adult offenders.

Prison sentences

Prison is only available for offenders aged 21 and over. For the crime of murder the only sentence possible is imprisonment for life. For other crimes Parliament sets out the maximum possible period of imprisonment for each crime, for example the maximum for theft is seven years while the maximum for rape is life imprisonment. While long prison sentences are given for serious assaults it is rare for an offender to be given the maximum sentence available, especially for theft and other crimes against property. The Criminal Justice Act 1991 states that a prison sentence should not be passed unless the court considers that the crime was so serious that only a prison sentence is justified or the case involves a violent or sexual offence and only a prison sentence would be adequate to protect the public from serious harm. In considering the seriousness of the offence the court may take into account previous convictions, and the fact that the offender was already on bail at the time he committed the offence automatically makes it more serious.

In the guidelines of suggested 'entry points' published by the Magistrates' Association a custodial sentence is advised for offences such as aggravated vehicle taking, assaulting a police officer and burglary of a residential property.

The United Kingdom has a higher percentage of its population in prison than any other European Union country. Many prisons are old, overcrowded, insanitary and lacking in facilities and critics point out that prison fails to deter or reform the majority of prisoners. Indeed there are frequent reports about the misuse of drugs in prison and the high levels of violence. Reformers argue that it is unnecessary for so many offenders to be imprisoned, particularly those who are not dangerous and have committed crimes such as petty theft.

Prisoners do not serve the whole of the sentence passed by the court. Anyone sent to prison for less than four years is automatically released after they have served half of the sentence and may be released before the half way point if they are electronically tagged. Long-term prisoners serving four years or more are automatically released after they have served two-thirds of their sentence, but they can be released earlier on licence, provided they have served at least half of the sentence.

Suspended prison sentences

An offender may be given a suspended prison sentence – of up to two years (six months maximum in the Magistrates' Court) – but the serving of that sentence is suspended for a period of time of up to two years. If during this period of suspension the defendant does not commit any further crimes the original period of imprisonment will not be served. If, however, the offender does commit another offence during the period of suspension the original sentence is 'activated', that is, he automatically serves that sentence plus any extra he is given for the new offence. The Criminal Justice Act 1991 provides that suspended prison sentences should only be given where the offence is so serious that an immediate custodial sentence would have been appropriate but there are exceptional circumstances in the case to justify suspending the sentence. Suspended sentences are often viewed as a soft option, even though they can be combined with a fine or compensation order. Many defendants who are given a suspended sentence commit further offences so that they end up serving a longer sentence eventually. A suspended sentence can only be used where the offender is aged 21 or over.

Young offenders' institutions

Under the Criminal Justice Act 1991 offenders aged 18 to 20 can be sent to a Young Offenders' Institution as a custodial sentence. The minimum sentence is 21 days and the maximum is the maximum allowed for the particular offence.

Detention and training orders

Under the Crime and Disorder Act 1998 offenders aged 15 to 17 can be sentenced to a detention and training order as a custodial sentence. The minimum is four months and the maximum 24 months. This sentence can also be given to those aged 12 to 14 but only if they are persistent offenders. The Act also allows for such an order to be made in the future for 10 and 11 years old. However, such a sentence will only be possible if the child is a persistent offender and only a custodial sentence would be adequate to protect the public from further reoffending.

Critics point out that custodial sentences are more likely to turn a child into a repeat offender. For very serious offences committed by people under the age of 18, the courts have, however, another power under the Children and Young Persons' Act 1933. This Act allows offenders to be detained for longer periods, provided that the crime they have committed carries a maximum prison sentence for adults of at least 14 years. The same Act also provides that any offender aged 10 to 17 who is convicted of murder shall be detained during Her Majesty's Pleasure.

12.3 Community penalties

There are four community penalties:

• Probation order

• Community service order
• Combination order
• Curfew order

The Criminal Justice Act 1991 sets out the details of these orders in sections 8–13. These orders can be used for offenders aged 16 and above.

Probation order

A probation order places the offender under the supervision of a probation officer for a period of between six months and three years. The offender must lead an honest and industrious life during this period and keep in contact with his probation officer. In addition the court can include in the order other provisions:

a as to residence, ordering the defendant to live at a certain address;
b that the defendant take part in specified activities up to a total of 60 days;
c that he attends a probation centre;
d that he attend for medical or psychiatric treatment, or undergo treatment for drug or alcohol abuse.

Community service order

A community service order requires the offender to do between 40 and 240 hours work on a scheme organised by the probation service. The type of work involved will vary, but is always aimed at benefiting the community as a whole. It might involve painting school buildings or fitting out a children's play area or gardening for elderly people. The offender will usually work an eight-hour day on Saturday or Sunday until he has completed the number of hours set by the court.

Combination order

This type of order combines a probation order with up to 100 hours community service.

Curfew orders

These orders are a new concept introduced by the Criminal Justice Act 1991. The offender can be ordered to remain at a certain address for between 2 and 12 hours in any 24 hours. The order may be imposed for a maximum of six months. The curfew will be monitored under local arrangements, which can include electronic tagging, provided the Home Secretary has been notified that the area has these facilities. Electronic tagging has been tried in some areas and proved fairly successful. In the first two years over 80% of such orders were completed without problems.

Under the Public Order Act 1986 the courts also have the power to exclude an offender from a particular place. This power has been used to ban football hooligans from going to matches.

12.4 Fines

The courts have the power to fine an offender for any crime. The Crown Court theoretically has no limits on the amount it can fine and in some company fraud cases there have been fines of over a million pounds. The Magistrates' Court is limited to a maximum fine of £5,000. For those under 18 years old there are lower maximum fines: for ages 10 to 13 the maximum is £250 and for ages 14 to 17 the maximum is £1,000. In deciding the amount of a fine the court must take into account both the seriousness of the offence and the financial circumstances of the offender. This requirement replaced the idea of 'unit fines' which were used briefly during 1992–3. To work out the amount of a unit fine the court had to calculate the disposable income of the offender, that is, the money left each week after paying rent/mortgage and all other household bills. This amount was then multiplied by the number of units that the seriousness of the offence merited. This method of calculating fines was intended to reflect not only the seriousness of the offence, but also the amount the offender could afford to pay. The system, however, produced some odd results, especially where the defendant failed to complete the form showing his financial commitments properly. One case that made headline news was where a young man was fined £1,200 for dropping a crisp packet. He had not given details of his income and was assessed at the top rate of £100 per unit. When he appealed and filled out the forms correctly the fine was reduced to £48, that is £4 per unit. Many magistrates were unhappy with the system and about 30 resigned in protest. However the principle that the amount of the fine should be proportionate to the amount the offender can afford to pay is sensible.

12.5 Discharges

For minor offences and particularly for first time offenders the courts can decide not to punish them but to discharge them, either conditionally or absolutely. A conditional discharge carries the condition that the offender must not re-offend within a certain time, up to three years; if he breaks this condition he can be re-sentenced for the original offence. An absolute discharge means that there are no conditions attached. The reason for using discharges is that the majority of first time offenders will be sufficiently punished by the fact that they have appeared in court and are unlikely to commit any further offences. Discharges can be used for offenders of any age (over the age of 10) and are very common for younger offenders.

Figure 12.2 shows in simple diagram form the seriousness of the different levels of punishment.

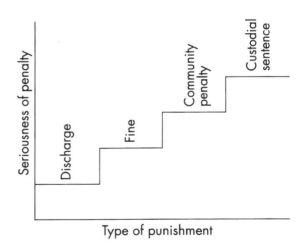

Figure 12.2   Levels of punishment

A C T I V I T Y

Make a collection of newspaper cuttings giving details of sentences passed on offenders by the courts. Compare the type of offence/offender and the nature of the sentence in each case.

(This work could be used towards coursework on sentencing.)

12.6 Young offenders

In addition to fines and discharges there are a number of other penalties for offenders under the age of 18. The main order is a supervision order where the offender is placed under the supervision of the local social services. The court can add extra 'strings' to this order, such as ordering that the offender live in a specified place or is subject to a night restriction order under which he will not be allowed out at night or that he take part in specified activities. Normally under a supervision order the young offender will continue to live at home, but the court can order that such an offender live in local authority accommodation for up to six months.

The court can also make an attendance centre order of up to 24 hours. This means that the young offender will have to go on a Saturday to a special centre for two or three hours and take part in organised leisure activities; in other words a type of compulsory youth club. Attendance centre orders can also be made for 18- to 20-year-olds for a maximum of 36 hours.

For those under 16 there is an emphasis on their parents being responsible for their behaviour and, when fining an offender the court can order the parents to pay that fine. Parents can also be bound over to keep their child under control for a certain length of time so that if the child commits another offence the parents will forfeit a sum of money up to a maximum amount of £1,000.

12.7 Mentally ill offenders

The law recognises that mentally ill offenders should not be punished but treated for their problems. Under the Mental Health Act 1983 those with severe mental problems who are dangerous can be sent to a secure hospital such as Broadmoor. Those with lesser problems can be placed under the guardianship of the local authority, so that suitable treatment, possibly as a residential patient, can be arranged. It is also possible for the court to make a probation order with a condition that the person attends for treatment.

12.8 Compensation

There are other measures available to the court where the emphasis is on compensating the victim. These measures are usually used as well as, and not instead of, punishment. The main one is a power to order the offender to pay a sum of money to his victim as compensation. Under section 104 of the Criminal Justice Act 1988 courts are under a duty to give reasons if they do not make a compensation order when they have power to do so. Where property has been recovered after a crime the courts can order restitution, that is, return of the property to its rightful owner. This order can also be made if the proceeds of a crime are traceable. There have also been some pilot schemes where offenders are ordered to work for their victim (with the victim's consent).

The court can also order that items used in committing a crime should be forfeited. This power has been used to take away cars and other vehicles used for transporting drugs and it has even been used to take away the car belonging to a man convicted of drink-driving.

APPLYING THE LAW

Suggest one suitable punishment for each of the following cases and explain what the aim of the punishment is.

1 Marie, aged 18, has been found guilty of stealing a pair of jeans from a shop. It is her first offence.
2 Peter, aged 27, has been found guilty of an assault causing grievous bodily harm. He has three previous convictions for violence.
3 Susan, aged 22, has been found guilty of taking and driving away a car without the consent of the owner and causing criminal damage to it. She has one previous conviction for a similar crime.

Examination question

See question 1(e) p. 118.

13 Law of contract

Contracts are very important, both in the business world and in everyday life. Businesses make multi-million pound deals, buy and sell factories and shops or lease buildings. All these arrangements would be recognised as contracts. However, ordinary people are just as likely to make contracts even if the amounts involved are smaller. Buying a car, renting a flat, hiring a video; all these situations involve contracts. Even everyday occurrences involve making contracts. How do you travel to school or college or work? If it is by train, then you make a contract when you buy the ticket. If it is by car, then you make a contract when you buy petrol. And what about all the other small items one buys? Even buying a packet of crisps creates a contract.

Since contracts play such a large part in daily life, it is not surprising that the law has several rules about them.

First, **what is a contract**? It is an agreement that is legally binding; a promise that can be enforced in the courts. This means that where there is a dispute over an agreement the courts are prepared to hear the case and give a judgment on it. In order for the courts to recognise an agreement as a contract four main elements must be present:

- offer and acceptance
- consideration
- capacity to make a contract
- intention to create legal relations

It is necessary to look at all these elements in detail.

13.1 Offer and acceptance

An offer is a proposition or suggestion put by one or more persons to another person or persons. An acceptance is an agreement to this suggestion. For example John offers to buy a car for £2,000 from Mr Smith and Mr Smith accepts this offer. John is making a suggestion that he should buy the car (an offer) and Mr Smith is agreeing to this suggestion (an acceptance).

As these two points are at the heart of any contract and there have been many cases in the courts, from the courts' decisions in these cases it is possible to draw up a series of 'rules' about offers and acceptance.

Offers

The courts will only recognise an offer as being a valid offer and capable of being accepted if it is intended as an offer. The law distinguishes between an offer and what it calls 'an invitation to treat'. An invitation to treat is where the other person is inviting you to make an offer, so that he can consider it and accept or reject it.

An invitation to treat can be seen in the case of *Gibson* v. *Manchester City Council* (1979). Mr Gibson was a council house tenant who wanted to buy his house from the council. After he had sent an initial form and administration fee to the council they wrote to him saying:

the corporation may be prepared to sell the house to you . . . If you would like to buy your council house please complete the enclosed

126

application form and return it as soon as possible.

Mr Gibson completed and returned the form, but soon afterwards there was a local election and the new Labour council refused to sell the house. Mr Gibson claimed that the council had made him an offer to sell so that when he returned the application form he had accepted their offer. However, the House of Lords ruled that the words used by the council in their letter were not an offer but an invitation to treat. The council were inviting Mr Gibson to apply to buy the house. The application by Mr Gibson was the offer and the council had not accepted that offer. Three important situations which are *always* invitations to treat and *not* offers are:

a   articles for sale on display in a shop window or on a shelf in a store;
b   advertisements of items for sale in newspapers, magazines or catalogues;
c   auction sales.

All these have been decided by the courts. *Fisher* v. *Bell* (1961) decided that a shop keeper who had a display of flick knives in a shop window was not offering them for sale. The display was an invitation to treat. In this situation the customer who went into the shop and asked to buy a knife would be making the offer. The sales person in the shop could accept that offer and sell the customer a knife or refuse the offer and not sell.

Pharmaceutical Society of Great Britain v. *Boots Chemists* (1953) decided that displaying items on shelves in a self-service store was only inviting customers to offer to buy them; that is, there was an invitation to treat and not an offer. The offer was made by the customer at the checkout and could be accepted or refused by the cashier. This decision was important for self-service stores as it meant that they could include items on their shelves which have by law to be supervised at the moment the contract of sale is made. This covers items such as bottles of wine and spirits. If the display of a bottle on a shelf was an offer this would mean that the customer would accept the offer when he picked the bottle off the shelf. The contract for sale would be complete at that moment and in order to comply with the law and supervise the sale, the store would need to have a member of staff standing by every customer when he or she picked up a bottle. As the law stands, the contract for sale is made at the checkout, making it easier for stores and supermarkets to supervise the sale.

In *Partridge* v. *Crittenden* (1968) advertising wild birds for sale in a magazine was held to be invitation to treat and not an offer. This decision avoids any problems that could arise if demand exceeded supply. Imagine an advertisement of 'six adorable puppies for sale at £20 each'. If this was an offer, then people writing in to buy the puppies would be accepting the offer. So if 10 people wrote on the same day it would lead to an impossible situation of 10 contracts but only six puppies. This illustration makes it easier to see why the courts have held that the original advertisement is not an offer. The person who responds to the advertisement is making the offer and the advertiser chooses whether to accept that offer or not. So if there is a situation of six puppies for sale and 10 people offering to buy them the advertiser can decide which, if any, of those 10 offers he will accept.

Payne v. *Cave* (1789) held that an auctioneer calling for bids at an auction was not making an offer. He was making an invitation to treat and the bid itself was the offer. This meant that, as an offer can be withdrawn at any time before it is accepted, the defendant, who was bidding, could withdraw his offer before the auctioneer accepted it by banging his hammer. In fact if the auctioneer's call for bids was an offer, then the first person to bid would be accepting that offer, the contract would be complete and the auction at an end. The whole idea of an auction would be lost.

Reward posters

Reward posters are, however, considered offers. They are different from advertising an item for sale. In *Carlill* v. *Carbolic Smoke Ball Co.* (1893) the company manufactured smoke balls which they claimed could prevent or cure a number of diseases. They published an advertisement which included the words '£100 reward' and offered this sum to anyone who bought one of their smoke balls, used it in the correct manner but still caught influenza. Mrs Carlill bought a smoke ball, used it as directed, but unfortunately became ill with 'flu. She claimed the reward from the company and when they refused to pay she sued them. The court held that the advertisement was an offer and Mrs Carlill had accepted that offer when she bought and used the smoke ball. This meant that there was a contract and Mrs Carlill could get her £100.

More common reward posters are ones which offer a sum of money to anyone finding and returning a lost pet. As with Mrs Carlill's case these posters are considered in law to be offers so that if you see such a poster, find and return the missing animal, you have a right to the amount offered.

Further rules about offers

1 *The offer must be certain*, that is, definite enough in its terms so that if it is accepted both parties know exactly what they have agreed to, i.e. what the terms of the contract are. An offer to employ a secretary and 'to pay a London salary' is not certain. The salary is not definite enough.

If the parties have written several letters before coming to an agreement, then all the letters are looked at to see if the terms are certain. If the final letter offered to employ a secretary 'at the rate already mentioned' and an earlier letter had mentioned an actual figure, then that offer would be definite.

2 *The offer may be by any method*, in writing, spoken or even by conduct.

Writing is not necessary. Just think of everyday contractual situations. A person buying a train ticket usually requests it verbally. Unless it is a season ticket it is very unlikely that the offer will be in writing. It is even less likely that anyone will write down their offer to buy an item in a shop.

In fact in a self-service shop it is possible that the contract may be completed without either party saying anything. The customer takes the item he wants to buy to the checkout and, without speaking, places it on the counter, thus making an offer to buy it by conduct. The cashier rings up the price of the item on the till, accepting the offer. Neither person has said anything but there is already a completed contract. A more common example of making an offer by conduct is at an auction, where the person making the bid (the offer) does so by nodding his head, raising his hand or making another signal to show that he is bidding.

3 *The offer can be to anyone*, that is, to an individual, or to a group of people or to the whole world. The person making the offer can decide whether he wants to make it to one person only or make it available to several persons, any one of whom can accept it. If Mr Jones offers to sell his car to Mr Robinson for £2,000, then Mr Brown who happens to hear what is said cannot accept that offer. It has not been made to him. However, if Mr Jones had said to a group of friends, which included Mr Brown, that he was willing to sell his car to any of them, Mr Brown can accept that offer. He is one of the group to which the offer was made.

It is also possible to make an offer to the world at large so that anyone who wishes can accept the offer. This was the position in *Carlill* v. *Carbolic Smoke Ball Co.* (1893), which we have already met (*see* p. 127). The offer was in such a form that anyone could accept it.

4 *The offer must be communicated before it is effective.* In other words the person who accepts must know about the offer when he does the conduct needed to accept it. For example if Mrs Carlill had not seen the advertisement saying '£100 reward' before she bought the smoke ball, the offer would not have been communicated to her and she could not have accepted it. Another situation is

where someone advertises a reward for the return of a lost cat (remember that reward posters are offers) and a neighbour finds and returns the cat without having seen the reward poster. The neighbour is doing the action required to accept, but the offer is not effective, as it has not been communicated to him. This is important because it means there is no contract and so the neighbour cannot claim the reward even if he later sees the poster. Where an offer is sent by post, it is communicated when it arrives.

5 *The offer must still be in existence when it is accepted.*

a this means that if there is a time limit, the offer ceases when the time limit runs out. It cannot be accepted after that. Where no time limit has been set, the courts will assume that the offer exists for a reasonable length of time, but not indefinitely. This was shown by *Ramsgate Victoria Hotel* v. *Montefiore* (1866) when an offer to buy shares was made on 8 June. The offeree (the person to whom the offer was made) tried to accept it on 25 November. The court decided that the offer no longer existed and so it could not be accepted. The delay between 8 June and 25 November was too great. What is considered a reasonable length of time for one case could be different in another. Where the offer is connected with buying and selling perishable goods, e.g. fruit, two days might be a reasonable time, whereas with electrical equipment, two weeks or even two months would be reasonable;

b an offer may also cease if the person making it withdraws it before it is accepted. It is said in this case that the offer is revoked. This is what happened in the auction case of *Payne* v. *Cave* (1789). The defendant made a bid (the offer) but withdrew it before the auctioneer accepted it. However the offeree must know that the offer has been revoked. In *Byrne* v. *van Tienhoven* (1880), the defendants had offered to sell 1,000 boxes of tinplate to the plaintiffs, who were in New York. The defendants then changed their mind and wrote on 8 October revoking their offer. This letter arrived at the plaintiffs' office on 25 October. In the meantime the plaintiffs telegraphed an acceptance on 11 October and confirmed this in a letter which they posted on 20 October. It was, therefore, important to decide on which date the offer ceased to exist. Did it cease on the 8th, the day the letter of revocation was posted or did it cease on the 25th, the day it arrived and was communicated to the plaintiffs? The court decided that the revocation of the offer occurred on 25 October, and therefore there was a contract between the parties, as the offer was in existence when the plaintiffs accepted it.

This sort of complicated date sequence is sometimes easier to understand if it is shown in a diagram form, as in Figure 13.1;

c the person who made the offer need not be the person to tell the offeree that it is revoked, provided the revocation is effectively and reliably communicated. In

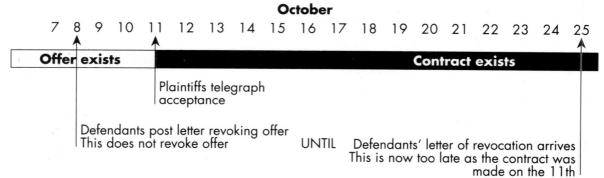

Figure 13.1   Byrne v. van Tienhoven: date sequence

Dickinson v. *Dodds* (1876) the offeree, who had been offered the chance to buy property, was told by a reliable third person that the property had been sold to someone else. The court decided that the revocation had been communicated to him; he knew the offer no longer existed and could not then try to accept it;

d if the offer was in the form of a reward poster, it can be revoked by taking the same steps to advertise the revocation as were taken to advertise the original offer. This means that if the reward poster offering £50 for the return of a lost pet was placed in a local shop window, then that offer can be revoked by placing a notice to that effect in the same shop window. This has to be done before the offer has been accepted by someone starting to perform the act required in the original offer. So if someone, who knows about the offer, has already found the pet before the withdrawal notice is placed in the window, the revocation is not effective. The reward can be claimed;

e an offer also ceases when it is rejected. Where Andrew offers to buy Bob's car for £2,000, but Bob says no, he does not want to sell, the offer ceases at the moment he says no. If Bob changes his mind and writes the next day to Andrew saying he agrees to sell, there is no offer for Bob to accept and so there is no contract. What has happened is that Bob is now making an offer of his own to Andrew that Andrew can accept or reject.

Again a diagram (Figure 13.2) can show this clearly.

f an offer also ceases to exist if the offeree makes a counter-offer. In the above example if Bob, instead of saying no, had said 'I'll sell for £2,100', this is a counter-offer. Its effect is the same as a rejection; it puts an end to the offer. A situation like this occurred in *Hyde* v. *Wrench* (1840). The defendant offered to sell his farm for £1,000. The plaintiff initially counter-offered to buy it for £950. The defendant refused this counter-offer. The plaintiff then said he would buy the farm for the original asking price of £1,000. The plaintiff claimed that there was now a contract; the defendant had made an offer to sell for £1,000 and he, the plaintiff, had accepted that offer. The court decided that the counter-offer of £950 terminated the offer, so there was no offer in existence when the plaintiff agreed to pay the original price and therefore no contract.

Figure 13.3 opposite shows this sequence in diagram form.

g the offer lapses if the goods involved are destroyed or damaged. This is obviously sensible. If you are offered the chance to buy a car and given a week to think about it, there is an offer which exists during that week. Two days into that week, the car is involved in an accident and badly damaged. You do not know about this and the day after the accident you write accepting the offer. If the car had not been damaged there would now be a contract, but it is clearly unfair to hold that you have to go ahead and pay for what is now a wreck. The courts would

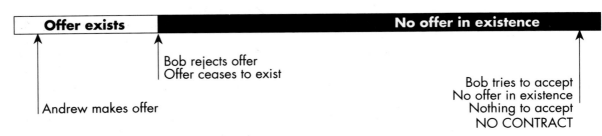

Figure 13.2 Rejection of offer: time sequence

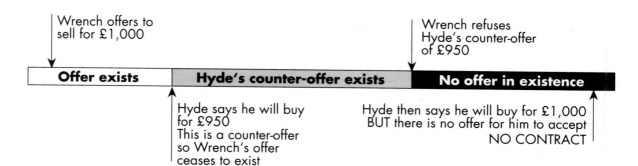

Figure 13.3   *Hyde v. Wrench: time sequence*

say that the offer lapsed when the car was damaged and so there was no offer for you to accept when you wrote your letter and therefore no contract;

h   the death of the offeror will normally bring any offer to an end.

Acceptance

As we have already said an acceptance is an agreement to the offer. The main rule about an acceptance is that it must agree to all the terms of the offer. It has to be absolute and unqualified. If the acceptance does not agree to the terms of the offer it is not an acceptance but a counter-offer. We have already seen this in *Hyde* v. *Wrench*. The difficulty sometimes is to distinguish between a request for information and a counter-offer. In *Stevenson* v. *McLean* (1880) the defendant offered to sell iron to the plaintiff, the offer to be open until Monday. The plaintiff replied by asking if he might buy the goods on credit. No reply was received from the defendant, so on Monday he telegraphed a full acceptance. The court held that asking if he could buy on credit was a mere request for information, so the offer remained open and was accepted by the telegram.

It is suggested that the test for distinguishing between enquiries and counter-offers is: could the 'enquiry' be accepted? If not it cannot be a counter-offer. In *Hyde* v. *Wrench* the counter-offer to buy for £950 could have been accepted by Wrench if he had wished to do so; it was quite clear and certain. In *Stevenson* v. *McLean* the request could not form a counter-offer; it was not specific enough. It did not state in detail what credit terms the plaintiff was suggesting.

An acceptance must be by the person to whom the offer was made, unless it is open to the whole world as in *Carlill* v. *Carbolic Smoke Ball Co.* (p. 127).

Communication of the acceptance

There are several rules about communicating acceptance to the person who made the offer.

1 The normal rule is that it must be *communicated to the offeror*. This means that staying silent is not an acceptance, a situation that is illustrated in *Felthouse* v. *Bindley* (1862). In this case the plaintiff wrote to his nephew offering to buy a horse for £30. 15s. (£30.75), following a discussion as to whether he should pay £30 or 30 guineas (one guinea being equal to £1.05). He said, 'If I hear no more about it I will consider the horse to be mine.' The nephew did not reply but ordered the auctioneer to withdraw the horse from open sale. By error the horse was auctioned and Felthouse sued for his loss, claiming that he had a contract with his nephew to buy the horse. It was held that as the nephew had not communicated his acceptance of the offer no contract existed.

2 There are, however, *exceptions to the normal rule*. It is possible to imply acceptance from conduct or for the need for it to be waived by

the person who has made the offer. This was the position in the *Smoke ball* case. The buying of the smoke ball indicated acceptance; it was not necessary for Mrs Carlill to do anything else to communicate her acceptance. In reward cases it is not only impractical to expect everyone seeing such a poster to communicate acceptance, but it is unlikely that the person offering the reward would want hundreds of people to write or telephone just to say that they had seen the poster and were intending to look for the lost item.

3 The person who makes the offer can lay down a *specific way for the offeree to accept*. If there is a prescribed way of communicating the acceptance then only that method or, possibly, one which places the offeror in a more advantageous position by arriving more quickly than the specified method will do. This is shown in *Eliason* v. *Henshaw* (1819) where the plaintiff offered to buy flour from Henshaw. The offer said that acceptance had to be given to the waggoner who delivered the offer. Instead of doing this Henshaw sent his acceptance by post and it arrived after the return of the waggoner. Because Henshaw had not communicated by the specified method there was no contract.

4 If there is no prescribed way of communicating then *any effective method will do*. The important point here is that the method must be *effective*. The effectiveness or otherwise was the subject of discussion in *Entores* v. *Miles Far East* (1955) when Lord Denning made obiter (non-binding) statements on this point.

So, for example, if A shouts an offer across a river but cannot hear B's reply because of noise from a passing aircraft, the reply is not communicated. Similarly, if a telephone line goes dead as B is accepting so that A does not hear the acceptance it is not effective.

5 *Postal acceptance* is an exception to the rule that the acceptance must be effectively communicated. If the use of post is a reasonable method of accepting then the acceptance is assumed to have been made the moment it is posted. This is a very old rule and its operation can be seen in the case of *Adams* v. *Lindsell* (1818).

On 2 September 1817 the defendants wrote to the plaintiff offering to sell some wool and requiring an answer in the course of post. Because the letter was incorrectly addressed, it did not arrive until 5 September and that same evening the plaintiff posted a letter of acceptance. This arrived on 9 September whereas in the normal course a reply would have been expected on 7 September. On 8 September the defendants sold the wool to someone else. It was held that a contract came into being on 5 September when the plaintiff posted the letter so the defendants were in breach of contract by selling on 8 September. Let's use a diagram (Figure 13.4 opposite) to make this sequence of events clearer.

In *Household Fire etc.* v. *Grant* (1879) it was decided that, even where the letter was lost in the post this rule would still be used and so there was held to be an effective acceptance. However, posting means placing the letter in a

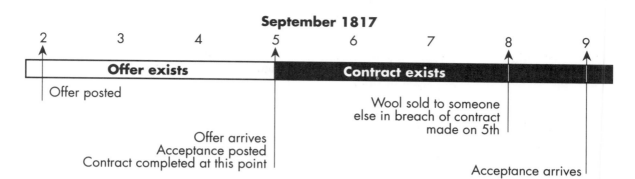

Figure 13.4 Adams v. Lindsell: date sequence

post box or into the hands of a Post Office employee authorised to receive letters. Handing a letter to a postman authorised to deliver letters is not 'posting' it and so does not count as a valid acceptance until the letter is delivered.

Telegrams are treated in the same way as letters; that is, an acceptance by telegram is held to be effective the moment the telegram is handed in at a post office.

6 *Telex* (and presumably fax or any other electronic mail system) are treated as being virtually instantaneous and therefore the normal rules of acceptance apply. That means that a telex is only communicated effectively when it arrives. This was decided in *Entores Ltd* v. *Miles Far East* (1955). However in *Brinkibon Ltd* v. *Stahag Stahl* (1982) when the House of Lords approved the decision in the *Entores* case they also said that it might not apply in every case, for example, if a telex arrived out of working hours, it would be effectively communicated at the beginning of the next working day.

Comments on the rule for postal acceptance

The normal rule that acceptance must be effectively communicated is common sense, but the rule that a letter of acceptance takes effect the moment it is placed in a post box does at first sight seem rather strange. How is the person who made the offer to know at what time a letter gets put in a post box, possibly hundreds or even thousands of miles away? Would it not be more sensible to say that the contract comes into being when he receives the acceptance? But this creates problems for the offeree; how does he know at what moment his letter arrives? So the courts have had to balance the needs of the two parties. This they have done by limiting the rule to situations where use of the post is reasonable. Also since the offeror can specify how an acceptance should be made he can always exclude the use of post as a means of acceptance. Two other points in support of the rule are that it is easier to prove postage than to prove receipt and it is argued that if an offer is sent by post then the offeror is using the postal service as his agent, so that when the person accepting puts his letter into a post box, he has given his acceptance to the offeror's agent. It was on this basis that *Household Fire etc.* v. *Grant* was decided.

The main argument against the rule is that it was created at a time when there was no other method of communicating directly with a person some miles away. Telephones had not been invented, let alone fax machines or electronic mail boxes. In a world of modern methods of communication, should the rule still apply?

APPLYING THE LAW

1 **Simon offers to sell his cricket bat to Andy for £20. Andy says he will buy it for £15, but Simon does not agree to this. Andy then says he will pay the £20, but Simon now refuses to sell the bat.**

Advise Andy whether he has a contract to purchase the bat.

2 **Angela receives a mail order catalogue from Smart Homes Ltd, advertising microwave ovens. Angela orders a 'Smart Special' Microwave oven, costing £175. Two weeks later she receives a letter from the company saying that they are unable to supply the model she ordered and returning her cheque. Angela believes that Smart Homes are in breach of contract.**

Advise Angela.

3 **Brian buys 'Take-off', a new brand of stain remover, having first seen an advertisement which included the words 'Take-off will remove all ink stains. £25 will be paid if it fails to work for you.' Brian uses the stain remover according to instructions but it does not remove ink stains from his shirt.**

Advise Brian whether he has a legal right to the £25.

4 **On Wednesday Gillian writes to Charles, offering to sell him an antique ring for £400. Charles receives the letter on Friday and immediately writes and posts a letter agreeing to buy the ring. On Sunday, while at an antique fair, Gillian is offered £500 for the ring by Nigel. On Monday morning Gillian telephones Charles and leaves a message on his answer phone, withdrawing her offer to him. Charles listens to the message that evening. His letter to Gillian arrives at her home on Tuesday morning.**

Advise Gillian as to her contractual liability.

13.2 Consideration

Consideration means that both parties must put something into the contract. Older cases stress the idea of a benefit or a detriment to the parties. In *Currie* v. *Misa* (1875) it was said:

A valuable consideration, in the sense of the law, may consist either in some right, interest, profit or benefit accruing to the one party or some forebearance, detriment, loss or responsibility given, suffered or undertaken by the other.

The idea of a benefit or detriment is outdated but has some use in understanding the idea of consideration. Take the following contract.

Marie agrees to buy Joanna's car for £1,500. In this simple situation we can see the following two parts to the contract:

1 Marie agrees to pay Joanna £1,500 – this is a benefit to Joanna, since she is going to get the money, but a detriment to Marie since she is paying out the money.
2 Joanna agrees to hand over her car to Marie – this is a benefit to Marie since she is getting the car, but a detriment to Joanna as she is handing over her car.

The consideration can also be thought of as the price in a bargain. The 'price' does not have to be money, but it must have some value. The important thing is that both sides must show that they have given something in return for the other's promise. In fact, the consideration in a contract is really the whole point of the contract. Looking back to the example of Marie agreeing to buy Joanna's car, obviously Marie is only going to agree to it because she wants the car and is prepared to pay £1,500 for it; while Joanna is only entering into the contract because she wants to sell her car and get money in exchange.

Executed and executory consideration

Where the parties are making a promise to each other about what they will do in the future, the consideration is called *executory consideration*. If, in the example of Marie and Joanna, Marie says that she will give Joanna the money next Thursday and Joanna says that she will hand over the car to Marie immediately she receives the money, both are promising to do something in the future and these promises are sufficient for the consideration in the contract. The contract comes into existence the moment those promises are exchanged.

In some contracts, however, the consideration is carried out as the contract is made. Reward cases illustrate this. When someone, having seen a reward poster about a lost dog, finds and returns that dog, he does the act he is required to do at the time he takes the dog to its owner's house. In this case the consideration is called *executed consideration*.

Rules about consideration

1 *Both sides must contribute something to the bargain.* A gift does not have any consideration in return for it, as, for example, when Uncle Tom promises to give Andrew £100. Andrew is not contributing anything so the law will not enforce this promise (unless it is contained in a special deed).

2 *The consideration has to be real,* i.e. have some value, but it need not be adequate. This means that the consideration given on either side need not match in value so long as something is given. So, for example, Uncle Tom promises to pay Andrew £100 if Andrew will give him a packet of cigarettes. In this situation both are putting something into the contract even though the values are not equal. This point was considered in *Chappell & Co. Ltd* v. *Nestlés Ltd* (1960) when the House of Lords held that three chocolate bar wrappers could be valuable consideration, in the situation where a customer sent in wrappers (and money) in return for goods (a record). Lord Somervell in this case said: 'A contracting party can stipulate what consideration he chooses. A peppercorn does not cease to be good consideration if it is established that the promisee does not like pepper and will throw away the corn.' In other words if the parties are happy with the agreement, it does not matter what the value is, provided there is some value.

Exceptions

There are three situations where there appears to be value but the courts have held it is not good or sufficient consideration. These are:

a consideration which does not come from the plaintiff;
b consideration which is in the past;
c consideration which is already a duty.

Let's look at each of these in turn.

1 *Consideration which does not come from the plaintiff.* Only parties to the contract have rights under it. If Andrew's two uncles each promise to pay him £100 on his twenty-first birthday, then the contract is between his two uncles. Andrew has put nothing into it. He is not a party to the agreement. So if one uncle pays and the other does not, Andrew cannot sue for the missing £100. However, one uncle can sue the other. This situation occurred in *Tweddle* v. *Atkinson* (1861) where the fathers of a couple who were getting married each promised to pay the bridegroom £500. One father paid, but the other died without paying. The bridegroom sued the estate of that father for the promised £500, but the court held he had no rights under the agreement since he (the bridegroom) had not given any consideration. This idea also involves the concept of *privity of contract,* that is, that only the parties to the contract have any rights under it.

2 *Consideration which is past.* Where the thing that you are offering to put into the contract has already occurred before the contract is made, it cannot be counted as consideration for the contract you are now making. This is shown by the case of *Re McArdle* (1951). In this case a widow had been left a house for her to live in during her lifetime. She repaired and decorated the property. After she had done this her children, who were the ultimate beneficiaries, that is, the house was going to be theirs after the widow died, promised to pay towards the improvements. However, they did not keep their promise to pay. It was decided that they could not be sued because the widow had already finished the work when the children made the promise. Her consideration was in the past.

There is an exception to this. This is when one party asks the other to act and payment is implied. When the other party later promises payment, the courts will enforce that promise. This idea comes from a very old case, *Lampleigh* v. *Braithwaite* (1615). In that case Braithwaite, who had been tried and sentenced to death, asked Lampleigh to travel to the King and seek a reprieve from hanging for him (a king's pardon). Lampleigh did this successfully. Braithwaite was so delighted that he then promised to pay Lampleigh £100, but failed to do so. It was decided that Lampleigh could claim the money as he had acted at Braithwaite's request.

3 *The promise must be more than a duty.* A

promise to do what you are already bound to do is not good consideration. This means that where you are already under an existing contractual duty, you cannot claim that by doing that duty you are putting anything into the new contract. This is illustrated by *Stilk* v. *Myrick* (1809) when it was decided that a sailor could not recover extra pay he was promised for carrying on working when two other sailors out of a crew of eleven deserted. He was only doing the work he had already agreed to do. However, in *Hartley* v. *Ponsonby* (1857) it was decided that a sailor on similar facts could sue because more than half the crew had deserted and he was being asked to do far more than his original duties.

Another case on this point is *Glasbrook Bros.* v. *Glamorgan County Council* (1925). The owners of a colliery asked for a police guard to protect it during a strike. The police thought that a mobile force would give sufficient protection but agreed to provide a fixed guard when the mine owner promised to pay £2,200 for the guard. The company subsequently refused to pay, claiming that the police were under a duty to provide protection, but it was held that the police had done more than their duty by providing the fixed guard and the mine owners had to pay.

A more recent case, *Williams* v. *Roffey* (1990) raises some doubts on the rule that an existing duty is not good consideration. The defendants had a contract to renovate a block of flats. They sub-contracted the carpentry work to the plaintiff for £20,000. The plaintiff ran into financial difficulties and got behind with the work. The defendants then promised to pay him an extra £575 for each flat he completed. The plaintiff did all the work in eight more flats, but the defendants only paid him an extra £1,500 instead of 8 × £575 (£4,600). The plaintiff sued for the difference and the Court of Appeal decided the case in his favour. The judges gave a very complicated judgment, but the main reason for the decision seems to be that in the new agreement between the parties, although the plaintiff was going to do no more than he already was under contract to do, the defendants were getting a benefit (or avoiding a disadvantage) from the new contract to pay the extra, since they would not be paid under their original contract unless the flats were completed. Reasonableness, fairness and commercial practicality were considered important.

Promises involving debts

The normal rule is that a promise to pay a smaller sum for an existing debt is not good consideration; even if the creditor does agree to it, he can later change his mind. This is the rule in *Pinnel's Case* (1602). But offering £800 plus a bike as repayment for an existing debt of £1000 will count. This is because the bike brings in a new element.

Should the need for consideration be retained?

Some judges dislike the bargain idea because it may defeat the parties' clear intentions. As far back as 1937 the Law Reform Committee recommended the abolition of many of the present principles of consideration, but these reforms have not been brought into effect. In particular the courts are reluctant to hold that a business transaction which has been satisfactory to the business people who made it is not a legally binding agreement because of the lack of consideration. This was the situation in *Williams* v. *Roffey* above.

It can also be argued that if one party acts to his detriment because of a promise, that should be sufficient to enforce the promise. Take an example where Uncle Tom promises to pay Andrew £500. Believing that he is going to get this £500 Andrew then makes a contract to buy a bike costing £1,000, which he is not able to afford without the £500 promised by Uncle Tom. If Uncle Tom then refuses to pay, should Andrew be entitled to claim the money? On the other hand, Uncle Tom did not know that Andrew was going to buy the bike.

The two main arguments for keeping the rule that there has to be consideration on both sides are: (1) there is a legal way of making a binding promise without consideration and that is by making a deed, a promise under seal and (2) the problems of proof: if I do not have to show that I have done anything in exchange, it is easy for me to make false claims that I have been promised money.

APPLYING THE LAW

1 Anthony pays Flowers Ltd £25 to deliver a bouquet of red roses to his girlfriend, Jane. Flowers Ltd send a bunch of dead daisies to Jane.

    Advise Jane as to whether she has a claim against Flowers Ltd.

2 Louise rents a flat belonging to Caroline. Louise repaints all the rooms and repairs a broken window. Caroline is delighted when she sees the improvements that Louise has made and promises to pay Louise the cost of the paint. Two months later Caroline has still not paid this cost.

    Can Louise claim the money?

3 Toby, who has just won a new car in a competition, promises to give Kevin his old car. A week later Kevin sees Toby's old car advertised for sale in the local garage.

    Advise Kevin.

13.3 Intention to create legal relations

There are some agreements where, even though there is a valid offer and acceptance and both sides have put in good consideration, the courts may still decide that they will not enforce the agreement. This is because, at the time the parties made their agreement, they did not intend it to be legally binding. In order to decide whether an agreement was meant to be legally binding the courts treat domestic and social agreements in a different way from business agreements.

Social and domestic agreements

Social and domestic agreements are agreements made within the family or on social matters between friends. Examples are a parent's agreement to pay a son money for cutting the lawn or an agreement that everyone coming to a party will bring a bottle of wine. The courts normally assume that if the agreement is a domestic or social one then the parties did not intend to be legally bound. So, in the case of *Balfour* v. *Balfour* (1919), the court decided that an agreement by a husband to pay his wife £30 a month, because she was unable through ill health to return with him to Sri Lanka where he worked, was not legally binding. When the husband stopped paying the money, the wife was not able to claim it. Similarly, in *Jones* v. *Padavatton* (1969) a daughter was not able to claim money from her mother, even though the mother had promised to support the daughter during her studies for the Bar. There are several reasons why the courts are reluctant to make such agreements legally binding. One is that many will involve minor matters and would be a waste of court time. Another is that family problems are best sorted out amicably and a court case will not help family relationships.

However, the courts may be persuaded by all the circumstances of the agreement that, even though it was between family or friends, it was meant as a legally binding contract. Clear examples are where a marriage is breaking up and the husband and wife come to a financial agreement. The surrounding circumstances of the marriage breakup make the situation different. This was seen in *Merritt* v. *Merritt* (1970), where the hus-

Figure 13.5 Intention to create legal relations

Domestic or social contract	Business contract
Court starts by presuming that the parties DO NOT intend to be legally bound BUT	Court starts by presuming that the parties DO intend to be legally bound BUT
If there is evidence that the parties DID intend to be legally bound, the court will enforce the contract	If there is evidence that the parties DID NOT intend to be legally bound, the court will not enforce the contract

band agreed, after he had left his wife for another woman, that he would transfer the family home to his wife if she paid the remaining mortgage payments. The court held that this was a legally binding contract. Another example is *Simpkins* v. *Pays* (1955) where the defendant, her granddaughter and the plaintiff, who was a lodger in the house, jointly entered a competition. The entry, which was sent in under the defendant's name, won £750, but the defendant refused to give the plaintiff any of the prize money. He sued for one-third of the money and the court decided that the arrangement had been intended as a legally binding contract, so he could get his share.

Business agreements

For business agreements the courts start with the presumption that such agreements are legally binding. This means the court assumes that the parties meant to enter into a contract that could be enforced through the courts if one of them did not carry out the contract. However, if one of the parties can show that this was not what was meant, then the courts may decide that there is not a legally binding contract. In *Rose & Frank Co.* v. *Crompton* (1925), the parties had included in their written agreement the words 'this agreement is not entered into ... as a formal or legal agreement and shall not be subject to legal jurisdiction in the law courts'. It was held that these words made it quite clear that the parties did not mean to be legally bound. The courts have also held that the phrase 'binding in honour only' means there is no intention to be legally bound. These words appear on football pools coupons, so that when a person enters the football pools competition, he is agreeing that there is no legally binding contract between him and the pools company. This, of course, means that even if he correctly forecasts the results, he cannot sue the company for any winnings if they refuse to pay him as happened in *Appleson* v. *Littlewoods Pools* (1939).

At the top of the next column a standing forecast agreement with Littlewoods is reproduced. Look for the words which show that the courts will not enforce the contract.

Figure 13.5 on p.137 summarises the way in which courts approach decisions on domestic and business contracts.

I agree to Littlewoods Football Pool Rules for each week, which govern all entries and I agree that this transaction (apart from the provisions about the Foundation referred to below) covering the whole period of my Standing Forecast Coupon also any extension to it which I might make, is binding in honour only (copies of the Rules can be had on request). I acknowledge that any Collector, Main Collector or Concessionaire through whom my coupon or any extension to it is submitted is my agent, and I agree with all such Collectors, Main Collectors and Concessionaires that any transaction between me and them (otherwise than in relation to the Foundation referred to below) is likewise binding in honour only. I am not under 18 years of age.

I also agree in respect of an effective transaction, for every £1.05 (and pro rata) of my remittance £1 is my stake and 5p is a donation to the Foundation for Sport and the Arts which I instruct you to hold in trust for, and send on to, that Foundation.

I understand that the numbers on my Standing Forecast Coupon serve to identify the matches appearing in the current coupon/fixture list for each week as published in certain newspapers.

Signature

APPLYING THE LAW

1 **Sarah promises to pay her daughter, Kylie, £20 per week if she will do the household cleaning. Kylie keeps her side of the bargain, but after five weeks Sarah has only paid Kylie £10.**

   Advise Kylie as to whether she can claim the money owed.
2 **John, a haulage contractor, signs an agreement with Quick Move Ltd under which he is to provide lorries for carrying office furniture. The agreement contains the words: 'This agreement is binding in honour only'.**

   Advise John as to the effect of this clause.

13.4 Capacity of minors

A minor is anyone under 18 years of age. This age was fixed by the Family Law Reform Act 1969. Prior to that Act anyone under 21 years of age was a minor, a fact which must be remembered when looking at old cases.

Minors can make contracts. This ability or legal capacity is necessary for everyday life. Minors make contracts about all sorts of things: paying for a bus or train ticket; paying the entrance price to go swimming or to a disco; buying sweets, magazines, books or other items in daily life; contracts of employment, either full-time or part-time; these are just some of the examples of contracts which are made every day. There is no legal minimum age for being able to make a contract. Chapter 14, which looks at contracts involving the sale of goods, cites the case of *Godley* v. *Perry* (1960) (p.152) where a boy aged six bought a catapult and was able to rely on the fact that he had a contract with the shop to claim damages.

The law, however, tries to protect minors and so there are some special rules about enforcing contracts against minors.

The law divides contracts made by minors into two types:

1 *Binding contracts*. These are recognised as valid contracts, which the other party can enforce against the minor. There are two categories of binding contracts:

a contracts for necessaries; and
b beneficial contracts of service.

Once the minor has made a binding contract he must go through with it or the other party can sue the minor for breach of contract.

2 *Voidable contracts*. This category covers all other contracts and such contracts cannot be enforced against a minor. The minor has the right to choose whether or not he or she wishes this type of contract to remain in force. If the minor does not want the contract to remain in force, it is said that the minor avoids (pulls out of) the contract and so the law calls this type of contract voidable.

Binding contracts

Contracts for necessaries

Necessaries can be goods such as food and clothing or services such as legal advice or housing. Contracts for education and training are also capable of being contracts for necessaries.

The Sale of Goods Act 1979 says that goods are necessaries if they are 'suitable to the condition in life of the ... [minor] and to his actual requirements at the time of sale and delivery'. This means that normal clothing needed by the minor will come under the heading of necessaries.

In the case of *Nash* v. *Inman* (1908) an undergraduate at Cambridge University ordered eleven fancy waistcoats from his tailor. It was held that these were not necessaries. He already had a large number of clothes and while one or two waistcoats might have been considered necessaries, eleven waistcoats certainly would not. He was not, therefore, bound by the contract.

Luxury items cannot be necessaries. In *Elkington & Co. Ltd* v. *Amery* (1936) a minor who was engaged to be married bought, on credit, an engagement ring and a wedding ring. These items were held to be necessaries, even though they were quite expensive, but a gold vanity bag that he also bought for his fiancée, was held to be a luxury and not a necessary.

In *Chapple* v. *Cooper* (1844) a widow (aged under 21) made a contract with an undertaker for the funeral of her husband. When she did not pay, the undertaker sued her. The court held the contract was for a necessary.

Where the goods are found to be necessaries, the minor is bound by the contract but the Minors' Contracts Act 1987 says that he need only pay a reasonable price for any items that are actually supplied to him. So if the original agreed price is excessive, the court will decide what a reasonable price would be and the minor will be ordered to pay that.

Beneficial contracts of service

Contracts of this type are those for work, education, training, apprenticeship or similar situations. Such a contract will be binding only if it is beneficial as a whole for the minor. So, if there is one clause in the contract that is not beneficial this does not matter, provided the contract when looked at as a complete package does benefit the minor.

This was seen in *Doyle* v. *White City Stadium* (1935) a case about a minor who was a professional boxer. He had a contract to fight under which he was to be paid £3,000, 'win lose or draw'. Clearly this was beneficial to him! However there was also a clause in the contract which said that he would not be paid if he was disqualified during the fight. When he was disqualified for a breach of boxing rules, he tried to claim that the contract was not binding. The court held that as a whole the contract was beneficial and therefore all of the contract applied and he could not claim any money for the fight.

The situation is different if the contract as a whole is 'oppressive'. This is shown by *De Francesco* v. *Barnum* (1890), where the minor had an apprenticeship contract to learn to dance. The contract stated that she would not be paid during the apprenticeship, was not to marry during the apprenticeship, nor was she allowed to dance professionally for any other person. When she agreed to dance for the defendant, the plaintiff sued saying she was in breach of her apprenticeship. The court decided that the terms of the apprenticeship were too harsh and it was not therefore a binding contract. Where the training is not of benefit to the minor the contract is not binding. Where a law student entered into a contract for flying lessons, it was held it was not a binding contract.

Voidable contracts

If the minor decides not to continue with a voidable contract, the other party cannot sue the minor for breach of contract. So if a 17-year-old books an expensive cruise as a holiday, the travel agent cannot claim any money if the minor cancels at the last minute. However, if the minor decides to go through with the contract and goes on the holiday, the minor has the right to sue the holiday company if the cruise is not up to the standard advertised.

The law does give the other party some limited rights in certain situations, even though the minor is entitled to cancel the contract. The Minors' Contracts Act 1987 says that where the minor has acquired property under a voidable contract, the court can order the minor to return that property or any property representing it, if it is 'just and equitable to do so'. This means that if a minor orders an expensive gold watch from a mail order company and that watch is delivered to the minor, the minor may still cancel the contract, but he or she will have to return the watch. If the minor has sold the watch without paying for it and used the money to buy a CD player, the court may decide it is 'just and equitable' (i.e., fair) to order the minor to hand over the CD player. If the CD player cost more than the money the minor got for the watch then it would be unfair to order the CD player to be handed over. This type of order can only be made if the original item or property representing it still exists. If the minor sells the watch and spends the money on a holiday, there is nothing left to represent the watch and the mail order company will be unable to make any claim.

The courts have also held that where a minor has deliberately lied about his or her age and pretended to be over 18, it is fair to allow the other party to reclaim any goods which have not been paid for.

Where there is an ongoing contract, as in renting a flat, the courts will allow the minor to cancel the contract at any time, but the minor must pay a reasonable amount for the period of time he rented the flat before he cancelled the contract. So if the contract is to rent a flat for one year, the minor is quite entitled to repudiate (pull out of) the contract after, say, four months and he will only have to pay a reasonable rent for those four months.

When the minor becomes 18 years old while the contract is still going on, he can ratify (confirm) the contract. This will then make the contract binding against him. So in the example of renting a flat for a year, if the minor becomes 18 one month after the start of the agreement and confirms the contract he will have to pay the rent for the rest of the year period.

Figure 13.6 shows by means of a flow chart the different types of minors' contracts.

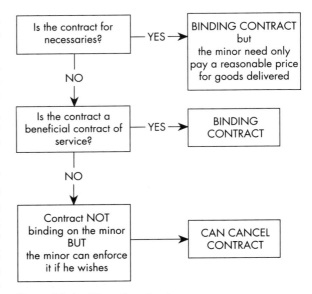

Figure 13.6 Minors' contracts

Guarantees

Because contracts cannot always be enforced against minors, the other party may want an adult to guarantee payment. Where an adult gives such a guarantee, the Minors' Contract Act 1987 states that the guarantee can be enforced even though the contract cannot be enforced against the minor.

APPLYING THE LAW

1 **Melanie, aged 16, goes into a jeweller's shop and orders a gold pendant, which she wants engraved with her name. The jeweller tells her it will take four days to do the engraving and she says she will pay for the pendant when she returns to collect it. One week later she returns to the jeweller's and tells him she no longer wants the pendant.**

    Advise the jeweller.

2 **Daniel, aged 17, orders a suit by mail order from Get Smart Ltd. When the suit arrives he decides to keep it but refuses to pay for it.**

    Advise Get Smart Ltd in the following situations:

    a **Daniel has just started work in a bank and has been told he must wear a suit for work;**

    b **Daniel is attending college and already has two other suits;**

    c **Daniel signed a form when he ordered the suit, declaring that he was over 18 years old.**

13.5 Contracts and writing

The general rule is that contracts do not have to be in writing. When the auctioneer accepts a bid at an auction, there is a valid contract at that moment even though nothing has been written. In fact it is quite probable that the other party to the contract may not have even spoken, since the bid is usually made by a nod or other sign.

Exceptions

Some contracts do have to be in writing. These are:

a   contracts to transfer shares in a registered company;

b   contracts for hire-purchase and other regulated consumer credit agreements;

c   bills of exchange and cheques;

d   promissory notes (commonly called IOUs);

e   contracts for marine insurance.

If these contracts are not in writing, the courts will refuse to enforce them.

   Some other contracts do not have to be completely in writing but there must be some written evidence of them. There are two main types:

1 *Contracts of guarantee.* A guarantee is a promise to pay for the debt or failure of another person to pay. There is a very old rule going back to the Statute of Frauds 1677, that a guarantee cannot be enforced unless there is evidence of it in writing which has been signed by the guarantor.

2 *Contracts for the sale of land.* Under the Law of Property (Miscellaneous Provisions) Act 1989 such a contract must have written evidence of all the important terms in one document (or two where contracts are exchanged) which has been signed by or on behalf of both parties. The details that must be included are:

a   the parties' names and description (i.e., lawyer, housewife);

b   the address of the property being sold;

c   the price or other consideration.

If there are any other special terms, such as the date when the property is to be vacated by the seller, this term must also be included.

Contracts made by deed

A deed is a very formal document. It has to be signed by the person making the deed and the signature must be witnessed by two witnesses. Very few contracts have to be made by a deed; the most important type of contract is the lease of land for three years or more. However it is possible to make any contract by a deed if the parties wish to do so. The main difference with a contract made by a deed is that there is no need for there to be consideration from both parties.

13.6 Terms of a contract

Express terms

Since a contract is an agreement, the parties may include in it any specific terms they wish. These may be in writing or agreed verbally. For example in a written contract for the sale of a house the price of the house will be included. This is a written express term. The buyer promises to pay the agreed amount. An example of an express verbal term might occur when buying an item in a shop. A shopper saying 'I want to buy a packet of glue suitable for use on china' is making that an express term of the contract even though it is not written down. It is a verbal express term.

Implied terms

In some contracts, however, not all the terms will be stated by the parties. Any term that is not specifically mentioned by the parties is called an implied term. Implied terms are usually included because an Act of Parliament states that all contracts of a particular type must include certain terms. This happens with contracts for the sale of goods. Sections 12–15 of the Sale of Goods Act 1979 imply several terms which are mainly aimed at consumer protection. (*See* Chapter 14.) There are also many other Acts of Parliament which imply terms, for example the Carriage of Goods by Sea Act 1971.

It is also possible for a term to be implied by the courts because it is needed to make the rest of the agreement make sense. This is rare but may occur in business contracts where the rest of the contract would not make sense without the implied term. An example of a case in which the courts implied a term into the contract is *The Moorcock* (1889). *The Moorcock* was a steamship and her owners had hired a mooring on the River Thames at a point where the Thames was tidal. When the tide went out the boat was grounded on the river bed and damaged. The contract did not include any term that the mooring was safe for the boat, but the court said that letting a river berth implied that the river bottom was safe to berth.

Conditions

Not all terms in a contract are of equal importance. A key term in a contract is called a condition. It is a term which is crucial to the contract. In the example of buying glue suitable for sticking china together, this is a condition, since it is the whole purpose of buying the glue. If one party breaks a condition the innocent party can cancel the contract if he wishes and may be able to claim damages as well.

Warranties

Less important terms are called warranties. If a warranty is broken the contract remains in force. The innocent party cannot cancel the contract, but he can still claim for damages for breach of warranty. In a contract to buy a car there is a breach of warranty if the side lights on the car do not work. The buyer cannot cancel the contract and reject the car because of such a minor fault, but he can claim the cost of putting the fault right.

APPLYING THE LAW

Decide whether there is a breach of condition or warranty in the following situations.

1 **Gary, a well-known pop star, has a contract with a recording company. The contract includes (a) a term that Gary will record three records; (b) a term that Gary will sing the songs on those records at his next concert. Gary records two records, but refuses to do the third. He does not sing the songs at his next concert.**
2 **Amanda orders a new washing machine after the salesman assures her that it is suitable for washing extra heavy loads. When the washing machine is delivered she notices that there is scratch on one side. The first time she uses the machine for a heavy load, it breaks down.**

Exclusion clauses

It is possible to include a term in a contract so that one party can avoid liability in the event of certain things happening. Most car parks have notices saying, 'Cars parked at owners' risk'. This is an exclusion clause in the contract the car driver made with the parking firm when he paid to park his car. If the car is damaged while in the car park, the owner will not be able to make a claim against the car park firm.

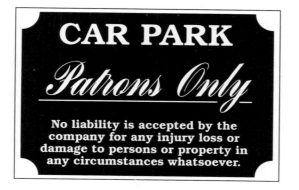

Neither the courts nor Parliament like the use of exclusion clauses and both have developed strict rules about their use. Parliament has passed the Unfair Contract Terms Act 1977 which limits the use of exclusion clauses. The most important limitations are:

a that an exclusion clause cannot restrict liability for death or serious injury resulting from negligence (s. 2(1));

b that liability for other loss or damage can only be restricted if the exclusion clause is reasonable (s. 2(2));

c that in consumer contracts (*see* Chapter 14) an exclusion clause cannot prevent liability for a breach where the contractual performance is substantially different from that which was reasonably expected (s. 3).

The fact that liability for death or serious injury cannot be excluded means that a car park firm could be liable if a car driver was seriously injured in their car park even though there was a notice saying, 'Cars parked at owners' risk'.

To avoid liability for other loss or damage the exclusion clause must be reasonable. An example of a clause being held to be unreasonable occurred in *Woodman* v. *Photo Trade Processing* (1981). Wedding photographs were ruined and the processing company tried to rely on a clause in the contract which said that their liability was limited to replacing the film. The court held that this clause was unreasonable and the plaintiff could recover damages for disappointment as well as the cost of the film.

The idea of contractual performance being substantially different from that which was reasonably expected can be illustrated by an example of a contract with a garage to respray the whole of your car. If the garage resprays all of the car but paints the roof a different colour to the rest of the car, this would be substantially different from what you expected them to do. The garage could not rely on any exclusion clause to avoid liability.

Another way in which Parliament has prevented the use of exclusion clauses is in section 6 of the Unfair Contract Terms Act 1977. This section stops sellers in consumer sales from excluding liability for breach of any of the implied terms in sections 12–15 of the Sale of Goods Act 1979.

Where the exclusion clause is not forbidden by Parliament, the courts have developed rules to try and control their use. The main rule is that the clause must be brought to the other party's notice before they enter into the contract. In *Olley* v. *Marlborough Court Hotel* (1949) a couple booked into a hotel. The contract with the hotel was formed at that point. After they had booked in they went to their room and in the room was a notice saying, 'the proprietors will not hold themselves responsible for articles lost or stolen unless handed to the manageress for safe custody'. The woman's furs were stolen from her hotel room. She claimed their value from the hotel and the hotel had to pay her. They could not rely on the exclusion notice since it had not been communicated to the couple before they made the contract.

Where a party signs a written contract he agrees to all the terms that are written down. This is so even if he does not read those terms. This means that if there is an exclusion clause printed in the contract, then unless it is one of those forbidden by Parliament, that exclusion clause will be valid. Sometimes this is referred to as the 'small print', since often the terms are printed in tiny letters. This does not matter. If you sign a contract you are assumed to be agreeing to all the terms written in it and will be bound by them.

A C T I V I T Y

Look at the two pictures on p. 143. Both are of notices excluding liability in car parks. Answer the following questions.

1 **What is the difference in the wording?**
2 **Does the Unfair Contract Terms Act 1977 limit either or both of these exclusion notices? Give reasons for your answer.**

13.7 Discharge of contracts

There are several ways in which a contract can come to an end (or be discharged):

- Performance
- Agreement
- Frustration
- Breach

Performance

Here the contract ends when both parties have done everything they agreed to do under the contract. If you ordered a freezer from a shop, the contract would end when the shop delivered the freezer and you paid for it. Both parties have done what they promised to do. The general rule is that the whole contract must be performed exactly as agreed. If there is a set time for performing the contract then it must be performed within that time. In the example above of ordering a freezer, the shop may promise to deliver it within two weeks. They are not performing their side of the contract if they do not deliver it in that time. Where the parties do not agree on a time limit, then the contract must be performed within a reasonable time. What is reasonable will depend on the type of contract. If the shop and the customer do not agree on a time limit in the freezer example, then it would be reasonable if the shop delivered it five weeks after the order was placed. However, in a contract to buy strawberries, five weeks might not be reasonable.

Part performance

Problems also occur where one party only performs part of the contract. Since the normal rule is that the whole contract must be performed, a party who only performs part of it cannot usually claim anything for that part. In *Sumpter* v. *Hedges* (1898) there was a contract in which the plaintiff agreed to build two houses and stables for the defendant for £565. The plaintiff did part of the work but then abandoned it and the defendant completed the work. The plaintiff tried to claim for the value of the work he had done, about £333, but the court held that he was not entitled to any money as he had not completed the contract.

The courts will only allow a claim for part performance where:

a the contract has almost been completed; in *Hoenig* v. *Isaacs* (1952), where a carpenter and decorator had a contract to do £750 worth of work, he nearly finished it, but did a small part badly. The court held he should be paid £694, i.e. £750 less the cost of finishing the work, which was £56;

b the contract can be divided up into different parts; in most building contracts today, there will be an agreement that the builder should be paid something when he completes the foundations of the building; a further sum when the walls and roof are complete and the final amount when the building is finished. In this type of contract, the builder will be able to claim the agreed amount for the foundations, even if he does no more work;

c the other party prevents full performance; for example, in a contract to decorate the inside of a house, the decorator will be able to claim for the work he has done if the occupier of the house without any reason stops him from finishing the decoration;

d where the other party is prepared to accept part performance; for example, if a supplier can only deliver 150 cricket bats instead of the 200 agreed, there is an acceptance of that part performance if the shop is willing to accept the 150. This means the shop will have to pay for those 150 bats.

Agreement

Contracts are brought into existence by agreement between the parties, so if the parties agree they can also bring the contract to an end. If the agreement to end the contract is made before either side has performed any part of it there is no problem. The only problem is when one party has already performed part of the contract but the other party has not. In this case the agreement to end the contract should include some compensation for the work already done or the agreement must be made in the form of a deed.

Frustration

This is the legal term used when something happens to make it impossible for the contract to take place. A contract can be frustrated because:

a   the property involved in the contract is destroyed; an example of this occurred in the case of *Taylor* v. *Caldwell* (1863) where there was a contract to hire a music hall to put on four concerts. The music hall was burnt down before the first concert;

b   the person due to perform the contract becomes too ill to do it; this will only apply where that particular person is crucial to the contract. If there is a contract to paint a house, it is probably not important who actually does the painting, so if the original painter becomes ill, another painter can replace him. However, if the contract is for a famous artist to paint a portrait, then the contract will be frustrated if that artist is too ill to paint. In *Condor* v. *Barron Knights* (1966), a drummer contracted to play with a well-known pop group was not well enough to do all the concerts agreed in the contract. It was held that his illness frustrated the contract;

c   after the contract has been made, a law is passed which makes the performance of the contract illegal; this has happened in wartime situations where laws about trade in certain goods have been passed.

Effects of frustration

Any contract which has been frustrated is held to have been discharged (ended). The courts will try to put the parties back in the position they were in before they made the contract. This means that any property or money handed over under the contract must be given back, although if one party has incurred expenses he will be able to claim those out of any money he has to hand back. Any party obtaining a benefit will have to pay what is reasonable for that benefit, thus if in *Taylor* v. *Caldwell* the hall had burnt down after the first concert instead of before, Taylor would have had to pay for the use of the hall for that one concert.

Breach

A serious breach of contract will allow the innocent party to treat the contract as at an end. In 13.6 we saw that important terms are called conditions. If a condition is broken the innocent party can decide whether he wants the contract to continue or whether he wants it brought to an end.

Anticipatory breach

In some contracts there is an agreement to do something in the future, for instance, a singer agrees to sing at a concert on 15 June next year. If, two months before that concert, the singer says he will not give the concert, this is called an anticipatory breach. The contract is not due to be performed until 15 June, but the other party need not wait until then to claim damages. He can claim once the singer has made it clear that he will not give the concert, that is, in anticipation of the breach.

13.8 Remedies for breach of contract

When there has been a breach of contract, the innocent party can start a court action and the court can award him certain remedies. The most important remedies are damages, specific performance, injunction and rescission.

Damages

Damages are an award of money to compensate the innocent party and put him in the same position financially as he would have been had the contract not been broken. Damages are a common law remedy and so available as of right to compensate for any direct and foreseeable loss. In a contract to purchase a pot of yoghurt, there is a direct and foreseeable loss of the cost of the pot if it turns out to be empty. This means that the purchaser can claim the purchase price as damages. If, however, the yoghurt has been contaminated with cleaning fluid, so that the purchaser becomes ill after eating it, the purchaser can claim damages (compensation) for the illness, as well as the return of the purchase price.

Remoteness of damage

The only restriction on claiming damages is that the law does not allow a claim for any loss that is considered to be too remote from the consequences of the breach. This rule comes from the case of *Hadley* v. *Baxendale* (1854). The plaintiff, Hadley, owned a mill and ordered a new driving shaft for it, which was to be delivered by the defendant. The defendant was late in delivering the shaft and the plaintiff sued for breach of contract. The plaintiff tried to claim for loss of profit as the mill had been out of action while awaiting the new shaft. It was held that as the defendant did not know that the mill could not operate without the shaft, the loss of profits was too remote and could not be claimed. The case decided that damages should be awarded where:

a they arose naturally from the breach of the contract; or

b they were reasonably in contemplation of both parties when they made the contract.

If the mill owner had told Baxendale that a quick delivery was necessary because the mill could not operate without the shaft, he would have been able to claim his loss of profit as it would have been 'reasonably in the contemplation of both parties'.

In *Anglia Television* v. *Reed* (1972) an American actor made a contract with the plaintiffs to play the leading role in a television film. The plaintiffs had already spent money on preparing for the filming and after the contract was made they spent more. The actor broke the contract and the plaintiffs were unable to find a suitable replacement. This meant that the money

spent on preparation had been wasted. They sued Mr Reed for all the wasted money, including that spent before he had entered into the contract. It was held that the defendant had to pay damages covering all the money wasted on preparation. The court said that the defendant must have contemplated that, if he broke his contract, all the expenditure would be wasted, whether it was incurred before or after the contract.

A case in which part of the damage was natural and foreseeable, but part was not is *Victoria Laundry* v. *Newman Industries Ltd* (1948). In this case the plaintiffs ordered a new boiler from the defendants. The defendants were five months late in delivering the boiler and Victoria Laundry sued them for loss of profits during that five months. The court held that they could claim for loss of normal profits during this time as these were reasonably foreseeable. However they could not claim for loss of extra profits on special dyeing contracts. They had not told the defendants about these contracts and without being told the defendants could not be expected to foresee the extra loss.

Specific performance

Specific performance is an equitable remedy. This means that the court does not have to grant the remedy if damages are sufficient. The remedy is discretionary; the court will only grant it where it is just and fair to do so. When it is granted, an order for specific performance orders the other party to carry out his side of the contract. Specific performance is not often ordered. It is never granted in contracts where:

a one of the parties is a minor;

b the contract is for lending money;

c the contract is for personal service; this covers such things as singing at a concert or acting in a film, painting a house or painting a picture, or working at any job. Specific performance will not be granted because it is clearly impossible to force a person to carry out such a service when they do not wish to do it.

Specific performance is not usually granted where the contract involves the sale of goods. In this type of contract damages will normally be an adequate remedy. If the seller refuses to go through with the sale, the buyer can buy a similar item from someone else and claim damages from the seller for any extra cost or inconvenience. So in a contract to buy a motor bike for £1,500, the buyer could buy the same make and model of bike from another person and if he had to pay £1,750 then he could claim the extra £250 from the original seller who broke the contract. In the same way if the buyer refuses to complete the contract, the seller can sell to another person and claim damages from the buyer if the sale price is less than that originally agreed.

The only time the court might order specific performance is in a sale of goods that are very rare, where it would be almost impossible to find the same type of item to buy anywhere else. This could happen with a rare stamp, where there might be only six known examples in the whole world. Specific performance is most often used in contracts for the sale of land since the courts take the view that damages will not properly compensate such a buyer.

Injunction

Injunction is another equitable remedy. An injunction will only be ordered if the court thinks that it is fair and just in all the circumstances. An injunction usually orders one party to a contract NOT to do something which is in breach of the contract. In *Warner Bros* v. *Nelson* (1937) the actress, Bette Davies, was ordered not to make a film for another company, as that would been a breach of her contract to act exclusively for Warner Brothers. However such an injunction will not be granted if it means that the defendant would have no reasonable alternative way of earning a living.

Rescission

Rescission is also an equitable remedy. Rescission has the effect of putting the parties back in the position they would have been in if they had never made a contract. In a contract for the sale of an item, the item would be returned to the seller and the purchase money to the buyer. Rescission is used where one party has been persuaded to make the contract through a misrepresentation (false statement) of the facts by the other party.

Examination questions

1 There are established rules in contract. One rule, relating to the formation of a contract, states that offers, revocation and acceptances all must be communicated to the other party. Another rule states that communication of acceptance is not necessary if the contract is unilateral, i.e. a promise in return for an act by the other party.

The problem

The Newtown Weekly News, a local newspaper, has recently been running a campaign to clean up the local environment.

The local canal has recently benefited from the clean up campaign and the paper, keen to advertise its success, one week places an advertisement offering '£100 to the first person to swim the half-mile section of the canal which runs through Newtown.'

That morning before breakfast, Peter, a keen swimmer, goes for his usual early morning swim in the canal, completing the half mile required. Peter does not read the local paper.

At about midday the local police inform the newspaper that swimming the canal can be dangerous. The newspaper decides to withdraw the offer and puts a notice to that effect in the window of the newspaper offices.

That afternoon Andrew, who has seen both the advertisement and the notice in the window, decides to swim the half mile anyway.

The following day Mary, who has seen the advertisement but not the notice, decides to swim the half mile, hoping to claim the reward.

a Peter claims that, as he was the first person to swim the canal, he is entitled to the £100. Advise him, giving your reasons.
(4 marks)

b Discuss the legal principles which apply to the newspaper's notice in its office window. *(4 marks)*

c In the light of these principles, advise
  i Andrew **and** (*4 marks*)
  ii Mary (*4 marks*)
  whether they would be entitled to claim
  the £100.

d Comment on what difference, if any, it
  would make if Andrew had not seen the
  notice in the window but had heard about
  the notice from a friend. (*4 marks*)

e The situation above could have been
  further complicated if any of the parties
  had decided to use the post.
  i Discuss what is meant by the postal
    rule as it applies to offers and
    acceptances sent by post. (*6 marks*)
  ii How appropriate is this rule in a
    modern society? (*4 marks*)

Total: 30 marks

SEG Sample Paper for 1996 (Higher Tier)

2 A contract consists of a legally binding
agreement between two or more people, under
which the parties must give or promise
something of value which the law will
recognise as consideration. The parties must
intend to create legal relations by their
agreement and, in addition, must have the
capacity to contract. For example, certain
restrictions are placed upon a minor's ability to
enter into a valid and binding contract.

The problem

Claire, aged 15, and her mother Rebecca,
decide to go shopping in town. Claire, who
is extremely fashion conscious, wants a new
pair of shoes to match a dress she bought
last week but knows she does not have
enough money on her. Rebecca knows that
Claire already has lots of pairs of shoes but
eventually agrees to lend her the £20 Claire
needs to buy them, provided Claire pays her
back.

When they return home, Claire reminds
her mother that she had to do all the cooking the previous month when Rebecca was
ill. Finally, Rebecca reluctantly agrees that
Claire need not repay her the £20 because of
the extra housework she had done.

---

a If a situation like this was to come to
  court, the law might be reluctant to
  enforce the agreement for a number of
  reasons. In the light of this statement,
  explain how the following issues
  influence the court:
  i the family relationship between the two
    parties; (*4 marks*)
  ii Claire's age. (*4 marks*)

b What difference, if any, could it have
  made if the shoes had been regulation
  school shoes and Claire had grown out of
  her previous pair? (*4 marks*)

c i Explain whether or not a court would
    view Claire's extra housework as valid
    consideration for Rebecca's promise
    not to insist on the return of her £20.
    (*4 marks*)
  ii How appropriate do you consider the
    law to be in this area? (*4 marks*)

d Comment on how well the law deals with
  i agreements between family members;
  ii agreements involving minors under the
    age of 18. (*10 marks*)

Total: 30 marks

SEG 1994

3 There are a number of established remedies
available to an injured party as a result of a
breach of contract. These include the common
law remedies of repudiation and damages, and
the equitable remedies of specific performance
and an injunction. Common law remedies are
available as a right, whereas equitable
remedies are discretionary.

The problem

Two months ago World Wide Pictures Ltd, a
film company, entered into a contract with
Michael J. Wolf, an actor, to play the leading
role in their latest film 'Teen-Fox III'. In the
contract, Wolf agreed to be available for one
year from the date of the contract for
rehearsals and shooting the film. He also
agreed not to undertake any other film or TV
work during that year.

Today World Wide Pictures received a
telegram from Mr Wolf stating that he has

---

signed a contract with an Australian TV station to star in an Australian soap opera and that he is no longer available to carry out his contract.

It would appear that, without Mr Wolf, the film is unlikely to be made as no suitable replacement actor is available, and that therefore World Wide Pictures Ltd looks likely to lose a great deal of money. In addition, the film's producer, Stephanie, looks likely to lose her job with World Wide Pictures if the film is not made.

a Damages may only be claimed by an injured party to a contract if the loss caused is both a direct and foreseeable consequence of the breach, i.e. the damage must not be too remote.

Explain with reasons whether:

i World Wide Pictures Ltd could sue Mr Wolf for the loss made on the film, including loss of expected profit;

ii Stephanie could sue Mr Wolf if she does in fact lose her job. (*8 marks*)

b The ideal solution for World Wide Pictures Ltd would be to force Mr Wolf to carry out his original contract with the company.

Explain whether or not such a remedy would be available. (*4 marks*)

c Alternatively, World Wide Pictures Ltd is considering trying to stop Mr Wolf working for the Australian TV station.

Explain what the remedy would be and whether it would be available to the company. (*6 marks*)

d The various remedies for breach of contract are not available in all circumstances to cover every loss. They are all restricted in one way or another.

Describe some of these restrictions.

Explain with reasons whether or not you consider these restrictions to be justified. (*12 marks*)

Total: 30 marks

SEG 1992

14 *Consumer law*

Many contracts involve the ordinary person buying goods for personal or family use from shops or other businesses. These are known as consumer contracts. There are also other types of consumer contracts, in particular, hire-purchase contracts, contracts to hire goods and contracts for services such as repairing a car or rewiring a house. The normal rules of contract about offer, acceptance, consideration and capacity apply. At the same time law recognises that it is necessary to make sure that the consumer is not at a disadvantage when dealing with a business and so there are a number of Acts of Parliament which imply terms into such contracts.

This idea of consumer protection is not new. One of the first Acts passed by Parliament was the Sale of Goods Act 1893. Since then there have been a number of Acts all designed to protect the consumer and in this chapter we are going to look at the main provisions in three of these: the Sale of Goods Act 1979, the Supply of Goods and Services Act 1982 and the Consumer Protection Act 1987.

14.1 Sale of Goods Act 1979

This Act defines a contract of sale of goods as:

a contract by which the seller transfers or agrees to transfer the property in goods to the buyer for a money consideration called the price. (s. 2)

The word 'goods' means physical items which are moveable, for example, furniture, food, cars, clothes, machinery and tools. In order to be cov-ered by the Act it must be intended that the ownership of the item is to be given to the buyer for a sum of money. It does not matter whether the contract is carried out straightaway, as in the case of buying food in a supermarket, or whether the transfer of the goods is to be carried out in the future, as might happen when furniture is ordered from a shop to be delivered and paid for in two weeks time. Both these situations are sales of goods covered by the Sale of Goods Act.

The most important sections are sections 12, 13, 14 and 15. These four sections imply certain terms into contracts of sale of goods. In 13.6 we saw that an implied term automatically becomes part of the contract even though the parties do not mention it. The terms in these four sections are therefore automatically part of any consumer contract for the sale of goods. Figure 14.1 summarises the implied conditions in these four sections (*see* p. 153).

Section 12(1) – the right to sell the goods

This section implies a condition that the seller has a right to sell the goods, in other words, that the seller can transfer the ownership in the goods to the buyer. This is clearly very important as no-one wants to buy goods only to be told that the goods do not belong to them. In *Rowland* v. *Divall* (1923) the plaintiff bought a car from the defendant. The plaintiff then discovered that the car had been stolen and so the defendant was not the owner of the car and had no right to sell it. The true owner reclaimed his car and the plaintiff sued the defendant for a breach of section 12. It was held that the plaintiff was entitled to get the purchase price back from the defendant. Section 12 applies to all sales of goods, even where the seller is not acting in the course of business, but is a private person selling just one item.

Section 13 – goods must match description

Where there is a contract for the sale of goods by description, there is an implied condition that the goods will correspond with (match) the description. This section covers situations where the buyer does not see the goods before he buys them but relies on what is said in an advertisement. It also covers situations where the buyer does see the goods but still relies to some extent on the description. This happened in *Beale* v. *Taylor* (1967) where a car was described in an advertisement as 'Herald, convertible white 1961'. The buyer went to see the car and agreed to buy it. The car was later discovered to be the back half of a 1961 model welded to the front half of an older car. Even though the plaintiff had looked at the car before he bought it, the court held that it was a sale by description and, since only half the car was a 1961 model, section 13 had been broken. The buyer was able to treat the contract as at an end and claim damages.

Section 13(3) adds that a sale can be a sale by description even in situations where the buyer selects the goods. This covers sales in supermarkets or other shops where the buyer picks the item off the shelf but still relies on the description on the label or the packaging. If a can of drink is labelled 'lemonade' the buyer is relying on that description. There is no other way the buyer can discover what is in the can and so if that can then turns out to contain an orange flavoured drink there is a breach of section 13.

Section 13 applies to all sales by description, private sales as well as those in the course of a business.

Section 14 – goods must be of satisfactory quality

Where goods are sold in the course of a business there is an implied condition that those goods will be of satisfactory quality. Until 1995 the phrase

used was 'of merchantable quality'. On 3 January 1995 the Sale and Supply of Goods Act 1994 made a change in the wording of the 1979 Sale of Goods Act. Where one Act changes an earlier Act in this way it is said that the earlier Act is amended. But remember that all cases decided before 1995 will be considering the old wording of merchantable quality.

Goods are of satisfactory quality if they meet the standard that a reasonable person would regard as satisfactory, taking account of any description of the goods, the price and any other relevant circumstances. So where jackets, for example, are marked 'seconds' and sold cheaply, they will be of satisfactory quality even if there is a minor fault in the weave of the material. However they would not be satisfactory if there was a major fault, such as one of the sleeves being missing! The test is an objective test because it is what a reasonable person would regard as satisfactory.

BUT IT WAS MARKED SECONDS, MADAM.

The Act goes on to say that in considering quality an important point is whether the goods are fit for all the purposes for which goods of the kind in question are commonly supplied. So in *Priest* v. *Last* (1903) where the item bought was a hot water bottle, the court held that the bottle had to be fit for its obvious purpose of warming a bed. Since the bottle burst when used it was not fit for its normal purpose. Similarly in *Godley* v. *Perry* (1960) when a boy aged six bought a catapult which broke when he used it, causing an injury to his eye, it was not fit for its normal purpose.

The Sale and Supply of Goods Act 1994 now also includes a list of other points which are covered by the word quality; these are appearance and finish, freedom from minor defects, safety and durability.

Section 14(3) says that if the buyer makes known to the seller a particular purpose for which the goods are being bought, then the goods must be fit for that purpose unless the buyer did not rely on the seller's skill and judgment or it is unreasonable for the buyer to rely on the seller's skill and judgment. In buying computer software from a specialist firm, if the buyer asks for a package that is suitable for a particular type of computer, then he has made the purpose of the goods known to the seller and it would be reasonable for him to rely on the seller's skill and judgment.

Section 14 does not apply to any defects to which the seller has specifically drawn the buyer's attention before the contract was made. Thus, where a secondhand car is for sale and the seller tells the buyer that the clutch is worn and will soon need replacing, the buyer cannot claim that the car is not of satisfactory quality if the clutch goes wrong a few days after the sale.

Section 14 does not apply either where the buyer examines the goods and the defects are ones which that examination ought to reveal. If a shopper before buying a new washing machine examines the outside of it, but fails to notice that there is a bad dent on the front panel, that shopper cannot claim that the dent is a breach of the condition of satisfactory quality. However, if the spinner will not work, the shopper can claim there is a breach of section 14 as a visual examination in the shop could not show the fault with the spinner.

Since section 14 only applies to sales in the course of a business, it does not apply to private sales. For example it would not apply where a private individual advertises his car for sale. In this case the law has a rule, *caveat emptor*, which means let the buyer beware.

Rejection of goods

Although section 14 implies a condition, the courts do not always hold that a breach of the condition means that the buyer can treat the contract as ended and reject the goods. In some cases the courts have held that by using an item for a few weeks the buyer has accepted the goods and lost his right to reject them. Of course the buyer can still claim damages for putting any fault right. In *Bernstein* v. *Pamson Motors* (1987) the plaintiff bought a brand new Nissan car. He used it for three weeks, but had only driven 143 miles when a piece of loose sealant caused the engine to seize up. The court held that the defect meant that the car was not of merchantable quality and there was a breach of section 14, but, because the plaintiff had had the car for three weeks he had accepted it and lost his right to treat the contract as at an end. This case contrasts with *Rogers* v. *Parish (Scarborough) Ltd* (1987) where a new Range Rover had a number of faults, but was still driveable. In this case the buyer complained about the faults quickly and the court held he was entitled to treat the contract as at an end and reject the car.

The Sale and Supply of Goods Act 1994 has tried to improve this area for purchasers. Buyers do not lose the right to reject goods just because they sign a delivery note. Nor do they lose the right to reject if they agree to let the seller try to repair them, if that repair does not work.

Section 15 – sale by sample

Where having examined a sample the buyer then orders goods, there are implied conditions that:

a   the goods must correspond with the sample
b   the buyer will have a reasonable opportunity of comparing the goods with the sample
c   the goods will not have a hidden defect which would make their quality unsatisfactory

This section will apply where a shopper chooses a carpet from seeing sample squares. It will also apply where a shop buys in bulk from a supplier after examining a sample. This occurred in *Godley* v. *Perry* (1960), the case where the young boy bought a catapult. The shop which had sold him the catapult claimed against the wholesaler because the shopkeeper had bought the catapults after looking at a sample. He successfully claimed that there was a breach of section 15 since the fault was a hidden defect which made them unmerchantable.

Excluding sections 12–15

Before 1977 shops and wholesalers often added exclusion clauses to contracts which said that sections 12–15 of the Sale of Goods Act did not apply. (At this time the 1893 Act was in force.) By excluding these sections from a contract the whole purpose of consumer protection in the Sale of Goods Act was lost. In order to make sure that consumers were protected Parliament passed the Unfair Contract Terms Act 1977. This Act, often called UCTA, says that section 12 of the Sale of Goods Act cannot be excluded from any contract for the sale of goods. UCTA also says that sections 13–15 of the Sale of Goods Act cannot be excluded from a consumer sale. A consumer sale is defined as a sale where the goods are of a type ordinarily supplied for private use or consumption and the seller is selling in the course of a business and the buyer is not buying in the course of business. So whenever a private individual buys goods which would be normally used for private use, such as a dining table and chairs, or for consumption, such as any food or drink, then this will be a consumer sale, provided the seller is selling in the course of business. However, if someone buys a secondhand car from his neighbour and not from a business, then this is not a consumer sale.

APPLYING THE LAW

Explain whether there is a breach of the Sale of Goods Act in each of the following situations and what remedy, if any, the buyer has.

1 **Andrew reads an advertisement in a newspaper of a car for sale. It says, 'Ford Fiesta 1993 model, low mileage'. Andrew telephones the seller and agrees to buy the car without seeing it for £4,000. When he takes delivery he finds that the car is an older model than stated in the advert.**

2 **Amelia agrees to buy some material from a shop after being assured by the sales assistant that the material will not shrink. In fact the material does shrink and is completely unsuitable for the purpose Amelia intended.**

3 **Bertram buys an umbrella, but when he tries to use it, he finds that the catch will not work so that the umbrella will not stay open.**

4 **Caroline buys a brand new car. After 235 miles the car breaks down because a piece of loose sealing compound in the engine cuts off the oil flow causing severe damage to the engine. The dealer offers to repair it free of charge. Caroline says she wants her money back.**

Figure 14.1 Summary of the implied conditions in the Sale of Goods Act 1979

Section	Implied condition	Comment
12	The seller has the right to sell the goods	Cannot be excluded from **any** contract
13	The goods match their description	Cannot be excluded from consumer sales Can be excluded from private sales
14	The goods are of satisfactory quality	Cannot be excluded from consumer sales
15	The goods match sample	Cannot be excluded from consumer sales Can be excluded from private sales

Ownership of goods

In a contract for the sale of goods it is important to know exactly when the ownership of goods passes from the seller to the buyer. There are usually no problems in sales in shops since the contract is formed at the checkout desk, the customer pays and takes the item with him within a matter of minutes or even seconds. In other situations where the goods are not immediately taken into the buyer's possession, there can be problems. What happens if a customer orders a car and arranges to collect it in three days' time? Is the car his or the garage's during those three days? What if the garage burnt down and the car was destroyed during that three-day period? The buyer needs to know when the ownership of the car passes to him so that he can insure against damage and loss.

Section 17 of the Sale of Goods Act says that the ownership passes when the parties intend it to pass. As in most consumer contracts the parties do not discuss when they intend ownership to pass, section 18 creates some rules for working out the parties' intentions. The main rules are:

1 In an unconditional contract for the sale of specific goods, the ownership passes when the contract is made. It does not matter that payment or delivery will take place later.
2 If the seller has to do something to specific goods to put them into a deliverable state, then the ownership passes when that has been done and the buyer has been notified that it has been done.

The effect of these two rules on the example of collecting a car in three days' time is that if there is no work to be done on the car, the ownership in it passes to the buyer at the moment the contract is made. If, however, the garage has to do some work on it and it will not be ready (in a deliverable state) until that third day, then the ownership of the car will not pass to the buyer until the work has been done and the buyer told the car is ready.

3 If goods have to be weighed, measured, tested or be subject to some such act before their price can be worked out, then the ownership does not pass to the buyer until this has been done and the buyer told it has been done.

4 Where goods are delivered to the buyer on approval or on sale or return, then ownership of the goods does not pass until the buyer signifies his acceptance of the goods to the seller or does some other act indicating his acceptance. If there is a time limit agreed and the buyer does not indicate his acceptance of the goods, then the goods become the buyer's when the time limit runs out.

The other important rule about transferring ownership in the goods is that the seller can only transfer the rights that he has. This means that if the seller does not own the goods and has not got the owner's consent to sell, he cannot transfer ownership to any buyer. The law says that no-one can give what he has not got. As the buyer cannot get ownership where the seller has no right to sell, the true owner is entitled to claim his property back. We have already met this situation in *Rowland* v. *Divall* (*see* p. 150). As the car was stolen the seller did not own the car and so was unable to transfer ownership to the plaintiff.

14.2 Supply of Goods and Services Act 1982

Transfer of goods

There are situations in which goods change hands but there is not a sale as defined in the Sale of Goods Act 1979. This can occur where goods are exchanged for each other and not for money; this is called barter. It also happens where goods are exchanged for tokens or labels from packets. Another situation is where goods are exchanged for a service, as, for example, receiving a free gift for introducing a new customer. None of these situations is covered by the Sale of Goods Act, so to protect the person acquiring goods in this way, Parliament passed the Supply of Goods and Services Act 1982. In all such transfers of goods this Act implies the same conditions as under the Sale of Goods Act:

a   that the person transferring the goods has the right to do so;
b   that the goods must correspond with any description;
c   that the goods are of satisfactory quality; and
d   that the goods will match any sample.

Contracts of hire

A contract of hire is an agreement that one person will have temporary possession of the other person's property for the payment of a sum of money. A common example is the hire of a TV set or video recorder. The hirer pays a sum of money each week for the use of the set, but the set is not his, nor is it ever intended that it will become his. The set belongs to the rental company. Other examples are hiring a car or van from a rental company. A contract to hire an item is not a sale of that item nor a permanent transfer of it. The Supply of Goods and Services Act 1982 gives the hirer similar rights to those in the Sale of Goods Act as to the goods matching their description, being of satisfactory quality and, where appropriate, matching any sample.

Supply of services

Contracts for the supply of services cover a very wide range of services. Some examples are repairs to a car by a garage, work done by a plumber or an electrician, painting and decorating, hairdressing, cleaning clothes or providing a hotel room. The Supply of Goods and Services Act 1982 implies three conditions into any contract for services where the supplier is acting in the course of a business. These are:

1 The supplier will carry out the service with reasonable care and skill.
2 Where the time for the service to be carried out is not fixed, the service will be carried out within a reasonable time.
3 Where the charge for the service has not been agreed, the supplier will be paid a reasonable charge.

These conditions apply whether or not any goods are supplied with the service. However, if goods are supplied then those goods are covered by the implied terms in the Sale of Goods Act 1979.

All three conditions use the word 'reasonable' and what is reasonable is a question of fact that may vary from one situation to another. Ruining a leather jacket which was sent for cleaning would hardly be 'carrying out the service with reasonable care and skill'; nor would rewiring a socket so badly that the wires shorted and caused a fire. What is a reasonable time will depend on the amount and difficulty of the work to be done and the length of time normally taken for such work. In *Charnock* v. *Liverpool Corporation* (1968) a garage took eight weeks to repair a car when a 'normally competent' repairer would have taken five weeks. It was held that the extra three weeks was an unreasonable delay and the plaintiff could claim damages from the repairer.

A reasonable charge is again a question of fact. If there is an estimate given before the work is done, then it is almost certainly unreasonable if the supplier tries to charge double the estimate. However if the supplier at the finish of the work charges 5 per cent more than the original estimate that is probably reasonable. If there is no estimate given before the work starts then what is reasonable may be judged by what other reputable firms charge for the same service.

14.3 Consumer Protection Act 1987

This Act was passed to bring into force the European Product Liability Directive. It affects both civil and criminal law since it gives consumers certain rights to sue the 'manufacturer' of a product and it makes breach of various safety regulations a criminal offence.

The Act is important because it allows claims by any consumer, not just by the buyer. This means that someone who has been given a present may be able to claim for damage caused by defects in the present, whereas under the Sale of Goods Act that person has no rights as he/she is not the buyer.

The Consumer Protection Act applies to 'defective products'. A product is defined as anything which has gone through a manufacturing process and it includes gas and electricity. Fresh food which has not been processed in any way is not covered by the Act. A product is defective if 'the safety of the product is not such as persons generally are entitled to expect'. The defect can be one of three types:

a a defect in design;
b a defect in processing or manufacturing;
c a defect in instructions or a lack of warning that means the product may be used, installed or assembled in an unsafe way.

Where there is a defect, the consumer has a right

to sue the 'producer'. This means the actual manufacturer or any company which labels goods under its own brand name, even if the goods were made for it by another company. It also includes any person who imports goods into the European Union countries when the goods were manufactured outside the European Union.

In order to claim the consumer must show that the product caused damage. Damage covers death or any injury caused by the defective product; it also includes loss or damage to property provided that loss or damage amounts to at least £275.

Apart from this restriction on claims, the Act also allows producers certain defences which will prevent a claim. For example, the producer has a defence if he can show that the state of scientific and technical knowledge at the time of production meant the defect could not possibly have been discovered.

These limitations in the Consumer Protection Act make it far from satisfactory, but it does provide those who have not bought the product with some protection which they would not otherwise have.

A comparison of the rights under the consumer protection Acts is set out in Figure 14.2.

Unfair Terms in Consumer Contracts Regulations 1994

These Regulations prevent businesses unfairly excluding liability in what are known as standard form contracts. These are contracts in which the business sets out all the terms which it always uses in that type of situation and the customer has to agree to those terms or not make a contract with that business.

The Regulations state that a term is unfair if:

- it is not in plain language
- the consumers' obligations are much heavier than those of the business
- the consumer does not have a real chance of seeing the goods before making the contract; for example, where goods are ordered by telephone

The Regulations only apply to contracts between businesses and consumers.

A C T I V I T Y

Try to find a standard form contract and look to see if it does use plain English. An example could be a contract for a mobile phone.

Examination questions

1 In general, people may make whatever contracts they wish. However, in situations involving consumers, certain terms are implied into contracts by statute. This means that these terms become part of a contract because of an Act of Parliament.

In a contract for the sale of goods, the law requires that the goods must match their description and also must be of merchantable

Figure 14.2 Comparing the rights under the consumer protection Acts

	Sale of Goods	Supply of Goods and Services	Consumer Protection
A buys a faulty iron, which causes a fire	Right against seller (s. 14)	–	Right against producer if damage more than £275
B's car is serviced badly and a defective brake pad is fitted causing a crash in which B is injured	Right against garage (s. 14) for brake pad	Right against garage for bad workmanship	Right against producer
C buys a doll for her child, D, who is injured by the wire used for attaching the arms of the doll	C has right against seller	–	D has right against producer

quality and fit for their intended use (the Sale of Goods Act 1979).

In a contract for the provision of services, the service must be provided within a reasonable time and for a reasonable price. In addition the service must be provided with reasonable care and skill (the Supply of Goods and Services Act 1982).

Explain how these Acts may apply in each of the following situations.

a   Rachel buys a coat from her local store. The coat is described as 'waterproof'. The first time Rachel wears the coat in the rain, it leaks. *(4 marks)*

b   Mandy takes her car to a local garage for a simple repair. The garage keeps the car for two weeks and then charges her double the original estimate. *(4 marks)*

Total: 8 marks

SEG Sample Paper for 1996 (Foundation Tier)

2 The Supply of Goods and Services Act 1982 has certain implied terms that will protect the customer.

a   Ms Smith ordered a new central heating system for her house. The boiler that was fitted as part of the system is not sufficiently powerful to heat the house.

   i Explain the relevant implied term and how it applies to this situation. *(3 marks)*

   ii Explain Ms Smith's rights in this situation. *(2 marks)*

b   Rachel goes to Abel Hair Styles to have her hair styled. Shortly after leaving the salon she meets a friend who tells her that the styling is totally inappropriate for her and that it has also started to drop out.

   i Explain the relevant implied term and how it applies to this situation. *(3 marks)*

   ii Explain whether or not Rachel would have any remedy in this situation. *(3 marks)*

c   George engages Rapid Mobile Car Engineers to come and service his car. He asks them to give him a telephone call to say when they will be coming. After three weeks they have still not called.

   i Explain the implied term that applies to this situation. *(2 marks)*

   ii What remedy is available to George in respect of the agreement he has made with Rapid Mobile Car Engineers? *(3 marks)*

d   If a visitor were to be injured by an item supplied under a contract for work and materials, the Supply of Goods and Services Act 1982 would not offer a remedy.

   i Name **two** avenues of law through which the injured visitor could claim compensation for their injury. *(2 marks)*

   ii Briefly state why **one** of these is likely to be more effective in achieving an award of compensation. *(2 marks)*

Total: 20 marks

AEB 1993

15

Tort

15.1 The nature of a tort

The law of tort covers a wide range of actions. A car passenger suing for injuries suffered in a car crash; a workman claiming compensation for injuries suffered at work; a libel case over the publication of an untrue statement in a paper; and a claim because someone has trespassed on your land are all examples of cases that could be brought.

A tort is regarded as a civil wrong. The word 'tort' is actually the French word for 'wrong'. Liability in tort comes from either a breach of duty owed by members of society to each other or the infringement of a right of another person. These rights and duties have been largely developed by the courts through case law, though there are some Acts of Parliament which create rights and duties, such as the Occupiers' Liability Act 1957 and the Torts (Interference with Goods) Act 1977.

The law of tort protects people, their property and their reputation. A claim in tort can be made if someone, through breach of duty or infringement of a right, injures you, your property or your reputation. There are several different torts recognised by English law and this chapter will consider some of the more common ones:

- negligence
- occupiers' liability
- trespass
- nuisance
- defamation

For some of these torts the plaintiff must prove that damage was caused; for other torts it is only necessary to show the infringement of a right. It is said that such torts are 'actionable per se'. This means the claimant can claim simply because his right has been infringed: he does not need to prove that he has suffered any damage.

Figure 15.1 Differences between crimes and torts

Crimes	Torts
A wrong against the State	A wrong against an individual
Case will usually be started by the State	Case will be started by the individual affected
Defendant will be prosecuted in the criminal courts	Defendant will be sued in the civil courts
If guilty the defendant will be punished	If liable the defendant will have to compensate the claimant (previously plaintiff)

It is important to realise the differences between torts and crimes as both can be considered 'wrongs'. A crime is an offence against society, even though it may only be directed against one individual. A tort is a wrong against an individual and does not affect society as a whole. The main function of criminal law is to keep law and order and protect the public. The main function of the law of torts is to provide the individual who has suffered with a way of enforcing his rights. A criminal case will take place in the criminal courts, while an action for tort will be in the civil courts. Finally the purpose of the criminal case is to punish anybody found guilty of a crime; the purpose of an action for tort is to compensate the claimant or enforce his rights in some other way such as granting an injunction. These differences are shown in Figure 15.1 on p. 158. In some cases the same action may be both a crime and a tort. Drunken driving both breaks the criminal law and, if it causes injury or damage to another person, can give rise to an action for the tort of negligence. This idea of double liability was considered in Chapter 1.

15.2 Negligence

The tort of negligence is one of the most often-used torts because it covers such things as car crashes, medical negligence and defective workmanship which causes damage.

To prove negligence you need to prove **three** things:

1 The other person owes you a duty of care.
2 There was a breach of that duty of care.
3 As a result of that breach you have suffered damage.

Duty of care

The tort of negligence has developed this century, largely as a result of the judgment in the case of *Donoghue* v. *Stevenson* (1932). The facts in *Donoghue* v. *Stevenson* were that Mrs Donoghue went to a café with a friend. The friend bought her a bottle of ginger beer. She drank part of the ginger beer and then as she poured out the remainder from the bottle she found it contained a dead and decomposing snail. As a result she became ill. She could not sue the shopkeeper under the law of contract since she had not bought the ginger beer. So she started a case against the manufacturers of the ginger beer. She claimed they were negligent in not making sure that bottles were properly cleaned and she won her case. Lord Atkin giving the judgment of the House of Lords defined negligence by saying: 'You must take reasonable care to avoid acts or omissions which you can reasonably foresee would be likely to injure your neighbours.' He went on to say that your neighbour was anyone who would be so directly affected by your act that you ought reasonably to have them in contemplation.

Although the *Donoghue* case was about a manufacturer's duty of care to the consumer of their products, a duty of care has since been held to exist in numerous other situations:

a a lift repairer owes a duty of care to anyone using that lift;
b an electricity company owes a duty of care to the public over the positioning of its electricity cables;
c a solicitor owes a duty of care to anyone likely to suffer financially if he fails to make sure a will is properly witnessed;
d a DIY enthusiast owes a duty of care to a fireman injured when he attended at a fire caused by the DIY man.

The neighbour test

All the above examples come from cases where the courts held that a duty of care was owed; the plaintiff came into the category of being the defendant's 'neighbour' as set out in Lord Atkin's judgment. *Haseldine* v. *Daw* (1941) decided that a plaintiff who was injured when using a lift as a result of the negligent repair of that lift could sue the repairer of the lift. In *Buckland* v. *Guildford Gas Light and Coke Co.* (1948) a 13-year-old girl was electrocuted when she climbed a tree and touched an overhead wire hidden in its branches. It was held that the electricity company should have foreseen this possibility and they owed a duty of care to the girl. *Ross* v. *Caunters* (1979) involved the situation of a solicitor owing a duty of care. The case is considered more fully on p. 161. The last example comes from a case called *Ogwu* v. *Taylor* (1987) where a do-it-yourself enthusiast had negligently used a blow lamp to burn off paint and set fire to the roof timbers of his house. The fire brigade had to be called out and one of the firemen was injured in the fire. The House of Lords decided that a duty of care was owed to the fireman.

In some cases the courts have decided that there is no duty of care because the plaintiff does not come into the category of being the defendant's 'neighbour'. The defendant cannot reasonably be expected to have that person in mind since he or she is not likely to be directly affected by the defendant's acts or omissions. This is shown in *Bourhill* v. *Young* (1943) where a motor cyclist crashed into a car and was killed. Mrs Bourhill, who was eight months pregnant, heard the crash but did not see it. She did, however, see blood from the accident on the road; she suffered shock and her baby was still-born. She sued the motor cyclist's estate, claiming that he had owed her a duty of care. The court decided that she was not owed a duty of care; she was not his 'neighbour'; the motor cyclist could not reasonably anticipate that she would be affected by his negligent driving. He did, of course, owe a duty of care to the car driver with whom he collided.

Nervous shock

This 'neighbour test' has been important in other cases where the plaintiff was not directly injured by the defendant's negligence, but suffered nervous shock as a result. Nervous shock means more than 'ordinary human emotion'; the defendant must cause the plaintiff to suffer an identifiable psychiatric condition. This was shown in *Reilly* v. *Merseyside Regional Health Authority* (1994) where there were two plaintiffs, husband and wife. They had gone to visit their new grandson in a maternity hospital when they were trapped in a lift. The husband, who already had a heart condition, suffered chest pains and insomnia after the incident. The wife, who was claustrophobic (had a fear of enclosed spaces), experienced acute distress while in the lift and afterwards had difficulty sleeping. The Court of Appeal held that these were just 'ordinary human emotion' suffered as a result of an unpleasant experience. There was no actual psychiatric illness caused by the incident and neither plaintiff could succeed in their claim.

In *McLoughlin* v. *O'Brien* (1982) a mother suffered nervous shock when one of her children was killed and her other two children and her husband injured in a road accident. She was not present at the accident but was told about it and saw her family in hospital before they had been attended to by medical staff. The House of Lords held that the driver who had caused the accident did owe her a duty of care. It was obvious that a mother in such circumstances would be affected. This decision was considered in what are known as the Hillsborough cases, which were claims following a tragedy at Hillsborough football ground in which nearly a hundred people were killed. The House of Lords had to rule on the cases of ten people who had lost relatives in the disaster. Some of the plaintiffs had been present at the ground, others had seen it on television, while others had been required to identify the body of a close relative following the tragedy. The House of Lords held that claims for nervous shock could only be made where:

a   there was a close relationship between the person killed and the person who suffered the shock; parent/child relationships and husband and wife would come into this category but others such as fiancées or grandparents could only claim if they could show that there was an especially close relationship;

b   the person claiming must have been present at the scene of the accident or seen its 'immediate aftermath'; and identifying a body in a mortuary a few hours after the incident did not count as 'immediate aftermath';

c   watching on television was not enough to establish a duty of care.

Economic loss

Cases where the plaintiff has suffered economic loss are approached by the courts in a different way from other cases involving negligence. This distinction was commented on by Lord Bridge in *Caparo Industries plc* v. *Dickman* (1990):

One of the most important distinctions always to be observed lies in the law's essentially different approach to the different kinds of damage which one party may have suffered in the consequence of the acts and omissions of another. It is quite one thing to owe a duty of care to avoid causing injury to the person or property of others. It is quite another to avoid causing others to suffer purely economic loss.

If the economic loss is caused by a negligent act or omission then the normal rule is that the plaintiff cannot claim. This is made clear in the decisions in the cases of *D & F Estates Ltd* v. *Church Commissioners for England* (1988) and *Murphy* v. *Brentwood District Council* (1990). The one exception where a plaintiff can claim for economic loss is shown by *Ross* v. *Caunters* (1979), where a solicitor was in breach of his professional duty when he failed to warn a testator that the husband of a legatee should not witness the will. As a result the legatee lost her inheritance and she successfully sued the solicitor for her economic loss. The case of *White* v. *Jones* (1995) stated that this decision is still good law. In White the solicitor failed to draw up a new will for his client, despite receiving clear instructions to do so. As a result the testator's two daughters were disinherited when their father died. They successfully claimed the financial loss from the solicitor. It was held that there was a special relationship between a solicitor and an intended beneficiary which should attract a liability if the solicitor was negligent.

Economic loss caused by a negligent statement

In *Hedley Byrne* v. *Heller & Partners* (1964) the courts, for the first time, recognised that a duty of care could be owed for negligent misstatement where there was a 'special relationship' between the parties. In *Hedley Byrne* the plaintiffs had asked the defendants, who were bankers, about the financial standing of a company with whom they were considering doing business. The defendants wrote in reply that the company was 'considered good for its ordinary business engagements'. Relying on this the plaintiffs made a contract with the company but lost £17,000 when the company went out of business. The plaintiffs tried to claim that loss from the bank. The court recognised that in special circumstances a duty of care would be owed, but the plaintiffs did not win their case because the defendant bank had made it clear that the statement was made 'without responsibility'.

The law has now been authoritatively stated by *Caparo Industries plc* v. *Dickman* (1990), which decided that knowledge that the plaintiff will rely on the accuracy of the statement is the key factor. To establish a duty of care there must be sufficient closeness between the two parties, a special relationship, the damage must be foreseeable and the situation must be one where it is fair, just and reasonable that the law should impose a duty of care.

Breach of duty

Where a duty of care exists the plaintiff must still show that that duty had been broken if the claim of negligence is to be successful. The defendant must take reasonable care. The standard of care expected from the defendant will vary with the situation. In *Paris* v. *Stepney Borough Council* (1951), the defendants knew that the plaintiff, an employee, was blind in one eye. They failed to provide him with protective goggles for his work and he was blinded when a chip of metal hit his good eye. The employers argued that it was not usual to provide goggles for the type of work the plaintiff was doing, but the court held that as the defendants knew their employee was blind in one eye, they had to take greater care for his safety than for that of normally sighted employees. If the risk is not known to anyone at the time of the injury, the defendant cannot be said to be in breach of his duty of care. This was seen in *Roe* v. *Minister of Health* (1954) where the plaintiff became paralysed because anaesthetic given to him during an operation was contaminated by disinfectant. The anaesthetic was kept in glass ampoules (small containers) which were stored in disinfectant. The disinfectant had got into the anaesthetic through invisible cracks in the glass. At the time of the operation in 1947, this risk was not known. It was held that the plaintiff had not proved that the hospital authorities had broken their duty of care and therefore he could not claim for negligence.

If the risk is very small then it may also be decided that the defendant is not in breach of the duty of care. This happened in *Bolton* v. *Stone* (1951) where the plaintiff was injured by a cricket ball hit into the street from a cricket ground. The evidence showed that the street was a hundred yards from the wicket and there was a 17-foot-high fence between the ground and the road and balls had been hit out of the ground on only six other occasions in 35 years. The plaintiff was unable to claim that the defendant was negligent.

The risk of a cricket ball landing in the street was so small that the defendant could not be expected to guard against it; the defendant was not in breach of the duty of care. The plaintiff was also unable to prove that there was a nuisance (*see* 15.7).

These cases show that the standard of care is the level of care a reasonable person would use. In cases where the defendant is an expert, e.g. a doctor, then the standard of care is the level of care to be expected from such an expert. Where the situation involves everyday occurrences then the level is that of the ordinary person. In car accident cases the standard is that of normal drivers; the fact that the defendant is a learner driver does not mean that the standard expected from him or her is lower than that expected from other drivers. This was decided in *Nettleship* v. *Weston* (1971) when it was said that a learner driver's 'incompetent best is not good enough'.

Resulting damage

Assuming that the plaintiff has proved that the defendant owes a duty of care and has broken that duty of care, the plaintiff must still prove that the damage suffered was caused by the breach of duty. This is largely a matter of fact as was shown in *Barnett* v. *Chelsea and Kensington Hospital Management Committee* (1968). In that case three nightwatchmen (one of whom was the plaintiff's husband) called at a hospital complaining of sickness after drinking tea at work. The nurse in the casualty department telephoned the doctor on duty, who did not come to examine the men but recommended that they should go home and see their own doctors. The plaintiff's husband went home and died a few hours later from arsenical poisoning. His widow sued the hospital alleging that the doctor was negligent in not examining her husband. She could easily show that the doctor owed her husband a duty of care and that by not examining him the doctor had broken that duty of care. However, the evidence showed that by the time the husband called at the hospital it was too late to save his life; the arsenic was already in his system in such a quantity that he would have died anyway. There was nothing the doctor could have done to save him. This meant that the damage (the death) was not a result of the doctor's breach of his duty of care and the widow could not succeed in her claim.

Remoteness of damage

Even if the plaintiff can prove that the damage was caused by the defendant's breach of duty, the plaintiff will not win the case if it is shown that damage was too remote. This means that if the damage is too far removed from the defendant's negligence the plaintiff will not be able to claim for that damage. This rule comes from an Australian case called *The Wagon Mound* (1961) where fuel oil had negligently been spilled onto the water in a harbour. Two days later the oil caught fire because of welding work being done on another ship and the plaintiff's wharf was burnt down. The damage done to the wharf was a result of the negligent spilling of the oil, but it was held that such a result was not reasonably foreseeable. This rule was followed in *Crossley* v. *Rawlinson* (1981) where the plaintiff in running towards a burning vehicle with a fire extinguisher tripped and was injured. It was held that as the plaintiff was only on the way to the danger created by the defendant, the injury was too remote. The plaintiff could not claim for it.

However if it is foreseeable that a certain type of damage may result then the defendant is liable for it. This is so even if the extent of the injury was unexpected. In *Smith* v. *Leech Brain & Co.* (1962) the plaintiff's husband was burnt on the lip by hot metal because of the defendant's negligence. The burn caused cancer and the man died. Since a burn was a foreseeable injury, the defendant was liable for the death. The defendant will also be liable if the type of injury was foreseeable, even though the exact way in which it happened was not. In *Hughes* v. *Lord Advocate* (1963) Post Office workmen left a manhole unattended and covered only with a tent and with paraffin lamps by the hole. The plaintiff was a boy aged eight, who, with a friend, climbed into the hole. On their way out the boys knocked one of the paraffin lamps into the hole and caused an explosion in which the plaintiff was badly burned. The boy was able to claim for his injuries since it was foreseeable that a child might explore the site and that a lamp might get broken and cause burns. The type of injury was foreseeable, even though it was not foreseeable that there would be an explosion, so the plaintiffs were liable.

Res ipsa loquitur

The general rule is that a plaintiff must prove all the three elements of negligence in order to win the case; that is, duty of care, breach of that duty and damage caused by that breach. In some cases the plaintiff is not able to say exactly what happened, but the facts clearly show that the defendant must have been negligent. If on the facts it is sufficiently obvious that there was negligence by the defendant, the plaintiff may rely on a rule of evidence called *res ipsa loquitur*, meaning the facts speak for themselves. The plaintiff has to show that:

a the defendant was in control of the situation which caused the plaintiff's injury; and

b the injury was more likely than not to have been caused by negligence.

If the plaintiff can show these, there is a *prima facie* case (case at first sight) of negligence and the burden of proof moves to the defendant who must now try to prove that he was not negligent. Examples of cases where the rule has been used include *Scott* v. *London & St Katherine Docks* (1865) in which the plaintiff had been hit on the head by six bags of sugar which fell from the defendant's warehouse. The plaintiff could not say why the bags had fallen, but the court held that in those circumstances it was for the defendant to show that there had not been negligence. The defendant was unable to do so and the plaintiff won the case. The rule was also used in *Mahon* v. *Osborne* (1939) where swabs were left inside a patient during an operation. The plaintiff, the patient, could not prove exactly what had happened, but the facts spoke for themselves.

The rule does not mean that the defendant is automatically proved to have been negligent; the defendant may still be able to show that he was not negligent. This happened in *Pearson* v. *N.W. Gas Board* (1968) where a gas explosion killed the plaintiff's husband and destroyed her home. The plaintiff could not prove how the explosion happened, but relied on res ipsa loquitur so that the defendants had to prove they were not negligent. The defendants were able to do this by showing that there had been an unusually severe

frost which had damaged a gas pipe and caused the gas leak. The defendants had not been negligent and so the plaintiff lost her case.

Contributory negligence

Contributory negligence means that the plaintiff has been partly to blame for the damage suffered. The plaintiff may still make a claim against the defendant but any damages awarded to the plaintiff will be reduced by the amount he was to blame. This rule comes from the Law Reform (Contributory Negligence) Act 1945. It is quite often used in cases arising from car crashes where both drivers may be partly to blame for the accident. The judge will decide how much each is at fault and then calculate the effect this has on the damages as in the example below:

Plaintiff 25 per cent to blame	
Damages would have been	£100,000
Take away 25 per cent	£25,000
Plaintiff awarded	£75,000

This happened in *Sayers* v. *Harlow UDC* (1957) where the plaintiff was unable to get out of a public toilet because of a faulty lock on the door. She shouted and tried to attract attention for about fifteen minutes, but when no-one came she tried to climb out. She stood on the toilet-roll holder which turned and caused her to fall and break her ankle. The defendants were held liable in negligence, but she was found to be 25 per cent to blame because she had stood on the toilet-roll holder. Her damages were reduced by 25 per cent.

In some cases the fact that the plaintiff has failed to take reasonable care for his own safety may make him contributorily negligent even though he did not cause the accident in any way. This is the position where a person working on a building site fails to wear his safety helmet and is hit on the head by a brick that has been negligently dropped by a workmate. In *Froom* v. *Butcher* (1976) the plaintiff was a front seat passenger in a car that was involved in an accident. As he was not the driver he obviously did not cause the accident, but he was held to be contributorily negligent because he did not wear a seatbelt. He contributed to the injuries he suffered when in the accident he was thrown through the windscreen and his damages were reduced by 20 per cent. In *Owens* v. *Brimmell* (1976) it was also decided that a person contributes to his own injuries if he travels in a car with a driver he knows to be drunk.

Remedies

The only remedy the court can award for injuries caused by negligence is an award of damages to try and compensate the plaintiff. Where the injury is to property, then the amount of damages can be worked out exactly. If a car is damaged in a crash then the damages would be the amount it cost the plaintiff to have it repaired, or if the car was a 'write-off', the cost of buying a similar car to replace it. Where the plaintiff was unable to use the car while it was being repaired, the plaintiff may also be able to claim the cost of hiring another car during that period, provided he needed to use a car and had no other means of transport.

Where the injury is to a person then it is more difficult to work out how much the plaintiff should receive as compensation. The courts award damages for pain and suffering and damages for loss of earnings, including future earnings. The amount for pain and suffering is decided by looking at cases where there have been similar injuries and trying to keep to a similar scale. Any amount for loss of earnings will depend on what

the plaintiff would have been likely to earn if he or she had not been disabled in some way. Where a person has died as a result of negligence, that person's dependants can also claim for future financial loss.

In March 1994 an award of £3.4 million was made to a 37-year-old woman who had been paralysed in a car crash. That award was the largest ever made and included compensation for her injuries, compensation for loss of future earnings and an amount for the cost of care as she needed two permanent nurses.

APPLYING THE LAW

1 Candy is given a box of chocolates by her boyfriend. When she eats one she is injured by a piece of glass inside the chocolate.

   Advise Candy.

2 Denver has the electrical fittings in his house rewired by Arthur, an electrician. Arthur wrongly connects the wires in the TV socket so that when Denver next switches on the TV, he suffers an electric shock and burns to his arm. The TV set is ruined beyond repair.

   Advise Denver.

3 Serena is walking down the street past some scaffolding when she is hit on the head by a spanner dropped by a worker on the scaffolding.

   Advise Serena. What special rule might help Serena in proving her case?

4 Zena, a pillion passenger on a motor bike, suffers head injuries in an accident caused by the negligence of the motor bike driver. Zena was not wearing a crash helmet.

   Advise Zena.

15.3 Occupiers' liability

Originally liability owed by an occupier to people visiting land came under the common law of negligence. However Parliament has passed two Acts which make the occupier, in certain circumstances, liable for injuries suffered by visitors so that in most cases a visitor will rely on these Acts. The first Act is the Occupiers' Liability Act 1957. This says that there are two categories of visitor: (a) lawful visitors and (b) persons who are not lawful visitors. This 1957 Act states that the occupier has:

a duty to take such care as in all the circumstances of the case is reasonable to see that the visitor will be reasonably safe in using the premises for the purposes for which he is invited to be there.

This duty is owed only to lawful visitors. A lawful visitor can be:

1 Someone invited to the premises by the occupier such as a friend invited to a party or to come round for coffee.
2 Someone who buys a ticket to come onto the land (e.g., to attend a football match or a concert).
3 Someone who has not been specifically invited but has implied permission to be there; this includes customers in a shop, a delivery person (e.g., delivering milk, papers or post to a house) and door-to-door salesmen.
4 Anyone who has the right in law to enter the premises (e.g., police officers with a search warrant or gas and electricity meter readers).

The duty is to take 'such care as is reasonable in all the circumstances' and so it will vary from case to case. The main rule is that an occupier must take greater care for child visitors, particularly young children, who are less careful and cannot always appreciate that something is dangerous. This is shown by *Glasgow Corporation* v. *Taylor* (1922) where a seven-year-old boy died after eating poisonous berries he had picked in a park belonging to the corporation. There was no warning notice about the berries, nor was there any fence to prevent children reaching them so the court held that the corporation was liable. It had failed to take reasonable care of child visitors to the park.

Where the visitors are adults or older children, it may be enough if the occupier puts up warning notices about any dangers on the land. In the case of shops a coloured warning triangle is usually placed on any wet or slippery floors to warn visitors of the danger.

An occupier will not usually be liable if the danger has been created by a specialist independent contractor carrying out work on the occupier's land. In *O'Connor* v. *Swan and Edgar* (1963), the defendant shop was not liable when some plaster fell from a ceiling and injured the plaintiff. The defendants had taken reasonable care in using independent specialist plasterers to do the work on the ceiling. In such a case the injured person should sue the independent contractor. However if the work done does not need any specialist knowledge to check on it, then the occupier will be liable. This happened in *Woodward* v. *Mayor of Hastings* (1945) when the plaintiff slipped on ice on a step. Independent contractors had been used to clean the steps but as it did not need any expert knowledge to check whether the steps were safe to use the occupier was liable for the injury to the plaintiff.

The Occupiers' Liability Act 1957 only applies to lawful visitors, so that under it an occupier does not owe any duty of care to a trespasser. This was also the rule at common law under a case called *Addie* v. *Dumbreck* (1929). This case involved a four-year-old boy being killed when he trespassed on land belonging to a colliery. The occupiers knew that children often played on their land, but despite this and even though the boy was only four years old, the judges in the House of Lords ruled that an occupier had no duty towards a trespasser. They said, 'the trespasser comes on to the premises at his own risk'. This rule was thought to be very harsh where young children were involved and eventually in *British Railways Board* v. *Herrington* (1972) the House of Lords changed the law. Herrington was a six-year-old boy who was badly burned when playing on a railway track. The Railway Board knew that the fence alongside the railway line was damaged and that children had been seen playing on the track for some weeks before the boy was injured. The House of Lords ruled that where an occupier knew of a danger and had not taken reasonable steps to prevent trespassers from entering the premises, they could be liable for injuries to a trespasser.

The Occupiers' Liability Act 1984 was passed to make this area of the law clearer. It states that an occupier owes a duty of care to 'non-visitors' (e.g. trespassers) if:

a he is aware of the danger or has reasonable grounds to believe that it exists; and

b he knows or has reasonable grounds to believe that there are 'non-visitors' in the vicinity of the danger or that 'non-visitors' may come into the vicinity; and

c the risk is one against which, in all the circumstances, he may be reasonably expected to offer the 'non-visitor' some protection.

The Occupiers' Liability Act 1984 allows a 'non-visitor' to claim for injury but not for damage to property.

15.4 Trespass to the person

All torts involving trespass are actionable *per se*, so that the plaintiff need only prove that the trespass occurred in order to succeed in a case. He does not have to show that the defendant caused any damage or injury. Trespass to the person takes three different forms. These are:

- assault
- battery
- false imprisonment

Assault

In law the word 'assault' has a technical special meaning which is different from its everyday use. We have already met this meaning in the criminal law (*see* 11.6). An assault in law is an act which causes another person to fear immediate and unlawful force will be used on them. This definition covers a wide variety of acts including raising a fist, threatening with a stick or other weapon, throwing something at a person and even spitting at a person. There must be an act; words alone are not enough.

Where the defendant makes it clear from what he says that he will not use force then there is no assault even though he has used a threatening gesture. So in *Turbervell* v. *Savadge* (1669), when the defendant put his hand on his sword in a threatening way, it was not an assault because he said, 'If it were not assize-time, I would not take such language from you'. It was assize-time (the time when special courts were held in the town), and so the words made it clear that the plaintiff need not fear the use of force.

Since it is a necessary part of an assault that the plaintiff reasonably fears immediate force will be used against him, there is not an assault if the defendant is too far away to carry out his threat. So if a person standing at a window on the fourth floor of a building raises his fist and threatens someone on the roadway outside the building that would not be an assault. Nor is it an assault if the plaintiff did not know about the threatening gesture, for example if the defendant pointed a gun at his back unknown to him.

Battery

Battery is the application of unlawful force to the body of another. The most obvious examples are slapping, punching or kicking another or hitting him with a stick or other weapon. The attacker does not have to personally touch the other, an indirect use of force is also a battery. So it is a battery if water is thrown over another or a chair is pulled from under a person causing him to fall.

Although the word force is used in the definition, this does not have to be a violent act. Any touching to which the other does not agree can be a battery. Surgical treatment by a doctor could be a battery if the patient did not agree to it. That was why in *Re S* (*see* Law Report on pp. 78–9) the doctors had to get the court's permission to operate. Even kissing another person who does not wish to be kissed can be a battery.

Often the defendant will commit an assault and a battery. This can happen where the defendant raises his fist (assault) and then punches (battery) the plaintiff. However in some situations there will be a battery without an assault first. This will happen where the plaintiff is unaware that he is going to be hit, for example if he is hit from behind or if he is hit when asleep.

Defences

There are some special defences to assault and battery. These are:

1 *Self-defence.* A person may use reasonable force to defend himself or another. What is reasonable will depend on the facts in each case. Pushing away an attacker is probably reasonable in almost every case, but using a weapon will only be reasonable if it is necessary. There is a saying that 'fists may be met with fists but not with a deadly weapon'. This is generally true, but there could be circumstances where there is a particularly vicious attack without a weapon and the only way the victim can protect himself adequately is by using a weapon.
2 *Lawful arrest.* Reasonable force may be used to make a lawful arrest. The law on arrests is set out in Chapter 10.
3 *Reasonable chastisement.* Parents and guardians may use reasonable force to chastise a child. The amount of force must not be large, but recent cases have decided that a smack is reasonable and even a smack with a slipper.

False imprisonment

False imprisonment occurs where, without a lawful reason, the plaintiff is prevented from moving freely as he wishes. It is the deprivation of personal liberty. False imprisonment, therefore, does not just cover situations where the plaintiff is wrongly put in prison or locked in a room. It also covers the following situations: handcuffing someone; refusing to allow a person to leave a house; refusing to stop a car and let a passenger get out. The false imprisonment can even take place in the open air by preventing someone from leaving a field or other place. The plaintiff need not know that he is unable to leave, the fact that he cannot leave is enough to prove this tort. In *Meering* v. *Grahame-White Aviation Co.* (1919) the plaintiff was being questioned in a room and, although he did not know it at the time, two men were standing outside the door to make sure that he did not leave. It was held he could still claim for false imprisonment.

If the person has a reasonable way out, then it is not false imprisonment. In *Bird* v. *Jones* (1845) the plaintiff insisted on trying to walk over a part of Hammersmith Bridge that was temporarily fenced off. The defendant stopped him going any further but told the plaintiff he could go back and then use the footpath on the other side of the bridge. Since the plaintiff had a reasonable alternative way out this was not false imprisonment.

In some situations detaining a person for a very short period of time is not false imprisonment. In *John Lewis & Co.* v. *Timms* (1952) the plaintiff and her daughter had been wrongly suspected of stealing. They were kept in an office against their will until the store manager had been informed. It was decided that the length of time they were held was not unreasonable and they could not claim for false imprisonment.

Defences

As with assault and battery there are some special defences to false imprisonment. These are:

1 *Lawful arrest.* Any person who has been lawfully arrested may be detained. The police can hold someone for up to 36 hours or longer if authorised by magistrates. The full rules are set out in Chapter 10.
2 *A court order of imprisonment.* Any sentence passed by a court allows a prisoner to be lawfully detained.
3 *A mental health order.* The Mental Health Acts allow a person to be held in a mental hospital under certain circumstances.
4 *Parental authority.* Parents and guardians have the right to prevent a child from leaving home or school in reasonable circumstances. So an hour's detention after school for serious misbehaviour is reasonable and not false imprisonment.

Remedies for trespass to the person

Damages

The main remedy of damages is available for all three forms of trespass to the person. Even if an assault or battery has not caused any injury, damages will be awarded although the amount of damages will be small. Where there is an injury then the amount of damages will increase with the seriousness of the injury. Similarly with false imprisonment, a plaintiff is entitled to damages even though he did not know at the time that he was not free to leave. However, where the false imprisonment causes the plaintiff distress, the amount of damages will increase. Also the longer the period of false imprisonment the higher the amount of damages.

Injunction

Where the trespass has occurred more than once and there is reason to think it might occur again in the future, then the court can grant an injunction ordering the defendant not to molest, assault or otherwise interfere with the plaintiff.

Habeas corpus

For the tort of false imprisonment there is another remedy available. This is the writ of habeas corpus and is used where the person is still being detained. Under this the plaintiff will apply to the Queen's Bench Divisional Court in the High Court for an order that the defendant explain the reason for the detention. If the defendant has no legal reason for detaining the plaintiff, the court will order the defendant to release the plaintiff. This writ is considered an important safeguard of the liberty of the individual. (*See* Chapter 19.)

APPLYING THE LAW

Explain whether the tort of trespass to the person has occurred in each of the following situations.

1 At an office party Amy throws her arms around Damien and kisses him. Damien is very annoyed as he has never liked Amy and has told her to leave him alone on previous occasions.

2 Barney aims a punch at Farouk. Farouk ducks out of the way so that Barney misses him and hits Julian on the back of the head instead.

3 Charlie refuses to let his girlfriend, Jane, leave her flat until she agrees to lend him £10.

15.5 Trespass to goods

Trespass to goods consists of direct and unlawful damage to, or interference with, goods in the possession of another person. Goods are moveable items of property such as clothes, jewellery, furniture, books, cars, cash and cheques. As with trespass to the person and trespass to land, the plaintiff can claim damages just because there has been an interference with his goods. The slightest touching is enough, there is no need to prove that the defendant damaged the goods. Nor does the plaintiff need to show that the defendant was acting in a spiteful way. In *Kirk* v. *Gregory* (1876) the defendant was genuinely worried that jewellery belonging to a man who had just died might be stolen and so decided to move it to a safer place in another room. Unfortunately the second room was not a good choice as the jewellery was then stolen from there by an unknown person. The defendant was held liable for trespass to the goods because she had interfered with the jewellery by moving it.

It is not necessary to own the goods to be able to sue for this tort. The person in possession can bring an action. In *Armory* v. *Delamirie* (1721) a boy chimney sweep found a jewel and took it to a goldsmith for it to be valued. The goldsmith refused to return the jewel to the boy, so the boy sued him successfully. A similar situation happened in a more modern setting in *Parker* v. *British Airways Board* (1982) when the plaintiff found a gold bracelet on the floor in the executive lounge at Heathrow Airport. He handed it in to an airline official and also left his name and address so that it could be returned to him if the true owner was not found. The owner was not found and British Airways sold the bracelet for £850. The plaintiff sued them successfully for the value of the bracelet.

Remedies

The main remedies for trespass to goods are damages and, where the defendant still has the goods, an order for the return of them to the plaintiff.

15.6 Trespass to land

Trespass to land is any unlawful entry onto land or buildings in the possession of another person. Remaining on land after the owner has withdrawn permission for you to be there is also a trespass; this could happen if a person decided to remain in a theatre after the end of a performance or in a football stadium after the match was finished. The original entry would not be a trespass, provided an entrance ticket had been bought, but the permission to be on the land only lasts while the play or game is going on. There can also be a trespass through an unlawful physical interference with land or buildings in the possession of another, for example by digging a tunnel underneath someone's land. Like trespass to the person and trespass to goods, trespass to land is actionable *per se*, so that the plaintiff does not have to prove the trespasser caused any damage. The fact of the trespass is enough to prove the case. An important point about trespass to land is that it is a direct interference with land. This is a major difference between trespass to land and nuisance (*see* 15.7 and Figure 15.3). To be liable for trespass, the defendant must have entered the land voluntarily. Where someone is pushed onto land, that person is not liable for trespass, but the person who pushed him would be.

Trespass to land can be committed in a number of different ways; the most common are by walking, riding or driving across another person's land. Other ways of committing trespass include sitting on someone's fence or wall; throwing objects onto the land; allowing one's animals to go onto the land; or, as already mentioned, digging a tunnel under another person's land or buildings. It is also possible for there to be a trespass in the air space immediately above land, even though the object is not touching the surface of the land in any way. This happened in *Kelsen* v. *Imperial Tobacco Co. Ltd* (1957) where an advertising sign projected over the plaintiff's land. The court granted the plaintiff an injunction ordering the defendant to remove the sign even though the

sign only projected by 20 centimetres. A crane swinging above another person's land was also held to be a trespass in *Woollerton and Wilson* v. *Costain* (1970). There is a problem, however, in deciding how far above the land the plaintiff can claim the air space. In *Lord Bernstein of Leigh* v. *Skyviews and General Ltd* (1977), it was decided that the plaintiff could not claim a trespass when the defendant's aircraft flew a few hundred feet above the plaintiff's house for the purpose of taking photographs of the house. The judge in that case said that the owner of land could only claim a right to the air space above it to such a height as was necessary for the ordinary enjoyment of land and buildings on it. The Civil Aviation Act 1982 also says that there cannot be an action for trespass (or nuisance) 'by reason only of the flight of an aircraft over any property at a height above the ground which having regard to wind, weather and all the circumstances of the case is reasonable'. The same Act provides that where anything falls from an aircraft onto land below and causes damage, there is a right to claim for that damage.

The plaintiff must be in possession of the land in order to have the right to sue for trespass. This means that the plaintiff has the right to exclude other people from the land; it does not only mean physical control. A person who is on holiday and not at home is still 'in possession' and could sue for trespass if anyone entered the house.

Defences

The main defences to trespass are that:

a the defendant had authority in law to be there; this applies to (among others) police with a search warrant, court bailiffs with a court order to seize goods and a neighbour who has obtained a court order under the Access to Neighbouring Land Act 1992 to go onto adjoining land in order to repair his own property;

b the defendant had a licence to be there; this is the position where the defendant has a valid ticket to watch a football match; but a licence can be withdrawn by the person in possession of the land (e.g. a football hooligan can be asked to leave);

c the defendant was on the land only to retake goods belonging to him and put on the land by the plaintiff;

d the trespass was necessary to save life (e.g. to rescue a child from a burning house);

e the defendant was abating a nuisance (*see* 15.7 below).

Remedies

Trespass to land is, like all other torts, a civil wrong so that the trespasser can be sued in the civil courts. Normally trespass is not a crime and notices that read 'Trespassers will be prosecuted' are wrong in law! Such notices should read 'Trespassers will be sued'.

However there are some exceptions where trespass is both a tort and a crime. In certain circumstances the Criminal Law Act 1977, the Public Order Act 1986 and the Criminal Justice and Public Order Act 1994 make trespass a crime. It is also a crime to trespass on premises such as railways where regulations (delegated legislation) have made it a crime.

Where a plaintiff takes a civil court action for trespass the court can:

1 *Award damages.* If there has been no harm to the land, the court awards nominal damages, i.e., a small amount of money. If there has been harm, perhaps crops have been destroyed or windows smashed, then the court awards damages to compensate for this.

2 *Grant an injunction.* An injunction may be granted if the trespass is continuing, as in *Kelsen* v. *Imperial Tobacco Co. Ltd.* The injunction in that case ordered the defendant to remove the sign that was causing the trespass. Where the defendant has frequently trespassed, e.g. by riding a horse across the land, the injunction would order him not to do it in the future.

3 *Order that the land be returned to the plaintiff.* This remedy will only be used where the defendant is staying on the land, perhaps living in a house, and refuses to leave. The court orders the defendant to leave the land and allow the plaintiff possession of it.

As well as these court orders, a plaintiff is allowed to use self-help and use such force as is reasonably necessary to eject the trespasser from the land. Force can only be used after the trespasser has been asked to leave and has refused to do so.

APPLYING THE LAW

1 **Nancy frequently takes her dog for a walk in a field belonging to a farmer. One day the farmer sees her, and without warning grabs hold of her, tearing the sleeve of her coat. He threatens to shoot her dog if he finds her on his land again.**

What types of trespass have been committed?

2 **Donald visits his friend Owen. While at Owen's house, he picks up an antique vase and carelessly drops it, smashing it.**

Advise Owen.

3 **Emily often throws rubbish from her garden into her neighbour, Sam's garden. She also often walks across Sam's garden as a short cut when coming home from the shops.**

Advise Sam on what remedies he may have.

15.7 Nuisance

The law recognises two different types of nuisance. These are private nuisance and public nuisance. The two types are quite different and must be considered separately.

Private nuisance

Private nuisance is something which unreasonably interferes with the plaintiff's use or enjoyment of his land. A nuisance can be caused by a wide variety of things and behaviour. In *Butler* v. *Standard Telephone and Cables Ltd* (1940) it was held that tree roots growing under a neighbour's land were in law a nuisance; while in *Lemmon* v. *Webb* (1894) overhanging branches were also considered to amount to a nuisance. Other types of nuisance may be less tangible but may equally affect the enjoyment of one's land. In *Bone* v. *Seal* (1975) smells coming from a pig farm were held to be a nuisance. Noise, vibration, fumes, gas and heat have all been held to be capable of being a nuisance in law.

Other behaviour which could amount to a nuisance would be blocking a person's driveway so that he was unable to get any vehicles in or out of

hand in *Castle* v. *St Augustine's Links* (1922), where golf balls were regularly hit into the road running alongside the thirteenth hole, it was held this was a nuisance.

2 *Unreasonableness.* To succeed with a claim for nuisance, the plaintiff must show not only that there was an interference with his use or enjoyment of his land, but also that such interference was unreasonable. The question of what is reasonable and what is unreasonable is one of fact. The court will consider the time, the place, the degree and way in which the act alleged to be a nuisance occurred.

a   *time:* the time of day may need to be considered; more noise will be allowed during the daytime than at night. The length of time could also be important since the longer the noise, fumes or other unpleasant interference lasts, the more likely it is a nuisance;

b   *place:* different standards may apply in different areas. A judge once said, 'What would be a nuisance in Belgrave Square would not necessarily be so in Bermondsey.' Clearly more noise, vibration etc. would be expected in an industrial estate than in a quiet residential street;

c   *sensitivity of the plaintiff:* the fact that the plaintiff or his property is extra-sensitive will not make reasonable behaviour a nuisance. In *Robinson* v. *Kilvert* (1889) the plaintiff stored some unusually sensitive brown paper in a room near the defendant's boiler. Heat from the boiler damaged the paper. It was held that this was not a nuisance since ordinary paper would not have been damaged;

d   *defendant's malice:* normally in tort cases the defendant's motive for his actions is not relevant. However in nuisance cases the fact that the defendant acted maliciously out of spite to annoy the plaintiff may make his behaviour unreasonable so that it becomes a nuisance. In *Christie* v. *Davey* (1893) the defendant disliked his neighbour giving music lessons and deliberately created a

the property. Also blocking light from entering through a window could be a nuisance as was shown in *Carr-Saunders* v. *Dick McNeil* (1986) where a two-storey addition to a building owned by the defendants blocked light from windows in the plaintiff's building.

To amount to a nuisance under the law several points will have to be considered: continuity, unreasonableness and what is or is not unreasonable.

1 *Continuity.* The normal rule is that a 'one-off' happening is not a nuisance. In *S.C.M. (UK) Ltd* v. *Whittal* (1970) a workman cut a power cable and stopped production in the plaintiff's factory. It was held that this could not be nuisance, since it was a single isolated event. However, if the single incident is caused by an ongoing state of affairs, there may be a nuisance. This happened in *Midwood* v. *Mayor of Manchester* (1905) where there was a gas explosion. This was a single event, but it had been caused by the build-up of gas on the defendant's land, which was an ongoing state of affairs, so the plaintiff was able to succeed with a claim for nuisance.

Even where the behaviour occurs more than once it will not always be a nuisance. In *Bolton* v. *Stone* (1951) the plaintiff was injured by a cricket ball hit into the roadway outside a cricket field. The evidence was that a cricket ball had only been hit into the roadway six times in 35 years and this was held to be too infrequent for it to be a nuisance. On the other noise during any lessons. He did this by blowing whistles, shouting, hammering and banging on trays. Each one of these on its own and done for a good purpose would probably not be a nuisance, but as he was acting out of spite the court held that it was a nuisance.

Who can sue for nuisance?

Since nuisance is interference with the use or enjoyment of land only someone with a legal right in the land can sue. This means the owner or tenant of the land can sue but a member of their family cannot. This was shown in *Malone* v. *Laskey* (1907) where vibration from machinery belonging to the defendants caused a lavatory cistern to come loose and fall on to the tenant's wife. She could not make a claim for nuisance since she did not have any legal right in the land; she was not the tenant. Of course if a lease is in joint names then both tenants could claim.

Who can be sued for nuisance?

The person who created the nuisance can be sued. The occupier of the land from which the nuisance comes can also be sued. This is so even if another person created the nuisance, provided the occupier knows about it or reasonably should have known of it. In *Sedleigh-Denfield* v. *O'Callaghan* (1940) a trespasser had laid a pipe in a ditch in such a way that the grating became choked with leaves and the next-door field was flooded. The defendants knew about the pipe and should have realised the possibility of a flood. They were therefore liable in nuisance even though they had not created the nuisance in the first place.

Defences

There are two special defences that apply to nuisance. The first is that the nuisance had been authorised by an Act of Parliament. This provides a complete defence. The second is called *prescription*. This can be claimed where the nuisance has been in existence and affecting the plaintiff for at least 20 years. This period of time gives the right to carry on the nuisance in the future. Where the nuisance existed but it did not originally affect the plaintiff, the period of 20 years will only start counting from the moment the plaintiff was affected. This happened in *Sturges* v. *Bridgman* (1879) where the plaintiff built a consulting room in his back garden. He then complained of the noise from the defendant's workshop. The defendant raised the defence of prescription claiming that the workshop had been there for over 20 years. The court decided that the time started counting from the moment the consulting room was built because it was only then that the noise became a nuisance.

Remedies

1 *Damages.* Where actual harm has been caused to the plaintiff or his property, the plaintiff can claim damages by way of compensation. If there has been no actual harm, then damages as a remedy is not available.

2 *Injunction.* In order to prevent the nuisance continuing the plaintiff may be able to obtain an injunction. Since an injunction is a discretionary remedy the court may decide not to grant one even though the plaintiff has proved that there is a nuisance. In *Miller* v. *Jackson* (1977) the plaintiff successfully proved that cricket balls which were frequently hit into his garden were a nuisance. He tried to get an injunction stopping the cricket club from playing on the village ground. The court refused to grant an injunction since the club had played there for 70 years and public enjoyment of the sport had to be balanced against the danger and inconvenience to the plaintiff. The plaintiff was awarded damages instead. However the opposite decision was reached in *Kennaway* v. *Thompson* (1981) where noise from motor-boat racing on a lake was found to be a nuisance. The plaintiff who lived by the lake was granted an injunction restricting the number of races that could be held.

3 *Abatement.* This is a 'self-help' remedy. A person affected by a nuisance has the right to abate (put an end to) the nuisance. There are no problems where this can be done without going on to the defendant's land, e.g. cutting off branches that overhang from a neighbour's land on to your own land. It must be noted, however, that the branches can only be cut off up to the boundary line and must be offered

back to your neighbour. If the abatement involves going on to the defendant's land, then notice of the intention to do this must be given, unless it is an emergency.

Public nuisance

A public nuisance is one which affects the comfort and convenience of a group or class of the public. It is much more widespread in its range than a private nuisance. As a result a public nuisance is considered a crime and the Attorney-General can prosecute the offender. Examples include blasting and quarrying operations, obstructing the highway, smoke from chimneys and golf balls frequently hit on to the roadway (*see Castle* v. *St Augustine's Links* (1922) on p. 171).

In *R.* v. *Shorrock* (1993) the defendant let a field on a farm for £2,000 for a weekend. The field was used for an 'acid house' party lasting 15 hours and with about 5,000 people attending it. The noise could be heard four miles away and a total of 275 people complained about the noise. The defendant was convicted of creating a public nuisance, even though he had not organised the party. The Court of Appeal said that he was guilty because he was the occupier of the land and he ought to have known of the consequences of letting the field.

Where a public nuisance affects one individual more than others, that individual can sue for the tort of private nuisance. So in *Castle* v. *St Augustine's Links*, where golf balls were frequently hit on to a road affecting all road users, a taxi driver, who was injured when a golf ball smashed his windscreen, was able to sue the golf club.

Figure 15.2 summarises the differences between private and public nuisance.

Figure 15.3 provides a comparison of nuisance and trespass to land.

APPLYING THE LAW

Explain whether the following situations would amount to a nuisance in law and suggest what remedies would be appropriate.

1 Robin, who lives in a quiet residential

Figure 15.2 Differences between private and public nuisance

Private nuisance	Public nuisance
Affects an individual	Affects a section of the community
Case started by the individual affected	Case started by the Attorney-General or the individual affected
Can never be a crime	Can be both a crime and a tort

Figure 15.3 Comparison of nuisance and trespass to land

Nuisance	Trespass to land
Indirect interference to land e.g. noise, smells etc.	Direct interference to land e.g. walking on land
Must be repetitive	One act enough
Must prove damage	No need to prove damage – actionable *per se* (of itself)
Can be a crime if it affects enough people	Normally not a crime

For both private nuisance and trespass to land only a person with an interest in the land can sue street, frequently gives noisy parties. The parties usually start at about 10 p.m. and go on until 3 or 4 o'clock in the morning.

2 Elliot and Mary are next-door neighbours. Elliot complains that the roots from one of Mary's trees are growing under his driveway and causing damage to the driveway. Because Mary refuses to do anything about this, Elliott starts having a bonfire every time Mary hangs her washing in the garden. Smoke and ash from the bonfire blow across Mary's garden, badly marking her washing.

15.8 Defamation

Defamation is making and publishing a false statement about another person which damages that person's reputation. Lord Atkin in 1936 defined defamation as a statement which tends 'to lower a person in the estimation of right-thinking members of society' or to cause those right-thinking members to 'shun or avoid' him. Defamation is either *libel* or *slander*.

1 *Libel*. This is defamation in a permanent form. Obvious examples include articles published in a newspaper or magazine or any other written material, pictures, paintings and statues, films and videos, records, CDs and cassettes. In *Monson* v. *Tussauds Ltd* (1894) it was even held that a waxwork model could be libel. In that case a model of the plaintiff had been placed near models of convicted murderers in a 'Chamber of Horrors'. Broadcasting on television or radio is defined as a permanent medium in the Defamation Act 1952 and words spoken on a stage during a play are also defined as a permanent form under the Theatres Act 1968. Libel is another tort that is actionable *per se*, that is, without having to prove that there was actual damage. Libel may be a crime if it is likely to cause a breach of the peace or if it is obscene.

2 *Slander*. This is defamation in a non-permanent form or a temporary form such as speech and gestures. Slander differs from libel in other ways as well: it cannot be a crime and it is not actionable *per se*. To prove slander the plaintiff must usually show that it has caused actual damage; for example that he lost his job as a result of what was said.

There are four exceptions where slander is actionable *per se* so that the plaintiff does not need to prove damage. These are where the slander implies that:

a a person has committed a crime punishable with imprisonment;
b a person has an existing infectious disease which would cause other people to shun him (e.g. AIDS or VD);
c a woman is unchaste or has committed adultery;
d a person is unfit to carry on his 'office, profession, calling, trade or business'.

We saw in Chapter 4 that defamation is one of the few civil actions where a jury may be used and that the jury decides the amount of damages.

To establish defamation it is necessary to prove three points. These are that:

a the statement was defamatory;
b the statement could reasonably be understood to refer to the plaintiff;
c the statement was published.

It is necessary to consider each of these points in a little detail. Figure 15.4 presents a flow chart for defamation (*see* p. 177).

The statement must be defamatory

The statement must be untrue. A true statement cannot be defamatory. It must also, as we have already seen, tend to lower a person in the estimation of right-thinking members of society. As public opinion changes, it can mean that different statements may become more or less likely to 'lower a person in the eyes of right-thinking members of society'. A statement that someone was illegitimate was very defamatory 50 years ago, but today it is unlikely to injure that person's reputation. The phrase 'right-thinking members of society' is shown in the case of *Byrne* v. *Dean* (1937) where, following a police raid on a golf club to remove an illegal gambling machine, a verse was put up on the club noticeboard. The verse included the lines:

But he who gave the game away
May he BYRNE in hell and rue the day.

Byrne sued for defamation, claiming that the verse suggested he had tipped off the police. The judge held that the words were not capable of being defamatory since they would not lower him in the estimation of 'right-thinking members of society'.

The meaning of some statements is clear; for example saying that someone is a thief. However in other cases the statement appears to be innocent at first look, but it has a hidden meaning which is defamatory. This hidden meaning is called an *innuendo*. In *Cassidy* v. *Daily Mirror Newspapers* (1929) a newspaper published a photograph of a man and woman saying, wrongly, they were engaged to be married. On the face of it this did not appear to be defamatory, but the man was already married and his wife sued for defamation, claiming that there was an innuendo that she was living with him without being married to him. Another case with a hidden meaning involved a cartoon of an amateur golfer and the mention of his name in an advertisement for chocolate. The innuendo was that he had been paid for the advertisement and so broken his amateur status.

The statement must refer to the plaintiff

Either the plaintiff must be named in the statement or else there must be a description which clearly identifies him. In the Cassidy case, the photograph of her husband was enough to identify Mrs Cassidy. If a statement is not meant to refer to the plaintiff but the description fits the plaintiff, he will be able to sue for defamation. This happened in *Newstead* v. *London Express Newspaper* (1939) when a statement that Harold Newstead, a 30-year-old Camberwell man, had been convicted of bigamy was published. This statement was true of one person called Harold Newstead, but not true of the plaintiff. Since the plaintiff was of the same name and age and lived in Camberwell it was held that the statement could reasonably be taken as referring to him.

Where a statement is made about a group of people, without mentioning specific names, it will depend on whether the group is so clearly defined that the statement could reasonably be taken as referring to the plaintiff. The larger the group is, the less likely that the plaintiff will be able to show that the statement could be taken as referring to him. So saying that 'all lawyers are crooks' cannot be taken as referring to any particular lawyer. However saying that 'all the staff in the Law department at X college are drug addicts' could be taken as referring to any one of the staff there.

A group cannot be defamed. In *Derbyshire County Council* v. *Times Newspapers Ltd* (1993) the House of Lords decided that a County Council had no right to sue for defamation.

The statement must be published

The statement must be published to a third party. Published does not just mean that it must be printed in a book or paper. Published in this context also has the meaning of the libel being made known or communicated to another person. If the statement is made only to the person concerned, then it has not been published. So, if Mr Green says to Mr Smith that Mr Smith is dishonest and has been stealing from him, that statement may be defamatory, but by saying it direct to Mr Smith and no-one else, it has not been published. But if one other person is present then it has been published. Where the defamatory statement is in a letter written and addressed to the person concerned, the statement has not been published, even if someone else wrongly opens the letter and reads the statement. This was shown in *Huth* v. *Huth* (1915) where a butler, without being authorised to do so, opened a letter addressed to his employer. The letter contained defamatory statements about the employer. It was held that it was not published as it was addressed to the person about whom the statements were made.

A postcard sent through the post is automatically assumed to be published. It is not necessary to show that anyone read it. The same is true of telegrams. Also where any libel is printed, for example in a book or paper, that is enough to show it was published. There is no need to prove that the book or paper was actually read by anyone. There are two exceptions where a third party may be told without the statement being considered published:

a where the plaintiff himself publishes it;
b where the defendant has told his/her own wife/husband.

Dissemination

Every repetition of the defamatory statement is a new publication, so that the person defamed can sue for each publication. This could happen where a statement is originally made by one person and then repeated in a newspaper article. The repetition by the newspaper is a publication and the person defamed can sue both the original maker of the statement and the newspaper.

Defences

The defendant in a defamation action can defend the case by:

a denying that the statement was defamatory; or
b denying that it referred to the plaintiff; or
c denying that it was published.

Apart from these there are some special defences available to the defendant.

Justification

Justification is a claim that the statement is true. To be a defence it is enough to show that the statement was substantially true. In other words if the facts said are mostly true then a small inaccuracy on one or two of the facts does not matter. In *Alexander* v. *North Eastern Railway Co.* (1865) the railway company, in an effort to stop people travelling without paying, published a sign which said that the plaintiff had been charged for 'riding in a train from Leeds for which his ticket was not available and refusing to pay the proper fare'. The sign went on to say that he had been convicted 'in the penalty of £9 1s 10d including costs, or three weeks' imprisonment'. This was inaccurate as it should have been 'two weeks' imprisonment', but the rest was accurate and true. The plaintiff sued for libel over the inaccurate statement of the number of weeks imprisonment. The court held that the statement was substantially true and he lost his case.

Absolute privilege

In some circumstances people are completely protected from being sued for defamation, regardless of what they have published. Absolute privi-

lege means that the following people have a total defence to an action for defamation:

a Members of the House of Commons or the House of Lords for any statement made in Parliament;
b reports of Parliamentary proceedings which have been authorised by Parliament, e.g. in Hansard, or which are reproduced in full in a broadcast on radio or television or in any paper; (if the original statements are not reproduced in full then the media can only claim qualified privilege – *see* below);
c people involved in court proceedings for anything said in the course of those proceedings; this includes judges, lawyers, the parties and witnesses;
d fair, accurate and contemporaneous reports in newspapers or on radio or television of any court proceedings; (this does not apply if the case is held in private);
e officers of State in any communication with each other about a matter of State; this category includes government ministers and very senior civil servants; it also includes military officers;
f husbands and wives in respect of anything they say or write to each other.

The main reason for allowing the defence of absolute privilege is that public interest outweighs the rights of the person defamed.

Qualified privilege

There are also situations where statements made will be privileged unless it is shown that the defendant acted out of malice or spite or some other improper motive. These are statements made:

a to protect an interest; this could occur where a shop manager reports to the managing director of the firm that he believes one of the employees is stealing. Provided this is not said out of malice the statement will be privileged. In such cases it is important that genuine suspicions are reported and investigated;
b to perform a duty; for example supplying a reference for an employee. An employer will be protected by privilege for what he states provided that he does not do it maliciously;

c as reports in media publications of any Parliamentary or judicial proceedings; this covers situations where abbreviated versions of the proceedings are published. Reports on the meetings of other public bodies such as local councils are also protected by qualified privilege.

As with absolute privilege it is argued that qualified privilege is needed in the public interest.

Fair comment

Fair comment applies to comments on matters which are of public interest. A statement will only be fair comment if it is a statement of opinion and not one of fact. The maker of the statement must honestly hold that opinion, although it does not mean that other people will agree with it. The test is: 'Was this an opinion, however exaggerated, obstinate or prejudiced, which was honestly held by the writer?', as Lord Diplock pointed out in *Silkin* v. *Beaverbrook Newspapers Ltd* (1958). If a statement is made maliciously then it cannot be fair comment.

Apology

Where a defendant has unintentionally published a defamatory statement in a newspaper or periodical, then, under the Defamation Act 1996, he will have a defence if he offers to publish a suitable correction and an apology as soon as possible and offers to pay a sum of money by way of compensation.

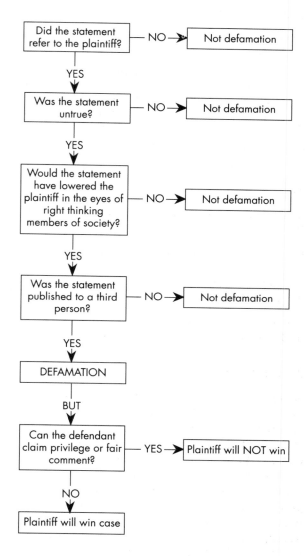

Figure 15.4   Flow chart for defamation

APPLYING THE LAW

1 Maggie tells her husband, Wesley, and a friend, Kate, that Dawn has been convicted of theft. In fact, although Dawn had been charged, the charges were dropped.

   Advise Dawn.

2 The *Daily Blare* newspaper publish a report of a trial in which they correctly state that: 'Jack Straw, a 25-year-old soldier, was dismissed from the army for repeatedly refusing to obey orders.' Unknown to them there is another soldier in a different regiment also called Jack Straw.

   He wishes to know if he can sue for libel.

3 Read the following newspaper article and answer the questions below.

Golfer sues partners over cheating claim

An amateur golfer who was accused by two fellow players of cheating took them to court yesterday in an attempt to win compensation.

John Buckingham, 57, a retired businessman, was accused of kicking his ball into a better position during a competition and twice dropping a ball from his pocket when his own was lost in trees.

Mr Buckingham, a 10-handicap golfer, of Elmton, Derbyshire, is claiming damages for libel from Reginald Dove, 50, and Graham Rusk, 33, both from the Mansfield, Nottinghamshire, area.

Patrick Milmo QC, for Mr Buckingham, told the jury at Nottingham County Court that he was accused of cheating at Sherwood Forest Golf Club near Mansfield in August 1990. 'This was not an accusation made informally over a pint of beer or a cup of tea after the game,' he said.

Letters signed by Mr Dove and Mr Rusk, making the allegations, were sent to the club secretary but the management committee found the claims were not proved.

The allegations centred on a club competition in which Mr Buckingham played an 'undistinguished' round of 86, reduced to 76 by his handicap, the court was told.

Mr Milmo told the jury that Mr Buckingham, who could have been expelled from the club if the charges had been proved, was seeking damages for injury to his reputation.

'Golf is a game that is based on honour and trust. Cheating is not only outlawed by the rules of the game, it is repugnant to the whole spirit and ethos of the game,' Mr Milmo said.

'It was a serious allegation and was treated as a serious allegation by the secretary and the committee.'

Mr Buckingham later told the hearing that golf played a significant part in his life. The former insurance company executive, who owned five insurance offices in the East Midlands, said: 'I enjoy my golf very much. It is a very important part of my social life. My life revolves around it.'

Mr Rusk and Mr Dove are using the defence of privilege and justification for their actions. The hearing is expected to last three days.

(Source: *The Times*, April 1994.)

a **In which court did this case take place?**

b **What is the defamatory statement in the case?**

c **Does the case involve libel or slander?**

d **To whom was the statement published?**

e **What two defences are the defendants using?**

f **How do you think these defences could apply in this case?**

15.9 Vicarious liability

Vicarious liability is the expression used when a person is liable for the torts of another. It means that one person who did not do the wrong act is automatically responsible for another's torts because the other is acting on his behalf. There must be a special relationship between the two people before one can be vicariously liable for the other's torts. The most common relationship is that of employer/employee, though it is possible for a partner in a business to be vicariously liable for acts done by another partner.

Vicarious liability for acts done by employees

Acting in the course of employment

The employee must be acting in the course of his employment.

1 It does not matter that an employee is using his employment to benefit himself, his employer will still be liable. This is shown by *Lloyd* v. *Grace, Smith & Co.* (1912) where a managing clerk in a firm of solicitors defrauded a client of some property, while advising her. It was held that the solicitors who employed him were liable for his actions since he was employed to advise clients and deal with property. The fact that he was the one to benefit from the fraud did not stop his employers from being liable.

2 An employer will be liable even if the employee does his work particularly carelessly. In *Century Insurance* v. *Northern Ireland Road Transport Board* (1942) the defendant's employee was delivering petrol to a garage. While petrol was being piped from his lorry into a tank he lit a cigarette and threw down the match, causing an explosion. His employer was held liable for the damage caused.

3 An employer may still be liable even if the employee does his work in a way in which he has been forbidden to. In *Limpus* v. *London General Omnibus Co.* (1862) the driver of a horse-driven bus had been forbidden to race other drivers; he did so and caused an accident in which another bus overturned. His employer was liable for the damage since the bus driver was acting in the course of his employment. The fact that the driver was doing his work in a forbidden way did not stop the employer from being liable. This same rule was used in *Rose* v. *Plenty* (1976) where a milkman was forbidden to let children help him with his milk round. The milkman broke this rule and allowed the plaintiff, a boy of 13 years old, to help with deliveries. The boy was injured as a result of an accident caused by the milkman's negligence. He was able to claim against the milkman's employers as the milkman was acting in the course of his employment, even though he should not have let the boy help him.

Not acting in the course of employment

Where an employee is not acting within the scope of his employment his employer is not liable for any tort he may commit.

1 Where the employee is doing something that is not part of his work, then the employer is not liable even if the incident happens at the workplace. In *Aldred* v. *Nanconco* (1987) the plaintiff, an employee, was in the washroom getting ready to leave work when another employee came in and pushed a washbasin that was loose against the plaintiff, causing an injury to the plaintiff's back. It was held that the employer was not vicariously liable since the second employee was not actually working at the time of the incident. Another case illustrating this point is *Beard* v. *London General Omnibus Co.* (1900) in which a bus conductor tried to drive the bus in order to turn it round at the end of the route. He was not employed to drive and so his employers were not liable for the accident he caused.

2 If an employee is on a 'frolic of his own' then the employer is not liable. This usually happens where an employee uses his employer's vehicle for his own purpose. An example is *Hilton* v. *Thomas Burton* (1961) where some demolition contractors used their employer's van to go to a café. On the return journey the driver crashed as a result of negligent driving and one of the other workmen was killed. They were allowed to drive the van, but on this occasion it was held that it was not part of their work as they were filling in time instead of working on the site. They were on a 'frolic of their own', so the plaintiff, the widow of the man killed, could not succeed in her claim against the employer.

3 Travelling to and from work is normally not part of the employment and the employer will not be liable for any torts committed by employees during the journey. However, where the journey is made during working time for the employer's benefit, then the employer will be vicariously liable. In *Smith* v. *Stages* (1989) two employees were sent from Staffordshire to Pembroke in South Wales to do urgent work for their employer. As the distance was so long, they were paid for two extra days to cover travelling time. One of the employees drove and took the other employee as a passenger. On the return journey the driver crashed, injuring himself and the other employee. The House of Lords decided that the employer was vicariously liable to the passenger for his injuries since the journey was part of their employment. The driver was acting in the scope of his employment.

Torts of independent contractors

An employer is only liable for torts committed by employees; he is not normally liable for torts committed by an independent contractor. There are exceptions to this rule: an employer is liable for the torts of independent contractors in the following situations:

a where the employer authorises the independent contractor to commit a tort;

b where the work involved is extra hazardous, that is, it involves an extra risk of damage being caused;

c where the work is being done on or over the highway, e.g. on a bridge crossing another road;

d where the law states that the employer is to remain liable; as where the employer has a duty to provide a safe system of work, he cannot avoid responsibility for torts committed by independent contractors.

Distinguishing between employees and independent contractors

Sometimes it can be difficult to decide whether someone is an employee or an independent contractor. The courts will consider several points in trying to make this decision. One test is whether the employer has overall control of the work done. Can the employer tell the other not only what to do, but also how to do it? The greater the degree of control the more likely it is that the other is an employee. However there are other points to consider:

1 How is the work to be paid for? An employee will receive regular wages, while an independent contractor will usually receive a lump sum.
2 How is income tax and national insurance dealt with? An employer must deduct these from an employee's wages, but will not make deductions from any monies paid to an independent contractor; an independent contractor must pay his own tax and insurance.
3 Who supplies the tools and equipment used? Independent contractors will usually provide their own.
4 Is the work being done as an integral part of the employer's business? If so, that person is probably an employee; an independent contractor is more likely to be doing work that is an accessory to the employer's business, but is not integrated into that business.

Justification for vicarious liability

At first sight it seems unfair to make one person responsible for a wrong done by another, particularly where the employer has expressly forbidden certain behaviour, as in *Limpus* v. *London General Omnibus Co.* set out above. However there are a number of reasons for this principle.

1 The main reason is that the employer is usually in a better financial position that the employee.

He will be more able to pay any compensation awarded to the injured person and will usually have insurance against the risk of accidents at work.
2 The employer is getting the profits from the work being done, so that he should also have to pay for losses.
3 The employer has control over choosing an employee and has the power to dismiss an incompetent employee. If he continues to employ someone who is known to create risks then it is fair that the employer should pay for any damage done by such an employee. *See Hudson* v. *Ridge Manufacturing Co.* on p. 186.
4 An employer will be encouraged to provide a safe system of work and to improve standards of training and supervision.

15.10 General defences in tort

General defences in tort are defences which are available for more than one tort. There are also special defences to individual torts which we have considered in the sections on each tort. An example of a specific defence is absolute privilege as a defence to the tort of defamation. In this section we will consider the most important general defences.

Consent

The Latin phrase that lawyers use for this defence is *volenti non fit injuria*. If a person consents to the risk of injury then he cannot claim for any injury done. In *Morris* v. *Murray* (1990) the plaintiff knew that Murray had drunk about 17 whiskies, but he still agreed to go for a joy ride in Murray's plane. The plane crashed, killing Murray and badly injuring the plaintiff. The plaintiff tried to sue Murray's estate but the Court of Appeal held that he had consented to the obvious risk of injury as he knew the pilot was drunk and he could not claim for his injuries.

Sporting activities

One of the most common areas of consent is in sporting activities. By implication players agree to risks which are normal in their chosen sport. A boxer cannot sue his opponent for trespass to the person even if he is badly injured in the course of the contest. Players in team games such as football, rugby and hockey know that they are likely to be tackled during the course of the match. Provided the tackle is within the rules of the game, an injured player cannot sue. However where the tackle goes beyond what is acceptable, a player can sue since he does not consent to illegal tackles. In *Condon* v. *Basi* (1985) the plaintiff was able to claim against another footballer who tackled him in a reckless and dangerous manner and broke his leg.

Spectators at sporting events are also assumed to consent to the risk of any damage occurring as a natural part of the game. In cricket matches where a ball is hit for six over the boundary into the spectators, it will not be possible to claim for any damage done by it. In *Hall* v. *Brooklands Auto Racing Club* (1933) a spectator who was injured when a car crashed off the track and into the railing where the spectator was standing, could not claim for his injuries. The court decided that the organisers of the race had taken reasonable precautions to protect spectators and, by standing near the railings, the plaintiff had consented to the risk of injury. It would have been different if the sports club had not taken reasonable precautions to protect spectators.

Exceptions

There are two types of situation where the plaintiff is held not to have consented even though he knew of the risk. These are:

1 *Rescue cases.* This is where a dangerous situation is created by the defendant's conduct and the plaintiff tries to rescue someone from that danger or prevent any damage occurring. In *Baker* v. *T.E. Hopkins & Son Ltd* (1959) a doctor went down a well to try to help men who had been overcome by fumes. The doctor himself was killed by the fumes. It was decided that the defendants were liable for the doctor's death since it was their negligence which had created the danger in the first place. The fact that the doctor had voluntarily gone into a dangerous situation to try to rescue other people did not mean he had consented to the risk.

In *Haynes* v. *Harwood* (1935) a horse and van had been left unattended. The horse bolted and a policeman was injured when he tried to stop the horse and prevent it injuring women and children nearby. Even though the policeman knew of the danger he could sue the defendants. He had a legal and moral duty to prevent other people being injured and he had not willingly consented to his own injuries.

2 *Employees.* Where an employee knows that there is a risk involved in his work but carries on working, he is not assumed to be agreeing to run that risk. This was seen in *Smith* v. *Baker* (1891) where the fact that the employee knew a crane was carrying rocks above his head did not mean that he had consented to the risk. He could still claim for injuries when rocks fell on to him. However where an employee fails to use safety equipment (e.g. a helmet) provided by his employer in this sort of situation, then he may be contributorily negligent. (*See* 15.2.)

Act of God

An Act of God is an act of nature which no-one could have foreseen. In other words, it is a natural happening which caused the damage; it was not caused by man. Further it was so unusual that no reasonable person would have thought of it happening. The hurricane which affected parts of southern England in October 1987 would come into this definition. Flash floods and extraordinary rainfall would also be within the definition as shown by the case of *Nichols* v. *Marsland* (1876), where a rainstorm 'greater and more violent than any within the memory of witnesses' caused an ornamental lake to overflow and cause damage to the plaintiff's land. The defendant was not liable for the damage since it was due to an Act of God.

Necessity

Where a defendant can show that the damage he caused was done to prevent a worse evil happening, he will have a defence. If a defendant had broken a window of the plaintiff's house in order to rescue the plaintiff's children from a fire, the defendant would have a defence to a claim of trespass to land. This, of course, is an extreme example. In *Cope* v. *Sharpe* (1912) the defendant was able to use the defence of necessity when a fire broke out on the plaintiff's land and he destroyed heather on another part of the plaintiff's land to prevent the original fire from spreading on to his employer's land, where there were pheasants.

Inevitable accident

It is a defence that the damage was caused by an inevitable accident. This is a happening which could not have been avoided by any reasonable care or precautions. It is different from Act of God in that a person will have started the chain of events in motion. In *Stanley* v. *Powell* (1891) the plaintiff was injured when the defendant fired a shot at a pheasant. The pellet hit a tree and glanced off almost at right angles, hitting the plaintiff. The defendant was not liable for the injury as he had not been negligent, the accident was inevitable.

Intervening act

Where the defendant has started a chain of events, but a new act by someone else has caused the final damage, then this may give the defendant a defence. The Latin phrase for this defence is *novus actus interveniens*. A good example is seen in the case of *Topp* v. *London Country Bus (South West) Ltd* (1993) where a minibus was left unattended with the keys in the ignition. The bus was stolen and the thief knocked down and killed the plaintiff's wife. The plaintiff tried to sue the bus company for the accident, claiming it was the negligence of the company's driver in leaving the bus unattended that led to the accident. This claim failed as the court held the accident was caused by the new act of the thief's negligent driving. It was a case of *novus actus interveniens*. However not all intervening acts will provide a defence. This was shown by the old case of *Scott* v. *Sheppard* (1773) in which the defendant threw a lighted squib onto a stall. Two other people in turn picked up the squib and threw it away from themselves in alarm for their own safety. After the second person had thrown the squib it exploded and injured the plaintiff. The defendant was held liable for the injury to the plaintiff, since the onward throwing of the squib was reasonably foreseeable and was only done in self-protection.

Statutory authority

If an Act of Parliament grants the defendant the right to do something, then the same Act may protect him from being sued for any damage done while exercising that right.

Examination questions

1 Negligence is a tort which involves the defendant causing damage to the plaintiff as a result of the defendant being in breach of a duty of care owed to the plaintiff.

   The plaintiff will then be awarded damages depending on the extent of the damage he has suffered, assuming the defendant was totally to blame.

   Where the tortfeasor (the person who commits the tort) happens to be an employee, the plaintiff may find, depending on the circumstances, that he has an alternative right of action against the employer.

The Problem

Elvis is employed as a bricklayer by Darratts Homes Ltd and is currently working on a new housing estate.

   On the day in question Elvis was working on the upstairs floor of a house when he carelessly dropped some bricks. One of the bricks struck Freddy, a fellow employee, on the head. Freddy was not wearing his safety helmet at the time, as he was required to do, and consequently suffered a fractured skull. Freddy is considering taking legal action in the tort of negligence.

---

a How would the court decide whether Freddy was owed a duty of care?
                                                                (6 marks)
b How might the principle of *res ipsa loquitur* (the facts speak for themselves) assist Freddy in his action?   *(4 marks)*
c Freddy has been advised that, if he pursues his action, he is unlikely to be awarded full compensation for his injuries.
     Explain why this is so.   *(6 marks)*

d Freddy has also been advised that he may have a right of action against Darratts Homes Ltd.

   i Explain what would need to be proved in court for Freddy to sue Darratts Homes Ltd successfully.   *(4 marks)*

   ii There are some who argue that it is not fair to make one person responsible for the torts of another.

     What, in your opinion, are the good and bad points regarding this principle of law, especially as it relates to the employer/employee relationship?

                    (10 marks)

                      Total: 30 marks

                      SEG 1993

2 A tort is a civil wrong against another. An injured party may sue in one of a number of different torts. These include negligence based on a breach of duty of care, and public or private nuisance. There is also trespass, either to land, property (goods) or the person.

In answer to an action in tort, the defendant can plead one of the general defences (which apply to most torts). These general defences include *volenti non fit injuria* (which means consent), inevitable accident, mistake and an act of God.

The problem

Jenny and David are playing their weekly round of golf. David is having a bad game. During the course of his round the following things happen.

1 On the first hole, David plays his shot but a sudden gust of wind carries the ball on to the next fairway, where it strikes and injures Terry, another golfer.

2 On the next hole, David's ball hits a tree, rebounds and strikes Jenny.

3 Later in the round, David hits the ball towards some bushes. The ball strikes Tony, a small boy who regularly comes on to the golf course without permission to look for balls to sell.

---

4 On the last hole, David hits the ball over a boundary hedge. The ball strikes Dorothy who is walking along a public footpath on the other side of the hedge.

---

a Both Terry and Jenny are considering suing David for negligence. Explain what **three** things they would have to prove in order to succeed in their action.

                      (6 marks)

b David has been told that he may have strong defences in both cases.

What defences could David plead if he were sued by

   i Terry **and**

   ii Jenny?

What would be the likely result of these cases?   *(6 marks)*

c Briefly explain which torts are being committed by Tony

   i by being on the golf course **and**

                    (2 marks)

   ii by taking and selling golf balls.

                    (2 marks)

d Dorothy is also considering suing David. She has been advised that an action for public nuisance may well succeed.

Do you think that Dorothy has been given good advice? Give reasons for your answer.   *(4 marks)*

e **i** Choose any **two** general defences in Tort. For **each** defence, describe a situation, different to the above situation on the golf course, where that defence could be pleaded.   *(6 marks)*

   ii Choose **one** of the situations you have described in your answer to i. Explain whether you consider the defence you have chosen to be justified.

                    (4 marks)

                      Total: 30 marks

            SEG Sample Paper for 1996
                  (Foundation Tier)

16 *Employment law*

16.1 Contracts of employment

The same main rules of contract that are discussed in Chapter 13 apply to contracts of employment. They are formed in the same way as any other contract; there must be an offer and an acceptance. There is consideration in that the employer is promising a job and the employee is promising his services. If the employee is under 18, the rules on beneficial contracts of service apply. The contract can be in writing or made orally or even by conduct. The difference between contracts of employment and other contracts is that the parties do not have the same freedom to include any terms they wish and, in particular, there are several rules about ending a contract of employment. Parliament has passed many laws affecting employment and most of these laws are designed to protect the employee. This chapter will consider some of the laws about employment.

Written particulars of employment

Although the contract does not have to be made in writing, the employer must provide the employee with a written statement of particulars of employment. This requirement comes from section 1 of the Employment Rights Act 1996. The particulars have to be given to any employee who works continuously for the employer for at least one month. This includes all part-time workers. The statement may be given in installments but all of the information must be given within two months of the employment starting. The idea of this requirement is that the employee should know exactly where he stands and the Act lists the information that has to be included. The main points that have to be included are:

a the names of the employer and the employee;

b the date when the employment began;

c the job title **or** a brief description of the work;

d the place of work **or** an indication that the employee is required to work at various places;

e normal working hours and any terms and conditions relating to working hours;

f the scale or rate of pay **or** the method of calculating it;

g the intervals at which the pay is paid (i.e. weekly, monthly etc.);

h holiday entitlement;

i sick pay provision, if any;

j pension and pension schemes, if any;

k the length of notice which the employee is obliged to give and entitled to receive to end his contract of employment;

l if the contract is for a fixed term, the date on which it ends;

m details of disciplinary rules;

n grievance procedure.

These particulars are NOT the contract of employment. By setting down all these points the employer is providing written evidence of the terms of the contract, but of course there may be other terms which the parties have agreed.

If the employer refuses to provide an employee with this written statement of particulars, the employee has the right under section 11 of the Employment Rights Act to apply to an Industrial Tribunal for an order that the employer give such particulars or to ask the Tribunal to decide the terms of the employment.

A C T I V I T Y

If you have written particulars of employment check that they contain the items set out in the list above.

16.2 Duties of employer

The common law and various Acts of Parliament state that an employer owes certain duties to his employee. The main duties are set out below.

To pay wages as agreed

It is a common law duty to pay wages as agreed. Where the rate, for some reason, was not agreed before starting work, the employer must pay a reasonable wage. Such a wage can be calculated by looking at any union rates for such work and/or the pay received by other employees doing similar work. If an employer does not pay wages that are due, the employee has the normal common law right of suing for damages (i.e. the amount owing) in the civil courts.

To provide an itemised pay slip

Section 8 of the Employment Rights Act 1996 states that an employer must provide every employee with an itemised pay slip. This must show:

a   the gross amount of pay;
b   any fixed deductions such as trade union subscriptions;
c   any variable deductions (e.g. income tax or National Insurance);
d   the net payment;
e   the method of payment (e.g. cash, cheque or paid into bank account).

If an employer does not provide an itemised pay slip, the employee has the right to make a complaint to an Industrial Tribunal.

To indemnify the employee against liability or loss

The duty to indemnify the employee includes refunding agreed expenses, such as travel expenses incurred within the course of the employment. Also, if an employee is sent out to purchase something for the employer's business, the employer must refund the purchase price. The employer must also indemnify the employee for any claims made by a third party as a result of the employee carrying out authorised work for the employer.

To provide work

The duty to provide work is not normally a duty imposed by the law on the employer. Provided the employer is prepared to pay full wages, the law does not demand that he provides any work for the employee to do. However, where the contract is for 'piece-work' or where commission is paid, then there may be a duty to provide work since, without it, the employee's income may be reduced below an acceptable level.

To provide a safe system of work

Both the common law and statute law place an employer under a duty to take safety precautions to protect employees. Under the common law an employer has a duty to take reasonable care for the safety of his employees. This duty includes providing:

• a competent staff
• proper equipment
• a safe place to work
• a safe system of work

The employee has the right to take an action for the tort of negligence (see Chapter 15) if he is injured as a result of a breach of this duty. An example of this occurred in the case of Paris v. Stepney Borough Council (1951) where a motor mechanic was able to claim for the loss of his sight. The employer knew that the employee had only one good eye so that any accident would have especially serious consequences, but failed to provide him with protective goggles when he was chipping rust from under a bus. A piece of metal flew into his good eye and blinded him.

An unusual case is *Hudson* v. *Ridge Manufacturing Co.* (1957) where an employee was injured as a result of a practical joke played by another employee. The employer knew that this other employee was a persistent practical joker and over a period of four years the employer had often reprimanded him for tripping up people and similar behaviour. As such behaviour could be dangerous it was held that the employer was liable to compensate the plaintiff when his wrist was broken as a result of a practical joke played on him. The employer had failed to provide competent fellow employees.

There are many Acts of Parliament and regulations which also place a duty on employers to provide safe systems of work. Some of these Acts cover specific types of workplace, for example the Factories Acts, which include a duty to fence all dangerous machinery. If there is a breach of a specific duty set out in a statute which results in an employee being injured, then the employee can bring an action in the courts to recover damages for the injury.

The most important statute is the Health and Safety at Work etc. Act 1974 which gives all employees in any place of work the right to claim for injuries suffered as a result of a breach of the Act. It also creates criminal liability for failure to maintain a safe system of work so that the employer may be prosecuted in the criminal courts as well for a serious breach of the Act. For example, in 1993 when a 26-year-old employee was crushed to death between two trains, the Channel Tunnel consortium was prosecuted and fined £200,000.

Under section 2 of the Health and Safety at Work Act an employer is under a general duty to ensure, so far as is reasonably practical, the health, safety and welfare at work of all his employees. The Act also specifies that, so far as is reasonably practical, an employer must:

a provide and maintain a safe plant, systems of work and workplace. This includes providing a safe means of entering and leaving work. In *Murphy* v. *Bradford Metropolitan Council* (1991) a teacher fell on a path leading into her school because the path had not been properly cleared of ice. It was held she was entitled to claim against her employers;

b ensure safety in the handling, storage and transport of articles and substances;

c provide such information, instruction, training and supervision as is necessary to ensure health and safety at work;

d provide a safe working environment (e.g. reduce or eliminate pollution or noise which could affect health).

New regulations are brought into force to protect employees as medical and technical knowledge improves and reveals new sources of potential danger to the health and safety of employees. Directives from the European Union can also lead to new health and safety requirements. The Health and Safety (Display Screen Equipment) Regulations 1992 is an example illustrating both these points. The Regulations lay down minimum requirements designed to protect the health of employees using Display Screen Equipment. One requirement is that the screen should be at least 90 per cent 'flicker-free'.

To treat with respect

As well as providing safe systems of work an employer must also treat employees with respect. This means that an employer who bullies staff, perhaps by shouting and swearing at them, or who sexually harasses staff has broken the contract of employment. Any employee who decides to leave work because of such behaviour is considered to have been dismissed from work (this is called constructive dismissal) and can claim for unfair dismissal. (*See* 16.5 for further information on unfair dismissal.)

To allow time off for public duties

Section 50 of the Employment Rights Act 1996 says that an employer must allow employees time off where this is necessary to carry out public duties. This includes time off to act as a lay magistrate, to sit on a local council or to act as a governor of a school or college. The Trade Union and Labour Relations (Consolidation) Act 1992 makes sure that trade union officials are allowed time off for their duties.

References

An employer is not obliged to provide an employee with a reference. If the employer does provide a reference he is, however, under a duty of care to make sure that its contents are accurate. This was decided in *Spring* v. *Guardian Assurance* (1994). The employee may also be able to sue the employer for defamation if it can be shown that the employer acted maliciously in giving wrong information. (*See* Chapter 15 for the tort of defamation.)

16.3 Duties of employee

Obedience

An employee has a duty to obey all reasonable lawful instructions in respect of his work. A serious breach of this duty is a breach of the contract of employment and the employer may have the right to dismiss the employee instantly. Persistent refusal to obey an order can also justify dismissal. In *Pepper* v. *Webb* (1969) the head gardener had frequently been insolent and finally, when asked to plant some flowers, said, 'I couldn't care less about your bloody greenhouse or your sodding garden'. His behaviour was held to be a breach of his duty to obey reasonable instructions.

An employee does not have to obey an order to do an illegal act or an order which would put him in danger.

To show good faith

There is an implied term in every contract of employment that the employee will give faithful service. In *BT* v. *Ticehurst* (1992) the Court of Appeal held that employees who had taken part in a 'rolling campaign of strategic strikes' were in breach of this implied term and so the employer was not obliged to pay them any of their wages during this period, even for the time they did work. In *Denco Ltd* v. *Joinson* (1991) an employee who misused a computer password at work by 'hacking' was not showing good faith and could be instantly dismissed from his job. Usually the employee's behaviour out of working hours will not involve a breach of his duty to show good faith. This means that 'moonlighting' by working for someone else during the employee's spare time is only a breach of this duty if it is likely to damage the employer's interests. A skilled person working for a rival firm in his spare time would be in breach of his duty to show good faith.

Confidentiality

An employee must not disclose trade secrets to rival companies; this is important in businesses where new designs or inventions are involved. Nor must an employee use information he has gained to make a profit for himself. In *Marshall* v. *Industrial Systems and Control Ltd* (1992) the Employment Appeal Tribunal held that an employer was justified in dismissing a managing director who intended starting up his own business and had approached his employer's main customer to try and take over their custom.

16.4 Termination of the contract

Giving notice

Both employers and employees must normally give notice if they wish to end the contract of employment. The exceptions to this rule are:

1 Fixed-term contracts, as these end automatically at the end of the fixed period. The date of the ending of a fixed-term contract must be included in the written particulars of employment.
2 Where there is a very serious breach of the employee's duty. In *Denco* v. *Joinson* (*see* above) the misuse of a computer password justified instant dismissal without notice.

The contract of employment may include a term about the amount of notice to be given by either the employer or the employee. Usually the more senior the position held by an employee the longer the period of notice required from either side. If there is no agreed term for giving notice the Employment Acts lay down minimum periods. An employee who has worked for at least four weeks must give a minimum of one week's notice. The amount of notice an employer must give increases with the length of the period of employment as set out below:

a   after four weeks' continuous service – one week's notice;

b   after two years' continuous service – two weeks' notice;

c   for every extra year's continuous service – one extra week's notice up to a maximum of 12 weeks' notice.

These are minimum periods and the courts may decide that a longer period is reasonable for certain types of employment. In one case a cinema manager was held to be entitled to six months' notice.

If an employer does not give the right amount of notice the dismissal is called wrongful dismissal and the employee has the right to claim damages for breach of contract. This claim will be for the amount of pay the employee would have been paid if he had worked the correct period of notice. So, if an employee is dismissed without any notice, when he should have received three weeks' notice, his claim is for three weeks' pay. The claim can be made in the civil courts, the small claims court in the County Court if the amount of lost pay is under £5,000 or the County Court or Queen's Bench Division of the High Court for larger claims or in an industrial tribunal.

An employer also has the right to take an action in court for breach of contract if his employee leaves without giving the correct notice and the employer can show that he has suffered loss or damage as a result.

APPLYING THE LAW

1 **Assuming there is no agreed period for giving notice, how much notice must the employer give in the following situations?**

    a **John has worked for Sainsways for two months;**

    b **Antonia has worked for Dogsbodies Ltd for five years.**

2 **Eddie, a newspaper editor on a salary of £80,000, has a contract under which he should be given three months' notice.**

The owner of the paper dismisses him without giving any notice.

    Advise Eddie as to what he can claim and where that claim should be made.

16.5 Unfair dismissal

Where an employee is protected by the Employment Acts, an employer must have good reason for dismissing that employee. A protected employee is one who has at least two years continuous service with the same employer. If the employer does not have a good reason for the dismissal it is an unfair dismissal and the employee can make a claim at an Industrial Tribunal.

The following employees CANNOT claim for unfair dismissal:

a   those who have worked for less than two years (except in discrimination cases);

b   those over retirement age;

c   those who work outside Great Britain.

A protected employee can make a claim even if the correct period of notice is given by the employer. A protected employee can also claim if he is forced to resign because of the employer's conduct.

Until 1994 an employee working between eight and 16 hours a week had to work for five years in order to become a protected employee and able to claim for unfair dismissal. In *R.* v. *Secretary of State for Employment, ex parte Equal Opportunities Commission* (1994) the House of Lords ruled that this was contrary to European law as it discriminated against women employees, who were more likely than men to work these type of hours. Following this case, in February 1995 the Government brought in new regulations which extended protected employee status to all workers who have completed two years continuous service. These regulations apply to all part-time staff, even those working fewer than 8 hours a week.

Automatically unfair reasons for dismissal

For protected employees the Employment Rights Act 1996 and the Trade Union and Labour Relations Act 1992 state that the following reasons for dismissal are considered automatically unfair:

a pregnancy, unless the pregnancy makes the woman unable to work and the employer has no other suitable work to offer her;

b trade union membership or taking part in trade union activities at 'appropriate times' (e.g. holding a meeting during a tea-break);

c going on strike, unless the employer dismisses all those on strike while the strike is continuing;

d taking action about health and safety matters; e.g. dismissal for refusing to operate a dangerous machine.

GET BACK TO WORK. THAT MACHINE IS NOT IN BREACH OF SAFETY REGULATIONS.

Potentially fair reasons for dismissal

Where the employer can show that the dismissal was because of the employee's 'misconduct, incapacity, breach of statutory duty, redundancy or other substantial reason' then the dismissal may be considered fair.

Misconduct covers a wide range of misbehaviour including persistent drunkenness at work, assaulting a fellow employee and disobedience. A criminal conviction for something which happened outside working hours is not a fair reason

for dismissal unless it affects the employee's work. So a conviction which leads to a driving disqualification could be a fair reason for dismissing a bus driver, but would not be a fair reason for dismissing a shop assistant.

If the reason for dismissal is *serious misconduct* by the employee, the employer is justified in dismissing that employee instantly (*see Denco* v. *Joinson* above) and that dismissal will be a fair dismissal. Where the reason is less serious, then the employer must follow a disciplinary procedure or the dismissal may be viewed as unfair. ACAS (the Advisory Conciliation and Arbitration Service) has issued a Code of Practice which indicates that a series of oral and written warnings should be given for minor misbehaviour and written warnings for more serious misconduct. Also, the employee must be given the chance to put his side of the case.

Incapacity must be assessed by considering the 'skill, aptitude, health or any other physical or mental quality' needed for the work. A lack of formal qualifications required for the work can also be a fair reason for dismissal. Wherever possible, though, the employee should be given a chance to train.

Redundancy is considered in 16.6.

Time limit

A claim for unfair dismissal must normally be started within three months of the last day on which the employee worked.

Powers of the tribunal

Where an employee successfully claims unfair dismissal, the tribunal can award financial compensation, which is usually made up of a basic award calculated according to the earnings, age and length of service of the employee and an amount for compensation for loss of earnings. There is to be a maximum limit on an award. However, for dismissals on the grounds of sexual or racial discrimination, this limitation was removed after the European Court of Justice ruled in *Marshall* (No. 2) that it was contrary to European law. In 1994 the removal of this limit allowed an award of nearly £300,000 to be made to Helen Homewood, an army major who had been forced to resign from the army when she

Figure 16.1 Differences between wrongful dismissal and unfair dismissal

	Wrongful dismissal	Unfair dismissal
Reason	No notice or insufficient notice given	No fair reason for dismissal
Qualifying period	4 weeks	2 years
Place for claim	Civil courts OR industrial tribunal	Industrial tribunal
Time limit on claim	6 years from date of dismissal	3 months from date of dismissal
What can be claimed	Damages for loss of pay	Compensation or reinstatement or re-engagement
Terminology	Plaintiff/defendant	Applicant/respondent
Legal aid	Available for claims over £5,000	Not available

became pregnant. Under the previous rules the maximum award she would have received was £10,000. Alternatively if the employee wishes and it is practicable in all the circumstances, the tribunal can order the employer to re-instate the employee in the same job or re-engage the employee in another suitable job. However this is only ordered in a small number of cases.

The differences between wrongful dismissal and unfair dismissal are shown in Figure 16.1.

16.6 Redundancy

When an employer has no work for an employee to do, the employer may fairly dismiss the employee. This is known as being made redundant. However the Employment Acts provide for protected employees to be paid 'redundancy pay'. An employee is entitled to a redundancy payment if he has worked for at least eight hours a week for a continuous period of at least two years. An employee who is over the normal retirement age for the work cannot claim for redundancy.

The amount of redundancy pay is calculated according to the employee's earnings, age and length of service, though there are limits. There is a gross maximum wage above which no additional payment is made, so an employee earning more than the set limit will not get full compensation. There is also a maximum period of 20 years' service for calculating the amount.

An employee will lose his right to redundancy pay if he is on strike at the time the redundancy notice is sent out.

An employee is not considered to be redundant if he accepts a different job or unreasonably refuses suitable alternative employment with the same firm.

If the alternative work is not suitable, the employee may claim redundancy. This occurred where a head teacher was offered a position as a supply teacher. It was held he could refuse the post even though he was still going to be paid at the same rate.

APPLYING THE LAW

Advise the following employees of their rights.

1 Ms Fogey, a receptionist aged 44, has worked for Gogetters Ltd for nine years. The managing director dismisses her, giving her nine weeks' notice, because he wants to establish a new image and employ younger and more glamorous staff.

2 Mr Sharp was employed as an accountant with the same firm for three years. His firm dismissed him without notice after learning that he had run up large gambling debts.

3 Tom and Jerry were employed as machine operators. They join an official strike called by their union. After they have failed to work for ten days their company dismisses them.

Would it make any difference if that dismissal was because the company had no work for them to do?

16.7 Freedom from discrimination

The Equal Pay Act 1970 makes it unlawful to discriminate between men and women in terms of payment including overtime, bonuses and piece-work payments. The Act has been extended to make it clear that this principle of non-discrimination applies not just where like or broadly similar work is being done but also where the work is of equal value. This means that if the work being done by a woman requires similar effort, skill etc. as a different job being done by a man, then the woman is entitled to equal pay.

The Sex Discrimination Act 1975 makes it unlawful for employers to discriminate in any other way on the grounds of sex including such areas as recruiting, promotion and training. Thus a male nursery nurse was able to prove discrimination when he was refused a job at a 'Tots' nursery in Liverpool. A teenage girl was awarded over £24,000 compensation in 1994 because she had been turned down for an apprenticeship as a motor mechanic because of her sex.

Genuine occupational qualification

Discrimination is allowed only if the sex of the person is a 'genuine occupational qualification'. This naturally covers modelling and acting but it also covers situations where for privacy or decency the sex of the worker is important, (e.g. a lavatory attendant). Other types of work where the sex of the employee may be a genuine occupational qualification include the provision of personal services and some welfare work (e.g. a counsellor to help rape victims).

Two other Acts make provisions about non-discrimination between men and women. These are the Sex Discrimination Act 1986 which widened the areas in which discrimination is forbidden to include retirement ages and the Employment Act 1989, which, among other things, abolished the rule that women were not allowed to work as miners.

The Race Relations Act 1976 forbids discrimination in employment on the grounds of a person's race. Again there are a few exceptions where a person's race can be a genuine occupational qualification, for example an acting role, modelling and waiters in national restaurants come within this.

Direct and indirect discrimination

Both the Sex Discrimination Act 1975 and the Race Relations Act 1976 make direct and indirect discrimination unlawful. Direct discrimination is where a person is treated differently because of race or sex, as in the cases of the male nursery nurse and the girl who wanted to be a motor mechanic. Indirect discrimination occurs when a condition is attached to a job that is likely to exclude one sex or one race more than others. Restricting applications for a job to those between the ages of 17 and 28 was held to be indirect discrimination against women, since many women are unavailable for work at this age due to child bearing and child-rearing commitments. Similarly a restriction on the size or height of job applicants could be indirect discrimination; although if height or size is a genuine occupational qualification due to the heaviness of the machinery involved in the work then it is not discriminatory.

Procedure

Any person who claims to have been unlawfully discriminated against in respect of work has the right to make a complaint to an Industrial Tribunal. Both the Sex Discrimination Act and the Race Relations Act also forbid discrimination in other areas of life. This is considered more fully in Chapter 19.

Disabled employees

The Disability Discrimination Act 1995 makes it unlawful for an employer to discriminate against a person with a disability. Employers must make reasonable adjustments to the work premises or to the working conditions to allow disabled persons to take up employment or promotion. This may mean that an employer will have to provide a ramp or a lift instead of steps so that there is wheelchair access to the premises. Or it may mean that the employer will have to be more flexible as regards working hours. Employers with less than 20 employees do not have to comply with the Act.

16.8 Trade unions

Trade unions are organisations which negotiate with management on pay and working conditions and generally try to protect workers' rights. Trade unions have a special status in law, which allows them to make contracts and to sue and be sued. Most workers have a right to belong to a trade union if they wish. The exceptions are those working in jobs where national security might be at risk. Employers, in general, cannot refuse to employ a worker either because that worker is or is not a trade union member.

Most of the law on trade unions is contained in the Trade Union and Labour Relations (Consolidation) Act 1992 and the Trade Union Reform and Employment Rights Act 1993. Since 1988 unions have had to hold a postal ballot of members and have a majority in favour before starting strike action. If a union does not hold a ballot it can be sued by anyone who is adversely affected by the strike.

Individual members of trade unions can apply to the Commissioner for the Rights of Trade Union Members if their rights as members are affected. Trade union membership has fallen steadily since 1979 when there were 13.2 million trade union members. In 1993 the membership was 7.3 million.

Examination questions

1 A contract of employment consists of a range of duties, many imposed by law, between employer and employee. The employer's duties include providing the employee with a written statement of the main terms of his contract of employment, paying wages as agreed, indemnifying (compensating) against liability and providing a safe system of work.

   In **each** of the following situations, **identify** the duty involved and **explain** what legal consequences may arise.

   a Megan starts a full-time job as a dental receptionist. Four months later her employer provides her with a statement identifying her job title and rates of pay.
   (4 marks)

   b John is employed as a machine operator in a factory. Due to a faulty safety guard, John traps and badly injures his hand.
   (4 marks)

   c Helen is employed as a full-time delivery

driver. During the course of her duties she negligently runs over and injures Sam.
(4 marks)

Total: 12 marks

SEG 1992

2 Read the four extracts below relating to **Sex Discrimination** and **Equal Pay**.

   Use the information they contain, and any other information you may have, to help you answer the questions which follow.

Extract A

> Employers are required to afford equal treatment in terms and conditions of employment to men and women who are employed on 'like work' or work rated as equivalent under a **Job Evaluation Study**. Equal pay is, therefore, not restricted to remuneration alone, but includes all terms of a contract other than those relating to death or retirement.

(*Source*: 'A Guide for Employers – Individual Rights of Employees', published by the Department of Employment, 1983.)

Extract B

> An individual can claim equal pay at an Industrial Tribunal for work which he or she considers to be of **Equal Value** to that done by a member of the opposite sex, employed by the same or an associated employer.

(*Source*: 'Guide to the Amended Equal Pay Act', published by the Equal Opportunities Commission.)

Extract C

> The 'like work' provisions of the Act ... state that a woman may bring an equal pay claim if she is engaged on 'like work' with a man. A woman is regarded as doing 'like work' not only where she is doing the same

work as a man, but also where their work is of a broadly similar nature.

There are three stages in a like work claim:

- you have to show that your work is the same or broadly similar to that of your male colleague,
- the Tribunal then has to decide whether any differences between the two jobs are of a practical importance,
- your employer may then be able to show that there is a material difference between the job holders which justifies the pay gap.

Different job titles, job descriptions and con-tractual obligations do not necessarily rule out a like work claim. It's what the job-hold-ers actually do that matters . . .

(*Source*: Adapted from 'Equal Pay for Work of Equal Value – A guide to the Amended Equal Pay Act', published by the Equal Opportunities Commission.)

a   Read Extracts A and B. What do you understand by the following?
  i   Equal Value   (*1 mark*)
  ii Job Evaluation Study   (*2 marks*)

b   Under what circumstances may a person claim Equal Pay with another?
What must be shown by a person claiming such a right?   (*6 marks*)

c   Look at Extract D.
  i   Where would you advise the woman to go for help and advice?
What advice would you expect her to receive?   (*3 marks*)
  ii Look at Extracts B and C. How might the court and tribunal system be used in bringing claims for equal pay and against sex discrimination?   (*8 marks*)

d   What do you think might be done to reduce the problems for those wishing to take action to secure their rights?
       (*5 marks*)

Total: 25 marks

Northern Examinations and Assessment Board 1992

Extract D

'I've just been sacked – the boss says that now I'm pregnant I can't do the work and I should let a man have the job instead.'

17 *Family law*

In 1866 a judge defined a marriage as 'the voluntary union for life of one man and one woman to the exclusion of all others'. Today increasing numbers of couples are choosing to live together without going through a formal ceremony of marriage. This is evidenced by the rise in births to 'single' mothers. In 1981 29 per cent of pregnancies were outside marriage, but by 1991 this figure had risen to 44 per cent. Many such births were registered by the mother and the father living at the same address. In other words the couple had a stable relationship but had not legally married. However there are still important legal distinctions between being married and merely cohabiting. These are considered under 17.4.

When a couple decide to marry formally there are several factors needed to make such a union into a valid marriage.

1 *Age*. The parties must be at least 16 years old. Anyone below that age who goes through a ceremony of marriage is not legally married. The age limit of 16 was set by the Age of Marriage Act 1929.
2 *No close blood relationship*. The law forbids people who are too closely related from marrying each other. This means that a man may not marry such close relatives as his mother, grandmother, daughter, granddaughter, or sister, while a woman may not marry her father, grandfather, son, grandson or brother. The full list of prohibited degrees of relationship is set out in the Marriage Act 1949 (as amended by the Marriage (Prohibited Degrees of Relationship) Act 1986). The main reasons for this prohibition are first, medical, since there is a great risk of genetic malformation in a child born to close relatives; and secondly public policy which stresses the importance of family life.
3 *Status*. The parties must be single, that is, not already married to someone else at the time of the ceremony of marriage. If a person goes through a second ceremony of marriage while already married, the second marriage is called a bigamous marriage and the person involved might be prosecuted for the crime of bigamy. The second marriage is not valid; the parties are not legally married. Where a party has been married but has legally been divorced then he/she is able to re-marry legally.
4 *Sex*. As seen in the definition given in 1866, the parties must be one man and one woman. If two people of the same sex go through a ceremony of marriage the law will not recognise that as a marriage. The sex registered on the birth certificate is regarded as the person's sex, even if a person has had a sex change operation in later life. This was shown by the case of *Corbett* v. *Corbett* (1970), where the 'wife' had been registered at birth as a male, but in adult life had had a sex change operation. The courts ruled that 'he' could not legally marry another male.
5 *Formalities*. In order for the marriage ceremony to be valid there are certain formalities which must be observed. The most

important of these are that the marriage is conducted by an authorised person (usually a priest or registrar) and that the ceremony must take place in an authorised building (this may be a church or other religious building, a register office or another building licensed for marriages). There are also some preliminary procedures which have to take place before the marriage. These will be different depending on where the marriage is going to take place and are set out in more detail on p. 196.

Void marriages

If one of the first four requirements (age, relationship, status, sex) set out above is absent, then the 'marriage' is always void. This means that although the parties went through a marriage ceremony they are not married to each other. The law under section 11 of the Matrimonial Causes Act 1973 will not recognise the 'marriage' as legal. This also means that any children born during the marriage are illegitimate, unless at the time of conception of the child or at the time of the ceremony of marriage (if later) one or both of the parties believed they were legally married.

The rules are a little different if the formalities are not observed. Here the law will only declare a marriage void if **both** parties knew that the formalities had not been observed. In other words, if one of them thought it was a genuine ceremony of marriage and believed that all the necessary formalities had been kept to, then the law will accept that it was a valid marriage.

Voidable marriages

The Matrimonial Causes Act 1973 (s. 12) also lists factors which will make a marriage voidable. A voidable marriage is valid at the time of the ceremony of marriage, but one or both of the parties may apply to the court later for the marriage to be annulled (that is, declared invalid). So when the ceremony of marriage has been completed the couple are legally regarded as married and will go on being legally married until a court annuls the marriage. An annulment of the marriage is not a divorce. The reasons for applying for an annulment are:

1 The marriage has not been consummated because of incapacity or wilful refusal. In other

words, the parties have never had sexual intercourse after the marriage because one of them was unable to do so or because one of them refused to.

2 One of the parties did not validly consent to the marriage because his/her consent was obtained by duress or mistake or because he/she was suffering from unsoundness of mind or otherwise. This means that if one of the parties did not genuinely consent to the marriage that party can ask for an annulment.

Duress is normally considered to be threats of death or injury which force the person to go through the marriage ceremony. However in *Hirani* v. *Hirani* (1982) where a 19-year-old Hindu girl was forced by her parents into an arranged marriage, one of the judges in the Court of Appeal said that the test for duress was whether the force experienced by the person was such as to overbear his will and destroy the reality of consent. This means that there does not always need to be a threat of physical injury.

Mistake is illustrated by the case of *Valier* v. *Valier* (1925) in which an Italian who understood very little English thought that the ceremony was only an engagement ceremony and not the actual marriage.

3 One of the parties, though capable of giving a valid consent, was suffering from mental disorder within the meaning of the Mental Health Act 1983 of such a kind as to be unfitted for marriage.

4 At the time of the marriage one of the parties, unknown to the other party, was suffering from venereal disease in a communicable form.

5 At the time of the marriage the bride was pregnant by some other man and the bridegroom did not know this.

Time limits

A petition for an annulment can be made immediately after the marriage. (In the case of a divorce the couple must be married for at least one year before divorce proceedings can be started.) However for reasons 2, 3, 4 and 5 above the proceedings for annulment must be made within three years of the marriage ceremony. This limit can be extended if the petitioner (the person starting the proceedings) has been suffering from a mental disorder.

Where the petitioner is seeking an annulment on the grounds of their partner's venereal disease or pregnancy, the petitioner must have been unaware of the fact at the time of the marriage ceremony.

The court has a discretion in deciding whether to grant an annulment; the court can always refuse to grant annulment if it is shown that the petitioner, knowing that he/she could get an annulment, behaved in such a way as to lead their partner to believe that they would not apply for an annulment. An example of this was a case where the husband, who knew his wife was incapable of having sexual intercourse and that he could get an annulment on this ground, had jointly with his wife adopted a child. The court refused to annul the marriage. The court can also refuse to annul the marriage if it feels that to do so would be unjust to the respondent.

Children of a voidable marriage are always regarded as legitimate, even after the marriage has been annulled.

17.2 Formalities of marriage ceremonies

The formalities of marriage ceremonies vary according to where the ceremony is to be held. Ceremonies may be Church of England weddings or marriages authorised by a superintendent registrar's certificate, which can take place in a register office or other authorised building, usually a building used for religious worship.

Church of England ceremonies

Before a Church of England wedding service can take place the couple must arrange for one of the following:

1 *Banns to be published.* Banns are an announcement that the marriage is going to take place and this announcement must be read out in the church of both of the parties on three Sundays in the three months immediately before the wedding is to take place.
2 *A common licence.* This licence is granted by a bishop and is an alternative to having the

banns read. In order to get such a licence the parties must swear that there is no impediment to their marriage (reason which would prevent their marrying) and one of the parties must live in the parish of the church to be used for at least 15 days before the wedding.
3 *A special licence.* This can only be granted by the Archbishop of Canterbury and it allows the couple to get married anywhere and at any time. All other methods mean there is at least a 15-day wait before the ceremony can take place. Also all the other methods mean that the ceremony must take place at a location that has a link with one of the parties.
4 *A superintendent registrar's certificate.* Any couple can give notice of their intended marriage to a register office. This notice is recorded in a book which is open to public inspection and after 21 days the couple will receive a certificate authorising their marriage.

Once one of these formalities has been observed, the wedding service can take place in a Church of England church. The service must be conducted by a qualified priest and should take place between 8 a.m. and 6 p.m. (unless the couple are being married by special licence). As well as the priest and the couple there must also be two witnesses present.

Other religious weddings

Where a couple wish to have a religious ceremony other than a Church of England ceremony, they need a superintendent registrar's certificate. This allows the ceremony to take place in a registered building (e.g. a chapel or synagogue). The ceremony must be conducted by an authorised person, usually a priest or minister of the couple's chosen religion. Alternatively, the registrar may be present.

The ceremony must be held between 8 a.m. and 6 p.m., there must be two witnesses and the building must be open to the public. The only exceptions are for Jewish marriages and Quaker marriages, which can take place at any time, without witnesses and behind closed doors.

Civil ceremonies

Where a couple do not wish to have a religious ceremony they may get married at a register office or other licensed building. In order to do this they need a superintendent registrar's certificate, obtained as described above. Such a certificate can also authorise a marriage to take place in hospital or at home if one of the parties is too ill or disabled to get to another building.

The ceremony must be conducted by a registrar and held between 8 a.m. and 6 p.m., there must be two witnesses and the building must be open to the public.

Originally, couples wanting a civil ceremony could only get married at their local register office. Since January 1995 it has become possible to marry in any register office. This change was made by the Marriage Act 1994. The same Act also allows any building to apply for a license for marriage ceremonies although the main types of building expected to be granted licenses are country houses and hotels.

Marriage of those aged 16 and 17

Where one of the parties to a marriage is over the age of 16, but under the age of 18, it is necessary for that person to obtain the consent of a parent or guardian before he or she can get married. If consent is refused then it is possible to apply to the local Magistrates' Court for permission to marry. The County Court and the High Court (Family Division) can also give consent, but it is more usual to go to the Magistrates' Court as the procedure will be quicker and cheaper. However where a person aged 16 or 17 gets married without obtaining consent, it must be noted that the marriage is valid. The parties concerned may be prosecuted for giving false information (either about their age or the consent) but the law still recognises the marriage as a valid one.

APPLYING THE LAW

In the following situations explain whether there is a valid marriage.

1 Gregory marries his niece, Rosalind aged 17, in a ceremony at a register office. Rosalind lies about her age, but the other formalities are complied with.
2 Because Terry and Susan want a quiet wedding Harold, a vicar, conducts the

marriage at the vicarage at 7 p.m. with his wife as witness.

17.3 Rights and duties of married partners

Maintenance

The original rule at common law was that a man was bound to maintain his wife; but a wife had no duty to maintain her husband. Statute law has altered this. Under the Matrimonial Causes Act 1973 both husbands and wives have the right to apply for a maintenance order. Usually, of course, it is the wife who applies but where a husband is unable to work, perhaps through illness, then a wife may be ordered to pay maintenance to him. The common law rule also included the point that the husband's duty to maintain his wife stopped if she deserted him or committed adultery. Again this has been changed by statute and desertion or adultery does not automatically bar a wife from getting maintenance; both are behaviour that a court may take into account along with everything else in deciding whether a wife should get maintenance or not.

At common law there is still a presumption that a wife has the right to use her husband's account for necessary household goods and that the husband will have to pay the shop concerned. However a husband can prevent himself from being liable for such debts by telling traders before any bill is run up that he will not pay his wife's debts.

Cohabitation

A married partner is entitled to expect the other partner to live with him/her. If one partner deserts the other the courts recognise this as a reason for divorce. However the law will not force one partner to live with the other. Since 1991 the courts have held that where a man forces his wife to have sexual intercourse with him against her will, he can be guilty of rape.

Right to inherit

On the death of one spouse where there is no will, the other spouse will inherit either all the estate, or a major part of it, depending on what other relatives there are. Even where a spouse has made a will disinheriting the other spouse, the law allows the surviving spouse to claim for a share of the estate. (*See* Chapter 18 for fuller details on inheritance.)

Duties to children

1 Both husband and wife have a duty to maintain their children while those children are under 16 years old (or older if still in full-time education). Where the children are living with the parent this means providing food and clothing and basic necessities. Any parent who 'wilfully neglects' a child can be charged with a criminal offence.

2 Parents must also make sure that children between the ages of 5 and 16 are educated. This does not mean that the child has to go to school; tuition at home is possible. Where a child is not attending school and not receiving any other satisfactory form of education, parents may be fined.

3 Parents must also protect their children from certain dangers or else risk being prosecuted. For example it is an offence to leave a child under the age of 12 in a room with an unguarded fire if death or serious injury results. The law tries to protect children from dangers of alcohol and so parents must not give any alcoholic drink to a child under five years old even if it is in the privacy of their own home. Also it is a criminal offence to be drunk in a public place while in charge of a child under the age of seven. The law protects children's moral welfare so that parents can be prosecuted if they are involved in the seduction or prostitution of a daughter under the age of 16. These are some examples; there are many others.

17.4 Cohabitation

As already noted in the opening paragraph of this chapter more couples are choosing to live together without going through a legal wedding ceremony than ever before. As a result Parliament has altered the law to give couples in a stable relationship some of the same rights and duties as married couples. For example unmarried partners can claim some social security benefits including family credit and income support. The Domestic Violence and Matrimonial Proceedings Act 1976 gives both married and unmarried people the right to protection from a violent partner. The Children Act 1989 makes no distinction between children born to legally married couples and illegitimate children; the same principles are applied to both. Similarly the Child Support Act 1991 makes the same provision for maintenance of legitimate and illegitimate children.

However there are still important differences between legally married couples and those who are cohabiting. These differences include:

1 Children of unmarried couples are illegitimate; this is not quite so important since the Family Law Reform Act 1987 removed many of the disadvantages of being illegitimate, in particular over the right to inheritance.

2 Some social security benefits such as a widow's benefit cannot be claimed.

3 A wife can claim a state pension relying on her husband's contribution while an unmarried partner cannot.

4 An unmarried partner has fewer rights over the home than a wife; unless the home is in joint names or the partner has contributed materially to it or it is protected under the Rent Acts, an unmarried partner will not have the same rights of occupation as a wife.

5 Inheritance between unmarried partners is not automatic; each partner must make a will if they want the other partner to inherit. This is in contrast to the position of married people; where there is no will husbands and wives automatically inherit the major part of each other's estate.

6 There is no need to apply for a divorce to end a cohabitation arrangement; couples who are legally married can only end their marriage by a divorce; however there may still be the same disputes over property, children and maintenance whether the couple were married or not!

17.5 Separation and divorce

Separation

The only legal way to end a marriage is by getting a decree of divorce from the courts. There are, however, other ways of having an official separation. These are:

1 *Separation agreements*. The couple can agree to live apart and may make a formal agreement about this but the marriage remains in existence and they are not free to remarry. A separation agreement may include an agreement about financial matters and arrangements about the care of children of the family. Any arrangements can be altered at a later date by a new agreement between the couple or by the courts if circumstances change.

2 *Matrimonial court orders*. The Domestic Proceedings and Magistrates' Court Act 1978 allows a husband or wife to apply to a Magistrates' Court for an order which will formally recognise that the couple are living apart and deal with maintenance. There are four reasons on which such an order can be obtained. These are that the party complained of has:

a failed to provide reasonable maintenance;
b failed to provide for, or make a proper contribution towards reasonable maintenance for a child of the marriage;
c behaved in such a way that the applicant cannot be expected to live with him/her;
d deserted the applicant.

Of these, the first three orders can be obtained even if the parties are living together.

3 *Judicial separation*. The County Court can also grant a judicial separation. This is a legal separation but the parties remain married to each other. In order to obtain a judicial separation a petitioner (the person seeking the separation) will need to prove one of the following facts:

a adultery by the other spouse and that the petitioner finds it intolerable to live with the other spouse;
b unreasonable behaviour by the other spouse;
c desertion by the other spouse for at least two years;
d that the parties have lived apart for a period of at least two years and the other party consents to a judicial separation;

e that the parties have lived apart for at least five years.

Parties apply for a judicial separation where they do not want a divorce but need a formal separation. This may be because they have religious beliefs which do not allow them to divorce. The court granting a judicial separation can also make orders about maintenance, property and children. The couple can have the judicial separation order rescinded (cancelled) if they later get back together. It is also possible to apply for a divorce later if the couple want the marriage ended.

Divorce

Although the definition of marriage given in the opening sentence of this chapter says it is the 'voluntary union for life', marriages do not always continue for life. The law allows couples to divorce. A divorce is a legal ending of the marriage and means that both partners are then free to marry another person.

Time limit

The Matrimonial and Family Proceedings Act 1984 states that no-one can apply for a divorce within a year of getting married. This rule is to try and encourage couples to work through any early difficulties in the marriage. However there may be situations where the behaviour of one of the parties is so violent or depraved that it seems wrong to prevent an early divorce. At least in such cases it is possible to apply for a judicial separation within the first year of the marriage or a matrimonial order or to make a separation agreement.

Applying for a divorce

To apply for a divorce one of the spouses must put in a document called a petition to the County Court. The spouse applying for a divorce is called the 'petitioner' and the other spouse is called the 'respondent'. The vast majority of divorce cases are undefended, that is, the respondent does not dispute the case. In such cases there is a simple procedure which means that neither party or their lawyers need personally go to court. The petitioner sets out the facts in a sworn document called an affidavit. Everything (except the arrangements for dependent children) is dealt with by posting documents to the court and so this is known as a 'postal divorce'. If the respondent wants to defend he/she must answer the petition and there will be a hearing at court to decide the case.

Irretrievable breakdown of marriage

Under the Matrimonial Causes Act 1973 the only grounds on which the court will grant a divorce is that the marriage has irretrievably broken down. In order to prove that this has happened the petitioner must establish one of five facts. These are:

a adultery by the other spouse and that the petitioner finds it intolerable to live with the other spouse;
b unreasonable behaviour by the other spouse;
c desertion for at least two years;
d that the parties have lived apart for a period of at least two years and the other party consents to a divorce;
e that the parties have lived apart for at least five years.

You will probably have noticed that these are the same facts that have to be proved in order to get a judicial separation. The important difference is that for a divorce these facts on their own are not enough; it must be shown that the marriage has irretrievably broken down. Let's look at what is meant by these five facts.

1 *Adultery.* This is when a married person has voluntary sexual intercourse with a person of the opposite sex. In order to get a divorce the petitioner must also show that he/she finds it intolerable to live with the respondent.

2 *Unreasonable behaviour.* The behaviour must be such that the petitioner cannot reasonably be expected to live with the respondent. This covers a wide range of behaviour including violence, child abuse, drunkenness, refusing to speak to the other spouse for long periods or being obsessively jealous. The court will take into account the whole of the circumstances in deciding whether the behaviour is such that the petitioner cannot reasonably be expected to live with the respondent.

3 *Desertion.* This is where one of the parties has left against the wishes of the other. Usually it will mean that the parties are living at different addresses, but the courts recognise that desertion is possible where the couple continue to live under the same roof but lead completely separate lives. This means they do not sleep in the same room nor do they eat together nor even sit in the same room watching TV together. The desertion must be for a minimum period of two years. The courts will ignore a period of up to six months living together during the desertion, provided the actual period of desertion lasts at least two years. So if Bill left his wife Mary on 1 May 1991 but returned on 1 September 1991 and they then lived together until 1 December 1991 when Bill left again, the courts will ignore that two-month period. Mary can apply for a divorce after 1 July 1993 because Bill will then have deserted her for a total of two years. (1 May 1991 to 1 July 1993 less the two months they lived together during that period.)

4 *Living apart for two years.* Both partners must agree to a divorce in this case. In working out the length of time the same rules apply as for desertion, that is, any period of six months will be ignored. Also as for desertion, the parties may be living in the same house provided they are living completely separate lives.

5 *Living apart for five years.* For this there is no need for the other spouse to agree to a divorce; the fact that the couple have lived apart for five years is enough proof that the marriage has broken down irretrievably. The respondent can oppose the granting of a divorce if it would cause grave financial or other hardship, for example that a respondent wife would lose rights to a pension from her husband's work. However, wherever possible the court prefers to grant a divorce and protect the respondent's financial position by making suitable financial orders. Clearly if the couple have been living apart for five years the marriage has irretrievably broken down.

Divorce decrees

When the court is satisfied that one of these facts is proved and that the marriage has irretrievably broken down, the court will grant a *decree nisi* of divorce. This does not end the marriage; it is only a stage on the way to the final divorce. Six weeks after a decree nisi is granted the petitioner can apply for the decree to be made absolute; this *decree absolute* ends the marriage. A decree absolute will only be given if the court is satisfied about the arrangements for the welfare of any children under the age of 16.

Reform of the divorce laws

In 1994 the Lord Chancellor started reviewing the divorce laws. One of the main criticisms of the present system is that most divorces are based on the fact that the breakdown of the marriage is due to the fault of one of the parties; (adultery, unreasonable behaviour and desertion all rely on this idea and in 1991 75 per cent of all divorces were on the grounds of either adultery or unreasonable behaviour). This does not reflect the fact that in many marriages the fault is not just on one side. Also it tends to make divorces more bitter, with disputes over finance and children. The Family Law Act 1996 was to bring in a no-fault based divorce system with the divorce process spread over a period of 12 months, giving the couple the chance for consideration and reflection.

Although it is sensible to make people think about their marriage and try to resolve problems there are arguments as to whether a one-year period is necessary for this. Many couples can sort things out more quickly and in these cases the extra waiting time could make matters more difficult. The move away from using lawyers to using mediators is again sensible in many cases, but in marriages where there is extreme violence or abuse mediation is possibly not the right way to deal with the problems. As a result of these criticisms the Lord Chancellor announced in 1999 that the reforms would be postponed.

17.6 Financial orders

Either spouse can apply for various financial orders to be made by the court. This can happen in proceedings for a decree of nullity, a judicial separation or a divorce.

The courts have the power to award:

a   maintenance (regular payments of money) by one spouse to the other;

b   maintenance payments for any dependent child;

c   a lump-sum payment to a spouse or to a child;

d   a transfer of property order; (this will usually be the family home).

Maintenance payments to a spouse

In deciding the amount of a payment to a spouse the court considers a number of things. These include the income, earning capacity and financial resources of both parties, the financial needs and obligations of both parties, their age and any disabilities (physical or mental) they have. In addition the court will look at the length of time they were married, the standard of living enjoyed by the family before the breakdown of the marriage and the contribution made by each party to the welfare of the family. In divorce proceedings the Matrimonial and Family Proceedings Act 1984 encourages a 'clean break' where possible, so that the 'financial obligations of each party to each other might be terminated as soon as is just and reasonable after the decree of divorce'. This is more likely to apply where the couple are young, there are no children of the marriage and both parties are capable of earning their own living. Where the court makes an order for maintenance payments it may work out the amount by what is called the 'one-third rule'. This means the income of both parties is added up and then divided by three; if the income of the spouse applying for maintenance (usually the wife) is less than that one-third, the other spouse will be ordered to pay an amount to make up the difference. This rule was first suggested in the case of *Wachtel* v. *Wachtel* (1973) and the working of the rule is shown below by using the income of the parties in that case.

Husband's annual income	£6,000
Wife's annual income	£750
	Total £6,750
Divide that total of £6,750 by 3 = £2,250	

The wife was already earning £750 so take that away from £2,250 = £1,500 and under the one-third rule the husband was ordered to pay maintenance of £1,500 per year to his wife.

This is not a rule which will be used in every case, but it is a flexible starting point for the courts to consider. Once an order has been made by the court either party can ask for it to be varied at a later date if circumstances change.

Maintenance payments for children

The courts will only make a maintenance order if the child or one of the parents lives outside Great Britain. Maintenance payments for children are now dealt with by the Child Support Agency. The parent with care of the child or children applies to the agency and the agency calculates the amount to be paid by the 'absent' parent. The Agency takes into account:

- the day-to-day cost of maintaining a child
- the income of both the parents (after making allowance for tax, national insurance and basic expenses such as rent or mortgage costs)
- any other children which either parent has

From this information the Agency works out the 'basic maintenance' requirement of the child and the 'assessable' income of the absent parent. The absent parent then has to pay 50 pence in every £1 of this assessable income until the basic maintenance level is met. So, if the basic maintenance is £75 per week and the absent parent has assessable income of £100, then a weekly payment of £50 must be made.

There are also provisions to make sure that the absent parent is left with enough money to live on. Where the absent parent is very well-off, an extra payment on top of the basic maintenance will be made.

Lump-sum payments

A lump-sum payment is a single payment of an amount of money. The court can order that a lump sum be paid to a spouse or to a child of the family. Such an order will only be made where one of the spouses has capital assets such as shares or building society savings or owns a business. A lump-sum payment can be ordered as well as or instead of maintenance.

Property-adjustment orders

In most marriages the only asset is the family home and the court can make orders about the transfer of ownership of the home. Usually it will be sold and the proceeds of the sale divided between the parties. Where the home was jointly owned by husband and wife during the marriage the court will usually order that it be divided evenly between them. Where the home was owned by only one of them, the usual order is that one-third be given to the other. However, as with maintenance, the court will consider all the needs and obligations of both parties and the contributions made by both during the marriage. Where there is a child under the age of 18, the court can order that the parent with care of that child should be allowed to remain living in the home until that child becomes 18.

17.7 Children

Where the parents cannot agree on what should happen to their children the courts have wide-ranging powers. All the law on welfare of children is now in the Children Act 1989. The key principle of this Act is that the welfare of the child is the most important consideration. The Act stresses that wherever possible children should be brought up and cared for within the family, but where there is a dispute the court will look at:

a   the child's own wishes;
b   the child's physical, emotional and educational needs;
c   the child's age, sex, background and other relevant considerations;
d   any harm which the child has suffered or might suffer in the future;
e   how able the child's parents are to meet his needs;
f   how the child might be affected by any change in circumstance.

The court can make a number of different orders, but will only make an order if it thinks that doing so would be in the best interests of the child. The available orders are:

1 *A residence order.* This says where and with whom the child should live. Usually it will be one of the parents but it is possible to order that the child live with another relative if that is in the child's best interests.
2 *A contact order.* This requires the person with whom the child is living to allow the child to

have contact with the person named in the order. The type of contact might be a weekly or fortnightly visit or a weekend stay but can include other matters such as telephone calls. The order is normally in favour of the parent with whom the child is not living, but the court can also make contact orders with other people such as grandparents.

3 *A prohibition order.* This will stop a parent from taking some action, such as taking the child abroad, without first getting the permission of the court.

4 *A specific issue order.* Where the parents cannot agree on a specific issue, for example which school the child should attend, the court can be asked to make an order about that specific issue.

These orders can be made whenever there is a dispute over the upbringing of a child and not just in divorce proceedings.

Public law

As well as resolving private disputes over the care of children, the Children Act 1989 also allows orders to be made where the child is not being properly cared for in some way. The Act expects local authorities to safeguard and promote the welfare of children in need in their area. As far as possible this is best achieved by providing services in partnership with the parents and helping them care for their children. Where necessary the local authority can apply to the court for one of the following orders:

1 *A supervision order.* The child is put under the supervision of a social worker for a period of one year; this period can be extended later. The important feature of a supervision order is that parents do not lose their responsibility for the child.

2 *An education supervision order.* This will be made where there is a problem over the child's attendance at school. The order will last for one year.

3 *A child assessment order.* The court will order the parents to cooperate with a medical or psychiatric assessment of the child. Such an order may be made where child abuse is suspected.

4 *A care order.* In extreme cases the court may

decide that a child is suffering or is likely to suffer significant harm through lack of parental care or control. In these cases the court will order that the child be placed in the care of the local authority, who will then make decisions about the welfare of the child including where the child should live.

5 *An emergency protection order.* As the name suggests this will only be granted in extremely urgent cases where the child's safety is immediately threatened in some way. The order places the child under the protection of the local authority for up to eight days. The authority may then apply for a care order.

17.8 The welfare state and the family

Since the setting up of a welfare state in the 1940s, the Government has provided financial benefits which are available for people in various situations. Some benefits are only payable if the person (or in some cases the husband) has been paying or been credited with National Insurance (NI) contributions. Other benefits are paid where a person's income is below a certain level. Finally there are some benefits to which everyone is entitled, regardless of their income level or whether they have paid NI contributions.

One of the main criticisms about the system is that there are so many different benefits available that people become confused. In fact it is estimated that many people who qualify for a benefit do not claim because they are unaware of their rights. An effort was made in 1987 to simplify the system, but to many people it is still confusing and daunting.

Benefits paid when NI contributions have been made

These are benefits which you can get only if you (or, for some benefits, your husband) have paid or been credited with enough contributions. They are:

1 *Jobseeker's allowance.* This is paid if a person has been working recently as an employee and is now out of work. The person must be available for work at short notice and be actively seeking employment.

2 *Sickness benefit.* In most cases a person who is unable to work because of illness will get statutory sick pay from his employer, but where someone has not worked for that employer for three months or where the person is self-employed then sickness benefit is payable for up to 28 weeks.

3 *Invalidity benefit.* This becomes payable where the person has been off work sick for more than 28 weeks. It will continue being paid as long as the person is unable to work.

4 *Retirement pension.* Women over the age of 60 and men over the age of 65 who have retired from work are entitled to a state retirement pension.

5 *Widows' benefits.* There are different benefits available for widows depending on the age of the widow and on whether she has dependent children.

Benefits paid to those on low incomes

Many of these benefits are aimed at providing families with a minimum level of income. The most important of these are:

1 *Income support.* This is a social security benefit to help people aged 18 or over and whose income is below a certain level. It is payable where the person is working less than 16 hours a week or is not in employment and is unable to work. It can be paid to top up other benefits or earnings from part-time work or where the person has no other income.

2 *Family credit.* To qualify for family credit, a person must be responsible for at least one child under 16 (or under 19 if in full-time education). The person claiming (or his/her partner) must be working at least 16 hours per week. The family's income must be below certain minimum levels. The amount of family credit payable depends on the family's income, how many children there are and their ages.

3 *Jobseeker's allowance.* For those actively seeking work.

Families on low incomes will also qualify for help with such things as rent payments, council tax payments and prescription charges.

Child benefit

This is payable to anyone who is responsible for a child under 16 (or if in full-time education under 19). A set amount is paid for each child regardless of the family's income. The amount paid for the first child in each family is slightly higher than the payments for other children.

Information and advice about claiming benefits is available from the Department of Social Security and Citizens Advice Bureaux will also be able to give information.

Examination questions

Note: This examination question was written before custody orders were renamed residence orders and access orders renamed contact orders.

1 Study the **five** extracts below. Use the information they contain and any other information which you may have to help you to answer the questions which follow.

Extract A

> *Divorce*
>
> A marriage is a legal contract until death, but divorce is possible after one year of marriage. If you want a divorce, you have to show a judge that your marriage has finally broken down.
>
> To get a divorce, you fill in a Petition Form and take it to the County Court. The Court sends a copy to your wife or husband who must reply to the Court and say what they want to do about it. There is a Court hearing. The person who wants the divorce does not normally go there, but writes an **Affidavit** instead. If the conditions for a divorce are met, the Judge grants a decree nisi. Six weeks later, you can ask for it to be made a decree absolute, and then you are divorced.
>
> If there are children of the marriage, the Court will decide who is to have **custody** of them and then may grant **access** to the other parent. The parent without **custody**

may be required to pay **maintenance** to the other.

Most divorces involve disagreements about children or property, and even if not, there should be legal advice before a divorce starts. With legal aid it does not cost very much.

Extract B

Extract C

'My wife and I were divorced two years ago. At first things worked out quite well. She kept the children, then aged seven and nine, and I saw them most weekends. But now I have met and moved in with a girl whom I intend to marry. My ex-wife has just "turned". She says it is not right that the children should come to my flat as I am "living in sin". She keeps finding reasons for the children not to come and won't let them leave her house if my girl-friend is with me – saying that the children are "naturally very distressed". I want the children to get to know my girl-friend since we are to be married but it just doesn't seem possible.'

Extract D

What to do if your Partner Takes the Children from you

Suppose on the other hand, that your partner decided to leave, and to take the children. Or imagine that you came home one day and found they had all gone. What would you do if you wanted the children back?

First of all, consider the situation. Who would the children be better off with? Courts are not too sympathetic towards a parent who has a history of mental illness, a criminal record or who has been violent towards the children. But otherwise, a court tends to give preference to the mother, especially if the children are under ten. Therefore, a woman in this situation, who wants her children back, must apply to Court immediately for custody. If she does nothing, the court will assume that she does not care all that much.

Extract E

a Look at Extract A. Explain in your own words what is meant by the following:
  i Custody, Access   *(2 marks)*
  ii Affidavit   *(2 marks)*
  iii Maintenance   *(2 marks)*
b What are the matters which may need to be sorted out during and after a divorce?
  What rights and duties do those involved have?   *(4 marks)*

c Look at Extract C. What sources of help, advice and information would you suggest might assist either of the parties in sorting out their problems? What would you advise them to do, and why?
(7 marks)

·**d** Look at the two cartoons (Extracts B and E). What problems and issues are they drawing attention to? What changes would you make to the process of divorce in order to reduce the difficulties which might arise? *(8 marks)*

Total: 25 marks

Northern Examinations
and Assessment Board 1990

2 A divorce can be granted provided the court is satisfied that the marriage has broken down completely or 'irretrievably'. This is proved by the petitioner who sues for divorce, on the basis of one of five facts set out in the Matrimonial Causes Act 1973. These 'facts' include both adultery and unreasonable behaviour.

Judicial separation is granted on the basis of these same five facts but the petitioner does not have to prove irretrievable breakdown.

Maintenance is a payment of money or other settlement usually from a husband to support his wife and family. Maintenance is usually claimed on the breakdown of a marriage.

The problem

George and Mildred have been married for 19 years and have a daughter Amy, aged 17, who is still in full-time education. George is an accountant, earning £250 per week. Mildred has a part-time job earning £80 per week.

Mildred is increasingly unhappy with her marriage to George. She claims that George never takes her out, that they have not been on holiday for seven years and that George is very mean with his money. She thinks that George is having an affair with his secretary.

Mildred has decided she wants to leave her husband. She has come to you, asking for your advice.

---

a Explain to Mildred **two** of the differences between divorce and judicial separation
(4 marks)

b Mildred has decided that she wishes to divorce her husband. A friend told her, 'There are two types of divorce, one following a decree nisi and the other following a decree absolute'.

i Explain to Mildred whether a court might grant her a divorce on the basis of her complaints set out in the above situation. Give reasons for your answer. *(8 marks)*

ii Mildred's friend is clearly not a legal expert! Describe to Mildred the **correct** difference between a decree nisi and a decree absolute. *(4 marks)*

iii In which courts could Mildred's case be heard? *(2 marks)*

c **i** The court has to consider a range of facts before a decision can be made about maintenance. Give an account of these facts and explain why they are important. *(8 marks)*

ii Explain whether you think the system of maintenance is justified. *(4 marks)*

Total: 30 marks

SEG Sample Paper for 1996
(Foundation Tier)

Inheritance 18

18.1 Making a will

A will is a formal declaration by a person of what he wants to happen to his property after he dies. Of course the will does not take effect until the person dies. This means that it is possible for that person to change his mind (perhaps several times!) about who should inherit his property and make another will (or wills) before he dies. If this happens it is the last will that counts when the person eventually dies.

The law provides several rules about making a will, though a will need not be complicated. In one case a will simply said 'All to mother'. It is possible to buy a standard form for a will from a stationers, but no particular words are needed, provided the will is clear. However, unless the situation is very straightforward, it is probably sensible to get legal advice on the wording of the will.

Another name for a will is a testament and the person making a will is called a testator (male) or testatrix (female). The law lays down several rules which must be satisfied for a will to be valid. These rules are about the capacity of the testator, in other words whether that person is legally able to make a will, his intention to make a will and about the formalities that are needed to make a legal will.

The testator must be:

a at least 18 years of age; the only exception is that those in the forces on active service and sailors at sea may make a will from the age of 14;

b of sound mind; this means that the testator must be able to understand that he is making a will and what effect it will have; where someone suffering from a mental illness has periods when he/she can understand, then a will made during such a period would be valid;

c acting of his own free will; if someone makes a will because of threats or fraud that will is not valid.

The formalities of making a will are set out in the Wills Act 1837 as amended by the Administration of Justice Act 1982 and are:

1 The will must be written; again there is an exception for those in the forces on active

MY LAST WILL AND TESTAMENT

WHY CAN'T YOU BE LIKE OTHER PEOPLE AND USE PAPER?

service and seamen at sea (*see* 18.2). It does not matter what the will is written on; in one case a will written on an egg shell was accepted as a valid will. But video wills are not legally valid since they are not written.

2 The will must be signed by the testator or another person in the presence of the testator and at his direction. If the testator cannot write, then he may make his mark instead of signing; this could be a cross, a rubber stamp or, as in the case of *Re Finn* (1936), the testator's thumb print. If the testator is physically unable to write, perhaps because of paralysis, the testator may tell someone else to sign the will for him.

3 The signature can be anywhere on the will, provided that it is intended to give effect to the will. Originally it had to be signed at the 'foot or end thereof', but this is no longer the rule. The signature may be anywhere on the will, provided the testator intended that signature to give effect to the will. In the case of *Wood* v. *Smith* (1993) the testator wrote a will two days before he died. He did not sign it at the bottom and when one of the witnesses pointed this out, the testator said 'I have signed it at the top. It can be signed anywhere.' In fact the testator had started the document by writing 'My Will by Percy Winterbone' and the Court of Appeal held that in writing his name at the top the testator had meant that to be his signature and the will was valid.

4 The signature or mark must be made or acknowledged in the presence of at least two witnesses who are present at the same time; (wills made by soldiers etc. again have special rules – *see* 18.2). The witnesses must see the signature or mark, but do not need to see it being made; it is enough if the testator acknowledges the signature as his. Nor do witnesses need to see the whole of the will; they do not need to know what is in it.

5 Those witnesses must be competent; that is, they must be able to understand that they are witnessing a signature, but there is no set age limit. A witness can be under the age of 18 provided he is old enough to understand. It was held in *Re Gibson* (1949) that a blind person could not be a witness, since he could not see the signature of the testator.

6 At least two witnesses must sign (or make

their marks on) the will. The witnesses must sign in the presence of the testator. It is not necessary, however, for the witnesses to sign in each other's presence, but, where they do so, a will drawn up by a lawyer will probably have an 'attestation clause' which says that both were present together. On p. 210 there is a draft will and at the end, just before the witnesses' signatures, there is an attestation clause.

7 The witnesses cannot benefit from the will; nor can the spouse of a witness. This was shown in *Ross* v. *Caunters* (1982) where the wife of one of the witnesses had been left £5,000 in the will and was not allowed to inherit that money. She sued the solicitor who had drawn up the will and had not checked that it had been witnessed properly.

The fact that a witness has been left property in the will does not make the will invalid. Only to the gift to the witness is affected; the rest of the will stands.

The other point to note is that if there are more than two witnesses then it is possible for some of the witnesses to inherit under the will, provided there are at least two other competent witnesses who do not benefit by the will. This rule was made by the Wills Act 1968 in order to change the law after the case of *Re Bravda* (1968) in which a father left property to his two daughters but they could not inherit it because they had witnessed the will. There were two other independent witnesses, but the father wanted the two daughters to sign as well so that they would know about the will. The change in the law did not help the two daughters but it made sure that anyone in the same position in future could inherit.

18.2 Privileged wills

While all the formalities set out above have to be followed for the great majority of wills, there are clearly some situations in which it is impracticable to make a formal will. A soldier in the middle of a battle, for example, or a sailor on a sinking ship cannot be expected to organise witnesses and follow the rules on attestation. The law recognises this by allowing soldiers and airmen who are on 'actual military service' and sailors who are at sea to make informal wills. For these the age limit for making a will is lowered to 14 years. If the will is written then there is no need for witnesses or the will can be unwritten provided two witnesses hear what the testator says. In *Re Jones* (1981) the testator was a soldier on duty in Northern Ireland. He was shot and taken to hospital. On the way to hospital he said in front of two officers 'If I don't make it, make sure that Anne gets all my stuff.' Anne was his fiancée and they were due to be married the following week. Jones died the day after he was shot and it was decided that his oral statement was a valid will and that his fiancée was entitled to inherit all his property.

The important point is that the soldier or airman must be on 'actual military service' when making the will. This depends on the facts of each case. In *Jones* there was not a state of war, but clearly he was on actual military service. For sailors the rule is that the sailor must be at sea when making the will. In *Rapley* v. *Rapley* (1983) a 19-year-old seaman made a written will and signed it while at home on leave, but the will was not witnessed. If he had been at sea when he made this will it would have come under the rules for privileged wills and been valid. Since he was at home when he made the will, it was not valid as it needed to be witnessed by two witnesses in the normal way. This was so even though he actually died at sea as a result of a ship sinking some 20 years later.

APPLYING THE LAW

In each of the following explain with reasons whether there is a valid will.

1 **Olive writes her will on the back of an old cheque book. She signs it at the top of the will. The will is then correctly witnessed by two people.**
2 **Maurice, who cannot write because of a physical disability, asks a friend, Trevor, to write out a will for him and to sign it on his behalf. The will is then witnessed by Jane, aged 17 and Bill, aged 21.**
3 **Dennis, who is a sailor, writes his will out on a will form he has bought from a stationers. He signs it at the bottom but does not get it witnessed.**

18.3 Changing a will

If a testator has made a will he can change or vary it or revoke (cancel) it. Any alteration to a will must be signed by the testator and witnessed in the same way as the original will. The rule on this is very strict, probably to make sure that there is no fraud by someone other than the testator altering the will. The strictness of the rule can be seen in *Re White* (1990) where amendments to the will were written on to the original will and at the end of the will the testator wrote 'Alterations to will dated 14.12.84. Witnessed.' and two witnesses signed below this. The court would still not accept these alterations as changing the original will since the actual alterations were not signed or initialled by the testator or the witnesses.

Codicils

A change can be made by making a codicil. This is a document which is used to add to, amend or partially revoke an existing will. A codicil must be written, witnessed and signed in the same way as a will. It then changes part of the will. For example, if the testator has made a will leaving all his property to his wife, he could later make a codicil in which he left £1,000 to his sister. The original will is then partly changed as the sister will now inherit £1,000 and the wife will inherit the remainder of the property.

18.4 Revoking a will

A testator can revoke a will at any time during his lifetime, provided he is still of sound mind, by any of the following methods:

1 *Making another will* in which he declares that all previous wills are revoked. If a new will does not expressly say that all previous wills are revoked then only the parts of the old will that conflict with the new will are revoked. This is more easily understood by looking at an example; if a testator in his first will has left his house to his wife, all the money in his bank account to his daughter and his car to his son;

THIS IS THE LAST WILL AND TESTAMENT

of me ...... Henry Horner ......

of ...... 10, High Street, Anytown, Blankshire ......

I hereby revoke all previous wills and codicils I have made. This is my last Will.

As executor(s) of this my will, I appoint: my wife Margaret Horner and my brother Jack Horner of 21 Station Road Anytown, Blankshire

I direct that all my debts and funeral and testamentary expenses be paid as soon as is convenient after my death.

I leave all my estate to my wife Margaret Horner of 10, High Street, Anytown, Blankshire, as long as she survives me by 28 days.

If she does not survive me by 28 days I leave all my estate to my son Thomas Horner of Honey Cottage, Beesfield, Mayshire.

H. Horner

Dated this 25th day of October 1994

Signed by the
testator/testatrix
in our presence and
by us in his/hers

...... Jack Spratt ...... (1st witness)
of 12 High Street, Anytown, Blankshire

...... John Smith ...... (2nd witness)
of 47 New Road, Anytown

then in a second will he leaves all the money in his bank account and the car to his brother, the second will does not mention the house so the wife still inherits the house, although the son and daughter do not inherit anything as the second will takes priority.

2 *Making a formal revocation of the will* without making another will. The formal revocation must be signed, witnessed etc. in the same manner as a will. It will then cancel the will.

3 *Deliberately destroying the will.* If a testator intentionally destroys his will or orders another person to destroy it in his presence then that will is revoked. The will can be destroyed by any means. The Wills Act 1837 says that a will is revoked by 'burning, tearing or otherwise destroying the same by the testator'. In *Re Adams* (1990) the testatrix telephoned her solicitor and told him to destroy her will. The solicitor sent the will to her and wrote that it would be better if she destroyed the will herself. After her death the will was found, but the testatrix had scribbled over parts of the will, in particular the signatures were heavily scored out. The court decided that, even though parts of the will could still be read, the testator had clearly intended to destroy the will and heavily scoring out the signatures was sufficient to revoke it.

Of course if the destruction is accidental then the will is not revoked and evidence of what it contained (possibly from a copy held by a solicitor) can be used to decide who should inherit.

4 *By marriage.* If a testator makes a will and later gets married, that marriage will automatically revoke the will. The only exception to this rule is where the will was made 'in contemplation of marriage'. In other words, the testator stated in the will that he intended marrying and also named the person he was going to marry, then when he married that named person the will would not be revoked.

5 *By divorce.* Where the testator makes a will and then later is divorced, any gift to the former spouse will fail but the rest of the will remains in effect. If the whole of the testator's property was left to the former spouse then the will does not take effect but the testator's property will be inherited by his nearest relations under the rules on intestacy (*see* 18.6). If the former spouse was named as executor (*see* 18.7), then that part of the will is also omitted and the spouse cannot be the executor.

18.5 Gifts of property

The law has different terms for gifts of property in a will. The first distinction is between leaving real property (land or a house) and personal property (any other property including money, cars, furniture, jewellery etc.). Where real property is left the technical term is a devise; where personal property is left it is called a legacy or a bequest.

There are also different types of legacy. These are:

1 *A specific legacy.* This is when the testator leaves a clearly identified thing to someone. The item or money that the legatee (person inheriting) is to get is a specific item or a specific sum of money. For example leaving 'my car, registration number . . .'. If the item no longer exists then the legatee will not be able to inherit it.

2 *A general legacy.* This is where the testator does not identify a specific thing but says (for example) 'I leave a painting from my collection to . . .'. The exact painting is not specified, the legatee has the right to choose one.

3 *A residuary legacy.* Quite often in a will the testator leaves specific things to a few people and then states, 'I leave all the rest of my property to . . .'. This means that the person named gets what, if anything, is left over. This is called the residue of the estate and the person inheriting is called the residuary legatee.

Sometimes a legatee who has been left a specific or a general legacy has died before the testator and in this case the legacy lapses and becomes part of the residue. The only exception to this is where the legacy was to a son or daughter of the testator and although that son or daughter has died they have left a child or children of their own. The legacy will then go to the child or, where there is more than one child, be divided equally between them, unless the testator has made it clear in the will that he does not wish this to happen. If the residuary legatee has died before the testator, then any residuary property is treated as though there was no will and distributed according to the rules of intestacy. The same exception applies where the legacy was to a son or daughter, the legacy goes to their children.

18.6 Intestacy

Not everyone makes a will; only about one-third of those who could make a will do so. Anyone

who dies without making a valid will is said to have died intestate and his/her property will be distributed according to the rules of intestacy. These rules are laid down by the Administration of Estates Act 1925 (as amended). The same rules apply whether it is a man or woman who has died and are as follows.

A surviving spouse

Where a person dies leaving a surviving spouse, the spouse will be entitled to inherit part or all of the estate depending on what other relatives there are:

Figure 18.1 The Bean family tree

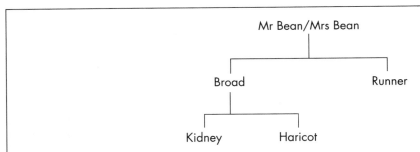

Situation 1
Mr Bean dies without making a will. He has a wife and two children alive. He also has two grandchildren. He leaves an estate worth £225,000.
• Mrs Bean will inherit the first £125,000 plus the personal items.
• This leaves £100,000 which will be divided into two (£50,000 + £50,000).
Mrs Bean will get a life interest in one half (£50,000) (although this will go to the children when she dies), as well as inheriting £125,000.
• The other £50,000 will be divided equally between the two children.
• This gives the following picture:

Mrs Bean has £125,000 plus the personal items (furniture, car etc. and a life interest in £50,000)

Broad £25,000   Runner £25,000

Kidney   Haricot

Situation 2
Mr Bean dies without making a will. He has a wife, one child, Runner, and two grandchildren alive. His other child, Broad, has already died.
• Mrs Bean gets exactly the same as in Situation 1.
• The remaining £50,000 is still divided into two and Runner gets one half.
• The other half is divided between Broad's two children.
• This gives the following picture:

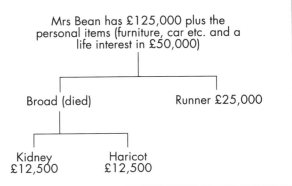

Mrs Bean has £125,000 plus the personal items (furniture, car etc. and a life interest in £50,000)

Broad (died)   Runner £25,000

Kidney £12,500   Haricot £12,500

1 *Surviving spouse and children* (or grandchildren/greatgrandchildren). The spouse will receive the first £125,000 of the estate and all the personal goods such as furniture, clothing, jewellery, car (personal goods do not include money or shares or other investments). Where there is more than £125,000 in the estate the remainder is divided into two parts and the spouse gets a life interest in one half (that means the spouse is entitled to the income from that half but when he/she dies it will belong to the children) while the other half goes to the children. If any child has died before its parent, then the issue of that child (grandchildren) would take that share. Illegitimate children have equal rights of inheritance to legitimate children.

Since this sounds complicated let's put it into practice with an example (Figure 18.1 opposite).

2 *Surviving spouse*, no children, but *surviving parent/s*. The spouse will receive the first £200,000 of the estate and all the personal goods. The remainder, if any, will be divided into two parts and the spouse will get one half outright, while the parent gets the other half. If both parents are still living they share this half between them. Step-parents are not counted as parents for this rule and do not inherit.

3 *Surviving spouse*, no children or parents, but *surviving brother/s, sister/s or nephew/s and niece/s*. The spouse will get the first £200,000 of the estate and all the personal goods. The remainder, if any, is divided into two parts and the spouse gets one half outright, while the brothers and sisters share the other half. If any brothers or sisters have already died their share goes to their children.

4 *Surviving spouse* but no children, grandchildren, parents, brother/s, sister/s, nephew/s or niece/s. The spouse will inherit the whole estate.

No surviving spouse

Where a person dies without leaving a surviving spouse, the nearest relatives inherit and the order is:

1 *Children*. If a child has already died then its children take that share.

2 *Parents*. If both parents are still alive they

share the estate equally, if only one parent survives that parent inherits the whole estate. (As before step-parents are not counted as parents for the rules of inheritance.)

3 *Brothers or sisters*. These divide the estate between them, so if there are two each will get a half, if there are three each will get a third, and so on. If any brother or sister has already died then their share goes to their children.

4 *Half-brothers and sisters*. The rules are the same as for brothers and sisters. Step-brothers and sisters do not inherit.

5 *Grandparents*.

6 *Aunts and uncles of the whole blood*. That is, aunts and uncles who had the same parents as your father or mother.

7 *Aunts and uncles of the half blood*. That is, aunts and uncles who had one parent in common with your father or mother. In other words your parents' half-brothers and sisters. (Again step-relatives do not inherit.)

If there are no surviving close relatives the estate is known as *bona vacantia* (goods without an owner) and the whole estate will go to the Crown. This means all the property will be sold and the proceeds paid into the Exchequer.

Figure 18.2 on p. 214 shows, by means of a flow chart, who inherits when there is no will.

APPLYING THE LAW

Assuming there is no will, explain who will inherit in the following situations.

1 Anthony dies leaving an ex-wife (he was divorced three years ago) and two sons. One of the sons is illegitimate. Anthony's estate is worth £150,000.

2 Brenda dies leaving a husband from whom she is separated, but not divorced. She also has one surviving son. Her daughter died two years ago but there are two grandchildren. Brenda's estate is worth £175,000.

3 Candice, who is not married and has no children, dies. Her mother is still alive and Candice has two brothers. Candice's estate is worth £60,000.

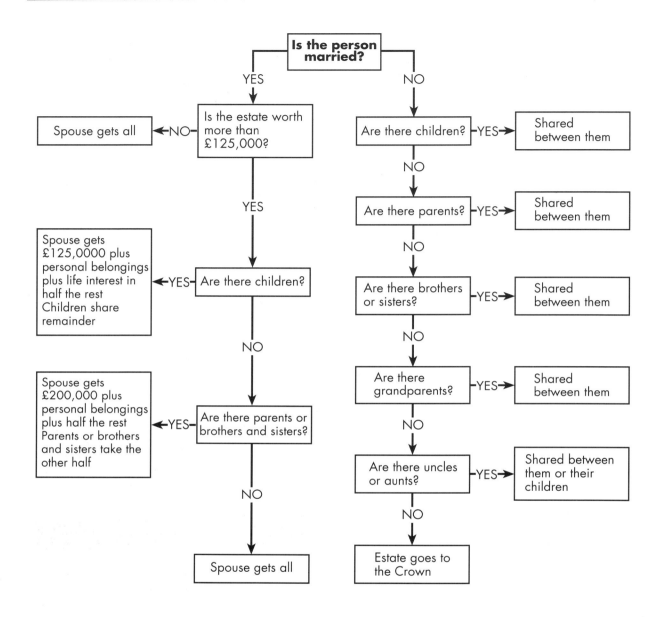

Figure 18.2   Who inherits when there is no will?

18.7 Personal representatives

When someone dies whether having made a will or not, someone has to deal with the estate and sort out all the property. The people who do this are called the deceased's *personal representatives*. If there is a will, the will may name the person or persons the deceased wanted to act as his personal representative (PR). In this case the PRs are known as executors. If there is no-one named in the will to act as executor or if there is no will, then the PRs are called administrators. The nearest relative has the right to apply to administer the estate. (Technically the female for executor is executrix and the female for administrator is administratrix.)

Applying for probate

The first thing a PR has to do is obtain the right to act. An executor has the right to act under the will but still has to apply for *probate*, that is, prove the will and his right to act. An administrator has to apply for *letters of administration* before he has the right to act. If the estate is small and only involves personal effects, cash or money in certain saving schemes such as building societies, and there is no dispute about who should inherit, then it is not necessary to apply for probate or letters of administration. However if the deceased owned a house or such items as shares, then it will be necessary to make an application. A solicitor can help the PR to make the application or the person can make it themselves. The Lord Chancellor's Department publishes a booklet called 'How to Obtain Probate' which explains the necessary procedure and helps PRs to act without a solicitor.

The Probate Registry will only issue probate or letters of administration once it is satisfied that full details of the deceased's estate have been given. The PRs must list all the debts that were owed at the time the deceased died; these could include mortgage payments or other household bills, credit card accounts or hire purchase payments. Expenses caused by the death are also listed; these will include the cost of the funeral as well as fees for the grant of probate and, where a solicitor is used, that bill.

The PRs must also list all the deceased's assets; that is, all the property owned by the deceased at the time of death. This could include money in a bank account or savings account, premium bonds, stocks and shares, as well as any house owned by the deceased and personal property, that is items such as clothing, furniture, jewellery and cars.

Once the PRs are sure that they have details of all debts and assets, then the PRs must:

a fill in a probate application form;
b fill in a form giving details of the estate;
c send or take those forms, together with the death certificate and the original will (if there is a will), to the local Probate Registry.

Where PRs are acting without a solicitor the Probate Registry will ask the PRs to attend for an interview and then to swear an oath that the information given is true to the best of their knowledge. Where a solicitor is instructed, then that solicitor will draw up the necessary forms, including the Executor's Oath and an Inland Revenue Affidavit for the PRs to swear on oath that the information is true to the best of their knowledge.

Caveats

Where there is an objection to probate or letters of administration being granted, the person who objects must inform the Probate Registry of the objection. This is called filing a caveat. A caveat might be filed because there is a challenge to the will; there might be a dispute as to whether the will is the last will made by the deceased or as to whether the will is valid. Any objection must be heard and decided upon before a grant of probate can be made.

Distributing the estate

Once probate or letters of administration have been granted the PRs can collect in all the deceased's assets. The PRs must first pay the debts, starting with the funeral expenses. If there is money left after all the debts, including any inheritance tax, have been paid, then the PRs distribute it to the people who are entitled to inherit.

18.8 Provision for family and dependants

Technically a person making a will can leave his property to anybody he wishes. This means that relatives could be disinherited and all the money could be left to a charity or someone else. A wife might have to move out of the family home and end up with no home and no money. Young children might have no provision made for them. It was felt that in some cases this was not right and so the Inheritance (Provision for Family and Dependants) Act 1975 gives the courts powers to make an award from the estate in cases where family, dependants or co-habitees have not been reasonably provided for by the will or intestacy.

The following people have the right to apply:

a the wife or husband of the deceased;
b a former wife or former husband of the

deceased, but only if the former spouse has not remarried;

c   a child of the deceased;

d   anyone who was treated as a child of the family by the deceased. This could include step-children;

e   any other person who was being maintained immediately before the death, partly or wholly, by the deceased. This could include elderly relatives or younger brothers and sisters;

f   and the Law Reform (Succession) Act 1995 also allows co-habitees to claim.

Reasonable financial provision

If the applicant is the husband or wife of the deceased, the court decides whether the financial provision under the will or intestacy is reasonable in all the circumstances, so that where the estate is large, a spouse may be given more money out of an estate, even though that spouse already has enough to live on.

Other applicants must show that they have not been left sufficient financial provision as is reasonable in all the circumstances for their maintenance.

The court will take into consideration:

a   the size of the estate;

b   the needs of the applicant;

c   the needs of those who do benefit under the will or intestacy;

d   the reasons why the deceased failed to leave money to the applicant;

e   the way in which the applicant had behaved towards the deceased during his life.

An application must be made within six months of probate or letters of administration being granted. The application is heard by the County Court or the Family Division of the High Court, depending on the amount of money involved.

18.9 The forfeiture rule

Normally the law rules that people cannot benefit from crimes they have committed. Where one person kills another, the killer should not inherit money or other property from his victim. This is called the forfeiture rule. The killer forfeits the

right to inherit. Where the killing is deliberate murder then this rule is obviously sensible, but in other situations the rule may appear unfair. For this reason the Forfeiture Act 1982 was passed. This Act allows people convicted of unlawful killing, other than murder, to claim for financial provision from the estate of the victim. It also allows such people to receive pensions and benefits such as a widow's allowance.

A claim must be made within three months of the conviction for the unlawful killing (this could be manslaughter or causing death by dangerous driving etc.). The court will only 'modify' the forfeiture rule and allow the claim if it is just in all the circumstances.

The first claim, *Re K* (1985), made under the Act illustrates this. In this case a battered wife killed her husband during a quarrel. She pleaded guilty to manslaughter and was placed on probation for two years. The court decided that it would be just to allow her to receive part of his estate.

Examination question

Generally a will must be in writing and signed by the testator who must be aged 18 or over. The testator's signature must be witnessed by at least two competent persons.

Witnesses who are also beneficiaries, either directly or indirectly, may well find that they lose their bequests.

The problem

Ivy Smith, aged 70, wrote and signed a will in which she left:

> £5,000 to her daughter-in-law, Gail;
> £2,000 to her friend, Vera.

The remainder of her estate was divided between her two grandchildren, Nicholas aged 18 and Sarah-Louise aged 15.

Ivy's husband, Bert, and her only child, Brian, are both dead.

Ivy also has a sister, Mabel aged 75, who lives in a nursing home. Ivy has for many years contributed towards the cost of Mabel's care in the nursing home.

Ivy's will was witnessed by:

1 Ivy's next door neighbour, Jack, who is Vera's husband;
2 Martin, Gail's new boyfriend;
3 Kevin and Sally, a handicapped young married couple who live in Ivy's street;

Kevin, aged 18, is blind; Sally, aged 17, is deaf.

a Comment on whether or not **each** of the above persons is competent to witness the will.   *(8 marks)*

b Discuss whether or not a valid will exists after all four witnesses have signed the will.
    In your answer, discuss whether or not all Ivy's bequests will be received by her beneficiaries.   *(8 marks)*

c Why do you think the law is so reluctant to allow a witness also to be a beneficiary?
                              (4 marks)

d If Ivy had died without making a will, the intestacy rules would have applied to her estate.
    Comment on how her estate would be distributed in this case   *(4 marks)*

e Explain how Mabel could establish an interest in Ivy's estate   *(6 marks)*

Total: 30 marks

SEG Sample Paper for 1996 (Higher Tier)

19 *Freedoms*

In developed countries today the rights and freedoms of the individual are regarded as important. In Britain we say that we live in a free society, meaning by this that everyone has certain basic rights and freedoms. These include freedom of speech, freedom to practise one's chosen religion, freedom from discrimination because of race or sex and the right to liberty. There are laws on particular points including racial and sexual discrimination, but some other rights are not written into our law. Even where our rights are set down in the law, there are limitations on these rights. Some limitations are needed in order to protect other people's rights or to protect society as a whole. To illustrate this, consider the right to liberty; clearly it is important that ordinary people have freedom of the person, the right not to be held prisoner; but there are situations where it is necessary to imprison violent and dangerous criminals to protect society from them.

There is also the Human Rights Act 1998 (due to come into effect in 2000). This Act incorporates the European Convention on Human Rights into British law making it unlawful for any public authority to act in a way that is incompatible with a Convention right. Citizens can take action for breach of a right.

19.1 European Convention on Human Rights

Even before the Human Rights Act came into effect the UK Government had signed this Convention. The European Convention on Human Rights was drawn up in order to try and protect people's rights after the horrors of the Second World War. It followed the Universal Declaration on Human Rights made by the General Assembly of the United Nations in 1948. Two years later in 1950 the Council of Europe adopted the European Convention on Human Rights. The Council of Europe is not part of the present European Union but a separate international organisation formed in 1949 and with a bigger membership than the European Union. In 1950 there were 21 members and 20 of these, including the United Kingdom, signed the European Convention on Human Rights. Since that date other European countries have joined the Council of Europe and signed the Convention, making 32 members in 1994.

The Convention sets out the rights and freedoms that the people of Europe should have. Article 2 states that everyone's right to life shall be protected by law; although the Article does recognise that States may impose the death penalty for those convicted of certain crimes. Article 3 says that no one shall be tortured and Article 4 declares that slavery is not allowed. Articles 3 and 4 are both very basic rights and it is probably surprising to realise that the United Kingdom has been found to be in breach of Article 3 in respect of treatment of prisoners in Northern Ireland. The other rights established by the Convention are dealt with in 19.3 to 19.7.

19.2 European Court of Human Rights

In order to protect the rights set out in the Convention, a Court of Human Rights was established in 1959. The procedure for applying to this court was simplified in 1994. A new permanent single European Court of Human Rights was established and individuals who feel their rights have been breached can apply direct to the Court. Member States can also report another Member State to the Court. A Chamber of the Court will consider whether the complaint is admissible and if it decides that it is, the Government of the State concerned is asked for its comments. There is the possibility of coming to a friendly negotiated settlement, but if this is not successful then the Court will hear the case in full and give a judgment. The European Court of Human Rights sits at Strasbourg.

19.3 Right to liberty

Article 5 of the European Convention on Human Rights sets out that everyone has the right to liberty and that no one shall be deprived of his liberty except where the law allows arrest or detention. Even in these cases the arrested person has the right to be told of the reason for his arrest and brought before a court within a reasonable time. In the English legal system this right to liberty has been important for centuries and was set out in the Magna Carta in 1215.

There are, as already pointed out, limitations on this right; but a person can only be detained on specific grounds set out in the law. The most widely used reasons for detaining people are:

a following a lawful arrest (*see* Chapter 10);
b on the order of a court while awaiting trial;
c a sentence of imprisonment after being found guilty of a crime;
d under the Mental Health Acts.

If a person has been unlawfully detained he may sue in the civil courts and claim damages for false imprisonment. Where the person is still being detained there is a special writ (court order) that can be obtained; this is the writ of *habeas corpus*. An application for this writ is made to the Queen's Bench Divisional Court and its effect is to order that the detained person be brought before the court immediately. An application for a writ of habeas corpus takes priority over any other case in court on that day and it will be heard first. The court will decide whether the detention is lawful

or not; if the court decides that there is no lawful reason for the detention it will order the immediate release of the prisoner.

There are two other Articles in the European Convention on Human Rights that are connected to the right to liberty and court proceedings.

Article 6 says there is a right to a fair and public hearing within a reasonable time; this is so for both criminal and civil cases. In *Darnell* v. *United Kingdom* (1993) the European Court of Human Rights held that a case about the unfair dismissal of a doctor had taken so long to be decided that the United Kingdom was in breach of Article 6. The doctor had been dismissed in 1984 but the final decision of the Employment Appeal Tribunal had not been made until 1993.

Article 7 states that no one shall be held guilty of a criminal offence if his act was not a crime at the time he did it. In other words the law may change between the time the defendant did the act and the time the case comes to court. In *R.* v. *R.* (1991) a man was convicted of marital rape. The House of Lords overruled previous decisions which held that this was not a crime. The defendant in the case has complained to the Council of Europe and a decision is awaited as to whether this is a breach of Article 7.

19.4 Freedom of religion

Under Article 9 everyone has the right to freedom of thought, conscience and religion. In the United Kingdom individuals have the right to follow any religion they choose. Generally today there is no discrimination against people because of their religion, although this was not always true. For example until 1829 a member of the Roman Catholic church was not allowed to be a Member of Parliament. The only exception to the principle of the freedom to worship is the Monarch who must be a member of the Church of England.

19.5 Freedom of speech

Article 10 states that everyone has the right to freedom of expression. This is the principle of freedom of speech and it is often regarded as being one of the key features of a democratic society. In this country it is possible to do such things as criticise the government and express opinions on current events. People in a country which does not have freedom of speech may be imprisoned for such activities. In some countries newspapers, television and radio are controlled by the Government and may only publish or broadcast material approved by that Government. In Britain the media are free to publish or broadcast almost any material or opinions; the Government does not interfere with the press.

However there are limitations, both on the freedom of individuals and on the media. These are designed to protect other people. The main restrictions are:

1 *Defamation*. As already seen in Chapter 15, defamation is a tort and anyone who has been defamed has the right to sue for damages. This protects people from having untrue statements made about them which could damage their reputation. Defamation can also be a crime if the statement is in a permanent form and likely to lead to a breach of the peace.

2 *National security*. Publishing information that could put the security of the country at risk is forbidden. The Official Secrets Acts create various criminal offences which forbid disclosing information. There is also the crime of treason which, among other things, prevents broadcasting enemy propaganda in times of war. Another offence which restricts freedom of speech is sedition. A person saying or publishing material which would bring the Government into hatred and contempt or encourage a rebellion could be prosecuted for sedition, although in practice prosecutions are very rare.

3 *Obscenity*. It is a criminal offence to publish anything which is likely to 'deprave or corrupt' people. This law is aimed at preventing the worst type of pornographic material from being published. However there are very few successful prosecutions. The law also forbids the taking or publishing of indecent pictures of young children under the Protection of Children Act 1978.

The law bans horror comics which are aimed at children and young persons from containing stories told mainly in pictures and showing violence, crimes, cruelty or incidents of a repulsive and horrible nature. In 1994 the Government started investigating ways of preventing children from obtaining violent computer games and video nasties.

4 *Contempt of court*. There are restrictions on reporting court proceedings; for example the names of children involved in court proceedings can only be published if the judge at the trial gives permission. Jurors are not allowed to publish any details of discussions in the jury room. There is also a general restriction on the press reporting of any material which might prejudice a fair trial. Newspapers have been fined very heavily for contempt of court.

5 *Discrimination*. The Public Order Act 1986 makes it an offence to publish or distribute any written work which is intended to stir up racial hatred.

19.6 Freedom of association and freedom of assembly

Article 11 gives the right to freedom of peaceful assembly and to freedom of association with others, including the right to join trade unions.

Association

In Britain most workers have the right to join a trade union, but there are some who have not. In 1984 the right to belong to a trade union was taken away from those working at the Government Communications Headquarters in Cheltenham. This limitation of rights was challenged in the English courts but it was held that the Government could withdraw trade union rights where national security was at risk.

There are also restrictions on associations where there is a crime involved; here the people concerned can be charged with the offence of conspiracy. Certain organisations are banned under the Prevention of Terrorism Act 1989.

Assembly

Meetings in private places are generally allowed, unless there is likely to be a crime. However there are a number of restrictions on meetings in public places. The main ones are:

1 The Highways Act 1980 makes it an offence to 'wilfully obstruct the free passage along the

highway'. A police constable can arrest anyone who commits this offence.

2 The Public Order Act 1986 creates two different offences about people using violent conduct in both public and private places. These are:

a *riot:* this is committed when 12 or more people present together use or threaten violence for a common purpose which would cause a person of reasonable firmness to fear for his personal safety;

b *violent disorder:* this is committed if there are three or more persons present together using or threatening violence in such a way that a person of reasonable firmness would fear for his personal safety.

3 The Public Order Act 1936 makes it a criminal offence to wear political uniforms in public except for ceremonial or special occasions when the wearing of uniform is not likely to provoke a breach of the peace.

4 It is unlawful for 50 or more persons to meet within one mile of the Houses of Parliament when Parliament is sitting.

5 The Criminal Justice and Public Order Act 1994 gives the police powers to intervene where:

a two or more people are trespassing on land with the common purpose of residing there and either they have threatened the owner of the land or they have six or more vehicles on the land. This is aimed at New Age Travellers;

b there is a gathering in the open air of 100 or more people at which amplified music is played during the night so loudly that it is likely to cause serious distress to local residents. This is aimed at so-called 'rave' parties.

In both these situations the police have powers to direct those involved to leave and if anyone refuses to leave the police may then arrest them. The Criminal Justice and Public Order Act 1994 also creates an offence called aggravated trespass and gives the police power to arrest anyone committing it. The offence occurs where a person trespasses on land in order to prevent some lawful activity on that land. It is aimed at demonstrations such as hunt saboteurs.

Processions

The Public Order Act 1986 makes several rules about processions. The organisers of a procession should give written notice to the local police of any intended procession at least seven days before it is due to take place. However annual processions such as local carnivals or May fairs are not included in this provision.

When a procession takes place, the most senior police officer present may impose any conditions necessary if he reasonably fears that serious public disorder is likely to result. So the police can change the proposed route of the procession.

Finally the Chief Constable for any area can apply to the district council for an order banning all (or certain types of) procession within a local area for up to three months.

19.7 Freedom from discrimination

Article 14 of the European Convention on Human Rights says that all these rights and freedoms should exist without any discrimination on any grounds such as sex, race, colour, language, religion, political or other opinion, national or social origin, national minority, property, birth or status.

We have already seen in Chapter 16 that the Sex Discrimination Acts and the Race Relations Act 1976 ban discrimination on the grounds of gender or race in employment. However both Acts cover a much wider area than employment.

Race Relations Act 1976

This Act covers discrimination in public places such as hotels, restaurants, theatres and transport. It also forbids discrimination in the supply of goods and services and education as well as all employment related areas. For example, refusal to allow someone to join a club because of their race would be a breach of the Act. The Act set up the Commission for Racial Equality which will give a complainant help, including where necessary legal representation to bring a case before the Race Relations Tribunal.

Public Order Act 1986

This Act creates various crimes for which people can be prosecuted. Such offences include committing acts and publishing material likely to stir up racial hatred.

Sex Equality Acts

As well as preventing discrimination in employment, these forbid discrimination on the basis of gender in education, transport, shops, banks and public places. The scope of the discrimination included is very wide and, for instance, it covers discrimination against women in sports so that women wrestlers and boxers cannot be banned. The Sex Discrimination Act 1975 set up the Equal Opportunities Commission which monitors sexual equality and, as well as helping complainants, it can take a case in its own name where it believes there is a breach of the law.

The Treaty of Rome is also important in protecting against discrimination in employment and related matters such as training, promotion and pension schemes.

19.8 Right to privacy

Although many of the freedoms set out in the European Convention on Human Rights are recognised in our law, the European Convention

on Human Rights is not part of English law. This is shown clearly by Article 8 which states that every person has a right to respect of his private and family life, his home and his correspondence. This part of the Convention is not part of our law. In England the law does not protect a person's private life; there is no rule against invasion of privacy. People in the public eye, such as the Royal family, film stars and sporting personalities often suffer from the intrusion of the media into their private lives.

19.9 Protection of rights

Ombudsmen

As already noted it is possible to go to the appropriate court or tribunal when there has been a breach of a person's rights. But to give people further protection the Government in 1967 created the post of the Parliamentary Commissioner for Administration (the Ombudsman). His responsibility is to investigate complaints about injustices suffered as a result of maladministration by government departments and agencies. There is also a Commissioner for the Health Service who investigates complaints about the health service. Such complaints must be referred to the Ombudsman by a member of the House of Commons. This means that a person with a grievance must first go to his/her Member of Parliament. Since 1974 there have been Ombudsmen appointed to investigate complaints against local authorities. There are three such Ombudsmen for England, each covering a different area and another for Wales.

Businesses have also established their own Ombudsmen, so that it is possible to complain about banks, building societies and insurance companies.

Examination question

We all live in a free society and individuals in the United Kingdom have certain rights and freedoms. These freedoms include freedom of movement, assembly, procession and speech, and freedom from discrimination. However, these freedoms are not absolute. In some situations they are restricted to protect the rights of citizens as a whole.

In each of the following situations:
Identify which right or freedom is involved. Explain how, if at all, it has been restricted and what action may then follow.

a Sally, a black qualified PE teacher with 10 years' experience, applies for a job at a boys' school. The headmaster refuses to interview her because he wants 'someone who can coach the school soccer team'. He eventually appoints Simon, who is qualified but has no teaching experience.

(4 marks)

b Humphrey is a civil servant who works for the Ministry of Defence. In the course of his job he comes across some classified information which the Government would prefer remain secret. Because of his political views, Humphrey passes the information to a national newspaper.

(4 marks)

c Martin, an offender with a criminal record and a history of violence, appears before the local Magistrates' Court charged with robbery. Martin is committed for trial to the Crown Court. On a previous occasion, Martin 'jumped' bail.   *(4 marks)*

Total: 12 marks

SEG 1992

Appendix

Coursework

For GCSE it is usual to have to do coursework which counts for 20 per cent of the final assessment. For Law the coursework required is usually two pieces of written work. Before starting coursework there are some important points to remember:

1 *Choosing a topic.* The topic covered by the coursework must be a topic from the subject content of the syllabus you are following. Of course it is sensible to choose a topic that particularly interests you but do check that your chosen topic is within the syllabus area.

2 *Choosing a title.* It is also important that the actual title of the piece of coursework is clear enough for you to know what issues you need to concentrate on. If the title is too wide it will be difficult to focus on a discussion; if the title is too narrow then it will not allow you to develop any worthwhile arguments.

In many cases teachers will suggest possible titles, but if you wish to select your own then it might be a good idea to use a two-part title, the first part involving describing or explaining the law and the second part asking for a discussion of how satisfactory that law is in some way. At the end of this appendix there are suggested titles for coursework.

3 *Researching your topic.* Try to use as many different sources as possible. The type of sources will vary depending on the nature of the topic. For example, if the topic is about the courts then visits to the appropriate court will be important; if the topic involves people in the legal system then a discussion with someone working in the law will be a valuable source. However it will also be necessary to read different textbooks to make sure you fully understand the background.

Where the topic is currently in the news it is worthwhile reading newspaper articles to develop an understanding of the issues.

It is possible to get leaflets on some topics such as legal aid, making a small claim in the County Court or social security benefits from Citizens Advice Bureaux. There are also other organisations that can give specialised information on areas such as race relations, equal opportunities, consumer protection.

Keep a record of the sources you use as these should be included in the presentation of your coursework.

4 *Writing the coursework.* Check how long the work should be; often the limit is 1,000 words. DO NOT write more than the required amount. The quality of the work is the important element. DO NOT copy large bits from books; try to put it into your own words. Make a plan before you start and then do a draft version. Try to explain clearly what the present position is before discussing the issues involved. Where suitable you might decide to include diagrams to explain points. If you do so, make sure the diagrams are clearly labelled. When discussing any points make sure that you think of both sides of the argument. Finish with a conclusion based on the points you have made.

Now read your draft through; check for spelling errors. Finally copy or type the work out as neatly as you can.

Suggested titles for coursework

The following titles are examples of suitable titles given by the Southern Examining Group.

1 **a** Describe how the system of delegated legislation operates.

    b Discuss the advantages and disadvantages of such legislation and consider whether or not the controls on delegated legislation are effective.

2 **a** Describe the training and work of barristers, solicitors and legal executives.

    b Discuss the arguments for and against the legal professions being fused into a single profession.

3 **a** Explain how a jury is formed and describe its function in relation to the judge.

    b Discuss the advantages and disadvantages of the system and consider the effects of a trial by a judge alone.

4 **a** Describe the main 'freedoms' for the subjects of this country.

    b Discuss whether or not the restrictions attached to these freedoms are necessary.

5 **a** Explain the law regarding the capacity of minors to make contracts.

    b Is there justification for treating all minors, regardless of age, differently from adults?

6 **a** Describe the law relating to sex and racial discrimination in employment and education.

    b Discuss its fairness, and make suggestions to improve the situation.

7 **a** Explain the law of libel.

    b Discuss the situation of the award of large sums of damages for libel, compared with damages awarded for physical injuries caused by the negligence of large organisations.

OR

    b Discuss the role of the jury in libel cases. Should the jury decide the amount of damages awarded? Should there be a jury?

8 **a** Explain the law regarding people under the age of 18 who wish to marry.

    b Discuss the arguments for and against minors below this age being able to marry without consent of adults.

9 **a** Describe the method of distribution of a dead person's estate under the rules of intestacy.

    b Discuss a fairer way of distribution.

10 **a** Explain the crime of murder and the importance of 'mens rea' and 'actus reus' to the crime.

    b Discuss the defences of diminished responsibility and provocation and consider whether the law concerning these defences should be changed with regard to women who have been the victims of physical abuse.

Table of Acts of Parliament

Table of Cases

Index

Additional Examination Questions

7. Tort

Defamation is defined as the publication of a defamatory statement which tends to lower a person in the estimation of right-thinking members of society. An action for defamation can be defended by using one or more of a range of special defences. These include justification, fair comment and privilege. Defamation is also unusual as a tort in that the case is usually decided by a jury and Legal Aid is not available to either party.

The Problem

Oliver is a government minister and has been a member of Parliament for over twenty years. He was widely regarded as honest and hard-working and some regarded him as a potential future Prime Minister. However, recently, some stories about Oliver have started to circulate in the House of Commons. It has been alleged that he was paid a large sum of money to favour a company bidding for a government contract. Rumours are also going round that he is having an affair with a House of Commons researcher.

These rumours have been picked up by a Sunday newspaper which wrote an article about Oliver, with a picture of him falling down the steps of a London hotel, under the headline,

"Oliver falls for Commons researcher after heavy night at top London hotel."

Oliver has denied all the allegations against him and claims that he was at the hotel for a genuine meeting on government business.

(a) Oliver is considering suing for defamation. Explain to him what he would need to prove.

(6 marks)

(b) Oliver has been advised that he has the potential right to sue in both libel and slander. Explain the differences between these two types of defamation. *(4 marks)*

(c) Following legal advice, Oliver has been told that he may have been the victim of **defamation by innuendo**. Explain and illustrate what is meant by this phrase. *(4 marks)*

(d) Oliver has also been warned by his solicitor that the newspaper is likely to contest his claim using one or more of the special defamation defences. Discuss how these defences may apply in this situation. *(6 marks)*

(e) (i) Identify **two** of the problems often associated with bringing an action in defamation.

(2 marks)

(ii) Discuss how **one** of these problems could be overcome. *(4 marks)*

(iii) Comment on how well the law of defamation protects the ordinary member of the public.

(4 marks)

Southern Examining Group 1997, Higher Tier, © SEG

Answer **one** question in this Section. Carefully read **all** questions before you make your choice. Where appropriate, support your answers by referring to relevant statutes, cases or examples.

5. Contract

There are established rules in contract. One rule states that a contract requires an offer by one party and an acceptance of that offer by the other. The law also distinguishes between an offer, which can be accepted, and an invitation to treat, which cannot. In addition, once the contract is entered into, only the two parties can sue or be sued under the contract.

In a contract for the sale or supply of goods or services, Parliament has passed a number of Acts, in 1979, 1982 and 1994, designed principally to protect consumers through the use of certain implied terms.

Following a breach of contract, an injured party will usually be entitled to sue for some form of remedy.

The Problem

Alma has gone shopping, looking for a birthday present for her husband Boris. In the window of the local camera shop, she sees a high quality camera priced at £25. Alma knows that the camera was priced at £250 last week.

Alma goes into the shop and insists on buying the camera for £25. The shop is reluctant to sell, pointing out that the price ticket was a mistake, but eventually the manager agrees to see the camera at the price in the window.

Boris is happy with his birthday present until he tries to use the zoom facility on his camera which, unknown to Boris, does not work. Boris finishes the roll of film and Alma takes it to the local camera shop for developing.

The shop takes six weeks to develop the film because of a problem with its developing machine. This problem also leads to Boris' film being over-exposed and the pictures ruined.

Boris has since discovered the problem with the camera and returns to the shop to complain. However, the manager refuses to refund the cost of the camera, saying that it is the "manufacturer's fault". The manager also refuses to compensate Boris for the ruined photographs.

(a) (i)   Explain and illustrate the difference between an offer and an invitation to treat.   *(4 marks)*
    (ii) Discuss whether or not the shop was legally obliged to sell the camera for £25.   *(4 marks)*
(b) Name the Act of Parliament which applies to the sale of a camera that does not work properly. Discuss how the Act could help the purchaser.   *(4 marks)*
(c) Name the Act of Parliament that would apply to the six week delay in developing the film. Discuss how this Act would help the customer.   *(3 marks)*
(d) Name the Act of Parliament that would apply to the ruined photographs. Discuss how this Act would help the customer.   *(3 marks)*
(e) Taking into account your answers to (b), (c) and (d), discuss whether
    (i)   Alma would have a right of action against the shop;   *(3 marks)*
    (ii) Boris would have a right of action against the shop.   *(3 marks)*
(f) (i)   State the most likely remedy available in a case such as this.   *(1 mark)*
    (ii) Name the court where this case would almost certainly be heard.   *(1 mark)*
    (iii) Comment on the advantages of using this court.   *(4 marks)*

Southern Examining Group 1997, Foundation Tier, © SEG

7. Criminal Law

A person is guilty of theft if he dishonestly appropriates property belonging to another with the intention of permanently depriving the other of it.

The crime of burglary can be committed in a variety of ways, all of which are charged under Section 9 of the Theft Act 1968. An intentional homicide is charged as murder, although manslaughter can be committed in a variety of circumstances.

The Problem

Harold lives alone in a large house which stands in its own grounds some distance from his neighbours.

During the last two years, Harold's house has been broken into on three separate occasions and he has lost thousands of pounds worth of his personal possessions. On the last occasion, Harold was attacked and knocked unconscious. No one has ever been caught for these offences.

Harold decided he needed some protection and bought himself a gun which he kept loaded in his bedroom. Shortly afterwards, Ian and James decided to break into Harold's house at night. Harold was asleep upstairs, but woke up when he heard a noise downstairs. Taking his gun, Harold went to the top of the stairs and called out, "Give yourself up or I will shoot." He then fired a shot in the dark which hit and seriously wounded Ian. James escaped, taking some money which he had found, using Harold's car which he later abandoned in a town centre car park.

Ian was taken to hospital where he was initially treated by Kim, a junior doctor. Owing to a lack of experience and excessive fatigue, Kim ordered the wrong treatment and Ian died shortly afterwards.

(a) Discuss the criminal liability of Ian and James as they enter Harold's house. *(4 marks)*

(b) Discuss James' criminal liability with respect to the following:
  (i) the money; *(4 marks)*
  (ii) Harold's car (ignoring any road traffic offences he may be committing). *(4 marks)*

(c) Harold has been told by the police that he is likely to be charged with a homicide offence.
  (i) Name the **two** alternative charges Harold could face. *(2 marks)*
  (ii) Ignoring the issue of the poor medical treatment, discuss which of these two offences Harold is more likely to be charged with. *(6 marks)*
  (iii) Discuss any possible defence(s) Harold could plead. *(4 marks)*

(d) (i) Briefly explain what effect the poor medical treatment will have on Harold's case. *(2 marks)*
  (ii) Comment on how appropriate you think the law is in this respect. *(4 marks)*

Southern Examining Group 1997, Higher Tier, © SEG

8. Family Law

A marriage is defined as the voluntary union for life of one man and one woman, to the exclusion of all others. The parties must meet the minimum age requirements, not fall within the prohibited degrees of relationship nor already have an existing marriage.

In addition, the parties must comply with various statutory or church requirements, otherwise the marriage may be either void or voidable.

Recent changes to the divorce law have introduced the concepts of mediation and no-fault divorce. However, the ground for divorce, irretrievable breakdown, has not changed.

The Problem

Simon and Tony are lifelong friends and both are aged 28. Both married about ten years ago, though Simon divorced his wife five years ago.

Tony has been separated from his wife Una for over two years, and she is now living with someone else. Both Simon and Tony are planning to re-marry. Simon is planning to marry his cousin Violet, aged 17. They are hoping to marry quietly one evening because of family disapproval of the marriage. Simon intends to use Tony as a witness and has told him to say nothing because no one in Simon's family has been told about the wedding arrangements.

Simon told Tony that when he was divorced five years ago, the divorce was based on two years' separation and that the divorce was "automatic". Tony therefore assumed that he was already divorced and went through a ceremony of marriage with Wilma. The ceremony took place at the local Registry office with Simon and Violet present as witnesses.

(a) (i)   In the context of marriage, explain what is meant by the terms **void** and **voidable**.   *(3 marks)*
    (ii) Identify **three** different situations where a marriage would be **voidable**.   *(3 marks)*
(b) Discuss the validity of Simon's intended marriage to Violet, taking into account
    (i)   whom Simon is intending to marry;
    (ii) the circumstances in which the ceremony is being planned.   *(6 marks)*
(c) (i)   Explain to Tony the legal differences between separation and divorce.   *(4 marks)*
    (ii) In the light of these differences, briefly discuss the validity of Tony's marriage to Wilma.   *(2 marks)*
(d) In the context of divorce,
    (i)   explain what is meant by the term "irretrievable breakdown";   *(4 marks)*
    (ii) name the **two** courts where divorce matters can be dealt with;   *(2 marks)*
    (iii) briefly explain what is meant by maintenance.   *(2 marks)*
(e) Comment on whether or not the changes to the divorce law are appropriate to meet the needs of a modern society.   *(4 marks)*

Southern Examining Group 1998, Foundation Tier, © SEG

Section B

Answer **two** questions from this section.

You are advised to spend about 40 minutes on each question.

B4 (a) Give a brief explanation of **three** welfare benefits that are available to those unable to work because of illness or disability and have families to look after. *(8)*

(b) What do you consider to be the problems in the current welfare benefit system? What improvements to the law, if any, would you suggest and why? *(13)*

Northern Examinations and Assessment Board 1998, Tier H, © NEAB